Fodor's 2009

SAN
FRANCISCO

Where to Stay and Eat
for All Budgets

Must-See Sights
and Local Secrets

Ratings You Can Trust

Fodor's Travel Publications   New York, Toronto, London, Sydney, Auckland
www.fodors.com

FODOR'S SAN FRANCISCO 2009

Editors: Michael Nalepa, Bethany Cassin Beckerlegge, Molly Moker

Editorial Production: Evangelos Vasilakis
Maps & Illustrations: David Lindroth, Mark Stroud, *cartographers*; Bob Blake, Rebecca Baer, and William Wu *map editors*
Design: Fabrizio La Rocca, *creative director*; Guido Caroti, Siobhan O'Hare, *art directors*; Tina Malaney, Chie Ushio, Ann McBride, Jessica Walsh, *designers*; Melanie Marin, *senior picture editor;*
Cover Photo: (Cyclist in front of the Unity Amongst Diversity mural.) Copyright 2004 Precita Eyes Muralists. 12' x60', Independent Living Skills Center, 225 Valencia Street, San Francisco, CA. Directed by Susan Cervantes and assisted by Christy Majano in collaboration with 15 students 16 and 17 years, from the Walden House youth rehabilitation group home. Funded by the Department of Human Services (DHS): Ty Milford/Aurora Photos
Production/Manufacturing: Matthew Struble

ISBN 978-1-4000-1961-8

ISSN 1525–1829

SPECIAL SALES

This book is available at special discounts for bulk purchases for sales promotions or premiums. Special editions, including personalized covers, excerpts of existing books, and corporate imprints, can be created in large quantities for special needs. For more information, write to Special Markets/Premium Sales, 1745 Broadway, MD 6-2, New York, New York 10019, or e-mail specialmarkets@randomhouse.com.

AN IMPORTANT TIP & AN INVITATION

Although all prices, opening times, and other details in this book are based on information supplied to us at press time, changes occur all the time in the travel world, and Fodor's cannot accept responsibility for facts that become outdated or for inadvertent errors or omissions. So **always confirm information when it matters,** especially if you're making a detour to visit a specific place. Your experiences—positive and negative—matter to us. If we have missed or misstated something, **please write to us.** We follow up on all suggestions. Contact the San Francisco editor at editors@fodors.com or c/o Fodor's at 1745 Broadway, New York, NY 10019.

PRINTED IN THE UNITED STATES OF AMERICA

10 9 8 7 6 5 4 3 2 1

Be a Fodor's Correspondent

Your opinion matters. It matters to us. It matters to your fellow Fodor's travelers, too. And we'd like to hear it. In fact, we need to hear it.

When you share your experiences and opinions, you become an active member of the Fodor's community. That means we'll not only use your feedback to make our books better, but we'll publish your names and comments whenever possible. Throughout our guides, look for "Word of Mouth," excerpts of your unvarnished feedback.

Here's how you can help improve Fodor's for all of us.

Tell us when we're right. We rely on local writers to give you an insider's perspective. But our writers and staff editors—who are the best in the business—depend on you. Your positive feedback is a vote to renew our recommendations for the next edition.

Tell us when we're wrong. We're proud that we update most of our guides every year. But we're not perfect. Things change. Hotels cut services. Museums change hours. Charming cafés lose charm. If our writer didn't quite capture the essence of a place, tell us how you'd do it differently. If any of our descriptions are inaccurate or inadequate, we'll incorporate your changes in the next edition and will correct factual errors at fodors.com immediately.

Tell us what to include. You probably have had fantastic travel experiences that aren't yet in Fodor's. Why not share them with a community of like-minded travelers? Maybe you chanced upon a beach or bistro or B&B that you don't want to keep to yourself. Tell us why we should include it. And share your discoveries and experiences with everyone directly at fodors.com. Your input may lead us to add a new listing or highlight a place we cover with a "Highly Recommended" star or with our highest rating, "Fodor's Choice."

Give us your opinion instantly at our feedback center at www.fodors.com/feedback. You may also e-mail editors@fodors.com with the subject line "San Francisco Editor." Or send your nominations, comments, and complaints by mail to San Francisco Editor, Fodor's, 1745 Broadway, New York, NY 10019.

You and travelers like you are the heart of the Fodor's community. Make our community richer by sharing your experiences. Be a Fodor's correspondent.

Happy Traveling!

Tim Jarrell, Publisher

CONTENTS

SAN FRANCISCO IN FOCUS

ABOUT THIS BOOK

Our Ratings

Sometimes you find terrific travel experiences and sometimes they just find you. But usually the burden is on you to select the right combination of experiences. That's where our ratings come in.

As travelers we've all discovered a place so wonderful and also so locally unique that superlatives don't do it justice: you just have to be there to know. These sights, properties, and experiences get our highest rating, **Fodor's Choice**, indicated by orange stars throughout this book.

Black stars highlight sights and properties we deem **Highly Recommended**, places that our writers, editors, and readers praise again and again for consistency and excellence.

By default, there's another category: any place we include in this book is by definition worth your time, unless we say otherwise. And we will.

Disagree with any of our choices? Care to nominate a place or suggest that we rate one more highly? Visit our feedback center at www.fodors.com/feedback.

Budget Well

Hotel and restaurant price categories from ¢ to $$$$ are defined in the opening pages of each chapter. For attractions, we always give standard adult admission fees; reductions are usually available for children, students, and senior citizens. Want to pay with plastic? **AE, D, DC, MC, V** following restaurant and hotel listings indicate if American Express, Discover, Diners Club, MasterCard, and Visa are accepted.

Restaurants

Unless we state otherwise, restaurants are open for lunch and dinner daily. We mention dress only when there's a specific requirement and reservations only when they're essential or not accepted—it's always best to book ahead.

Hotels

Hotels have private bath, phone, TV, and air-conditioning and operate on the European Plan (aka EP, meaning without meals), unless we specify that they use the Continental Plan (CP, with a Continental breakfast), Breakfast Plan (BP, with a full breakfast), or Modified American Plan (MAP, with breakfast and dinner) or are all-inclusive (AI, including all meals and most activi-

ties). We always list facilities but not whether you'll be charged an extra fee to use them, so when pricing accommodations, find out what's included.

Many Listings
★	Fodor's Choice
★	Highly recommended
✉	Physical address
✛	Directions
⌂	Mailing address
☎	Telephone
🖷	Fax
⊕	On the Web
✐	E-mail
🎫	Admission fee
☉	Open/closed times
Ⓜ	Metro stations
🚍	Credit cards

Hotels & Restaurants
🏨	Hotel
⊷	Number of rooms
⌓	Facilities
❘⊙❘	Meal plans
✕	Restaurant
⌔	Reservations
↘	Smoking
⌑⌑	BYOB
✕🏨	Hotel with restaurant that warrants a visit

Outdoors
🏌	Golf
⚠	Camping

Other
☾	Family-friendly
⇨	See also
✉	Branch address
☞	Take note

Experience San Francisco

Cable car on Russian Hill, Hyde Street line

WORD OF MOUTH

"San Francisco is about diversity. There's room for [those who like] the Wharf and Victorians and the Castro and North Beach and the Mission and Chinatown and even Union Square. Something for everyone."

—Catbert

SAN FRANCISCO TODAY

The quintessential boomtown, San Francisco has been alternately riding high and crashing since the gold rush. Those bearish during the heady days of the dot-com bubble had barely finished dancing on the grave of the Internet economy when biotech rode into town, turning bust to boom once again (today's housing market downturn has graciously sidestepped the city). So which San Francisco will you find when you come to town? A reversal of fortune is always possible, but here's a snapshot of what the city's like—for now, anyway.

Today's San Francisco:

. . . is just as liberal as you've heard. Baghdad by the Bay, Sodom by the Sea: prudish types have been pegging San Francisco as a bastion of sexy liberalism since the town first rolled out the welcome mat. And we do tend to espouse a pretty live-and-let-live attitude here. Health insurance for city employees has covered gender-reassignment surgery since 2001. We voted in 2005 to ban handguns, and women run both the police and fire departments (Heather Fong and Joanne Hayes-White, respectively). Our biggest bash of the year is June's gay pride celebration, when roughly a million people descend on the city to party.

Our dashing young Mayor Gavin Newsom, himself a raging metrosexual, won the eternal devotion of gay San Franciscans when he decided to issue marriage licenses to same-sex couples in 2004. And in this town, he's considered a moderate. Newsom enjoys the city's tolerance as well. Following the 2007 revelation that he had a fling with his social secretary—who was also the wife of his good friend and campaign manager—and Newsom's admission that he has a drinking problem, his approval rating topped 70% and he went on to win a second term virtually unopposed.

. . . embraces its eccentrics. If a 6-foot-tall transvestite in evening wear doesn't merit a second look, just what does it take to stand out in this town? If history serves, it takes quirkiness and staying power. For instance, back in the 19th century, a San Francisco businessman declared himself Norton I, Emperor of the United States and Protector of Mexico. Instead of shipping him off to a nice, quiet place, San Franciscans became his willing subjects, police officers saluted him, and newspa-

WHAT WE'RE TALKING ABOUT

The sparring match between Mayor Gavin Newsom's office and the *San Francisco Chronicle* continues over homeless folks living in Golden Gate Park. The mayor sends in city workers offering services, then the paper follows the trail at night and uncovers camp after thriving camp, compelling the mayor to send in city workers. . . .

We love to hate Muni. Grousing about Muni's slow service and accident rates is a rite of passage. Commuters unite on Web sites like munioutrage.com and www.rescuemuni.org.

What are the results of City Hall's controversial Care Not Cash program? This significantly cut welfare checks to the chronically homeless, replacing them with housing and social services. Thousands of formerly-homeless people are newly housed, but panhan-

pers printed his proclamations (among them that the Democrats and Republicans be abolished for bickering).

Today the Brown Twins, ladies of a certain age who dress alike in eye-catching outfits and are always together, have their own place on the list of San Francisco icons. There's also Pink Man, who rides on a unicycle wearing a hot pink unitard. (He says you can tell someone's a local when "they don't balk at Pink Man.")

One of the most celebrated eccentrics is Frank Chu, a middle-aged guy in a frumpy suit who's been faithfully carrying a picket sign around the Financial District since the 1990s. He accuses various politicians of being in cahoots and keeping millions of dollars from him and the population of the "12 galaxies." The city's response? Politicians buy ad space on the back of his sign and fans named a Mission District bar 12 Galaxies in tribute. Chu eats and drinks on the house there.

. . . is losing residents. At 46 square mi, San Francisco is twice the size of Manhattan but has only half the population: about 744,000 and dropping. In fact, more people lived in San Francisco in 1950 (775,000) than do today. The city main-tained its population until the dot-com boom of the 1990s drove young families to the East Bay in search of lower housing prices. When the bubble burst, there was a second purge as many of those high-tech Johnny-come-latelies scrambled for cheaper ground out of town.

. . . is reshaping its downtown. Limited by its geography, San Francisco simply has nowhere to go but up. The sprawling area south of Market Street was long an industrial center, but since that industry has dried up, new high-rise developments are underway. Plot the nascent high-rises on a map and you can see a radical shift southward, stretching from Mission Street to Mission Bay (where UCSF's 43-acre medical and biotech campus is rising). More than 20 towers are in the works, several of which will eclipse the city's current tallest building, the 853-foot Transamerica Pyramid.

Got your bearings? Then join the locals as they constantly check the pulse of the city. Although the frenzied adrenaline rush of the dot-com era has died down, a new wave of energy is gathering.

---

dling has become even more prevalent.

Mayor Newsom thrust the issue of same-sex marriage into the national spotlight when he ordered the city registrar to issue marriage licenses to same-sex couples in 2004. With the issue back before the court, Newsom is basking in the love—backed by strong public support—so much nicer than the intractable issues of homelessness and housing shortages.

There's lots of hand-wringing and gnashing of teeth in the Bay Area these days over the slipping housing market, but city residents are still sitting pretty. While housing prices in most counties here continue to drop, San Francisco's keep sneaking up—with a median home price of $800,000.

EXPERIENCE SAN FRANCISCO PLANNER

When to Go

You can visit San Francisco comfortably any time of year. Possibly the best time to visit San Francisco is September and October, when the city's most summerlike weather packs the calendar with outdoor concerts and festivals. The climate here always feels Mediterranean and moderate—with a foggy, sometimes chilly bite. The temperature rarely drops below 40°F, and anything warmer than 80°F is considered a heat wave. Be prepared for rain in winter, especially December and January. Winds off the ocean can add to the chill factor, so pack warm clothing. That old joke about summer in SF feeling like winter is true at heart, but once you move inland, summers are warmer.

SAN FRANCISCO
TEMPERATURES

How's the Weather?

Thanks to its proximity to the Pacific Ocean, San Francisco has remarkably consistent weather throughout the year. The average high is 63°F and the average low is 51°F. Summer comes late in San Francisco, which sees its warmest days in September and October. On average, the city gets 20 inches of rainfall a year, most of it in the December–March period.

Getting Around

Walking: San Francisco dearly rewards walking, and the areas that most visitors cover are easy (and safe) to reach on foot. However, many neighborhoods have steep—make that *steep*—hills. In some areas the sidewalk is carved into steps; a place that seems just a few blocks away might be a real hike, depending on the grade. When your calves ache, you're that much closer to being a local. Check the Safety section for a recap on areas to avoid walking.

By Subway: BART is San Francisco's subway, limited to one straight line through the city. Within the city, it's a handy way to get to the Mission or perhaps Civic Center. BART is most useful for reaching the East Bay or the airport. There are no special visitor passes for BART; within town a ticket runs $1.50.

On Muni: Muni includes the city's extensive system of buses, electric streetcars, nostalgic E- and F-line trolleys, and cable cars. The trolleys and cable cars are a pleasure for the ride alone and they run in well-traveled areas like Market Street and, in the case of the cable cars, the hills from Union Square to Fisherman's Wharf. Basic fare for the bus, streetcars, and trolleys is $1.50; cable car tickets cost $5 one-way. At $11, a one-day Muni Passport that includes cable car rides is a great deal.

By Car or Taxi: Considering its precipitous hills, one-way streets, and infuriating dearth of parking, San Francisco is not a good place to drive yourself. Taxis, however, can come in very handy. Call one or hail one on the street; they tend to cluster around downtown hotels.

Safety

Like any large city, San Francisco has its share of sketchy or downright troubled areas, but overall it's a relatively safe urban area. If you use common sense and follow basic precautions (sticking to well-lighted streets after dark, holding onto your bags rather than leaving them next to you), all should be well.

Even with forewarning, some visitors are taken aback by the high number of homeless people in the city's central areas, like the Civic Center. There's also a certain residual counter-culture effect—the lingering visions of the 1960s scene bring in a few thousand street kids every summer. (These teens and twentysomethings tend to hang out in the Haight and camp in the city's parks.) Although most homeless people are no threat, some panhandle aggressively. If you feel uncomfortable, simply don't engage them and move away.

Below is a list of the central city areas that you may want to avoid for safety's sake. Other parts of town, like the Haight, may look a bit scuzzy with graffiti or litter, but are basically safe during the day.

The Tenderloin. Named for a cut of steak, this neighborhood west of Union Square and above Civic Center is a particularly seedy part of town, with drug dealers, homeless and mentally ill people, hustlers, and X-rated joints. It's roughly bordered by Taylor, Polk, Geary, and Market streets. Avoid coming here after dark, especially if you're walking.

Western Addition. An actively dangerous neighborhood, even in daytime, with outbreaks of gun violence. Don't stray down Fillmore Street south of Geary Boulevard.

Civic Center. If you're hoofing it after a show, go west to Gough Street; don't head north, east, or south from the Civic Center on foot, and avoid Market Street between 6th and 10th.

Parts of the Mission District. The flat blocks of the Mission range from a bit scruffy to edgy to truly sketchy, with some gang activity. Steer clear of the areas east of Mission Street and south of 24th Street, especially after dark. If you have to walk between 16th and 24th streets, head west to Valencia, which runs parallel to Mission.

Some areas in Golden Gate Park. These include the area near the Haight Street entrance, where street kids often smoke and deal pot, and around the pedestrian tunnels on the far west end of the park. *See Chapter 8* for more details.

Parts of SoMa: You'll be in an empty industrial neighborhood if you drift more than five blocks or so south of Market.

5 Helpful SF Web Sites

Check out these online options—besides our own www.fodors.com!

www.onlyinsanfrancisco.com for the San Francisco visitors bureau.

www.sfgate.com/chronicle from the major daily newspaper, especially www.sfgate.com/traveler (for Bay Area travel) and www.sfgate.com/eguide (for entertainment articles and listings).

www.sfist.com for a daily feed of local news, gossip, and preoccupations.

http://mistersf.com for a passionate local's rundown on favorite local spots and city FAQs.

www.sfstation.com for daily listings on all sorts of events, restaurants, clubs, etc. Want to find a high volume of local comments on these places? Try www.yelp.com.

. . . and 3 more just for ha-has

www.burritoeater.com for opinionated reviews of Bay Area burritos.

http://munihaiku.com for poetic plaints about the Muni system.

www.lizhickok.com for photos of a model of SF made from Jell-O.

WHAT'S WHERE

1 Union Square. Home to a tourism trifecta: hotels, public transportation, and shopping. There are more hotel beds here than in any other neighborhood in the city; several transit options converge, including the cable cars. The square itself is dominated by flagship stores—but if you're not a shopper, this area may bore you.

2 Chinatown. Live fish flopping around on ice; the scent of incense, cigarettes, and vanilla; bargains announced in myriad Chinese dialects...you'll feel like you should have brought your passport.

3 SoMa. Anchored by SFMOMA and Yerba Buena Gardens, SoMa is a once-industrial neighborhood that's in transition. Luxury condos are going up and there are several cool dance clubs and restaurants, but some parts are still quite gritty.

4 Civic Center. Monumental city government buildings and performing arts venues, but also a chronic homeless magnet. Locals love Hayes Valley, the chic little neighborhood to the west.

5 Nob Hill. Topped by staid and elegant behemoths, hotels that ooze reserve and breeding, Nob Hill is old-money San Francisco.

6 Russian Hill. These steep streets hold a vibrant, classy neighborhood that's very au courant. Locals flock to Polk and Hyde streets, the hill's main commercial avenues, for excellent neighborhood eateries and fantastic window-shopping.

7 North Beach. The city's small Italian neighborhood makes even locals feel like they're on holiday. In the morning, fresh foccacia beckons, and there are few better ways to laze away an afternoon than in one of North Beach's cafés.

8 The Embarcadero. The city's northeastern waterfront is anchored at the foot of Market Street by the exquisitely restored Ferry Building. The promenade that starts in back has great views of the bay and the Bay Bridge.

9 The Northern Waterfront. Wandering the shops and so-called attractions of Fisherman's Wharf, Pier 39, and Ghirardelli Square, the only locals you'll meet will be a reluctant few with visitors in tow. Almost every business here is designed for tourists, so if you're looking for a souvenir shop...

10 Jackson Square. For history buffs and antiques lovers, this upscale corner of the Financial District is a pleasant diversion.

WHAT'S WHERE

11 The Marina. With fine-wine shops, trendy boutiques, fashionable cafés and restaurants, and pricey waterfront homes, the Marina is San Francisco's yuppiest neighborhood. It's also home to the exquisite 1915 Palace of Fine Arts.

12 The Presidio. Locals come to the Presidio, the wooded shoreline park just west of the Marina, for a quick in-town getaway, the spirit-lift only an amble on the sand in the shadow of the Golden Gate Bridge can provide.

13 Golden Gate Park. Covering more than 1,000 acres of greenery, with sports fields, windmills, museums, gardens, and a few buffalo thrown in for good measure, Golden Gate Park is San Francisco's backyard.

14 The Western Shoreline. A natural gem underappreciated by locals and visitors alike, the city's windswept Pacific shore stretches for miles.

15 The Haight. If you're looking for '60s souvenirs, you can find them here, along with some of the loveliest Victorians in town (and aggressive panhandling). Hip locals come for the great secondhand shops, cheap brunch, and low-key bars and cafés.

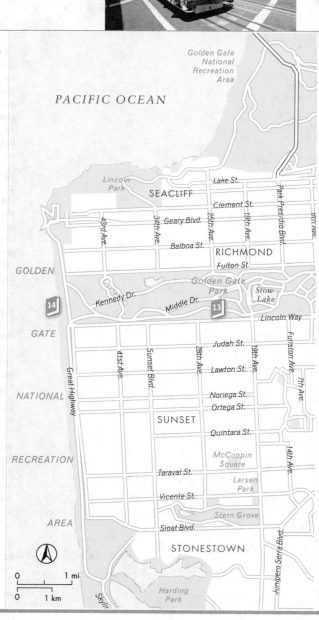

16 The Castro. Even with its rainbow-flag-waving, in-your-face style, the Castro is a friendly neighborhood that welcomes visitors of all stripes. Shop the trendy boutiques, and catch a film at the truly noteworthy Castro Theatre.

17 Noe Valley. Noe Valley is a cute, pricey neighborhood favored by young families. The main strip, 24th Street, is lined with coffee shops, eateries, and boutiques selling fancy bath products and trendy children's clothing.

18 The Mission District. When the sun sets, people descend on the Mission from all over the Bay Area for destination restaurants, excellent bargain-priced ethnic eateries, and the hippest bar scene around.

19 Pacific Heights. This neighborhood has some of San Francisco's most opulent real estate—but in most cases, you'll have to be content with an exterior view.

20 Japantown. Though a tight-knit Japanese-American population supports this area, there is little of interest to outsiders. If you do end up in Japantown, stick to the small streets north of Japan Center.

TOP SAN FRANCISCO ATTRACTIONS

Alcatraz

(A) Considering how many movies have been set here, you might feel like you've already "been there, done that"—but you really shouldn't miss a trip to America's most infamous federal pen. Husky-throated onetime inmates and grizzled former guards bring the Rock to life on the wonderful audio tour; you'll hear yarns about desperate escape attempts and notorious crooks like Al Capone while you walk the cold cement cellblock. But it's not all doom and gloom: you'll enjoy stunning views of the city skyline on the ferry ride to and from the island.

Golden Gate Bridge

(B) San Francisco's signature International Orange span is the city's majestic background, and about 10 million people a year head to the bridge for an up-close look. Walking the 1.7 mi to Marin County—inches from roaring traffic, steel shaking beneath your feet, and a far-too-low railing between you and the water 200 feet below—is much more than a superlative photo op (though it's that, too).

Fisherman's Wharf

(C) Once part of a thriving fishing industry, Fisherman's Wharf has deteriorated into a giant harpoon aimed straight at your wallet. Throngs from all over the world come to watch the flopping, barking, or napping sea lions; buy cheap T-shirts; and chow down on overpriced, mediocre food. It's all an utter mystery to locals, who don't come here. Ever. See the magnificent historic ships at the Hyde Street Pier, then take your money and run.

Golden Gate Park

(D) It may be world famous, but first and foremost the park is the city's backyard. Come here any day of the week, and you'll find a microcosm of San Francisco, from the Russian senior citizens feeding

the pigeons at Stow Lake to the moms pushing strollers through the botanical gardens to the arts boosters checking out the latest at the de Young Museum. Be sure to visit the park's iconic treasures, including the serene Japanese Tea Garden and the beautiful Victorian Conservatory of Flowers. If you have the time to venture farther into this urban oasis, you'll discover less-accessible gems like the Beach Chalet and the wild western shores of Ocean Beach.

Palace of Fine Arts

(E) Perched on a swan-filled lagoon near the Marina's yacht harbor, this stirringly beautiful terra-cotta-color dome has an otherworldly quality about it. Built for the 1915 Panama-Pacific International Exhibition, the palace is a San Francisco architect's version of a Roman ruin, and it's been eliciting gasps for almost a century. Try to see it from the water.

Coit Tower

(F) Most people assume that this stubby white tower atop Telegraph Hill is supposed to look like a fire hose. And considering that a fire truck–chasing, cross-dressing 19th-century socialite donated the funds to build it in honor of firefighters, maybe it is. The tower itself is of vague interest—it does house the history of San Francisco in murals—but the "park"(ing lot) at its base gives fantastic views of the city and the bay. The tower sits at the top of Telegraph Hill's Filbert Steps, a steep stairway through glorious gardens with vistas of transcendent beauty, an only-in–San Francisco spot locals cherish.

Cable Cars

(G) You've already seen them (on the big screen, in magazines, and, admit it, on the Rice-a-Roni™ box). And considering a ticket costs $5 a pop, do you really

need to ride a cable car? Yes, you do, at least once during your visit. Flag down a Powell–Hyde car along Powell Street, grab the pole, and clatter and jiggle up mansion-topped Nob Hill. Crest the hill, and hold on for the hair-raising descent to Fisherman's Wharf, with sun glittering off the bay and Alcatraz bobbing in the distance. Don't deny it—this would be a deal at twice the price.

AT&T Park

(H) One of the finest examples of modern "retro" ballparks, the Giants coastal digs are the perfect place to spend a sunny afternoon enjoying the national pastime. Grab a dog and some garlic fries, and revel in the bay views. If you're lucky, you'll get to see someone drill a splash hit into McCovey Cove.

Ferry Building

(I) Foodies rejoice! The historic Ferry Building is stuffed to the brim with all things tasty, including cafés, restaurants, a farmers' market, and merchants peddling everything from wine and olive oil to oysters and mushrooms. The building backs up to the bay, so the views are great—but they're even better from the decks of the departing ferries.

Wine Country

(J) You don't need to be a connoisseur to enjoy a trip to Napa or Sonoma...or both (hey, you're on vacation). But there's more to a wine country visit than vineyard tours and tastings: landmark restaurants, breathtaking scenery, fantastic artwork, hot air balloon rides, and secluded boutique hotels. And when you're ready for a break, a great glass of wine is never that far out of reach.

LOCAL FOR A DAY

Want to get a slice of local life by just hanging out, skipping the sightseeing? These experiences will let you pretend you're a San Franciscan, without a whopping rent check.

Shop the Ferry Plaza Farmers' Market
Roll out of bed and make your way to the Ferry Building—preferably on a Saturday—to join locals and celebrity chefs on a taste bud–driven raid. Out front and in back of the main building, farmer-run stands showcase the Bay Area's finest organic, free-range, low-food-mile goods. The indoor stalls will keep your mouth watering with artisanal cheeses, chocolates, and luscious pastries. Snag some takeaway food plus some perfectly ripe fruit for a picnic.

Stretch Your Legs in the Presidio
Spend a few hours wandering around this former military base at the foot of the Golden Gate Bridge. The park is redeveloping the old military buildings, along with ballfields and other rec areas. Join people walking their dogs on the wooded hiking trails or the paths of Crissy Field. On the waterfront, get in line for a cocoa at the Warming Hut.

Hang Out in Hayes Valley
Long beloved of artsy, cutting-edge locals, this quarter of cool cafés and high-design boutiques is either coming into its own or getting too big for its britches, depending on whom you ask. The renovation of Octavia Boulevard, one of this neighborhood's main arteries, makes Hayes Valley even busier. Grab a coffee from local cult microroasters Blue Bottle Coffee and check out the latest temporary art installation in Patricia's Green, the petite community park.

Find a Quiet Beach
Leave the beach near Fisherman's Wharf far behind and seek out these two instead. Breezy Baker Beach, tucked against the cliffs just south of the Golden Gate Bridge, is known for its bridge and ocean views—and its nudists, those hardy souls. A bit farther south, nestled in ultrapricey Seacliff, is China Beach, a smaller, more secluded spot that's never crowded.

Linger Over Breakfast
Notoriously food-centric San Franciscans are big on the most important meal of the day. The lines at popular breakfast places can be just as long as those at the hottest nightspots. Some longtime favorites include:

Mama's tried-and-true diner, where the line forms early (1701 Stockton St., at Filbert St., North Beach, 415/362–6421).

Kate's Kitchen, where heaping plates of Southern-inspired fare take the edge off a hairy-tongued Lower Haight morning after (471 Haight St., near Fillmore St., Lower Haight, 415/626–3984).

Ella's, where oatmeal and chicken hash are served alongside gussied-up standbys like brandied French toast (500 Presidio St., at California St., Pacific Heights, 415/441–5669).

Nurse a Coffee
Spend a few hours in the right independent café or coffeehouse and you'll feel like you're in a neighborhood living room. Come for a jolt of java, sometimes a reasonably priced meal, and usually Wi-Fi. Stay all afternoon—nobody minds—and you'll see the best reflection of a micro-community.

SAN FRANCISCO WITH KIDS

On the Move

Cable Cars. This one's a no-brainer. But don't miss the **Cable Car Terminus** at Powell and Market streets, where conductors push the iconic cars on giant turntables, and the **Cable Car Museum,** where you can see how cable cars work.

Adventure Cat Sailing. Them: playing on the trampoline at the bow of this 55-foot catamaran. You: enjoying a drink and the bay sunset on the stern deck.

F-Line Trolleys. Thomas the Tank Engine fan in tow? Hop on one of the F-line's neat historic streetcars. ■TIP➔ **Bonus: this line connects other kid-friendly sights, like Fisherman's Wharf and the Ferry Building.**

Sneak in Some Culture

Stern Grove Festival. Enjoying a delicious picnic in a eucalyptus grove, your kids might not even complain that they're listening to—gasp—classical music.

ODC/San Francisco. Best known for their holiday production of *The Velveteen Rabbit,* the dance troupe also holds other performances throughout the year.

San Francisco Mime Troupe. We know, it sounds lame. But these aren't your father's mimes.

The Great Outdoors

Muir Woods. If these massive trees look tall to you, imagine seeing them from two or three feet lower.

Stow Lake. When feeding bread to the ducks gets old (like that's ever going to happen), you can rent a rowboat, paddleboat, or electric motorboat.

Golden Gate Promenade. If your kids can handle a 3.3-mi walk, this one's a beauty—winding from Aquatic Park Beach, through the Presidio, to Fort Point Pier near the base of the Golden Gate Bridge.

Aquatic Park Beach. Does your brood include a wannabe Michael Phelps? Then head to this popular beach, one of the few places around the city where it's safe to swim. ■TIP➔ **Many other Bay Area beaches have powerful currents that make swimming dangerous.**

Just Plain Fun

AT&T Park. Emerald grass, a sun-kissed day, a hot dog in your hand...and suddenly, you're 10 again, too.

Dim Sum. A rolling buffet for which kids point and pick—likely an instant hit.

Fisherman's Wharf, Hyde Street Pier, Ghirardelli Square, and Pier 39. The phrase "tourist trap" may come to mind, but in this area you can get a shrimp cocktail, clamber around old ships, snack on chocolate, and laugh at the sea lions.

Musée Mécanique. How did people get by before PS3? Come here to find out.

Rooftop @ Yerba Buena Gardens. Head here for ice-skating, bowling, a carousel, a playground, and Zeum, an interactive arts and technology center.

San Francisco Zoo. Between Penguin Island, Lemur Forest, and Koala Crossing, you can make a day of it. Don't tease the animals.

Learn a Thing or Two

California Academy of Sciences. Dinosaurs, penguins, giant insects, snake feedings... what's not to like?

Exploratorium. A very hands-on science museum, including the full-immersion Tactile Dome.

GREAT
ITINERARIES

Bring Your Appetite

Start the day at the Ferry Building, which is stuffed with tempting produce, cafés, and artisanal treats. Nab a little something for breakfast, then take the California line cable car uphill to Chinatown. Walk along Grant Avenue and Stockton Street, peeking into mysterious herb apothecaries, live-seafood stores, and sweet-smelling tea shops before having a dim sum lunch or a steamed-bun snack.

Then head to North Beach for an espresso and pastry at one of the classic outdoor cafés. The Italian delis, bakeries, and pasta houses are worth visiting even if you can't eat another bite. Get your appetite back by making your way uphill to Coit Tower for sweeping views of the bay. (Climbing the steep stairways is a tough but scenically stunning way to do this.)

At the end of the day, either head back to North Beach's Columbus Avenue and let one of the restaurant hawkers talk you into coming in for pasta, or make the trip to the Mission District for fantastic, inexpensive ethnic food.

Work the Wharf

Fisherman's Wharf and the surrounding attractions may be touristy with a capital T, but there are some fun experiences to be had. With your prereserved ticket in hand (do this in advance since tours frequently sell out), set out for Alcatraz. When the ferry docks back at Pier 33, head north along the waterfront to Pier 39. If you're on a kitschy-souvenir hunt, browse through the pier's overpriced stores. Otherwise, check out the hundreds of sea lions basking on floating platforms next to the pier. Take a step back in time to early-20th-century San Francisco at

delightful Musée Mécanique, then grab an Irish coffee at the Buena Vista.

As tempting as it might be to dine on the water, most Fisherman's Wharf restaurants have less-than-spectacular food (Gary Danko is an exception). A better and cheaper option is to pick up some to-go Dungeness crab from one of the outdoor vendors and eat as you stroll along the waterfront. Or hop the Powell–Hyde or Powell–Mason cable-car line for better dining in Russian Hill and North Beach, respectively.

Art & Retail Therapy

Beat the crowds in the morning at SFMOMA (remember that it's closed Wednesday). The modern art collection is SoMa's main magnet, but there are several other museums to consider, too, such as the new Contemporary Jewish Museum, the Museum of the African Diaspora, and the San Francisco Craft and Folk Art Museum.

Take a break from exhibits across the street from SFMOMA in the expansive Yerba Buena Gardens. If you have kids in tow, drop by Metreon. Otherwise, head up 4th Street and join the masses at the Bloomingdale's-anchored Westfield San Francisco Shopping Centre and the shops around Union Square. This area isn't known for great restaurants, so when you get peckish, head to Belden Place. This bistro-lined alley (many places here are closed Sunday) is one of the few places around Union Square where locals dine.

To top off the evening, gaze down on the city lights from one of the square's skyview lounges like Harry Denton's Starlight Lounge.

Golden Gate Park

Golden Gate Park is better than usual on Sunday, when its main arteries are closed to cars (a more limited closure occurs on Saturday from April to September). Start your day at the glorious Conservatory of Flowers (closed Monday). Be sure to take in the scenes ingeniously rendered in flowers out front. Pace the wooden bridges and stone pathways of the Japanese Tea Garden before hitting the San Francisco Botanical Garden at Strybing Arboretum. Next up: the striking, controversial de Young Museum (closed Monday) and the glorious reopened California Academy of Sciences. Make your way west, stopping at Stow Lake, where you can rent a boat and paddle near Strawberry Hill. Back on land, continue west toward Ocean Beach and the endless Pacific. Cap off your tour by kicking back with a pint to enjoy the sunset ocean view at the Beach Chalet.

Find the Funky Neighborhoods

Ride the antique trolleys to the western end of the F-line in the Castro. Stroll down Castro Street, past the Art Deco Castro Theatre, window-shopping and stopping at any café that tempts you. Head east on 16th Street to Dolores Street and Mission Dolores, and wander rows of centuries-old gravestones in its tiny cemetery.

Then hit the "Valencia Corridor" (Valencia Street between 16th and 20th streets), dipping into independent bookstores, hipster cafés, and quirky shops. Seek out the area's vibrant, often politically charged murals, either on your own or on a tour with the Precita Eyes organization. Stay in the Mission for dinner and drinks; this is one of the city's best restaurant neighborhoods.

Take It to the Bridge

Start with a stroll and a search for picnic supplies in the Marina, before heading to the gorgeous Palace of Fine Arts. If you're traveling with kids, be sure to visit the Exploratorium (closed Monday) next door. Don't miss its bizarre-but-cool Tactile Dome.

Continue west into the Presidio park and make for Crissy Field, the marshland and sandy beach along the northern shore, for your picnic. With the Golden Gate Bridge view to inspire you, head onto or over the bridge itself. Be sure to wear comfortable shoes; the bridge is 1.7 mi across. Save this for a sunny day—and don't forget your jacket!

Bay Views & Real Estate Envy

Start at terraced Ina Coolbrith Park on Russian Hill for broad vistas of the bay. Ascend the Vallejo Steps and you're within easy reach of many of Russian Hill's hidden lanes. Explore famous Macondray Lane; then head around the corner to Leavenworth Street just north of Union Street and look left for the steps to equally lovely but virtually unknown Havens Place. Continue north to zigzag down crooked Lombard Street. If you still have some stamina, head west to Pacific Heights, where you can check out the Haas-Lilienthal House, a Queen Anne treasure, and scads of other Victorians. Want to snap a picture of that iconic row of "painted ladies" with the city's skyline in the background? You'll need to head to Alamo Square in the Western Addition (Hayes and Steiner streets). Finally, head back to Hyde Street for dinner at one of Russian Hill's trendy eateries.

TOP WALKING TOURS

- **All About Chinatown** (☎415/982–8839 ⊕*www.allaboutchinatown.com*). A delightful "behind-the-scenes" look at the neighborhood. Owner Linda Lee and her guides stop in Ross Alley and at a Buddhist temple. At herbal and food markets, you'll learn the therapeutic yield of fish stomachs and ponder uses for live partridges.

- **Chinatown Alleyway Tours** (☎415/984–1478 ⊕*www.chinatownalleyway tours.org*). To learn about the modern Chinatown community, join up with one of these young guides. Tour leaders, who all grew up here, discuss not only Chinatown's history but also current social issues.

- **Don Herron's Dashiell Hammett Tour** (⊕*www.donherron.com*). Brush up on your noir slang and join trench-coated guide Herron for a walk by the mystery writer's haunts and the locations from some of Hammett's novels.

- **Foot! Comedy Walking Tours** (☎415/793–5378 ⊕*www.foottours.com*). You'll likely find yourself breathless with laughter, not just gasping after a steep hill. The tour leaders are all moonlighting pro comedians; they've got offerings like "Nude, Lewd and Crude" North Beach.

- **Local Tastes of the City Tours** (☎415/665–0480 or 888/358–8687 ⊕*www.localtastesofthecitytours.com*). If you want to aggressively snack your way through a neighborhood as you walk it, consider hanging with cookbook author Tom Medin. You'll learn why certain things just taste better in San Francisco—like coffee and anything baked with sourdough—and you'll get tips about how to find good food

once you get back home. Along the way, you'll gradually gorge yourself into oblivion: the North Beach tour, for instance, might include multiple stops for coffee and baked goods.

- **Precita Eyes Mural Walks** (☎415/285–2287 ⊕*www.precitaeyes.org*). For an insider's look at the vibrant murals in the Mission District, this is the place to call. The nonprofit organization has nurtured this local art form from the get-go and they stay on top of all the latest additions. *See* the Mission District *chapter* for more details.

- **San Francisco City Guides** (☎415/557–4266 ⊕*www.sfcityguides.org*). An outstanding free service supported by the San Francisco Public Library. Walking tour themes range from individual neighborhoods to local history (the Gold Rush, the 1906 quake, ghost walks) to architecture. Each May and October additional walks are offered. Although the tours are free and the knowledgeable guides are volunteers, it's appropriate to make a $5 donation for these nonprofit programs. Tour schedules are available at library branches and the **San Francisco Visitor Information Center** (✉*Hallidie Plaza, lower level, Powell and Market Sts., Union Sq.* ☎415/391–2000, 415/392–0328 TDD ⊕*www.sfvisitor.org*).

- **Wok Wiz Chinatown Tour** (☎650/355–9657 ⊕*www.wokwiz.com*). Cookbook author Shirley Fong-Torres and her team lead these walks. Conversation topics include folklore and, of course, food. One version called "I Can't Believe I Ate My Way Through Chinatown!" includes breakfast and lunch.

FREE & ALMOST FREE

Despite—or perhaps because of—the astronomical cost of living here, San Francisco offers loads of free diversions. Here are our picks for the best free things to do in the city, in alphabetical order. (That is, in addition to the free theater that is life in San Francisco's neighborhoods, parks, beaches, churches, and other public spaces.)

Museums & Galleries That Are Always Free

Chinese Culture Center
Creativity Explored
Fort Point National Historic Site
Museo Italo-Americano
Octagon House
Randall Museum
San Francisco Cable Car Museum
San Francisco Railway Museum
SFMOMA Artists Gallery
Tattoo Art Museum
Walter & McBean Galleries at the San Francisco Art Institute
Wells Fargo History Museum

Free Museum Times

The first week of every month is a bonanza of free museum times.

Asian Art Museum, first Tuesday of every month

California Academy of Sciences, first Wednesday of every month

Cartoon Art Museum, first Tuesday of every month is pay-what-you-wish

Chinese Historical Society of America, first Thursday of every month

Contemporary Jewish Museum, third Monday of every month

de Young Museum, first Tuesday of every month

Exploratorium, first Wednesday of every month

Legion of Honor, first Tuesday of every month

Museum of Craft and Folk Art, first Tuesday of every month

San Francisco Museum of Craft + Design, first Thursday of every month, 5–7 PM

San Francisco Museum of Modern Art, first Tuesday of every month

Yerba Buena Center for the Arts (galleries), first Tuesday of every month

Free Concerts

■ Stern Grove Festival concerts, held on Sunday afternoons from June through August, are a longstanding city tradition. Performances range from opera to jazz to pop music. The amphitheater is in a beautiful eucalyptus grove, so come early and picnic before the show.

■ The Golden Gate Park Band plays free public concerts on Sunday afternoons, April through October, on the Music Concourse in the namesake park. You might hear anything from Sousa marches to showtunes.

■ The San Francisco Conservatory of Music offers frequent free recitals year-round.

■ Yerba Buena Gardens Festival hosts many concerts and events from May through October (sometimes almost daily), including Latin jazz, global music, dance, even puppet shows.

Free Tours

- The San Francisco City Guides walking tours are easily one of the best deals going. Knowledgeable, enthusiastic guides lead walks that focus on a particular neighborhood, theme, or historical period, like Victorian architecture in Alamo Square or the bawdy days of the Barbary Coast. The tours are free, though a $5 donation is welcome.

- City Hall offers free tours of its grandiose HQ on weekdays.

More Great Experiences for $5 or Less

- See some baseball at AT&T Park, for free! Go to the stadium's Portwalk, beyond the outfield wall, and you'll have a standing-room view of the game through the open fence. The fans who watch here are known as the Knothole Gang. BYO peanuts.

- Visit the Golden Gate Fortune Cookie Factory in Chinatown. This is technically free, although you'll have to resist the temptation to take photos (a 50¢ fee) and buy cookies. There are several nearby spots where you can get a delicious snack for just a dollar or two, like the custard tarts at Golden Gate Bakery. Stop in one or two of Chinatown's incense-filled temples, too—it's best to give a small donation, but you'll feel a world away.

- Do your own walking tour of the Mission District's fantastic outdoor murals, then grab a bite at a taqueria or taco truck.

- Walk across the Golden Gate Bridge—an obvious but breathtaking choice.

- Choose a perfect treat at the Ferry Building's fabulous marketplace—maybe a scoop of Ciao Bello gelato or a croissant from Miette—and stroll the waterfront promenade toward the Bay Bridge to Cupid's Span, the giant bow and arrow sculpture impaling Rincon Park.

- Visit the Diego Rivera mural at the San Francisco Art Institute, then sip a cuppa at the school's café and check out the million-dollar view from its North Beach perch.

- Tour the grounds around the Palace of Fine Arts, circling its swan-filled lagoon. Next, walk through the Presidio to the Letterman Digital Arts Center campus. Visit the Yoda fountain, then peek inside the building beyond to see a life-size Darth Vader figure. To further explore the Presidio, you can hop the free PresidiGo shuttle. (The Presidio also has lots of free parking.)

- Check out the offerings at lively El Rio bar in the Mission District. They often have free live music and very cheap drink specials.

- Hike up to the top of Telegraph Hill for sweeping city and bay views. Since the surrounding trees aren't trimmed back, the view isn't quite as terrific as the one from the hill's Coit Tower, but it's still a knockout.

- If you're in town on the second Thursday of the month, head to the Mission for Dolores Park Movie Night. Screenings, which start at dusk, are free—check the schedule at www.doloresparkmovie.org.

- Ride a cable car. We hate to harp on this, but you gotta do it at least once.

OFFBEAT SF

Looking for an unusual San Francisco experience that'll give you bragging rights? Try one of these quirky choices—even a local would be impressed.

- **ATA.** Dedicated to getting anyone's art in front of an audience, Artists' Television Access has been showing films by local artists for more than 20 years. An open-minded crowd comes to ATA's tiny space, where $5 gets you a peek at what might be the next groundbreaker. *www.atasite.org*

- **Audium.** Billed as a "theater of sound-sculptured space," Audium is an experience like no other. Every Friday and Saturday, a few dozen participants sit in concentric circles in a completely soundproofed room in utter darkness, and music plays over the 169 speakers strategically placed, well, everywhere. *www.audium.org*

- **Mt. Davidson.** Ask most San Franciscans what the highest point in town is and they'll likely say Twin Peaks, but it's actually this "mountain," the next hill over. Visible from all over town but rarely visited, Mt. Davidson is topped with a eucalyptus-filled park. Finding the road up here is tricky (entrance at Dalewood and Myra ways), but once you get there you'll have amazing views—while all those tourists are still waiting for a parking space on Twin Peaks.

- **Qoöl at 111 Minna.** The granddaddy of the gallery-cum-house-party scene, this hip SoMa loft is packed to the gills on Wednesday with a friendly, artsy crowd. The art is edgy, the DJ sets are potent, the drinks are stiff, and the party kicks off at 5 PM. *www.qoolsf.com*

- **16th Avenue Steps.** Just standing at the base of this glorious mosaic of a stairway in the Inner Sunset is a treat: its underwater theme gives way to daytime dragonflies and butterflies, eventually transitioning to a starry, bat-studded night sky. Hike to the top, and you may have tiny Grand View Park all to yourself. The view is, well, grand. Moraga St., between 15th and 16th Aves.

- **Slides at AT&T Park.** The massive Coke bottle looming over the AT&T ballpark is a familiar sight, but most people don't know that you can slide inside. The Coca-Cola Superslide has a series of slides twisting and turning down the bottle's contours. Kids aren't the only ones who get a kick out of the 56-foot "Guzzlers" and the 20-foot "Twist-Offs." It's open for free on some nongame days.

- **The Tamale Lady.** It's impossible to pin down her location but if you're out and about in the Mission of an evening, keep an eye peeled for this San Francisco legend. Her tamales are terrific but the real reason that she's revered is her supernatural ability to show up in a bar and provide protein at the critical moment in a bender.

- **Third Thursdays at the Cal Academy of Sciences.** Supersized snakes, waddling penguins, and taxidermy are cool anytime, but throw in a cash bar and this science club gets even cooler. Join an in-the-know crowd knocking back drinks and handling wild animals (with help from the academy's staffers) from 5 PM to 9 PM. *www.calacademy.org*

GET OUTTA TOWN

Marin County

Marin County beckons from the other side of the Golden Gate Bridge—the ultimate playground for anyone who likes being outdoors. Hordes of visitors crane their necks at the huge redwoods in Muir Woods National Monument; mountain bikers zoom down Mt. Tamalpais; and scenery buffs head to the Marin Headlands, Stinson Beach, and the Point Reyes National Seashore to gaze at the vast Pacific. Over 40% of Marin County is parkland, so there are plenty of places to hike and reconnect with nature.

The towns in Marin are small and low-key, with varying degrees of chic. There's Sausalito with its yachts and boutiques; Tiburon with its gallery-lined Main Street; and Mill Valley with its redwood groves and reclusive rock stars. Places like Stinson Beach and Bolinas, meanwhile, are for those who truly want to get away from anything urban. Lots of bed-and-breakfasts and hotels in Marin are geared for weekend retreats—it's the perfect place to drop out of sight for a few days. Taking a ferry here from San Francisco will make your getaway even more romantic.

East Bay (Berkeley & Oakland)

To San Franciscans, the East Bay is shorthand for Berkeley and Oakland, both across the Bay Bridge from the city. Berkeley is defined by its University of California campus and its liberal-to-radical politics. Ever since the Free Speech Movement ignited at the Cal campus in the 1960s, Berkeley has been the place for renegade spirits, bursting bookstores, and caffeine-fueled debates. It's not all intellectual-politico jargon, though; there are plenty of creature comforts, too. Most famously, there's Chez Panisse, the restaurant that embodies seasonal, simple, local cooking—but there are countless tasty treasures to be sampled in Berkeley's Gourmet Ghetto. Or you could shop for indie tracks at Amoeba Music, obscure tomes at Cody's Books, and the perfect bottle of Sancerre at Kermit Lynch Wine Merchant.

Oakland is grittier and even more diverse, with a buzzing arts scene. Small pockets of the city are pretty dodgy, so it's important to know where you're going. Old Oakland has a concentration of evocative Victorian buildings, now full of cafés and shops; the Rockridge neighborhood is home to lovely Market Hall, a European-style market. Jack London Square may be the best place to get a sense of Oakland's role as a major port, but it feels pretty sterile. Head to a jazz joint like Yoshi's or a gallery-bar like Café van Kleef, though, and you'll feel the city's indomitable energy.

Wine Country

With rolling, vine-covered hills, warm weather, and incredibly good restaurants, hotels, and spas, the Sonoma and Napa valleys are the places to indulge yourself. Whether you're passionate about wine or a curious newcomer, you'll find dozens upon dozens of tasting rooms and wineries that are right for you. Some of the world's most high-profile vintners work here, but there are also plenty of under-the-radar local stars to discover. Don't overlook the towns in your rush to the vineyards, though. Places like Napa, Sonoma, Healdsburg, Glen Ellen, and Calistoga have lovely, historic centers, farmers' markets, and tempting shops. You can get to the Wine Country in less than two hours by car—but the experience does not come cheap.

FESTIVALS & PARADES

San Francisco's major parades and festivals are notoriously creative, energetic, and often off-the-wall. Among the hundreds of events on the city's annual calendar, here are the ones that are especially characteristic and fun.

- **Chinese New Year, February.** This celebration in North America's largest Chinatown lasts for almost three weeks. The grand finale is the spectacularly loud, crowded, and colorful Golden Dragon Parade, which rocks with firecrackers. If you don't want to wait on the sidewalk for hours in advance, buy bleacher seats. Contact the Chinese Chamber of Commerce (☎415/982–3071 ⊕www.chineseparade.com) for more info.

- **St. Patrick's Day, March.** Held on the Saturday closest to March 17, the festival (⊕www.sfstpatricksdayparade.com) includes snake races and a parade through downtown. Local bars get in the spirit by selling green-tinted beer (urp).

- **St. Stupid's Day Parade, April.** The First Church of the Last Laugh (⊕www.saintstupid.com) holds this fantastically funny event on—when else—April 1. It wanders through the Financial District, with hundreds of people dressed up in elaborate costumes (although there are fewer drag queens than on Halloween). Parade-goers toss socks at the Stock Exchange, throw pennies at the angular sculpture in front of the Bank of America building called the "banker's heart," and sing their way down Columbus Avenue.

- **San Francisco International Film Festival, April–May.** The country's longest-running film festival packs in audiences with premieres, international films, and rarities. Check their listings (☎415/561–5000 ⊕www.sfiff.org) well in advance for tickets.

- **Cinco de Mayo Festival, May.** On the Sunday closest to May 5, the Mission District boils with activity, including a vibrant parade, Mexican music, and dancing in the streets.

- **Lesbian, Gay, Bisexual, and Transgender Pride Celebration, June.** More than half a million people come to join the world's largest pride event, with a downtown parade roaring to a start by leather-clad Dykes on Bikes. If you're visiting around this time, book your hotel *far* ahead (☎415/864–3733 or 415/677–7959 ⊕www.sfpride.com).

- **San Francisco Open Studios, October.** More than 700 artists open their studios to the public. It's a great window into the local fine arts scene (☎415/861–9838 ⊕www.artspan.org).

- **Dance-Along Nutcracker, December.** This fabulous holiday tradition, part spoof and part warmhearted family event, was started by the San Francisco Lesbian/Gay Freedom Band (⊕www.sflgfb.org). You can join the dancers onstage for some free-form choreography, or simply toss snowflakes from the audience.

CABLE CARS

The moment it dawns on you that you severely underestimated the steepness of the San Francisco hills when setting out for a stroll will likely be the same moment you look down and realize those tracks aren't just for show—or just for tourists.

Sure, locals rarely use the cable cars for commuting these days. (That's partially due to the recent fare hikes—hear that, Muni?) So you'll likely be packed in with plenty of fellow sightseers. You may even be approaching cable car fatigue after seeing its image on so many souvenirs. But if you fear the magic is gone, simply climb on board and those jaded thoughts will dissolve. Grab the pole and gawk at the view as the car clanks down an insanely steep grade toward the bay. Listen to the humming cable, the clang of the bell, and the occasional quip from the gripman. It's an experience you shouldn't pass up, whether on your first trip or your fiftieth.

HOW CABLE CARS WORK

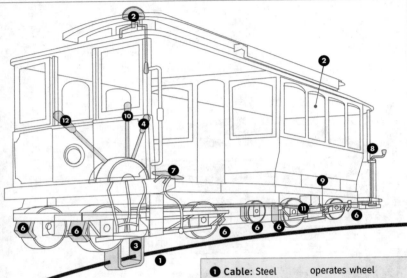

The mechanics are pretty simple: cable cars grab a moving subterranean cable with a "grip" to go. To stop, they release the grip and apply one or more types of brakes. Four cables, totaling 9 miles, power the city's three lines. If the gripman doesn't adjust the grip just right when going up a steep hill, the cable will start to slip and the car will have to back down the hill and try again. This is an extremely rare occurrence—imagine the ribbing the gripman gets back at the cable car barn!

Gripman: Stands in front and operates the grip, brakes, and bell. Favorite joke, especially at the peak of a steep hill: "This is my first day on the job folks..."

Conductor: Stands in the back, deals with tickets, alerts the grip about what's coming up, and operates the rear wheel brakes.

❶ Cable: Steel wrapped around flexible sisal core; 2 inches thick; runs at a constant 9½ mph.

❷ Bells: Used for crew communication; alerts other drivers and pedestrians.

❸ Grip: Vice-like lever extends through the center slot in the track to grab or release the cable.

❹ Grip Lever: Left-hand lever; operates grip.

❺ Car: Entire car weighs 8 tons.

❻ Wheel Brake: Steel brake pads on each wheel.

❼ Wheel Brake Lever: Foot pedal; operates wheel brakes.

❽ Rear Wheel Brake Lever: Applied for extra traction on hills.

❾ Track Brake: 2-foot long sections of Monterey pine push down against the track to help stop the car.

❿ Track Brake Lever: Middle lever; operates track brakes.

⓫ Emergency Brake: 18-inch steel wedge, jams into street slot to bring car to an immediate stop.

⓬ Emergency Brake Lever: Right-hand lever, red; operates emergency brake.

ROUTES

Cars run at least every 15 minutes, from around 6 AM to about 1 AM.

Powell–Hyde line: Most scenic, with classic Bay views. Begins at Powell and Market streets, then crosses Nob Hill and Russian Hill before a white-knuckle descent down Hyde Street, ending near the Hyde Street Pier.

Powell–Mason line: Also begins at Powell and Market streets, but winds through North Beach to Bay and Taylor streets, a few blocks from Fisherman's Wharf.

California line: Runs from the foot of Market Street, at Drumm Street, up Nob Hill and back. Great views (and aromas and sounds) of Chinatown on the way up. Sit in back to catch glimpses of the Bay. ■ TIP→ **Take the California line if it's just the cable-car experience you're after—the lines are shorter, and the grips and conductors say it's friendlier and has a slower pace.**

RULES OF THE RIDE

Tickets. A whopping $5 each way. There are ticket booths at all three turnarounds, or you can pay the conductor after you board (they can make change). Try not to grumble about the price—they're embarrassed enough as it is.

■ TIP→ **If you're planning to use public transit a few times, or if you'd like to ride back and forth on the cable car without worrying about the price, consider a one-day Muni passport ($11). You can get passports online, at the Powell Street turnaround, the TIX booth on Union Square, or the Fisherman's Wharf cable-car ticket booth at Beach and Hyde streets.**

All Aboard. You can board on either side of the cable car. It's legal to stand on the running boards and hang on to the pole, but keep your ears open for the gripman's warnings. ■ TIP→ **Grab a seat on the outside bench for the best views.**

Most people wait (and wait) in line at one of the cable car turnarounds, but you can also hop on along the route. Board wherever you see a white sign showing a figure climbing aboard a brown cable car; wave to the approaching driver, and wait until the car stops.

Taking a spin on the Hyde St. turntable.

CABLE CAR HISTORY

HALLIDIE FREES THE HORSES

In the 1850s and '60s, San Francisco's streetcars were drawn by horses. Legend has it that the horrible sight of a car dragging a team of horses downhill to their deaths roused Andrew Smith Hallidie to action. The English immigrant had invented the "Hallidie Ropeway," essentially a cable car for mined ore, and he was convinced that his invention could also move people. In 1873, Hallidie and his intrepid crew prepared to test the first cable car high on Russian Hill. The anxious engineer peered down into the foggy darkness, failed to see the bottom of the hill, and promptly turned the controls over to Hallidie. Needless to say, the thing worked...but rides were free for the first two days because people were afraid to get on.

SEE IT FOR YOURSELF

The **Cable Car Museum** is one of the city's best free offerings and an absolute must for kids. (You can even ride a cable car there, since all three lines stop between Russian Hill and Nob Hill.) The museum, which is inside the city's last cable-car barn, takes the top off the system to let you see how it all works.

Eternally humming and squealing, the massive powerhouse cable wheels steal the show. You can also climb aboard a vintage car and take the grip, let the kids ring a cable-car bell (briefly), and check out vintage gear dating from 1873.

✉ *1201 Mason St., at Washington St., Nob Hill* ☎ *415/474–1887* ⊕ *www.cablecarmuseum.com* ✉ *Free* ⊗ *Oct.–Mar., daily 10–5; Apr.–Sept., daily 10–6*

■ **TIP→** The gift shop sells cable car paraphernalia, including an authentic gripman's bell for $600 (it'll sound like Powell Street in your house every day). For significantly less, you can pick up a key chain made from a piece of worn-out cable.

CHAMPION OF THE CABLE CAR BELL

Each July the city's best and brightest come together to crown a bell-ringing champion at Union Square. The crowd cheers gripmen and conductors as they stomp, shake, and riff with the rope. But it's not a popularity contest; the ringers are judged by former bell-ringing champions who take each ping and gong very seriously.

Union Square & Chinatown

Chinatown gate at Grant Avenue

WORD OF MOUTH

"I've been in Chinatown a few times recently, and I'm seeing changes on Grant. While many of the old, kitschy souvenir shops are still around, some have been refurbished and it looks like the next generation has taken over. . . . I know everyone says this stretch of Chinatown is horrible and touristy, and while it still seems touristy, I was surprised by how much I found that I honestly liked."

—wandergrrl

GETTING ORIENTED

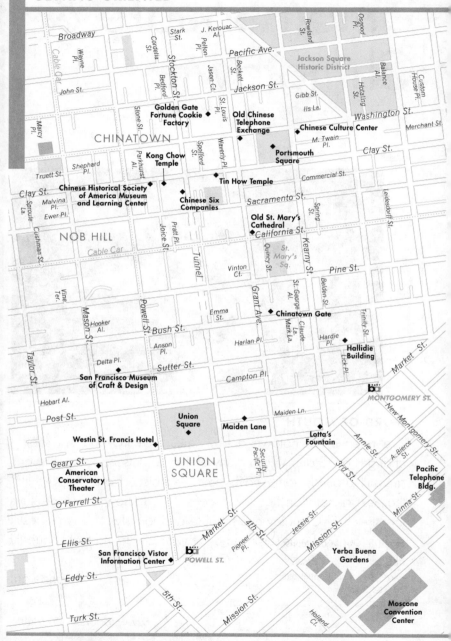

TOP 5 REASONS TO GO

Ross Alley, Chinatown: Breathe deep as you watch the nimble hands at Golden Gate Fortune Cookie Factory, then relax with a cocktail at Li Po around the corner, rumored to be haunted by the ghost of an opium junkie still looking to score.

Return to noir San Francisco: Have a late martini lunch at John's Grill, then swing through the lobby of the Flood Building and nod to the Maltese Falcon.

Shop the Square: Prime your credit cards and dive right in, from Bloomie's to the boutiques of Maiden Lane.

Tin How Temple: Climb the narrow stairway to this space with hundreds of red lanterns, then step onto the tiny balcony and take in the alley scene below.

Elevator at the St. Francis: Ride a glass elevator to the sky (or the 32nd floor) for a gorgeous view of the cityscape, especially in the evening when the lights come up.

QUICK BITES

If your blood sugar's low, head into the Virgin Megastore and upstairs to **Citizen Cupcake** (⊠ *2 Stockton St., Union Square* ☎ *415/399–1565*) for a namesake sweet, either classic (chocolate) or modern (rose-saffron, date-toffee). There are some savories, too, like tamales and grilled sandwiches. The big-city views out the tall windows are a bonus.

Eastern Bakery (⊠ *720 Grant Ave., Chinatown* ☎ *415/433–7973*) claims to be the oldest bakery in Chinatown. The packed little space has become a must-stop on the tourist trail. But it's not just a tourist trap, since the dirt-cheap steamed pork buns make a terrific quick lunch on the go.

If you're after a substantial bite to eat, duck into the **Irish Bank** (⊠ *10 Mark La., Union Square* ☎ *415/788–7152*), across from the Chinatown Gate, for fish-and-chips.

GETTING THERE

In these two neighborhoods, cars equal hassle. Traffic is slow and parking is pricey. Save yourself the frustration and take advantage of the confluence of public transit at Powell and Market streets; buses, BART (Powell Street station), cable cars, and F-line streetcars run here.

For the love of Buddha, don't drive in Chinatown! The steep, narrow, one-way streets are notoriously difficult to navigate by car. Both Powell lines of the cable car system pass through. You can also take the 30—Stockton bus; this route is a virtual "Chinatown Express," running from Fisherman's Wharf down Stockton Street through Chinatown to Union Square.

If you're determined to drive, there are several garages available. *See* "Where Can I Find" later in this chapter.

MAKING THE MOST OF YOUR TIME

Set aside at least an hour to scope out the stores and sights in and around Union Square—or most of the day if you're a shopper—but don't bother arriving before 10 AM, when the first shops open. Sunday is a bit quieter.

Give yourself at least two hours to see compact Chinatown. If possible, come on a weekday (less crowded) and before lunchtime (busiest with locals). You won't need more than 15 or 20 minutes at any of the sights themselves, but exploring the shops and alleys is, indeed, the whole point.

UNION SQUARE & CHINATOWN

Sightseeing
☆☆★★★

Nightlife
☆☆☆☆★

Dining
☆☆★★★

Lodging
☆★★★★

Shopping
★★★★★

By Denise M. Leto

The Union Square area bristles with big-city bravado, while just a stone's throw away is a place that feels like a city unto itself, Chinatown. The two areas share a strong commercial streak, although manifested very differently. In Union Square, the crowds zigzag among international brands, trailing glossy shopping bags. A few blocks north, people dash between small neighborhood stores, their arms draped with plastic totes filled with groceries or souvenirs.

In Union Square, the city's finest department stores put on their best faces, along with such exclusive emporiums as Tiffany & Co. and Prada, and such big-name franchises as Niketown, Apple Store, Virgin Megastore, H&M, and Barney's. Visitors lay their heads at several dozen hotels within a three-block walk of the square, and the downtown theater district and many fine arts galleries are nearby. By any measure, Union Square is shop-centric; if you're not that into shopping, you can find little beyond buildings of vague historical interest to entice you here.

A few blocks uphill is the abrupt beginning of dense and insular Chinatown—the oldest such community in the country. When the street signs have Chinese characters, produce stalls crowd pedestrians off the sidewalk, and folks scurry by with telltale pink plastic shopping bags, you'll know you're there. (The neighborhood huddles together in the 17 blocks and 41 alleys bordered roughly by Bush, Kearny, and Powell streets and Broadway.) Chinatown has been attracting the curious for more than 100 years, and no neighborhood in the city absorbs as many tourists without seeming to forfeit its character. Join the flow and step into another world. Good-luck banners of crimson and gold hang beside dragon-entwined lampposts and pagoda roofs, while honking cars chime in with shoppers bargaining loudly in Cantonese or Mandarin.

WHAT TO SEE IN UNION SQUARE

American Conservatory Theater. The 1906 earthquake destroyed all eight of downtown San Francisco's theaters, and this one, a neoclassical stunner, stepped up to the plate a year later. Today it's inextricably linked with its eponymous repertory company, known for award-winning productions by major playwrights such as Tony Kushner (*Angels in America*) and Tom Stoppard (premieres of *Indian Ink*, *The Invention of Love*) and cutting-edge works such as *The Black Rider* by Tom Waits, William S. Burroughs, and Robert Wilson. Damaged heavily in the 1989 earthquake, the building has been beautifully restored. ⊠ *415 Geary St., box office at 405 Geary St., Union Square* ☎ *415/749–2228.*

CABLE CAR TERMINUS

Two of the three cable car lines begin and end their runs at Powell and Market streets, a couple of blocks south of Union Square. These two lines are the most scenic, and both pass near Fisherman's Wharf, so they're usually clogged with first-time sightseers. The wait to board a cable car at this intersection is longer than at any other stop in the system. If you'd rather avoid the mob, board the less-touristy California line at the bottom of Market Street, at Drumm Street. For more info on the cable cars, *see the Experience chapter.*

Hallidie Building. Named for cable-car inventor Andrew S. Hallidie, this 1918 structure is best viewed from across the street. Willis Polk's revolutionary glass-curtain wall—believed to be the world's first such facade—hangs a foot beyond the reinforced concrete of the frame. The reflecting glass, decorative exterior fire escapes that appear to be metal balconies, and Venetian Gothic cornice are notably lovely. ⊠ *130 Sutter St., between Kearny and Montgomery Sts., Union Square.*

Lotta's Fountain. Saucy gold rush–era actress, singer, and dancer Lotta Crabtree so aroused the city's miners that they were known to shower her with gold nuggets and silver dollars after her performances. The peculiar, rather clunky fountain was her way of saying thanks to her fans. Given to the city in 1875, the fountain became a meeting place for survivors after the 1906 earthquake. Each April 18, the anniversary of the quake, San Franciscans—including an ever-dwindling handful of survivors—gather at this quirky monument. You can see an image of Lotta herself in one of the Anton Refregier murals in Rincon Center. ⊠ *Traffic triangle at intersection of 3rd, Market, Kearny, and Geary Sts., Union Square.*

Maiden Lane. Known as Morton Street in the raffish Barbary Coast era, this former red-light district reported at least one murder a week during the late 19th century. Things cooled down after the 1906 fire destroyed the brothels, and these days Maiden Lane is a chic, boutique-lined pedestrian mall stretching two blocks, between Stockton and Kearny streets. Wrought-iron gates close the street to traffic most days between 11 and 5, when the lane becomes a patchwork of umbrella-shaded tables.

At **140 Maiden Lane** you can see the only Frank Lloyd Wright building in San Francisco. Walking through the brick archway and recessed entry feels a bit like entering a glowing cave. The interior's graceful, curving ramp and skylights are said to have been his model for the Guggenheim Museum in New York. Xanadu Tribal Arts, a gallery showcasing Baltic, Latin-American, and African folk art, now occupies the space. ⊠ *Between Stockton and Kearny Sts., Union Square.*

San Francisco Museum of Craft + Design. You could be forgiven for walking by this museum, thinking that it's a private office or boutique. No one expects a front garden—a garden!—in this pack-in-every-square-foot neighborhood. It's a serene welcome to this stark three-room space, which opened in 2004. Quarterly exhibits focus on modern design of all sorts, from fanciful furniture to designer toys to wine labels. Whether you should visit depends entirely on the exhibit: if the theme grabs you, it's well worth coming by. ⊠ *550 Sutter St., Union Square* ☎ *415/773–0303* ⊕ *www. sfmcd.com* ⊠ *$3 donation* ☉ *Tues., Wed., Fri., and Sat. 10–5, Thurs. 10–7, Sun. noon–5.*

San Francisco Visitor Information Center. A multilingual staff operates this facility below the cable-car terminus. Staffers answer questions and provide maps and pamphlets. You can also pick up discount coupons—the savings can be significant, especially for families—and hotel brochures here. ⊠ *Hallidie Plaza, lower level, Powell and Market Sts., Union Square* ☎ *415/391–2000 or 415/283–0177* ⊕ *www.onlyinsan francisco.com* ☉ *Weekdays 9–5, Sat. 9–3; also Sun. 9–3 in May–Oct.*

Union Square. The heart of San Francisco's downtown since 1850, a 2½-acre square surrounded by department stores and the St. Francis Hotel, is about the only place you can sit for free in this part of town. The public responded to Union Square's 2002 redesign with a resounding shrug. With its pretty landscaping, easier street access, and the addition of a café (welcome, but nothing special), it's certainly an improvement over the old concrete wasteland, but no one's beating a path downtown to hang out here. Four globular lamp sculptures by the artist R. M. Fischer preside over the space; there's also an open-air stage, a visitor information booth, and a front-row seat to the cable-car tracks. And there's a familiar kaleidoscope of characters: office workers sunning and brown-bagging, street musicians, shoppers taking a rest, kids chasing pigeons, and a fair number of homeless people.

LITTLE SAIGON

The best Vietnamese food in the city is west of Union Square, along Larkin Street between Eddy and O'Farrell streets, where 80% of the businesses are owned by Vietnamese-Americans. Marketing types call this corridor Little Saigon; locals call it the Tenderloin, AKA the hood. If working girls and drug dealers can't come between you and your *pho* (beef-broth noodle soup), you can find cheap, often fantastic food here. Check out Pho Hoa for pho, Saigon Sandwiches for *bánh mì* (unsurprisingly, Vietnamese sandwiches), and Pagolac for excellent everything. And if you come for dinner, take a cab.

The square takes its name from the violent pro-union demonstrations staged here before the Civil War. At center stage, Robert Ingersoll Aitken's *Victory Monument* commemorates Commodore George Dewey's victory over the Spanish fleet at Manila in 1898. The 97-foot Corinthian column, topped by a bronze figure symbolizing naval conquest, was dedicated by Theodore Roosevelt in 1903 and withstood the 1906 earthquake.

FANTASY FOUNTAIN

In front of the Grand Hyatt hotel at 345 Stockton Street gurgles an intricate bronze fountain depicting San Francisco. It's one of many local public works by Ruth Asawa, the city's "fountain lady." Look closely at this one and you can find an amorous couple behind one of the Victorian bay windows.

After the earthquake and fire of 1906, the square was dubbed Little St. Francis because of the temporary shelter erected for residents of the St. Francis Hotel. Actor John Barrymore, the grandfather of actress Drew Barrymore and a notorious carouser, was among the guests pressed into volunteering to stack bricks in the square. His uncle, thespian John Drew, remarked, "It took an act of God to get John out of bed and the United States Army to get him to work."

On the eastern edge of Union Square, **TIX Bay Area** (☎*415/433–7827 info only* ⊛*www.theatrebayarea.org*) provides half-price day-of-performance tickets (cash or traveler's checks only) to all types of performing-arts events, as well as regular full-price box-office services. Union Square covers a convenient but expensive four-level underground garage. ⊠*Bordered by Powell, Stockton, Post, and Geary Sts., Union Square.*

Westin St. Francis Hotel. The second-oldest hotel in the city, established in 1904, was conceived by railroad baron and financier Charles Crocker and his associates as a hostelry for their millionaire friends. Swift service and sumptuous surroundings have always been hallmarks of the property. After the hotel was ravaged by the 1906 fire, a larger, more luxurious Italian Renaissance–style residence was opened in 1907 to attract loyal clients from among the world's rich and powerful. The hotel's checkered past includes the ill-fated 1921 bash in the suite of the silent-film comedian Fatty Arbuckle, at which a woman became ill and later died. Arbuckle endured three sensational trials for rape and murder before being acquitted, by which time his career was kaput. In 1975 Sara Jane Moore, standing among a

---

PUT YOUR HANDS TOGETHER

For a rockin' gospel concert and inclusive, feel-good vibe, head to **Glide Memorial Church** (⊠*Ellis and Taylor Sts.*) on the edge of the sketchy Tenderloin, Sunday mornings at 9 and 11. Reverend Cecil Williams, a bear of a man, is a local celeb do-gooder who leads a hand-clapping, shout-it-out, get-on-your-feet "celebration" that attracts a diverse and enthusiastic crowd. Visitors—gay and straight, all colors of the rainbow, religious or not—are welcome (and plentiful). You might recognize the church from the film *Pursuit of Happyness*.

crowd outside the hotel, attempted to shoot then-president Gerald Ford. As might be imagined, no plaques in the lobby commemorate these events. ■TIP➔ **One of the best views in the city is from the glass elevators here—and best of all, it's free. Zip up to the 32nd floor for a bird's-eye view; the lights of the nighttime cityscape are particularly lovely.** Don't be shy if you're not a guest: some visitors make this a stop every time they're in town. ✉ *335 Powell St., at Geary St., Union Square* ☎ *415/397–7000* ⊕ *www.westinstfrancis.com.*

> **LOOK UP!**
>
> When wandering around Chinatown, don't forget to look up! Above the chintziest souvenir shop might loom an ornate balcony or a curly pagoda roof. The best examples are on the 900 block of Grant Avenue (at Washington Street) and at Waverly Place.

WHAT TO SEE IN CHINATOWN

Chinatown Gate. This is the official entrance to Chinatown. Stone lions flank the base of the pagoda-topped gate; the lions, dragons, and fish up top symbolize wealth, prosperity, and other good things. The four Chinese characters immediately beneath the pagoda represent the philosophy of Sun Yat-sen (1866–1925), the leader who unified China in the early 20th century. Sun Yat-sen, who lived in exile in San Francisco for a few years, promoted the notion of friendship and peace among all nations based on equality, justice, and goodwill. The vertical characters under the left pagoda read "peace" and "trust," the ones under the right pagoda "respect" and "love." The whole shebang usually telegraphs the internationally understood message of "photo op." ✉ *Grant Ave. at Bush St., Chinatown.*

Chinese Culture Center. Mostly a place for the community to gather for calligraphy and Mandarin classes, the center also houses a gallery with occasionally interesting temporary exhibits by Chinese and Chinese-American artists. Heritage walks ($18; make reservations a day ahead) focus on the history of the Chinese in San Francisco; four participants required. ✉ *Hilton, 750 Kearny St., 3rd fl., Chinatown* ☎ *415/986–1822* ⊕ *www.c-c-c.org* ✉ *Free* ⊙ *Tues.–Sat. 10–4.*

Chinese Historical Society of America Museum and Learning Center. This airy, light-filled gallery has displays about the Chinese-American experience from 19th-century agriculture to 21st-century food and fashion trends, including a poignant collection of racist games and toys. A separate room hosts rotating exhibits by contemporary Chinese-American artists. ✉ *965 Clay St., Chinatown* ☎ *415/391–1188* ⊕ *www.chsa.org* ✉ *$3, free 1st Thurs. of month* ⊙ *Tues.–Fri. noon–5, Sat. 11–4.*

Chinese Six Companies. Once the White House of Chinatown, this striking building has balconies and lion-supported columns. Begun as an umbrella group for the many family and regional *tongs* (mutual-aid and fraternal organizations) that sprang up to help gold-rush immigrants, the Chinese Six Companies functioned as a government within

CLOSE UP

Chinatown Tongs

If you take it from Hollywood, Chinese *tongs* (secretive fraternal associations) rank right up there with the Italian mafia and the Japanese yakuza. The general public perception is one of an honor-bound brother-hood with an impenetrable code of silence; fortunes amassed through prostitution and narcotics; and dis-putes settled in a hail of gunfire, preferably in a crowded restaurant. In fact, the tongs began as an innocent community service—but for roughly a century there's been more than a little truth to the sensational image.

When Chinese immigrants first arrived in San Francisco during the gold rush, they made a beeline for an appropri-ate tong. These benevolent organiza-tions welcomed people from specific regions of China, or those with certain family names, and helped new arriv-als get a foothold. For thousands of men otherwise alone in the city, these tongs were a vital social connection. It didn't take long, however, until offers of protection services ushered in a new criminal element, casting a sinister shadow over all the tongs, legitimate or not.

As gambling parlors, illegal lotter-ies, opium dens, and brothels took root, many tongs became the go-to sources for turf protection and retribution. Early on, the muscles behind the tongs became known as "hatchet men" for their weapons of choice. (They believed guns made too much noise.)

"Tong wars" regularly broke out between competing groups, with especially blood-soaked periods in the 1920s and 1970s. Today the tongs are less influential than at the turn of the 20th century, but they remain a major part of Chinatown life as they own large swaths of real estate and pro-vide care for the elderly. The criminal side is alive and well, profiting from prostitution and drugs and doing a brisk business in pirated music and DVDs. Violence still erupts, too. In early 2006, Allen Leung, a prominent community leader, was shot dead in his shop on Jackson Street. Among his activities, Leung was a very influential "dragon head" of the Hop Sing tong, a group involved in prostitution, the heroin trade, and other underground activities. And just like in the movies, no one's talking.

—Denise M. Leto

Chinatown, settling disputes among members and fighting against anti-Chinese laws. The business leaders who ran the six companies (which still exist) dominated the neighborhood's political and economic life for decades. The building is closed to the public. ✉ *843 Stockton St., Chinatown.*

Golden Gate Fortune Cookie Factory. Follow your nose down Ross Alley to this tiny cookie factory. Workers sit at circular motorized griddles and wait for dollops of batter to drop onto a tiny metal plate, which rotates into an oven. A few moments later out comes a cookie that's pli-able and ready for folding. It's easy to peek in for a moment, and hard to leave without a few free samples. A bagful of cookies—with mildly racy "adult" fortunes or more-benign ones—costs about $3. You can also purchase the cookies "fortuneless" in their waferlike unfolded

Where can I find. . .?

PARKING	**Sutter-Stockton Garage** ✉444 Stockton St. Reasonable prices and not too crowded.	**North Beach Parking Garage** ✉735 Vallejo St. Relatively clean and roomy.
A DRUGSTORE	**Walgreens** ✉459 Powell St. Open 24 hours.	**Rite-Aid Pharmacy** ✉776 Market St. Open from 7 AM to 9 PM.
A NIGHTCAP	**The Hidden Vine Wine Bar** ✉620 Post St. A quiet spot that pours mostly California wines.	**Bourbon & Branch** ✉501 Jones St. Worth following the rules to sip such outstanding cocktails.

state, which makes snacking that much more efficient. Being allowed to photograph the cookie makers at work will set you back 50¢. ✉56 *Ross Alley, west of and parallel to Grant Ave. between Washington and Jackson Sts., Chinatown* ☎*415/781–3956* ✉*Free* ⊙*Daily 9–8.*

Kong Chow Temple. This ornate temple sets a somber, spiritual tone right away with a sign warning visitors not to touch *anything*. The god to whom the members of this temple pray represents honesty and trust. Chinese stores and restaurants often display his image because he's thought to bring good luck in business. Chinese immigrants established the temple in 1851; its congregation moved to this building in 1977. Take the elevator up to the fourth floor, where incense fills the air. You can show respect by placing a dollar or two in the donation box and by leaving your camera in its case. Amid the statuary, flowers, and richly colored altars (red wards off evil spirits and signifies virility, green symbolizes longevity, and gold connotes majesty), a couple of plaques announce that MRS. HARRY S. TRUMAN CAME TO THIS TEMPLE IN JUNE 1948 FOR A PREDICTION ON THE OUTCOME OF THE ELECTION . . . THIS FORTUNE CAME TRUE. The temple's balcony has a good view of Chinatown. ✉*855 Stockton St., Chinatown* ☎*No phone* ✉*Free* ⊙*Mon.–Sat. 9–4.*

Old Chinese Telephone Exchange. After the 1906 earthquake, many Chinatown buildings were rebuilt in western style with pagoda roof and fancy balconies slapped on. This building—today the Bank of Canton—is the exception, an example of top-to-bottom Chinese architecture. The intricate three-tier pagoda was built in 1909. The exchange's operators were renowned for their prodigious memories, about which the San Francisco Chamber of Commerce boasted in 1914: "These girls respond all day with hardly a mistake to calls that are given (in English or one of five Chinese dialects) by the name of the subscriber instead of by his number—a mental feat that would be practically impossible to most high-schooled American misses." ⊠ *Bank of Canton, 743 Washington St., Chinatown.*

> **YEAR OF THE OX**
>
> During Chinese New Year in February, Chinatown explodes with activity. The three-week festival peaks with the crazy-popular Chinese New Year's Parade, ushering in the Year of the Ox in 2009.

Old St. Mary's Cathedral. Dedicated in 1854, this served as the city's Catholic cathedral until 1891. The verse below the massive clock face beseeched naughty Barbary Coast boys: "Son, observe the time and fly from evil." Behind the church in **St. Mary's Square,** a statue of Sun Yat-sen towers over the site of the Chinese leader's favorite reading spot during his years in San Francisco. ⊠ *Grant Ave. and California St., Chinatown.*

Portsmouth Square. Chinatown's living room buzzes with activity. The square, with its pagoda-shaped structures, is a favorite spot for morning tai chi; by noon dozens of men huddle around Chinese chess tables, engaged in not-always-legal competition. Kids scamper about the square's two grungy playgrounds (warning: the bathrooms are sketchy). Back in the late 19th century this land was near the waterfront and Robert Louis Stevenson, the author of *Treasure Island,* often dropped by, chatting up the sailors who hung out here. Some of the information he gleaned about life at sea found its way into his fiction. A bronze galleon sculpture, a tribute to Stevenson, is anchored in a corner of the square. ⊠ *Bordered by Walter Lum Pl. and Kearny, Washington, and Clay Sts., Chinatown.*

Tin How Temple. Duck into the inconspicuous doorway, climb three flights of stairs—on the second floor is a mah-jongg parlor whose patrons hope the spirits above will favor them—and be assaulted by the aroma of incense in this tiny, altar-filled room. Day Ju, one of the first three Chinese to arrive in San Francisco, dedicated this temple to the Queen of the Heavens and the Goddess of the Seven Seas in 1852. In the temple's entryway, elderly ladies can often be seen preparing "money" to be burned as offerings to various Buddhist gods or as funds for ancestors to use in the afterlife. Hundreds of red-and-gold lanterns cover the ceiling; the larger the lamp, the larger its donor's contribution to the temple. Gifts of oranges, dim sum, and money left by the faithful, who kneel mumbling prayers, rest on altars to various gods. Tin How presides over the middle back of the temple, flanked by one red and one green lesser god. Take a good look around, since taking photographs is not allowed. ⊠ *125 Waverly Pl., Chinatown* ☎ *No phone* ⊠ *Free, donations accepted* ☉ *Daily 9–4.*

Dining in Union Square & Chinatown

BUDGET

Great Eastern, Chinese, 649 Jackson St.

Naan 'N' Curry, Indian, 533 Jackson St.

R&G Lounge, Chinese, 631 Kearny St.

MODERATE

B44, Spanish, 44 Belden Pl.

Café Claude, French Bistro, 7 Claude La.

Canteen, American, Commodore Hotel, 817 Sutter St.

Cortez, Mediterranean, Hotel Adagio, 550 Geary St.

Jeanty at Jack's, French, 615 Sacramento St.

Le Colonial, Vietnamese, 20 Cosmo Pl.

Millennium, Vegetarian, Savoy Hotel, 580 Geary St.

Plouf, French, 40 Belden Pl.

Restaurant Jeanne D'Arc, French, Cornell

Hotel de France, 715 Bush St.

Rubicon, American, 558 Sacramento St.

Scala's Bistro, Italian, Sir Francis Drake Hotel, 432 Powell St.

EXPENSIVE

Farallon, Seafood, 450 Post St.

Fleur de Lys, French, 777 Sutter St.

Michael Mina, American, 335 Powell St., in Westin St. Francis Hotel

CHINATOWN

Chinatown's streets flood the senses. Incense and cigarette smoke mingle with the scents of briny fish and sweet vanilla. Rooflines flare outward, pagoda-style. Loud Cantonese bargaining and honking car horns rise above the sharp clack of mah-jongg tiles and the eternally humming cables beneath the street.

Most Chinatown visitors march down Grant Avenue, buy a few trinkets, and call it a day. Do yourself a favor and dig deeper. This is one of the largest Chinese communities outside Asia, and there is far more to it than buying a back-scratcher near Chinatown Gate. To get a real feel for the neighborhood, wander off the main drag. Step into a temple or an herb shop and wander down a flag-draped alley. And don't be shy: its residents welcome guests warmly, though rarely in English.

Whatever you do, don't leave without eating something. Noodle houses, bakeries, tea houses, and dim sum shops seem to occupy every other storefront. There's a feast for your eyes as well: in the market windows on Stockton and Grant, you'll see hanging whole roast ducks, fish and shellfish swimming in tanks, and strips of shiny, pink-glazed Chinese-style barbecued pork. (For the scoop on dim sum, *see* the Union Square & Chinatown spotlight in the Where to Eat chapter.)

CHINATOWN'S HISTORY

The Street of Gamblers (Ross Alley), 1898 (top).
The first Chinese telephone operator in Chinatown (bottom).

Sam Brannan's 1848 cry of "Gold!" didn't take long to reach across the world to China. Struggling with famine, drought, and political upheaval at home, thousands of Chinese jumped at the chance to try their luck in California. Most came from the Pearl River Delta region, in the Guangdong province, and spoke Cantonese dialects. From the start, Chinese businesses circled around Portsmouth Square, which was conveniently central. Bachelor rooming houses sprang up, since the vast majority of new arrivals were men. By 1853, the area was called Chinatown.

COLD WELCOME
The Chinese faced discrimination from the get-go. Harrassment became outright hostility as first the gold rush, then the work on the Transcontinental Railroad petered out. Special taxes were imposed to shoulder aside competing "coolie labor." Laws forbidding the Chinese from moving outside Chinatown kept the residents packed in like sardines,

with nowhere to go but up and down—thus the many basement establishments in the neighborhood. State and federal laws passed in the 1870s deterred Chinese women from immigrating, deeming them prostitutes. In the late 1870s, looting and arson attacks on Chinatown businesses soared.

The coup de grace, though, was the Chinese Exclusion Act, passed by the U.S.

Chinatown's Grant Avenue.

Women and children flooded in to the neighborhood after the Great Quake

Congress in 1882, which slammed the doors to America for "Asiatics." This was the country's first significant restriction on immigration. The law also prevented the existing Chinese residents, including American-born children, from becoming naturalized citizens. With a society of mostly men (forbidden, of course, from marrying white women), San Francisco hoped that Chinatown would simply die out.

OUT OF THE ASHES

When the devastating 1906 earthquake and fire hit, city fathers thought they'd seize the opportunity to kick the Chinese out of Chinatown and get their hands on that desirable piece of downtown real estate. Then Chinatown businessman Look Tin Eli had a brainstorm of Disneyesque proportions.

He proposed that Chinatown be rebuilt, but in a tourist-friendly, stylized, "Oriental" way. Anglo-American architects would design new buildings with pagoda roofs and dragon-covered columns. Chinatown would attract more tourists—the curious had been visiting on the sly

for decades—and add more tax money to the city's coffers. Ka-ching: the sales pitch worked.

PAPER SONS

For the Chinese, the 1906 earthquake turned the virtual "no entry" sign into a flashing neon "welcome!" All the city's immigration records went up in smoke, and the Chinese quickly began to apply for passports as U.S. citizens, claiming their old ones were lost in the fire. Not only did thousands of Chinese become legal overnight, but so did their sons in China, or "sons," if they weren't really related. Whole families in Chinatown had passports in names that weren't their own; these "paper sons" were not only a windfall but also an uncomfortable neighborhood conspiracy. The city caught on eventually and set up an immigration center on Angel Island in 1910. Immigrants spent weeks or months being inspected and interrogated while their papers were checked. Roughly 250,000 people made it through. With this influx, including women and children, Chinatown finally became a more complete community.

A GREAT WALK THROUGH CHINATOWN

■ Start at the Chinatown Gate and walk ahead on Grant Avenue, entering the souvenir gauntlet. (You'll also pass Old St. Mary's Cathedral.)

■ Make a right on Clay Street and walk to Portsmouth Square. Sometimes it feels like the whole neighborhood's here, playing chess and exercising.

■ Head up Washington Street to the elaborately pagodaed Old Chinese Telephone Exchange building, now the Bank of Canton. Across Grant, look left for Waverly Place. Here Republic of China flags flap over some of the neighborhood's most striking buildings, including Tin How Temple.

■ At the Sacramento Street end of Waverly Place stands the oddly beautiful brick First Chinese Baptist Church of 1908. Just across the way, the Clarion Music Center is chock-full of unusual instruments, as well as exquisite lion-dance sets.

■ Head back to Washington Street and check out the herb shops, like the Superior Trading Company (No. 839) and the Great China Herb Co. (No. 857).

■ Follow the scent of vanilla from Washington Street down Ross Alley (entrance across

from Superior Trading Company) to the Golden Gate Fortune Cookie Factory. Then head across the alley to Sam Bo Trading Co., where religious items are stacked chockablock in the narrow space. Tell the friendly owners your troubles and they'll prepare a package of joss papers, joss sticks, and candles, and tell you how and when to offer them up.

■ Turn left on Jackson Street; ahead is the real Chinatown's main artery, Stockton Street. This is where most residents do their grocery shopping; if it's Saturday, get ready for throngs (and their elbows). Look toward the back of stores for Buddhist altars with offerings of oranges and grapefruit. From here you can loop one block east back to Grant.

ALL THE TEA IN CHINATOWN

Preparing a perfect brew at the Imperial Tea Court

San Francisco's close ties to Asia have always made it more tea-conscious than other American burgs, but these days the city is in the throes of a tea renaissance, with new tasting rooms popping up in every neighborhood. Below are our favorite Chinatown spots for every tea under the sun.

Red Blossom Tea. A light and modern shop—the staff really know their stuff. It's a favorite among younger tea enthusiasts, who swear by its excellent bang-for-the-buck value. While Red Blossom doesn't do formal tastings or sell tea by the cup, they'll gladly brew up perfect samples of the teas you're interested in. ✉ *831 Grant Ave.* ☎ *415/395–0868*

Vital Tea Leaf. Tastings here work like those for wine—one of the gregarious, knowledgeable servers chooses the teas and describes them as you sample. It's a great spot for tea newbies to get their feet wet without a hard sell, but local connoisseurs grumble about the high prices and the self-promotion. ✉ *1044 Grant Ave.* ☎ *415/981–2388.*

Imperial Tea Court. If you want to visit the most respected of traditional tea purveyors, you'll need to venture outside of Chinatown. Imperial Tea Court's serene Powell Street oasis closed unexpectedly in 2007, but you'll find the same great selection and expertise at their fancy new digs in the Ferry Building. ☎ *415/544–9830.*

WAITING FOR CUSTARD

As you're strolling down Grant Avenue, past the plastic Buddhas and yin/yang balls, be sure to stop at the **Golden Gate Bakery** (No. 1029) for some delicious eggy *dan tat* (custard tarts). These flaky-crusted treats are heaven for just a buck. There's often a line, but it's worth the wait.

DON'T-MISS SHOPS

Locals snap up flowers from an outdoor vendor

If you're in the market for a pair of chirping metal crickets (oh you'll hear them, trust us), you can duck into any of the obvious souvenir-stuffed storefronts. But if you're looking for something special, head for these tempting sources.

■TIP➤ **Fierce neighborhood competition keeps prices within reason, but for popular wares like jade, it pays to shop around before making a serious investment. Many stores accept cash only.**

Chinatown Kite Shop. Family-run shop selling bright, fun-shaped kites—dragons, butterflies, sharks—since the 1960s. ⊠ *717 Grant Ave.* ☎ *415/989–5182.*

Dragon House. A veritable museum: the store sells authentic, centuries-old antiques like ivory carvings. ⊠ *455 Grant Ave.* ☎ *415/421–3693.*

Jade Galore. Not the cheapest place to pick up jade figures and jewelry, but locals trust its quality and adore its wide selection of Chinese bling. ⊠ *1000 Stockton St.* ☎ *415/982–4863.*

Old Shanghai. One of the largest selections of hand-painted robes, formal dresses, and jackets in Chinatown, plus chic Asian-inspired pieces. ⊠ *645 Grant Ave.* ☎ *415/986–1222.*

CHINATOWN WITH KIDS

It can be tough for the little ones to keep their hands to themselves, especially when all sorts of curios spill out onto the sidewalk at just the right height. To burn off some steam (in them) and relieve some stress (in you), take them to the small but spruce playground directly behind Old St. Mary's at Grant Avenue and California Street. If that setting's too tranquil, head to the more boisterous Willie Wong Playground, on Sacramento Street at Waverly Place.

SoMa & Civic Center

Skylight in the Museum of Modern Art

WORD OF MOUTH

"If your children get tired and need a little greenery take them to Yerba Buena [Gardens]. Most children love the "shaking man" statue at the park. There is also the MLK memorial at one end; you go behind the waterfall to see it and little ones always seem to enjoy."

—LoveItaly

GETTING ORIENTED

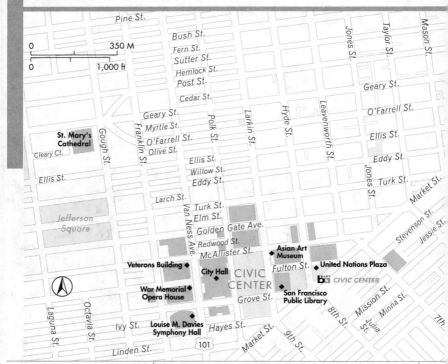

GETTING THERE

For most SoMa visitors, who stick close to SFMOMA and the Yerba Buena Gardens, getting here is a matter of walking roughly 10 minutes from Union Square, less from Market Street transit.

It's best to reach Civic Center by BART, bus, or F-line. Hoofing it from Union Square requires walking through the unsavory Tenderloin area, and from SoMa it's a long, ugly haul.

After dark, safety dictates a cab for both neighborhoods.

QUICK BITES

Above the Martin Luther King Jr. memorial in the Yerba Buena Gardens, the **Samovar Tea Lounge** (✉ *730 Howard St., SoMa* ☎ *415/227–9400*) is a serene retreat with glass walls overlooking an infinity pool. Especially on a blustery day, the organic and fair trade teas hit the spot.

Metreon's **Taste of San Francisco** (✉ *101 4th St., between Mission and Howard Sts., SoMa*) is the perfect spot to grab all the fixings for an alfresco lunch. Choose wood-fired pizza from the Firewood Café or a generous burrito from Luna Azul and stake out a spot in the Yerba Buena Gardens.

If you see a clutch of people gathered around what looks like a garage in Hayes Valley, chances are you've stumbled upon **Blue Bottle Coffee** (✉ *315 Linden St., Hayes Valley* ☎ *415/252–7535*), a tiny stand selling what many claim is the best organic coffee on the planet. The "artisanal micro-roasting" philosophy says that all coffee should be brewed within 24 hours of roasting, and yes, they are Very Serious.

3

MAKING THE MOST OF YOUR TIME

You could spend all day museum-hopping in SoMa. Allow two hours to see SFMOMA; if there's a big show on, avoid the line by buying tickets online and arrive early to beat the throngs. An hour each should do it for Museum of the African Diaspora, the Contemporary Jewish Museum, and the Center for the Arts, less than that for the minor museums.

SoMa after dark is another adventure entirely. More interested in merlot or megaclubs than Matisse? Start here around 8 PM for dinner, then move on to a bar or dance spot. *See* the Where to Eat and Nightlife & the Arts chapters for our top recommendations.

Don't be suckered by visions of grand architecture and "important" performing-arts venues in Civic Center. Unless you have tickets to the opera, ballet, or a concert, there's no good reason for you to spend much time there.

TOP 5 REASONS TO GO

SFMOMA: Big-name modern art exhibits in a durably cool building.

Asian Art Museum: Stand face-to-face with a massive gold Buddha in one of the world's largest collections of Asian art.

Club-hopping in SoMa: Shake it with the cool, friendly crowd that fills SoMa's dance clubs until the wee hours, and all weekend long at the EndUp.

Yerba Buena Gardens: Gather picnic provisions and choose a spot on the grass in downtown's oasis.

Hanging out at Patricia's Green: Grab a cup of coffee (Blue Bottle's just around the corner) and head to the narrow swath of park that serves as hopping Hayes Valley's living room. Check out the monumental temporary art exhibit—it always has an interactive element—and the little ones clambering on the fantastic climbing dome.

SOMA & CIVIC CENTER

Sightseeing
☆☆★★★

Nightlife
☆☆★★★

Dining
☆☆★★★

Lodging
☆☆☆★★

Shopping
☆☆☆☆★

To a newcomer, SoMa (short for "south of Market") and Civic Center may look like cheek-by-jowl neighbors—they're divided by Market Street. To locals, though, these areas are firmly separate entities, especially since Market Street itself is considered such a strong demarcation line. Both neighborhoods have a core of cultural sights but more than their share of sketchy blocks.

By Denise M. Leto

SoMa is less a neighborhood than it is a sprawling area of wide, traffic-heavy boulevards lined with office high-rises and pricey live-work lofts. Aside from the fact that many of them work in the area, locals are drawn to the cultural offerings, smattering of destination restaurants, and concentration of dance clubs. In terms of sightseeing, SoMa holds a few points of interest—SFMOMA and the Yerba Buena Gardens top the list—and these are conveniently close together.

SoMa was once known as South of the Slot (read: the Wrong Side of the Tracks) in reference to the cable-car slot that ran up Market Street. Ever since gold-rush miners set up their tents in 1848, SoMa has played a major role in housing immigrants to the city. Industry took over much of the area when the 1906 earthquake collapsed most of the homes into their quicksand bases.

SoMa's emergence as a focal point of San Francisco's cultural life was more than three decades in the making. Huge sections of the then-industrial neighborhood were razed in the 1960s, and alternative artists and the gay leather crowd set up shop. A dozen bars and bathhouses frequented by the latter group cropped up; some survive today, and the legacy of that time is the still-raucous annual Folsom Street Fair. The neighborhood lost many artists to the far reaches of SoMa and to the Mission District when urban renewal finally began in earnest in the 1970s; still more fled when the dot-com heyday sent prices here skyrocketing.

Life in the SoMa of the mid- to late 1990s was what the gold rush must have felt like. Young prospectors flooded in to take their pick of well-paying jobs at high-tech start-ups. Companies with hot (or not) ideas filled their $100-plus-per-square-foot offices with recent college grads, foosball tables, $1,000 ergonomic chairs, and free catered meals. Gaggles of gadget-toting twentysomethings spent their evenings wandering from launch party to marketing event, loading up on swag. Rents—commercial in SoMa and residential citywide—went through the roof, but the dot-commers could still pony up while waiting for the holy grail of the IPO. South Park, the green oval anchored by high-tech hangout Caffè Centro, briefly became the center of the universe.

HAYES VALLEY

Hayes Valley, right next door to the Civic Center, is an offbeat neighborhood with terrific eateries, cool watering holes, and great browsing in its funky clothing and home decor boutiques. Swing down main drag Hayes Street, between Franklin and Laguna, and you can hit the highlights, including two very popular restaurants, Absinthe and Suppenküche. Comfy Place Pigalle (at Hayes and Octavia streets) is also a favorite for its living-room atmosphere, wines, and microbrews. Locals love this quarter, but without any big-name draws, it remains off the radar for most visitors.

The electric buzz of the dot-com boom, when venture capitalists couldn't give their money away fast enough, changed the face of the neighborhood forever. Today's post-boom SoMa is sobered up and on the rise; the thousands of kids rich on paper have been replaced with substantially wealthy people staking out luxury high-rises. Jackhammers herald the impending arrival of a handful of luxury residential towers that will dwarf what are now the city's tallest buildings. The area may still have more than its share of seedy pockets, but you'd be lucky to nab a condo here for less than $1 million.

Across Market Street from the western edge of SoMa is another of the city's patchy neighborhoods, the Civic Center, between McAllister and Grove streets and Franklin and Hyde streets. The optimistic "City Beautiful" movement of the early 20th century produced the beaux-arts-style complex for which this area is named, including the War Memorial Opera House, the Veterans Building, and the old public library, now home of the Asian Art Museum. The centerpiece is the eye-catching, gold-domed City Hall. The current main library on Larkin Street between Fulton and Grove streets is a modern variation on the Civic Center's architectural theme.

The Civic Center area may have been set up on City Beautiful principles, but illusion soon gives way to reality. The buildings are grand, but there's a stark juxtaposition of the powerful and the powerless here. On the streets and plazas of Civic Center, many of the city's most destitute residents eke out an existence.

Despite the evidence of social problems, there are areas of interest on either side of City Hall. East of City Hall is United Nations Plaza, which hosts a poor man's version of the Ferry Building's glorious farmers' market twice weekly. On the west side of City Hall are the opera house, the symphony hall, and other cultural institutions. A few upscale restaurants in the surrounding blocks cater to the theater-symphony crowd. Tickets to a show at one of the grand performance halls are the main reason to venture here. Otherwise, unless you have a hankering to gawk at gray-stone, monumental structures, a glimpse of the gold-veined dome of City Hall as you drive down the street should be enough, especially for first-time visitors.

WHAT TO SEE IN SOMA

California Historical Society. If you're not a history buff, the CHS might seem like an obvious skip—who wants to look at fading old photographs and musty artifacts? If the answer is an indignant "I do!" or if you're just curious, these airy galleries are well worth a stop. A rotating selection draws from the society's vast repository of Californiana—hundreds of thousands of photographs, publications, paintings, and gold-rush paraphernalia. ■TIP→ **From out front, take a look across the street: this is the best view of MoAD's three-story photo mosaic.** ⊠*678 Mission St., SoMa* ☎*415/357–1848* ⊕*www.californiahistoricalsociety.org* ⊠*$3* ☉*Wed.–Sat. noon–4:30; galleries close between exhibitions.*

OFF THE BEATEN PATH

GLBT Historical Society Museum. Tucked away in a small exhibit space on the third floor, the Gay, Lesbian, Bisexual, and Transgender (GLBT) Historical Society Museum presents rotating multimedia exhibits on themes such as the Gay Olympics, Harvey Milk, and GLBT military service. Though perhaps not for the faint of heart (those offended by photos of lustily frolicking naked people may, well, be offended), this thoughtful display offers an inside look at these communities so integral to the fabric of San Francisco life. The upstairs location and tiny space mean you may well be the only visitor; a helpful docent from the GLBT Historical Society's office next door will gladly show you around and answer any questions. ⊠*657 Mission St., 3rd fl., SoMa* ☎*415/777–5455* ⊕*www.glbthistory.org* ⊠*$4 donation* ☉*Tues.–Sat. 1–5.*

Cartoon Art Museum. Krazy Kat, Zippy the Pinhead, Batman, and other colorful cartoon icons greet you at the Cartoon Art Museum, established with an endowment from cartoonist-icon Charles M. Schulz. The museum's strength is its changing exhibits, which explore such topics as America from the perspective of international political cartoons, and the output of women and African-American cartoonists. Serious fans of cartoons—especially those on the quirky underground side—will likely enjoy the exhibits; those with a casual interest may be disappointed. The museum store carries lots of cool books. ⊠*655 Mission St., SoMa* ☎*415/227–8666* ⊕*www.cartoonart.org* ⊠*$6, pay what you wish 1st Tues. of month* ☉*Tues.–Sun. 11–5.*

Contemporary Jewish Museum. Stand on the Mission Street border of Yerba Buena Gardens and look across the way—rising next to St. Patrick's is the new home of the latest major museum to land in this neighborhood. "Starchitect" Daniel Libeskind's state-of-the-art building opened in summer 2008. The new structure joins a 1906 power station with giant, blocky shapes sheathed in bright blue steel panels. Inside, you'll find a series of temporary exhibits that often focus on political themes. These can be controversial but offer insight to anyone interested in contemporary Jewish life. ⊠*Mission St., between 3rd and 4th Sts., SoMa* ☎*415/591–8800* ⊕*www.jmsf.org* ⊠*$5, free 3rd Mon. of month* ☉*Sun.–Thurs. noon–6.*

Metreon. Child's play meets the 21st century at this high-tech mall, adored by gearheads and teenage boys obsessed with tabletop games. Tilt is a high-tech interactive arcade. At Kamikaze Pop, pick up anime and manga DVDs and cute gear, or head to Things From Another World for a huge selection of comic books, graphic novels, and related novelties. A 15-screen multiplex and IMAX theater, retail shops such as PlayStation and Sony Style, and outposts of some of the city's favorite restaurants are all part of the complex. It's a good place to pick up lunch for a picnic in the Yerba Buena Gardens, right outside; if you forgot your blanket, head to the patio tables outside Metreon's second floor. ⊠*101 4th St., between Mission and Howard Sts., SoMa* ☎*800/638–7366* ⊕*www.metreon.com.*

Museum of the African Diaspora (MoAD). Dedicated to the influence that people of African descent have had all over the world, MoAD provokes discussion from the git-go with the question, "When did you discover you are African?" painted on the wall at the entrance. With no permanent collection, the museum is light on displays and heavy on interactive exhibits. For instance, you can sit in a darkened theater and listen to the moving life stories of slaves; hear snippets of music that helped create genres from gospel to hip-hop; and see videos about the Civil Rights movement or the Haitian Revolution. Some grumble that sweeping generalities replace specific information, but almost everyone can appreciate the museum's most striking exhibit, in the front window. The three-story mosaic, made from thousands of photographs, forms the image of a little girl's face. Walk up the stairs inside the museum and view the photographs up close—Malcolm X is there, Muhammad Ali, too, along with everyday folks—but the best view is from across the street. ⊠*685 Mission St., SoMa* ☎*415/358–7200* ⊕*www.moadsf. org* ⊠*$10* ☉*Wed.–Sat. 11–6, Sun. noon–5.*

OFF THE BEATEN PATH

Mint Plaza. Arising from what had long been a gritty, windswept cut-through behind the abandoned Old Mint, L-shaped Mint Plaza is shaping up to be that vibrant mix that urban planners always aim for but often miss: stylish urban residences (that are actually occupied) cheek-by-jowl with thriving local businesses, all combining to produce a happening street scene. The secret, tucked-away feel of the alley—which is mere feet from Mission Street—will make you feel like an insider when you visit. You can already stop by Blue Bottle Café for coffee and a nosh, and by the time you read this you'll be able to grab a table at Chez Papa, one of the city's favorite French bistros. Betting pools are forming now to wager how long those orange chairs—meant to encourage the public-space feel—will survive. Even the mint itself is being reinvented: the Museum of San Francisco is slated to open inside the structure in 2011. ⊠ *Jessie and Mint Sts., near Mission and Fifth Sts., SoMa.*

Museum of Craft and Folk Art. If you're in the area, this one-room museum is a great way to spend a half hour. This bright space hosts five rotating exhibits per year showcasing American folk art, tribal art, and contemporary crafts. One exhibit saw the museum transformed into a forest of paper, all created by hand from plants, trees, and river water by an artisan in Japan. Another was devoted entirely to the art of the ukulele. Its tiny front space houses a shop with high-end, sometimes whimsical crafts from around the world. ⊠ *51 Yerba Buena La., SoMa* ☎ *415/227–4888* ⊕ *www.mocfa.org* ⊠ *$5, free 1st Tues. of month* ⊙ *Tues.–Fri. 11–6, weekends 11–5.*

Palace Hotel. The city's oldest hotel, a Sheraton property, opened in 1875. Fire destroyed the original Palace after the 1906 earthquake, despite the hotel's 28,000-gallon reservoir; the current building dates from 1909. President Warren Harding died at the Palace while still in office in 1923, and the body of King Kalakaua of Hawaii spent a night here after he died in San Francisco in 1891. The managers play up this ghoulish past with talk of a haunted guest room. **San Francisco City Guides** (☎ *415/557–4266* ⊙ *Tours Tues. and Sat. at 10, Thurs. at 2*) offers free guided tours of the Palace Hotel's grand interior. You see the glass-dome Garden Court restaurant, mosaic-tile floors in Oriental rug designs, and Maxfield Parrish's wall-size painting *The Pied Piper,* the centerpiece of the Pied Piper Bar. Glass cases off the main lobby contain memorabilia of the hotel's glory days. ⊠ *2 New Montgomery St., SoMa* ☎ *415/512–1111* ⊕ *www.sfpalace.com.*

Rincon Center. The only reason to visit what is basically a modern office building is the striking Works Project Administration mural by Anton Refregier in the lobby of the streamline moderne–style former post office on the building's Mission Street side. The 27 panels depict California life from the days when Native Americans were the state's sole inhabitants through World War I. Completion of this significant work was interrupted by World War II (which explains the swastika in the final panel) and political infighting. The latter led to some alteration in Refregier's "radical" historical interpretations; they exuded too much populist sentiment for some of the politicians who opposed the artist. A permanent exhibit below the murals contains photographs and artifacts of life in the Rincon area in the 1800s. A sheer five-story column of water resembling a mini-rainstorm is the centerpiece of the indoor arcade around the corner from the mural. ⊠ *Bordered by Steuart, Spear, Mission, and Howard Sts., SoMa.*

Fodor'sChoice **San Francisco Museum of Modern Art** *(SFMOMA)*. With its brick facade
★ and a striped central tower lopped at a lipstick-like angle, architect Mario Botta's SFMOMA building fairly screams "modern-art
museum." Indeed it is. The stripes continue inside, from the black
marble and gray granite of the floors right up the imposing staircase to
the wooden slats on the ceiling.

■TIP➔ **Taking in all of SFMOMA's four exhibit floors can be overwhelming,
so having a plan is helpful. Keep in mind that the museum's heavy hitters
are on floors 2 and 3.** Floor 2 gets the big-name traveling exhibits and
collection highlights such as Matisse's *Woman with the Hat,* Diego
Rivera's *The Flower Carrier,* and Georgia O'Keeffe's *Black Place 1.*
Photography buffs should hustle up to floor 3, with its works by Ansel
Adams and Alfred Stieglitz. The large-scale contemporary exhibits on
floors 4 and 5 can usually be seen quickly (or skipped). If it's on display, don't miss sculptor Jeff Koons' memorably creepy, life-size gilded
porcelain *Michael Jackson and Bubbles,* on the fifth floor at the end
of the Turret Bridge, a vertiginous catwalk dangling under the central
tower. The window at the bridge's other end offers a great view over the
Yerba Buena Gardens below. At this writing, a new fifth-floor, garage-
top sculpture garden was to be added at the end of 2008.

Seating in the museum can be scarce, so luckily Caffè Museo, accessible
from the street, provides a refuge for quite good, reasonably priced
drinks and light meals. It's easy to drop a fortune at the museum's
large store, chockablock with fun gadgets, artsy doodads of all kinds,
very modern furniture, and possibly the best selection of kids' books
in town. ■TIP➔ **No ticket is required to visit the lobby, so if it's the architecture you're interested in, save yourself the admission and have a gander for free.** ⊠*151 3rd St., SoMa* ☎*415/357–4000* ⊕*www.sfmoma.
org* 🗐*$12.50, free 1st Tues. of month, ½ price Thurs. 6–9* ☉*Labor
Day–Memorial Day, Fri.–Tues. 11–5:45, Thurs. 11–8:45; Memorial
Day–Labor Day, Fri.–Tues. 10–5:45, Thurs. 10–8:45.*

Yerba Buena Center for the Arts. If MOMA's for your parents, the Center
is for you. You never know what's going to be on at this facility in the
Yerba Buena Gardens, but whether it's an exhibit of Mexican street
graphics (graffiti to laypeople), innovative modern dance, or baffling
video installations, it's likely to be memorable. The productions here
tend to draw a young, energetic crowd and lean hard toward the cutting edge. ⊠*701 Mission St., SoMa* ☎*415/978–2787* ⊕*www.ybca.
org* 🗐*Galleries $7, free 1st Tues. of month* ☉*Galleries and box office
Tues., Wed., and Fri.–Sun. noon–5, Thurs. noon–8.*

★ ☺ **Yerba Buena Gardens.** There's not much South of Market that encourages
lingering outdoors, or indeed walking at all, with this notable exception. These two blocks encompass the **Center for the Arts, Metreon,
Moscone Convention Center,** and the convention center's rooftop
Zeum, but the gardens themselves are the everyday draw. Office workers escape to the green swath of the East Garden. The memorial to
Martin Luther King Jr. is the focal point here. Powerful streams of
water surge over large, jagged stone columns, mirroring the endur-

ing force of King's words that are carved on the stone walls and on glass blocks behind the waterfall. Moscone North is behind the memorial, and an overhead walkway leads to Moscone South and its rooftop attractions. ■TIP→ **The gardens are liveliest during the week and especially during the Yerba Buena Gardens Festival (May–October, www.ybgf.org), when free performances run from Latin music to Balinese dance.**

Atop the Moscone Convention Center perch a few lures for kids. The historic **Looff carousel** ($3 for two rides) twirls daily 11–6. South of the carousel is **Zeum** (☎415/820–3320 ⊕www.zeum.org), a high-tech, interactive arts-and-technology center ($8, 3–18 $6) geared to children ages eight and over. Kids can make Claymation videos, work in a computer lab, and view exhibits and performances. Zeum is open 1–5 Wednesday through Friday and 11–5 weekends during the school year and Tuesday through Sunday when school's out. Also part of the rooftop complex are gardens, an ice-skating rink, and a bowling alley. ✉*Bordered by 3rd, 4th, Mission, and Folsom Sts., SoMa* ☎*No phone* ⊕*www.yerbabuena.org* ⊠*Free* ☉*Daily sunrise–10* PM.

WHAT TO SEE IN CIVIC CENTER

★ **Asian Art Museum.** Expecting a building full of Buddhas and jade? Well, yeah, you can find plenty of those here. Happily, though, you don't have to be a connoisseur of Asian art to appreciate a visit to this splendidly renovated museum, whose monumental exterior conceals a light, open, and welcoming space. The fraction of the museum's items on display (about 2,500 pieces from a 15,000-plus-piece collection) is laid out thematically and by region, making it easy to follow developments.

Begin on the third floor, where highlights of Buddhist art in Southeast Asia and early China include a large, jewel-encrusted, exquisitely painted 19th-century Burmese Buddha and clothed rod puppets from Java. On the second floor you can find later Chinese works, as well as pieces from Korea and Japan. Look for a cobalt tiger jauntily smoking a pipe on a whimsical Korean jar and delicate Japanese tea implements. The ground floor displays rotating exhibits, including contemporary and traveling shows. ■TIP→ **If you'd like to attend one of the bimonthly tea ceremonies and tastings at the Japanese Teahouse, call ahead, since preregistration is required.** ✉*200 Larkin St., between McAllister and Fulton Sts., Civic Center* ☎*415/581–3500* ⊕*www.asianart.org* ⊠*$12, free 1st Sun. of month; $5 Thurs. 5–9; tea ceremony $20, includes museum* ☉*Tues., Wed., and Fri.–Sun. 10–5, Thurs. 10–9.*

City Hall. This imposing 1915 structure with its massive gold-leaf dome—higher than the U.S. Capitol's—is about as close to a palace as you're going to get in San Francisco. (The metal detectors take something away from the grandeur, though.) The classic granite-and-marble behemoth was modeled after St. Peter's cathedral in Rome. Architect Arthur Brown Jr., who also designed Coit Tower and the War Memorial Opera House, designed an interior with grand columns and a sweeping central staircase. San Franciscans were thrilled, and probably a bit surprised, when his firm built City Hall in just a few years. The building it replaced, dubbed "the new City Hall ruin," had lined the pockets of corrupt builders and politicians during its 27 years of construction. That 1899 structure collapsed in about 27 seconds in the 1906 earthquake, revealing trash and newspapers mixed into the building materials.

City Hall was spruced up and seismically retrofitted in the late 1990s, but the sense of history remains palpable. Some noteworthy events that have taken place here include the marriage of Marilyn Monroe and Joe DiMaggio (1954); the hosing—down the central staircase—of civil-rights and freedom-

WORD OF MOUTH

"City Hall is one of the most beautiful public buildings I have ever seen. Open to the public and the free tour is worth an hour of your time."   –QC

of-speech protesters (1960); the murders of Mayor George Moscone and openly gay supervisor Harvey Milk (1978); the torching of the lobby by angry members of the gay community in response to the light sentence given to the former supervisor who killed the men (1979); and the registrations of scores of gay couples in celebration of the passage of San Francisco's Domestic Partners Act (1991). February 2004 has come to be known as the Winter of Love: thousands of gay and lesbian couples responded to Mayor Gavin Newsom's decision to issue marriage licenses to same-sex partners, turning City Hall into the site of raucous celebration and joyful nuptials for a month before the state Supreme Court ordered the practice stopped. Free tours are offered weekdays at 10, noon, and 2.

The South Light Court houses a modest, rotating display from the collection of the **Museum of the City of San Francisco** (⊕*www.sfmuseum.org*), including historical items, maps, and photographs. That enormous, 700-pound iron head once crowned the *Goddess of Progress* statue, which topped the old City Hall building when it crumbled during the 1906 earthquake. Unlike the building, the statue survived the earthquake in one piece, but the subsequent removal proved too much for it.

Across Polk Street is **Civic Center Plaza,** with lawns, walkways, seasonal flower beds, a playground, and an underground parking garage. This sprawling space is generally clean but somewhat grim. A large part of the city's homeless population hangs out here, despite frequently being shunted away, so the plaza can feel dodgy. ⊠*Bordered by Van Ness Ave. and Polk, Grove, and McAllister Sts., Civic Center* ☎*415/554–6023* ⊕*www.sfgov.org/site/cityhall* ⊠*Free* ☉ *Weekdays 8–8.*

Once exclusively a bakery and sandwich joint, star pastry chef Elizabeth Falkner's Citizen Cake (✉ *399 Grove St., Civic Center* ☎ *415/861–2228*) is now a full-fledged restaurant, but it's still a very worthwhile detour. Choose a sweet—cookies, pastries, chocolates, even house-made ice cream—to go from the patisserie case, or stake out a table in the urban-industrial space.

Louise M. Davies Symphony Hall. Fascinating and futuristic looking, this 2,750-seat hall is the home of the San Francisco Symphony. The glass wraparound lobby and pop-out balcony high on the southeast corner are visible from outside. Henry Moore created the bronze sculpture that sits on the sidewalk at Van Ness Avenue and Grove Street. The hall's 59 adjustable Plexiglas acoustical disks cascade from the ceiling like hanging windshields. Concerts range from typical symphonic fare to more unusual combinations, such as performers like Al Green and Arlo Guthrie. Scheduled tours (75 minutes), which meet at the Grove Street entrance, take in Davies and the nearby opera house and Herbst Theatre. ✉ *201 Van Ness Ave., Civic Center* ☎ *415/552–8338* ⊕ *www.sfwmpac.org* ☜ *Tours $5* ⊙ *Tours Mon. on the hr 10–2.*

San Francisco Public Library. Topped with a swirl like an Art Deco nautilus, the library's seven-level glass atrium fills the building with light. Opened in 1996, the New Main (as Herb Caen dubbed it) is a modernized version of the old beaux-arts-style library. Local researchers take advantage of centers dedicated to gay-and-lesbian, African-American, Chinese, and Filipino history, and everyone appreciates the basement-level café, Wi-Fi, and 15-minute Internet terminal access. On the sixth floor, an exhibit inside the San Francisco History Center includes doodads from the 1894 Mid-Winter Fair and the 1915 Pan-Pacific Exhibition, as well as the "valuable emeralds" philanthropist Helene Strybing left to the city—alas, green glass. ■ TIP→ **Noir fans should head to the back of the center; you can see a "Maltese Falcon" statue in the Flood Building but this is the only place to see novelist Dashiell Hammett's typewriter.** Free tours of the library are conducted the second Wednesday of the month at 2:30. ✉ *100 Larkin St., at Grove St., Civic Center* ☎ *415/557–4400* ⊕ *sfpl.lib.ca.us* ⊙ *Mon. and Sat. 10–6, Tues.–Thurs. 9–8, Fri. noon–6, Sun. noon–5.*

United Nations Plaza. Locals know this plaza for two things: its Wednesday and Sunday farmers' market—cheap and earthy to the Ferry Building's pricey and beautiful—and its homeless population, which seems to return no matter how many times the city tries to shunt them aside. Brick pillars listing various nations and the dates of their admittance into the United Nations line the plaza, and its floor is inscribed with the goals and philosophy of the United Nations charter, which was signed at the War Memorial Opera House in 1945. ✉ *Fulton St. between Hyde and Market Sts., Civic Center.*

War Memorial Opera House. During San Francisco's Barbary Coast days, operagoers smoked cigars, didn't check their revolvers, and expressed their appreciation with "shrill whistles and savage yells," as one observer put it. All the old opera houses were destroyed in the 1906 quake, but lusty support for opera continued. The San Francisco

Where can I find . . .?

PARKING	Civic Center Plaza Garage	Jesse Square Garage
	✉355 McAllister St.	✉223 Stevenson St.
	Most convenient place to use if youre here for a performance.	A SoMa secret with good rates and plenty of space.
A GAS STATION	**76**	**Chevron**
	✉390 1st St.	✉1298 Howard St.
	Near I80, with middling prices.	In SoMa but relatively close to Civic Center.
PRE-THEATER DRINKS	**Hôtel Biron**	**Jade Bar**
	✉45 Rose St.	✉650 Gough St.
	Have a glass of wine in this tiny, arty Hayes Valley spot.	Va-voom lounge with great happy hour specials.

Opera didn't have a permanent home until the War Memorial Opera House was inaugurated in 1932 with a performance of *Tosca*. Modeled after its European counterparts, the building has a vaulted and coffered ceiling, marble foyer, two balconies, and a huge silver art-deco chandelier that resembles a sunburst. The San Francisco Opera performs here from September through December and in summer; the opera house hosts the San Francisco Ballet from February through May, with December *Nutcracker* performances. ✉*301 Van Ness Ave., Civic Center* ☎*415/621–6600* ⊕*www.sfwmpac.org.*

War Memorial Veterans Building. Performing- and visual-arts organizations occupy much of this 1930s structure. **Herbst Theatre** (☎*415/392–4400*) hosts classical ensembles, dance performances, and City Arts and Lectures events. Past City Arts speakers have included author Salman Rushdie and comedian and author Al Franken. Also in the building are two galleries that charge no admission. The street-level **San Francisco Arts Commission Gallery** (☎*415/554–6080* ✉*Free* ☉ *Wed.–Sat. noon–5*) displays the works of Bay Area artists. The **Museum of Performance & Design** (☎*415/255–4800* ✉*Free* ☉*Library Wed.–Sat. noon–5, Sat. 1–5; gallery Tues.–Sat. noon–5*) occupies part of the fourth floor. A small gallery hosts interesting exhibitions, but the organization functions mainly as a library and research center for the San Francisco Bay Area's rich performing-arts legacy. ✉*401 Van Ness Ave., Civic Center* ⊕*www.sfwmpac.org.*

Dining in SoMA & Civic Center

AT A GLANCE

BUDGET

Chaat Café, Indian, 320 3rd St.

Suppenküche, German, 601 Hayes St.

MODERATE

Absinthe, French, 398 Hayes St.

Bar Jules, French, 609 Hayes St.

Coco500, American, 500 Brannan St.

Hayes Street Grill, Seafood, 320 Hayes St.

LuLu, Mediterranean, 816 Folsom St.

Orson, American, 508 Fourth St.

Salt House, American, 545 Mission St.

Town Hall, American, 342 Howard St.

Two, American, 22 Hawthorne St.

Yank Sing, Chinese, 1 Rincon Center, 101 Spear St.

Zuni Café, Mediterranean, 1658 Market St.

EXPENSIVE

Acme Chophouse, Steak, 24 Willie Mays Plaza

Ame, Eclectic, St. Regis Hotel, 689 Mission St.

Bacar, American, 448 Brannan St.

Fifth Floor, American, Palomar Hotel, 12 4th St.

Garden Court, American, Palace Hotel, 2 New Montgomery St.

Jardinière, American, 300 Grove St.

Nob Hill & Russian Hill

Lombard street

WORD OF MOUTH

"Are you familiar with our famous hills? Pacific Heights, Nob Hill & Russian Hill can be monster climbs if you don't study the terrain before you head out."

—StuDudley

GETTING ORIENTED

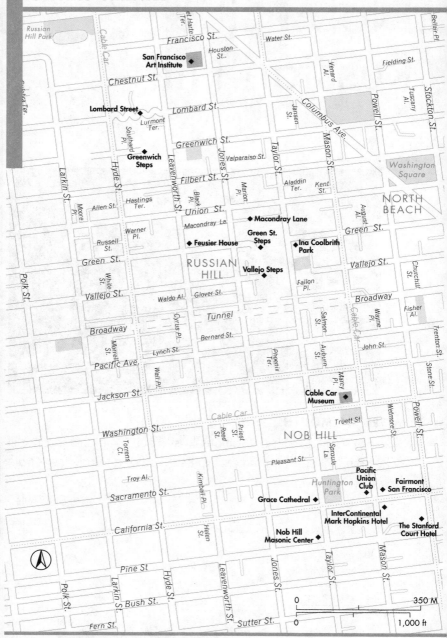

Russian Hill Park

Cable Car

Colaho Ter.

Harte Ter.

Francisco St.

Houston St.

Water St.

San Francisco Art Institute

Venard Al.

Fielding St.

Chestnut St.

Stockton St.

Tuscany Al.

Lombard Street

Lombard St.

Lurmont Ter.

Columbus Ave.

Powell St.

Larkin St.

Hyde St.

Southard Pl.

Greenwich Steps

Greenwich St.

Jansen St.

Taylor St.

Mason St.

Washington Square

Leavenworth St.

Jones St.

Valparaiso St.

Filbert St.

Moore Pl.

Allen St.

Hastings Ter.

Black Pl.

Marion Pl.

Aladdin Ter.

Kent St.

NORTH BEACH

Warner Pl.

Union St.

Russell St.

Macondray La.

Macondray Lane

August Al.

Feusier House

Green St. Steps

Green St.

Ina Coolbrith Park

White St.

RUSSIAN HILL

Vallejo Steps

Vallejo St.

Churchill St.

Green St.

Green St.

Vallejo St.

Polk St.

Vallejo St.

Waldo Al.

Glover St.

Fallon Pl.

Broadway

Tunnel

Fisher Al.

Cyrus Pl.

Bernard St.

Salmon St.

Wayne Pl.

Trenton St.

Broadway

Morrell St.

Lynch St.

Cable Car

John St.

Pacific Ave.

Wall Pl.

Auburn St.

Stone St.

Jackson St.

Phoenix Ter.

Marcy Pl.

Cable Car Museum

Wetmore St.

Cable Car

Priest St.

Reed St.

Truett St.

Powell St.

Washington St.

NOB HILL

Torrens Ct.

Sproule La.

Troy Al.

Pleasant St.

Pacific Union Club

Fairmont San Francisco

Sacramento St.

Kimball Pl.

Huntington Park

Grace Cathedral

InterContinental Mark Hopkins Hotel

California St.

Helen St.

The Stanford Court Hotel

Nob Hill Masonic Center

Pine St.

Larkin St.

Hyde St.

Leavenworth St.

Jones St.

Taylor St.

Mason St.

Polk St.

Bush St.

Fern St.

Sutter St.

0   350 M

0   1,000 ft

TOP 5 REASONS TO GO

Macondray Lane: Duck into this secret, lush garden lane and walk its narrow, uneven cobblestones.

Vallejo Steps area: Make the steep climb up to lovely Ina Coolbrith Park, then continue up along the glorious garden path of the Vallejo Steps to a spectacular view at the top.

San Francisco Art Institute: Contemplate a Diego Rivera mural and stop at the café for cheap organic coffee and a priceless view of the city and the bay. It may be the best way to spend an hour for a buck in town.

Cable Car Museum: Ride a cable car all the way back to the barn, hanging on tight as it clack-clack-clacks its way up Nob Hill, then go behind the scenes at the museum.

Play "Bullitt" on the steepest streets: For the ride of your life, take a drive up and down the city's steepest streets on Russian Hill. A trip over the precipice of Filbert or Jones will make you feel like you're falling off the edge of the world.

QUICK BITES

A harpist plays the classics and other tunes during afternoon tea at the **Ritz-Carlton, San Francisco** (⌂ *600 Stockton St., at California St., Nob Hill* ☎ *415/296–7465* ⊕ *www.ritzcarlton.com*). Hours vary throughout the year, but seatings are usually available 3:30–4:30 on weekdays and 1–4:30 on weekends.

Take a break from walking the hills at the original **Swensen's Ice Cream** (⌂ *1999 Hyde St., at Union St., Russian Hill* ☎ *415/775–6818*), a neighborhood favorite since it opened in 1948. An antique sign still fronts the tiny shop, which has just a single counter inside, but concessions to the times include such ice-cream flavors as green tea and lychee.

GETTING THERE

The thing about Russian Hill and Nob Hill is that they're both especially steep hills. If you're not up for the hike, a cable car is certainly the most exciting way to reach the top. Take the California line for Nob Hill and the Powell–Hyde line for Russian Hill. There is some bus service as well, such as the 1–California bus for Nob Hill, but the routes only run east–west. Only the cable cars tackle the steeper north–south streets. Driving yourself is a hassle, since parking is a challenge on these crowded, precipitous streets.

MAKING THE MOST OF YOUR TIME

Since walking Nob Hill is (almost) all about gazing at exteriors, touring the neighborhood during daylight hours is a must. The sights here don't require a lot of visiting time—say a half hour each at the Cable Car Museum and Grace Cathedral—but allow plenty of time for the walk itself. An afternoon visit is ideal for Russian Hill, so you can browse the shops. You could cover both neighborhoods in three or four hours. If you time it just right, you can finish up with a sunset cocktail at one of the über-swanky hotel lounges or the quirky Tonga Room.

NOB HILL & RUSSIAN HILL

Sightseeing
☆☆☆★★

Nightlife
☆☆☆☆★

Dining
☆☆★★★

Lodging
☆☆★★★

Shopping
☆☆☆★★

By Denise M. Leto

In place of the quirky charm and cultural diversity that mark other San Francisco neighborhoods, Nob Hill exudes history and good breeding. Topped with some of the city's most elegant hotels, Gothic Grace Cathedral, and private blue-blood clubs, it's the pinnacle of privilege. One hill over, across Pacific Avenue, is another old-family bastion, Russian Hill. It may not be quite as wealthy as Nob Hill, but it's no slouch—and it's known for its jaw-dropping views.

Nob Hill was officially dubbed during the 1870s when "the Big Four"—Charles Crocker, Leland Stanford, Mark Hopkins, and Collis Huntington, who were involved in the construction of the transcontinental railroad—built their hilltop estates. The lingo is thick from this era: those on the hilltop were referred to as "nabobs" (originally meaning a provincial governor from India) and "swells," and the hill itself was called Snob Hill, a term that survives to this day. By 1882 so many estates had sprung up on Nob Hill that Robert Louis Stevenson called it "the hill of palaces." But the 1906 earthquake and fire destroyed all the palatial mansions, except for portions of the Flood brownstone. History buffs may choose to linger here, but for most visitors, a casual glimpse from a cable car will be enough.

Essentially a tony residential neighborhood of spiffy pieds-à-terre, Victorian flats, Edwardian cottages, and boxlike condos, Russian Hill also has some of the city's loveliest stairway walks, hidden garden ways, and steepest streets—brave drivers can really have some fun here—not to mention those bay views. Several stories explain the origin of Russian Hill's name. One legend has it that Russian farmers raised vegetables here for Farallon Islands seal hunters; another attributes the name to a Russian sailor of prodigious drinking habits who drowned when he fell into a well on the hill. A plaque at the top of the Vallejo Steps gives credence to the version that says sailors of the Russian-American company were buried here in the 1840s. Be sure to visit the sign for yourself—its location offers perhaps the finest vantage point on the hill.

WHAT TO SEE IN NOB HILL

For details on the ♺ **Cable Car Museum,** *see* the Cable Cars feature in the Experience chapter.

Fairmont San Francisco. The hotel's dazzling opening was delayed a year by the 1906 quake, but since then the marble palace has hosted presidents, royalty, movie stars, and local nabobs. Things have changed since its early days, however: on the eve of World War I you could get a room for as low as $2.50 per night, meals included. Nowadays, prices go as high as $8,000, which buys a night in the eight-room, Persian-art-filled penthouse suite that was showcased regularly in the 1980s TV series *Hotel.* Swing through the opulent lobby on your way to tea (served daily 2:30–4:30) at the **Laurel Court** restaurant. Don't miss an evening cocktail (a mai tai is in order) in the kitschy **Tonga Room,** complete with tiki huts, a sporadic tropical rainstorm, and a floating bandstand. ✉ *950 Mason St., Nob Hill* ☎ *415/772–5000* ⊕ *www. fairmont.com.*

Grace Cathedral. Not many churches can boast a Keith Haring sculpture and not one but two labyrinths. The seat of the Episcopal Church in San Francisco, this soaring Gothic-style structure, erected on the site of Charles Crocker's mansion, took 53 years to build, wrapping up in 1964. The gilded bronze doors at the east entrance were taken from casts of Lorenzo Ghiberti's incredible Gates of Paradise, which are on the baptistery in Florence, Italy. A black-and-bronze stone sculpture of St. Francis by Beniamino Bufano greets you as you enter.

The 35-foot-wide labyrinth, a large, purplish rug, is a replica of the 13th-century stone maze on the floor of the Chartres cathedral. All are encouraged to walk the ¼-mi-long labyrinth, a ritual based on the tradition of meditative walking. There's also a terrazzo outdoor labyrinth on the church's north side. The AIDS Interfaith Chapel, to the right as you enter Grace, contains a metal tryptich sculpture by the late artist Keith Haring and panels from the AIDS Memorial Quilt. ■ TIP→ **Especially dramatic times to view the cathedral are during Thursday-night evensong (5:15) and during special holiday programs.** ✉ *1100 California St., at Taylor St., Nob Hill* ☎ *415/749–6300* ⊕ *www.grace cathedral.org* ⊙ *Weekdays 7–6, Sat. 8–6, Sun. 7–7.*

InterContinental Mark Hopkins Hotel. Built on the ashes of railroad tycoon Mark Hopkins's grand estate (constructed at his wife's urging; Hop-

LOOK FAMILIAR?

The grand Brocklebank Apartments, on the northeast corner of Sacramento and Mason streets across from the Fairmont hotel, might look eerily familiar. In 1958 the complex was showcased in Alfred Hitchcock's *Vertigo* (Jimmy Stewart starts trailing Kim Novak here) and in the 1990s it popped up in the miniseries *Tales of the City.*

kins himself preferred to live frugally), this 19-story hotel went up in 1926. A combination of French château and Spanish Renaissance architecture, with noteworthy terra-cotta detailing, it has hosted statesmen, royalty, and Hollywood celebrities. The 11-room penthouse was turned into a glass-walled cocktail lounge in 1939: the **Top of the Mark** is remembered fondly by thousands of World War II veterans who jammed the lounge before leaving for overseas duty. Wives and sweethearts watching the ships depart gave the room's northwest nook its name—Weepers' Corner. With its 360-degree views, the lounge is a wonderful spot for a nighttime drink. ✉ *999 California St., at Mason St., Nob Hill* ☎ *415/392–3434* ⊕ *www.markhopkins.net.*

Nob Hill Masonic Center. Erected by Freemasons in 1957, the hall is familiar to locals mostly as a concert and lecture venue, where such notables as Van Morrison and Al Gore have appeared. The recent Dan Brown–led spate of interest in the Masons and other secret fraternities unfortunately hasn't done anything to improve the sightlines or the seats here, but those interested in Masonic history can check out the impressive lobby mosaic. "How the hell did I do that?" wondered artist Emile Norman in 2005 on the eve of his mosaic's renovation. Mainly in rich greens and yellows, the mosaic depicts the Masons' role in California history. There's also an intricate model of King Solomon's Temple in the lobby. ✉ *1111 California St., Nob Hill* ☎ *415/776–4702* ⊕ *www. sfmasoniccenter.com* ⊗ *Lobby weekdays 8–5.*

Pacific Union Club. The former home of silver baron James Flood cost a whopping $1.5 million in 1886, when even a stylish Victorian like the Haas-Lilienthal House cost less than $20,000. All that cash did buy some structural stability. The Flood residence (to be precise, its shell) was the only Nob Hill mansion to survive the 1906 earthquake and fire. The Pacific Union Club, a bastion of the wealthy and powerful, purchased the house in 1907 and commissioned Willis Polk to redesign it; the architect added the semicircular wings and third floor. (The ornate fence design dates from the mansion's construction.) West of the house, Huntington Park is the site of the Huntington mansion, destroyed in 1906. Mrs. Huntington donated the land to the city for use as a park; the Crockers purchased the Fountain of the Tortoises, based on the original in Rome. ■ TIP→ **The benches around the fountain offer a welcome break after climbing Nob Hill.**

It's hard to get the skinny on the club itself; its 700 or so members allegedly follow the directive "no women, no Democrats, no reporters." Those who join usually spend decades on the waiting list and undergo a stringent vetting process, the rigors of which might embarrass the NSA. Needless to say, the club is closed to the public. ✉ *1000 California St., Nob Hill.*

The Stanford Court Hotel. In 1876 trendsetter Leland Stanford, a California governor and founder of Stanford University, was the first to build an estate on Nob Hill. The only part that survived the earthquake was a basalt-and-granite wall that's been restored; check it out from the eastern side of the hotel. In 1912 an apartment house was built on the site of the former estate, and in 1972 the present-day hotel was constructed from the shell of that building. The lobby has a stained-glass dome and sepia-tone murals depicting scenes of early San Francisco. ✉ *905 California St., Nob Hill* ☎ *415/989–3500* ⊕ *www.renaissancehotels.com.*

WHAT TO SEE IN RUSSIAN HILL

Feusier House. Octagonal houses were once thought to make the best use of space and enhance the physical and mental well-being of their occupants. A brief mid-19th-century craze inspired the construction of several in San Francisco. Only the Feusier House, built in 1857, and the Octagon House remain standing. A private residence, the Feusier House is easy to overlook unless you look closely—it's dwarfed by the large-scale apartments around it. Across from the Feusier House is the **1907 Firehouse** (✉ *1088 Green St., Russian Hill*). Louise M. Davies, the local art patron for whom symphony hall is named, bought it from the city in 1957. The firehouse is closed to the public, but it's worth taking in the exterior. ✉ *1067 Green St., Russian Hill.*

★ **Ina Coolbrith Park.** If you make it all the way up here, you may have the place all to yourself, or at least feel like you do. The park's terraces are carved from a hill so steep that it's difficult to see if anyone else is there or not. Locals love this park because it feels like a secret no one else knows about—one of the city's magic hidden gardens, with a meditative setting and spectacular views of the bay peeking out from among the trees. A poet, Oakland librarian, and niece of Mormon prophet Joseph Smith, Ina Coolbrith (1842–1928) introduced Jack London and Isadora Duncan to the world of books. For years she entertained literary greats in her Macondray Lane home near the park. In 1915 she was named poet laureate of California. ✉ *Vallejo St. between Mason and Taylor Sts., Russian Hill.*

Lombard Street. The block-long "Crookedest Street in the World" makes eight switchbacks down the east face of Russian Hill between Hyde and Leavenworth streets. Residents bemoan the traffic jam outside their front doors, and occasionally the city attempts to discourage drivers by posting a traffic cop near the top of the hill, but the determined can find a way around. If no one is standing guard, join the line of cars waiting to drive down the steep hill, or avoid the whole mess and walk down the steps on either side of Lombard. You take in super views of North Beach and Coit Tower whether you walk or drive—though if you're the one behind the wheel, you'd better keep your eye on the road lest you become yet another of the many folks who ram the garden barriers.

Where can I find . . .?

PARKING	State Garage	Lombardi Parking Garage
	✉818 Leavenworth St.	✉1600 Jackson St.
	Wont get you to the top of Nob Hill, but decent rates.	Relatively close to parking desert of Russian Hill.

A CUP OF COFFEE	Nook	Chameleon Cafe
	✉1500 Hyde St.	✉1299 Pacific Ave.
	Coffee, chai tea, and healthy light meals.	Retro Russian Hill spot with potent coffee and free Wi-Fi.

A DRUGSTORE	Rite Aid	Walgreens
	✉1300 Bush St.	✉1524 Polk St.
	Stop for a bandage or a drink if the hills are getting to you.	Open Mon.Sat. until midnight, Sun. until 11 PM.

■TIP➡ **Can't stand the throngs? Thrill seekers of a different stripe may want to head two blocks south of Lombard to Filbert Street. At a gradient of 31.5%, the hair-raising descent between Hyde and Leavenworth streets is the city's steepest. Go slowly!** ✉*Lombard St. between Hyde and Leavenworth Sts., Russian Hill.*

Fodor'sChoice ★ **Macondray Lane.** San Francisco has no shortage of impressive, grand homes, but it's the tiny fairy-tale lanes that make most folks want to move here, and Macondray Lane is the quintessential hidden garden. Enter under a lovely wooden trellis and proceed down a quiet, cobbled pedestrian lane lined with Edwardian cottages and flowering plants and trees. ■TIP➡ **Watch your step—the cobblestones are quite uneven in spots.** A flight of steep wooden stairs at the end of the lane leads to Taylor Street—on the way down you can't miss the bay views. If you've read any of Armistead Maupin's *Tales of the City* books, you may find the lane vaguely familiar. It's the thinly disguised setting for part of the series' action. ✉*Between Jones and Taylor Sts., and Union and Green Sts., Russian Hill.*

★ **San Francisco Art Institute.** A Moorish-tile fountain in a tree-shaded courtyard draws the eye as soon as you enter the institute. The number-one reason for a visit is Mexican master Diego Rivera's *Making of a Fresco Showing the Building of a City* (1931), in the student gallery to your immediate left inside the entrance. Rivera himself is in the fresco—his broad behind is to the viewer—and he's surrounded by his assistants. They in turn are surrounded by a construction scene, laborers, and city notables such as sculptor Robert Stackpole and architect Timothy Pfleuger. *The Making of a Fresco* is one of three San Francisco murals painted by Rivera. The number-two reason to come here is the café, or more precisely the eye-popping, panoramic view from the café, which serves surprisingly decent food for a song.

AT A GLANCE

Dining in Nob Hill & Russian Hill

MODERATE
Antica Trattoria, Italian, 2400 Polk St.

EXPENSIVE
La Folie, French, 2316 Polk St.

Masa's, French, Hotel Vintage Court, 648 Bush St.

Ritz-Carlton Dining Room and Terrace, French, 600 Stockton St.

4

The older portions of the Art Institute, including the lovely Mission-style bell tower, were erected in 1926. To this day, otherwise pragmatic people claim that ghostly footsteps can be heard in the tower at night. Ansel Adams created the school's fine-arts photography department in 1946, and school directors established the country's first fine-arts film program. Notable faculty and alumni have included painter Richard Diebenkorn and photographers Dorothea Lange, Edward Weston, and Annie Leibovitz. The **Walter & McBean Galleries** (☎*415/749–4563* ☉*Tues.–Sat. 11–6*) exhibit the often provocative works of established artists. ✉*800 Chestnut St., North Beach* ☎*415/771-7020* ⊕*www. sfai.edu* ☜*Galleries free* ☉*Student gallery daily 8:30–8:30.*

Vallejo Steps area. Several Russian Hill buildings survived the 1906 earthquake and fire and remain standing. Patriotic firefighters saved what's come to be known as the **Flag House** (✉*1652–56 Taylor St., Russian Hill*) when they spotted the American flag on the property and doused the flames with seltzer water and wet sand. The owner, a flag collector, fearing the house would burn to the ground, wanted it to go down in style, with "all flags flying."

The Flag House, at the southwest corner of Ina Coolbrith Park, is one of a number of California Shingle–style homes in this neighborhood, several of which were designed by Willis Polk. Polk also laid out the Vallejo steps, which climb the steep ridge across Taylor Street from the Flag House. If the walk up the steps themselves is too steep for you, it's possible to park at the top of the steps by heading east on Vallejo from Jones. The **Polk-Williams House** (✉*Taylor and Vallejo Sts., Russian Hill*) was designed by Polk, who lived in one of its finer sections. The architect also designed **1034–1036 Vallejo,** across the street from the Polk-Williams House. ✉*Taylor and Vallejo Sts., steps lead up toward Jones St., Russian Hill.*

7–10 AM All available troops report to Mayor Eugene Schmitz and begin rescuing civilians.

10:30 AM "Ham and Egg Fire" is started by a family cooking breakfast. This fire destroys City Hall and advances south down Mission Street.

2:30 PM Soldiers begin dynamiting buildings around 5th and Mission streets to create firebreaks.

8:15 AM A major aftershock hits; many damaged buildings collapse.

1 PM The entire Financial District is in flames.

3 PM Mayor Schmitz issues "shoot to kill" order to police to quell looting and other crimes.

WEDNESDAY, APRIL 19, 1906

5:12 AM The brunt of the earthquake hits, with sharp shocks and violent shaking lasting up to a minute. Fifty-two fires start across the city.

EARTHQUAKE CITY

San Franciscans know that they are, quite literally, living on the edge. Multiple fault lines run through the Bay Area. Small, undetectable earthquakes rumble beneath the surface here every few days; a few each year are strong enough to feel. Yet residents are willing to tempt fate to live in this vibrant city, and usually the gamble pays off. But if you roll the dice often enough, eventually they come up snake eyes.

9 PM Firefighters attempt to stop fires from advancing up Nob Hill; they are unsuccessful.

5 AM Nob Hill mansions are engulfed in flames. Fire reaches Van Ness, where the army has dynamited mansions along the wide avenue to create a firebreak.

Firebreak at Van Ness is successful in the early morning, and the fire's westward movement is halted.

FRIDAY, APRIL 20

THURSDAY, APRIL 19

4 AM Secretary of War William Howard Taft orders rations, supplies, and "all the tents in the U.S. Army" sent to San Francisco.

SATURDAY, APRIL 21

Fire in the Mission is stopped at 20th and Dolores streets.

1906: THE GREAT QUAKE & FIRE

Looking down Sacramento Street as the fire rages

It was dark at 5:12 AM on Wednesday, April 18, 1906 —a peaceful midweek morning. A few early risers had just rolled out of bed to put a kettle on. High-society revelers, having attended the much-anticipated Metropolitan Opera of New York performance of *Carmen* Tuesday night, had only just shut their eyes. Night-shifters were still trudging home along the cobblestone avenues.

Seconds later, the face of San Francisco would change forever, after the most severe urban earthquake in known history and four days of uncontrollable fires ravaged the city. The toll would be massive: 28,188 buildings destroyed; $500 million in damages ($8–$12 billion in today's dollars); more than 3,000 dead; and, in a city of 400,000, approximately 225,000 residents left homeless.

Contrary to popular belief, the 1906 earthquake left many landmarks relatively unharmed—it was the subsequent fires that reduced San Francisco to rubble. Nearly all of the city's water mains were severed by the quake, leaving fires to rage unchecked for four days. By the time the flames subsided on Saturday, April 21, burned areas of the city extended more than 500 city blocks, from the bay west to Van Ness and south to 7th and Townsend streets. SoMa, the Financial District, North Beach, and other center-city neighborhoods were beyond repair. The death toll was estimated at just under 500 people—a number that stood until quite recently. But over the past 20 years, dogged research has upped that number to about 3,400. Most of the disaster's victims were consumed by the fires, buried in rubble, or were left uncounted because of their immigrant status.

BY THE NUMBERS

Magnitude: Estimated 7.9 on the moment magnitude scale. The energy unleashed was roughly the equivalent of 15 million tons of dynamite.

Area: Felt in an area of approximately 375,000 square miles, from Coquille, Oregon in the north (390 mi), to Los Angeles in the south (370 mi), to central Nevada in the east (340 mi).

Epicenter: 2 mi offshore, under the Pacific Ocean.

"As soon as I reached the curb a second shock hit.... I was thrown flat and the cobblestones danced like corn in a popper."

—Thomas Jefferson Chase, a Ferry Building ticket clerk

AREA DESTROYED BY FIRE

(top) Fire on Market Street
(bottom) Clay Street in ruins

4

IN FOCUS: EARTHQUAKE CITY

LANDMARKS THAT REMAIN

Lotta's Fountain, at the intersection of Kearny and Market streets, was dedicated to the city in 1875; it's the oldest standing monument in San Francisco. A ceremony commemorating the Great Quake is held here every April 18 at 5:12 AM.

The 1889 **Audiffred Building** (Mission St. and the Embarcadero) was the only waterfront structure standing after the fires.

The exterior wall of the 42-room brownstone **Flood mansion** (1000 California St.), now the private Pacific Union Club, is the only intact pre-1906 building on Nob Hill.

The Italian renaissance palazzo–style **U.S. Post Office** (7th and Mission Sts.), completed in 1905, still stands.

Employees dramatically rescued the 1874 **Old U.S. Mint** (88 5th St.)—and the $300,000,000 in its vaults—from within, pumping water from an artesian well.

"The glass in our windows ... melted down like butter; the sandstone and granite, of which the building was constructed, began to flake off with explosive noises like the firing of artillery."

—U.S. Mint Superintendent Frank Aleomon Leach

THE LITTLE HYDRANT THAT COULD

On Friday, April 20, 1906, fires raged through the Mission. The situation looked bleak, until locals alerted firemen to a working hydrant at 20th and Church streets. With help from refugees and "the Little Giant," firefighters were able to halt the fire's advance at 20th and Dolores streets, steps from the Mission Dolores. Each April, locals paint the hydrant gold in celebration.

Removing debris at Third, Kearney, and Market streets

LOST TREASURES

The **Palace Hotel** (Market and Montgomery Sts.), built in 1876, was the city's most elegant and prestigious hotel, with 800 rooms, marble balconies, and elevators.

The huge, Beaux-Arts **City Hall**, finished in 1899, took 26 years and $6 million (about $130 million in today's dollars) to build. It collapsed in about a minute.

The most ostentatious displays of wealth in San Francisco were the **Nob Hill mansions** owned by railroad magnates Charles Crocker, Mark Hopkins, Leland Stanford, and Collis Huntington—San Francisco's "Big Four." Some considered the homes' destruction to be retribution for the millionaires' corrupt dealings.

REBUILDING

Grand plans to re-create San Francisco in the image of Paris or Washington were short-lived. Residents and business-owners, eager to erase the scars of the disaster, hastily rebuilt the city. Formerly opulent structures, such as City Hall, were reconstructed quickly, with simpler designs and cheaper materials. Graft scandals engulfed Mayor Schmitz, who was removed from office in summer 1907. By then, the last refugee houses were being pulled down. Two years later, about 20,000 new buildings had gone up.

LEARN MORE

The Bancroft Library, at UC Berkeley, has an excellent digital collection titled **"The 1906 San Francisco Earthquake and Fire"** (⊕ http://bancroft.berkeley.edu/collections/earthquakeandfire), with an interactive map and hundreds of photographs of the earthquake and fire.

The Virtual Museum of the City of San Francisco (⊕ www.sfmuseum.org) has the city's best collection of photographs and information about the event; it's available online only, except during special exhibitions.

The *San Francisco Chronicle*'s coverage (⊕ www.sfgate.com/greatquake/) includes first-person accounts, overview articles, and current-day assessments.

San Francisco City Guides (☏ 415/577–4266, ⊕ www.sfcityguides.org) gives earthquake and fire walking tours year-round.

> "They held on longest to their trunks, and over these trunks many a strong man broke his heart that night. The hills of San Francisco are steep, and up these hills, mile after mile, were the trunks dragged."
>
> —Jack London, for *Collier's* national weekly

1989: THE LOMA PRIETA QUAKE

Smashed cars on the collapsed section of the Bay Bridge

Excitement filled the Bay Area on October 17, 1989—it was Game 3 of the World Series between the Oakland Athletics and the San Francisco Giants. But as the players took the field of Candlestick Park, exhilaration turned to shock when, at 5:04 pm, a 6.9-magnitude earthquake shook the region.

At first, the thousands of fans in the ballpark thought it might be a joke, but then the field began to roll. The Giants' pitcher, Mike Krukow, said "It felt like a 600-pound gopher going underneath my feet at 40 miles an hour."

The Giants' stadium resisted damage, as did much of San Francisco, but the Marina district was not so lucky. It was built on filled-in marshland, which liquefied as it shook. (Liquefaction occurs when un-compacted soil is jolted and loosens, sinks, and shifts.) Parking garages below buildings collapsed. Fires broke out. To the east, a fifty-foot section of the Bay Bridge collapsed onto the lower deck, claiming one motorist's life. In Oakland, the top deck of the Cypress freeway crashed down, killing 42 drivers. In all, 62 people lost their lives in the earthquake, and 12,000 lost their homes.

The lack of damage from Loma Prieta was mainly due to luck. A blimp covering the World Series game filmed the Marina fires, alerting the fire chief to their existence since phone lines were down. Water lines were ruptured, but the Marina fires were put out by a fireboat that happened to be in the harbor. Winds were light, so the fires didn't spread. And traffic was light on the Bay Bridge, thanks to the World Series.

BY THE NUMBERS

Magnitude: 6.9 on the moment magnitude scale—about ⅓₂ the force of the 1906 quake. The shaking lasted for about 15 seconds.

Area: Felt throughout central California and into western Nevada.

Epicenter: About 60 mi south-southeast of San Francisco, near Loma Prieta peak in the Santa Cruz Mountains.

Cost: Over $6 billion in damages (about $3 billion in San Francisco alone).

> "It was like something out of a Godzilla movie. There were people screaming, hollering, waving, every hellish sight you could imagine, every rescue you could imagine."
>
> —Oakland firefighter Mike Hill

SCIENTIFICALLY SPEAKING

Modern earthquake science was born after the 1906 quake. Geologists were stunned by the size and the massive north/south shift of the earth (nearly 20 feet in places), which could not be explained by the prevailing scientific belief that earthquakes themselves created faults. Subsequent studies lead to the development of the theory of plate tectonics in the 1950s and 60s, now generally accepted as the cause of the 1906 earthquake.

THE NEXT BIG ONE

In 2002, the U.S. Geological Survey reported that there was a 62% chance that an earthquake of magnitude 6.7 or higher would hit the Bay Area before 2032, most likely occurring at the San Andreas Fault (which cuts the peninsula at its "neck") or at the Hayward Fault (which runs through Oakland and Berkeley).

Small quakes hit the Bay Area every few days, but are usually only magnitude 2 or 3, which most people don't even feel. Fewer than five quakes per year are large enough to be felt, but these are usually akin to the rumble of a tractor-trailer passing, and last only a few seconds. Since 1800, only four quakes have been categorized as "major," at a magnitude of 7.0 or higher.

Berkeley Digital Seismic Network, Northern California Seismic Network, USGS Low-Frequency Physical Network, and Parkfield High-Frequency Seismic Network all have instruments spread around the Bay Area: surface motion sensors, borehole geophones and accelerometers, tensor strain meters, GPS receivers, and ocean-bottom observatories are monitoring the area's shaky ground.

WHAT HAVE WE LEARNED?

Every earthquake teaches engineers a bit more, and modern building codes are such that it's unlikely that a new building would topple in an earthquake. In the Loma Prieta quake, newer up-to-code structures like the Transamerica Pyramid survived with barely a scrape. Unfortunately,

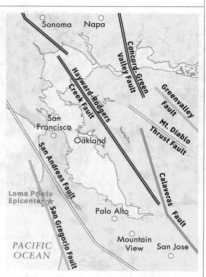

modern building codes don't apply to older buildings unless they undergo renovation.

BART tunnels under the bay are not strong enough to withstand a major quake. The new, earthquake-ready eastern section of the Bay Bridge isn't scheduled for completion until 2013—more than 20 years after the Loma Prieta quake. Water pipeline upgrades are a work in progress, but are far from done. About 85% of the city's hospitals are not retrofitted. The entire Sunset neighborhood is on unstable ground and could collapse in a major quake, as buildings did in 1989. And an earthquake on the Hayward fault could destroy the Delta levee system, which supplies water to at least a third of the state of California.

Progress is being made, albeit slowly. Schools have been retrofitted for the most part, and other public buildings, like hospitals, have deadlines for retrofitting. By 2030, all hospitals must be fully functional in an earthquake.

The U.S. Geological Survey posts real-time earthquake maps and 24-hour forecasts on its Web site (⊕ http://quake.wr.usgs.gov/recent/index.html).

North Beach

Italian bakery, North Beach

WORD OF MOUTH

"To me, walking [in North Beach] always makes me feel like I'm on vacation. On sunny days, the sidewalk tables are full of folks sipping wine or cappuccino. The food might not be the absolute best in town, but the place has a great relaxed vibe. The famous boho café Trieste is always a treat, very old school with folks sketching instead of plugged into laptops."

—wandergrrl

GETTING ORIENTED

Pier 43

Pier 41

Pier 39

Pier 35

Pier 33

Pier 31

Pier 29

Pier 27

San Francisco Bay

◆ Fishermans Wharf

Beach St.

NORTH
BEACH

North Point St.

The Embarcadero

Bay St.

Taylor St. Cable Car

Mason St.

Powell St.

Stockton St.

Kearny St.

Pfeiffer St.

Chestnut St.

Chestnut St.

TELEGRAPH
HILL

Lombard St.

Lombard St.

Telegraph Hill ◆

Levi Strauss
Headquarters ◆

◆ Tatoo Art
Museum

Jansen St.

◆ Coit Tower

Greenwich St.

Alta St.

Saints Peter and
Paul Catholic Church ◆

Union St.

Jones St.

Filbert St.

Washington
Square ◆

Varennes St.

Sonoma St.

Green St.

Sansome St.

Battery St.

Macondray La.

Union St.

Columbus Ave.

Grant Ave.

Kearny St.

Montgomery St.

Taylor St.

Green St.

Vallejo St.

Broadway

Beat Museum ◆

City Lights
Bookstore ◆

Tunnel

Stockton St.

Sentinel
Building ◆

Jackson
Square
Historic
District

Bernard St.

Pacific Ave.

Cable Car

John St.

Jackson St.

Cable Car

Cable Car
Museum ◆

CHINATOWN

Washington St.

Portsmouth
Square

M. Twain
Pl.

Clay St.

Commercial St.

0   350 M

0   1,000 ft

TOP 5 REASONS TO GO

Espresso, espresso, espresso: Or cappuccino, Americano, mocha—however you take your caffeine, this is the neighborhood for it. Hanging out in a café constitutes sightseeing here, so find a chair and get to work.

Colorful watering holes: The high concentration of bars with character, like Tosca Café, makes North Beach the perfect neighborhood for a pub crawl.

Filbert Steps: Walk down this dizzying stairway from Telegraph Hill's Coit Tower, past lush private gardens and jaw-dropping bay views—and listen for the hill's famous screeching parrots.

Grant Avenue: Check out vanguard boutiques, rambling antiques shops, and cavernous old-time bars, all chockablock on narrow Grant Avenue. The best stuff is crowded into the four blocks between Columbus Avenue and Filbert Street.

Browsing books at City Lights: Illuminate your mind at this Beat-era landmark. Its great book selection, author events, and keen staff make it just as cool as ever.

QUICK BITES

Many consider the fresh-from-the-oven focaccia from **Liguria Bakery** (⊠*1700 Stockton St., at Filbert St., North Beach* ☎*415/421–3786*) to be the best in the neighborhood. Get there early, before noon—when the focaccia is gone, the place usually closes.

The friendly *paesans* behind the counter at **Molinari's Deli** (⊠*373 Columbus Ave., North Beach* ☎*415/421–2337*) serve up the most delicious, and quite possibly the biggest, sandwiches in town. Take a number, grab your bread from the bin, and gaze upon the sandwich board. If you want to eat in, say a prayer to the patron saint of table nabbing—there are all of three tables, outside. Fortunately, Washington Square park is close by.

GETTING THERE

The Powell–Mason cable car line can drop you within a block of Washington Square park, in the heart of North Beach. The 30–Stockton and 15–3rd Street buses run to the neighborhood from Market Street. Once you're here, North Beach is a snap to explore on foot. It's mostly relatively flat—but climbing Telegraph Hill to reach Coit Tower is another story entirely.

MAKING THE MOST OF YOUR TIME

There's no bad time of day to visit this quarter. The cafés buzz morning to night, the shops along main drags Columbus Avenue and Broadway tend to stay open until at least 6 or 7 PM, and late-night revelers don't start checking their watches until about 2 AM. Sunday is quieter since some shops close (though City Lights is open daily, until midnight).

Plan to spend a few hours here— it's all about lingering and the only major "sightseeing" spot is Coit Tower. The walk up to the tower is strenuous but rewarding; if you can tough it, make time for it. If you're driving, keep in mind that parking is difficult, especially at night.

5

NORTH BEACH

San Francisco novelist Herbert Gold calls North Beach "the longest-running, most glorious American bohemian operetta outside Greenwich Village." Indeed, to anyone who's spent some time in its eccentric old bars and cafés, North Beach evokes everything from the Barbary Coast days to the no-less-rowdy beatnik era. Italian bakeries appear frozen in time, homages to Jack Kerouac and Allen Ginsberg pop up everywhere, and the modern equivalent of the Barbary Coast's "houses of ill repute," strip joints, do business on Broadway. With its outdoor café tables, throngs of tourists, and holiday vibe, this is probably the part of town Europeans are thinking of when they say San Francisco is the most European city in America.

By Denise M. Leto

The neighborhood truly was a beach at the time of the gold rush—the bay extended into the hollow between Telegraph and Russian hills. Among the first immigrants to Yerba Buena during the early 1840s were young men from the northern provinces of Italy. The Genoese started the fishing industry in the newly renamed boomtown of San Francisco, as well as a much-needed produce business. Later, Sicilians emerged as leaders of the fishing fleets and eventually as proprietors of the seafood restaurants lining Fisherman's Wharf. Meanwhile, their Genoese cousins established banking and manufacturing empires.

Once almost exclusively Italian-American, today North Beach is a mixture of Italian (many of them elderly), Chinese, and San Francisco yuppie, the last among the few able to afford moving here after neighborhood real estate prices began their steep ascent in the late 1990s.

But walk down narrow Romolo Place (off Broadway east of Columbus) or Genoa Place (off Union west of Kearny) or Medau Place (off Filbert west of Grant) and you can feel the immigrant Italian roots of this neighborhood. Locals know that most of the city's finest Italian restaurants are elsewhere, but North Beach is the place that puts folks in mind of Italian food, and there are many decent options to choose from. Bakeries sell focaccia fresh from the oven; eaten warm or cold, it's the perfect portable food. Many other aromas fill the air: coffee beans, deli meats and cheeses, Italian pastries, and—always—pungent garlic. For more on the North Beach food scene, *see* the Where to Eat chapter.

WHAT TO SEE

Beat Museum. It's hard to tell whether the folks who opened this small museum in 2006 are serious—what would the counterculture say about the $18 "Beat beret"? But if you're truly Beat-curious, stop by. Check out the "Beat pad," a mockup of one of the cheap, tiny North Beach apartments the writers and artists populated in the 1950s, complete with bongos and bottle-as-candleholder. Memorabilia includes the shirt Neal Cassady wore while driving Ken Kesey's Merry Prankster bus, "Further." An early photo of the legendary bus is juxtaposed with a more current picture showing it covered with moss and overgrowth, labeled "Nothing lasts." Indeed. There are also manuscripts, letters, and early editions by Jack Kerouac, Allen Ginsberg, and Lawrence Ferlinghetti. The gift store has a good selection of Beat philosophy, though it's nothing you won't find across the street at City Lights. ✉ *540 Broadway, North Beach* ☎ *415/399–9626* ⊕ *www.thebeat museum.org* ✍ *$5* ☉ *Mon. noon–8, Tues.–Sun. 10–10.*

★ **City Lights Bookstore.** Take a look at the exterior of the store: the replica of a revolutionary mural destroyed in Chiapas, Mexico, by military forces; the poetry in the windows; and the sign that says "Turn your sell [sic] phone off. Be here now." This place isn't just doling out best sellers. Designated a city landmark, the hangout of Beat-era writers—Allen Ginsberg and store founder Lawrence Ferlinghetti among them—remains a vital part of San Francisco's literary scene. Browse the three levels of sometimes haphazardly arranged poetry, philosophy, politics, fiction, history, and

CLOSE UP

A Good Walk in North Beach

To hit the highlights of the neighborhood, start off with a browse at Beat landmark City Lights Bookstore. For cool boutique shopping, head north up Grant Avenue. Otherwise, it's time to get down to the serious business of hanging out. Make a left onto Columbus Avenue when you leave the bookstore and walk the strip until you find a café table or pastry display that calls your name.

Fortified, continue down Columbus to Washington Square, where you can walk or take the 39 bus up Telegraph Hill to Coit Tower's views. Be sure to take in the gorgeous gardens along the Filbert Steps on the way down. Finally, reward yourself by returning to Columbus Avenue for a drink at one of the atmosphere-steeped watering holes like Tosca, which is run by a woman Sean Penn calls "the last of the great saloon mistresses."

local zines, to the tune of creaking wood floors. ■TIP→ **Be sure to check their calendar of literary events.**

Back in the day, the basement was a kind of literary living room, where writers like Ginsberg and Kerouac would read and even receive mail. Ferlinghetti cemented City Lights' place in history by publishing Ginsberg's *Howl and Other Poems* in 1956. The small volume was ignored in the mainstream . . . until Ferlinghetti and the bookstore manager were arrested for corruption of youth and obscenity. In the landmark First Amendment trial that followed the judge exonerated both, saying a work that has "redeeming social significance" can't be obscene. *Howl* went on to become a classic.

Kerouac Alley, branching off Columbus Avenue right near City Lights, was rehabbed in 2007. Embedded in the pavement are quotes from Lawrence Ferlinghetti, Maya Angelou, Confucius, John Steinbeck, and of course, the namesake himself. ⊠*261 Columbus Ave., North Beach* ☎*415/362–8193* ⊕*www.citylights.com* ⊘*Daily 10 AM–midnight.*

★ **Coit Tower.** Whether you think it resembles a fire hose or something more, ahem, adult, this 210-foot tower is among San Francisco's most distinctive skyline sights. Although the monument wasn't intended as a tribute to firemen, it's often considered as such because of the donor's special attachment to the local fire company. As the story goes, a young gold rush–era girl, Lillie Hitchcock Coit (known as Miss Lil), was a fervent admirer of her local fire company—so much so that she once deserted a wedding party and chased down the street after her favorite engine, Knickerbocker No. 5, while clad in her bridesmaid finery. She became the Knickerbocker Company's mascot and always signed her name "Lillie Coit 5." When Lillie died in 1929 she left the city $125,000 to "expend in an appropriate manner . . . to the beauty of San Francisco."

You can ride the elevator to the top of the tower—the only thing you have to pay for here—to enjoy the view of the Bay Bridge and the Golden Gate Bridge; due north is Alcatraz Island. ■TIP→ **The views**

CLOSE UP

The Birds

While on Telegraph Hill, you might be startled by a chorus of piercing squawks and a rushing sound of wings. No, you're not about to have a Hitchcock bird-attack moment. These small, vivid green parrots with cherry-red heads number in the hundreds; they're descendants of former pets that escaped or were released by their former owners. (The birds dislike cages and they bite if bothered . . . must've been some disillusioned owners along the way.)

The parrots like to roost high in the aging cypress trees on the hill, chattering and fluttering, sometimes taking wing en masse. They're not popular with most residents, but they did find a champion in local bohemian Mark Bittner, a former street musician. Bittner began chronicling their habits, publishing a book and battling the homeowners who wanted to cut down the cypresses. A documentary, *The Wild Parrots of Telegraph Hill*, made the issue a cause célèbre. In 2007, City Hall, which recognizes a golden goose when it sees one, stepped in and brokered a solution to keep the celebrity birds in town. The city will cover the homeowners' insurance worries and plant new trees for the next generation of wild parrots.

—Denise M. Leto

from the base of the tower are also expansive—and free. Parking at Coit Tower is limited; in fact, you may have to wait (and wait) for a space. Save yourself some frustration and take the 39 bus which goes all the way up to the tower's base or, if you're in good shape, hike up. For more details on the lovely stairway walk, *see* Telegraph Hill, below.

Inside the tower, 19 Depression-era murals depict California's economic and political life. The federal government commissioned the paintings from 25 local artists, and ended up funding quite a controversy. The radical Mexican painter Diego Rivera inspired the murals' socialist-realist style, with its biting cultural commentary, particularly about the exploitation of workers. At the time the murals were painted, clashes between management and labor along the waterfront and elsewhere in San Francisco were widespread. ⊠*Telegraph Hill Blvd. at Greenwich St. or Lombard St., North Beach* ☎*415/362–0808* ✉*Free; elevator to top $3.75* ☉*Daily 10–6.*

OFF THE BEATEN PATH

Tattoo Art Museum. Legendary tattoo artist and historian Lyle Tuttle's collection of tattoo memorabilia fills half his crowded tattoo parlor on the edge of North Beach. Exhibits, including equipment, photographs, newspaper clippings, and a stuffed bat, cover everything from primitive tattooing in Samoa (where the bat comes in) to tattooing in San Francisco in the 1960s. ⊠*841 Columbus Ave., near Lombard St., North Beach* ☎*415/775–4991* ✉*Free* ☉*Daily noon–9.*

Grant Avenue. Originally called Calle de la Fundación, Grant Avenue is the oldest street in the city but it's got plenty of young blood. Here dusty bars such as the Saloon and perennial favorites like the Savoy Tivoli mix with hotshot boutiques, odd curio shops like the antique jumble that is Aria, atmospheric cafés such as the boho haven Caffè

3 Reasons To Love the Espresso in North Beach

Cafés are a way of life in North Beach, and if you're as serious about your coffee as the average San Franciscan or Fodor's editor, you might want to stop in at all three of these spots.

The Giotta family celebrates the art of a good espresso as well as a good tune at **Caffe Trieste** (⊠ *601 Vallejo St., at Grant Ave., North Beach* ☎ *415/392–6739*). Every Saturday (as they have since 1971) from noon to 2 PM, the family presents a weekly musical. Arrive early to secure seats. The program ranges from Italian pop and folk music to operas, and patrons are encouraged to participate. If you're one of the few people in creation who haven't gotten started on a screenplay, you may take inspiration from the fact that Francis Ford Coppola reportedly wrote the screenplay for *The Godfather* here.

Intimate, triangular **Mario's Bohemian Cigar Store** (⊠ *566 Columbus Ave., North Beach* ☎ *415/362–0536*) serves up great hot focaccia sandwiches and North Beach–worthy

espresso at its few tables and beautiful antique oak bar under old-time posters. On sunny days, take your order across the street to Washington Square for a classic San Francisco picnic.

A glance at the menu board— "Espresso: $1.80, Espresso with lemon: $10"—will clue you in that **Caffé Roma** (⊠ *526 Columbus Ave., North Beach* ☎ *415/296–7942*) takes its coffee a lot more seriously than it takes itself. And if you've got a problem with that, owner Tony Azzollini will convince you, from his refusal to make your coffee extra hot to his insistence that you drink your espresso the moment it's brewed. Airy and decidedly undistracting—black and white marble is the predominant theme—Roma is a no-nonsense coffee drinker's pit stop for a hot cup as well as coffee drinks, pastries, and wine. Spot the massive red roaster in the window and you'll know you're there. And if you insist on the lemon twist, you deserve to pay.

Trieste, and authentic Italian delis. While the street runs from Union Square through Chinatown, North Beach, and beyond, the fun stuff in this neighborhood is crowded into the four blocks between Columbus Avenue and Filbert Street. ⊠ *North Beach.*

Levi Strauss headquarters. The carefully landscaped complex appears so collegiate that it's affectionately known as LSU—short for Levi Strauss University. Lawns complement the redbrick buildings, and gurgling fountains drown out the sounds of traffic, providing a perfect environment for brown-bag and picnic lunches. The lobby visitor center has six displays focusing on the history of the company, including a vintage ad exhibit and the latest Levi products. The Filbert Steps to Coit Tower are across the street. ⊠ *Levi's Plaza, 1155 Battery St., North Beach.*

Saints Peter and Paul Catholic Church. Camera-toting visitors focus their lenses on the Romanesque splendor of what's often called the Italian Cathedral. Completed in 1924, the church has Disneyesque stone-white towers that are local landmarks. Mass reflects the neighborhood; it's given in English, Italian, and Chinese. Following their 1954 City

Hall wedding, Marilyn Monroe and Joe DiMaggio had their wedding photos snapped here. ■TIP➜ **On the first Sunday of October a mass followed by a parade to Fisherman's Wharf celebrates the Blessing of the Fleet. Another popular event is the Columbus Day pageant in North Beach, with a parade that ends at the church.** ⊠*666 Filbert St., at Washington Sq., North Beach* ☎*415/421–0809* ⊕*www.stspeter paul.san-francisco.ca.us/church.*

> ## O PIONEERS!
>
> The corner of Broadway and Columbus Avenue witnessed an unusual historic breakthrough. Here stood the Condor Club where, in 1964, Carol Doda became the country's first dancer to break the topless barrier. A bronze plaque honors the milestone (only in SF). And Doda, naturally, now owns a lingerie store in Cow Hollow.

Sentinel Building. A striking triangular shape and a gorgeous green patina make this 1907 building at the end of Columbus Avenue a visual knockout. In the 1970s, local filmmaker Francis Ford Coppola bought the building to use for his production company. The ground floor is now Coppola's stylish wine bar, **Café Zoetrope**. Stop in for wines from the Coppola vineyards in Napa and Sonoma, simple Italian dishes, and foodie gifts. ⊠*916 Kearny St., at Columbus Ave.*

Fodor's Choice ★ **Telegraph Hill.** Hill residents have some of the best views in the city, as well as the most difficult ascents to their aeries. The hill rises from the east end of Lombard Street to a height of 284 feet and is capped by Coit Tower (*see above*). Imagine lugging your groceries up that! If you brave the slope, though, you can be rewarded with a "secret treasure" SF moment. Filbert Street starts up the hill, then becomes the Filbert Steps when the going gets too steep. You can cut between the Filbert Steps and another flight, the Greenwich Steps, on up to the hilltop. As you climb, you can pass some of the city's oldest houses and be surrounded by beautiful, flowering private gardens. In some places the trees grow over the stairs so they feel like a green tunnel; elsewhere, you'll have wide-open views of the bay. And the telegraphic name? It comes from the hill's status as the first Morse code signal station back in 1853. ⊠*Bordered by Lombard, Filbert, Kearny, and Sansome Sts., North Beach.*

OFF THE BEATEN PATH

1360 Montgomery Street. In the 1947 film *Dark Passage*, Humphrey Bogart plays an escaped prisoner from San Quentin convicted of killing his wife. His real-life wife, Lauren Bacall, befriends him and lets him hole up in her apartment, inside this fantastic Art Deco building. From the street you can view the etched-glass gazelles and palms counterpointing a silvered fresco of a heroic bridge worker. ⊠*Montgomery St. between Union and Filbert Sts., near top of Filbert Steps, North Beach.*

Washington Square. Once the daytime social heart of Little Italy, this grassy patch has changed character numerous times over the years. The Beats hung out in the 1950s, hippies camped out in the 1960s and early '70s, and nowadays you're just as likely to see kids of Southeast Asian descent tossing a Frisbee as Italian men or women chatting

AT A GLANCE

Dining in North Beach

BUDGET
L'Osteria del Forno,
Italian, 519 Columbus
Ave.

MODERATE
Capp's Corner, Italian,
1600 Powell St.

El Raigón, Steak, 510
Union St.

Maykadeh, Middle Eastern, 470 Green St.

Moose's, American,
1652 Stockton St.

Rose Pistola, Italian,
532 Columbus Ave.

Tommaso's, Pizza, 1042
Kearny St.

EXPENSIVE
Coi, American, 373
Broadway

about their children and the old country. In the morning elderly Asians perform the motions of tai chi, but by mid-morning groups of conservatively dressed Italian men in their 70s and 80s begin to arrive. Any time of day, the park may attract a number of homeless people, who stretch out to rest on the benches and grass, and young locals sunbathing or running their dogs. Lillie Hitchcock Coit, in yet another show of affection for San Francisco's firefighters, donated the statue of two firemen with a child they rescued. ■TIP➔ **The North Beach Festival, the city's oldest street fair, celebrates the area's Italian culture here each June.** ✉*Bordered by Columbus Ave. and Stockton, Filbert, and Union Sts., North Beach.*

On the Waterfront

Fisherman's Wharf

WORD OF MOUTH

"I know that there are a lot of tacky things about the Wharf, but how about the cruises, the bike rentals, and the great central location for visiting some really great neighborhoods? And wow, the physical beauty of the bay, I can't imagine taking a trip to San Francisco and not visiting the Wharf at least once."

—don512

GETTING ORIENTED

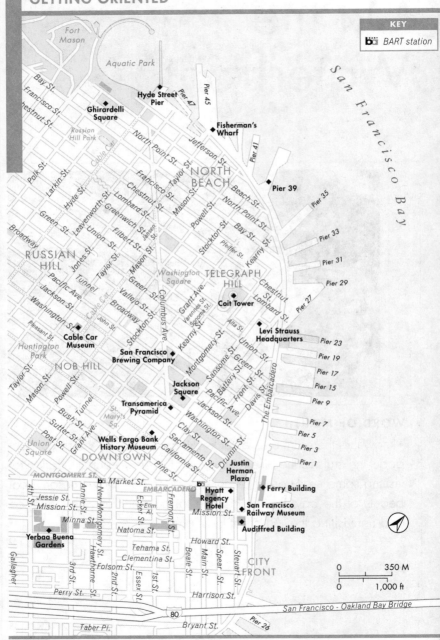

KEY

🚉 BART station

Fort Mason

Aquatic Park

Bay St.
Francisco St.
Chestnut St.

Ghirardelli Square

Hyde Street Pier

Pier 47

Pier 45

Fisherman's Wharf

Russian Hill Park

Jefferson St.

North Point St.

Taylor St.

NORTH BEACH

Beach St.

Pier 41

Polk St.
Larkin St.
Hyde St.
Leavenworth St.
Greenwich St.
Lombard St.

Francisco St.
Chestnut St.
Mason St.
North Point St.

Pier 39

Pier 35

Green St.
Union St.
Filbert St.

Jackson St.

Bay St.
Kearny

Stockton St.
Powell St.

Pier 33

Broadway

RUSSIAN HILL

Jones St.

Taylor St.

Mason St.

Columbus Ave.

Green St.

Washington Square

TELEGRAPH HILL

Pfeiffer St.

Pier 31

Pier 29

Pacific Ave.
Jackson St.
Washington St.

Tunnel

Vallejo St.

Broadway

Grant Ave.

Varennes St.
Sonoma St.

Coit Tower

Chestnut

Lombard St.

Pier 27

Pleasant St.

Cable Car Museum

John St.

Stockton St.

Kearny St.

Alta St.

Levi Strauss Headquarters

Pier 23

Huntington Park

Taylor St.
Mason St.

NOB HILL

Powell St.

Tunnel

San Francisco Brewing Company

Montgomery St.

Union St.

Green St.

Sansome St.

Pier 19

Pier 17

Bush St.

Grant Ave.

St. Mary's Sq.

Jackson Square

Battery St.

Front St.

Davis St.

Pier 15

Pier 9

Sutter St.
Post St.

Transamerica Pyramid

Pacific Ave.

Washington St.

The Embarcadero

Pier 7

Union Square

Clay St.

Jackson St.

Pier 5

DOWNTOWN

Wells Fargo Bank History Museum

Sacramento St.

California St.

Drumm St.

Pier 3

Pine St.

Justin Herman Plaza

Pier 1

MONTGOMERY ST.

Market St.

EMBARCADERO

Hyatt Regency Hotel

Ferry Building

4th St.

Jessie St.
Mission St.

Annie St.

New Montgomery St.

Ecker St.

Elim Al.

Fremont St.

Mission St.

San Francisco Railway Museum

Minna St.

Natoma St.

Audiffred Building

Yerbaa Buena Gardens

Hawthorne St.

Tehama St.

Howard St.

Clementina St.

Beale St.

Main St.

Spear St.

Steuart St.

CITY FRONT

Gallagher

3rd St.

2nd St.

Folsom St.

Essex St.

1st St.

0 — 350 M

0 — 1,000 ft

Perry St.

Harrison St.

80

San Francisco - Oakland Bay Bridge

Taber Pl.

Bryant St.

Pier 26

San Francisco Bay

GETTING THERE

The Powell–Hyde and Powell–Mason cable car lines both end near Fisherman's Wharf. The walk from downtown through North Beach to the northern waterfront is lovely, and if you stick to Columbus Avenue, the incline is relatively gentle. F-line trolleys, often packed to capacity, run all the way down Market to the Embarcadero, then north to the Wharf.

TOP 5 REASONS TO GO

Ferry Building: Join locals eyeing luscious produce and foods prepared by some of the city's best chefs at San Francisco's premier farmers' market.

Hyde Street Pier: Feel the rocking of the waves aboard the gorgeously restored 19th-century *Balclutha,* where park rangers teach visitors to sing sea chanteys and raise the sails, then head to the Buena Vista for an Irish coffee.

Alcatraz: Go from a scenic bay tour to "the hole"—solitary confinement in absolute darkness—while inmates and guards tell you stories about what life was really like on the Rock.

F-line: Grab a polished wooden seat aboard one of the city's lovingly restored vintage streetcars and clatter down the tracks toward the Ferry Building's spire.

Musée Mécanique: Take a pocketful of quarters and step through the gaping mouth of Laffing Sal to this arcade of vintage machines.

FERRIES

The bay is a huge part of San Francisco's charm, and getting out on the water gives you an attractive and unique (though windy) perspective on the city. Keep in mind that a ride on a commuter ferry is cheaper than a cruise, and just as lovely. The **Red and White Fleet** (⊠ *Pier 43½, Fisherman's Wharf* ☎ *415/447–0591 or 800/229–2784* ⊕ *www.redandwhite.com*) has the widest range of tour options, including sunset cruises from April to October. The **Ferry Building Line** (⊠ *1 Ferry Plaza, Embarcadero* ☎ *415/901–5253* ⊕ *www.ferrybuildingline.com*) offers bay cruises with three different audio tours—natural history, architecture, and Native American—on a limited schedule from the Ferry Building. The tours are longer and twice as expensive as other lines' bay cruises. The **Blue & Gold Fleet** (⊠ *Pier 41, Fisherman's Wharf* ☎ *415/705–5555* ⊕ *www.blueandgoldfleet. com*) is essentially a ferry company, with service to Oakland, Alameda, Tiburon, Sausalito, Vallejo, and Angel Island.

MAKING THE MOST OF YOUR TIME

If you're planning to go to Alcatraz, be sure to buy your tickets in advance, as tours frequently sell out. Alcatraz ferries now leave from Pier 33—so there isn't a single good reason to suffer Pier 39's tacky, overpriced attractions. If you're a sailor at heart, definitely spend an hour with the historic ships of Hyde Street Pier.

QUICK BITES

The Ferry Building is everyone's favorite spot for a bite on the Embarcadero. Gather bread, cheese, and fruit for a picnic, or grab something to go from **Out the Door** (⊠ *1 Ferry Plaza, Embarcadero* ☎ *415/861–8032*), beloved Vietnamese restaurant Slanted Door's takeout counter. If you need a sweet treat, head to pink **Miette** (⊠ *1 Ferry Plaza, Embarcadero* ☎ *415/837–0300*), where the cakes and pastries are absolute organic perfection.

6

Sightseeing
☆☆☆★★

Nightlife
☆☆☆☆☆

Dining
☆☆★★★

Lodging
☆★★★★

Shopping
☆☆☆★★

San Francisco's waterfront neighborhoods have fabulous views and utterly different personalities. Kitschy, overpriced Fisherman's Wharf struggles to maintain the last shreds of its existence as a working wharf, while Pier 39 is a full-fledged consumer circus. The Ferry Building draws well-heeled locals with its culinary pleasures, firmly reconnecting the Embarcadero to downtown. Between the Ferry Building and Pier 39, a former maritime no-man's land is filling in a bit—especially near Pier 33, where the perpetually booked Alcatraz cruises depart—with a waterfront restaurant here and a restored pedestrian-friendly pier there.

By Denise M. Leto

Today's shoreline was once Yerba Buena Cove, filled in during the latter half of the 19th century when San Francisco was a brawling, extravagant gold-rush town. Jackson Square, now a genteel and upscale corner of the inland Financial District, was the heart of the Barbary Coast, bordering some of the roughest wharves in the world. Below Montgomery Street (in today's Financial District), between California Street and Broadway, lies a remnant of these wild days: more than 100 ships abandoned by frantic crews and passengers caught up in gold fever lie under the foundations of buildings here.

WHAT TO SEE

Angel Island. For an outdoorsy adventure, consider a day at this island northwest of Alcatraz. Discovered by Spaniards in 1775 and declared a U.S. military reserve 75 years later, the island was used as a screening ground for Asian immigrants—who were often held for months, even years, before being granted entry—from 1910 until 1940. Starting in 2009, you can visit the restored Immigration Station; from the dock where detainees landed to the barracks you can see the poems in Japanese script they etched onto the walls. In 1963 the government designated Angel Island a state park. Today people come for picnics, hikes along the scenic 5-mi path that winds around the island's perimeter, and tram tours that explain the park's history. Twenty-five bicycles are permitted on the ferry on a first-come, first-served basis, and you can rent mountain bikes for $10 an hour or $30 a day at the landing (daily April–October; call during other times). There are also a dozen primitive campsites. Blue and Gold Fleet is the only Angel Island ferry service with departures from San Francisco. Boats leave Pier 41 weekdays at 10 and return at 4; on weekends they sail at 10:35 and return at 4:55. ⊠ *Pier 41, Fisherman's Wharf* ☎ *415/435–1915 park information and ferry schedules, 415/705–5555, 800/426–8687 tickets* ⊕ *www. angelisland.org* 🎫 *$14.50* ☉ *Angel Island open daily 8 AM to sunset.*

> ### F-LINE TROLLEYS
>
> The F-line, the city's system of vintage electric trolleys, gives the cable cars a run for their money as San Francisco's best-loved mode of transportation. These beautifully restored streetcars—some dating from the 19th century—run from the Castro all the way down Market Street to the Embarcadero, then north to Fisherman's Wharf. Each car is unique, restored to the colors of its city of origin, from New Orleans and Philadelphia to Moscow and Milan. The line is so popular that there's talk of extending it to Fort Mason. Purchase tickets on board; exact change is required. ⊕ *www.street car.org* 🎫 *$1.50.*

6

NEED A BREAK?
Even locals love the cheery Buena Vista Café (⊠ *2765 Hyde St., Fisherman's Wharf* ☎ *415/474–5044*), which claims to be the first place in the U.S. to have served Irish coffee. The café opens at 9 AM weekdays (8 AM weekends) and dishes up a great breakfast. They serve about 2,000 Irish coffees a day, so it's always crowded; try for a table overlooking nostalgic Victorian Park and its cable-car turntable.

Fodor's Choice ★ **Ferry Building.** Renovated in 2003, the Ferry Building is the jewel of the Embarcadero. The beacon of the port area, erected in 1896, has a 230-foot clock tower modeled after the campanile of the cathedral in Seville, Spain. On the morning of April 18, 1906, the tower's four clock faces, powered by the swinging of a 14-foot pendulum, stopped at 5:17—the moment the great earthquake struck—and stayed still for 12 months.

Today San Franciscans flock to the street-level Market Hall, stocking up on supplies from local favorites such as Acme Bread, Scharffen Berger Chocolate, and Cowgirl Creamery. Lucky diners claim a coveted table at Slanted Door, the city's beloved high-end Vietnamese restaurant. The seafood bars at Hog Island Oyster Company and Ferry Plaza Seafood have fantastic city panoramas—or you can take your purchases around to the building's bay side, where benches face views of the Bay Bridge. Saturday mornings, the plaza in front of the building buzzes with an upscale, celebrity-chef-studded farmers' market. Extending from the piers on the north side of the building south to the Bay Bridge, the waterfront promenade is a favorite among joggers and picnickers, with a front-row view of the sailboats slipping by. The Ferry Building also serves actual ferries: from behind the building they sail to Sausalito, Larkspur, Tiburon, and the East Bay. ⊠*Embarcadero at foot of Market St., Embarcadero* ⊕*www.ferrybuildingmarketplace.com.*

🕲 **Fisherman's Wharf.** It may be one of the city's best-known attractions, but the wharf is a no-go zone for most locals, who shy away from the difficult parking, overpriced food, and cheesy shops at third-rate shopping centers like the Cannery at Del Monte Square. If you just can't resist a visit here, come early to avoid the crowds and get a sense of the wharf's functional role—it's not just an amusement park replica.

Most of the entertainment at the wharf is schlocky and overpriced, with one notable exception: the splendid **Musée Mécanique** (☎*415/346–2000* ⊙ *Weekdays 10–7, weekends 10–8*), a time-warped arcade with antique mechanical contrivances, including peep shows and nickelodeons. Some favorites are the giant and rather creepy "Laffing Sal" (you enter the museum through his gaping mouth), an arm-wrestling machine, the world's only steam-powered motorcycle, and mechanical fortune-telling figures that speak from their curtained boxes. Keep your eyes open for depictions of race that betray the prejudices of the time: stoned Chinese figures in the "Opium-Den" and clown-faced African-Americans eating watermelon in the "Mechanical Farm." Admission is free, but you'll need quarters to bring the machines to life.

Among the two floors of exhibits at **Ripley's Believe It or Not! Museum** (⊠*175 Jefferson St., Fisherman's Wharf* ☎*415/771–6188* ⊕*www.ripleysf.com*) is an 8-foot-long scale model of a cable car, made entirely of matchsticks. Admission to Ripley's, open Sunday through Thursday 10–10 and Friday and Saturday 10 AM–midnight, is $14.99. Notables from local boy Robin Williams to Jesus await at the **Wax Museum** (⊠*145 Jefferson St., Fisherman's Wharf* ☎*415/439–4305* ⊕*www.waxmuseum.com*), open weekdays 10–9, weekends 9 AM–11 PM. Admission is $12.95.

The **USS Pampanito** (⊠*Pier 45, Fisherman's Wharf* ☎*415/775–1943* ⊙*Oct.–Memorial Day, Sun.–Thurs. 9–6, Fri. and Sat. 9–8; Memorial Day–Sept., Thurs.–Tues. 9–8, Wed. 9–6*) provides an intriguing if mildly claustrophobic glimpse into life on a submarine during World War II. The sub sank six Japanese warships and damaged four others. Admission is $9; the family pass is a great deal at $20 for two adults and up to four kids. ⊠*Jefferson St. between Leavenworth St. and Pier 39, Fisherman's Wharf.*

OFF THE BEATEN PATH

S.S. Jeremiah O'Brien. A participant in the D-day landing in Normandy during World War II, this Liberty Ship freighter is one of two such vessels (out of 2,500 built) still in working order. To keep the 1943 ship in sailing shape, the steam engine—which appears in the film *Titanic*—is operated dockside seven times a year on special "steaming weekends." Cruises take place several times a year between May and October. ⊠*Pier 45, Fisherman's Wharf* ☎*415/544–0100* ⊕*www.ssjeremiahobrien.org* ▤*$9* ⊙*Daily 9–4.*

Ghirardelli Square. Most of the red-brick buildings in this early-20th-century complex were once part of the Ghirardelli factory. Tourists come here to pick up the famous chocolate, but you can purchase it all over town and save yourself a trip to what is essentially a mall. (If you're a shopaholic, though, it definitely beats the Cannery.) There are no less than three Ghirardelli stores here, as well as gift shops and a couple of restaurants—including Ana Mandara—that even locals love. Placards throughout the square describe the factory's history. ✉ *900 N. Point St., Fisherman's Wharf* ☎ *415/775–5500* ⊕ *www.ghirardellisq.com.*

> ### ALCATRAZ'S FUTURE
>
> Alcatraz is currently undergoing an extensive restoration, and funds are being raised to renovate and reopen outbuildings that have been closed for years. The jail cells' vintage locks are also slated to be repaired. Tours of the island once included briefly locking members into cells—but this hasn't been a part of the program since corroded lock mechanisms began sticking, *really* locking some people in!

Hyatt Regency. John Portman designed this hotel noted for its 17-story hanging garden, a delightful green space you'd never expect from the unwelcoming, imposing exterior. The garden glows at Christmas, when strands of tiny white lights dangle over the cavernous atrium lobby. The four glass elevators facing the lobby are fun to ride, unless you suffer from vertigo. Head all the way up to the hotel's expensive and mediocre revolving restaurant, Equinox, for a drink (but just a drink) and a look at the 360-degree rotating view. ✉ *5 Embarcadero Center, Embarcadero* ☎ *415/788–1234* ⊕ *sanfranciscoregency.hyatt.com.*

☉ ★ **Hyde Street Pier.** Cotton candy and souvenirs are all well and good, but if you want to get to the heart of the Wharf—boats—there's no better place to do it than this pier, by far one of the Wharf area's best bargains. Depending on the time of day, you might see boat builders at work or children pretending to man an early-1900s ship.

Don't pass up the centerpiece collection of historic vessels, part of the **San Francisco Maritime National Historic Park,** almost all of which can be boarded. The *Balclutha,* an 1886 full-rigged three-masted sailing vessel that's more than 250 feet long, sailed around Cape Horn 17 times; kids especially love the *Eureka,* a side-wheel passenger and car ferry, for her onboard collection of vintage cars; the *Hercules* is a steam-powered tugboat. The *C. A. Thayer,* a three-masted schooner, recently underwent a painstaking restoration and is back on display. Across the street from the pier and almost a museum in itself is the San Francisco Maritime National Historic Park's **Visitor Center** (✉ *499 Jefferson St., at Hyde St., Fisherman's Wharf* ☎ *415/447–5000* ☉ *Memorial Day–Sept., daily 9:30–7; Oct.–Memorial Day, daily 9:30–5*), happily free of mind-numbing, text-heavy displays. Instead, fun, large-scale exhibits, such as a huge First Order Fresnel lighthouse lens and a shipwrecked boat, make this an engaging and relatively quick stop. ✉ *Hyde and Jefferson Sts., Fisherman's Wharf* ☎ *415/561–7100* ⊕ *www.nps.gov/safr*

6

🚢*Ships* $5 🕐*Memorial Day–Sept., daily 9:30–5:30; Oct.–Memorial Day, daily 9:30–5.*

Jackson Square. This was the heart of the Barbary Coast of the Gay '90s (the 1890s, that is). Although most of the red-light district was destroyed in the fire that followed the 1906 earthquake, old redbrick buildings and narrow alleys recall the romance and rowdiness of San Francisco's early days. The days of brothels and bar fights are long gone—now Jackson Square is a genteel, quiet corner of the Finan-

> ## WHISKEY RHYME
>
> The Italianate Hotaling building survived the disastrous 1906 quake and fire—a miracle considering the thousands of barrels of inflammable liquid inside. A plaque on the side of the structure repeats a famous query: IF, AS THEY SAY, GOD SPANKED THE TOWN FOR BEING OVER FRISKY, WHY DID HE BURN THE CHURCHES DOWN AND SAVE HOTALING'S WHISKEY?

cial District. It's of interest to the historically inclined and antiques-shop browsers, but otherwise safely skipped.

Some of the city's first business buildings, survivors of the 1906 quake, still stand between Montgomery and Sansome streets. After a few decades of neglect, these old-timers were adopted by preservation-minded interior designers and wholesale-furniture dealers for use as showrooms. In 1972 the city officially designated the area—bordered by Columbus Avenue on the west, Broadway and Pacific Avenue on the north, Washington Street on the south, and Sansome Street on the east—San Francisco's first historic district. When property values soared, many of the fabric and furniture outlets fled to Potrero Hill. Advertising agencies, attorneys, and antiques dealers now occupy the Jackson Square–area structures. Restored 19th-century brick buildings line Hotaling Place, which connects Washington and Jackson streets. The lane is named for the head of the **A.P. Hotaling Company whiskey distillery** (✉*451 Jackson St., at Hotaling Pl.*), which was the largest liquor repository on the West Coast in its day. (Hotaling whiskey is still made in the city, by the way; look for their single malts for a sip of truly local flavor.)

It takes a bit of conjuring to evoke the wild Barbary Coast days when checking out the now-gentrified gold-rush-era buildings in the 700 block of **Montgomery Street.** But this was an especially colorful block. Author Mark Twain was a reporter for the spunky *Golden Era* newspaper, which occupied No. 732 (now part of the building at No. 744). From 1959 to 1996, the late ambulance-chaser extraordinaire, lawyer Melvin Belli, had his headquarters there. There was never a dull moment in Belli's world; he represented clients from Mae West to Gloria Sykes (who in 1964 claimed that a cable car accident turned her into a nymphomaniac) to Jim and Tammy Faye Bakker. Whenever he won a case, he fired a cannon and raised the Jolly Roger. Belli was also known for receiving a letter from the never-caught Zodiac killer. It seems fitting that the building sat for years, deteriorating and moldering, while the late attorney's sons fought wife number five (joined with Belli in holy matrimony just three months before his death). She even-

NATIVE LAND

In the 1960s, Native Americans attempted to reclaim Alcatraz, citing an 1868 treaty that granted Native Americans any surplus federal land. Their activism crested in 1969, when several dozen Native Americans began a 19-month occupation, supported by public opinion and a friendly media.

The group offered to buy the island from the government for $24 worth of beads and other goods—exactly what Native Americans had been paid for Manhattan in 1626. In their Proclamation to the Great White Father and His People, the group laid out the 10 reasons that Alcatraz would make an ideal Indian reservation, among them: "There is no industry and so unemployment is very great," and "The soil is rocky and nonproductive, and the land does not support game." The last holdouts were removed by federal agents in 1971, but today's visitors are still greeted with the huge graffitied message: "Indians Welcome. Indian Land."

tually won, and the building is finally being renovated. ⊠ *Jackson Sq. district bordered by Broadway and Washington, Kearny, and Sansome Sts., Financial District.*

Market Street buildings. The street, which bisects the city at an angle, has consistently challenged San Francisco's architects. One of the most intriguing responses to this challenge sits diagonally across Market Street from the Palace Hotel. The tower of the **Hobart Building** (No. 582) combines a flat facade and oval sides and is considered one of Willis Polk's best works in the city. East on Market Street is Charles Havens's triangular **Flatiron Building** (No. 540–548), another classic solution. At Bush Street, the **Donahue Monument** holds its own against the skyscrapers that tower over the intersection. This homage to waterfront mechanics, which survived the 1906 earthquake (a famous photograph shows Market Street in ruins around the sculpture), was designed by Douglas Tilden, a noted California sculptor. The plaque in the sidewalk next to the monument marks the spot as the location of the San Francisco Bay shoreline in 1848. Telltale nautical details such as anchors, ropes, and shells adorn the gracefully detailed **Matson Building** (No. 215), built in the 1920s for the shipping line Matson Navigation. ⊠ *Between New Montgomery and Beale Sts., Financial District.*

San Francisco National Maritime Museum. You'll feel as if you're out to sea when you step aboard, er, inside this sturdy, round, ship-shaped structure dubbed the Bathhouse. Part of the **San Francisco Maritime National Historical Park,** the museum has three floors that exhibit intricate ship models, beautifully restored figureheads, photographs of life at sea, and other artifacts chronicling the maritime history of San Francisco and the West Coast. The views from the top floor are stunning, and be sure to step onto the first-floor balcony, which overlooks the beach, and check out the lovely WPA-era tile designs on your way to the steamships exhibit. At this writing the museum was closed,

Where can I find . . .?

PARKING	**Beach and Hyde Garage** ⊠655 Beach St. Steps away from Fishermans Wharf attractions.	**Embarcadero Center** ⊠Battery St., near Broadway Four hours free on nights and weekends with validation.
A DRUGSTORE	**Walgreens** ⊠320 Bay St. Stop in for sunscreen on your way to your Alcatraz cruise.	**Safeway** ⊠145 Jackson St. Need some aspirin after walking the Embarcadero?
A DRINK	**Harrington's** ⊠245 Front St. Irish saloon with a good selection of imported beers.	**Hog Island Oyster Bar** ⊠Ferry Building Wine and oysters with a bay view.

but it was expected to open in the second half of 2009 (call ahead to check before visiting). ⊠*Aquatic Park foot of Polk St., Fisherman's Wharf* ☎*415/561-7100* ⊕*www.nps.gov/safr* ⊠*Donation suggested* ⊙ *Daily 10–5.*

Ⓒ **Pier 39.** The city's most popular waterfront attraction draws millions of visitors each year who come to browse through its vertiginous array of shops and concessions hawking every conceivable form of souvenir. The pier can be quite crowded, and the numerous street performers may leave you feeling more harassed than entertained. Arriving early in the morning ensures you a front-row view of the sea lions, but if you're here to shop—and make no mistake about it, Pier 39 wants your money—be aware that most stores don't open until 9:30 or 10 (later in winter).

Pick up a buckwheat hull–filled otter neck wrap or a plush sea lion to snuggle at the **Marine Mammal Store** (☎*415/289–7373*), whose proceeds benefit Sausalito's respected wild-animal hospital, the Marine Mammal Center. Sales of the excellent books, maps, and collectibles—including a series of gorgeous, distinctive Art Deco posters for Alcatraz, the Presidio, Fort Point, and the other members of the Golden Gate National Recreation Area—at the **National Park Store** (☎*415/433–7221*) help to support the National Park Service. Brilliant colors enliven the double-decker **San Francisco Carousel** (⊠*$3 per ride*), decorated with images of such city landmarks as the Golden Gate Bridge and Lombard Street. Follow the sound of barking to the northwest side of the pier to view the hundreds of sea lions that bask and play on the docks. At **Aquarium of the Bay** (☎*415/623–5300 or 888/732–3483* ⊕*www.aquariumofthebay. com* ⊠*$14.95*), moving walkways transport you through a space surrounded on three sides by water filled with indigenous San Francisco Bay marine life, from fish and plankton to sharks. Many find the aquarium overpriced; if you can, take advantage of the family rate ($37.95 for two adults and two kids under 12). The aquarium is open

BRAVING THE WATERS

Federal prison officials liked to claim that it was impossible to escape Alcatraz, and for the most part, that assertion was true. For seasoned swimmers, though, the trip has never posed a problem—in fact, it's been downright popular.

In the 1930s, in an attempt to dissuade the feds from converting Alcatraz into a prison, a handful of schoolgirls made the swim to the city. At age 60, native son Jack LaLanne did it (for the second time) while shackled and towing a 1,000-pound rowboat. Every year a couple thousand participants take the plunge during the annual Escape from Alcatraz Triathlon. Heck, a dog made the crossing in 2005 and finished well ahead of most of the (human) pack. And in 2006, seven-year-old Braxton Bilbrey became the youngest "escapee" on record. Incidentally, those reports of shark-infested waters are true—but the sharks aren't dangerous species.

June through September daily 9–8; during the rest of the year it's open Monday through Thursday 10–6 and Friday through Sunday 10–7.

The **California Welcome Center** (☎ *415/981–1280 ◷ Daily 10–5 ⊕ www. visitcwc.com*), on Pier 39's second level, includes an Internet café. Expensive parking (free with validation from a Pier 39 restaurant) is at the Pier 39 Garage, off Powell Street at the Embarcadero. ⊠ *Beach St. at Embarcadero, Fisherman's Wharf ⊕ www.pier39.com.*

San Francisco Brewing Company. Built in 1907, this pub looks like a museum piece from San Francisco's Barbary Coast days. An old upright piano sits in the corner under the original stained-glass windows. Take a seat at the mahogany bar, where you can look down at the white-tile spittoon. An adjacent room holds the handmade copper brewing kettle used to produce a dozen beers—with names such as Pony Express—by means of old-fashioned gravity-flow methods. ⊠ *155 Columbus Ave., North Beach ☎ 415/434–3344 ⊕ www.sfbrewing.com ◷ Mon.–Sat. 11:30–1 AM, Sun. noon–1 AM.*

☉ **San Francisco Railway Museum.** A labor of love brought to you by the same vintage-transit enthusiasts responsible for the F-line's revival, this one-room museum and store celebrates the city's storied streetcars and cable cars with photographs, models, and artifacts. The permanent exhibit will eventually include the (replicated) end of a streetcar with a working cab for kids to explore. In the meantime, little ones will have to content themselves with operating the cool, antique Wiley birdcage traffic signal and viewing (but not touching) models and display cases. Right on the F-line track, just across from the Ferry Building, this is a great quick stop. ⊠ *77 Steuart St., in Hotel Vitale, Embarcadero ☎ 415/974–1948 ⊕ www.streetcar.org ⊡ Free ◷ Wed.–Sun. 10–6.*

Transamerica Pyramid. It's neither owned by Transamerica nor is it a pyramid, but this 853-foot-tall obelisk *is* the most photographed of the city's high-rises. Excoriated in the design stages as "the world's largest architectural folly," the icon was quickly hailed as a masterpiece when

Dining On the Waterfront

BUDGET

Hog Island Oyster Company, Seafood, Ferry Bldg., Embarcadero at Market St.

Mijita Cocina Mexicana, Mexican, Ferry Bldg., Embarcadero at Market St.

MODERATE

Fog City Diner, American, 1300 Battery St.

Kokkari, Greek, 200 Jackson St.

McCormick & Kuleto's, Seafood, Ghirardelli Sq., Beach and Larkin Sts.

One Market, American, 1 Market St.

Perbacco, Italian, 230 California St.

Piperade, Spanish, 1015 Battery St.

Tadich Grill, Seafood, 240 California St.

Slanted Door, Vietnamese, Ferry Bldg., Embarcadero at Market St.

Yank Sing, Chinese, 1 Rincon Center, 101 Spear St.

EXPENSIVE

Aqua, Seafood, 252 California St.

Boulevard, American, 1 Mission St.

Epic Roasthouse, Steakhouse, 369 Embarcadero

Gary Danko, American, 800 N. Point St.

Waterbar, Seafood, 399 Embarcadero

it opened in 1972. Today it's probably the city's most recognized structure after the Golden Gate Bridge. A fragrant redwood grove along the east side of the building, replete with benches and a cheerful fountain, is a placid patch in which to unwind. ✉ *600 Montgomery St., Financial District* ⊕ *www.transamerica.com.*

Wells Fargo Bank History Museum. There were no formal banks in San Francisco during the early years of the gold rush, and miners often entrusted their gold dust to saloon keepers. In 1852 Wells Fargo opened its first bank in the city, and the company soon established banking offices in mother-lode camps throughout California. Stagecoaches and pony-express riders connected points around the burgeoning state, where the population boomed from 15,000 to 200,000 between 1848 and 1852. The museum displays samples of nuggets and gold dust from mines, a mural-size map of the Mother Lode, mementos of the poet bandit Black Bart (who signed his poems "Po8"), and an old telegraph machine on which you can practice sending codes. The showpiece is a red Concord stagecoach, the likes of which carried passengers from St. Joseph, Missouri, to San Francisco in just three weeks during the 1850s. ✉ *420 Montgomery St., Financial District* ☎ *415/396–2619* ⊕ *www.wellsfargohistory.com* 🎟 *Free* ☉ *Weekdays 9–5.*

ALCATRAZ

"They made that place purely for punishment, where men would rot. It was designed to systematically destroy human beings . . . Cold, gray, and lonely, it had a weird way of haunting you—there were those dungeons that you heard about, but there was also the city . . . only a mile and a quarter away, so close you could almost touch it. Sometimes the wind would blow a certain way and you could smell the Italian cooking in North Beach and hear the laughter of people, of women and kids. That made it worse than hell."

–Jim Quillen, former Alcatraz inmate

Gripping the rail as the ferryboat pitches gently in the chilly breeze, you watch formidable Alcatraz rising ahead. Imagine making this trip shackled at the ankle and waist, the looming fortress on the craggy island ahead waiting to swallow you whole. Thousands of visitors come every day to walk in the footsteps of Alcatraz's notorious criminals. The stories of life and death on "the Rock" may sometimes be exaggerated, but it's almost impossible to resist the chance to wander the cellblock that tamed the country's toughest gangsters and saw daring escape attempts of tremendous desperation.

LIFE ON THE ROCK

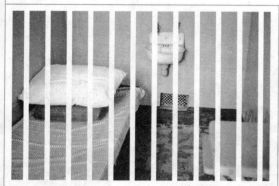

The federal penitentiary's first warden, James A. Johnston, was largely responsible for Alcatraz's (mostly false) hell-on-earth reputation. A tough but relatively humane disciplinarian, Johnston strictly limited the information flow to and from the prison when it opened in 1934. Prisoners' letters were censored, newspapers and radios were forbidden, and no visits were allowed during a convict's first three months in the slammer. Understandably, imaginations ran wild on the mainland.

A LIFE OF PRIVILEGE

Monotony was an understatement on Alcatraz; the same precise schedule was kept daily. The rulebook stated, "You are entitled to food, clothing, shelter, and medical attention. Anything else you get is a privilege." These privileges, from the right to work to the ability to receive mail, were earned by following the prison's rules. A relatively minor infraction meant losing privileges. A serious breach, like fighting, brought severe punishments like time in the Hole (a.k.a. the Strip Cell, since the prisoner had to strip) or the Oriental (an absolutely dark, silent cell with a hole in the ground for a toilet).

THE SPAGHETTI RIOT

Johnston knew that poor food was one of the major causes of prison riots, so he insisted that Alcatraz serve the best chow in the prison system. But the next warden at Alcatraz slacked off, and in 1950, one spaghetti meal too many sent the inmates over the edge. Guards deployed tear gas to subdue the rioters.

A PRISONER'S DAY

6:30 AM: Wake-up call. Prisoners get up, get dressed, and clean cells.

6:50 AM: Prisoners stand at cell doors to be counted.

7:00 AM: Prisoners march single-file to mess hall for breakfast.

7:20 AM: Prisoners head to work or industries detail; count.

9:30 AM: 8-minute break; count.

11:30 AM: Count; prisoners march to mess hall for lunch.

12:00 PM: Prisoners march to cells; count; break in cells.

12:20 PM: Prisoners leave cells, march single-file back to work; count.

2:30 PM: 8-minute break; count.

4:15 PM: Prisoners stop work, two counts.

4:25 PM: Prisoners march into mess hall and are counted; dinner.

4:45 PM: Prisoners return to cells and are locked in.

5:00 PM: Prisoners stand at their doors to be counted.

8:00 PM: Count.

9:30 PM: Count; lights out.

12:01 AM—5 am: Three counts.

INFAMOUS INMATES

Fewer than 2,000 inmates ever did time on the Rock; though they weren't necessarily the worst criminals, they were definitely the worst prisoners. Most were escape artists while others, like Al Capone, had corrupted the prison system from the inside with bribes.

Name Al "Scarface" Capone

On the Rock 1934–1939

In for Tax evasion

Claim to fame Notorious Chicago gangster and bootlegger who arranged the 1929 St. Valentine's Day Massacre.

Hard fact Capone was among the first transfers to the Rock and arrived smiling and joking. He soon realized the party was over. Capone endured a few stints in the Hole and Warden Johnston's early enforced-silence policy; he was also stabbed by a fellow inmate. The gangster eventually caved, saying "it looks like Alcatraz has got me licked," thus cementing the prison's reputation.

Name Robert "The Birdman" Stroud

On the Rock 1942–1959

In for Murder, including the fatal stabbing of a prison guard

Claim to fame Subject of the acclaimed but largely fictitious 1962 film *Birdman of Alcatraz*.

Hard fact Stroud was actually known as the "Bird Doctor of Leavenworth." While incarcerated in Leavenworth prison through the 1920s and 30s, he became an expert on birds, tending an aviary and writing two books. The stench and mess in his cell discouraged the guards from searching it—and finding Stroud's homemade still. His years on the Rock were birdless.

Name George "Machine Gun" Kelly

On the Rock 1934–1951

In for Kidnapping

Claim to fame Became an expert with a machine gun at the urging of his wife, Kathryn. Kathryn also encouraged his string of bank robberies and the kidnapping for ransom of oilman Charles Urschel. Insert "ball and chain" joke here... While stashed in Leavenworth on a life sentence, Kelly boasted that he would escape and then free Kathryn. That got him a one-way ticket to Alcatraz.

Hard fact Was an altar boy on Alcatraz and was generally considered a model prisoner.

NO ESCAPE

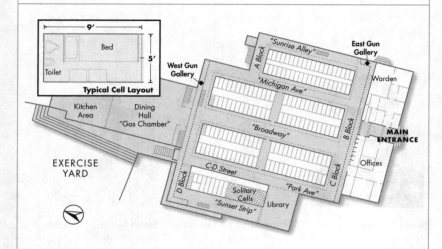

Alcatraz was a maximum-security federal penitentiary with one guard for every three prisoners. The biggest deterrent to escape, though, was the 1.4-mi of icy bay waters separating the Rock from the city. Only a few prisoners made it off the island, and only one is known to have survived. And that story about the shark-infested waters? There are sharks in the bay, but they're not the man-eating kind.

Bloodiest Attempt: In 1946, six prisoners hatched a plan to surprise a guard, seize weapons, and escape through the rec yard. They succeeded up to a point, arming themselves and locking several guards into cells, but things got ugly when the group couldn't find the key that opened the door to the prison yard. Desperate, they opened fire on the trapped guards. Warden Johnston called in the Marines, who shelled the cell house for two days in the so-called Battle of Alcatraz. Three ringleaders were killed in the fighting; two were executed for murder; and one, who was just 19 years old, got 99 years slapped on to his sentence.

Craftiest Attempt: Over six months, three convicts stole bits and pieces from the kitchen and machine shop to make drills and digging pieces. They used these basic tools to widen a vent into the utility corridor. They also gathered bits of cardboard, toilet paper, and hair from the prison's barbershop to make crude models of their own heads. Then, like teenagers sneaking out, they put the decoy heads in their cots and walked away—up the pipes in the utility corridor to the roof, then down a drainpipe to the ground. They apparently swam for it, equipped with life vests made from prison raincoats, and are officially presumed dead.

Most Anticlimactic: In 1962, one prisoner spent an entire year loosening the bars in a window. Then he slipped through and managed to swim all the way to Fort Point, near the Golden Gate Bridge. He promptly fell asleep there and was found an hour later by some teenagers.

6 TIPS FOR ESCAPING TO ALCATRAZ

Walking down "Broadway," once the cell blocks' busiest corridor

1. Buy your ticket in advance. Visit the Web site for Alcatraz Cruises (☎ 415/981–7625 ⊕ www.alcatrazcruises.com) to scout out available departure times for the ferry. Prepay by credit card and keep a receipt record; the ticket price covers the boat ride and the audio tour. Pick up your ticket at the "will call" window at Pier 33 up to an hour before sailing and experience just a touch of schaden-freude as you overhear attendants tell scores of too-late passengers that your tour is sold out.

2. Dress smart. Bring that pullover you packed to ward off the chill from the boat ride and Alcatraz Island. Also: sneakers. Some Alcatraz guides are fanatical about making excellent time.

3. Go for the evening tour. You'll get even more out of the experience if you do it at night. The evening tour has programs not offered during the day, the bridge-to-bridge view of the city twinkles at night, and your "prison experience" will be amplified as darkness mourn-fully falls while you shuffle around the cell block.

4. Unplug and go against the flow. If you miss a cue on the excellent audio tour and find yourself out of synch, don't sweat it—use it as an opportunity to switch off the tape and walk against the grain of the people following the tour. No one will stop you if you walk back through a cell block on your own, taking the time to listen to the haunt-ing sound of your own footsteps on the concrete floor.

5. Be mindful of scheduled and limited-capacity talks. Some programs only hap-pen once a day (the schedule is posted in the cell house). Certain talks have limited capacity seating, so keep an eye out for a cell house staffer handing out passes shortly before the start time.

6. Talk to the staff. One of the island's greatest resources is its staff, who prac-tically bubble over with information. Pick their brains, and draw them out about what they know.

PRACTICALITIES

An Alcatraz Cruises ferry picks up (willing) visitors to "Uncle Sam's Devil's Island"

GETTING THERE

All cruises are operated by Alcatraz Cruises, the park's authorized concessionaire.

✉ *Pier 33, Fisherman's Wharf* ☎ *415/981–7625* 🖂 *$24.50, including audio tour; $31.50 evening tour, including audio* ☿ *Ferry departures every 30–45 mins Sept.–late May, daily 9:30–2:15, 4:20 for evening tour Thurs.–Mon. only; late May–Aug., daily 9:30–4:15, 6:30 and 7:30 for evening tour* ⊕ *www.nps.gov/alca, www.parksconservancy.org/visit/alcatraz.php, www.alcatrazcruises.com*

TIMING

The boat ride to Alcatraz is only about 15 minutes long, but you should allow about three hours for your entire visit. The delightful F-line vintage streetcars are the most direct public transit to the dock; on weekdays the 10-Townsend bus will get you within a few blocks of Pier 33.

FOOD

The prisoners might have enjoyed good food on Alcatraz, but you won't—unless

you pack a picnic. Food is not available on the island, so be sure to stock up before you board the boat. The Ferry Building's bounty is just a 20-minute walk from Pier 33. In a pinch, you can also pony up for the underwhelming snacks on the boat.

KIDS ON THE ROCK

Parents should be aware that the audio tour, while engaging and worthwhile, includes some startlingly realistic sound effects. (Some children might not get a kick out of the gunshots from the Battle of Alcatraz—or the guards' screams, for that matter.) If you stay just one minute ahead in the program, you can always fast forward through the violent moments on your little one's audio tour.

STORM TROOPER ALERT!

When he was filming *Star Wars*, George Lucas recorded the sound of Alcatraz's cell doors slamming shut and used the sound bite in the movie whenever Darth Vader's star cruiser closed its doors.

The Marina & the Presidio

The Palace of Fine Arts

WORD OF MOUTH

"Crissy Field . . . a perfect combination of natural beauty (the bay, the Marin headlands) and man-made beauty (the bridges, the city skyline). Where people of all kinds are out enjoying it. Add the fact that you can get a fantastic cup of coffee, lunch, etc., at the Warming Hut and I am in heaven."

—sfmaster

GETTING ORIENTED

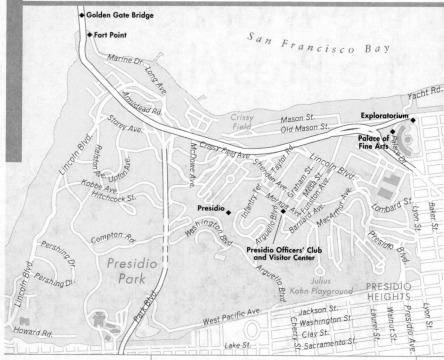

MAKING THE MOST OF YOUR TIME

Allow two hours for the Exploratorium, plus a half hour to stroll around the Palace of Fine Arts. Walking across the Golden Gate Bridge takes about 30 minutes, but leave some time to take in the view on the other side. If you aren't in a hurry, plan to spend at least two to three hours in the Presidio. In a pinch, make a 30–45 minute swing through for the views. Shoppers can burn up an entire day browsing the Marina's Chestnut Street and Cow Hollow's Union Street. Weekends are liveliest, while Mondays are quiet since some shops close.

TOP 5 REASONS TO GO

Golden Gate Bridge: Get a good look at the iconic span from the Presidio, then bundle up and walk over the water.

Shop Cow Hollow and the Marina: Browse hip boutiques and lavish antiques shops on Union Street, Cow Hollow's main drag. Then head north across Lombard Street to the Marina's shopping hot spot, Chestnut Street.

Exploratorium and the Palace of Fine Arts: The hands-on Exploratorium is a perennial kids' fave. Just outside is the stunning, Romanesque Palace of Fine Arts.

Crissy Field: Try to spot egrets and herons from the bayside wooden boardwalk over this restored tidal marshland under the Golden Gate Bridge.

Presidio wanderings: Lace up your walking shoes and follow one of the wooded trails; the city will feel a hundred miles away. If you've got a car, take a meandering drive, stopping at any and all ocean lookouts—Inspiration Point and Immigrant Point will take your breath away.

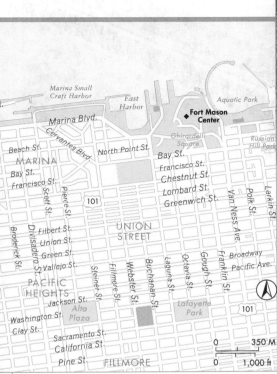

GETTING THERE

The only public transportation that operates to this part of town is the bus, so if you don't have your own wheels, take the 30–Stockton to Chestnut and Laguna in the Marina, two blocks south of Fort Mason.

The Marina and the Presidio are great for biking (though the Presidio has some hills) and easily reached along the Embarcadero.

The Presidio, vast and with plenty of free parking, is one area where it pays to have a car. If you're driving to either the Marina or the Presidio, parking isn't too bad—the Exploratorium and the Palace of Fine Arts, Crissy Field, and Fort Mason all have free lots.

For those without wheels, the free year-round shuttle PresidiGo, which loops through the Presidio every half hour, is a dream; ride the whole route for a good 45-minute overview. Pick it up at the transit center, at Lincoln Boulevard and Graham Street. For a map and schedule, check www.presidio.gov/directions/presidigo.

QUICK BITES

Greens to Go (⊠ *Fort Mason, Bldg. A, Marina* ☎ *415/771–6330*), the take-out wing of the famous Greens vegetarian restaurant, carries mouthwatering premade salads, sandwiches, and soups. There aren't any seats, but a steep flight of stairs leads up to a grassy picnicking area with splendid views of the Marina.

If you're after something sweet, look for the periwinkle awning at **La Boulange** (⊠ *1909 Union St., Cow Hollow* ☎ *415/440–4450*), which serves tartines (open-faced sandwiches) in addition to perfect pastries and cakes. Free refills of organic coffee and a welcoming interior encourage lingering.

Sightseeing
☆★★★

Nightlife
☆☆★★

Dining
☆☆★★

Lodging
☆☆★★

Shopping
☆★★★

Yachts bob at their moorings, satisfied-looking folks jog along the Marina Green, and multimillion-dollar homes overlook the bay in this picturesque, if somewhat sterile, neighborhood. Does it all seem a bit too perfect? Well, it got this way after the hard knock of Loma Prieta—the current pretty face was put on after hundreds of homes collapsed in the 1989 earthquake. Just west of this waterfront area is a more natural beauty: the Presidio. Once a military base, this beautiful, sprawling park is mostly green space, with hills, woods, and the marshlands of Crissy Field.

By Denise M. Leto

It's often said that the Marina's 1989 disaster was literally built on the legacy of the Great Quake. Local legend has it that rubble from the 1906 catastrophe was used to fill in the area—unstable landfill that then liquefied when the Loma Prieta temblor struck. That story was disproved in 2004, but regardless of the origin of Marina land, its shaky character stays the same. The district suffered the worst damage in the city from the 1989 quake, and many residents fled in search of more-solid ground. Others stayed put. "I realize that we're sitting on Jell-O," said one local. "[But] how many areas are as beautiful as the Marina? At some point, you just have to pick your poison...."

Well-funded postcollegiates and the nouveau riche quickly replaced those who left, changing the tenor of this formerly low-key neighborhood. The number of yuppie coffee emporiums skyrocketed, a bank became a Williams-Sonoma, and the local grocer gave way to a Pottery Barn. On weekends, a young, fairly homogeneous, well-to-do crowd floods the cafés and bars. (Some things don't change—even before the quake, the Marina Safeway was a famed pickup place for straight singles, hence the nickname "Dateway.") One unquestionable improvement has been the influx of contemporary cuisine into this former bastion of outdated Italian fare. South of Lom-

bard Street is the Marina's affluent neighbor, Cow Hollow, whose
main drag, Union Street, has some
of the city's best boutique shopping and a good selection of fun,
fine restaurants and cafés. Joggers
and kite-flyers head to the Marina
Green, the strip of lawn between
the yacht club and the mansions
of Marina Boulevard.

The Presidio, meanwhile, is going
through some shakeups, too. In
1996, President Clinton signed
a bill placing the Presidio in the
hands of a trust corporation as
part of a novel money-generat-

> **DON'T LOOK DOWN**
>
> Armed only with helmets, safety
> harnesses, and painting equip-
> ment, a full-time crew of 38 paint-
> ers keeps the Golden Gate Bridge
> clad in International Orange.
> Contrary to a favorite bit of local
> lore, they don't actually sweep on
> an entire coat of paint from one
> end of the bridge to the other, but
> instead scrape, prime, and repaint
> small sections that have rusted
> from exposure to the elements.

ing experiment. The trust manages most of the Presidio land, leasing
buildings and allowing limited development with the goal of making
enough money to cover the Presidio's operating costs. The National
Park Service oversees the coastal sections. Whether this arrangement
is a worthy model for national parks of the future, or the first step in
the crass commercialization of a public resource, remains to be seen.
Whatever the outcome, the Presidio will still have superb views and
the best hiking and biking areas in San Francisco; a drive through the
lush area is also a treat.

WHAT TO SEE IN THE MARINA

★ **Exploratorium.** Walking into this fascinating "museum of science, art,
and human perception" is like visiting a mad scientist's laboratory.
Most of the exhibits are super-size, and you can play with everything.
You can feel like Alice in Wonderland in the distortion room, where
you seem to shrink and grow as you walk across the slanted, checkered
floor. In the shadow room, a powerful flash freezes an image of your
shadow on the wall; jumping is a favorite pose. "Pushover" demon-
strates cow-tipping, but for people: stand on one foot and try to keep
your balance while a friend swings a striped panel in front of you (trust
us, you're going to fall).

More than 650 other exhibits focus on sea and insect life, computers,
electricity, patterns and light, language, the weather, and much more.
"Explainers"—usually high-school students on their days off—demonstrate cool scientific tools and procedures, like DNA sample-collection
and analysis. One surefire hit is the pitch-black, touchy-feely Tactile
Dome. In this geodesic dome strewn with textured objects, you crawl
through a course of ladders, slides, and tunnels, relying solely on your
sense of touch. Not surprisingly, lovey-dovey couples sometimes linger
in the "grope dome," but be forewarned: the staff will turn on the
lights if they have to. ■TIP→ **Reservations are required for the Tactile
Dome and will get you 75 minutes of access. You have to be at least seven**

years old to go through the dome, and the space is not for the claustrophobic. ⊠*3601 Lyon St., at Marina Blvd., Marina* ☎*415/561–0360 general information, 415/561–0362 Tactile Dome reservations* ⊕*www.exploratorium.edu* ✐*$14, free 1st Wed. of month; Tactile Dome $3 extra* ⊙*Tues.–Sun. 10–5.*

OFF THE BEATEN PATH

Wave Organ. Conceived by environmental artist Peter Richards and fashioned by master stonecutter George Gonzales, this unusual wave-activated acoustic sculpture gives off subtle harmonic sounds produced by seawater as it passes through 25 tubes. The sound is loudest at high tide. The granite and marble used for walkways, benches, and alcoves that are part of the piece were salvaged from a gold-rush-era cemetery. ⊠*North of Marina Green at end of jetty by Yacht Rd., park in lot north of Marina Blvd. at Lyon St., Marina.*

Fort Mason Center. Originally a depot for the shipment of supplies to the Pacific during World War II, the fort was converted into a cultural center in 1977. Here you can find the vegetarian restaurant Greens and shops, galleries, and performance spaces, most of which are closed Monday. There's also plentiful free parking—a rarity in the city.

You have to be seriously into Italian-American culture to appreciate the text- and photograph-heavy exhibits at the **Museo Italo-Americano** (⊠*Bldg. C* ☎*415/673–2200* ⊙*Tues.–Sun. noon–4*), but depending on the exhibit, it might be worth a glance if you're already at Fort Mason. Plus, it's free. The temporary exhibits downstairs at the free **SFMOMA Artists Gallery** (⊠*Bldg. A* ☎*415/441–4777*) can be great, but head upstairs and check out the paintings, sculptures, prints, and photographs for sale and for rent. It's a fun scene, with folks flipping through the works like posters. You won't find a Picasso or a Rembrandt here, but you can find works of high quality by emerging Northern California artists—and where else can you get a $50,000 work of art to hang on your wall for $400 (a month)? It's open Tuesday through Saturday 11:30–5:30. ⊠*Buchanan St. and Marina Blvd., Marina* ☎*415/979–3010 event information* ⊕*www.fortmason.org.*

Fodor's Choice
★

Palace of Fine Arts. At first glance this stunning, rosy rococo palace seems to be from another world, and indeed, it's the sole survivor of the many tinted-plaster structures (a temporary classical city of sorts) built for the 1915 Panama-Pacific International Exposition, the world's fair that celebrated San Francisco's recovery from the 1906 earthquake and fire. The expo buildings originally extended about a mile along the shore. Bernard Maybeck designed this faux Roman Classic beauty, which was reconstructed in concrete and reopened in 1967.

A victim of the elements, the palace is currently undergoing a piece-by-piece renovation; stand under the rotunda and look up to see the net that's protecting you from falling debris. The massive columns (each topped with four "weeping maidens"), great rotunda, and swan-filled lagoon have been used in countless fashion layouts, films, and wedding photo shoots. After admiring the lagoon, look across the street to the house at 3460 Baker Street. If the maidens out front look familiar, they should— they're original casts of the lovely "garland ladies" you can see in the Palace's colonnade. The house was on the market in 2007; if you'd had a cool $8 million, it could've been yours. ⊠ *Baker and Beach Sts., Marina* ☎ *415/561–0364 palace history tours* ⊕ *www.exploratorium. edu/palace* ☜ *Free* ⊙ *Daily 24 hrs.*

WHAT TO SEE IN THE PRESIDIO

☙ **Fort Point.** Dwarfed today by the Golden Gate Bridge, this brick fortress constructed between 1853 and 1861 was designed to protect San Francisco from a Civil War sea attack that never materialized. It was also used as a coastal-defense-fortification post during World War II, when soldiers stood watch here. This National Historic Site is now a sprawling museum filled with military memorabilia, surrounding a lonely, windswept courtyard. The building has a gloomy air and is suitably atmospheric. (It's usually chilly and windy, too, so bring a jacket.) On days when Fort Point is staffed, guided group tours and cannon drills take place. The top floor affords a unique angle on the bay. ■ TIP➜ **Take care when walking along the front side of the building, as it's slippery and the waves have a dizzying effect.** Though it's only open Friday through Sunday, Fort Point may soon be open during the week; call ahead for hours. Southeast of this structure is the **Fort Point Mine Depot,** an army facility that functioned as the headquarters for underwater mining operations throughout World War II. Today it's the Warming Hut, a National Park Service café and bookstore. ⊠ *Marine Dr. off Lincoln Blvd., Presidio* ☎ *415/556–1693* ⊕ *www.nps.gov/fopo* ☜ *Free* ⊙ *Fri.–Sun. 10–5.*

Fodor'sChoice
★ **Golden Gate Bridge.** The suspension bridge that connects San Francisco with Marin County has long wowed sightseers with its simple but powerful Art Deco design. Completed in 1937 after four years of construction, the 2-mi span and its 750-foot towers were built to withstand winds of more than 100 mph. It's also not a bad place to be in an earthquake: designed to sway up to 27.7 feet, the Golden Gate Bridge, unlike the Bay Bridge, was undamaged by the 1989 Loma Prieta quake. (If you're on the bridge when it's windy, stand still and you can feel it swaying a bit.) Though it's frequently gusty and misty—always bring a jacket, no matter what the weather's like—the bridge provides unparalleled views of the Bay Area. Muni buses 28 and 29 make stops at the Golden Gate Bridge toll plaza, on the San Francisco side. However, drive to fully appreciate the bridge from multiple vantage points in and around the Presidio; you'll be able to park at designated areas.

> ### WORD OF MOUTH
>
> "I would highly recommend a bike ride over the Golden Gate Bridge and down into Sausalito. It is a tough ride in some spots but it was amazing. The view from the bridge was incredible! The hill down into Sausalito is steep and long but very fun!"
>
> –Kerry392

7

Where can I find . . .?

PARKING	**Marina Green Park** ✉Marina Blvd. The price is right: free!	**Lombard Street Garage** ✉2055 Lombard St. City-owned, with reasonable rates.
A DRUGSTORE	**Walgreens** ✉3201 Divisadero, at Lombard St. Open 24 hours.	**Safeway** ✉15 Marina Blvd. The infamous "Dateway" has a pharmacy.
A BAR	**MatrixFillmore** ✉3138 Fillmore St. On the prowl and looking fabu- lous? Stop in for a martini.	**Bus Stop** ✉1901 Union St. Not dressed up? Drop by this Cow Hollow sports bar.

From the bridge's eastern-side walkway—the only side pedestrians are allowed on—you can take in the San Francisco skyline and the bay islands; look west for the wild hills of the Marin Headlands, the curving coast south to Land's End, and the Pacific Ocean. On sunny days, sailboats dot the water, and brave windsurfers test the often-treacherous tides beneath the bridge. ■TIP→ **A vista point on the Marin side gives you a spectacular city panorama.**

But there's a well-known, darker side to the bridge's story, too. The bridge is perhaps the world's most popular suicide platform, with an average of about 20 jumpers per year. (The first leaped just three months after the bridge's completion, and the official count was stopped in 1995 as the 1,000 jump approached.) Signs along the bridge read "There is hope. Make the call," referring the disconsolate to the special telephones on the bridge. Bridge officers, who patrol the walkway and watch by security camera to spot potential jumpers, successfully talk down two-thirds to three-quarters of them each year. Documentary filmmaker Eric Steel's controversial 2006 movie *The Bridge* once again put pressure on the Golden Gate Bridge Highway and Transportation District to install a suicide barrier, and a study is currently underway. ✉*Lincoln Blvd. near Doyle Dr. and Fort Point, Presidio* ☎*415/921–5858* ⊕*www.goldengatebridge.org* ☉*Pedestrians Mar.–Oct., daily 5* AM–9 PM; *Nov.–Feb., daily 5* AM–6 PM; *hrs change with daylight saving time. Bicyclists daily 24 hrs.*

★ **Presidio.** When San Franciscans want to spend a day in the woods, they head here. The Presidio has 1,400 acres of hills and majestic woods, two small beaches, and—the one thing Golden Gate Park doesn't have—stunning views of the bay, the Golden Gate Bridge, and Marin County. ■TIP→ **The best lookout points lie along Washington Boulevard, which meanders through the park.**

Part of the **Golden Gate National Recreation Area,** the Presidio was a military post for more than 200 years. Don Juan Bautista de Anza and

The Presidio with Kids

CLOSE UP

If you're in town with children (and you have a car), the sprawling, bayside Presidio offers enough kid-friendly diversions for one very full day. Start off at **Julius Kahn Park**, on the Presidio's southern edge, which has a disproportionate number of structures that spin. Swing by George Lucas's **Letterman Digital Arts Center** to check out the Yoda fountain; then head to the **Immigrant Point Lookout** on Washington Boulevard, with views of the bay and the ocean. Children love the pet cemetery, with its sweet, leaning headstones; it's near the stables, where you might glimpse some of the park police's equestrian members. The last stop is **Crissy Field**, where kids can ride bikes, skate, or run along the beach and clamber over the rocks; the view of the Golden Gate Bridge from below is captivating. Two nature centers here have fun, hands-on exhibits for kids. Finally, stop by the **Warming Hut**, at the western end of Crissy Field, for sandwiches and hot chocolate. You can also do a version of this day using the PresidiGo shuttle, but you'll need to adapt your route according to the shuttle stops.

a band of Spanish settlers first claimed the area in 1776. It became a Mexican garrison in 1822 when Mexico gained its independence from Spain; U.S. troops forcibly occupied the Presidio in 1846. The U.S. Sixth Army was stationed here until October 1994, when the coveted space was transferred into civilian hands.

Today, after much controversy, the area is being transformed into a self-sustaining national park with a combination of public, commercial, and residential projects. In 2005, Bay Area filmmaker George Lucas opened the **Letterman Digital Arts Center,** his 23-acre digital studio "campus," along the eastern edge of the land. Seventeen of those acres are exquisitely landscaped and open to the public, but not even landscaping this perfect can compete with the wilds of the Presidio. A lodge at the Main Post is in the planning stages.

The battle over the fate of the rest of the Presidio is ongoing. Many older buildings have been reconstructed; the issue now is how to fill them. The original plan described a nexus for arts, education, and environmental groups. Since the Presidio's overseeing trust must make the park financially self-sufficient by 2013, which means generating enough revenue to keep afloat without the federal government's monthly $20 million checks, many fear that money will trump culture. The Asian-themed SenSpa has opened, a Walt Disney museum is on the way, and Donald Fisher—founder of the Gap clothing chain—wants to build a home for his huge modern-art collection near the parade ground (this has become a compelling and controversial proposal). With old military housing now repurposed as apartments and homes with rents up to $10,000 a month, there's some concern that the Presidio will become an incoherent mix of pricey real estate. Still, the $6 million that Lucas shells out annually for rent does plant a lot of saplings....

Dining in the Marina & the Presidio

MODERATE

A-16, Italian, 2355 Chestnut St.

Betelnut, Asian, 2030 Union St.

Greens Restaurant, Vegetarian, Bldg. A, Fort Mason

Isa, French, 3324 Steiner St.

Laïola, Spanish, 2031 Chestnut St.

Rose's Café, Italian, 2298 Union St.

Terzo, Mediterranean, 3011 Steiner St.

The Presidio also has two beaches, a golf course, a visitor center, and picnic sites; the views from the many overlooks are sublime.

★ ♿ Especially popular is **Crissy Field,** a stretch of restored marshlands along the sand of the bay. Kids on bikes, folks walking dogs, and joggers share the paved path along the shore, often winding up at the Warming Hut, a combination café and store at the end of the path, for a hot chocolate in the shadow of the Golden Gate Bridge. Midway along the Golden Gate Promenade path that winds along the shore is the Gulf of the Farallones National Marine Sanctuary Visitor Center, where kids can get a close-up view of small sea creatures and learn about the rich ecosystem offshore. Toward the promenade's eastern end, Crissy Field Center offers great children's programs and has cool science displays. West of the Golden Gate Bridge is sandy **Baker Beach,** beloved for its spectacular views and laid-back vibe (read: you'll see naked people here). This is one of those places locals like to show off to visitors. ✉ *Between Marina and Lincoln Park, Presidio* ⊕ *www.nps.gov/prsf and www.presidio.gov.*

Presidio Officers' Club and Visitor Center. A remnant of the days when the Presidio was an army base, this Mission-style clubhouse now doubles as a temporary visitor center and exhibit space. Hit the visitor center for maps, schedules of the walking and biking tours, recaps of the Presidio's history, and a good selection of Bay Area books and souvenirs.

The club's temporary art exhibitions explore the unique cultural identity of the American West and the Pan-Pacific, such as Japanese wood-block prints. The space also sometimes offers dance performances, lectures, and theater. And a bonus that's rare in San Francisco: ample free parking. In one of the Presidio's most exciting projects, the parade ground parking lot (on what's known as the Main Post) is slated to become a lodge—most likely a swank and green one—and a swath of restored habitat that will stretch all the way to Crissy Field. ✉ *50 Moraga Ave., Presidio* ☎ *Visitor center 415/561–4323, 415/561–5500 for exhibits* ⊕ *www.presidiotrust. gov* ☉ *Visitor center daily 9–5; exhibit space Wed.–Sun. 11–5.*

Golden Gate Park & the Western Shoreline

WORD OF MOUTH

"Definitely go up in the de Young tower—great view! And I really enjoyed walking around the botanical gardens in addition to the Japanese garden."

—NWWanderer

GETTING ORIENTED

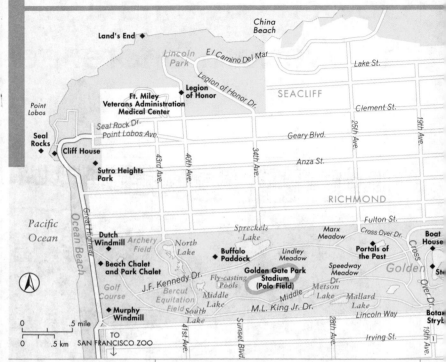

SAFETY IN THE PARK

Although Golden Gate Park is essentially safe, avoid walking here after dark and use common sense if you venture away from the busier areas. Here are the few zones that can be dodgy.

Hippie Hill (aka "the marijuana fields"): near the Haight Street entrance

Horseshoe Pits (closed): in the northeast corner of the park

Lily Pond (aka Hobo Lake): in the east end near the Australian Tree Fern Dell

Windmills: on the park's western edge, especially around the pedestrian tunnels

TOP 5 REASONS TO GO

Conservatory of Flowers: Stand at the top of the steps, across the lawn from the conservatory, and take in the sheer beauty of the white, wood-and-glass domed structure.

de Young Museum and Japanese Tea Garden: Scale the steep humpback bridge in the perfectly groomed Japanese Tea Garden. Then head to the observation floor at the copper-covered de Young and take in the sweeping view.

Lands End: Head down the freshly restored Coastal Trail near the Cliff House; you'll quickly find yourself in a forest with unparalleled views of the Golden Gate Bridge.

Toast the sunset at the Beach Chalet: Top off a day of exploring with a cocktail overlooking Ocean Beach.

San Francisco Botanical Garden: Wander through a landscape of horsetails, gingko trees, and other dinosaur-era plants at the arboretum's Primitive Plant Garden, then stretch out on the grass and watch turtles sunning themselves at the pond.

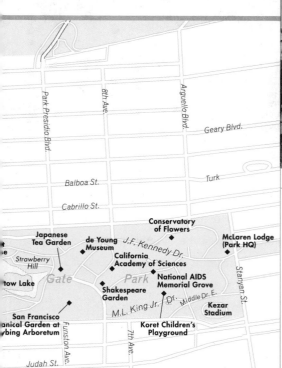

Map labels: Park Presidio Blvd., 8th Ave., Arguello Blvd., Geary Blvd., Balboa St., Turk, Cabrillo St., Conservatory of Flowers, Japanese Tea Garden, de Young Museum, J.F. Kennedy Dr., McLaren Lodge (Park HQ), Strawberry Hill, California Academy of Sciences, tow Lake, Gate, Park, Stow Lake, National AIDS Memorial Grove, Shakespeare Garden, M.L. King Jr. Dr., Middle Dr. E., Stanyan St., Kezar Stadium, San Francisco Botanical Garden at Strybing Arboretum, Funston Ave., 7th Ave., Koret Children's Playground, Judah St.

QUICK BITES

Dining options within Golden Gate Park are extremely limited. The gorgeous setting often overshadows the upscale comfort food at the **Beach Chalet** and **Park Chalet** (✉ *1000 Great Hwy.* ☎ *415/386–8439*), on the western edge. The **de Young Café** (✉ *50 Hagiwara Tea Garden Dr.* ☎ *415/750–2614*), which has an outdoor sculpture garden, has a good seasonal menu created from local ingredients. Step into the Japanese Garden's serene, open-air **Tea House** (✉ *Tea Garden Dr. off John F. Kennedy Dr.*) for tea and cookies. Snack bars at Stow Lake and the children's playground sell prepackaged cookies, chips, and ice cream.

For a quick, supply-gathering jaunt outside the park, your best bets are Haight Street (east of the park) or 9th Avenue (just south of the park). Try unbelievable veggie pizza at co-op **Arizmendi** (✉ *1331 9th Ave.* ☎ *415/566–3117*). Or scarf down burritos at **Gordo** (✉ *1239 9th Ave.* ☎ *415/566–6011*).

GETTING THERE

The 5–Fulton bus runs to and along the north side of Golden Gate Park from Civic Center. The N–Judah buses run frequently from downtown to the corner of 9th Avenue and Irving Street, just south of the park. If you're just heading to the eastern end of the park, the 21–Hayes bus will get you there.

There's plenty of parking at the park, much of it free. On Sunday (and Saturday spring through fall), John F. Kennedy Drive is closed to cars, so it can be hard to find an inroad into the park then. Crossover Drive, which cuts north–south through the park, is strictly a thoroughfare, with no park access.

To reach the Western Shoreline from downtown by bus, nab the 38–Geary, which runs all the way to 48th and Point Lobos avenues, just east of the Cliff House. Along the Western Shoreline, the 18–46th Avenue bus runs between the Legion of Honor and the zoo (and beyond).

8

Sightseeing
☆☆★★★

Nightlife
☆☆☆☆☆

Dining
☆☆☆☆★

Lodging
☆☆☆☆☆

Shopping
☆☆☆☆☆

Jogging, cycling, skating, picnicking, going to a museum, checking out a concert, dozing in the sunshine...Golden Gate Park is the perfect playground for fast-paced types, laid-back dawdlers, and everyone in between. More than 1,000 acres, stretching from the Haight all the way to the windy Pacific coast, the park is a vast patchwork of woods, trails, lakes, lush gardens, sports facilities, museums—even a herd of buffalo. You can hit the highlights in a few hours, but it would literally take days to fully explore the entire park.

By Denise M. Leto

There's more natural beauty beyond the park's borders, along San Francisco's wild Western Shoreline. Few other American cities provide a more intimate and dramatic view of the power and fury of the surf attacking the shore. From Lincoln Park in the north, along Ocean Beach from the Richmond south to the Sunset, a different breed of San Franciscan chooses to live in this area: surfers who brave the heaviest fog to ride the waves; writers who seek solace and inspiration in this city outpost; dog lovers committed to giving their pets a good workout each day.

From Lands End in Lincoln Park you have some of the best views of the Golden Gate (the name was given to the opening of San Francisco Bay long before the bridge was built) and the Marin Headlands. From the historic Cliff House south to the sprawling San Francisco Zoo, the Great Highway and Ocean Beach run along the western edge of the city. (If you're here in winter or spring, keep your eyes peeled for migrating gray whales.) The wind is often strong along the shoreline, summer fog can blanket the ocean beaches, and the water is cold and usually too rough for swimming. Don't forget your jacket!

WHAT TO SEE ON THE WESTERN SHORELINE

Cliff House. A meal at the Cliff House isn't about the food—the spectacular ocean view is what brings folks here. The vistas, which include offshore Seal Rock (the barking marine mammals who reside there are actually sea lions), can be 30 mi or more on a clear day—or less than a mile on foggy days. ■TIP➔ **Come for drinks just before sunset; then head back into town for dinner.**

Three buildings have occupied this site since 1863. The current building dates from 1909; a 2004 renovation has left a strikingly attractive restaurant and a squat concrete viewing platform out back. The complex, owned by the National Park Service, includes a gift shop.

Sitting on the observation deck is the **Giant Camera,** a cute yellow-painted wooden model of an old-fashioned camera with its lens pointing skyward. Built in the 1940s and threatened many times with demolition, it's now on the National Register of Historic Places. Step into the dark, tiny room inside (for a rather steep $5 fee); a fascinating 360-degree image of the surrounding area—which rotates as the "lens" on the roof rotates—is projected on a large, circular table. ■TIP➔ **In winter and spring, you may also glimpse migrating gray whales from the observation deck.**

■ **BATH-ROOM BREAKS**

In Golden Gate Park, free public restrooms are fairly common and mostly clean, especially around the eastern end's attractions. The San Francisco Botanical Garden has numerous facilities, including inside each gate. Enter the de Young Museum at the sculpture garden and café patio and you can use the public restrooms there. Farther west, behind Stow Lake's boathouse and near the Koret Children's Quarter are facilities. Near the ocean, there are public restrooms at the Beach Chalet–Park Chalet. And you can always duck into the bar at the Cliff House (immediate left inside the door) and enjoy historic black-and-white photos on the way to the snazzy bathrooms there.

8

To the north of the Cliff House are the ruins of the once-grand glass-roof **Sutro Baths,** which you can explore on your own (they look a bit like water-storage receptacles). Adolf Sutro, eccentric onetime San Francisco mayor and Cliff House owner, built the bath complex, including a train out to the site, in 1896, so that everyday folks could enjoy the benefits of swimming. Six enormous baths (some freshwater and some seawater), more than 500 dressing rooms, and several restaurants covered 3 acres north of the Cliff House and accommodated 25,000 bathers. Likened to Roman baths in a European glass palace, the baths were for decades

The Boss Gardner

Fiery Scotsman John McLaren reigned as park superintendent from 1890 to 1943, ruling with an iron fist and often taking on City Hall to defend "his" park. When government officials planned to build a trolley line through the park, McLaren cursed "the rascals at City Hall" and marched downtown to challenge the decision, complaining that many plantings would be destroyed. The city planner assured him that the rail line would cut through a sparsely planted area of the park, but McLaren dragged the man to the site—which had miraculously bloomed into a lush flower garden overnight. When park police wanted to remove a tree that was too close to their stationhouse,

McLaren allegedly replied, "I'm a reasonable man. Let's compromise, and you move the station."

McLaren hated statues and planted around them so vigorously that some, long forgotten, were only excavated after his death. Some say he hid the one of himself in the stables; discovered and installed posthumously, it strolls McLaren's beloved Rhododendron Dell. When he reached retirement age, instead of a gold watch he got the title Superintendent for Life, and finally died peacefully at home, in the park building now known as McLaren Lodge.

—Denise M. Leto

the favorite destination of San Franciscans in search of entertainment. The complex fell into disuse after World War II, was closed in 1952, and burned down (under officially questionable circumstances, wink wink) during demolition in 1966. ⊠*1090 Point Lobos Ave., Outer Richmond*☎*415/386–3330* ⊕*www.cliffhouse.com* ⊠*Free* ☉ *Weekdays 9* AM*–9:30* PM*, weekends 9* AM*–10* PM.

Legion of Honor. You can't beat the location of this museum of European art—situated on cliffs overlooking the ocean, the Golden Gate Bridge, and the Marin Headlands. A pyramidal glass skylight in the entrance court illuminates the lower-level galleries, which exhibit prints and drawings, English and European porcelain, and ancient Assyrian, Greek, Roman, and Egyptian art. The 20-plus galleries on the upper level display the permanent collection of European art (paintings, sculpture, decorative arts, and tapestries) from the 14th century to the present day.

The noteworthy Auguste Rodin collection includes two galleries devoted to the master and a third with works by Rodin and other 19th-century sculptors. An original cast of Rodin's *The Thinker* welcomes you as you walk through the courtyard. As fine as the museum is, the setting and view outshine the collection and make a trip here worthwhile.

The **Legion Café,** on the lower level, serves tasty light meals (soup, sandwiches, grilled chicken) inside and on a garden terrace. (Unfortunately, there's no view.) Just north of the museum's parking lot is George Segal's *The Holocaust,* a stark white installation that evokes life in concentration camps during World War II. It's haunting at night, when backlighted by lights in the Legion's parking lot. ■**TIP→ Admission to the Legion also counts as same-day admission to the de Young Museum.** ⊠*34th Ave. at Clement St., Outer Richmond* ☎*415/750–3600* ⊕*www.thinker.org* ⊡*$10, $2 off with Muni transfer, free 1st Tues. of month* ⊘*Tues.–Sun. 9:30–5:15.*

WORD OF MOUTH

"The Legion of Honor is in the most terrific setting with its views to the Golden Gate Bridge and the headlands. The porcelain on the lower level is beautifully displayed—sort of like being at Gump's except you can't buy anything!"

–dovima

★ **Lincoln Park.** Although many of the city's green spaces are gentle and welcoming, Lincoln Park is a wild 275-acre park with windswept cliffs and sweeping views. The newly renovated Coastal Trail, the park's most dramatic, leads out to **Lands End**; pick it up west of the Legion of Honor (at the end of El Camino del Mar) or from the parking lot at Point Lobos and El Camino del Mar. Time your hike to hit Mile Rock at low tide, and you might catch a glimpse of two wrecked ships peeking up from their watery graves. **Do be careful if you hike here; landslides are frequent, and many people have fallen into the sea by standing too close to the edge of a crumbling bluff top.**

On the tamer side, large Monterey cypresses line the fairways at Lincoln Park's 18-hole golf course, near the Legion of Honor. At one time this land was the Golden Gate Cemetery, where the dead were segregated by nationality; most were indigent and interred without ceremony in the potter's field. In 1900, the Board of Supervisors voted to ban burials within city limits, and all but two city cemeteries (at Mission Dolores and the Presidio) were moved to Colma, a small town just south of San Francisco. When digging has to be done in the park, bones occasionally surface again. ⊠*Entrance at 34th Ave. at Clement St., Outer Richmond.*

Ocean Beach. Stretching 3 mi along the western side of the city from the Richmond to the Sunset, this sandy swath of the Pacific coast is good for jogging or walking the dog—but not for swimming. The water is so cold that surfers wear wet suits year-round, and riptides are strong. As for sunbathing, it's rarely warm enough here; think meditative walking instead of sun worshipping.

Paths on both sides of the Great Highway lead from Lincoln Way to Sloat Boulevard (near the zoo); the beachside path winds through landscaped sand dunes, and the paved path across the highway is good for biking and in-line skating. (Though you have to rent bikes elsewhere.) The **Beach Chalet** restaurant and brewpub is across the Great Highway from Ocean Beach, about five blocks south of the Cliff House. ⊠*Along Great Hwy. from Cliff House to Sloat Blvd. and beyond.*

☺ **San Francisco Zoo.** Awash in bad press since one of its tigers escaped its enclosure and killed a visitor on Christmas day 2007, the city's zoo is struggling to polish its image, update its habitats, restore its reputation

8

Where can I find...?

A PARKING SPACE	**Metered Lots** ⊠Irving St. and 6th, 7th, and 8th Near the parks east side.	**Metered Lot** ⊠Irving St. and 20th This city-owned lot is a block from central Golden Gate Park.
A GAS STATION	**Sunset 76** ⊠1700 Noriega St. Head here to get a flat patched, or to gas up.	**19th Ave 76 Station** ⊠1401 19th Ave. Stop by for gas and auto re- pairs.
A DRUGSTORE	**Walgreens** ⊠5411 Geary Blvd., at 18th Ave. Open 24 hours.	**Walgreens** ⊠199 Parnassus Ave. Just two blocks from Golden Gate Parks southeast corner.

with animal welfare organizations, and avoid the direct oversight of the city's Board of Supervisors. Nestled onto prime oceanfront property, the zoo—which some have accused of caring more about human entertainment than the welfare of its wards—is touting its metamorphosis into the "New Zoo," a wildlife-focused recreation center that inspires visitors to become conservationists. Integrated exhibits group different species of animals from the same geographic areas together in enclosures that don't look like cages. More than 250 species reside here, including endangered species such as the snow leopard, Sumatran tiger, and grizzly bear.

The zoo's superstar exhibit is **Grizzly Gulch,** where orphaned sisters Kachina and Kiona enchant visitors with their frolicking and swimming. When the bears are in the water, the only thing between you and them is (thankfully thick) glass. Grizzly feedings are 10:30 AM daily.

The **Lemur Forest** has five varieties of the bug-eyed, long-tailed primates from Madagascar. You can help hoist food into the lemurs' feeding towers and watch the fuzzy creatures climb up to chow down. African Kikuyu grass carpets the circular outer area of **Gorilla Preserve,** one of the largest and most natural gorilla habitats of any zoo in the world. Trees and shrubs create communal play areas.

Ten species of rare monkeys—including colobus monkeys, white ruffed lemurs, and macaques—live and play at the two-tier **Primate Discovery Center,** which contains 23 interactive learning exhibits on the ground level.

Magellanic penguins waddle about the rather sad **Penguin Island,** splashing and frolicking in its 200-foot pool. Feeding time is 3 PM (2:30 on Thursday). Koalas peer out from among the trees in **Koala Crossing,** and kangaroos and wallabies headline the **Australian Walkabout** exhibit. The 7-acre **Puente al Sur** (Bridge to the South) re-creates habitats in South America, replete with giant anteaters and capybaras.

Creating Golden Gate Park

In the 1860s, San Francisco was booming. The California gold rush and the transcontinental railroad had swelled the city's population, and San Francisco needed a magnificent public green space to emulate its older, eastern siblings.

City Hall chose an unlikely location: a vast expanse of sand dunes on the western side of the city. The local government cut a deal with the squatters who lived in the area, and in 1870, Golden Gate Park was born . . . on paper, anyway.

William Hammond Hall, a civil engineer first hired to survey the land, became the park's intrepid first superintendent and began to create an urban oasis. In five years he managed to plant 60,000 trees—a feat on its own, considering that 75% of the park was covered in sand. Legend has it that after many plants failed to take root, a spilled sack of horse feed saved the day. Hall noticed that the toppled barley sprouted, so he mixed lupine with the grain, and voila—greenery.

—Denise M. Leto

An **African Savanna** exhibit mixes giraffe, zebra, kudu, ostrich, and many other species, all living together in a 3-acre section with a central viewing spot, accessed by a covered passageway.

The 7-acre **Children's Zoo** has about 300 mammals, birds, and reptiles, plus an insect zoo, a meerkat and prairie-dog exhibit, a nature trail, a nature theater, a restored 1921 Dentzel carousel, and a mini–steam train. A ride on the train costs $3, and you can hop astride one of the carousel's 52 hand-carved menagerie animals for $2. ⊠*Sloat Blvd. and 47th Ave., Sunset* ✢ *Muni L–Taraval streetcar from downtown* ☎*415/753– 7080* ⊕*www.sfzoo.org* ⊠*$11, $1 off with Muni transfer, free 1st Wed. of month* ⊙*Daily 10–5. Children's zoo 10–4:30.*

Sutro Heights Park. Crows and other large birds battle the heady breezes at this cliff-top park on what were once the grounds of the home of Adolph Sutro, an eccentric mining engineer and former San Francisco mayor. An extremely wealthy man, Sutro may have owned about 10% of San Francisco at one point, but he couldn't buy good taste: a few remnants of his gaudy, faux-classical statue collection still stand (including the lions at what was the main gate). Monterey cypresses and Canary Island palms dot the park, and photos on placards depict what things looked like before the house burned down in 1896, from the greenhouse to the ornate carpet-bed designs.

All that remains of the main house is its foundation. Climb up for a sweeping view of the Pacific Ocean and the Cliff House below (which Sutro owned), and try to imagine what the perspective might have been like from one of the upper floors. San Francisco City Guides (☎415/557–4266) runs a free Saturday tour of the park that starts at 2 (meet at the lion statue at 48th and Point Lobos avenues). ⊠*Point Lobos and 48th Aves., Outer Richmond.*

8

Dining in Golden Gate & the Western Shoreline

BUDGET

Dragonfly, Vietnamese, 420 Judah St.

Park Chow, American, 1240 9th Ave.

Pho Hoa Clement, Vietnamese, 239 Clement St.

San Tung No. 2, Chinese, 1031 Irving St.

Ton Kiang, Chinese, 5821 Geary Blvd.

MODERATE

Aziza, Moroccan, 5800 Geary Blvd.

Katia's, Russian, 600 5th Ave.

GOLDEN GATE PARK

Golden Gate Park is the yin to downtown's yang. Like New York's Central Park, San Francisco's most beloved green space is about getting away from the frenetic pace of urban life. Walk 100 yards into the park from any direction and look around: you'll see towering trees, meandering paths, and maybe an isolated lake—but you probably won't see the cityscape. And that's the whole idea.

Stretching more than 1,000 acres from the ocean to the Haight, this is a place to slow down and smell the eucalyptus. Stockbrokers and gadget-laden parents stroll the Music Concourse, while speedy tattooed cyclists and wobbly, training-wheeled kids cruise along shaded paths. Stooped seniors warm the garden benches, hikers search for waterfalls, and picnickers lounge in the Rhododendron Dell. San Franciscans love their city, but this is where they come to breathe.

(opposite page) People exercising in the park (top)
Rowing on Stow Lake

ORIENTATION

The park breaks down naturally into three chunks. The eastern end attracts the biggest crowds with its cluster of block-buster sights. It's also the easiest place to dip into the park for a quick trip. Water hobbyists come to the middle section's lake-speckled open space, home to fly-casting pools and the Model Yacht Club. Sporty types head west to the coastal end for its soccer fields, golf course, and archery range. This windswept western end is the park's least visited and most naturally landscaped part. Most of the park is relatively flat, though cyclists will feel the rise pedaling east.

🕑 *Daily 6 am—10pm*
🌐 *www.parks.sfgov.org*

WALKING TOURS

San Francisco Botanical Garden (☎ 415/661–1316) has free botanical tours every day. Tours start at the book-

IN FOCUS GOLDEN GATE PARK

8

store weekdays at 1:30 PM, weekends at 10:30 AM and 1:30 PM. Meet at the Friend Gate (at the northern entrance) Wednesday, Friday, and Sunday at 2 PM. **San Francisco Parks Trust** (☎ 415/263–0991) offers historically minded tours of the Japanese Tea Garden Wednesday and Sunday at 1. The 45-minute tours are free but don't include garden admission.

BEST TIMES TO VISIT

Time of day: It's best to arrive early at the Conservatory of Flowers, the de Young Museum, and the Japanese Tea Garden to avoid crowds. At sunset, the only place to be is the park's western end, watching the sun dip into the Pacific.

Time of year: Come to the eastern end of the park on a sunny weekend, and you'll think the whole Bay Area is here with you—visit during the week if you can. The long, Indian summer days of September and October are the warmest times to

visit, and many special weekend events are held then.

Blooms: The rhododendrons burst into billowy bloom between February and May. The Queen Wilhelmina Tulip Garden blossoms in February and March. Cherry trees in the Japanese Tea Garden bloom in April, and the Rose Garden is at its best from mid-May to mid-June, in the beginning of July, and during September.

BEST PLACES TO PICNIC

■ Lawn in front of the Conservatory of Flowers.

■ By the pond in the San Francisco Botanical Garden.

■ The benches overlooking the Rustic Bridge at Stow Lake.

■ Rhododendron Dell.

DON'T-MISS SIGHTS

CONSERVATORY OF FLOWERS

Whatever you do, be sure to at least drive by the Conservatory of Flowers—it's just too darn pretty to miss. The gorgeous, white-framed, 1878 glass structure is topped with a 14-ton glass dome. Stepping inside the giant greenhouse is like taking a quick trip to the rainforest; it's humid, warm, and smells earthy. The undeniable highlight is the Aquatic Plants section, where lily pads float and carnivorous plants dine on bugs to the sounds of rushing water. On the east side of the conservatory (to the right as you face the building), cypress, pine, and redwood trees surround the **Dahlia Garden,** which blooms in summer and fall. To the west is the **Rhododendron Dell,** which contains 850 varieties, more than any other garden in the country. It's a favorite local Mother's Day picnic spot.

✉ *John F. Kennedy Dr. at Conservatory Dr.* ☎ *415/666–7001* 🎟 *$5, free 1st Tues. of month* ⊙ *Tues.–Sun. 9–5* ⊕ *www.conservatoryofflowers.org.*

DE YOUNG MUSEUM

It seems that everyone in town has a strong opinion about the new museum, unveiled in 2005. Some adore the striking copper facade, while others grimace and hope that the green patina of age will mellow the effect. Most maligned is the 144-foot tower, but the view from its ninth-story observation room, ringed by floor-to-ceiling windows, is a must-see, and free to boot.

The building almost overshadows the de Young's respected collection of American, African, and Oceanic art. Works by Wayne Thiebaud, John Singer Sargent, Winslow Homer, and Richard Diebenkorn are the painting collection's highlights. The museum's 2009 schedule includes *Warhol Live.*

■TIP→ Note that a ticket here is also good for same-day admission to the Legion of Honor.

✉ *50 Hagiwara Tea Garden Dr.* ☎ *415/750–3600* ⊕ *www.thinker.org/deyoung* 🎟 *$10, free 1st Tues. of month* ⊙ *Tues.–Sun. 9:30–5, Fri. 9:30–8:45.*

SAN FRANCISCO JAPANESE TEA GARDEN

As you amble through the manicured landscape, past Japanese sculptures and perfect miniature pagodas, over ponds of carp that have been there since before the 1906 quake, you may be transported to a more peaceful plane. Or maybe the shrieks of kids clambering over the almost vertical "humpback" bridges will keep you firmly in the here and now. Either way, this garden is one of those tourist spots that's truly worth a stop (a half-hour will do). And at 5 acres, it's large enough that you'll always be able to find a bit of serenity, even when the tour buses drop by.

■TIP→ The garden is especially lovely in April, when the cherry blossoms are in bloom.

✉ *Hagiwara Tea Garden Dr. off John F. Kennedy Dr.* ☎ *415/752–4227* 🎫 *$4, free Mon., Wed., and Fri. 9 am– 10am* ☼ *Mar.–Oct., daily 9–6; Nov.– Feb., daily 9–4:45.*

CALIFORNIA ACADEMY OF SCIENCES

At this writing, San Francisco's newest star attraction was set to open on September 27, 2008. Renzo Piano's audacious, prescient design for this natural history museum completes the dramatic transformation of the park's Music Concourse. An eco-friendly, energy-efficient adventure in biodiversity and green architecture, it's equipped with a rainforest, a planetarium, a retractable ceiling over the central courtyard, and a "living roof" that's covered with native plants. Dotted with large mounds and hills—Piano's tribute to the local topography—the roof looks like an alien launch pad. ✉ *55 Music Concourse Dr.* ☎ *415/379–8000* ⊕ *www.calacademy.org* 🎫 *$24.95* ☼ *Mon.–Sat. 9:30–5, Sun. 11–5.*

ALSO WORTH SEEING

Paddle boats on Stow Lake near the Rustic Bridge

San francisco Botanical Garden at Strybing Arboretum One of the best picnic spots in a very picnic-friendly park, the 55-acre arboretum specializes in plants from areas with climates similar to that of the Bay Area. Walk the Eastern Australian garden to see tough, pokey shrubs and plants with cartoon-like names, such as the hilly-pilly tree. Kids gravitate toward the large shallow fountain and the pond with ducks, turtles, and egrets. ⊠ *Enter the park at 9th Ave. at Lincoln Way* ☎ *415/661–1316* ⊕ *www.sfbotanicalgarden.org* ⊡ *Free* ☉ *Weekdays 8–4:30, weekends 10–5.*

Koret Children's Quarter. The country's first public children's playground reopened in 2007 after a spectacular renovation, with wave-shaped climbing walls. Old-fashioned cement slides, and a 20-plus-foot rope climbing structure that kids love and parents fear. Thankfully, one holdover is the beautiful, handcrafted 1912 Herschell-Spillman Carousel. ⊠ *Bowling Green Dr., off Martin Luther King Jr. Dr.* ☎ *415/831–2700* ⊡ *Playground free, carousel $1.50 kids 6–12, $.50* ☉ *Playground daily dawn–dusk;*

carousel Memorial Day–Labor Day, daily 10–4:30, Labor Day–Memorial Day, Fri.–Sun. 10–4:30.

National AIDS Memorial Grove. This lush, serene 7-acre grove was conceived as a living memorial to the disease's victims. Coast live oaks, Monterey pines, coast redwoods, and other trees flank the grove. There are also two stone circles, one recording the names of the dead and their loved ones, the other engraved with a poem. Free 20-minute tours are available some Saturdays. ⊠ *Middle Dr. E, west of tennis courts* ☎ *415/765-0497* ⊕ *www.aidsmemorial.org.*

Stow Lake. This placid body of water surrounds Strawberry Hill. Cross one of the bridges—the 19th-century stone bridge on the southwest side is lovely—and ascend the hill, topped with a waterfall and an elaborate Chinese Pavilion. ⊠ *Off John F. Kennedy Dr.* ☎ *Boat rental 415/752–0347; surrey and bike rental 415/668–6699* ☉ *Boat rentals daily 10–4, surrey and bicycle rentals daily 9–dusk.*

BEST WAYS TO SPEND YOUR TIME

A new perspective from the de Young Museum

The park stretches 3 mi east to west and is a half-mile wide, so it's possible to cover the whole thing in a day—by car, public transportation, bike, or even on foot. But to do so might feel more like a forced march than a pleasure. Weigh your time and your interests, choose your top picks, then leave at least an extra hour to just enjoy being outdoors.

Two hours: Swing by the exquisite Conservatory of Flowers for a 20-minute peek, then head to the de Young Museum. Spend a few minutes assessing its controversial exterior and perhaps glide through some of the galleries before heading to the observation tower for a panoramic view of the city. Cross the music concourse to the spectacular Academy of Sciences.

Half day: Spend a little extra time at the sights described above, then head to the nearby Japanese Tea Garden to enjoy its perfectionist landscape. Next, cross the street to the San Francisco Botanical Garden at Strybing Arboretum and check out the intriguing Primitive Garden. If you brought supplies, this is a great place for a picnic; you can also grab lunch at the de Young Café.

Full day: After the half-day (above) continue on to the children's playground if you have kids in tow. Once your little ones see the playground's tree house–like play structures and climbing opportunities, you may be here for the rest of the day. Alternatively, make your way to the serene National AIDS Memorial Grove. Then head west, stopping at Stow Lake to climb Strawberry Hill. Wind up at the Beach Chalet for a sunset drink.

WALKING THE PARK

The most convenient entry point is on the eastern edge at Stanyan and Kezar streets, which points you directly toward the Conservatory of Flowers. It's a 10-minute walk there; allow another 10–15 minutes to reach the California Academy of Sciences, de Young Museum, Japanese Tea Garden, and San Francisco Botanical Garden. Stow Lake is another 10 minutes west from these three sights.

■TIP➔ Carry a map—the park's sightlines usually prevent you from using city landmarks as reference points. Posted maps in the park are few and far between, and they're often out of date too. Paths aren't always clear here, so stick to well-marked trails. See this chapter's Getting Oriented feature for safety tips.

Taking a break in the Japanese Tea Garden

GETTING AROUND ON WHEELS

Rollerbladers in Golden Gate Park

GETTING AROUND BY BIKE

The park is fantastic for cycling, especially on Sunday when cars are barred from John F. Kennedy Drive. Biking the park round trip is about a 7-mi trip, which usually takes 1–2 hours. The route down John F. Kennedy Drive takes you past the prettiest, well-maintained sections of the park on a mostly flat circuit. The most popular route continues all the way to the beach. Keep in mind that the ride is downhill toward the ocean, uphill heading east.

Golden Gate Park Bike & Skate (✉ 3038 Fulton St. ☎ 415/668–1117). On the northern edge of the park; has good deals on rentals.

Blazing Saddles (✉ 1095 Columbus Ave., North Beach ☎ 415/202–8888). The biggest rental outfit in town. Although their branches aren't close to the park, the company is worth considering since they have tons of bikes in good condition. They're very helpful when it comes to route recommendations, too.

GETTING AROUND BY CAR

If you have a car, you'll have no trouble hopping from sight to sight. (But remember, the main road, John F. Kennedy Drive, is closed to cars on Sunday and, April–September, on Saturday.) Parking within the park is often free and is usually easy to find, especially beyond the eastern end. On Sundays or anytime the eastern end is crowded, head for the residential streets north of the park or the underground parking lot; enter on 10th and Fulton (northern edge of the park) or MLK and Concourse (in the park).

GETTING AROUND BY SHUTTLE

If you're visiting on a weekend between May and October, you can ride the free Golden Gate Park shuttle. This loops through the park every 15 minutes, roughly between 10 AM and 6 PM, stopping at 15 sights from McLaren Lodge to the Beach Chalet. Maps are posted at each stop.

The Haight, The Castro & Noe Valley

WORD OF MOUTH

"The Haight neighborhood is less 'kooky' than the Haight Street, although the street is certainly interesting. There are a lot of lovely Victorian houses in this area. . . . A perfect Sunday would be a visit to the Haight in the morning (all the weekend hippies are there on Sunday), followed by an afternoon bicycling in Golden Gate Park."

—StuDudley

GETTING ORIENTED

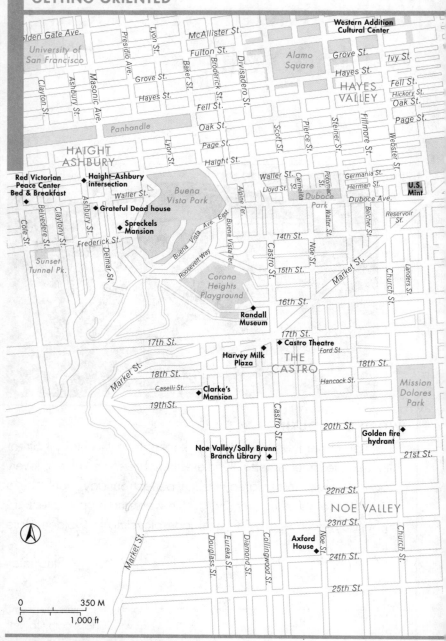

MAKING THE MOST OF YOUR TIME

The Upper Haight is only a few blocks long, and although there are plenty of shops and amusements, an hour or so should be enough. Many restaurants here cater to the morning-after crowd, so this is a great place for brunch. With the prevalence of panhandling and street kids in this area, you may be most comfortable here during the day.

The Castro, with its fun storefronts and gay-theme shops, invites unhurried exploration; allot at least 60–90 minutes. Visit in the evening to check out the lively nightlife, or in the late morning—especially on weekends.

A loop through Noe Valley takes about an hour. With its popular breakfast spots and cafés, this neighborhood is a good place for a morning stroll. After you've filled up, browse the upscale, offbeat, and whimsical shops along 24th and Castro streets.

TOP 5 REASONS TO GO

Castro Theatre: Take in a film at this gorgeous throwback and join the audience shouting out lines, commentary, and songs. Come early and let the Wurlitzer set the mood.

Sunday brunch in the Castro: Recover from Saturday night (with the entire community) at one of the Castro's brunch destinations; Lime, 2223 Market, and Luna are good bets.

Vintage shopping in the Haight: Find the perfect chiffon dress at La Rosa, a pristine faux-leopard coat at Held Over, or the motorcycle jacket of your dreams at Buffalo Exchange.

24th Street stroll: Take a leisurely ramble down loveable Noe Valley's main drag, lined with unpretentious cafés, comfy eateries, and cute one-of-a-kind shops.

Cliff's Variety: Stroll the aisles of the Castro's "hardware" store for lightbulbs, hammers, and pipes (as well as false eyelashes, tiaras, and feather boas) to get a feel for what makes this neighborhood special.

QUICK BITES

Lovejoy's Antiques & Tea Room (✉ *1351 Church St., at Clipper St., Noe Valley* ☎ *415/648–5895*) is a homey jumble, its lace-covered tables, couches, and mismatched chairs set among the antiques for sale. High tea and cream tea are served, along with traditional English-tearoom "fayre."

Get a jolt of organic fair-trade caffeine and a bit of revolutionary spirit at book-filled **Coffee to the People** (✉ *1206 Masonic Ave., Haight* ☎ *415/626–2435*).

The aroma alone might lure you into **Philz Coffee** (✉ *4023 18th St., Castro* ☎ *415/552–8378*), just off the main drag of Castro Street. Its fedora-hung, cramped space gives off a casual vibe, but don't be fooled: the city's second most popular place for the über-serious coffee drinker (after Blue Bottle) serves up the strongest handcrafted cup of joe in town.

9

GETTING THERE

The Castro is the end of the line for the F-line, and both the Castro and Noe Valley are served by the J–Church Metro. The only public transit that runs to the Haight is the bus; take the 7–Haight from Civic Center or the 6–Parnassus from Polk and Market. If you're on foot, keep in mind that the hill between the Castro and Noe Valley is very steep.

Sightseeing
☆☆☆☆★

Nightlife
☆☆★★★

Dining
☆☆★★★

Lodging
☆☆☆☆★

Shopping
☆☆★★★

Once you've seen the blockbuster sights and you're getting curious about the neighborhoods where the city's heart beats, come out to these three areas. They wear their personalities large and proud, and all are perfect for just strolling around. You can move from the Haight's residue of 1960s counterculture to the Castro's connection to 1970s and '80s gay life to 1990s gentrification in Noe Valley. Although history thrust the Haight and the Castro onto the international stage, both are anything but stagnant—they're still dynamic areas well worth exploring. Noe Valley may lack the headlines, but a mellow morning walk here will make you feel like a local.

By Denise M. Leto

During the 1960s, the siren song of free love, peace, and mind-altering substances lured thousands of young people to the Haight, a neighborhood just east of Golden Gate Park. By 1966 the area had become a hot spot for rock artists, including the Grateful Dead, Jefferson Airplane, and Janis Joplin. Some of the most infamous flower children, including Charles Manson and People's Temple founder Jim Jones, also called the Haight home.

Today the '60s message of peace, civil rights, and higher consciousness has been distilled into a successful blend of commercialism and progressive causes: the Haight Ashbury Free Medical Clinic, founded in 1967, survives at the corner of Haight and Clayton, while throwbacks like Bound Together Books (the anarchist book collective), the head shop Pipe Dreams, and a bevy of tie-dye shops all keep the Summer of Love alive in their own way. The Haight's famous political spirit—it was the first neighborhood in the nation to lead a freeway revolt, and it continues to host regular boycotts against chain stores—survives alongside some of the finest Victorian-lined streets in the city. And the kids continue to come: this is where young people who end up on San Francisco's streets most often gather. Visitors tend to find the Haight either edgy and exhilarating or scummy and intimidating (the panhandling here can be aggressive).

Just over Buena Vista Hill from Haight Street, nestled at the base of Twin Peaks, lies the brash and sassy Castro District—the social, political, and cultural center of San Francisco's thriving gay (and, to a lesser extent, lesbian) community. This neighborhood is one of the city's liveliest and most welcoming,

> ### SISTER ACT!
>
> If you're lucky enough to happen upon a cluster of cheeky cross-dressing nuns while in the Castro, meet the legendary Sisters of Perpetual Indulgence. They're decked out in white face-paint, glitter, and fabulous jewels. Renowned for their wit and charity fund-raising bashes, the Sisters—Sister Mary MaeHimm, Sister Bea Attitude, Sister Farrah Moans, and the gang—are the pinnacle of Castro color.

especially on weekends. Streets teem with folks out shopping, pushing political causes, heading to art films, and lingering in bars and cafés. Hard-bodied men in painted-on tees cruise the cutting-edge clothing and novelty stores, and pairs of all genders and sexual persuasions hold hands. Brightly painted, intricately restored Victorians line the streets here, making the Castro a good place to view striking examples of the architecture San Francisco is famous for.

Still farther south lies Noe Valley—also known as Stroller Valley for its relatively high concentration of little ones—an upscale but relaxed enclave that's one of the city's most desirable places to live. Church Street and 24th Street, the neighborhood's main thoroughfares, teem with laid-back cafés, kid-friendly restaurants, and comfortable, old-time shops. You can also see remnants of Noe Valley's agricultural beginnings: Billy Goat Hill (at Castro and 30th streets), a wild-grass hill often draped in fog, is named for the goats that grazed here right into the 20th century.

9

WHAT TO SEE IN THE HAIGHT

Buena Vista Park. If you can manage the steep climb, this eucalyptus-filled park has great city views. Be sure to scan the stone rain gutters lining many of the park's walkways for inscribed names and dates; these are the remains of gravestones left unclaimed when the city closed the Laurel Hill cemetery around 1940. You might also come across used needles and condoms; definitely avoid the park after dark, when these items are left behind. ⊠*Haight St. between Lyon St. and Buena Vista Ave. W, Haight.*

Grateful Dead house. On the outside, this is just one more well-kept Victorian on a street that's full of them—but true fans of the Dead may find some inspiration at this legendary structure. The three-story house (closed to the public) is tastefully painted in sedate mauves, tans, and teals (no bright tie-dye colors here). ⊠*710 Ashbury St., just past Waller St., Haight.*

Haight-Ashbury intersection. On October 6, 1967, hippies took over the intersection of Haight and Ashbury streets to proclaim the "Death of Hip." If they thought hip was dead then, they'd find absolute confirmation of it today, what with the only tie-dye in sight on the Ben & Jerry's storefront on the famed corner.

Everyone knows the Summer of Love had something to do with free love and LSD, but the drugs and other excesses of that period have tended to obscure the residents' serious attempts to create an America that was more spiritually oriented, more environmentally aware, and less caught up in commercialism. The Diggers, a radical group of actors and populist agitators, for example, operated a free shop a few blocks off Haight Street. Everything really was free at the free shop; people brought in things they didn't need and took things they did. (The group also coined immortal phrases like "Do your own thing.")

> ### WORD OF MOUTH
>
> "I climbed to the top of Buena Vista Park which is near the old Haight-Ashbury area, then dipped down and then up again to Corona Heights. Talk about the seven hills of Rome! Someone should mention the seven hills of San Francisco . . . Then there's the absolutely fantastic view up on Twin Peaks."
>
> –easytraveler

Among the folks who hung out in or near the Haight during the late 1960s were writers Richard Brautigan, Allen Ginsberg, Ken Kesey, and Gary Snyder; anarchist Abbie Hoffman; rock performers Marty Balin, Jerry Garcia, Janis Joplin, and Grace Slick; LSD champion Timothy Leary; and filmmaker Kenneth Anger. If you're keen to feel something resembling the hippie spirit these days, there's always Hippie Hill, just inside the Haight Street entrance of Golden Gate Park. Think drum circles, guitar players, and whiffs of pot smoke.

WHICH HAIGHT?

The Haight is actually composed of two distinct neighborhoods: the Lower Haight runs from Divisadero to Webster; the Upper Haight, immediately east of Golden Gate Park, is the part tourists tend to call Haight-Ashbury (and the part that's covered here). San Franciscans come to the Upper Haight for the dozens of vintage clothing stores concentrated in its few blocks, bars with character, restaurants where huge breakfast portions take the edge off a hangover, and Amoeba, the best place in town for new and used CDs and vinyl. The Lower Haight is a lively, grittier stretch with several well-loved pubs and a smattering of niche music shops.

Red Victorian Peace Center Bed & Breakfast. By even the most generous accounts, the Summer of Love quickly crashed and burned, and the Haight veered sharply away from the higher goals that inspired that fabled summer. In 1977 Sami Sunchild acquired the Red Vic, built as a hotel in 1904, with the aim of preserving the best of 1960s ideals. She decorated her rooms with 1960s themes—one chamber is called the Flower Child Room—and opened the Peace Art Center on the ground floor. Here you can buy her paintings, T-shirts, and "meditative art,"

Hanging Out in the Haight

There's no finer way to ease into a lazy day in the Haight than with a towering stack of cornmeal pancakes at **Kate's Kitchen.** After conquering that mountain of chow, stagger over six blocks to another challenge: the hike up **Buena Vista Park,** a dodgy green space with a payoff of sweeping city and bridge views. Back on Haight Street, 1960s flashbacks await at vintage head shop **Pipe Dreams** and the brightly colored tie-dye shop **Positively Haight Street.** The fabled Haight-Ashbury intersection is anticlimactic; walk a block south to the **Grateful Dead house.**

Back in the here and now, head to **Behind the Post Office** for dreamy duds, and stop in at **Happy Trails** to admire the whimsical, kitschy doodads. After ambling through the **Wasteland** to scope out vintage leather jackets, you'll be ready for **Amoeba,** the used-vinyl-and-CD mecca. When you eventually emerge, you can do some shoe-gazing at **John Fluevog** before schlepping your finds back to **Cha Cha Cha** to indulge in some sangria and spicy Caribbean-ish fare. Then it's off to retro-swank **Zam Zam** for a nightcap.

—Denise M. Leto

along with books about the Haight and prayer flags. Simple, cheap vegan and vegetarian fare is available in the Peace Café, and there's also a meditation room. ⊠*1665 Haight St., Haight* ☎*415/864–1978* ⊕*www.redvic.com.*

Boisterous Cha Cha Cha (⊠*1801 Haight St., at Shrader St., Haight* ☎*415/386–5758*) serves island cuisine, a mix of Cajun, Southwestern, and Caribbean influences. The decor is Technicolor tropical plastic, and the food is hot and spicy. Try the fried calamari or chili-spiked shrimp, and wash everything down with a pitcher of Cha Cha Cha's signature sangria. Reservations are not accepted, so expect a wait for dinner.

Spreckels Mansion. Not to be confused with the Spreckels Mansion of Pacific Heights, this house was built for sugar baron Richard Spreckels in 1887. Later tenants included Jack London and Ambrose Bierce. The boxy, putty-color Victorian—today a private home—is in mint condition. ⊠*737 Buena Vista Ave. W, Haight.*

WHAT TO SEE IN THE CASTRO

★ **Castro Theatre.** There are worse ways to while away an afternoon than catching a flick at this gorgeous, 1,500-seat art-deco theater; opened in 1922, it's the grandest of San Francisco's few remaining movie palaces. The neon marquee, which stands at the top of the Castro strip, is the neighborhood's great landmark. The Castro's elaborate Spanish baroque interior is fairly well preserved. Before many shows the theater's pipe organ rises from the orchestra pit and an organist plays pop and movie tunes, usually ending with the Jeanette McDonald standard "San Francisco" (go ahead, sing along). The crowd can be enthusiastic and vocal, talking back to the screen as loudly as it talks to them. Clas-

Hippie History

The eternal lure for twentysome-things, cheap rent, first helped spawn an indelible part of SF's history and public image. In the early 1960s, young people started streaming into the sprawling, inexpensive Victorians in the area around the University of San Francisco. The new Haight locals earnestly planned a new era of communal living, individual empowerment, and expanded consciousness.

Golden Gate Park's Panhandle, a thin strip of green on the Haight's northern edge, was their public gathering spot—the site of protests, concerts, food giveaways, and general hanging out. In 1967 George Harrison strolled up the park's Hippie Hill, borrowed a guitar, and played for a while before someone finally recognized him. He led the crowd, Pied Piper-style, into the Haight.

At first, the counterculture was all about sharing and taking care of one another—a good thing, considering most hippies were either broke or had renounced money. They hadn't renounced food, though, and the daily free "feeds" in the Panhandle were a staple for many. The Diggers, an anarchist street theater group, were known for handing out bread shaped like the big coffee cans they baked it in. (The Diggers also gave us immortal phrases such as "Do your own thing.")

At the time, the U.S. government, Harvard professor Timothy Leary, a Stanford student named Ken Kesey, and the kids in the Haight were all experimenting with LSD. Acid was legal, widely available, and usually given away for free. At Kesey's all-night parties, called "acid tests," a buck got you a cup of "electric" Kool-Aid, a preview of psychedelic art, and an earful of

the house band, the Grateful Dead. LSD was deemed illegal in 1966, and the kids responded by staging a Love Pageant Rally, where they dropped acid tabs en masse and rocked out to Janis Joplin and the Dead.

Things crested early in 1967, when between 10,000 and 50,000 people ("depending on whether you were a policeman or a hippie," according to one hippie) gathered at the Polo Field in Golden Gate Park for the Human Be-In of the Gathering of the Tribes. Allen Ginsberg and Timothy Leary spoke, the Dead and Jefferson Airplane played, and people costumed with beads and feathers waved flags, clanged cymbals, and beat drums. A parachutist dropped onto the field, tossing fistfuls of acid tabs to the crowd. America watched via satellite, gape-mouthed—it was every conservative parent's nightmare.

Later that year, thousands heeded Scott McKenzie's song "San Francisco," which promised "For those who come to San Francisco, Summertime will be a love-in there." The Summer of Love swelled the Haight's population from 7,000 to 75,000; people came both to join in and to ogle the nutty subculture. But degenerates soon joined the gentle people, heroin replaced LSD, crime was rampant, and the Haight began a fast slide.

Hippies will tell you the Human Be-In was the pinnacle of their scene, while the Summer of Love came from outside—a media creation that turned their movement into a monster. Still, the idea of that fictional summer still lingers, and to this day pilgrims from all over the world come to the Haight to search for a past that never was.

sics such as *Who's Afraid of Virginia Woolf?* take on a whole new life, with the assembled beating the actors to the punch and fashioning even snappier comebacks for Elizabeth Taylor. Head here to catch classics, a Fellini film retrospective, or the latest take on same-sex love. ✉*429 Castro St., Castro* ☎*415/621–6120.*

Clarke's Mansion. Built for attorney Alfred "Nobby" Clarke, this 1892 off-white baroque Queen Anne home was dubbed Clarke's Folly. (His wife refused to inhabit it because it was in an unfashionable part of town—at the time, anyone who was anyone lived on Nob Hill.) The greenery-shrouded house (now apartments) is a beauty, with dormers, cupolas, rounded bay windows, and huge turrets topped by gold-leaf spheres. ✉*250 Douglass St., between 18th and 19th Sts., Castro.*

> **PINK TRIANGLE PARK**
>
> On a median near the Castro's huge rainbow flag stands this memorial to the gays, lesbians, and bisexual and transgender people whom the Nazis forced to wear pink triangles. Fifteen triangular granite columns, one for every 1,000 gays, lesbians, bisexual, and transgender people estimated to have been killed during and after the Holocaust, stand at the tip of a pink-rock-filled triangle—a reminder of the gay community's past and ongoing struggle for civil rights. ✉*Corner of Market, Castro, and 17th Sts., Castro.*

NEED A BREAK? Sometimes referred to as Café Floorshow because it's such a see-and-be-seen place, Café Flore (✉*2298 Market St., Castro* ☎*415/621–8579*) serves coffee drinks, beer, and café fare. It's a good place to catch the latest Castro gossip.

Harvey Milk Plaza. An 18-foot-long rainbow flag, a gay icon, flies above this plaza named for the man who electrified the city in 1977 by being elected to its Board of Supervisors as an openly gay candidate. In the early 1970s, Milk had opened a camera store on the block of Castro Street between 18th and 19th streets. The store became the center for his campaign to gain thorough inclusion for gays in the city's social and political life.

The liberal Milk hadn't served a full year of his term before he and Mayor George Moscone, also a liberal, were shot in November 1978 at City Hall. The murderer was a conservative ex-supervisor named Dan White, who had recently resigned his post and then became enraged when Moscone wouldn't reinstate him. Milk and White had often been at odds on the board, and White thought Milk had been part of a cabal to keep him from returning to his post. Milk's assassination shocked the gay community, which became infuriated when the infamous "Twinkie defense"—that junk food had led to diminished mental capacity—resulted in a manslaughter verdict for White. During the so-called White Night Riot of May 21, 1979, gays and their sympathizers stormed City Hall, torching its lobby and several police cars.

9

Children of the Rainbow Revolution

San Francisco's gay community has been a part of the city since its earliest days. As a port city and a major hub during the 19th-century gold rush, it became known for its sexual openness along with all its other liberalities. But the major catalyst for the rise of a gay community was World War II.

During the war, hundreds of thousands of servicemen cycled through "Sodom by the Sea," and for most, San Francisco's permissive atmosphere was an eye-opening experience. The army's "off-limits" lists of forbidden establishments unintentionally (but effectively) pointed the way to the city's gay bars. When soldiers were dishonorably discharged for homosexual activity, many stayed on.

Scores of these newcomers found homes in what was then called Eureka Valley. When the war ended, the predominantly Irish-Catholic families in that neighborhood began to move out, heading for the 'burbs. The new arrivals snapped up the Victorians on the main drag, Castro Street.

The establishment pushed back. In the 1950s, San Francisco's police chief vowed to crack down on "perverts," and the city's gays, lesbians, bisexuals, and transgender residents lived in fear of getting caught in police raids. (Arrest meant being outed in the morning paper.) But harassment helped galvanize the community. The Daughters of Bilitis lesbian organization was founded in the city in 1955; the gay male Mattachine Society, started in Los Angeles in 1950, followed suit with an SF branch.

By the mid-1960s, these clashing interests gave the growing gay population a national profile. The police

upped their policy of harassment, but overplayed their hand. In 1965, they dramatically raided a New Year's benefit event, and the tide of public opinion began to turn. The police were forced to appoint the first-ever liaison to the gay community. Local gay organizations began to lobby openly. As one gay participant noted, "We didn't go back into the woodwork."

The 1970s—thumping disco, raucous street parties, and gay bashing—were a tumultuous time for the gay community. Thousands from across the country flocked to San Francisco's gay scene. Eureka Valley had more than 60 gay bars, the bathhouse scene in SoMa (where the leather crowd held court) was thriving, and graffiti around town read "Save San Francisco—Kill a Fag." When the Eureka Valley Merchants Association refused to admit gay-owned businesses in 1974, Harvey Milk founded the Castro Valley Association, and the neighborhood's new moniker was born. Milk was elected to the city's Board of Supervisors in 1977, its first openly gay official.

San Francisco's gay community was getting serious about politics, civil rights, and self-preservation, but it still loved a party: 350,000 people attended the 1978 Gay Freedom Day Parade, where the rainbow flag debuted. But on November 27, 1978, Milk and Mayor George Moscone were gunned down in City Hall by enraged former city council member Dan White. Thousands marched in silent tribute out of the Castro down to City Hall.

When the killer got a relatively light conviction of manslaughter, the next march was not silent. Another crowd of thousands converged on City Hall, this time smashing windows, burn-

ing 12 police cars, and fighting with police in what became known as the White Night Riots. The police retaliated by storming the Castro.

The gay community recovered, even thrived—especially economically—but in 1981, the first medical and journalistic reports of a dangerous new disease surfaced. A notice appeared in a Castro pharmacy's window, warning people about "the gay cancer," later named AIDS. By 1983, the populations most vulnerable to the burgeoning epidemic were publicly identified as gay men in San Francisco and New York City.

San Francisco gay activists were quick to mobilize, starting foundations as early as 1982 to care for the sick, along with public memorials to raise awareness nationwide. By 1990, the disease had killed 10,000 San Franciscans. Local organizations lobbied hard to speed up drug development and FDA approvals. In the past decade, the city's network of volunteer organizations and public outreach has been recognized as one of the best global models for combating the disease.

Today the Castro is still the heart of San Francisco's gay life—though many young hetero families have also moved in. As the ur-gay mecca starts to get diluted, new neighborhood coalitions are forming to debate its character and future. In the meantime, a Harvey Milk bust was unveiled in City Hall on May 22, 2008, Milk's birthday.

9

Milk, who had feared assassination, left behind a tape recording in which he urged the community to continue the work he had begun. His legacy is the high visibility of gay people throughout city government. A plaque at the base of the flagpole lists the names of past and present openly gay and lesbian state and local officials. ✉*Southwest corner of Castro and Market Sts., Castro.*

🔄 **Randall Museum.** The best thing about visiting this free nature museum for kids may be its tremendous views of San Francisco. Younger kids who are still excited about petting a rabbit, touching a snakeskin, or seeing a live hawk will enjoy a trip here. (Many of the creatures here can't be released into the wild due to injury or other problems). The museum sits beneath a hill variously known as Red Rock, Museum Hill, and, correctly, Corona Heights; hike up the steep but short trail for great, unobstructed city views. ■TIP➡ **It's a great resource for local families, but if you're going to take the kids to just one museum in town, make it the Exploratorium.** ✉*199 Museum Way, off Roosevelt Way, Castro* ☎*415/554–9600* ⊕*www.randallmuseum.org* ✉*Free* 🕓*Tues.–Sat. 10–5.*

> **FAIR & BALANCED?**
>
> If you think San Francisco is full of loopy liberals, you're not alone: witness the proprietor of Twin Peaks Realty in Noe Valley, a veritable one-man right-wing movement in the city. He updates his window display continually; longtime exhibits include faded photos of Ronald Reagan in his glory days, conservative bumper stickers, and images of Richard Nixon and Joe DiMaggio. For a chuckle, stop and read the messages in the window; they often begin with greetings to "Left-wing loonies" and "Looney Valley liberals."

CASTRO & NOE WALK

The Castro and Noe Valley are both neighborhoods that beg to be walked—or ambled through, really, without time pressure or an absolute destination. Hit the Castro first, beginning at Harvey Milk Plaza under the gigantic rainbow flag. If you're going on to Noe Valley, first head east down Market Street for the cafés, bistros, and shops, then go back to Castro Street and head south, past the glorious art-deco Castro Theatre, checking out boutiques and cafés along the way. To tour Noe Valley, go east down 18th Street to Church (at Dolores Park), and then either strap on your hiking boots and head south over the hill or hop the J-Church to 24th Street, the center of this rambling neighborhood.

WHAT TO SEE IN NOE VALLEY

Axford House. This mauve house was built in 1877, when Noe Valley was still a rural area, as evidenced by the hayloft in the gable of the adjacent carriage house. The house is perched several feet above the sidewalk. Various types of roses grow in the well-maintained garden that surrounds the house, which is a private home. ✉*1190 Noe St., at 25th St., Noe Valley*

Where can I find . . .?

A NIGHTCAP	**Trax** ✉ **1437** Haight St. A laid-back place with good beer specials.	**Pilsner Inn** ✉ 225 Church St. A casual neighborhood joint with a nice patio.
A CUP OF COFFEE	**Peet's** ✉ 2257 Market St. One cup, and you could become a Peetnik.	**Cole Valley Cafe** ✉ 701 Cole St., at Waller St. Good coffee and free Wi-Fi. Whats not to like?
A PARKING SPACE	**Metered Lot** ✉ Castro St. and 17th St. City-owned lot.	**Metered Lot** ✉ Collingwood St. and 18th St. City-owned lot.

TWIN PEAKS

Windswept and desolate Twin Peaks yields sweeping vistas of San Francisco and the neighboring east and north bay counties. You can get a real feel for the city's layout here; arrive before the late-afternoon fog turns the view into pea soup during the summer. To drive here, head west from Castro Street up Market Street, which eventually becomes Portola Drive. Turn right (north) on Twin Peaks Boulevard and follow the signs to the top. Muni Bus 37–Corbett heads west to Twin Peaks from Market Street. Catch this bus above the Castro Street Muni light-rail station on the island west of Castro at Market Street.

Golden fire hydrant. When all the other fire hydrants went dry during the fire that followed the 1906 earthquake, this one kept pumping. Noe Valley and the Mission District were thus spared the devastation wrought elsewhere in the city, which explains the large number of prequake homes here. Every year on April 18 (the anniversary of the quake), the famous hydrant gets a fresh coat of gold paint. ✉ *Church and 20th Sts., southeast corner, across from Dolores Park, Noe Valley.*

Noe Valley/Sally Brunn Branch Library. In the early 20th century, philanthropist Andrew Carnegie told Americans he would build them elegant libraries if they would fill them with books. A community garden flanks part of the yellow-brick library Carnegie financed (completely renovated and reopened in 2008), and there's a deck (accessed through the children's book room) with picnic tables where you can relax and admire Carnegie's inspired structure. ✉ *451 Jersey St., Noe Valley* ☎ *415/355–5707* ◷ *Tues. 10–9, Wed. 1–9, Thurs. and Sat. 10–6, Fri. 1–6.*

9

> **WORD OF MOUTH**
>
> "Laidley Street has some very interesting architecture. If you are interested in unique architecture, turn right (southeast) at the bottom of the stairs & walk up & back 'lovely' Laidley a bit."
>
> –StuDudley

Dining in the Haight, the Castro & Noe Valley

BUDGET

Chow, American, 215 Church St.

Thep Phanom, Thai, 400 Waller St.

MODERATE

2223 Restaurant, American, 2223 Market St.

Home, American, 2100 Market St.

Incanto, Italian, 1550 Church St.

Indian Oven, Indian, 233 Fillmore St.

La Ciccia, Italian, 291 30th St.

Nopa, American, 560 Divisidero St.

Poleng Lounge, Asian, 1751 Fulton St.

RNM, American, 598 Haight St.

Mission District

Mission Street

WORD OF MOUTH

"The [Mission] neighborhood is either dicey or colorful, depending on your point of view. . . . Speaking of point of view, you will learn all about combining a tube top and hot pants with high heels if you get a window seat at Maverick (to think I'd been doing it wrong all these years!)."

—dovima

GETTING ORIENTED

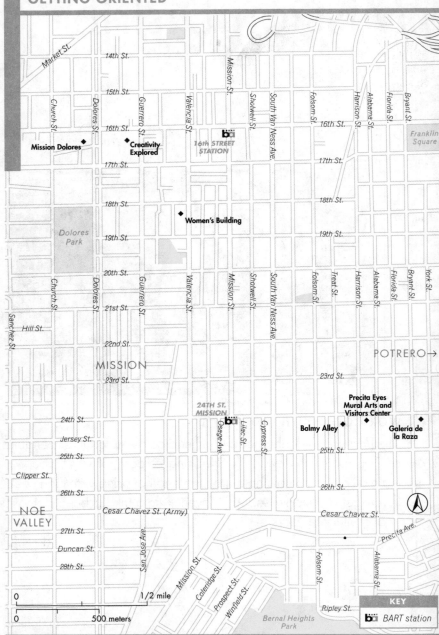

Market St.

14th St.

15th St.

Church St.

Dolores St.

Guerrero St.

16th St.

Valencia St.

Mission St.

Shotwell St.

South Van Ness Ave.

Folsom St.

Harrison St.

Alabama St.

Florida St.

Bryant St.

16th St.

Franklin Square

Mission Dolores ◆

◆ **Creativity Explored**

🅑 **16th STREET STATION**

17th St.

18th St.

◆ **Women's Building**

Dolores Park

19th St.

18th St.

19th St.

Church St.

Dolores St.

Guerrero St.

20th St.

21st St.

Valencia St.

Mission St.

Shotwell St.

South Van Ness Ave.

Folsom St.

Treat St.

Harrison St.

Alabama St.

Florida St.

Bryant St.

York St.

Sanchez St.

Hill St.

22nd St.

MISSION

23rd St.

POTRERO→

23rd St.

Precita Eyes Mural Arts and Visitors Center

24th St.

Jersey St.

24TH ST. MISSION

🅑

Osage Ave.

Lilac St.

Cypress St.

Balmy Alley ◆

◆

◆ **Galería de la Raza**

25th St.

25th St.

Clipper St.

26th St.

26th St.

NOE VALLEY

Cesar Chavez St. (Army)

San Jose Ave.

Cesar Chavez St.

27th St.

Duncan St.

28th St.

Precita Ave.

•

Alabama St.

Folsom St.

Mission St.

Coleridge St.

Prospect St.

Winfield St.

Ripley St.

Bernal Heights Park

0 ———————— 1/2 mile

0 ———————— 500 meters

TOP 5 REASONS TO GO

Bar-hop: Embrace your inner (or not so inner) hipster. Start off at Medjool's rare rooftop deck, then move up to the stylish Nihon Whisky Lounge or pull up a chair in no-pretension Truck. Round the night off in the company of the 100 beers available at Monk's Kettle.

Chow down on phenomenal, cheap ethnic food: Keen appetites and thin wallets will meet their match here. Just try to decide between deliciously fresh burritos, garlicky falafel, thin-crust pizza, savory crepes, and more.

One-of-a-kind shopping: Barter for buried treasure at 826 Valencia and its Pirate Supply Store, then hop next door and say hello to the giraffe's head at the mad taxidermy-cum-garden store hodgepodge that is Paxton Gate.

Vivid murals: Check out dozens of energetic, colorful public artworks in alleyways and on building exteriors.

Hang out in Dolores Park: Join Mission locals and their dogs on this hilly expanse of green with—wait for it—a glorious view of downtown and, if you're lucky, the Bay Bridge.

QUICK BITES

Latin-American pastries are the specialty at **La Victoria** (⊠ *2937 24th St., at Alabama St., Mission* ☎ *415/642–7120*). You can also pick up a coffee, piñatas, and votive candles.

For an old-fashioned soda or homemade ice cream, stop into the **St. Francis Fountain and Candy Store** (⊠ *2801 24th St., at York St.* ☎ *415/826–4200*).

Muddy Waters (⊠ *521 Valencia St., at 16th St.* ☎ *415/863–8006*) is a welcome stop near the 16th Street Mission BART station. You'll get an eyeful of the neighborhood culture here—some oddball characters and very casual housekeeping—but the coffee, chai, and wireless crackle at full capacity.

GETTING THERE

If your muscles are aching from climbing the hills downtown, you can find the Mission to be welcomingly flat terrain. BART's two Mission District stations drop you right in the heart of the action. Get off at 16th Street for Mission Dolores, shopping, nightlife, and restaurants, or 24th Street to see the neighborhood murals. The busy 14–Mission bus runs all the way from downtown into the neighborhood, but BART is a much faster and more direct route. Parking can be a drag, especially on weekend evenings. If you're heading out in the evening, your safest bet would be taking a cab, since some blocks of this area are pretty sketchy.

MAKING THE MOST OF YOUR TIME

A walk that includes Mission Dolores and your own amble past the neighborhood's murals takes about two hours. If you plan to go on a mural walk with the Precita Eyes organization or if you're a window-shopper, add at least another hour. The Mission is a neighborhood that sleeps in; about the only thing to do here before 9 AM is gaze at the outdoor murals. In the afternoon and evening the main drags really come to life.

Sunday through Tuesday is relatively quiet here, especially in the evening—a great time to get a café table with no wait. If you're getting bummed out by fog elsewhere in the city, come here—the Mission wins out in San Francisco's system of microclimates.

10

Sightseeing
☆☆☆★★

Nightlife
★★★★★

Dining
★★★★★

Lodging
☆☆☆☆☆

Shopping
☆☆★★★

The Mission has a number of distinct personalities: it's the Latino neighborhood, where working-class folks raise their families and where gangs occasionally clash; it's the hipster hood, where tattooed and pierced twenty- and thirtysome-things hold court in the coolest cafés and bars in town; it's a culinary epicenter, with the strongest concentration of destination restaurants and affordable ethnic cuisine; and it's the artists' quarter, where murals adorn literally blocks of walls. It's also the city's equivalent of the Sunshine State— this neighborhood's always the last to succumb to fog.

By Denise M Leto

The eight blocks of Valencia Street between 16th and 24th streets— what's come to be known as the Valencia Corridor—typify the neighborhood's diversity. Businesses on the block between 16th and 17th streets, for instance, include an upscale Peruvian restaurant, the Bombay Ice Cream parlor (try a scoop of the zesty cardamom ice cream) and adjacent Indian grocery and sundries store, a tattoo parlor, the yuppie-chic Blondie's bar, a handful of funky home decor stores, a pizzeria, a taquería, a Turkish restaurant, a sushi bar, bargain and pricey thrift shops, and the Puerto Allegre restaurant, a hole-in-the-wall with pack-a-punch margaritas locals revere. On the other hand, Mission Street itself, three blocks east, is mostly a down-in-the-mouth row of check-cashing places, dollar stores, and residential hotels—but there are more than a few great taquerías. And the farther east you go, the sketchier the neighborhood gets.

Italian and Irish in the early 20th century, the Mission became heavily Latino in the late 1960s, when immigrants from Mexico and Central America began arriving. An influx of Chinese, Vietnamese, Arabic, and other immigrants, along with a young bohemian crowd enticed by cheap rents and the burgeoning arts-and-nightlife scene, followed in the 1980s and early 1990s. The skyrocketing rents of the late 1990s have leveled off and the district is yet again in transition. The Mission is still quite scruffy in patches, so as you plan your explorations take into account your comfort zone. ■ TIP ➡ **If raucous barhoppers are a bit intimidating to you, an afternoon trip to the Valencia Corridor may be your best bet.**

WHAT TO SEE

Balmy Alley. Mission District artists have transformed the walls of their neighborhood with paintings, and Balmy Alley is one of the best-executed examples. Murals fill the one-block alley, with newer ones continually filling in the blank spaces. Local children working with adults started the project in 1971. Since then dozens of artists have steadily added to it, with the aim of promoting peace in Central America, as well as community spirit and AIDS awareness. **Be alert here: the 25th Street end of the alley adjoins a somewhat dangerous area.** ⊠ *24th St. between and parallel to Harrison and Treat Sts., alley runs south to 25th St., Mission.*

Creativity Explored. Joyous, if chaotic, creativity pervades the workshops of this art-education center and gallery for developmentally disabled adults. Several dozen adults work at the center each day—guided by a staff of working artists—painting, working in the darkroom, producing videos, and crafting prints, textiles, and ceramics. On weekdays you can drop by and see the artists at work. The art produced here is striking, and some of it is for sale; this is a great place to find a unique San Francisco masterpiece to take home. ⊠ *3245 16th St., Mission* ☎ *415/863–2108* ⊕ *www.creativityexplored.org* ⊠ *Free* ☉ *Weekdays 10–3, Sat. 1–6.*

Galería de la Raza. San Francisco's premier showcase for contemporary Latino art, the gallery exhibits the works of local and international artists. Events include readings and spoken word by local poets and writers, screening of Latin American and Spanish films, and theater works by local minority theater troupes. Just across the street, take a gander at the amazing art festooning the 24th Street Minipark, a tiny urban playground. A mosaic-covered Quetzalcoatl serpent plunges into the ground and rises, creating hills for little ones to clamber over, and mural-covered walls surround the space. ⊠ *2857 24th St., at Bryant St., Mission* ☎ *415/826–8009* ⊕ *www.galeriadelaraza.org* ☉ *Gallery Wed.–Sat. noon–6.*

10

CLOSE UP

Murals with a Mission

San Francisco fairly teems with murals. Since the 1970s, groups of artists have worked to transform the city's walls into canvases, art accessible to everyone. Muralists here fall into two loose categories: those in the Latin American tradition of addressing political and social justice issues through art, and everyone else (those who simply paint on a large scale and like lots of people to see it).

Rediscovering the work of Mexican liberal artist and muralist Diego Rivera in the 1960s, Latino muralists began to address public issues on the community's walls. Heavily Latino since the 1970s, the Mission District became the collective canvas for these artists. The Precita Eyes Mural Arts Center emerged to support those artists and galvanize collaborative projects in the neighborhood. Early on, the San Francisco Arts Commission hired the center to create murals all over town. Of the 800-plus murals that adorn city surfaces, a good quarter of them were painted by muralists associated with Precita Eyes.

Bright Sunbelt colors reflect the medium's historical geography; in contemporary work, look for anime and woodblock cuts along with traditional Latino symbols. Murals are considered permanent, and aren't painted over without consulting the artist first. Keep your eyes peeled as you wander the city and you'll begin to discover art almost everywhere you look. Here are the best and brightest of the Mission District:

■ **Balmy Alley.** The most famous of the Mission's murals—a vivid sweep from end to end. This group series began in 1971 and still gets new additions.

■ **Clarion Alley.** A new generation of muralists is creating a fresh alley-cum-gallery here, between Valencia and Mission streets by 17th and 18th streets. The loosely connected artists of the Clarion Alley Mural Project (CAMP) represent a broad range of style and imagery. Carpet-draped Indonesian elephants plod calmly down the block; kung fu movie-style headlines shout slogans. The works here offer a dense glimpse at the Mission's contemporary art scene; combine this with a visit to Balmy Alley for an overview of art from the 1970s to today.

■ **24th Street.** Several murals on the buildings along 24th Street, including St. Peter's (at Alabama Street) and even McDonald's (at Mission Street).

■ **Women's Building.** *Maestrapeace—the impressive, towering mural that seems to enclose this building*—celebrates women around the world who work for peace.

■ **826 Valencia.** Fans of graphic novelist Chris Ware will want to take a good look at the facade here. Ware designed the intricate mural for the storefront, a meditation on the evolution of human communication.

■ **Shotwell Street grocery.** A bit off the beaten path but well worth the detour is Brian Barneclo's gigantic *Food Chain*. This adorns the grocery store on Shotwell Street between 14th and 15th streets. It's a retro, 1950s-style celebration of the city's many neighborhoods (and the food chain), complete with an ant birthday party and worms finishing off a human skull. But in a cute way. Barneclo fans can see more of his work at cool watering hole Rye and hipster restaurant Nopa.

—Denise M. Leto

Where can I find . . .?

CAFÉ WITH FREE WI-FI	**Maxfield's** ✉ 398 Dolores St. Coffees mediocre but plenty of power sources.	**Ritual Roasters** ✉ 1026 Valencia St. Strong coffee, very sceney.	
A GAS STATION	**Arco** ✉ 1798 Mission St. Close to the neighborhood core.	**Potrero Hill 76** ✉ 401 Potrero Ave. Average prices; near the 101.	
A DRUGSTORE	**Community Pharmacy** ✉ 2462 Mission St. All the OTC standbys.	**Walgreens** ✉ 1979 Mission St. Right by the 16th Street BART station.	

OFF THE BEATEN PATH

Vermont Street. With a similar series of switchbacks, this Potrero Hill street is a kind of blue-collar Lombard Street, but minus the throngs (and the spectacular gardens and views). It's on the east side of the 101 from the Mission. To check it out, head down 24th Street to the end, go left on Vermont, right on 23rd Street past the freeway, left on Rhode Island Street, left on 20th Street, and finally head left down the curvy stretch of Vermont. Bring a city map along! ✉ *Between 20th and 22nd Sts., Potrero Hill.*

★ **Mission Dolores.** Two churches stand side-by-side at this mission, including the small adobe **Mission San Francisco de Asís,** the oldest standing structure in San Francisco. Completed in 1791, it's the sixth of the 21 California missions founded by Father Junípero Serra in the 18th and early 19th centuries. Its ceiling depicts original Ohlone Indian basket designs, executed in vegetable dyes. The tiny chapel includes frescoes and a hand-painted wooden altar. There's a hidden treasure here, too. In 2004, an archaeologist and an artist crawling along the ceiling's rafters opened a trap door behind the altar and rediscovered the mission's original mural, painted with natural dyes by Native Americans in 1791. The centuries have taken their toll, so the team photographed the 20-by 22-foot mural and has begun digitally restoring the photographic version. Among the images is a dagger-pierced Sacred Heart of Jesus. Check out the project at www.missiondoloresmural.com.

There's a small museum covering the mission's founding and history,

10

WORD OF MOUTH

"I so fell in love with [Dolores Park] I tried to make it there every day . . . the combination of the SF skyline in the distance, the beautiful Spanish colonial turret of Mission High School (right there), the occasional "J" streetcar, combined with the ever-charming and diverse SF row homes and the peaceful, relaxed ambience of San Franciscans enjoying the park . . ."

–Daniel Williams

and the pretty little mission cemetery (made famous by a scene in Alfred Hitchcock's *Vertigo*) maintains the graves of mid-19th-century European immigrants. (The remains of an estimated 5,000 Native Americans lie in unmarked graves.) Services are held in both the Mission San Francisco de Asís and next door in the handsome multidome basilica. ✉ *Dolores and 16th Sts., Mission* ☎ *415/621–8203* ⊕ *www.missiondolores.org* ✉ *$5 donation, audio tour $7* ☉ *Nov.–Apr., daily 9–4; May–Oct., daily 9–4:30.*

Precita Eyes Mural Arts and Visitors Center. Founded by muralists, this nonprofit arts organization designs and creates murals. The artists themselves lead informative guided walks of murals in the area. Most tours start with a 45-minute slide presentation. The bike and walking trips, which take between one and three hours, pass several dozen murals. May is Mural Awareness Month, with visits to murals-in-progress and presentations by artists. You can pick up a map of 24th Street's murals at the center and buy art supplies, T-shirts, postcards, and other mural-related items. Bike tours are available by appointment; Saturday's 11 AM walking tour meets at Cafe Venice, at 24th and Mission streets. (All other tours meet at the center.) ✉ *2981 24th St., Mission* ☎ *415/285–2287* ⊕ *www.precitaeyes.org* ✉ *Center free, tours $10–$12* ☉ *Center weekdays 10–5, Sat. 10–4, Sun. noon–4; walks weekends at 11 and 1:30 or by appointment.*

Women's Building. The cornerstone of the female-owned and -run businesses in the neighborhood, this place has held workshops and conferences of particular interest to women since 1979. The exterior is the reason to visit: its two stories are completely covered with an impressive mural, *Maestrapeace*, depicting women's peacekeeping efforts over the centuries. Inside are offices for many social and political organizations; the center also sponsors talks and readings by writers such as Alice Walker and Angela Davis. Head inside to pick up a key to the murals' figures and symbols. ✉ *3543 18th St., Mission* ☎ *415/431–1180* ☉ *Mon.–Thurs. 9–5, Fri. 10–6.*

SAFETY IN THE MISSION

The Mission is a vibrant area but it does have dodgy zones. The safest area is bordered by Mission, Dolores, 16th, and 20th streets—where everything is happening anyway. Plenty of homeless people crash in doorways, and robberies and assaults are not uncommon. After dark, the areas east of Mission Street and south of 24th Street can feel unsafe, with empty stretches or groups of loitering toughs. If you're in this area after dark, stick to main drags like Mission and 24th streets. If you keep your wits about you and stick to well-lighted areas, you're unlikely to run into trouble.

Reel-Life San Francisco

With its spectacular cityscape, atmospheric fog, and a camera-ready iconic bridge, it's little wonder that San Francisco has been the setting for hundreds of films. While you're running around town, you might have the occasional sense of déjà vu, sparked by a scene from a Hitchcock or Clint Eastwood thriller. Below are a few of the city's favorite cinematic sites.

■ *Zodiac*, a 2007 drama about a legendary Bay Area serial killer, filmed scenes at the real-life locations where victims were gunned down. It also recreated the San Francisco Chronicle offices, but down south in L.A.

■ City Hall shows up in the Clint Eastwood cop thrillers *Dirty Harry* and *Magnum Force* and is set aflame in the James Bond flick *A View to a Kill*. Its domed interior became a nightclub for Robin Williams' *Bicentennial Man* and a courthouse in *Tucker: The Man and His Dream*.

■ Streets in Russian Hill, Potrero Hill, and North Beach were used for the supreme car-chase sequence in *Bullitt*. The namesake detective, played by Steve McQueen, lived in Nob Hill at 1153–57 Taylor Street. And the "King of

Cool" did much of his own stunt driving, thank you very much.

■ Brocklebank Apartments, at Mason and Sacramento streets in Nob Hill, appears in several films, most notably as the posh residence of Kim Novak in Alfred Hitchcock's *Vertigo*. Other key *Vertigo* locations include the cemetery of Mission Dolores and the waterfront at Fort Point.

■ The great Bogie-and-Bacall noir film *Dark Passage* revolves around the Art Deco apartment building at 1360 Montgomery Street and the nearby Filbert Steps.

■ Dashiell Hammett's "Thin Man" characters, Nick and Nora Charles, do much of their sleuthing in the city, especially in films like *After the Thin Man*, in which the base of Coit Tower stands in as the entrance to the Charles' home.

■ North Beach's Tosca Café, at 242 Columbus Avenue, is the bar where Michael Douglas unwinds in *Basic Instinct*.

■ The Hilton Hotel at 333 O'Farrell Street became the "Hotel Bristol," the scene of much of the mayhem caused by Barbra Streisand in *What's Up, Doc?*

■ At 2640 Steiner Street in Pacific Heights is the elegant home that Robin Williams infiltrates while disguised as a nanny in *Mrs. Doubtfire*.

■ And, of course, there are plenty of movies about the notorious federal prison on Alcatraz Island, including Burt Lancaster's redemption drama *Birdman of Alcatraz*, Clint Eastwood's suspenseful *Escape from Alcatraz*, the goofy *So I Married an Axe Murderer*, and the Sean Connery and Nicolas Cage action flick, *The Rock*.

—Jim Van Buskirk

10

Dining in the Mission District

AT A GLANCE

BUDGET
Andalu, American, 3198 16th St.

Angkor Borei, Cambodian, 3471 Mission St.

Burger Joint, American, 807 Valenica St.

Dosa, Indian, 995 Valencia St.

La Santaneca de la Mission, Latin American, 2815 Mission St.

Los Jarritos, Mexican, 901 Van Ness Ave.

Ti Couz, French, 3108 16th St.

MODERATE
Chez Spencer, French, 82 14th St.

Ducca, Italian, 50 Third St.

Farina, Italian, 3560 18th St.

Foreign Cinema, American, 2534 Mission St.

Charanga, Latin American, 2351 Mission St.

Delfina, Italian, 3621 18th St.

Limón, Peruvian, 524 Valencia St.

Luna Park, American, 694 Valencia St.

Range, American, 842 Valencia St.

Pacific Heights & Japantown

Cherry Blossom festival at Japantown

WORD OF MOUTH

"In Japantown, the Kinokuniya Bookstore is a great stop not just for books but for calendars, anime comic books, etc. Across the hallway from Kinokuniya is a little restaurant . . . called Maki, and it's on my VERY short list of authentic Japanese restaurants."

—dovima

GETTING ORIENTED

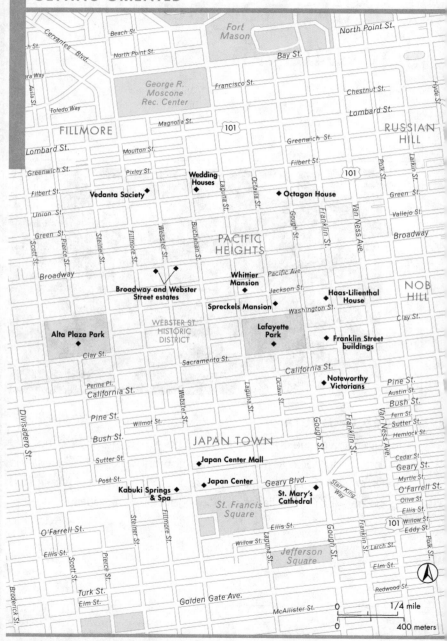

11

TOP 5 REASONS TO GO

Chic shopping on Fillmore Street: Browse the superfine shops along Pacific Heights' main drag.

Picnic with a view at Lafayette Park: Gather supplies along Fillmore Street and climb to the top of this park. It's surrounded by grand homes and has a sweeping view of the city.

Asian food galore in the Japan Center: Graze your way through the mall, from sushi boat offerings at Isobune to quick bean-paste snacks at May's Coffee Stand, decked out like an open-air Japanese restaurant.

Spa serenity at Kabuki Springs: Enter the peaceful lobby and prepare to be transported at the Japanese-style communal baths.

See how the other half lives: Check out the grand, historic homes along the tree-lined streets of Pacific Heights.

QUICK BITES

Swing by **Boulangerie Bay Bread** (✉ *2325 Pine St., at Fillmore St., Pacific Heights* ☎ *415/440–0356*), an oh-so-French bakery and patisserie whose patrons swoon for its perfect baguettes, rounds, croissants, and tartlets. Flaky-crusted savory tarts filled with veggies and cheese or leeks and prosciutto make perfect picnic fare for Lafayette Park.

Red-and-white lanterns adorn the room at the Japan Center's **Isobune** (✉ *Kintetsu Bldg., 1737 Post St., Japantown* ☎ *415/563–1030*), where "sushi boats" float around the counter. Crowds of customers take what they want and pay per dish at the end of the meal.

MAKING THE MOST OF YOUR TIME

Give yourself an hour to wander Fillmore Street, more if you're planning to have a meal here or picnic in Lafayette or Alta Plaza parks. Checking out the stunning homes in Pacific Heights is best done by car, unless you have serious stamina; a half hour should be enough.

Since the Japan Center is the only real highlight of Japantown, plan a daytime visit for a meal and some window-shopping; lunchtime is ideal.

GETTING THERE

Steep streets in Pacific Heights make for impressive views and rough walking; unless you're in decent shape, consider taking a car or taxi to this neighborhood.

The only public transit that runs through the area is the bus. For Pacific Heights proper, take the 12 to the area just north of Lafayette Park. For shopping on Union Street in Cow Hollow (lower Pacific Heights), catch the 41– or the 45–Union bus.

Buses that run to Japantown from downtown include the 2–, 3–, and 4– to Sutter Street and the very busy 38–Geary.

Sightseeing
☆☆☆☆★

Nightlife
☆☆☆☆★

Dining
☆☆★★★

Lodging
☆☆☆☆★

Shopping
☆☆★★★

Pacific Heights and Japantown are something of an odd couple: privileged, old-school San Francisco and the workaday commercial center of Japanese-American life in the city, stacked virtually on top of each other. The sprawling, extravagant mansions of Pacific Heights gradually give way to the more modest Victorians and unassuming housing tracts of Japantown. The cool boutiques and cafés of northern Fillmore Street fade into salons and pizzerias farther south. The most interesting spots in Japantown huddle in the Japan Center, the neighborhood's two-block centerpiece, and along Post Street. You can find plenty of authentic Japanese treats in the shops and restaurants, but unless you have a special interest in these, the area likely won't make it onto your must-see list.

By Denise M. Leto

Pacific Heights defines San Francisco's most expensive and dramatic real estate. Grand Victorians line the streets, mansions and town houses are priced in the millions, and there are magnificent views from almost any point in the neighborhood. Old money and new, personalities in the limelight, and those who prefer absolute media anonymity live here, and few outsiders see anything other than the pleasing facades of Queen Anne charmers, English Tudor imports, and baroque bastions. Nancy Pelosi and Dianne Feinstein, Larry Ellison and Gordon Getty all own impressive homes here, but not even pockets as deep as those can buy a large garden—space in the city is simply at too much of a premium. The boutiques and restaurants along Fillmore, which range from glam to funky but are somehow all cool, have become a draw for the whole city.

Japantown, on the other hand, feels somewhat adrift. (Also called Nihonmachi, it's centered on the southern slope of Pacific Heights, north of Geary Boulevard between Fillmore and Laguna streets.) The Japan Center mall, for instance, comes across as rather sterile—it's nothing like the active street scene of Chinatown. Where Chinatown is densely populated and still largely Chinese, Japantown struggles to retain its unique character.

The Japanese community in San Francisco started around 1860; after the 1906 earthquake and fire, many of these newcomers settled in the Western Addition. By the 1930s they had opened shops, markets, meeting halls, and restaurants and established Shinto and Buddhist temples. But during World War II, the area was virtually gutted when many of its residents, including second- and third-generation Americans, were forced into so-called relocation camps. During the 1960s and '70s, redevelopment further eroded the neighborhood, and most Japanese-Americans now live elsewhere in the city.

Still, when several key properties in the neighborhood were sold in 2007, a vocal group rallied to "save Japantown," and some new blood may finally be infusing the neighborhood with energy: Robert Redford's Sundance corporation turned the venerable Kabuki Theatre into a destination cinema-restaurant combo, local hotel guru Joie de Vivre took over the Hotel Kabuki, and a new J-Pop Center promises to bring Japanese pop culture to the neighborhood sometime in the next few years.

Japantown is a relatively safe area, but the Western Addition, south of Geary Boulevard, can be dangerous even during the daytime. Avoid going too far west of Fillmore Street on either side of Geary.

WHAT TO SEE IN PACIFIC HEIGHTS

Alta Plaza Park. Golden Gate Park's fierce longtime superintendent, John McLaren, designed Alta Plaza in 1910, modeling its terracing on the Grand Casino in Monte Carlo, Monaco. From the top you can see Marin to the north, downtown to the east, Twin Peaks to the south, and Golden Gate Park to the west. Little ones like the small, enclosed playground at the top; everywhere else is dog territory. ⊠ *Bordered by Clay, Steiner, Jackson, and Scott Sts., Pacific Heights.*

Broadway and Webster Street estates. Broadway uptown, unlike its garish North Beach stretch, has plenty of prestigious addresses. The three-story palace at 2222 Broadway, which has an intricately filigreed doorway, was built by Comstock silver-mine heir James Flood and later donated to a religious order. The Convent of the Sacred Heart purchased the **Grant House** at 2220 Broadway. These two build-

> **WORD OF MOUTH**
>
> "Fillmore Street (farther up the hill toward Pacific Heights) is an interesting neighborhood—not as yuppy as the Marina/Cow Hollow, but not as counterculture as the Haight."
>
> —waldrons

A PACIFIC HEIGHTS WALK

Start at **Broadway and Webster Street,** where four notable estates stand within a block of one another. Two are on the north side of Broadway to the west of the intersection, one is on the same side to the east, and the last is half a block south on Webster Street. Head south down Webster and hang a right onto Clay to **Alta Plaza Park,** or skip the park and turn left on Jackson to the **Whittier Mansion,** on the corner of Jackson and Laguna streets. Head south down Laguna and cross Washington Street to **Lafayette Park.** Walk on Washington along the edge of Lafayette Park, past the formal French **Spreckels Mansion** at the corner of Octavia Street, and continue east two more blocks to Franklin Street. Turn left (north); halfway down the block stands the handsome **Haas-Lilienthal House.** Head back south on Franklin Street, stopping to view several **Franklin Street buildings.** At California Street, turn right (west) to see more **noteworthy Victorians** on that street and Laguna Street. Beyond Laguna, continue three blocks west back to Fillmore Street.

ings, along with a Flood property at 2120 Broadway, are used as school quarters. A gold-mine heir, William Bourn II, commissioned Willis Polk to build the nearby brick mansion at 2550 Webster Street.

Franklin Street buildings. What at first looks like a stone facade on the **Golden Gate Church** (✉ *1901 Franklin St.*) is actually redwood painted white. A Georgian-style residence built in the early 1900s for a coffee merchant sits at 1735 Franklin. On the northeast corner of Franklin and California streets is a **Christian Science church;** built in the Tuscan Revival style, it's noteworthy for its terra-cotta detailing. The **Coleman House** (✉ *1701 Franklin St., Pacific Heights*) is an impressive twin-turreted Queen Anne mansion that was built for a gold-rush mining and lumber baron. Don't miss the large, brilliant-purple stained-glass window on the house's north side. ✉ *Franklin St. between Washington and California Sts., Pacific Heights.*

Haas-Lilienthal House. A small display of photographs on the bottom floor of this elaborate, gray 1886 Queen Anne house makes clear that despite its lofty stature and striking, round third-story tower, the house was modest compared with some of the giants that fell victim to the 1906 earthquake and fire. The Foundation for San Francisco's Architectural Heritage operates the home, whose carefully kept rooms provide an intriguing glimpse into late-19th-century life through period furniture, authentic details (antique dishes in the kitchen built-in), and photos of the family who occupied the house until 1972. Volunteers conduct one-hour house tours three days a week and informative two-hour walking tours ($8) of the Civic Center, Broadway, and Union Street areas on Saturday afternoons, and of the eastern portion of Pacific Heights on Sunday afternoons (call or check Web site for schedule). ✉ *2007 Franklin St., between Washington and Jackson Sts., Pacific Heights* ☎ *415/441–3004* ⊕ *www.sfheritage.org* ▱ *Entry $8* ⊙ *1-hr tour Wed. and Sat. noon–3, Sun. 11–4, 2-hr tour Sun. at 12:30.*

Lafayette Park. Clusters of trees dot this four-block-square oasis for sunbathers and dog-and-Frisbee teams. During the 1860s a tenacious squatter, Sam Holladay, built himself a big wooden house in the center of the park. Holladay even instructed city gardeners as if the land were his own and defied all orders to leave. The house was finally torn down in 1936. On the south side of the park, squat but elegant **2151 Sacramento,** a private condominium, is the site of a home occupied by Sir Arthur Conan Doyle in the late 19th century. Coats of arms blaze in the front stained-glass windows. The park itself is a lovely neighborhood space, where Pacific Heights residents laze in the sun or exercise their pedigreed canines while gazing at downtown's skyline in the distance. ⊠*Bordered by Laguna, Gough, Sacramento, and Washington Sts., Pacific Heights.*

Noteworthy Victorians. Two **Italianate Victorians** (⊠*1818 and 1834 California St., Pacific Heights*) stand out on the 1800 block of California. A block farther is the Victorian-era **Atherton House** (⊠*1990 California St., Pacific Heights*), whose mildly daffy design incorporates Queen Anne, Stick-Eastlake, and other architectural elements. Many claim the house—now apartments—is haunted by the ghosts of its 19th-century residents, who regularly whisper, glow, and generally cause a mild fuss. The oft-photographed **Laguna Street Victorians,** on the west side of the 1800 block of Laguna Street, cost between $2,000 and $2,600 when they were built in the 1870s. No bright colors here though—most of the paint jobs are in soft beiges or pastels. ⊠*California St. between Franklin and Octavia Sts., and Laguna St. between Pine and Bush Sts., Pacific Heights.*

Octagon House. This eight-sided home sits across the street from its original site on Gough Street; it's one of two remaining octagonal houses in the city (the other is on Russian Hill), and the only one open to the public. White quoins accent each of the eight corners of the pretty blue-gray exterior, and a colonial-style garden completes the picture. Inside, it's full of antique American furniture, decorative arts (paintings, silver, rugs), and documents from the 18th and 19th centuries. A deck of Revolutionary-era hand-painted playing cards takes an antimonarchist position: in place of kings, queens, and jacks, the American upstarts substituted American statesmen, Roman goddesses, and Indian chiefs. ⊠*2645 Gough St., Pacific Heights* ☎*415/441–7512* ⊠*Free, donations encouraged* ☉*Feb.–Dec., 2nd Sun. and 2nd and 4th Thurs. of month noon–3; group tours weekdays by appointment.*

Spreckels Mansion. Shrouded behind tall juniper hedges at the corner of lovely winding, brick Octavia Street, overlooking Lafayette Park, the estate was built for sugar heir Adolph Spreckels and his wife, Alma. Mrs. Spreckels was so pleased with her house that she commissioned George Applegarth to design another building in a similar vein: the Legion of Honor. One of the city's great iconoclasts, Alma Spreckels was the model for the bronze figure atop the Victory Monument in Union Square. Today the house belongs to prolific romance novelist Danielle Steel. ⊠*2080 Washington St., at Octavia St., Pacific Heights.*

Vedanta Society. A pastiche of colonial, Queen Anne, Moorish, and Hindu opulence, lavender with turrets battling red-topped onion domes and Victorian detailing everywhere, this 1905 structure was the first Hindu temple in the West. Vedanta, an underlying philosophy of Hinduism, maintains that all religions are paths to one goal. Although the Vedanta Society's main location is the temple at Vallejo and Fillmore streets (closed Tuesday), *this* temple (open only Friday evening from 8 to 9) is the organization's heart. ⊠*2963 Webster St., Pacific Heights* ☎*415/922–2323* ⊕*www.sfvedanta.org.*

Wedding Houses. These identical white double-peak homes (joined in the middle) were erected in the late 1870s or early 1880s by dairy rancher James Cudworth as wedding gifts for his two daughters. These days, the buildings house businesses and an English-style pub. ⊠*1980 Union St., Pacific Heights.*

Whittier Mansion. With a Spanish-tile roof and scrolled bay windows on all four sides, this is one of the most elegant 19th-century houses in the state. An anomaly in a town that lost most of its grand mansions to the 1906 quake, the Whittier Mansion was built so solidly that only a chimney toppled over during the disaster. ⊠*2090 Jackson St., Pacific Heights.*

WHAT TO SEE IN JAPANTOWN

Japan Center. The noted American architect Minoru Yamasaki created this 5-acre complex, which opened in 1968. Architecturally the development hasn't aged well, and its Peace Plaza, where seasonal festivals are held, is an unwelcoming sea of cement. The Japan Center includes the shop- and restaurant-filled Kintetsu and Kinokuniya buildings; the excellent Kabuki Springs & Spa; the Hotel Kabuki; and the Sundance Kabuki, Robert Redford's fancy, reserved-seating cinema/restaurant complex.

The Kinokuniya Bookstores, in the Kinokuniya Building, has an extensive selection of Japanese-language books, *manga* (graphic novels), books on design, and English-language translations and books on Japanese topics. Just outside, follow the Japanese teenagers to Pika Pika, where you and your friends can step into a photo booth and then use special effects and stickers to decorate your creation. On the bridge connecting the center's two buildings, check out Shige Antiques for *yukata* (lightweight cotton kimonos) for kids and lovely silk kimonos, and Asakichi and its tiny incense shop for tinkling wind chimes and display-worthy tea kettles. Continue into the Kintetsu Building for a selection of Japanese restaurants.

Between the Miyako Mall and Kintetsu Building are the five-tier, 100-foot-tall **Peace Pagoda** and the Peace Plaza. The pagoda, which draws on the 1,200-year-old tradition of miniature round pagodas dedicated to eternal peace, was designed in the late 1960s by Yoshiro Taniguchi to convey the "friendship and goodwill" of the Japanese people to the people of the United States. The plaza itself is a shadeless, unwelcoming

Where can I find . . .?

A DRUGSTORE	**Walgreens** ⊠1899 Fillmore St. Open until 10 PM Mon.Sat., 9 PM on Sun.	**Safeway** ⊠1335 Webster St., at Geary St. Open daily until midnight.
A COFFEE SHOP	**Peet's Coffee and Tea** ⊠2197 Fillmore St. The Berkeley Peets was the inspiration for Starbucks.	**White Crane Tea Company** ⊠1737 Post St. #337 Japanese tea thats actually from Japan.
A PARKING SPACE	**Japan Center Garage** ⊠1610 Geary Blvd. Validation available through many Japan Center proprietors.	**California and Steiner** ⊠2450 California St. Outdoor parking lot with metered spaces.

stretch of cement with little seating. Continue into the Miyako Mall to Ichiban Kan, a Japanese dollar store where you can pick up fun Japanese kitchenware, tote bags decorated with hedgehogs, and erasers shaped like food. ⊠*Bordered by Geary Blvd. and Fillmore, Post, and Laguna Sts., Japantown* ☎*No phone.*

Japan Center Mall. The buildings lining this open-air mall are of the shoji school of architecture. The mall's many good restaurants draw a lively crowd of nearby workers for lunch, but the atmosphere remains weirdly hushed. The shops are geared more toward locals—travel agencies, electronics shops—but there are some fun Japanese goods stores. Arrive early in the day and you may score some fabulous mochi (a soft, sweet Japanese rice treat) at **Benkyodo** (⊠*1747 Buchanan St., Japantown* ☎*415/922–1244*). It's easy to spend hours among the fabulous origami and craft papers at **Paper Tree** (⊠*1743 Buchanan St., Japantown* ☎*415/921–7100*), open since the 1960s. Be sure to swing around the corner, just off the mall, to **Super 7** (⊠*1628 Post St., Japantown* ☎*415/409–4700*), home of many large plastic Godzillas, glow-in-the-dark robots, and cool graphic tees. You can have a seat on local artist Ruth Asawa's twin origami-style fountains, which sit in the middle of the mall; they're squat circular structures made of fieldstone, with three levels for sitting and a brick floor. ⊠*Buchanan St. between Post and Sutter Sts., Japantown* ☎*No phone.*

★ **Kabuki Springs & Spa.** This serene spa is one Japantown destination that draws locals from all over town, from hipster to grandma, Japanese-American or not. Balinese urns decorate the communal bath area of this house of tranquility, and you're just as likely to hear soothing flute or classical music as you are Kitaro.

The massage palette has also expanded well beyond traditional Shiatsu technique. The experience is no less relaxing, however, and the treatment regimen includes facials, salt scrubs, and mud and seaweed

AT A GLANCE

Dining in Pacific Heights & Japantown

BUDGET

Mifune, Japanese, Japan Center, Kintetsu Bldg., 1737 Post St.

MODERATE

Florio, French Bistro, 1915 Fillmore St.

O Izakaya Lounge, Japanese, 1625 Post St.

Vivande Porta Via, Italian, 2125 Fillmore St.

Maki, Japanese, Japan Center, Kinokuniya Bldg., 1825 Post St.

SPQR, Italian, 1911 Fillmore St.

Yoshi's, Japanese, 1300 Fillmore St.

EXPENSIVE

Quince, Italian, 1701 Octavia St.

Spruce, American, 3640 Sacramento St.

wraps. You can take your massage in a private room with a bath or in a curtained-off area. The communal baths ($20 weekdays, $25 weekends) contain hot and cold tubs, a large Japanese-style bath, a sauna, a steam room, and showers. Bang the gong for quiet if your fellow bathers are speaking too loudly.

The clothing-optional baths are open for men only on Monday, Thursday, and Saturday; women bathe on Wednesday, Friday, and Sunday. Bathing suits are required on Tuesday, when the baths are coed. Men and women can reserve private rooms daily. An 80-minute massage-and-bath package with a private room costs $105; a package that includes a 50-minute massage and the use of the communal baths costs $95. ⊠*1750 Geary Blvd., Japantown* ☎*415/922–6000* ⊕*www.kabukisprings.com* ⊗*Daily 10–10.*

EYE ON ARCHITECTURE

San Francisco's architecture scene has been going through a dramatic growth spurt—with the growing pains to match. Bold-face international architects seem to be everywhere, spearheading major projects like the de Young Museum (Herzog & de Meuron of Switzerland), the California Academy of Sciences (Renzo Piano of Italy), and the Contemporary Jewish Museum (Polish–New Yorker Daniel Libeskind). As the hard hats multiply, so do the heated local debates.

The development flurry is thrown into relief by the previous decades spent carefully preserving the city's historic buildings. Genteel Victorian homes are a city signature, and this residential legacy has been fiercely protected. But some critics complain of the lack of a current, strong, homegrown style and the trend for "imported talent."

San Francisco Museum of Modern Art (SFMOMA)

Residents aren't shy about voicing opinions on the "starchitect" plans, either. As high-profile designs unfold and new condo neighborhoods break ground, criticism will surely escalate. (One thing that gratifies everyone: The impressive advances made in eco-friendly building practices.) As *Chronicle* columnist John King put it, SF is getting "a crash course in contemporary architecture. One that is long, long overdue."

SAN FRANCISCO'S SIGNATURE BUILDINGS

❶ OCTAGONAL HOUSES
c. 1850—60s

Only a few examples of this fad remain; the preserved home on Gough Street is a prime specimen. The style was promoted as being particularly healthy, as it would bring in more light and fresh air. Inside the Gough Street house (open to the public) are square rooms divided by triangular storage spaces. The builder, William McElroy, hid a "time capsule" letter under its stairway.

Octagonal Houses

❷ QUEEN ANNE HOUSES
c. 1885—1890s

The most richly decorated, over-the-top style for Victorian town houses. Known for steep, shingled roofs, slanted bay windows, gingerbread adornments, and "witch's-cap" towers. (The ornamentation was mostly mass-produced, then added to façades.) One of the best is the Haas-Lilienthal home in Pacific Heights, now a public museum.

Queen Anne Houses

❸ PAINTED LADIES
c. 1870—1900, paint jobs in the 1960s

Name for Victorian houses with vivid, polychrome paint jobs. The original colors were neutrals, but hippies slathered on buttercup yellow, purple, fuschia, you name it. Examples of all the Victorian architectural variations have gotten the Easter-egg treatment, from the pointed arches of the Gothic Revival to the angular bay windows of the Stick-Eastlake look. The most scenic collection of painted ladies can be found along "Postcard Row," a stretch of six candy-colored homes on Steiner Street opposite Alamo Square.

Painted Ladies

WALKING TOURS

For architecture-centric walking tours, check out the offerings from **San Francisco Architectural Heritage** (☎ 415/441–3000 ⊕ www.sfheritage.org.) **San Francisco City Guides** (☎ 415/557–4266 ⊕ www.sfcityguides.org) has some cool tours focusing on specific buildings, like the Ferry Building or the Yerba Buena Complex.

Transamerica Pyramid

❹ TRANSAMERICA PYRAMID
c. 1972

At 853 feet, this tapering skyscraper, designed by William Pereira, is the tallest building in San Francisco's skyline. Its elevator shafts flare out like jug-ears. The tower first sparked a storm of protest, with opponents picketing and then-Assemblyman John Burton claiming that it would "rape the skyline."

Now it's considered an icon. Although the building isn't open to the public, you can spend time in the lovely grove of redwood trees on the east side of the tower.

SFMOMA

❺ SFMOMA
c. 1995

Renowned Swiss architect Mario Botta's first shot at designing a museum. The sturdy, geometric, symmetrical forms have become his characteristic style. Here a black-and-white striped cylindrical tower anchors the brick building. Botta called the huge, slanted skylight the city's "eye, like the Cyclops."

de Young Museum of Fine Art

❻ DE YOUNG MUSEUM OF FINE ART
c. 2005

Love it or hate it, this structure is a must-see spot in Golden Gate park, as well as one of the city's new landmarks. The museum's original Egyptian-revival edifice was rendered structurally unsafe by the Loma Prieta quake, and the Pritzker prize-winning Swiss team Herzog & de Meuron won the commission to rebuild. Their design's copper facade and 144 ft. observation tower—a twisted parallelogram poking above the treetops—drew fire from critics, who compared the design to a "rusty aircraft carrier." But the museum's copper hue is mellowing with age, and the panoramic view from the tower is a hit—shifting any controversy to the museum's internal politics.

NEAR MISS

The Union Square area almost got a way-out building by hot-button Dutch architect Rem Koolhaas in 2001. The plan: a 10-story Prada store clad in steel, with thousands of porthole windows. The *Chronicle*'s architecture critic imagined it as a giant cheese grater... but the dot-com-era economic bust scuttled the project.

NEW STARS & COMING ATTRACTIONS

❼ MISSION BAY, RINCON HILL, AND THE TRANSBAY DISTRICT
Ongoing

Tremendous changes are coming to San Francisco's cityscape, especially moving south from Market Street along the waterfront, where these high-density residential communities are underway. Don't expect old-school gingerbread. Instead, glass-sheathed, condo-crammed high-rises are taking over what was a working-class area of warehouses and lofts, studded by the AT&T Ballpark. A new UCSF campus is springing up in Mission Bay, with a blocky Campus Community Center by Mexican architect Ricardo Legorreta now open for business.

❽ PRESIDIO
Ongoing

The development of this parkland continues at a relatively slow pace. Its historic military-base buildings are being put to new uses—everything from a printing press to a spa. Filmmaker George Lucas built a digital arts center here, and a Walt Disney museum is in the works.

❾ CONTEMPORARY JEWISH MUSEUM
Opened summer 2008

Daniel Libeskind, best known for his work on the World Trade Center site, is behind this newcomer in the Yerba Buena Cultural District. An extension in blue stainless steel meshes with the previous building, Willis Polk's 1907 power substation. Together, they form Hebrew letters that mean "to life!" See www.jmsf.org for more info.

❿ CALIFORNIA ACADEMY OF SCIENCES
Due to open in late 2008

The new natural history museum faces the controversial de Young Museum in Golden Gate Park. Renzo Piano's design is also a "green building" pilot project, with environmentally friendly materials and energy strategies. Its knockout element is the living roof, covered in native California plants.

The UCSF Community Center

Contemporary Jewish Museum

California Academy of Sciences

ARCHI-FEST

Are you craving more? The American Institute of Architects' SF chapter organizes an **Architecture and the City festival** each September. The event includes tours, lectures, films, and what's been called "domestic modernist porn," a home-tour weekend. Check www.aiasf.org for details.

For an incredibly rich trove of architecture and design publications, head to **William Stout Architectural Books** (⇨ the Shopping chapter).

Where to Eat

Café in North Beach

WORD OF MOUTH

"Where do you go for fresh oysters in San Francisco?"

—Sharon

"Swan Oyster Depot. They're only open for lunch, only counter seating. Everything's fresh, they serve 'em till they run out. It's a cool place and the shuckers are very friendly. Go at 2:00 to avoid lines."

—Mike

THE SCENE

Updated by
Sharon Silva

You can find just about any food in San Francisco, a place where trends are set and culinary diversity rules. Since the 1849 gold rush flooded the city with foreign flavors, residents' appetites for exotic eats haven't diminished by even one bite.

Today San Francisco remains a vital culinary crossroads, with nearly every ethnic cuisine represented, from Afghan to Vietnamese. You don't just go out for Chinese here: regional offerings range from the classic Cantonese to the obscure Hakka cuisine of southern China. And although locals have long headed to the Mission District for Latin food, Chinatown for Asian food, and North Beach for Italian food, they also know that every part of the city offers dining experiences beyond the neighborhood tradition.

As for restaurant trends, small plates—à la Spanish tapas—have become the eating experience *du jour*. Now a slew of Italian, Asian, Latin, Mediterranean, and even American restaurants, as well as Spanish spots, are satisfying locals' hunger for myriad small tastes in a single sitting. At the same time, Italian restaurants, which once typically put dishes from all over the boot on their menus, are now focusing on the traditions of just one region, such as Liguria, Lazio, Campania, or Sardinia.

Diners also have grown increasingly serious about what they're sipping. In response, restaurateurs are offering more sophisticated wine lists, emphasizing new vintners, lesser-known varietals, and emerging winemaking regions. And "cocktailians" have been treated to an explosion of innovative drinks that are keeping mixologists busy pouring, stirring, and shaking from one end of town to the other.

San Francisco Bay

NORTHERN WATERFRONT

MARINA
busy bar scene, upscale eats

NORTH BEACH
red-sauce eateries

Bay St.

Columbus Ave.

The Embarcadero

RUSSIAN HILL

TELEGRAPH HILL

Lombard St.

FILLMORE

Broadway (tunnel)

CHINATOWN
dim-sum palaces, noodle shops, Asian bakeries

Polk St.

Larkin St.

Hyde St.

Broadway

Washington St.

FINANCIAL DISTRICT

PACIFIC HEIGHTS

NOB HILL
deluxe dining rooms

California St.

Powell St.

Grant Ave.

Sacramento St.

1st St.

Pine St.

Van Ness Ave.

Franklin St.

Gough St.

Laguna St.

2nd St.

JAPANTOWN
Ramen shops and sushi restaurants

Bush St.

Post St.

UNION SQUARE
Posh noshing

3rd St.

Geary St.

Geary St.

4th St.

Steiner St.

Turk St.

CIVIC CENTER

5th St.

Market St.

6th St.

Folsom St.

HAYES VALLEY

Mission St.

7th St.

Golden Gate Ave.

SOMA

Harrison St.

Fulton St.

Divisadero St.

WESTERN ADDITION

Hayes St.

Fell St.

8th St.

9th St.

Bryant St.

Brannan St.

Townsend St.

HAIGHT

Haight St.

10th St.

HAYES VALLEY
hipster hangouts, great brunch spots

King St.

Berry St.

Buena Vista Park

Duboce Ave.

Market St.

Van Ness Ave.

Mission St.

CASTRO
swanky lounges, lively bistros

Harrison St.

Mariposa St.

POTRERO HILL

17th St.

Potrero Ave.

Castro St.

Mission Dolores Park

Guerrero St.

Dolores St.

20th St.

MISSION
burrito joints and trendy eateries

0   1 mi

0   1 km

NOE VALLEY

WHERE TO EAT PLANNER

Eating Out Strategy

Where should we eat? With hundreds of San Francisco eateries competing for your attention, it may seem like a daunting question. But don't worry. Our expert writers and editors have done most of the legwork. The 130-plus selections here represent the best this city has to offer—from hot dogs to haute cuisine. Search "Best Bets" for top recommendations by price, cuisine, and experience. Sample local flavor in the neighborhood features. Or find a review quickly in the alphabetical listings. Delve in, and enjoy!

Hours

Unless otherwise noted, the restaurants listed in this guide are open daily for lunch and dinner. Prime time for dinner is around 7:30 or 8 PM, and although places for night owls to fuel up are plentiful, most restaurants stop serving around 10 PM. Restaurants, along with bars and clubs, may serve alcohol between the hours of 6 AM and 2 AM. The legal age to buy alcoholic beverages in California is 21 years old.

What to Wear

In general, San Franciscans are neat but casual dressers; only at the top-notch dining rooms do you see a more formal style. But the way you look can influence how you're treated—and where you're seated. Generally speaking, jeans will suffice at most table-service restaurants in the $ to $$ range. Moving up from there, many pricier restaurants require jackets, and some insist on ties. In reviews, we mention dress only when men are required to wear a jacket or a jacket and tie. Note that shorts, sweatpants, and sports jerseys are rarely appropriate. When in doubt, call the restaurant and ask.

Reservations

Plan ahead if you're determined to snag a sought-after reservation. Some renowned restaurants are booked weeks or even months in advance. But you can get lucky at the last minute if you're flexible—and friendly. Most restaurants keep a few tables open for walk-ins and VIPs. Show up for dinner early (5:30 PM) or late (after 9 PM) and politely inquire about any last-minute vacancies or cancellations. If you're calling a few days ahead of time, ask if you can be put on a waiting list. Occasionally, an eatery may ask you to call the day before your scheduled meal to reconfirm.

Wine

Some of the city's top restaurants still automatically stock historic French vintages, but most wine lists respect the origin of the cuisine being served, with Italian restaurants primarily pouring Italian labels, Spanish restaurants pouring Spanish, and so on. Of course, California wines are commonly in the mix, too, with those from limited-production, lesser-known wineries on the better lists. Some restaurants even deliberately keep their wine lists small, so they can change them frequently to match the season and the menu. Half bottles are becoming more prevalent, and good wines by the glass are everywhere. Don't hesitate to ask for recommendations.

Tipping & Taxes

In most restaurants, tip the waiter 16%–20%. (To figure the amount quickly, just double the tax noted on the check—it's 8.5% of your bill—and add a bit more if the service merited it.) Bills for parties of six or more sometimes include the tip. Tip at least $1 per drink at the bar. Tipping the maître d' is not necessary unless you're trying to pave your way to being a regular. Also be aware that many restaurants, now required to fund the city's new universal health care ordinance, are passing these costs along to their customers—usually in the form of a 3%–4% surcharge or a $1–$1.50-per-head charge.

Parking

Most upper-end restaurants offer valet parking—worth considering in crowded neighborhoods such as North Beach, Union Square, Civic Center, and the Mission. There's often a nominal charge and a time restriction on validated parking.

Prices

If you're watching your budget, be sure to ask the price of daily specials recited by the waiter or captain. The charge for these dishes can sometimes be out of line with the other prices on the menu. And always review your bill. If you eat early or late you may be able to take advantage of a prix-fixe deal not offered at peak hours. Many upscale restaurants offer lunch deals with special menus at bargain prices. Credit cards are widely accepted, but some restaurants (particularly smaller ones) accept only cash. If you plan to use a credit card, it's a good idea to double-check its acceptability when making reservations or before sitting down to eat. Some restaurants are marked with a price range ($$–$$$, for example). This indicates one of two things: either the average cost straddles two categories, or if you order strategically, you can get out for less than most diners spend.

WHAT IT COSTS AT DINNER

¢	$	$$	$$$	$$$$
under $10	$10–$14	$15–$22	$23–$30	over $30

Prices are per person for a typical main course or equivalent combination of smaller dishes. Note: if a restaurant offers only prix-fixe (set-price) meals, it has been given the price category that reflects the full prix-fixe price.

In This Chapter

12

SMOKING

Smoking is banned in all city restaurants and bars.

CHILDREN

Dining with youngsters in the city does not have to mean culinary exile. Many of the restaurants reviewed in this chapter are excellent choices for families and are marked with a ☾ symbol.

BEST BETS FOR SAN FRANCISCO DINING

With thousands of restaurants to choose from, how will you decide where to eat? Fodor's writers and editors have selected their favorite restaurants by price, cuisine, and experience in the Best Bets lists below. In the first column, Fodor's Choice designations represent the "best of the best" in every price category. You can also search by neighborhood for excellent eats—just peruse the following pages. Or find specific details about a restaurant in the full reviews, listed alphabetically later in the chapter.

FODOR'S CHOICE ★

A16, $$
Boulevard, $$$$
Delfina, $$-$$$
Gary Danko, $$$$
Jardinière, $$$$
L'Osteria del Forno, $
Michael Mina, $$$$
Swan Oyster Depot, $
Zuni Café, $$$

By Price

¢

Burger Joint
Mijita Cocina Mexicana
Naan 'N' Curry
Pho Hoa Clement

$

L'Osteria del Forno
Park Chow
Swan Oyster Depot
Ti Couz

$$

A16
Dosa
Nopa
Range
Ton Kiang

$$$

Canteen
Delfina
One Market
Perbacco
Zuni Café

$$$$

Boulevard
Gary Danko
Jardinière
Michael Mina
Quince

By Cuisine

AMERICAN

Canteen, $$-$$$
One Market, $$$
Nopa, $$
Town Hall, $$-$$$
Two, $$-$$$

CHINESE

R&G Lounge, $-$$
Ton Kiang, $
Yank Sing, $$

FRENCH

Bar Jules, $$$
Café Claude, $$-$$$
Chez Papa, $$
La Folie, $$$$
Ti Couz, $

INDIAN

Dosa, $$
Indian Oven, $$

ITALIAN

A16, $$
Delfina, $$-$$$
Incanto, $$
La Ciccia, $$
SPQR, $$

JAPANESE

Maki, $$
Mifune, $
O Izakaya Lounge, $$
Yoshi's, $$$

LATIN AMERICAN

Charanga, $$
La Santaneca de la Mission, ¢-$
Limón, $$
Mijita Cocina Mexicana, ¢

MEDITERRANEAN

Cortez, $$$
LuLu, $$$
Terzo, $$
Zuni Café, $$$

12

MEXICAN

Los Jarritos, ¢
Mijita Cocina Mexicana, ¢

SEAFOOD

Aqua, $$$$
Hog Island Oyster Company, $
Plouf, $$$
Swan Oyster Depot, $

STEAK HOUSE

Acme Chophouse, $$$$
Epic Roasthouse, $$$$
Harris', $$$$

VIETNAMESE

Bodega Bistro, $$
Pagolac, ¢-$
Slanted Door, $$-$$$

By Experience

BAR MENU

Absinthe, $$$
Epic Roasthouse, $$$$
Farallon, $$$$
Kokkari, $$$

BAY VIEWS

Epic Roasthouse, $$$$
Greens, $$
Slanted Door, $$-$$$
Waterbar, $$$$

BRUNCH

Foreign Cinema, $$$
Rose's Café, $$-$$$
Suppenküche, $$

BUSINESS DINING

Boulevard, $$$$
One Market, $$$
Rubicon, $$$

CHILD-FRIENDLY

Burger Joint, ¢
Capp's Corner, $$
Mijita Cocina Mexicana, ¢
Park Chow, $
Yank Sing, $$

COMMUNAL TABLE

Bocadillos, $
Nopa, $$
Salt House, $$$
Tommaso's, $$
Two, $$-$$$

HISTORIC INTEREST

Boulevard, $$$$
Jeanty at Jack's, $$
Swan Oyster Depot, $
Tadich, $$-$$$
Tommaso's, $$

HOTEL DINING

Ame, $$$$
Canteen, $$-$$$
Ducca, $$$
O Izakaya Lounge, $$

HOT SPOTS

Nopa, $$
Range, $$
Spruce, $$$-$$$$
Town Hall, $$-$$$
Yoshi's, $$$

LATE-NIGHT BITES

Absinthe, $$$
Chow, $
Great Eastern, $-$$
Nopa, $$
Zuni Café, $$$

PRE-THEATER MEAL

Cortez, $$$
Farallon, $$$$
Le Colonial, $$
Scala's Bistro, $$$

QUIET MEAL

Acquerello, $$$$
Bodega Bistro, $$
Coi, $$$$
Fleur de Lys, $$$$

SINGLES SCENE

Laïola, $$
Nopa, $$
Poleng, $$
Salt House, $$$

SMALL PLATES

Bocadillos, $
Coco500, $$
Laïola, $$
O Izakaya Lounge, $$
Poleng, $$

SPECIAL OCCASION

Boulevard, $$$$
Gary Danko, $$$$
Jardinière, $$$$
Michael Mina, $$$$

UNION SQUARE, FINANCIAL DISTRICT & CHINATOWN

Fashion, business, and history collide in this broad swatch of the city, where you can eat for pennies or spend your rent in a single sitting.

Around Union Square, pictured above, department stores and boutiques rule, and hotels—from Campton Place to the Sir Francis Drake—pull diners in for pricey lunches and pricier dinners. Amid the towers of the Financial District, CEOs find a bounty of smart dining rooms, including **Jeanty at Jack's** (615 Sacramento St., 415/693–0941), **Rubicon** (558 Sacramento St., 415/434–4100), and Alfred's Steak House (659 Merchant St., 415/781–7058).

But budget-minded locals know to slip into sandwich shops that line the alleys off Kearny, Montgomery, and Bush streets, or to head to Sutter and Post streets, where modest storefronts dish up well-priced Burmese, Japanese, Thai, and Indonesian plates. Or you can hotfoot it over to the narrow lanes of Chinatown, where a bowl of wonton soup or a rice plate in dozens of storefront eateries along Jackson, Clay, or Washington streets will bring change from a five-dollar bill.

EURO FLAVOR

San Franciscans like to brag about their city's European atmosphere, citing Belden Alley as evidence of that claim. The charming pedestrians-only street is anchored by the historic **Sam's Grill** (374 Bush St., 415/421–0594), a seafood institution for more than 70 years. Beyond Sam's, the possibilities are a delicious mix of European tables, with French favorites like **Plouf** (40 Belden Pl., 415/986–6491) and **Café Bastille** (22 Belden Pl., 415/986–5673), the Italian **Brindisi Cucina di Mare** (88 Belden Pl., 415/593–8000), and the Spanish **B44** (44 Belden Pl., 415/986–6287).

DIVING INTO DIM SUM

The popular Cantonese midday custom of going out for dim sum—small dishes, both savory and sweet, hot and cold—can be explored on nearly every block in Chinatown. In big restaurants, servers push dish-laden carts around the dining room, and diners select what they want as the offerings roll by. Smaller places dispense with the carts in favor of more easily managed trays. You won't always know what you're choosing, so embrace the mystery—it's half the fun of dim sum.

12

New Asia (772 Pacific Ave., 415/391–6666) is perfect for dim sum newbies—English is spoken here, and the sprawling room means you won't stick out like a sore thumb. For the best selection, try for a table near the kitchen; by the time the carts make their way upstairs, they're picked over.

For more adventurous spirits, **Dol Ho** (808 Pacific Ave., 415/392–2828) is a hole-in-the-wall serving up good dim sum at great prices. Neighborhood regulars fill the small space, snapping up the best items from the single cart. There's not much English spoken here, but the high authenticity factor and low tab make any sign-language efforts pay off.

When you walk downstairs into out-of-the-way **Hang Ah** (1 Pagoda Pl., at Stockton St., 415/982–5686), you'll feel like you've discovered a hidden gem (even though this "discovery" is actually 120 years old) where you can fill up on respectable dim sum for a song. If you're in a rush, stop at friendly You's (675 Broadway, 415/788–7028), a busy takeout spot famous for its barbecued pork buns.

Many locals like **Great Eastern** (649 Jackson St., 415/986–2500) because they can check off what they want on dim sum menus instead of waiting for a cart. Others, especially Financial District workers on weekdays and families on weekends, migrate to **City View Restaurant** (622 Commercial St., 415/398–2838) for its relatively quiet dining room, ample choices, and atmospheric location on one of the neighborhood's quaint cobblestone blocks.

RESTAURANTS IN THIS AREA

AMERICAN
Canteen, $$-$$$
Michael Mina, $$$$
Rubicon, $$$
CHINESE
Great Eastern, $-$$
R&G Lounge, $$
Yank Sing, $$
FRENCH
Jeanty at Jack's, $$
Plouf, $$-$$$
Restaurant Jeanne D'Arc, $$$
Fleur de Lys, $$$$
FRENCH
Café Claude, $$
GREEK
Kokkari, $$$
INDIAN
Naan 'N' Curry, ¢
ITALIAN
Perbacco, $$-$$$
Scala's Bistro, $$$
MEDITERRANEAN
Cortez, $$$
SEAFOOD
Aqua, $$$$
Farallon, $$$$
Tadich Grill, $$-$$$
SPANISH
B44, $$-$$$
Bocadillos, $$
VEGETARIAN
Millennium, $$
VIETNAMESE
Le Colonial, $$

SOMA, CIVIC CENTER & HAYES VALLEY

These areas prove that terrific restaurants can spring up in gritty surroundings—and often, they'll help spur a general neighborhood improvement. This serving of gentrification comes with tempting menus and stylish dining rooms.

The hip SoMa neighborhood lies south of Market Street and east of Van Ness, running all the way to the bay. It once was a warehouse district punctuated by blue-collar households, many of them immigrant families. Nowadays, the same streets—especially Brannan, Folsom, and Fourth streets, and the area around AT&T Park—are chockablock with residential lofts, trendy bars and clubs, and scores of restaurants that fuel the mostly young, mostly single local crowd.

The Civic Center, which embraces a handful of blocks around Van Ness Avenue north of Market Street, and bleeds into Hayes Valley, is heavy with government buildings and grand performance spaces. Its dining scene is geared for people grabbing a bite before or after *La Bohème* or Mahler.

SWEET TREATS

For high-style desserts, head to **Citizen Cake** (399 Grove St., at Gough St., 415/861–2228), pictured above, where star pastry chef Elizabeth Falkner turns out such creative concoctions as upside-down pineapple parfait, with vanilla mochi cake, coconut cream, and vanilla gelato, and rosebud crème brûlée, with caramel crisps and saffron pistachio cookies. Citizen Cake also serves lunch and dinner, with the classic tuna salad sandwich reigning at mid-day and grass-fed flank steak with potato gratin and horseradish ice cream for dinner. For a quick fix, cruise the small pastry counter just next door.

EAT CHEAP OR DINE CHIC

SNACKING AROUND...

SoMa: Tree-lined South Park, pictured below, is a charming green oasis, complete with a swing set for kids, benches for adults, and cute cafés that both will enjoy. The park is bordered by Second and Third streets, and Brannan and Bryant streets. One of our favorite cafés is **The Butler & the Chef** (155 South Park St., 415/896–2075) which offers organic breakfast and lunch items, including croissants and *croque monsieurs* that will make you think you're in Paris.

Civic Center: For something quick before a show at the symphony hall or opera house, head to **Arlequin** (384 Hayes St., near Gough St., 415/626–1211), the café offshoot of the classy Absinthe restaurant. Arlequin is famous for its grilled ham and Gruyère cheese sandwich on *pain levain*. Order at the counter, then grab a table indoors or in the back garden. Nearby, East Coast transplants stop into **Max's in Opera Plaza** (601 Van Ness Ave., 415/771–7300) for pastrami sandwiches, or a bowl of soul-satisfying matzo ball soup.

Hayes Valley: Gyros are the kind of walk-away quick meals that make **Hayes & Kebab** (406 Hayes St., at Gough St., 415/861–2977) a popular neighborhood stop anytime. Fans also rave about the falafel sandwiches and hummus and pita. At **Modern Tea** (602 Hayes St., at Laguna St., 415/626–5406), you can sip the house namesake with a slab of dreamy buttermilk pudding cake.

SOMA SOPHISTICATES

The area around Brannan and Fourth streets has several classy restaurants. We like the wine-savvy **Bacar** (448 Brannan St., 415/904–4100) and the lively **Coco500** (500 Brannan St., 415/543–2222), a small-plates star. A second stretch on Folsom Street, near Fourth Street, is home to the lively Mediterranean **LuLu** (816 Folsom St., 415/495–5775) and **Oola** (860 Folsom St., 415/995–2061), a hot American bistro.

RESTAURANTS IN THIS AREA

AMERICAN
Bacar, $$$$
Coco500, $$
Fifth Floor, $$$$
Jardinière, $$$$
Orson, $$$
Salt House, $$$
Town Hall, $$-$$$
Two, $$-$$$

ECLECTIC
Ame, $$$$

FRENCH
Absinthe, $$$
Bar Jules, $$$
Ducca, $$$

GERMAN
Suppenküche, $$

ITALIAN
Acquerello, $$$$

MEDITERRANEAN
LuLu, $$$
Zuni Café, $$$

SEAFOOD
Hayes Street Grill, $$-$$$
Swan Oyster Depot, $-$$

STEAK HOUSE
Acme Chophouse, $$$$
Harris', $$$$

VIETNAMESE
Bodega Bistro, $$
Pagolac, $

THE WATERFRONT

Locals and visitors alike flock here for gorgeous bay views, a world-class waterfront esplanade, and a ferry building that is much better known for its food than its boat rides.

Not surprisingly, both restaurateurs and diners appreciate proximity to the water, and a slew of restaurants, including the award-winning **Boulevard** (1 Mission St., 415/543–6084), Hotel Vitale's sleek **Americano** (8 Mission St., 415/278–3777), the splashy **Waterbar** (399 Embarcadero, 415/284–9922), the meat-driven **Epic Roasthouse** (369 Embarcadero, 415/369–9955), and the Zen-tranquil **Ozumo** (161 Steuart St., 415/882–1333), are just steps from the shore.

To the north of the Ferry Building lies Fisherman's Wharf, a jumbled mix of seafood dining rooms, sidewalk vendors, and trinket shops that visitors religiously trudge through and San Franciscans invariably dismiss as a tourist trap. But even disdainful locals are sometimes seen making their way home from the Wharf with a cracked crab tucked under one arm and a loaf of sourdough bread under the other.

DUNGENESS CRAB

The local Dungeness season runs from November through June, which is when San Franciscans descend on the more than half-dozen crab stands at the wharf. Buy an expertly cracked Dungeness at the nearly century-old **Guardino's** (corner of Jefferson and Taylor Sts., 415/775–3669), pick up a loaf of sourdough bread, and feast on a true San Francisco tradition.

If you happen to be in town in February, you're in for a treat: events honoring the celebrated crustacean occur throughout the month at restaurants citywide, as part of the annual San Francisco Crab Festival. Check local listings.

A MOVEABLE FEAST

The **Ferry Building Marketplace** (1 Ferry Bldg., Embarcadero), pictured at left, is located at the foot of Market Street on the Embarcadero, with a magnetic pull that makes even the most jaded foodies go weak in the knees. It has just about everything: you can sit down to a three-course meal at **Marketbar** (415/434–1100), snack on tacos at **Mijita** (415/399–0814) or beluga caviar at **Tsar Nicoulai** (415/288–8630), or stock up on amazing fresh ingredients.

Hungry for Asian fare? The Japan-based **Delica rf1** (415/834–0344) offers an irresistible daily bento. Looking for rotisserie chicken and ratatouille? The Provencal-inspired **Mistral** (415/399–9751) has both. Happy with a cheese sandwich? Stop in at **Cowgirl Creamery** (415/362–9354) for a wedge of artisanal blue, and then grab a crusty baguette at the **Acme Bread Company** (415/288–2978) a few steps away. Or order a burger at **Taylor's Refresher** (415/328–3663), a bowl of clam chowder at **Hog Island** (415/391–7117), a Vietnamese spring roll at **Out the Door** (415/321–3740), or a glass of vintage cabernet at the **Wine Merchant** (415/391–9400).

Have a sweet tooth? There are chocolates at **Recchiuti Confections** (415/834–9494), cupcakes at **Miette** (415/837–0300), and creamy gelato at **Ciao Bella** (415/834–9330). And that's not everything, so bring your appetite and leave your calorie counter at home.

LOCAL FAVORITE: BOULETTE'S LARDER

Long before you get to **Boulette's Larder** (Ferry Bldg., 415/399–1155) you know something is cooking. The aromas that rise from this retail food shop and daytime dining spot waft through the Ferry Building Marketplace, pulling people to the southern end of the complex. Breakfast might be poached eggs and Dungeness crab, or piping-hot beignets, while lunch is whatever is on the stove that day—chard and squash gratin, chicken ragout with Indian spices, homey lamb stew, guinea hen . . . it's all delicious.

12

RESTAURANTS IN THIS AREA

AMERICAN
Boulevard, $$$$
Fog City Diner, $$
Gary Danko, $$$$
One Market, $$$
CHINESE
Yank Sing, $$
MEXICAN
Mijita Cocina Mexicana, ¢
SEAFOOD
Hog Island Oyster Company, $
Waterbar, $$$$
STEAK HOUSE
Epic Roasthouse, $$$$
SPANISH
Piperade, $$-$$$
VIETNAMESE
Slanted Door, $$-$$$

NORTH BEACH, NOB HILL & RUSSIAN HILL

One of the city's oldest neighborhoods, North Beach continues to speak Italian, albeit in fewer households than it did when Joe DiMaggio was hitting home runs at the local playground. But the Italian presence in the markets and cafés is deliciously unmissable.

For great people-watching, snag a sidewalk table at Calzone's, a pizza eatery at 430 Columbus Ave., near Vallejo St.

Columbus Avenue, North Beach's primary commercial artery, and nearby side streets boast dozens of moderately priced Italian restaurants and coffee bars that San Franciscans flock to for a dose of strong community feeling.

Nob Hill, the most famous hill in a city of hills, is known for its iconic hotels—the Fairmont, the Mark, Ritz-Carlton, the Huntington—though their dining rooms are not winning stars nowadays.

Nearby Russian Hill, which rises from Columbus Avenue, has few restaurants on its peak and higher slopes, but packs in scores of kitchens and cafés, especially around Polk and Larkin streets, as it descends to Van Ness Avenue.

BOB'S DONUTS

Everyone knows they shouldn't eat doughnuts. But that doesn't stop anyone from biting into the award-winning dough rings at **Bob's Donuts** (1621 Polk St., near Clay St., 415/776-3141). However you like 'em—cake, glazed, raised, sugared, or apple-studded—Bob's makes them 24 hours a day. They're fried in small batches, guaranteeing that every bite is both fresh and delicious.

ON THE CHEAP: BIG FLAVORS IN...

LITTLE ITALY

North Beach is awash in restaurants, most of them more lively and fun than food-worthy. But casual bites in this neighborhood are almost always first-rate. Two delicatessens, the century-old **Molinari's** (373 Columbus Ave., at Vallejo St., 415/421–2337) and the six-year-old **Palermo** (1556 Stockton St., near Green St., 415/362–9892), make delicious Italian sandwiches to order—mortadella, salami, prosciutto—that are great for toting to a bench in nearby Washington Square park. If you prefer to eat indoors, grab a table at the modest **Mario's Bohemian Cigar Store** (566 Columbus Ave., at Union St., 415/362–0536), which no longer sells cigars but does offer a legendary meatball sandwich on focaccia.

Time for a sweet treat? Browse the cases at two neighborhood institutions, **Victoria Pastry** (1362 Stockton St., at Vallejo St., 415/781–2015) and **Stella** (446 Columbus Ave., near Green St., 415/986–2914), or plant yourself at a sidewalk table at **Caffè Greco** (423 Columbus Ave., near Vallejo St., 415/397–6261), pictured below, to enjoy espresso and tiramisu.

LITTLE SAIGON

The northern edge of Nob Hill bleeds into the mean streets of the Tenderloin, a mixed neighborhood of Southeast Asians, Latinos, and countless others who struggle to get by. But hidden in among the hardscrabble corner groceries, smoke shops, and shady bars are some Vietnamese culinary gems, especially on Larkin Street. That's where you can find **Bodega Bistro** (607 Larkin St., 415/921–1218), the neighborhood's best Vietnamese restaurant, along with **Pagolac** (655 Larkin St., 415/776–3234), **Turtle Tower** (631 Larkin St., 415/409–3333), and the fluorescent-bright **Baguette Express** (668 Larkin St., 415/345–8999), an outsized sandwich emporium. Just a block away is the tiny, homier—and some say better—**Saigon Sandwiches** (560 Larkin St., 415/474–5698).

RESTAURANTS IN THIS AREA

AMERICAN
Coi, $$$$
FRENCH
La Folie, $$$$
Masa's, $$$$
ITALIAN
Antica Trattoria, $$
Capp's Corner, $$
L'Osteria del Forno, $
Rose Pistola, $$-$$$
MIDDLE EASTERN
Maykadeh, $$
STEAK HOUSE
El Raigón, $$$

THE MISSION, THE CASTRO & NOE VALLEY

You'll never go hungry here, in some of San Francisco's most jam-packed restaurant neighborhoods. From dirt-cheap taquerias to hip tapas joints, city dwellers know this sector (especially the Mission) as the go-to area for a great meal.

The city's best Mexican food can be found in the Mission. A pile of hot, salty chips and fiery salsa will run you $2. A filling burrito meal goes for about $5.

Head over to the Mission to dig into Mexican and Latin American menus. In recent years, the Latino community has been sharing the neighborhood with legions of twenty- and thirtysomethings who pack the affordable eateries along Valencia Street, between 16th and 24th streets, and Mission Street, from 19th to 24th streets. East of the Mission, Potrero Hill is home to a cluster of casual dining rooms in the blocks around Connecticut and 18th streets.

The Castro neighborhood, the epicenter of the city's gay community, is chockablock with restaurants and bars. Market Street between Church and Castro streets is a great stretch for people-watching and restaurant hopping.

Just south, in Noe Valley, everyone seems to be pushing a baby carriage, but they're all eating out too, mostly along 24th Street from Church to Castro, and on Church from 24th to 30th streets.

GLOBAL SCOOPS

The Mission has ice cream in every flavor imaginable. **Bombay Ice Creamery** (552 Valencia St., near 16th St., 415/861–3995) has dreamy cardamom. **Bi-Rite Creamery** (3692 18th St., near Valencia St., 415/626–5600) balances orbs of salted caramel in organic cones. And the venerable **Mitchell's** (668 San Jose St., at 29th St., 415/648–2300) has been scooping out creamy lemon custard for over 50 years.

12

MISSION DINING TWO WAYS

	Mexican:	Italian:
Grab-and-go	Two silver **El Toyanese Taco Trucks** (19th St. and Harrison St.; 22nd St. and Harrison St.) serve up the city's most authentic tacos, stuffed with pork or beef and fiery salsa.	The no-frills **Arinell** (509 Valencia St., near 16th St., 415/255–1303) is famous for its floppy New York–style slices handed across a walk-up counter.
Cheap eats	**Pancho Villa Taqueria** (3071 16th St., between Mission and Valencia Sts., 415/864–8840) is a Mission institution. The bulging burritos, heavy with beans, rice, meat, and salsa, are just $5.	The super-busy **Little Star** (400 Valencia St., at 15th Street, 415/551–7827) doles out cornmeal-crusted pizzas, deep-dish or thin, with toppings like spinach and feta, pesto, and chicken.
Casual chic	**Velvet Cantina** (3349 23rd St., at Bartlett St., 415/648–4142) offers a modern take on Mexican cuisine, in a dimly lighted, bordello-theme room filled with hipsters. Try the avocado-cactus enchiladas with cilantro pesto, washed down with a memorable margarita.	Stop in at **Pizzeria Delfina** (3611 18th St. at Guerrero St., 415/437–6800), the casual offshoot of upscale Delfina, for paper-thin Neapolitan pies, antipasto (eggplant caponata, fresh-stretched mozzarella), and some 15 wines by the glass.

MEXICAN VS. ITALIAN

For years, the Mission was where San Franciscans went to eat burritos and tacos, enchiladas, and tamales. But in the mid-1990s, new Italian eateries began to open up in this Mexican stronghold, with Parmesan and pasta threatening to outshine queso fresco and frijoles. The culinary turf struggle continues today. Thankfully for diners, there are plenty of tasty choices on both sides of the menu.

RESTAURANTS
IN THIS AREA

AMERICAN
Andalu, $$
Chow, $
Foreign Cinema, $$$
Home, $$
Luna Park, $$
Range, $$
BURGER
Burger Joint, ¢
CAMBODIAN
Angkor Borei, $
FRENCH
Chez Papa, $$$
Chez Spencer, $$$$
Ti Couz, $
INDIAN
Dosa, $$
ITALIAN
Delfina, $$$
Farina, $$-$$$
Incanto, $$
La Ciccia, $$
LATIN AMERICAN
Charanga, $$
La Santaneca de la Mission, ¢-$
MEDITERRANEAN
Baraka, $$-$$$
MEXICAN
Los Jarritos, ¢-$
PERUVIAN
Limón, $$-$$$

PACIFIC HEIGHTS, THE MARINA & JAPANTOWN

One of the city's best public transit rides is on the 22–Fillmore trolley, from the edge of Japantown at Geary Boulevard and Fillmore Street, up through mansion-lined Pacific Heights, then down to Cow Hollow and the Marina. We recommend jumping on and off the trolley, stopping for treats along the way.

In Japantown, which covers about six city blocks, start with a green tea latte at the pillbox-size **Café Tan Tan** in the Japan Center (Kinokuniya Bldg., 415/346–6260), or an ice cream-and-fruit-filled crepe next door at **Sophie's Crepes** (415/929–7732).

Up the hill, Lower Pacific Heights is all about shopping. But growling stomachs can find relief in a bag of madeleines at **Bay Bread Boulangerie** (2325 Pine St., 415/440–0356). Climb back on the trolley for a spectacular view as it crests the hill on Broadway. On your way down, you'll travel past upscale restaurants and no-frills diners, swank saloons and dimly lighted bars along Union, Lombard, and Chestnut streets. Just jump off when something catches your eye.

ITALIAN WINE BAR

A simple bite and a glass of Dolcetto d'Alba may be all you want after a long day of scaling San Francisco's hills. The small, delightfully rustic **Ottimista Enoteca** (1838 Union St., 415/674–8400), pictured at upper right, offers just that, with more than two dozen wines by the glass and small plates like saffron-scented *arancine* (deep-fried fontina-stuffed rice balls) and grilled prosciutto-wrapped asparagus with a poached egg. For something more substantial, try the braised pork with rosemary-mascarpone polenta. If you're out late, end on a sweet note with a glass of *vin santo* and biscotti, served until 2 AM on weekends.

12

TASTE OF TOKYO, WEST-COAST STYLE

At San Francisco's three-building Japan Center mall, bordered by Geary Boulevard and Post, Fillmore, and Laguna streets, you can eat like they do in Tokyo, stopping in at the sleek **Juban** (Kinokuniya Bldg., 415/776–5822) for *yakiniku*, meat grilled at your table, including prized Wagyu beef at $60 a serving; at the homey **Izumiya** (Kinokuniya Bldg., 415/441–6867), where *okonomiyaki*, a design-your-own savory pancake studded with pork or squid, is the draw; or at the refined **Ino Sushi** (Mikyako Bldg., 415/922–3121), with its 10-seat sushi bar and handful of tables.

RESTAURANTS IN THIS AREA

Noodle aficionados will want to try the house-made ramen at **Sapporo-ya** (Kinokuniya Bldg., 415/563–7400), the soba and udon at **Mifune** (Kintetsu Bldg., 415/922–0337), and all three varieties at the small, penny-wise **Suzu** (Kinokuniya Bldg., 415/346–5083). If your group wants a mix of specialties, wend your way to **Taraka** (Miyako Bldg., 415/921–2000), a *shokuji dokoro*, or Japanese bistro, which offers a mix of items, from sushi to tempura. But even Taraka has a specialty: a traditional sukiyaki prepared at your table, just as it would be in Japan.

BRUNCHING LIKE A LOCAL

Don't be surprised on weekend mornings to find San Franciscans of all ages waiting in line—rain or shine—at eateries around town. Like attending church or watching Sunday football, going out to brunch is a revered weekend ritual here, a time for friends and family to gather and gab. And, of course, to eat.

For biscuits with sausage gravy and cinnamon-scented French toast, head to **Elite Café** (2049 Fillmore St., 415/673–5483). The wildly popular **Ella's** (500 Presidio Ave., 415/441–5669) is home to some of the city's best sticky buns and chicken hash with eggs. For classic diner flavor, grab a seat at **Home Plate** (2274 Lombard St., 415/922–4663), where the scones are free and the atmosphere is low-key.

AMERICAN
Spruce, $$$-$$$$
ASIAN
Betelnut, $$
FRENCH
Florio, $$-$$$
Isa, $$$
ITALIAN
A-16, $$
Quince, $$$$
Rose's Café, $$-$$$
SPQR, $$
Vivande Porta Via, $$-$$$
JAPANESE
Maki, $$
Mifune, $
O Izakaya Lounge, $$
Yoshi's, $$$
MEDITERRANEAN
Terzo, $$
VEGETARIAN
Greens Restaurant, $$

HAIGHT, RICHMOND & SUNSET

The Haight-Ashbury was home base for the country's famed 1960s counterculture, and its café scene still reflects that colorful past. For ethnic flavors, go to the neighborhoods on either side of Golden Gate Park.

Over time, the Haight has become two distinct neighborhoods. The Upper Haight is an energetic commercial stretch from Masonic to Stanyan, where head shops and tofu-burger joints still thrive. A few upscale boutiques and restaurants, like the sizzling Caribbean kitchen of **Cha Cha Cha** (1801 Haight St., 415/386–5758), pictured below right, give the blocks a whiff of class. Meanwhile, the modestly gritty Lower Haight has emerged as a lively bohemian quarter of sorts, with hip, mostly ethnic eateries lining the blocks between Webster and Pierce streets.

The Richmond and Sunset neighborhoods encompass the land on both sides of Golden Gate Park, running all the way to the ocean's edge. Both districts have welcomed a dramatic increase in Asian families. And not surprisingly, scores of Asian restaurants have opened to serve them.

HAUTE PIES

The shoebox-size **Pizzetta 211** (211 23rd Ave., near Clement St., Richmond, 415/379–9880), pictured above, puts together thin-crust pies topped with the kinds of ingredients that will make you swoon. The selection changes daily—the tomato, basil, and mozzarella pizza is the only constant—but our favorites include the pancetta, Gorgonzola, and fig pizza, and the Sardinian cheese, pine nut, and rosemary pie. There are a couple of leafy salads and some nice wines, too, but the pizza is why everybody is here. Pizzetta 211 is open for lunch and dinner Wednesday through Sunday, and doesn't take reservations. Go early to avoid a long wait.

EXPLORING THE RICHMOND DISTRICT

NEW CHINATOWN

Since the early 20th century, the Richmond District has been a desirable family address. Today, those families are primarily Asian, and the neighborhood has been dubbed New China-town, though its dining choices go far beyond the People's Republic. Locals in search of a meal head to three main areas: Clement Street from Arguello Boulevard to 26th Avenue; Geary Boulevard from Masonic to 26th Avenue, and Balboa Street from 33rd to 39th avenues. Clement Street is a sea of temptation. If you'd like to try the complex curries and sal-ads at the always-busy **Burma SuperStar** (309 Clement St., near 3rd Ave., 415/387–2147), put your name and cell phone number on the waiting list as soon as you get to the neigh-borhood. There's also the venerable **Ocean Restaurant** (726 Clement St., near 8th Ave., 415/668–8896), a homey Canton-ese kitchen that promises good food at great prices. A cluster of plain-jane storefronts fire up smoky charcoal braziers on Geary Boulevard between Arguello Boulevard and 10th Avenue, including the **Wooden Charcoal Barbecue House** (4609 Geary Blvd., 415/751–6336), which serves up Korean *bulkogi*, or grilled beef ribs.

OLD RUSSIA

Nostalgia hangs heavy in the dining room of the half-cen-tury-old **Cinderella Bakery and Restaurant** (436 Balboa St., near 5th Ave., 415/751–9690), where diners tuck into borscht and cabbage rolls, while sipping *kvass,* or beer brewed from bread. Be sure to stop at the bakery counter on your way out for a flaky napoleon or cheese pastries. Not far away, at **Mos-cow and Tblisi Bakery** (5540 Geary Blvd., near 19th Ave., 415/668–6959), locals line up for some of those same old-country tastes, including *piroshki,* meat- and vegetable-filled pastries, and poppy-seed rolls that will both turn back the clock and recharge your batteries for the touring ahead.

12

RESTAURANTS IN THIS AREA

American
Nopa, $$
Park Chow, $
RNM, $$-$$$
Asian
Poleng Lounge, $$
Chinese
San Tung No. 2, ¢-$
Ton Kiang, $$
Indian
Indian Oven, $$
Moroccan
Aziza, $$-$$$
Russian
Katia's, $$
Thai
Thep Phanom, $$
Vietnamese
Dragonfly, $-$$
Pho Hoa Clement, ¢

RESTAURANT REVIEWS (ALPHABETICAL)

$$–$$$
Fodor'sChoice
★
ITALIAN
Marina

✕**A16.** Marina residents—and, judging from the crowds, everybody else—gravitate to this lively trattoria, named for the autostrada that winds through Italy's sunny south. The kitchen serves the food of Naples and surrounding Campania, such as mozzarella *burrata* (cream-filled) with olive oil and crostini, and crisp-crusted pizzas, including a classic Neapolitan Margherita (mozzarella, tomato, and basil). Among the regularly changing mains are veal meatballs with braised radicchio and house-made lamb sausage. A big wine list of primarily southern Italian with some Californian wines suits the fare perfectly. The long space includes an animated bar scene near the door; ask for a table in the quieter alcove at the far end. Reservations are easier to snag mid-week. ⊠*2355 Chestnut St., Marina* ☎*415/771–2216* ⊟*AE, MC, V* ☾*No lunch Sat.–Tues.*

$$$–$$$$
FRENCH
Hayes Valley

✕**Absinthe.** In 2007, this restaurant's long-notorious namesake could once again be poured legally in the United States, after nearly a century in exile. Not surprisingly, regular customers turned up in big numbers to sample the legendary Green Fairy, and then stayed on to enjoy Absinthe's brasserie-inspired fare of onion soup, cold seafood platters, slow-cooked rabbit, duck confit, and braised lamb shank. The late-night bar menu—oysters, *croque monsieur, croque madame* (grilled ham-and-cheese sandwiches), and *steak frites*—fuels neighborhood night owls. ⊠*398 Hayes St., Hayes Valley* ☎*415/551–1590* ⊟*AE, DC, MC, V* ☾*Closed Mon.*

$$$–$$$$
STEAK HOUSE
SoMa

✕**Acme Chophouse.** Dine here and you'll agree that cows shouldn't eat corn. Grass-fed beef, served up as a filet mignon and tartare, is the specialty at this old-style chophouse next door to the Giants baseball park. The kitchen stocks only naturally-raised local meats and poultry, including a 22-ounce rib eye that's sized to satisfy a sumo wrestler and priced for an emperor. All the familiar chophouse sides—creamed spinach, onion rings, scalloped potatoes—will keep traditionalists smiling. The setting is suitably casual, with lots of wood; TV monitors in the bar area mean no inning is missed. The lunch menu is more casual, with burgers, a crab and shrimp salad, pastrami on rye, and a flatiron steak that won't break the bank. ⊠*24 Willie Mays Plaza, SoMa* ☎*415/644–0242* ⊟*AE, DC, MC, V* ☾*Closed Sun. and Mon. No lunch Sat.*

$$$$
ITALIAN
Van Ness/Polk

✕**Acquerello.** Sometimes you need to pamper yourself, and this is a great place to do it. For years, devotees of chef-owner Suzette Gresham-Tognetti's Italian cooking have been swooning over what emerges from her kitchen: nettle-filled ravioli, potato gnocchi with lamb and beef *ragù*, duck breast with seared escarole. Dinners are prix fixe, with three, four, or five courses and choices within each course. Tognetti also tempts with an eight-course tasting menu ($168, with wine pairings). Co-owner Giancarlo Paterlini oversees the service and the list of Italian wines, both of which are superb. The room, with its vaulted ceiling and pale gold and ocher palette, suits both the refined food and Michelin, which awarded the restaurant one star in 2008. ⊠*1722 Sacramento*

St., Van Ness/Polk ☎415/567–5432 ▭*AE, D, MC, V* ☉*Closed Sun. and Mon. No lunch.*

$$$$ ✕**Ame.** America and Japan, along with France and Italy, converge in
ECLECTIC high style on the plates of chef Hiro Sone. Indeed, his food, from *cha-*
SoMa *wan mushi* (egg custard) with lobster and shiitake and tuna tartare
with sea urchin to pork cheeks with soft polenta, is almost too beautiful to eat. He serves it in an equally stunning, modern space in the
handsome St. Regis, which shelters both hotel guest rooms and condominium residences, including one that Al Gore makes his West Coast
home. Not surprisingly, the space and the plates attract members of the
local—and, some would say, stuffy—elite who know food and have the
means to pay a lofty price for it. ✉*St. Regis Hotel, 689 Mission St.,
SoMa* ☎*415/284–4040* ▭*AE, D, DC, MC, V* ☉*No lunch.*

¢–$ ✕**Andalu.** You can feast on some two dozen globe-circling small plates
ECLECTIC here, from tuna-tartare-filled miniature tacos (just a buck apiece on
Mission Tuesday) and cambozola cheese fondue to curly polenta fries and flatiron steak with Argentine *chimichurri* sauce. Average appetites should
plan on two plates per person. The equally global wine list has dozens
of intriguing offerings and seven carefully assembled flights, tempting
curious palates. The good-looking bi-level North Mission dining room
has a sky-blue ceiling and aquamarine-and-black tables. Save room for
the dessert of doughnut holes and thick hot cocoa topped with whipped
cream. Weekend brunch features a handful of the nighttime classics
plus corned beef hash, eggs Benedict, and French toast. ✉*3198 16th
St., Mission* ☎*415/621–2211* ▭*AE, MC, V* ☉*No lunch.*

¢–$ ✕**Angkor Borei.** Aromatic Thai basil, lemongrass, and softly sizzling
CAMBODIAN chilies perfume this modest neighborhood restaurant, opened by
Mission Cambodian refugees in the late 1980s. The menu includes an array
of curries, salads of squid or cold noodles with ground fish, a crisp,
pork-and-sprout-filled crepe, and lightly curried fish mousse cooked
in a banana leaf. Chicken grilled on skewers and served with mild
pickled vegetables is a house specialty, as are the green papaya salad
and the panfried catfish. Vegetarians will be happy to discover two full
pages of selections. Service is friendly though sometimes languid, so
don't stop here when you're in a hurry. ✉*3471 Mission St., Mission*
☎*415/550–8417* ▭*MC, V* ☉*Closed Tues.*

$$ ✕**Antica Trattoria.** The dining room—pale walls, dark-wood floors, a
ITALIAN partial view of the kitchen—reflects a strong sense of restraint. The
Russian Hill same no-nonsense quality characterizes the authentic Italian food of
owner-chef Ruggero Gadaldi. A small, regularly shifting, honestly
priced menu delivers archetypal dishes such as carpaccio with capers
and Parmesan, *pappardelle* (wide flat noodles) with wild boar, *tagliata
di manzo* (beef fillet slices) with arugula, and panna cotta with fresh
berries. The wine list is fairly priced, and the genial service is polished
but not stiff. ✉*2400 Polk St., Russian Hill* ☎*415/928–5797* ▭*DC,
MC, V* ☉*Closed Mon. No lunch.*

$$$$
SEAFOOD
Financial District

✗ **Aqua.** Quietly elegant, heavily mirrored and bouqueted, and playing mostly to a society crowd, this spot is among the city's most lauded seafood restaurants—Michelin laid two stars at its door—and among the most expensive. The kitchen, known for using exquisite ingredients, assembles beautiful preparations that are seriously fancy but not too fussy: tuna tartare with Moroccan spices, sturgeon and veal cheek bourguignon, Atlantic cod with polenta. Lunch is à la carte, but dinner is a $75 three-course prix-fixe affair with plenty of choice in each category. Lottery winners can opt for the seven-course tasting menu for $55 more. Service is as smooth as silk, desserts are showy, and the wine list is as high-class as the clientele. And if you find the house olive oil particularly tasty, Aqua sells it by the bottle. ✉ *252 California St., Financial District* ☎ *415/956–9662* ⚖ *Reservations essential* ▭ *AE, D, DC, MC, V* ◷ *No lunch weekends.*

$$–$$$
MOROCCAN
Richmond

✗ **Aziza.** Chef-owner Mourad Lahlou's Moroccan food boasts a healthy dose of modernity that keeps locals coming back for his unique flavors. Diners enjoy first courses like spicy lamb sausage with goat's-milk yogurt dipping sauce or a trio of luscious spreads (eggplant, pomegranate-almond, and yogurt-cucumber) with flatbread. The main courses, such as quail with a cumin-orange glaze accompanied with a bread salad, and a fork-tender lamb shank with spiced prunes, tend to be more audacious. The attractive three-room dining area, done in blue, saffron, and white, is a warm, inviting sea of tiles, arches, and candlelight. The wine list is skillfully geared to North African flavors (waiters can advise on the best choices), while cocktail enthusiasts can pick one of 20 inspired potions. ✉ *5800 Geary Blvd., Richmond* ☎ *415/752–2222* ▭ *MC, V* ◷ *Closed Tues. No lunch.*

$$–$$$
SPANISH
Financial District

✗ **B44.** Going to restaurant-lined Belden Place is like visiting your favorite candy store: There are just too many choices. But this spare, modern Spanish restaurant, which draws locals and visitors alike with its Catalan tapas and paellas, won't disappoint. The open kitchen sends out appealing small plates: white anchovies with pears and Idiazabal cheese, sherry-scented fish cheeks, warm octopus with tiny potatoes, and blood sausage with white beans. The paellas, individually served in an iron skillet, bring together inviting combinations such as chicken, rabbit, and mushrooms, or mixed seafood with squid ink. ✉ *44 Belden Pl., Financial District* ☎ *415/986–6287* ▭ *AE, MC, V* ◷ *No lunch weekends.*

$$$–$$$$
AMERICAN
SoMa

✗ **Bacar.** Hidden inside an understated brick-and-glass exterior is one of the city's most wine-savvy restaurants. Oenophiles mustn't forget their reading glasses: Bacar's by-the-glass options, which number about 60, preface an epic-length list of bottles. The food menu is humbler—in size though not price—with a handful of raw-bar options; a nice selection of appetizers, such as wood oven–roasted bone marrow and clams with shoestring potatoes, and half a dozen straightforward mains, like crisp-skinned roasted chicken with chanterelles and an outsized mesquite-grilled rib eye. The tri-level dining room allows for a mix of vantage points. On weekends, conversationalists should ask for a table

CALIFORNIA CUISINE CONTROVERSY

In late 2005, in a culinary op-ed piece in the *New York Times,* San Francisco chef Daniel Patterson, currently of the fashionable **Coi**, accused his local colleagues of a lack of imagination. He charged them with larding their menus with look-alike plates, and he blamed their timid offerings on their allegiance to Alice Waters, the recognized high priestess of California cuisine and, of course, of Berkeley's **Chez Panisse**. Patterson declared that hers was the "only voice speaking out on . . . the mission of that cuisine."

Not surprisingly, many of the assailed toques didn't cower behind their stoves. They came out swinging, loudly denouncing Patterson's characterization of them as cookie-cutter chefs.

This wasn't the first dustup over California cuisine, which was born in the early 1970s. From the beginning, folks have fought over who deserves credit for inventing what has become a highly marketable style. Waters, who opened Chez Panisse in 1971, gets the most votes. But chef Jeremiah Tower, who worked alongside Waters in those early days and later opened San Francisco's once wildly popular but now-shuttered Stars, has his partisans, as does Los Angeles chef Wolfgang Puck, creator of **Spago** restaurants.

What's all the finger-pointing about? First and foremost, California cuisine is about using the best local seasonal ingredients, sustainably raised, in ways that showcase, rather than smother, them. In other words, simplicity, not complexity, rules. But it's also about celebrating the state's cultural diversity, from slipping Thai basil into an Italian sauté to adding lemongrass to a pot of French steamed mussels. Fresh, local, and imaginative are key descriptive words, and a kind of "eat local, think global" ethos drives the kitchen.

Critics insist that though the basic principles are sound, there's too much copycat cuisine—too many warm goat cheese salads, thin-crust pizzas, and grilled fish riding alongside garlic mashed potatoes. Patterson describes it as "comfortable home cooking with no particular point of view," with the minds of its makers taken hostage by whatever Alice Waters says. And nearly everyone agrees that this self-conscious simplicity doesn't come cheap. Dinner for two without wine can easily run $150, making California cuisine the fuel of the elite.

Other pundits insist that chefs like Gary Danko and Michael Mina, both of them California cuisine advocates, are not sheep, but are instead risk takers who tinker constantly in pursuit of new and exciting tastes, and that they're not alone. For now, this culinary rumble is guaranteed to continue, with plenty of partisans arguing both sides. But what's new and what isn't is always relative, as the curiously titled *How to Keep a Husband or Culinary Tactics,* printed in San Francisco in 1872, illustrates. It was the first cookbook written and published in the Golden State, and its authors were already touting the wonders of Northern California's pristine produce.

12

away from the live jazz on the first floor. ⊠*448 Brannan St., SoMa* ☎*415/904–4100* ☐*AE, D, DC, MC, V* ☻*No lunch Sat.–Thurs.*

$$$
FRENCH
Hayes Valley

✕**Bar Jules.** An open kitchen, a counter lined with red-topped stools, a dozen or so small tables, and a generally young crowd are tucked into this cozy, bright eatery on the edge of trendy Hayes Valley. The daily-changing blackboard menu is small and invariably appealing, with dishes like leeks in vinaigrette dressed with sieved hard-cooked egg and capers, a buttery crab omelet, braised short ribs with pureed potatoes, and lamb chops with white beans. Desserts range from lemon tart to butterscotch pudding to apple crisp. Sunday brunch draws a neighborhood crowd to the sunny storefront. On the downside: service can be slow and sketchy, and the sea of hard surfaces can make quiet conversation impossible. ⊠*609 Hayes St., Hayes Valley* ☎*415/621–5482* ⌂*Reservations only for groups of six or more* ☐*AE, MC, V* ☻*No lunch Sun. and Tues. No dinner Sun. Closed Mon.*

$$–$$$
MEDITERRANEAN
Potrero Hill

✕**Baraka.** Partisans of Moroccan fare will enjoy a few of their favorite plates at the cozy Potrero Hill restaurant. Boldly spiced highlights include meatballs with goat's-milk yogurt and lamb *tagine* (traditional meat braise) with cinnamon-scented couscous. Other choices from around the Mediterranean include prosciutto-wrapped dates with Cabrales cheese, seared octopus, warm pistachio-crusted goat cheese, and crisp fries with harissa aioli. Copper-top tables, crimson banquettes, and scores of flickering candles give Baraka an appealing air of mystery. Come before 6:30 Sunday through Wednesday and before 6 the rest of the week and enjoy a three-course prix-fixe supper for under $25. ⊠*288 Connecticut St., Potrero Hill* ☎*415/225–0370* ☐*AE, MC, V* ☻*No lunch.*

$$
ASIAN
Cow Hollow

✕**Betelnut.** Most of the primarily young, hip crowd that packs this Union Street landmark probably don't know what a betel nut is (the seed of an Asian palm, chewed for the mild high it delivers). But they do know they like the pan-Asian cuisine and adventurous drinks (everything from martinis to house-brewed rice beer and sake flights). The menu, divided into big and small plates, noodles, dumplings, and salads, includes chili-crusted calamari, spicy Szechuan green beans, firecracker shrimp with a sizzling sambal dip, and aromatic short ribs with Thai basil and garlic. Lacquered walls, bamboo ceiling fans, and period posters create a comfortably exotic mood that matches the food. Patience is required to cope with long wait times and sluggish service. ⊠*2030 Union St., Cow Hollow* ☎*415/929–8855* ☐*D, DC, MC, V.*

$$
SPANISH
Financial District

✕**Bocadillos.** The name means "sandwiches," but that's only half the story here. You'll find 11 bocadillos at lunchtime: plump rolls filled with everything from serrano ham to Catalan sausage with arugula. But at night, chef-owner Gerald Hirigoyen, who also owns the high-profile Piperade, focuses on tapas, offering some two dozen choices, including a delicious grilled quail, an equally superb pig's trotters with herbs, and calamari with *romesco* (a thick combination of red pepper, tomato, almonds, and garlic) sauce. His wine list is well matched to the food. A youngish crowd typically piles into the modern, red-brick-walled dining space, so be prepared to wait for a seat. A large communal table is a good perch for singles. ✉ *710 Montgomery St., Financial District* ☎ *415/982–2622* ⌖ *Reservations not accepted* ▭ *AE, MC, V* ✆ *Closed Sun. No lunch Sat.*

$–$$
VIETNAMESE
Van Ness/Polk

✕ **Bodega Bistro.** With just one taste of his green papaya salad, you'll be hooked on the inspired cooking of North Vietnam–born Jimmy Kwok. His casual bistro, located on the mildly sketchy edge of the Tenderloin, brims at lunchtime with savvy eaters from Civic Center offices. For dinner, Kwok draws devotees from over the city who come not only for the salad, but also for his roast squab, *bun cha Hanoi* (broiled pork, herbs, rice vermicelli, and lettuce wrapped in rice paper), and salt-and-pepper Dungeness crab with garlic noodles. Kwok punctuates his Asian menu with a handful of French dishes. Cap your meal with crème caramel or a bowl of lemongrass ice cream. ✉ *607 Larkin St., Van Ness/Polk* ☎ *415/921–1218* ▭ *MC, V.*

$$$$
Fodor'sChoice
★
AMERICAN
Embarcadero

✕ **Boulevard.** Two of San Francisco's top restaurant celebrities—chef Nancy Oakes and designer Pat Kuleto—are responsible for this high-profile, high-priced eatery in the magnificent 1889 Audiffred Building, a Parisian look-alike and one of the few downtown structures to survive the 1906 earthquake. Kuleto's Belle Epoque interior and Oakes's sophisticated American food with a French accent attract well-dressed locals and flush out-of-towners. The menu changes seasonally, but count on generous portions of dishes like sweetbreads wrapped in bacon with lobster salad, frog legs with black truffles, pan-roasted petrale sole stuffed with scallop mousse, and suckling pig three ways (belly, chop, loin). Save room (and calories) for one of the dynamite desserts, such as the buttery almond cake with extra-dark hot cocoa ice cream. There's counter seating for folks too hungry to wait for a table. ✉ *1 Mission St., Embarcadero* ☎ *415/543–6084* ▭ *AE, D, DC, MC, V* ✆ *No lunch weekends.*

¢
☻
BURGER
Mission

✕ **Burger Joint.** Cross the threshold here and you're back in the days of sock hops and big Chevy sedans. Dressed in red and turquoise, with checkered floors and comfy booths, the retro Burger Joint serves Niman Ranch beef burgers, thick and creamy milk shakes, big root beer floats, and crisp, stocky fries. Every burger comes with tomatoes, lettuce, onion, and pickles, a toasted sesame bun, and a pile of fries. Cheeseburger partisans can dress up their patties with American, cheddar, Swiss, or Monterey jack. Non–beef eaters can opt for veggie or chicken-breast burgers. ✉ *807 Valenica St., Mission* ☎ *415/824–3494* ▭ *No credit cards.*

$$–$$$
FRENCH
Financial District

✕ **Café Claude.** If you think this place looks like it could be in Paris, you're right. Nearly everything, from the zinc bar and the banquettes to the light fixtures and cinema posters, was shipped from a defunct café in the City of Light to this atmospheric downtown alley. Order a *croque monsieur* or niçoise salad at lunchtime. The francophone kitchen sends out even more French staples for dinner, like escargots, steak tartare, coquilles Saint Jacques, and roast lamb. Stop by Thursday, Friday, and Saturday nights to enjoy live music along with your

12

food. ⊠ *7 Claude La., Financial District* ☎ *415/392–3515* ⊟ *AE, DC, MC, V* ⊘ *No lunch Sun.*

$$–$$$
☾
AMERICAN
Union Sq.

✕**Canteen.** Blink and you'll miss this place. Chef-owner Dennis Leary has transformed this narrow coffee shop into one of the most sought-after dinner reservations in town. The homey place has just 20 counter seats and a quartet of wooden booths. But that's all Leary, with a modest open kitchen and a single assistant, can handle. The dinner menu, which changes often, offers only four first courses, four mains, and three desserts. A typical meal might start with a delicious celery root soup with salt cod and bacon, followed by spice-crusted venison or pan-roasted rockfish with pumpkin seeds, and then a dreamy lemon or vanilla soufflé. On Tuesday night, a three-course prix-fixe menu is in force (no choices within each course) for $38. Because this is a one-man band, your food arrives at a leisurely pace. If a dinner reservation is elusive, try for lunch on weekdays or weekend brunch. ⊠ *Commodore Hotel, 817 Sutter St., Union Sq.* ☎ *415/928–8870* ⚄ *Reservations essential* ⊟ *AE, MC, V* ⊘ *Closed Mon. No lunch Tues. or weekends.*

$$–$$$
☾
ITALIAN
North Beach

✕**Capp's Corner.** One of North Beach's last family-style trattorias, Capp's is steadfastly old-fashioned. The men at the bar still roll dice for drinks, celebrity photos line the walls, and diners sit elbow-to-elbow at long, oilcloth-covered tables. The fare is packaged in bountiful five-course dinners for $20, with the roast lamb a good choice for the main (the tasty osso buco and polenta is $5 more). The food isn't award-winning, but a meal here won't break the bank either. A three-course option, good for smaller appetites—and smaller budgets ($17.50)—includes minestrone, salad, and choice of pasta. For $4 more, you can finish with an order of spumoni. Kids under 10 will be happy with their own menu priced at $13. ⊠ *1600 Powell St., North Beach* ☎ *415/989–2589* ⊟ *AE, DC, MC, V.*

$–$$
LATIN AMERICAN
Mission

✕**Charanga.** It's hard to resist the tropical vibe that weaves its way through this animated tapas depot, with its eclectic mix of Caribbean-inspired flavors. Some tapas stay true to their Spanish ancestry, like patatas bravas, which are twice-fried potatoes with roast-tomato sauce. Others, like fried yucca with chipotle aioli, are a mix of the Old and the New World, and some, like picadillo, Cuban-style minced beef dish studded with green olives and raisins, are firmly rooted on this side of the Atlantic. The dining room, with walls of exposed brick and soothing green, is small and friendly, so grab—or make—some friends, order a pitcher of sangria or a round of margaritas, and enjoy yourselves. ⊠ *2351 Mission St., Mission* ☎ *415/282–1813* ⚄ *Reservations not accepted* ⊟ *AE, D, MC, V* ⊘ *Closed Sun. and Mon. No lunch.*

$$$–$$$$
FRENCH
Potrero Hill

✕**Chez Papa.** France arrived on Potrero Hill with Chez Papa, which delivers food, waiters, and charm that would be right at home in Provence. The modest corner restaurant, with a Mediterranean blue awning, big windows overlooking the street, and a small heated patio, caters to a lively crowd that makes conversation difficult. Small plates include mussels in wine, brandade de morue (salt cod gratin), and caramelized onion tart with anchovies. Big plates range from rack of lamb and salmon with braised endives to homey lamb daube. Leave a bit of space for a typically Gallic crème brûlée or wedge of lemon tart. If you're penny-wise, sit down before six for a three-course prix-fixe supper priced at $25. To accommodate the overflow of Hill residents who have packed this place since Day One, the owners opened the tiny (and more casual) Chez Maman (crepes, burgers with blue cheese, salads) halfway down the block. ⊠ *1401 18th St., Potrero Hill* ☎ *415/255–0387* ▤ *AE, DC, MC, V* ☾ *No lunch Sun.*

$$$–$$$$
FRENCH
Mission

✕ **Chez Spencer.** A semi-industrial neighborhood, with an OfficeMax outlet a nearby neighbor, is an unlikely location for an upmarket French restaurant. Yet that's where you'll find Chez Spencer. Tucked into a former warehouse, it boasts arching beamed ceilings, polished concrete floors, a wood-burning oven, and a steady flow of devotees from all over the city. The menu—foie gras torchon, grilled steak with morels and truffled butter, pan-seared venison, smoked duck-breast salad with a poached egg at its center—is meticulously prepared. The wine list, small and mostly French, is carefully crafted to match the food. There's patio dining, too, with plenty of heaters to keep you warm. A six-course tasting menu will set you back $80, or $120 with wine pairings. The downside of Chez Spencer? The chef needs to tinker with the menu occasionally to keep regulars interested. ⊠ *82 14th St., Mission* ☎ *415/864–2191* ▤ *AE, D, DC, MC, V* ☾ *Closed Sun. No lunch.*

$–$$
☺
AMERICAN
Castro

✕ **Chow.** Wildly popular and consciously unpretentious, Chow is a funky yet savvy diner where soporific standards like hamburgers, pizzas, and spaghetti and meatballs are treated with culinary respect. A magnet for penny pinchers, the restaurant has built its top-notch reputation on honest fare made with fresh local ingredients priced to sell. Salads, pastas, and mains come in two sizes to accommodate big and small appetites, there's a daily sandwich special, and kids can peruse their mini-menu. Because reservations are restricted to large parties, folks hoping to snag seats usually surround the doorway. Come early (before 6:30) or late (after 10) to reduce the wait, and don't even think about leaving without trying the ginger cake with caramel sauce. ⊠ *215 Church St., Castro* ☎ *415/552–2469* ▤ *MC, V.*

$–$$$
AMERICAN
SoMa

✕ **Coco500.** Chef-owner Loretta Keller knows how to change with the times. She shuttered her long-admired Bizou restaurant and reopened in the same spot with this up-to-the-minute small-plates venue. Menu categories like "small starts," "leaf (salads)," and "California dirt (local organic vegetables)" reflect Keller's modern outlook, as do dishes like the "COCOmole taco," which pairs tortilla triangles with beef cheeks and a chili-chocolate sauce. You'll also find duck liver terrine, truffled flatbread, sizzling shrimp, and a signature *vacherin* (crème anglaise, Swiss meringue, coffee ice cream, and chocolate sauce) from Bizou days. For a simpler and smaller sweet ending, order the chocolate-dipped frozen banana. That delicious menu mix pulls in young hipsters and sophisticated oldsters, all cheerfully grazing the menu. ⊠ *500 Brannan St., SoMa* ☎ *415/543–2222* ▤ *AE, MC, V* ☾ *Closed Sun. No lunch Sat.*

$$$$
AMERICAN
North Beach

✕**Coi.** Daniel Patterson, who has made a name for himself both as a chef and as a pundit on contemporary restaurant trends, has had a restless career, but seems to have settled in at this intriguing 50-seat spot on the gritty end of Broadway. Coi (pronounced *kwa*) is really two restaurants. One is a 30-seat formal dining room—ascetic gold-taupe banquettes on two walls—that offers an 11-course tasting menu ($115). The food matches the space in sophistication, with such inspired dishes as nettle soup with ricotta and oxalis flowers, caramelized endive tart, a raviolo filled with a trio of mushrooms, and monkfish with pea shoots and truffle. The menu in the more casual—and more casually priced—lounge is à la carte, with less than a dozen items, including a crisp-skinned roast chicken, a bowl of udon noodles, and slow-cooked pork with shelling beans. ✉373 *Broadway, North Beach* ☎415/393–9000 ♻*No reservations accepted for lounge* ▤*AE, MC, V* ⊘*Closed Sun. and Mon. No lunch.*

$$$
MEDITERRANEAN
Union Sq.

✕**Cortez.** Young, well-dressed hipsters with just-cashed paychecks clog this bright, modern space in the Hotel Adagio. In the past, Cortez was one of the town's premier destinations for small plates, but nowadays the menu is a healthy mix of small and large, and folks don't seem to mind the change. The menu is always in flux—and in recent years, the chef's toque has been, too—but you can find such dishes as shrimp with creamy crab rice and pork short ribs with cauliflower mousse under small plates, and black cod with wilted rapini and duck breast with buttered chestnuts under big plates. Cap off the meal with sugar and spice beignets with chocolate fondue and you'll go home happy. If you're in a rush, enjoy crispy fries with harissa-spiked aioli chased by a martini in the bar. ✉*Hotel Adagio, 550 Geary St., Union Sq.* ☎415/292–6360 ▤*AE, MC, V* ⊘*No lunch.*

$$–$$$
Fodor'sChoice
★
ITALIAN
Mission

✕**Delfina.** "Irresistible." That's how countless die-hard fans describe Delfina. Such wild enthusiasm has made patience the critical virtue for anyone wanting a reservation here. The interior is comfortable, with hardwood floors, aluminum-top tables, a tile bar, and a casual, friendly atmosphere. The menu changes daily, but among the usual offerings are salt cod *mantecato* (whipped with olive oil) with fennel flatbread; grilled squid with warm white bean salad; spaghetti with tomatoes and garlic, and roast chicken with trumpet mushrooms. On warm nights, try for a table on the outdoor heated patio. The storefront next door is home to pint-size Pizzeria Delfina. ✉*3621 18th St., Mission* ☎415/552–4055 ♻*Reservations essential* ▤*MC, V* ⊘*No lunch.*

¢–$$
INDIAN
Mission

✕**Dosa.** Like Indian food but crave more than tandoori chicken and naan? Dosa is your answer. This temple of south Indian cuisine, done in cheerful tones of tangerine and turmeric, serves not only the large,

12

thin savory pancake for which it is named, but also curries, uttapam (open-faced pancakes), and various starters, breads, rice dishes, and chutneys. You can select from about 10 different dosa fillings, ranging from traditional potatoes, onions, and cashews to nontraditional cheddar, mozzarella, and onion. Each comes with tomato and fresh coconut chutneys and sambar (lentil curry) for dipping. Lamb curry with fennel and potatoes and prawn coconut masala are popular, as are starters like Chennai chicken (chicken marinated in yogurt and spices and lightly fried), fried chile-dusted prawns, and mung sprout salad. The wine and beer lists are top drawer and both include some Indian labels. ✉ *995 Valencia St. at 21st St., Mission* ☎*415/642–3672* ⚑*Reservations only for five or more* ⊟*AE, D, MC, V* ⊘*No lunch.*

$$$–$$$$
ITALIAN
SoMa

✕**Ducca.** Nowadays some of the city's best restaurants are in hotel dining rooms, and Ducca, resting smartly in a busy neighborhood of museums, movie houses, and theater spaces, is part of that welcome trend. Start off right with an aperitif and little fried rice balls concealing truffled cheese, or a handful of fried green olives stuffed with Gorgonzola. Follow that up with chef Richard Corbo's dreamy lobster sformato (a custardy soufflé) or rustic—and delicious—whole-wheat pasta tossed with sardines and caramelized fennel. Mains are split nearly evenly between meats and fish, including chicken riding alongside mascarpone polenta flecked with chanterelles and peas. Just looking to rest your feet? Join the after-work crowd at the alfresco bar (wisely heated) for a drink and a snack. ✉ *50 Third St., in the Westin San Francisco Market Street, SoMa* ☎*415/977–0271* ⊟*AE, D, DC, MC, V.*

¢–$$
VIETNAMESE
Inner Sunset

✕**Dragonfly.** Refined Vietnamese fare draws droves of locals to this modestly decorated, bi-level restaurant each night. They return for intriguing dishes like rice and frogs' legs steamed in bamboo, fork-tender pork and egg in coconut juice, and crunchy lotus root salad. Even the rice offerings go beyond the ordinary, with four types offered: coconut, Hainan (cooked in chicken stock with ginger and garlic), white, or brown jasmine. Wash down the meal with one of three refreshing Vietnamese beers, and cap it all off with a cup of inky coffee. Lunchtime brings more casual dishes, including *pho,* rice plates, and noodles. The staff makes up for its inexperience and for the slow arrival of your order with a cheerful attitude. ✉ *420 Judah St., Inner Sunset* ☎*415/661–7755* ⊟*AE, MC, V.*

$$$–$$$$
STEAK HOUSE
North Beach

✕**El Raigón.** Gauchos—and beef eaters from everywhere—will feel right at home in this Argentine steak house, complete with cowhide bar and open wood-beam ceiling. The range-raised beef steaks are expertly charred over a wood and charcoal fire; diners add the traditional *chimichurri* sauce to taste. Truly serious carnivores will want to start with beef empanadas, grilled chorizo, or blood sausage. Sautéed spinach and grilled asparagus are good sides, pancakes filled with *dulce de leche* caramel is a decadent dessert, and the Argentine Malbecs go with everything. ✉ *510 Union St., North Beach* ☎*415/291–0927* ⊟*AE, D, DC, MC, V* ⊘*Closed Sun. No lunch.*

$$$–$$$$
STEAK HOUSE
Embarcadero

✕**Epic Roasthouse.** "Epic" describes it all: the outsized dining room, the seven-foot flywheel and pulley that sits in the middle of it (an homage to old bayside pump houses), the mile-wide bay view, the huge metal fireplace, the hearty slabs of meat and, alas, the prices. This is the latest venture, along with the seafood-themed Waterbar right next door, of famed restaurant architect-owner Pat Kuleto. Chef Jan Birnbaum, who made his name first in San Francisco and later in the Napa Valley, is in charge of putting $54 porterhouses and $25 burgers on the fire. For sides, he has opted for sautéed spinach with garlic confit over classic creamed spinach, and truffled cauliflower over scalloped potatoes. If you don't have a Texas-sized wallet but still want an Epic experience, head upstairs to the Quiver bar and graze from the bar menu. ✉*369 Embarcadero between Folsom and Harrison, Embarcadero* ☎*415/369–9955* ▤*AE, D, DC, MC, V* ⊘*No lunch weekends.*

$$$$
SEAFOOD
Union Sq.

✕**Farallon.** Sculpted jellyfish chandeliers, kelp-covered columns, and sea-urchin lights give this swanky Pat Kuleto–designed restaurant a decidedly quirky look. But there's nothing quirky about chef Mark Franz's impeccable seafood, which reels in serious diners from coast to coast. The menu changes daily, but rotating dishes include prawn and scallop shui mai (dumplings) with oyster mushrooms, cornmeal-crusted fried squid with risotto nero (squid-ink risotto), California halibut with chestnut spaetzle, and, for meat eaters, braised beef cheeks with foie gras and lobster. If you want to enjoy the surroundings but not pay the price, you can take a seat at the newly installed French-style oyster bar and fill up on lobster sliders, crab cakes, french fries with aioli, and more from the cheaper bar menu. Or, if you're feeling a bit more flush, dine before 6:30 on a three-course prix-fixe supper for $48. ✉*450 Post St., Union Sq.* ☎*415/956–6969* ▤*AE, D, DC, MC, V* ⊘*No lunch.*

$$–$$$$
ITALIAN
Mission

✕**Farina.** Locals shed a tear when the longtime Anna's Danish Cookies closed in this spot, and cookie lovers are still mourning. But anyone who craves the Ligurian fare of northern Italy—the home of pesto, focaccia, and delicate pastas—is cheering the arrival of Farina. Here, they fill up on such iconic dishes as focaccia di Recco (paper-thin pizzalike focaccia sandwiching melted stracchino cheese), "handkerchief" pasta dressed with pesto, corzetti ("stamped" pasta rounds) with tomato meat sauce, and raviolini stuffed with borage and ricotta. Those with slim pocketbooks should stay away from the pricier secondi and instead choose from the regularly changing array of Ligurian carbs and small dishes of sautéed greens, roasted peppers, or other vegetables. ✉*3560 18th St. at Dearborn, Mission* ☎*415/565–0360* ▤*AE, D, DC, MC, V* ⊘*No lunch weekends.*

$$$$
FRENCH
SoMa

✕**Fifth Floor.** A clubhouse for well-off diners, this swanky spot is tucked away in the Palomar Hotel. Dressed up in the bold Art Moderne look of the 1930s and 1940s, the dining room is the stylish setting for chef Laurent Manrique's menu that celebrates the kitchens of southwest France, including such dishes as polenta and rabbit stew with hazelnuts, poached chicken with foie gras stuffing, and roasted pork shoulder with boudin (blood sausage), apples, and wilted spinach. For dessert, there's a luscious creamed-filled almond cake with black cherry marmalade. Dining here is like a trip to France, so allow for plenty of time—and money. ⊠*Palomar Hotel, 12 4th St., SoMa* ☎*415/348–1555* ▤*AE, DC, MC, V* ⊘*Closed Sun. No lunch.*

$$$$ **✕Fleur de Lys.** The creative cooking of chef-owner Hubert Keller has
FRENCH brought every conceivable culinary award to this romantic spot, includ-
Union Sq. ing a Michelin star. His three-, four-, and five-course prix-fixe menus (each course with many choices) include plenty of foie gras, squab, lobster, and truffles to satisfy palates geared to fancy French plates. The dining room, with its dramatic tented ceiling of 900 yards of draped and swathed fabric, is an ideal setting for the food. These days, some regulars have grumbled that Keller is paying more attention to his growing gourmet burger bar and steak house chain than his San Francisco dining room, citing less-than-stellar service and stagnant menu evidence of their claims. ⊠*777 Sutter St., Union Sq.* ☎*415/673–7779* ⌂*Reservations essential, jacket required* ▤*AE, D, DC, MC, V* ⊘*Closed Sun. No lunch.*

$$–$$$ **✕Florio.** San Franciscans have always had a weakness for little French
FRENCH bistros, which helped make Florio a hit from the day it opened. It had
Lower Pacific all the elements: a space that looked like a Paris address, classic char-
Heights cuterie and roast chicken, and reasonably priced French wines. Since then, this neighborhood favorite has picked up an Italian accent, with ravioli stuffed with butternut squash lining up next to steamed mussels and *steak frites* on the menu. Save room for the kitchen's crème caramel, a neighborhood favorite. The room can get noisy, so don't come here hoping for a quiet tête-à-tête. ⊠*1915 Fillmore St., Lower Pacific Heights* ☎*415/775–4300* ▤*AE, MC, V* ⊘*No lunch.*

$$ **✕Fog City Diner.** This fully chromed destination is a far cry from the
☾ no-frills diner of Edward Hopper's "Nighthawks." Fog City has all the
AMERICAN trappings of a luxurious railroad car: wood paneling, huge windows,
Embarcadero and comfortable booths. The menu is both classic and contemporary and includes memorable mac-and-cheese made with Gouda, ham, and peas; fried salt-and-pepper squid with chili-lime sauce; red curry mussel stew; thick burgers with fries; a towering lemon-meringue pie; and a sinful rum coconut layer cake with cream cheese frosting. Locals complain of too many out-of-towners, but plenty of folks who call San Francisco home fill the booths at lunch and dinner. ⊠*1300 Battery St., Embarcadero* ☎*415/982–2000* ▤*D, DC, MC, V.*

$$–$$$ **✕Foreign Cinema.** Forget popcorn. In this hip, loftlike space, "dinner
☾ and a movie" become one joyous event. Classic and contemporary
AMERICAN films like Fellini's Nights of Cabiria and Schnabel's The Diving Bell
Mission and the Butterfly are projected on a wall in a large inner courtyard while you're served oysters on the half shell, house-cured sardines, grilled squid with peppers and garlic, or steak with Argentine salsa. Fussy filmgoers should call ahead to find out what's playing and arrive in time for a good seat. Kids aren't forgotten, with celery and carrot sticks, pasta with butter and cheese, and two scoops of ice cream for

just $7. The weekend brunch brings big crowds. ✉*2534 Mission St., Mission* ☎*415/648–7600* ▭*AE, MC, V* ⊘*No lunch.*

$$$$
Fodor's Choice
★
AMERICAN
Fisherman's
Wharf

✕**Gary Danko.** Be prepared to wait your turn for a table behind chef Gary Danko's legion of loyal fans, who typically keep the reservation book chock-full here. The cost of a meal ($65–$96) is pegged to the number of courses, from three to five. The menu, which changes seasonally, may include pancetta-wrapped frogs' legs, seared foie gras with Fuji apples, lemon-crusted yellowfin tuna with roasted pepper, and quail stuffed with wild mushrooms and foie gras. A diet-destroying chocolate soufflé with two sauces is usually among the desserts. The wine list is the size of a small-town phone book, and the banquette-lined room, with beautiful wood floors and stunning (but restrained) floral arrangements, is as memorable as the food. ✉*800 N. Point St., Fisherman's Wharf* ☎*415/749–2060* ⌖*Reservations essential* ▭*D, DC, MC, V* ⊘*No lunch.*

$–$$$
☾
CHINESE
Chinatown

✕**Great Eastern.** Don't be tempted to order a Szechuan or Beijing dish here or you'll leave unhappy. This is a Cantonese restaurant, and that means fresh, simply prepared seafood, quickly cooked vegetables and meats, clear soups, and no fiery chilies. Tanks filled with crabs, black bass, catfish, shrimp, and other freshwater- and saltwater creatures occupy a corner of the street-level main dining room. Look to them for your meal, but check prices, as swimming seafood isn't cheap. Kids will find their Chinese-restaurant favorites here: stir-fried noodles, cashew chicken, fried rice. Avoid the basement dining room, which is brightly lighted but also claustrophobic. Toward midnight, Chinese night owls drop in for a plate of noodles or a bowl of *congee* (rice porridge). ✉*649 Jackson St., Chinatown* ☎*415/986–2550* ▭*AE, MC, V.*

$$–$$$
VEGETARIAN
Marina

✕**Greens Restaurant.** Owned and operated by the San Francisco Zen Center, this nonprofit vegetarian restaurant gets some of its fresh produce from the center's famous Green Gulch organic farm. Floor-to-ceiling windows give diners a sweeping view of the marina and the Golden Gate Bridge. Despite the lack of meat, hearty dishes like the Vietnamese yellow curry with cashew jasmine rice are designed to satisfy. Other standouts include thin-crust pizza with braised greens, sun-dried tomatoes, and three cheeses and fresh pea ravioli with saffron butter. An à la carte menu is offered on Sunday and weeknights, but on Saturday a $49 four-course prix-fixe dinner is served. Sunday brunch is a good time to watch boaters on the bay. A small counter just inside the front door stocks sandwiches, soups, and sweets for easy takeout. ✉*Bldg. A, Fort Mason, enter across Marina Blvd. from Safeway, Marina* ☎*415/771–6222* ▭*AE, D, MC, V* ⊘*No lunch Sun and Mon.*

$$$–$$$$
STEAK HOUSE
Van Ness/Polk

✕**Harris'.** Red-meat connoisseurs will appreciate this old-school restaurant, home to some of the best dry-aged steaks from corn-fed beef in town, including pricey Japanese Kobe rib eye. Harris' ages all of its beef for 21 days; proof of the process is visible from the street through a window where large cuts can be seen hanging. There are a dozen steaks to choose from, plus grilled chops, chicken, and a couple of seafood dishes for anyone who wants to steer clear of beef. Don't overlook the classic sides: creamed spinach, caramelized onions, and sautéed mushrooms. If you're a martini drinker, take this opportunity to enjoy an artful example of the legendary cocktail. ⊠*2100 Van Ness Ave., Van Ness/Polk* ☎*415/673–1888* ▭*AE, D, DC, MC, V* ⊘*No lunch.*

$$–$$$
SEAFOOD
Hayes Valley

✕**Hayes Street Grill.** Arrive here just as local music lovers are folding their napkins and heading off for the 8 PM curtain at the nearby opera house and you'll snag a table and some perfectly fresh seafood. Much of the fish—Pacific bluenose, yellowfin tuna, swordfish—is simply grilled and served with a choice of sauces from beurre blanc to tomato salsa. A pile of crisp, thin Belgian frites rides alongside the grilled offerings. Brass coat hooks, white tablecloths, a long bar, and a mix of banquettes and tables define the traditional San Francisco look of this three-decade-old seafood stronghold. Folks who eschew water-based fare will be happy to know grass-fed beef steak and thick pork chops are on the menu. ⊠*320 Hayes St., Hayes Valley* ☎*415/863–5545* ▭*AE, D, MC, V* ⊘*No lunch weekends.*

$–$$
MIDDLE EASTERN
Van Ness/Polk

✕**Helmand Palace.** In late 2007, this popular restaurant moved from a scruffy block of Broadway in North Beach (a rock slide forced its exit) to a smaller Van Ness address and added "Palace" to its name, but kept everything else—authentic Afghan cooking and a handsomely outfitted dining room—intact. Highlights of the reasonably priced menu include *aushak* (leek-filled ravioli served with yogurt and ground beef), pumpkin with yogurt-and-garlic sauce, and any of the lamb dishes, in particular the kebab strewn with yellow split peas and served on Afghan flatbread. Basmati rice pudding, perfumed with cardamom and pistachio, is an exotic—and satisfying—finish. ⊠*2424 Van Ness Ave., Van Ness/Polk* ☎*415/362–0641* ▭*AE, MC, V* ⊘*No lunch.*

$–$$$
SEAFOOD
Embarcadero

✕**Hog Island Oyster Company.** Hog Island, a thriving oyster farm in Tomales Bay, north of San Francisco, serves up its harvest at this attractive raw bar and retail shop in the busy Ferry Building. The U-shaped counter and a handful of tables seat no more than three dozen diners, who come here for impeccably fresh oysters or clams (also from Hog Island) on the half shell. Other mollusk-centered options include a first-rate oyster stew, clam chowder, and Manila clams with white beans. The bar also turns out what is arguably the best grilled cheese sandwich (with three artisanal cheeses on artisanal bread) this side of Wisconsin. You need to eat early, however, as the bar closes at 8 on weekdays and 6 on weekends. Happy hour, 5 to 7 on Monday and Thursday, is an oyster lover's dream: sweetwaters for a buck apiece and beer for $3.50. ⊠*Ferry Bldg., Embarcadero at Market St., Embarcadero* ☎*415/391–7177* ▭*AE, MC, V* ⊘*Closed Sun.*

$–$$
☺
AMERICAN
Castro

✕**Home.** If you're hungry for home cooking but don't want to stir the pots yourself, this big, noisy eatery is a good solution. Service can be sluggish, but the fresh, all natural ingredients and classic fare compensate heartily. Happiest at Home are comfort-food seekers who dream of macaroni and cheese, corn dogs, sloppy joes with coleslaw, Cobb salad, and meat loaf and potatoes. The lively Backyard Bar, a heated rear patio, roars until late in the night. On weekends, there's ham and

CLOSE UP

Eating with Kids

Kids can be fussy eaters, but parents can be, too, so picking places that will satisfy both is important. Fortunately, plenty of excellent possibilities exist all over town.

If you're downtown for breakfast, stop at the venerable **Sears Fine Foods** (⊠ *439 Powell St., near Post St.* ☎ *415/986–0700*), home of "the world-famous Swedish pancakes." Eighteen of the silver-dollar-size beauties cost less than a movie ticket. Nearby in Chinatown, **City View Restaurant** (⊠ *662 Commercial St., near Kearny St.* ☎ *415/398–2838*) serves a varied selection of dim sum, with tasty pork buns for kids and more exotic fare for adults.

Even if you skip the art at SFMOMA, you can still sit down in its adjoining **Caffè Museo** (⊠ *151 3rd St., between Mission and Howard Sts.* ☎ *415/357–4000*), where the kitchen offers a kids' pizza built from house-baked focaccia, mozzarella cheese, and tomato sauce. Try **Pluto's** (⊠ *627 Irving St., between 7th and 8th Sts.* ☎ *415/753–8867*) after a visit to Golden Gate Park. Small kids love the chicken nuggets, which arrive with good-for-you carrot and celery sticks, whereas bigger kids will likely opt for one of the two-fisted sandwiches. Everyone will want a s'more for dessert. **Barney's Gourmet Burgers** (⊠ *3344 Steiner St., near Union St.* ☎ *415/563–0307*), not far from Fort Mason and the Exploratorium, caters to older kids and their parents with mile-high burgers and giant salads. But Barney's doesn't forget "kids under 8," who have their own menu featuring a burger, an all-beef frank, chicken strips with ranch dressing, and more.

Nearly everybody loves pasta, and **Pasta Pomodoro** (⊠ *655 Union St., near Powell St.* ☎ *415/399–0300*) in North Beach, provides plenty of plates to choose from, including a kids' only menu that let's youngsters match up any one of three pasta shapes with five different sauces.

The Mission has dozens of no-frills taco-and-burrito parlors; especially worthy is the bustling, friendly **La Corneta** (⊠ *2731 Mission St., between 23rd and 24th sts.* ☎ *415/252–9560*), which has a baby burrito. Banana splits and hot fudge sundaes are what **St. Francis Fountain** (⊠ *2801 24th St., at York St.* ☎ *415/826–4200*) is known for, along with its vintage decor. Opened in 1918, it recalls the early 1950s, and the menu, with its burgers, BLT, grilled cheese sandwich, and chili with corn bread, is timeless. In Lower Haight, the small **Rosamunde Sausage Grill** (⊠ *545 Haight St., between Steiner and Fillmore Sts.* ☎ *415/437–6851*) serves just that—a slew of different sausages, from Polish to duck to weisswurst (Bavarian veal). Grilled onions, sauerkraut, and chili are extra, and since there are only six stools, plan on takeout. Carry your meal to nearby Duboce Park, with its charming playground.

Finally, both kids and adults love to be by the ocean, and the **Park Chalet** (⊠ *1000 Great Hwy., at Fulton St.* ☎ *415/386–8439*), hidden behind the two-story Beach Chalet, offers pizza, sticky ribs, a big banana split, and, on sunny days, outdoor tables and a wide expanse of lawn where kids can play while parents relax.

–Sharon Silva

eggs, brisket hash, and serious Bloody Marys for brunch-goers. Every night, the thrifty can sit down to the early-bird special—three courses and a glass of wine for $12—while the late-night crowd can dine until midnight. ⊠*2100 Market St., Castro* ☎*415/503–0333* ▤*AE, D, MC, V* ⊗*No lunch.*

$$
ITALIAN
Noe Valley

✕**Incanto.** The people who run Incanto are thoughtful. They filter, chill, and carbonate the very good local tap water and serve it in eco-friendly reusable glass carafes. They use sustainably grown and harvested ingredients produced by local farmers. They even grow many of their own herbs in their rooftop garden. That same thoughtfulness extends to a daily-changing menu that invariably includes tasty dishes not found at any other restaurant in town: pig's trotter with foie gras, bacon, and pear; cardoons with lemon and anchovy; bucatini (thick, spaghetti-like pasta) with cured tuna, egg, and parsley; bay leaf panna cotta. The consciously rustic interior—faux stone walls, tile floors, dark-wood tables and sideboards—is the perfect setting for the inspired fare, while the wine list of obscure Italian makes everything taste even better. ⊠*1550 Church St. at Duncan, Noe Valley* ☎*415/641–4500* ▤*AE, MC, V* ⊗*No lunch.*

$–$$
INDIAN
Lower Haight

✕**Indian Oven.** This Victorian storefront draws diners from all over the city who come for the tandoori specialties—chicken, lamb, breads. The *saag paneer* (spinach with Indian cheese) and *bengan bartha* (roasted eggplant with onions and spices) are also excellent. On Friday and Saturday nights, famished patrons overflow onto the sidewalk as they wait for open tables. If you try to linger over a *lassi* on one of these nights, you'll invariably be hurried along by a waiter. For better service, come on a slower weeknight. ⊠*233 Fillmore St., Lower Haight* ☎*415/626–1628* ▤*AE, D, DC, MC, V* ⊗*No lunch.*

¢–$$
FRENCH
Marina

✕**Isa.** A tiny storefront dining room, a talented chef, and a heated, candlelighted patio—Isa has all the trappings of a great night out whether it's the first date or the 50th. The menu of French-inspired tapas changes seasonally but regularly offers such crowd-pleasers as seared foie gras, flatiron steak topped with blue cheese, and potato-wrapped sea bass. Portions are petite, so hearty appetites will run up a good-size tab. A good way to keep your costs down is to opt for the two-course prix-fixe menu offered Monday through Thursday for just $22. The wine list, smartly crafted and including plenty of by-the-glass choices, complements the food. ⊠*3324 Steiner St., Marina* ☎*415/567–9588* ▤*MC, V* ⊗*Closed Sun. No lunch.*

$$$$
Fodor'sChoice
★
AMERICAN
Hayes Valley

✕**Jardinière.** A special anniversary? An important business dinner? A fat tax refund? These are the reasons one books a table at Jardinière. The restaurant takes its name from its chef-owner, Traci Des Jardins, and the sophisticated interior, with its eye-catching oval atrium and curving staircase, fills nightly with locals and out-of-towners alike. The equally sophisticated French-cum-Californian dining-room menu, served upstairs in the atrium, changes daily but regularly includes such high-priced adornments as caviar, foie gras, and truffles. Downstairs, the lounge menu, with smaller plates and smaller prices ($9 to $33), is

12

ideal for when you want to eat light while visiting with friends or tame your hunger before the opera or symphony. Cheese lovers will appreciate the wide variety of choices—both old world and new—housed in the glassed-in cheese-aging chamber in the rear of the restaurant. ✉ *300 Grove St., Hayes Valley* ☎ *415/861–5555* ⚐ *Reservations essential* ➼ *AE, DC, MC, V* ✆ *No lunch.*

$$–$$$$
FRENCH
Financial District

✗ **Jeanty at Jack's.** Chef Philippe Jeanty, who made a name for himself in the wine country (first at Domaine Chandon and then at his Bistro Jeanty and Père Jeanty), oversees this brass-and-wood, three-story brasserie located in what was Jack's restaurant, a San Francisco destination for steaks and chops since 1864. The food today is as French as the chef, with cassoulet, *steak frites,* rabbit terrine, steak tartare, and *coq au vin* among the offerings. The tomato soup with puff pastry will make you forget the bland canned stuff of your childhood. Business types stream in at lunch; dinnertime is quieter. This is the place to bring anyone who really eats what the French eat: pigs' feet, lambs' tongues, veal kidneys—they're all here. ✉ *615 Sacramento St., Financial District* ☎ *415/693–0941* ➼ *AE, MC, V* ✆ *No lunch weekends.*

$–$$
RUSSIAN
Inner Richmond

✗ **Katia's.** This bright Richmond District gem serves Russian food guaranteed to make former Moscovites smile. Order the deep purple borscht, crowned with a dollop of sour cream. Small dishes of eggplant caviar, marinated mushrooms, blini and smoked salmon, and meat- or vegetable-filled *piroshki* are delicious ways to start a meal. Follow up with hearty beef Stroganoff, delicate chicken cutlets, or homey *pelmeni,* meat-filled dumplings in broth. If you can put together a group, make a reservation for one of Katia's afternoon tea parties, complete with sweets and savories and tea dispensed from a handsome samovar. ✉ *600 5th Ave., Inner Richmond* ☎ *415/668–9292* ➼ *AE, D, MC, V* ✆ *Closed Mon. and Tues. No lunch weekends.*

$$–$$$$
GREEK
Financial District

✗ **Kokkari.** The interior of this classy restaurant won't recall homey tavernas just steps from the Acropolis. But its menu will satisfy your craving for good Greek taverna food—albeit at steak house prices. Most savvy diners start off with a trio of dips—eggplant, yogurt, and cucumber, and *taramasalata,* fish roe pureed with olive oil and bread crumbs. Main courses showcase such Athenian standards as moussaka, a mixed seafood grill, braised lamb shank, and grilled lamb chops. A bar menu of small plates—crispy smelts, feta-stuffed phyllo, grilled octopus—satisfies weekday afternoon customers. Desserts like semolina custard wrapped in phyllo, and yogurt with walnuts and honey, make for a light, sweet finish. ✉ *200 Jackson St., Financial District* ☎ *415/981–0983* ➼ *AE, D, DC, MC, V* ✆ *Closed Sun. No lunch Sat.*

$–$$
Fodor'sChoice
★
☯
ITALIAN
North Beach

✗ **L'Osteria del Forno.** A staff chattering in Italian and seductive aromas drifting from the open kitchen make customers who pass through the door of this modest storefront, with its sunny yellow walls and friendly waitstaff, feel as if they've stumbled into a homey trattoria in Italy. The kitchen produces small plates of simply cooked vegetables, a few pastas, some daily specials, milk-braised pork, a roast of the day, creamy polenta, and thin-crust pizzas—including a memorable "white" pie topped with porcini mushrooms and mozzarella. At lunch try one of North Beach's best focaccia sandwiches. ⊠ *519 Columbus Ave., North Beach* ☎ *415/982–1124* ⊟ *No credit cards* ⊗ *Closed Tues.*

$$
ITALIAN
Noe Valley

✕ **La Ciccia.** Chef Massimiliano Conti quickly won a loyal following after opening this charming neighborhood trattoria serving Sardinian food. The island's classics are all represented—seafood salad dressed with olive oil and lemon, seared lamb chops, pasta with *bottarga* (salted mullet roe); and *fregola* (pebble-shaped pasta) with an aromatic tomato sauce—and recommended. The space came with a pizza oven, so Conti also turns out a quartet of respectable thin-crusted pies. Opt for one of the Sardinian gems on the large wine list. ⊠ *291 30th St., Noe Valley* ☎ *415/550–8114* ⊟ *MC, V* ⊗ *Closed Mon. No lunch.*

$$$$
FRENCH
Russian Hill

✕ **La Folie.** This small, *très* Parisian establishment, has long been a favorite of Francophiles (and anyone who loves foie gras). The restaurant, outfitted in warm woods and white linens, is smartly designed to let the cuisine take center stage. Choose from well-apportioned prix-fixe menus of three, four, or five courses. The dishes, like pancetta-wrapped venison loin and a terrine of lobster, are artfully presented and always delicious. Vegetarians will be happy to discover a menu of their own. Such rarefied preparation is costly, of course, so you may want to save La Folie for a special occasion. ⊠ *2316 Polk St., Russian Hill* ☎ *415/776–5577* ⚖ *Reservations essential* ⊟ *AE, D, DC, MC, V* ⊗ *Closed Sun. No lunch.*

$$
SPANISH
Marina

✕ **Laïola.** San Franciscans never seem to tire of tapas, as the crowds—mostly young—at this new, smart, compact Marina outpost of Spanish small plates prove. Try for a seat at the long copper-topped bar or at a window table, and then contemplate the seasonally shifting menu that boasts some two dozen tempting tapas, such as lamb meatballs with cumin yogurt, chorizo-stuffed Medjool dates, potatoes with pepper-spiked aioli, roasted mushrooms with a poached egg, olive oil–poached albacore salad, chickpea croquettes, and grilled octopus. Most regulars seem to skip the four large plates but save room for pan con chocolate, a creamy chocolate pudding sprinkled with sea salt and olive oil. The nearly all-Spanish wine list includes some well-priced options. ⊠ *2031 Chestnut St., Marina* ☎ *415/346–5641* ⊟ *AE, D, MC, V* ⊗ *No lunch.*

¢–$
⊙
LATIN-AMERI-
CAN
Mission

✕ **La Santaneca de la Mission.** Lots of El Salvadorans live in the Mission, and here they find the *pupusa,* a stuffed cornmeal round that is more or less the hamburger of their homeland. It usually comes filled with beans, cheese, or meat—sometimes in combination—and is eaten with seasoned shredded cabbage. The kitchen at this friendly, family-run place also makes the more unusual rice-flour pupusa, as well as other dishes popular in Central America, including fried plantains, seafood soup, tamales filled with chicken or pork, *chicharrones* (fried pork skins), and yucca. Accompany your meal with *horchata,* a cooling rice-based drink flavored with cinnamon. ⊠ *2815 Mission St., Mission* ☎ *415/285–2131* ⊟ *MC, V.*

12

$$–$$$$
VIETNAMESE
Union Sq.

✕**Le Colonial.** This is high-style Vietnamese food served up in a French-colonial time machine: stamped tin ceiling, period photographs, slow-moving fans, and tropical plants. Local society types come for the sea bass steamed in banana leaves, tiger prawns in coconut curry, and lamb chops with grilled eggplant salad. They also like to pick from among the big selection of fried or fresh appetizer rolls, filled with everything from shredded duck to Dungeness crab. Downstairs are two large and rather formal dining rooms. Anything goes upstairs in the lively lounge: you can eat (so-called Vietnamese street food at indoor prices—$9 to $14), you can dance (Wednesday through Saturday nights), or you can just sip a cocktail at the bar and unwind. ✉ *20 Cosmo Pl., Union Sq.* ☎ *415/931–3600* ☰ *AE, D, MC, V* ✆ *No lunch.*

$$–$$$
PERUVIAN
Mission

✕**Limón.** Cooks in Peru and Ecuador have long argued over which country invented *ceviche,* a dish consisting of raw fish marinated in citrus juices. Most diners at Limón would probably line up with the Peruvians after eating the myriad, delicious versions here (try the impeccably fresh halibut or prawn with red pepper varieties), all accompanied by yucca and corn, and prepared by chef-owner Martin Castillo. They also like the *empanadas,* flaky pastries filled with minced beef, olives, and raisins; the hearty *lomo saltado,* beef strips sautéed with onions, tomatoes, and potatoes; the *arroz con mariscos,* mixed seafood with saffron rice; and the crispy whole snapper with coconut rice. Choose from a list of Peruvian beers for sipping with your meal. ✉ *524 Valencia St., Mission* ☎ *415/252–0918* ☰ *MC, V* ✆ *No lunch Mon.*

¢–$
♻
MEXICAN
Mission

✕**Los Jarritos.** A *jarrito* is an earthenware cup used for drinking tequila and other beverages in Mexico. You'll see plenty of these small traditional mugs hanging from the ceiling and decorating the walls in this old-time, sun-filled, family-run restaurant. At brunch, try the hearty *chilaquiles,* made from day-old tortillas cut into strips and cooked with cheese, eggs, chilies, and sauce. Or order eggs scrambled with cactus or with chicharrones (crisp pork skins) and served with freshly made tortillas. Soup offerings change daily, with Tuesday's albondigás (meatballs) comfort food at its best. On weekend evenings adventurous eaters may opt for *birria,* a spicy goat stew, or *menudo,* a tongue-searing soup made from tripe, calf's foot, and hominy. The latter is a time-honored hangover cure. Bring plenty of change for the jukebox loaded with Latin hits. ✉ *901 Van Ness Ave., Mission* ☎ *415/648–8383* ☰ *MC, V.*

> **WORD OF MOUTH**
>
> "One of my favorite places is LuLu. I guess you would call it Californian with a definite Provençal twist. Not specifically seafood but they can do wondrous things with sole and trout on the rotisserie (the menu changes daily, so not every night). The best thin-crust pizzas, too. Excellent salads. Extensive wine list. The place is a very large open-plan, loft-like, warehousey space with an enormous wood-burning oven. It's located on Folsom just west of 4th Street, in SoMa."
>
> –bluestar

$$–$$$
MEDITERRANEAN
SoMa

✕**LuLu.** In its early years, LuLu was a magnet for dot-commers, who jammed the place every night. When

12

the high-tech industry buckled, LuLu cooled, but never lost its appeal. Nowadays many of the same uncomplicated dishes—fried artichokes, fennel, and lemon slices; mussels roasted in an iron skillet; wood-oven roasted poultry, meats, and shellfish; a small selection of pizzas and pastas—fuel a more mixed clientele. There is a well-supplied raw bar, and main-course specials include a rotisserie-cooked main course that changes daily; Friday brings a succulent suckling pig. Sharing dishes is the custom here. Wine drinkers will appreciate the long list of choices by the glass. When LuLu is packed, service occasionally suffers. ⊠*816 Folsom St., SoMa* ☎*415/495–5775* ▤*AE, D, DC, MC, V.*

$–$$$
AMERICAN
Mission

✕**Luna Park.** It's a tight fit on weekend nights in this clangorous American bistro in the trendy Mission district. The youngish crowd is here to sip mojitos and Long Islands and nosh on steamed mussels or goat cheese fondue with apple wedges. Most of the mains are homey—mac-and-cheese, barbecued spareribs with fries and slaw, grilled hangar steak—and easy on the pocketbook. An order of s'mores includes cups of melted chocolate and marshmallows and a handful of house-made graham crackers to customize the campfire classic. On weekends, a slew of popular brunch dishes are added to the weekday lunch list of salads and sandwiches. ⊠*694 Valencia St., Mission* ☎*415/553–8584* ▤*MC, V.*

$–$$$
JAPANESE
Japantown

✕**Maki.** *Wappa-meshi,* rice topped with meat or fish and steamed in a bamboo basket, is the specialty at this diminutive restaurant featuring the refined Kansai cuisine of Osaka and Kyoto. The sashimi, sukiyaki, and freshwater eel on rice in a lacquer box are also first-rate. Everything is served on beautiful tableware, from the smallest *sunomono* salad to a big lunchtime *donburi,* protein-topped rice. Maki stocks an impressive assortment of sakes, which it serves in exquisite decanters. If you don't know your sake, the helpful staff will lead you in the right direction. ⊠*Japan Center, Kinokuniya Bldg., 1825 Post St., Japantown* ☎*415/921–5215* ▤*MC, V* ⊗*Closed Mon.*

$$$$
FRENCH
Nob Hill

✕**Masa's.** Although the toque has been passed to several chefs since the death of founding chef Masataka Kobayashi, this 25-year-old restaurant, with its chocolate-brown walls, white fabric ceiling, and red-silk-shaded lanterns, is still one of the country's most celebrated food temples. Chef Gregory Short, who worked alongside Thomas Keller at the famed French Laundry for seven years, is at the helm these days, and his tasting menus of six and nine courses ($90–$150, including a vegetarian option) are pleasing both diners and critics. The food is classic French with some contemporary touches and all the dishes are laced with fancy ingredients, leaving diners struggling to choose between pan-seared foie gras with poached mango and chilled foie gras with rhubarb "cobbler." ⊠*Hotel Vintage Court, 648 Bush St., Nob Hill* ☎*415/989–7154* ⚛*Reservations essential, jacket required* ▤*AE, D, DC, MC, V* ⊗*Closed Sun. and Mon. No lunch.*

$$–$$$
MIDDLE EASTERN
North Beach

✕**Maykadeh.** Although it sits in an Italian neighborhood, this authentic Persian restaurant has a large and faithful following of homesick Iranian émigrés. Lamb dishes with rice are the specialties, served in an attractive but not showy dining room. Among the many appetizers are traditional dishes such as eggplant with mint sauce and spiced lamb tongue. Along with the requisite—and tasty—kebabs, the restaurant serves a variety of poultry and meats marinated in olive oil, lime juice, and herbs. Anyone looking for a hearty, traditional main dish should order *ghorme sabzee,* lamb shank braised with a bouquet of Middle Eastern spices. Give yourself plenty of time here, as service occasionally slows to a crawl. ⊠*470 Green St., North Beach* ☎*415/362–8286* ▤*MC, V.*

$$$$
Fodor's Choice
★
AMERICAN
Union Sq.

✗**Michael Mina.** Decorated in celadon and ivory with stately columns and a vaulted ceiling, this elegant space is a match for chef Michael Mina's highly refined fare. His three-course prix-fixe (multiple choices for each course) includes a trio of tastes on each plate—for example, three preparations of quail for a first (quail thigh meat on marinated red beets, quail breast on beet greens and soft polenta, and quail breast on fried polenta resting in a pool of puréed golden beets), or "chocolate in three guises" for a dessert. Folks who prefer one taste rather than triple bites can opt for one of Mina's signature dishes, such as black mussel soufflé. Deep-pocketed diners can splurge on a six-course tasting menu. ⊠*335 Powell St., in Westin St. Francis Hotel, Union Sq.* ☎*415/397–9222* ⚑*Reservations essential* ▤*AE, D, DC, MC, V* ☾*No lunch.*

¢–$$
☾
JAPANESE
Japantown

✗**Mifune.** Thin brown soba and thick white udon are the stars at this long-popular North American outpost of an Osaka-based noodle empire. A line regularly snakes out the door, but the house-made noodles, served both hot and cold and with a score of toppings, are worth the wait. Seating is at wooden tables, where diners of every age can be heard slurping down big bowls of such traditional Japanese combinations as *nabeyaki udon,* wheat noodles topped with tempura, chicken, and fish cake; and *tenzaru,* cold noodles and hot tempura with gingery dipping sauce served on lacquered trays. ⊠*Japan Center, Kintetsu Bldg., 1737 Post St., Japantown* ☎*415/922–0337* ▤*AE, D, DC, MC, V.*

¢
☾
MEXICAN
Embarcadero

✗**Mijita Cocina Mexicana.** Famed local chef Traci Des Jardins is the culinary powerhouse behind two of the city's best-known white-tablecloth restaurants, Jardinière and Acme Chophouse. But to honor her Latin roots, she chose Mexican hot chocolate over martinis when she opened this casual taquería and weekend brunch spot. The tacos feature handmade corn tortillas and fillings like *carnitas* (slow-cooked pork), mahimahi, and *carne asada* (grilled strips of marinated meat). The superb meatball soup and Oaxacan chicken tamales are served daily, and the weekend brings such favorites as *huevos rancheros,* fried corn tortillas topped with fried eggs and salsa. Kid-size burritos (beans and cheese) and quesadillas will keep your niños happy. Seating is simple— wooden tables and benches—but a perfect perch for watching gulls on the bay. Plan to eat dinner early; Mijita closes at 7 on weekdays, 8 on weekends. ⊠*Ferry Bldg., Embarcadero at Market St., Embarcadero* ☎*415/399–0814* ▤*MC, V* ☾*No dinner Sun.*

12

$$–$$$
VEGETARIAN
Union Sq.

✕**Millennium.** This big, wood-lined dining room in the Savoy Hotel is *the* gourmet dining destination for visiting vegans. The seasonal menu of "animal-free" dishes made with organic ingredients includes pink grapefruit and endive salad with sweet and spicy cashews, seared rice cake with red coconut curry root vegetables, and maple-glazed smoked tempeh (fermented soybean cake) with garlic-horseradish mashed potatoes. All of the dishes are dressed up with bold flavors that won't disappoint omnivores. Come dessert, you may find the chocolate almond midnight (mocha chocolate filling in an almond-cashew crust) hard to resist. A long list of organic wines is available, and a tasting menu ($65) is offered for when your wallet is full. ⊠*Savoy Hotel, 580 Geary St., Union Sq.* ☎*415/345–3941* ☰*AE, D, DC, MC, V* ⊗*No lunch.*

¢
INDIAN
Financial District

✕**Naan 'N' Curry.** You will find no frills here—and minimal service and housekeeping—but you will find food fresh off the fire at rock-bottom prices. This is just one location in a local minichain of Indian-Pakistani eateries that cater primarily to starving students, poorly paid office workers, local South Asians, and anyone else who likes spicy food but doesn't give a damn about ambience. The tandoor-fired chicken *tikka masala,* bhindi (okra with onion and spices), and tongue-scorching tandoori lamb chops are favorites. The Bollywood music is too loud, but the naan is the size of a hubcap and the chai (milk) tea is free. ⊠*533 Jackson St., Financial District* ☎*415/693–0449* ☰*MC, V.*

$–$$$
AMERICAN
Haight

✕**Nopa.** In 2006, North of the Panhandle became the city's newest talked-about neighborhood in part because of the big, bustling Nopa, which is cleverly named after it. This casual space, with its high ceilings, concrete floor, long bar, and sea of tables, suits the high-energy crowd of young suits and neighborhood residents that fills it every night. They come primarily for the rustic fare, like an irresistible flatbread topped with bacon, caramelized leeks, and cheese; duck with farro (an ancient cereal grain similar to wheat) and vegetables; smoky, crisp-skinned rotisserie chicken; and a juicy grass-fed hamburger with thick-cut fries; and pecan pie with salted caramel ice cream. But they also love the lively spirit of the place. Unfortunately, that buzz sometimes means raised voices are the only way to communicate with fellow diners. ⊠*560 Divisidero St., Haight* ☎*415/864–8643* ☰*MC, V* ⊗*No lunch.*

¢–$$
JAPANESE
Japantown

✕**O Izakaya Lounge.** San Francisco has been hit by a mini-tsunami of izakaya spots, Japanese-style pubs where folks gather to drink and share small plates. The good-looking O Izakaya delivers that tradition plus big flat-screen TVs so that no one misses an inning. The walls are covered with oversized baseball cards, and seating is a mix of booths and tall communal tables. The menu is a wild ride of noodles (soba, yam), skewers (pork belly, hamachi belly, chicken), tempura, dumplings, salads, raw and cooked fish—even burgers. Sake aficionados will find plenty to choose from, including a trio of flights, plus there's lots of beer, shochu (a distilled spirit made from sweet potato, rice, or barley; similar to vodka), and cocktail choices to ensure no one goes thirsty. ⊠*1625 Post St., in the Hotel Kabuki, Japantown* ☎*415/614–5431* ☰*AE, D, DC, MC, V* ⊗*No lunch weekdays.*

$$–$$$$
AMERICAN
Embarcadero

✕**One Market.** A giant among American chefs, Bradley Ogden runs an upscale mini-restaurant chain that stretches from Marin County to San Diego. This large space with a bay view and a grown-up ambience is his well-known San Francisco outpost. (He also boasts a steak house in the downtown Westfield Centre.) The two-tier dining room seats 170—many of them suits brokering deals—and serves a seasonal, wonderfully homey yet imaginative menu that might include tender bacon-wrapped pork tenderloin with dandelion greens, potato-crusted petrale sole, and duck breast with black trumpet mushrooms. Hearty appetites will appreciate the three-course market menu for just $45. Folks who want only a small sweet to finish can choose from a half dozen mini-desserts, such as chocolate toffee almond cake, mint chip ice cream bar, or butterscotch pudding. The wine list includes the best California labels, many by the glass. ⊠*1 Market St., Embarcadero* ☎*415/777–5577* ♠*Reservations essential* ▭*AE, DC, MC, V* ⊗*Closed Sun. No lunch Sat.*

¢–$$
AMERICAN
SoMa

✕**Orson.** Edgy California cuisine—that's what chef Elizabeth Falkner, who made eating cupcakes fashionable at her popular Citizen Cake in Hayes Valley, has dubbed the mostly small-plate fare at Orson, her newest venture. This self-proclaimed edginess translates into some off-beat combinations, such as short ribs, spinach, and espresso; butterfish brûlée, caviar, and watercress; and smoked fish, black rice, and bacon. The stunning two-story space, an old warehouse done up with a circular marble bar, an eclectic mix of dining spaces, soaring ceilings, and catwalks, would be right at home in Tribeca. Don't bring a healthy appetite here unless you bring a fat wallet, too. Or, stop in for some duck-fat french fries and a snazzy cocktail or a fanciful Falkner dessert with coffee to enjoy the lively scene without squandering your rent. ⊠*508 Fourth St. at Bryant, SoMa* ☎*415/777–1508* ▭*AE, MC, V* ⊗*Closed Sun. No lunch.*

¢–$$
VIETNAMESE
Van Ness/Polk

✕**Pagolac.** Savvy diners know that Pagolac serves a great "seven-way beef" dinner, the classic south Vietnamese feast of seven different beef dishes, from soup to salad to spring rolls and more, for an unbelievable $16 per person. This is also a good place for lotus root salad with pink shrimp, all kinds of rolls (both fried and fresh), aromatic clay pots, and noodles or rice topped with protein of all types—pork, beef, shrimp, chicken—in all forms—fried, shredded, grilled. The narrow space is attractively decorated in dark wood tables and chairs and a few nice pieces of Vietnamese art, and the service, though sometimes a little ragged, is always friendly. Of course, such low prices and good food haven't remained a secret, so come before six or after nine to avoid a long wait for a table. ⊠*655 Larkin St., Van Ness/Polk* ☎*415/776–3234* ▭*No credit cards* ⊗*Closed Mon. No lunch.*

¢–$$
☺
AMERICAN
Inner Sunset

✕**Park Chow.** What do spaghetti-and-meatballs, Thai noodles with chicken and shrimp, and big burgers have in common? They're all on the eclectic comfort food menu at Park Chow, and offered at unbeatable prices. This neighborhood favorite is also known for its desserts: fresh-fruit cobblers and ginger cake with pumpkin ice cream are standouts. In cool weather, there's a roaring fire in the dining room fireplace;

in warm weather, get there early to snag an outdoor table. Up early? You can sit down to breakfast on weekdays and brunch on weekends. The original location is in the Castro neighborhood. ⊠ *1240 9th Ave., Inner Sunset* ☎ *415/665–9912* ▤ *MC, V.*

$$–$$$
ITALIAN
Financial District

✕ **Perbacco.** With its long marble bar and open kitchen, this brick-lined two-story space oozes big-city charm. The arrival of skinny, brittle bread sticks is the first sign that the kitchen understands the cuisine of northern Italy, specifically Piedmont. And if the breadbasket doesn't convince you, try the antipasto of house-made cured meats or burrata (cream-filled mozzarella) with peppers and anchovies, the delicate *agnolotti dal plin,* veal-stuffed pasta with a cabbage-laced meat sauce, or *pappardelle* with full-flavored short rib *ragù.* The clientele, a mix of business types and Italian food aficionados, appreciates the big, smart wine list along with the superb food. ⊠ *230 California St., Financial District* ☎ *415/955–0663* ▤ *AE, D, DC, MC, V* ⊗ *Closed Sun. No lunch Sat.*

¢–$
VIETNAMESE
Inner Richmond

✕ **Pho Hoa Clement.** The menu at this homey Formica-and-linoleum spot is big and remarkably cheap. You can order everything from sandwiches and salads to rice dishes and noodle plates. But the soups are what shine, from the two dozen varieties of *pho,* rice noodles in beef broth, to a dozen types of *hu tieu,* seafood and pork noodle soups. All of them are served in three sizes, small, medium, and large, with the sizes separated by just 50¢ and no bowl skimpy. Regulars, many of whom hail from Southeast Asia, favor the shrimp, fish ball, and pork slices soup with clear noodles and the special combo *pho* with rare steak, well-done brisket, tendon, and tripe. ⊠ *239 Clement St., Inner Richmond* ☎ *415/379–9008* ▤ *MC, V.*

$$–$$$
SPANISH
Embarcadero

✕ **Piperade.** Longtime San Francisco chef Gerald Hirogoyen serves a French Basque menu full of the rustic dishes of his childhood. Among them are *piquillo* peppers stuffed with salt cod, foie gras with quince paste, *pipérade* (cooked peppers and tomatoes served with serrano ham and poached egg), warm sheep's milk cheese-and-ham terrine, and grilled lamb chops marinated in thyme and sherry vinegar. Try a Basque wine from the impressive list and don't miss the featherweight orange-blossom beignets. Service in the typically packed dining room is professional without being stuffy. Hirogoyen has also opened a small café and take-out operation around the corner. ⊠ *1015 Battery St., Embarcadero* ☎ *415/391–2555* ▤ *AE, D, MC, V* ⊗ *Closed Sun. No lunch Sat.*

$$–$$$
FRENCH
Financial District

✕ **Plouf.** Plouf is a gold mine for mussel lovers, with seven preparations to choose from. Among the best are *marinière* (white wine, garlic, and parsley) and one combining coconut milk, lime juice, and chili. Add a side of the skinny fries and that's all most appetites need. The menu changes seasonally and includes roast lamb and steak to satisfy any unrepentant

> **WORD OF MOUTH**
>
> "You want 'funky'? Try the Clement Street area, which abounds with great budget restaurants, at least two on every block. Vietnamese, Thai, Peruvian, Korean, Burmese, Chinese, Argentinean, Russian, Indian—you name it. Cool bars, too." –LucieV

12

carnivores. Many of the appetizers—oysters on the half shell, calamari with fennel tempura, tuna tartare—stick to seafood, as well. The tables are squeezed together in the bright, lively dining room, so you might share in neighboring conversations. On temperate days and nights, try for one of the outdoor tables. ☒*40 Belden Pl., Financial District* ☎*415/986–6491* ☰*AE, MC, V* ⊘*Closed Sun. No lunch Sat.*

¢–$$
ASIAN
Haight

✕**Poleng Lounge.** At once a restaurant, nightclub, and tearoom, this captivating space hosts a young, diverse crowd that is happy to graze on Poleng's two dozen modern pan-Asian small plates. The food delivers a satisfying mix that keeps you ordering more: panfried vegetable-filled dumplings dusted with green tea powder, spicy-sweet adobo chicken wings, crab noodles, and crispy salt-and-pepper squid with green chili sauce. No one goes thirsty here, with dozens of cocktails, teas (including alcohol-infused teas), sakes, and wines to choose from. The dining space, with a communal table, batik accents, and water gently flowing down a limestone-tile wall, is comfortably separated from the nightclub, which doesn't tune up until 10. ☒*1751 Fulton St., Haight* ☎*415/441–1751* ☰*MC, V* ⊘*Closed Mon. No lunch.*

$$$–$$$$
ITALIAN
Lower Pacific
Heights

✕**Quince.** This is no place for anyone living paycheck to paycheck. In one of San Francisco's most fashionable residential neighborhoods, this small, smart eatery, housed in a former apothecary, caters to folks with fat pocketbooks who can make reservations weeks in advance. Michael Tusk, who has cooked at the legendary Chez Panisse and Oliveto, oversees the kitchen, where he uses only the finest local ingredients to turn out his Italian-inspired cuisine. The menu changes daily, featuring a delicious selection of seasonal dishes, such as saffron chitarra (thin pasta) with artichokes and squid; ricotta-stuffed ravioli with nettle pesto; or petrale sole roasted on fig leaves. The wine list is top-notch but pricey (the $35 corkage means you won't save much by bringing your own bottle), and the service is professional and friendly. ☒*1701 Octavia St., Lower Pacific Heights* ☎*415/775–8500* ⌗*Reservations essential* ☰*AE, MC, V* ⊘*Closed Mon. No lunch.*

$–$$$
⟳
CHINESE
Chinatown

✕**R&G Lounge.** The name conjures up an image of a dark, smoky bar with a piano player, but this Cantonese restaurant is actually as bright as a new penny. On the lower level (entrance on Kearny Street) is a no-tablecloth dining room that's packed at lunch and dinner. The classy upstairs space (entrance on Commercial Street) is a favorite stop for Chinese businessmen on expense accounts and special-occasion banquets. The street-level room on Kearny is a comfortable spot to wait for a table to open. A menu with photographs helps you pick from the many wonderful, sometimes pricey, always authentic dishes, such as salt-and-pepper Dungeness crab, roast squab, and shrimp-stuffed tofu. You can sip a lychee- or watermelon martini while waiting for your table. ☒*631 Kearny St., Chinatown* ☎*415/982–7877 or 415/982–3811* ☰*AE, D, DC, MC, V.*

$$–$$$
AMERICAN
Mission

✕**Range.** The name sounds strictly down-home, but the place looks and feels big city. Just across the threshold is a full bar stocked with the best bottles—and plenty of people to appreciate them. An open

12

kitchen with a line of tables opposite comes next, and then the dining room furnished with roomy banquettes. The compact, changing menu is a nice mix of homey and high-end, with raw yellowfin with citrus and fennel oil sharing space with coffee-rubbed pork shoulder on hominy grits. On the sweeter side, you'll find a memorable Meyer lemon tart with anise cream and a bittersweet chocolate soufflé. Service is smooth—informative but not gushy—in both the dining room and the bar. Adventurous cocktail-drinkers will want to dip into the specialty drinks menu before dinner. ⊠*842 Valencia St., Mission* ☎*415/282–8283* ⊟*MC, V* ⊘*No lunch.*

$$$
FRENCH
Union Sq.

✕**Restaurant Jeanne D'Arc.** When San Franciscans want a big, bourgeois French dinner, but their wallets hold only enough for a top-end main course, they head to Restaurant Jeanne D'Arc, quietly tucked into the lower level of the charming Cornell Hotel de France. Surrounded by faux 15th-century tapestries and fresh flowers is the largest collection of Joan of Arc memorabilia in the United States, so says the management. Dig into a four-course supper for $29.25, with a dozen main course options, like rabbit in white wine, duck confit, or filet mignon with mushroom sauce ($4 extra). For dessert there's apple tart or Grand Marnier soufflé, capping off a meal that you might find in a small town in Provence. ⊠*Cornell Hotel de France, 715 Bush St., Union Sq.* ☎*415/421–3154* ⊟*AE, D, DC, MC, V* ⊘*Closed Sun. No lunch.*

$–$$$
AMERICAN
Lower Haight

✕**RNM.** A small, glamorously lighted bar, a big LCD screen, and tablefuls of well-heeled hipsters make RNM look more like a cozy dinner house in New York's SoHo than in the endearingly scruffy Lower Haight. The menu, which changes seasonally, is divided into "small" and "larger" plates and delivers American food with French and Italian accents. In cooler months, you might find carrot soup with mint oil, grilled hearts of romaine with Fuji apples and blue cheese, and venison loin on kohlrabi gratin. The pizzas ($14) are generally good, as are the molten chocolate cake and butterscotch pot de crème. Portions can be petite, so plan on at least two small plates per person. Folks watching their pennies know to come before 7 for the $28 three-course prix-fixe dinner. ⊠*598 Haight St., Lower Haight* ☎*415/551–7900* ⊟*MC, V* ⊘*Closed Sun. and Mon. No lunch.*

$$–$$$$
ITALIAN
North Beach

✕**Rose Pistola.** This busy spot is named for one of North Beach's most revered barkeeps, while the food celebrates the neighborhood's early Ligurian settlers. The menu changes daily, but a large assortment of antipasti—grilled octopus with butter beans and arugula; bruschetta with asparagus, prosciutto, and truffle oil—and pizzas from the wood-burning oven are favorites, as are the cioppino and the fresh fish of the day, served in various ways. A big bar area opens onto the sidewalk, and an exhibition kitchen lets you keep an eye on your order. Even though the kitchen has had trouble holding onto a good chef and the service sometimes arrives with attitude, the crowds keep coming. ⊠*532 Columbus Ave., North Beach* ☎*415/399–0499* ⊟*AE, D, DC, MC, V.*

Coffee with a Shot of Local Flavor

North Beach may have the highest coffee profile, but fantastic brews can be found all over town. Tear yourself away from Columbus Avenue and head to Hayes Valley's **Blue Bottle Coffee** (⊠ 315 Linden St., near Gough St. ☎ 415/252–7535), a modest kiosk where the organic beans (no more than two days from the roaster) are ground for each cup and the espresso is automatically *ristretto*—a short shot. (Although traditionalists stick to the quirky kiosk, in early 2008 Blue Bottle opened a "proper café" downtown in the newly minted Mint Plaza.) In the Mission District, the owners of the inviting **Ritual Coffee Roasters** (⊠ 1026 Valencia, between 21st and 22nd Sts. ☎ 415/641–1024) have plunked their roaster in middle of the café, so you know where your beans—usually single-origin, rather than a blend—were roasted when you order your cap or latte. While you're sipping your inky strong cup at friendly **Farley's** (⊠ 1315 18th St., at Texas ☎ 415/648–1545), a neighborhood institution on sunny Potrero Hill,

you can play chess, check out the eclectic magazine selection, or catch up on the local gossip. Cubans are serious coffee drinkers, and **Café Lo Cubano** (⊠ 3401 California St., in Laurel Village ☎ 415/831–4383), with its *cafecito* (strong, sweet espresso) and other coffee drinks and grilled Cuban sandwiches, is the perfect introduction to a venerable tradition. In the Lower Haight, sun seekers grab an outside table at **Café du Soleil** (⊠ 200 Fillmore St., at Waller ☎ 415/934–8637) and sip bowls of café au lait brewed from organic beans with their morning croissant. And anyone looking for a real cup of joe in a bare-bones pine shack should join the savvy dock workers, carpenters, and young suits at the 80-year-old **Red's Java House** (⊠ Pier 30, between Embarcadero and Bryant St. ☎ 415/777–5626), where the coffee typically follows a cheeseburger and a Bud and the gorgeous view of the East Bay is priceless.

–Sharon Silva

$$–$$$
☺
ITALIAN
Cow Hollow

✕ **Rose's Café.** Sleepy-headed locals turn up at Rose's for the breakfast pizza of ham, eggs, and fontina; house-baked scones and muffins; or soft polenta with mascarpone and jam. Midday is time for a roasted chicken and fontina sandwich; pizza with mushrooms, feta, and thyme; or pasta with clams. Evening hours find customers eating their way through more pizza and pasta, a sirloin steak, or maybe steamed mussels. Seating is in comfortable booths, at tables, and at a counter. At the outside tables, overhead heaters keep you toasty when the temperature dips. Expect long lines for Sunday brunch. ⊠ 2298 Union St., Cow Hollow ☎ 415/775–2200 ▭ AE, D, DC, MC, V.

$$$–$$$$
AMERICAN
Financial District

✕ **Rubicon.** Robin Williams and Robert De Niro were among the first backers of this clubby, cherrywood-lined restaurant, part of the Drew Nieporent empire, but this is no Hollywood-style hot spot. And even though good chefs have come and gone, the kitchen always seems to be in talented hands. The loyal clientele—mostly older suits, male and female—appreciates the sophisticated after-work bar atmosphere, topnotch (though pricey) food, and the big, smart wine list. The seasonal menu—crispy spiced quail with lemon confit, beef short ribs with roasted mushrooms, clementine financier with olive oil ice cream—suits Rubicon's understated glamour. Try for a seat in the handsome downstairs room; the upstairs space is plainer. ✉ *558 Sacramento St., Financial District* ☎ *415/434–4100* 🖃 *AE, D, DC, MC, V* ⊘ *Closed Sun. No lunch Mon., Tues., or Thurs.–Sat.*

12

$$$
AMERICAN
SoMa

✕**Salt House.** A boisterous crowd—coworkers at the end of the day, folks in from the avenues, conventioneers from nearby Moscone Center—packs this high-ceilinged, brick-lined dining space that once housed a printing press. Rusted girders, chandeliers fashioned from old postcard racks, and water poured from vintage milk bottles set a casual mood. The small plates, like crisp shrimp atop spicy green beans, almonds, and serrano ham, are so appealing that most diners find it hard to move to the mains. Such flawed logic means missing out on a first-rate roast chicken with preserved lemon and garlic. Single diners can grab a seat at the big communal table. ✉ *545 Mission St., SoMa* ☎ *415/543–8900* 🖃 *AE, MC, V* ⊘ *No lunch weekends.*

$–$$
☾
CHINESE
Inner Sunset

✕**San Tung No. 2.** Many of the best chefs in Beijing's imperial kitchens hailed from China's northeastern province of Shandong. San Franciscans, with or without imperial ancestry, regularly enjoy dishes of the same province at this bare-bones storefront restaurant. Specialties include steamed dumplings—shrimp and leek dumplings are the most popular—and hand-pulled noodles, in soup or stir-fried. Among the typical accompaniments are a salad of jellyfish, seaweed, or sliced cucumbers and a plate of cold, poached chicken marinated in Shaoxing wine. Parents and kids regularly fight over platters of dry-fried chicken wings. To get a table without a wait, come before or after the noon rush. ✉ *1031 Irving St., Inner Sunset* ☎ *415/242–0828* 🖃 *MC, V.*

$$$
ITALIAN
Union Sq.

✕**Scala's Bistro.** Smart leather-and-wood booths, a pressed-tin ceiling, a menu of Italian (and a few French) dishes, a steady hum of activity—it's hard not to like the big-city feel of this hotel dining room at breakfast, lunch, and dinner. Fritto misto of shrimp, squid, and fennel, rigatoni with duck bolognese sauce, and salmon with buttermilk mashed potatoes are among the evening choices. The room is open late, making it a welcome dessert destination—with sweet successes like burnt caramel *panna cotta* and chocolate I.V. (mousse, pecan crust, gelato, sauce)—after the theater. ✉ *Sir Francis Drake Hotel, 432 Powell St., Union Sq.* ☎ *415/395–8555* 🖃 *AE, D, DC, MC, V.*

$$–$$$$
VIETNAMESE
Embarcadero

✕**Slanted Door.** If you're looking for homey Vietnamese food served in a down-to-earth dining room at a decent price, *don't* stop here. Celebrated chef-owner Charles Phan has mastered the upmarket, Western-accented Vietnamese menu. To showcase his cuisine, he chose a big space with sleek wooden tables and chairs, white marble floors, a cocktail lounge, a bar, and an enviable bay view. Among his popular dishes are green papaya salad, cellophane crab noodles, chicken clay pot, and shaking beef (tender beef cubes with garlic and onion). Alas, the crush of fame means that no one speaking in a normal voice can be heard. To avoid the midday and evening crowds (and to save some bucks), stop in for the afternoon-tea menu (spring rolls, grilled pork over rice noodles), or visit Out the Door, Phan's take-out counter around the corner from the restaurant. ⊠ *Ferry Bldg., Embarcadero at Market St., Embarcadero* ☎ *415/861–8032* ⚓ *Reservations essential* ▤ *AE, MC, V.*

$$–$$$$
AMERICAN
Pacific Heights

✗ **Spruce.** One of the hottest reservations in town from the day it opened, Spruce caters to the city's social set, with the older crowd sliding into the mohair banquettes in the early hours and the younger set taking their places after eight. The large space, a former 1930s auto barn, shelters a high-style dining room and a more casual bar-cum-library lounge, and the menu, which boasts burgers and foie gras, beer and Champagne, is served in both. Charcuterie, bavette steak with bordelaise sauce and duck-fat fries, and boudin blanc with sauerkraut reflect the French slant of the modern American menu. If you can't wrangle a table, stop in at the take-out café next door, which carries not only sandwiches, salads, and pastries but also anything from the dining room menu to go. ⊠ *3640 Sacramento St., Pacific Heights* ☎ *415/931–5100* ⚓ *Reservations essential* ▤ *AE, D, DC, MC, V* ☻ *No lunch weekends.*

$$
ITALIAN
Lower Pacific
Heights

✗ **SPQR.** If you know your Italian history, you know this acronym roughly translates to the senate and people of Rome—and in this case, the food, too. Brought to you by the same team that operates the Marina's wildly popular A16, SPQR is a casual, friendly spot—bare-topped tables, open kitchen, old travel posters on the walls—with a dedicated neighborhood following of all ages. Of course, that dedication usually means a long wait for a table. The loyalists come here for the nearly 20 antipasti (hot, cold, and fried), half a dozen pastas, and quartet of mains. Share a selection of antipasti (three for $18, five for $28), move on to spaghetti carbonara (eggs, bacon, and pecorino) or amatriciana (tomatoes and bacon), and finish with almond milk granita and you'll feel like the Coliseum could be just outside. ⊠ *1911 Fillmore St., Lower Pacific Heights* ☎ *415/771–7779* ⚓ *Reservations not accepted* ▤ *AE, MC, V* ☻ *No lunch weekends.*

$–$$
GERMAN
Hayes Valley

✗ **Suppenküche.** Nobody goes hungry—and no beer drinker goes thirsty—at this lively, hip outpost of simple German cooking in the trendy Hayes Valley corridor. When the room gets crowded, which it regularly does, strangers sit together at unfinished pine tables. The food—bratwurst and red cabbage, potato pancakes with house-made applesauce, meat loaf, sauerbraten, schnitzel, strudel—is tasty and easy on the pocketbook, and the imported brews are first-rate. There's also a popular Sunday brunch, with appealing fare such as gravlax with mustard-dill sauce and pancakes with brandied raisins. ⊠ *601 Hayes St., Hayes Valley* ☎ *415/252–9289* ▤ *AE, MC, V* ☻ *No lunch.*

¢–$$
Fodor'sChoice
★
SEAFOOD
Van Ness/Polk

✗ **Swan Oyster Depot.** Here is old San Francisco at its best. Half fish market and half diner, this small, slim seafood operation, open since 1912, has no tables, only a narrow marble counter with about a dozen and a half stools. Most people come in to buy perfectly fresh salmon, halibut, crabs, and other seafood to take home. Everyone else—locals and out-of-towners—hops onto one of the rickety stools to enjoy a bowl of clam chowder—the only hot food served—a dozen oysters, half a cracked crab, a big shrimp salad, or a smaller shrimp cocktail. Come early or late to avoid a long wait. ✉*1517 Polk St., Van Ness/Polk* ☎*415/673–1101* ▭*No credit cards* ⊘*Closed Sun. No dinner.*

$$–$$$
SEAFOOD
Financial District

✕**Tadich Grill.** Locations and owners have changed more than once since this old-timer started as a coffee stand on the waterfront in 1849, but the crowds keep coming. Generations of regulars advise that simple grills, sautés, and panfries are the best choices. Try the cioppino during crab season (November to May), and the Pacific halibut between January and May. Happily, the old-fashioned house-made tartar sauce doesn't change with the seasons. There's counter seating, a few tables, and private booths (complete with a bell to summon the waiter), and a long line of business types at noon is inevitable. The crusty, white-coated waiters are a throwback to another time, and the old-school bartenders serve up martinis as good as the mollusks. ✉*240 California St., Financial District* ☎*415/391–1849* ▭*MC, V* ⊘*Closed Sun.*

$$–$$$
MEDITERRANEAN
Cow Hollow

✕**Terzo.** With its zinc tapas bar, fireplace, big communal table, and mix of leather banquettes and oak tables, Terzo has what it takes to pull in the neighborhood social set and everyone else who appreciates expertly prepared Mediterranean fare. Although the restaurant debuted with a small-plates menu, it has since added entrées to the mix. On the compact, seasonally shifting menu, you might find creamy hummus and pita, pricey but good black truffle and scrambled egg bruschetta, chicken spiedini, and sea bass with garbanzos and romesco sauce. But a plate of seriously addictive onion rings is available year-round. The pricey wine list is loaded with interesting vintners and varietals. Choosing from a handful of aperitifs—Lillet, Dubonnet, sherry, vermouth—is a good way to start your meal. ✉*3011 Steiner St., Cow Hollow* ☎*415/441–3200* ▭*AE, D, DC, MC, V* ⊘*No lunch.*

$–$$
THAI
Lower Haight

✕**Thep Phanom.** Long ago, local food critics and restaurant-goers began singing the praises of Thep Phanom. The tune hasn't stopped, except for an occasional sour note on rising prices. Duck is deliciously prepared in several ways—atop a mound of spinach, in a fragrant curry, minced for salad. Seafood (in various guises) is another specialty, along with warm eggplant salad, stuffed chicken wings, spicy beef salad, fried quail, and rich Thai curries. The lengthy regular menu is supplemented by a list of daily specials, which makes it only harder to make a decision. At least you'll be pondering your choices in comfortable surroundings: the cozy dining room is lined with Thai art and artifacts that owner Pathama Parikanont has collected over the years. ✉*400 Waller St., Lower Haight* ☎*415/431–2526* ▭*AE, D, DC, MC, V* ⊘*No lunch.*

¢–$
☾
FRENCH
Mission

✕**Ti Couz.** Big, thin, square buckwheat crepes just like those found in Brittany are the specialty here, filled with everything from ham to Gruyère to ratatouille to sausage to scallops. You can begin with a green salad, oysters on the half shell, a plate of charcuterie, or a bowl of soup. Then, order a savory crepe from the long list of possibilities—you create your own filling combination—and end with a divine white chocolate or chestnut crepe. Or, you can skip the sweet crepe and order a gelato doused with espresso or liqueur. The self-consciously rustic dining room—sturdy wood tables, mismatched cutlery, white-washed walls—welcomes an eclectic crowd late into the night. A full bar serves mixed drinks, but the best—and the traditional—beverage is French hard cider, served in pottery bowls. ⊠ *3108 16th St., Mission* ☎ *415/252–7373* ⊟ *MC, V.*

$$
☾
PIZZA
North Beach

✕ **Tommaso's.** This is the site of San Francisco's first wood-fire pizza oven, installed in the 1930s when the restaurant opened. The oven is still here, and the restaurant, with its coat hooks, boothlike dining nooks, and communal table running the length of the basement dining room, has changed little since those early days. The pizzas' delightfully chewy crusts, creamy mozzarella, and full-bodied house-made sauce—for sale in jars, too—have kept legions of happy eaters returning for decades. Pair one of the hearty pies with a salad of grilled sweet peppers or of broccoli dressed in lemon juice and olive oil and a bottle of the house wine. ⊠ *1042 Kearny St., North Beach* ☎ *415/398–9696* ⊟ *AE, D, DC, MC, V* ☾ *Closed Mon. No lunch.*

$–$$$
☾
CHINESE
Richmond

✕ **Ton Kiang.** This restaurant introduced the lightly seasoned Hakka cuisine of southern China, rarely found in this country and even obscure to many Chinese. Salt-baked chicken, stuffed bean curd, steamed fresh bacon with dried mustard greens, chicken in wine sauce, and clay pots of meats and seafood are among the hallmarks of the Hakka kitchen, and all of them are done well here, as the tables packed with local Chinese families and others prove. Don't overlook the excellent seafood offerings like salt-and-pepper shrimp, catfish in black bean sauce, or stir-fried crab, for example. Some of the finest dim sum in the city brings in the noontime rush (a small selection is available at night, too). ⊠ *5821 Geary Blvd., Richmond* ☎ *415/387–8273* ⊟ *MC, V.*

$$–$$$
AMERICAN
SoMa

✕ **Town Hall.** Well-known chefs Mitchell and Steven Rosenthal are the brains behind this way station for the city's powerbrokers and their acolytes. The fare is sophisticated American—roasted veal meatballs; slow-roasted duck with gingersnap gravy; rib-eye steak with spicy creamed corn; cedar-planked salmon; butterscotch and chocolate *pots de crème*—with plenty of variety to satisfy nearly everyone. The converted-warehouse space, with dark-wood floors, exposed brick walls, white wainscoting, and contemporary art, comfortably blends old with new. You can cool your heels with a cocktail on the heated patio while you wait for your table. Locals travel across town for the lobster roll that occasionally turns up on the lunch menu. ⊠ *342 Howard St., SoMa* ☎ *415/908–3900* ⊟ *AE, MC, V* ⚱ *Reservations essential* ☾ *No lunch weekends.*

$$–$$$$
AMERICAN
SoMa

✕ **Two.** In a matter of just weeks, Hawthorne Lane, one of the city's best-known upmarket eateries, became Two, a more casual spot, with a big concrete and copper bar, a large table with benches for communal dining, and plenty of comfy banquettes. The menu, put together by the same staff that made Hawthorne Lane a destination, matches the more relaxed ambience. Enjoy the luxury of sea urchin spaghettini or the rich flavor of the devilishly good roasted marrowbones. The list of sides includes mac and cheese made with truffled cheese, while dessert traditionalists will appreciate the root beer float with a chocolate swizzle stick and the trio of ice cream sandwiches. Old-timers who remember the Hawthorne Lane bread basket as the best in town won't be disappointed—the kitchen still bakes up those coveted herbed biscuits. Cocktail fans will appreciate the old-school mixologists' work. Good house wines by the glass and carafe are a godsend to budgeters. ⊠ *22 Hawthorne St., SoMa* ☎ *415/777–9779* ⊟ *AE, D, DC, MC, V* ⊘ *No lunch Sat. Closed Sun.*

$$–$$$
ITALIAN
Lower Pacific Heights

✕**Vivande Porta Via.** The secret of how this quarter-century-old Italian delicatessen-restaurant, operated by well-known chef and cookbook author Carlo Middione, has outlasted many of its competitors is simple: authentic, carefully made trattoria dishes served by an engaged staff. The regularly changing menu includes simple fare at lunchtime—frittatas, sandwiches, pastas—and classier plates at night—prosciutto with figs, grilled Belgian endive wrapped in pancetta with lemon vinaigrette, fresh fettuccine with house-made fennel sausage, and risotto with shrimp and lemon. Counter seating lets you enjoy an antipasto and a glass of wine, or one of the excellent house-made desserts—lemon tart, cannoli, biscotti—and an espresso before or after a movie at the nearby Clay Theater. ⊠ *2125 Fillmore St., Lower Pacific Heights* ☎ *415/346–4430* ⊟ *AE, D, DC, MC, V.*

$$$–$$$$
SEAFOOD
Embarcadero

✕**Waterbar.** When you walk in the door of Waterbar, there's no mistaking what's on the menu. The 200-seat dining room is dominated by sky-high aquariums filled with candidates—or at least cousins of candidates (the kitchen has its own aquariums)—for your dinner plate. Every fin and shell is sustainably sourced, so there's no guilt in sitting down to a plate of poached petrale sole, wood oven–roasted striped bass, or seared haddock. Waterbar, like its next-door neighbor, Epic Roasthouse, is part of the steadily expanding empire of high-energy architect-restaurateur Pat Kuleto. Chef Parke Ulrich, who spent a decade at the city's celebrated seafood palace Farallon, dishes up the catch raw, cured, and cooked in dozens of ways, while nationally acclaimed pastry chef Emily Luchetti handles the sweet end of the menu. If you want to experience this watery world and not pay $50 for a whole lobster, grab seat in the bar, where you can snack off the bar menu and take in the drop-dead bay view. ⊠ *399 Embarcadero (between Folsom and Harrison), Embarcadero* ☎ *415/284–9922* ⊟ *AE, D, DC MC, V.*

¢–$$
CHINESE
Financial District

✕**Yank Sing.** This is the granddaddy of the city's dim sum teahouses. It opened in a plain-Jane storefront in Chinatown in 1959 but left its Cantonese neighbors behind for the high-rises of downtown by the 1970s. This brightly decorated location on quiet Stevenson Street (there's also a big, brassy branch in the Rincon Center) serves some of San Francisco's best dim sum to office workers—bosses and clerks alike—on weekdays and to big, boisterous families on weekends. The kitchen cooks up some 100 varieties of dim sum on a rotating basis, offering 60 different types daily. These include both the classic (steamed pork buns, shrimp dumplings, egg custard tartlets) and the creative (scallion-skewered prawns tied with bacon, lobster and tobiko roe dumplings, basil seafood dumplings). A take-out counter makes a meal on the run a satisfying and penny-wise compromise when office duties—or touring—won't wait. ⊠*49 Stevenson St., Financial District* ☎*415/541–4949* ▤*AE, DC, MC, V* ⊘*No dinner* ⊠*1 Rincon Center, 101 Spear St., Embarcadero* ☎*415/957–9300* ▤*AE, DC, MC, V* ⊘*No dinner.*

$$–$$$
JAPANESE
Japantown

✕**Yoshi's.** San Franciscans were long envious of Oakland jazz lovers who had Yoshi's restaurant and nationally known jazz club at their doorstep. But with the late 2007 opening of Yoshi's in San Francisco's slowly rising jazz district on the edge of Japantown, that envy quickly became history. While talented musicians do their thing in a separate space, the equally talented chef Shotaro Kamio serves some of the city's finest—and priciest—Japanese food: exquisite sashimi, memorable robata, crisp tempura, exotic maki-sushi (rolls), pristine nigiri sushi. A wood-burning oven delivers an unforgettable big-eye red snapper, a tender rib eye, cedar paper–wrapped vegetables, and more. The big, handsome restaurant harbors stylish booths, a sushi bar, small tables, a tatami room, a mezzanine lounge, and a bar, ensuring a comfortable perch for every diner. ⊠*1300 Fillmore St., Japantown* ☎*415/655–5600* ▤*AE, D, C, MC, V* ⊘*No lunch.*

$$$
Fodor'sChoice
★
MEDITERRANEAN
Hayes Valley

✕**Zuni Café.** After one bite of chef Judy Rodgers' succulent brick-oven-roasted whole chicken with Tuscan bread salad, you'll understand why she's a national star. Food is served here on two floors; the rabbit warren of rooms on the second level includes a balcony overlooking the main dining room. The crowd is a disparate mix that reflects the makeup of the city: casual and dressy, young and old, hip and staid. At the long copper bar, trays of briny-fresh oysters on the half shell are dispensed along with cocktails and wine. The southern French–Italian menu changes daily (though the signature chicken, prepared for two, is a fixture). Rotating dishes include house-cured anchovies with Parmigiano-Reggiano, crostini with tuna confit, nettle and onion soup with a poached egg, and grilled grouper with artichokes and white beans. Desserts are simple and satisfying and include crumbly crusted tarts and an addictive cream-laced coffee granita. ⊠*1658 Market St., Hayes Valley* ☎*415/552–2522* ▤*AE, MC, V* ⊘*Closed Mon.*

San Francisco Dining & Lodging Atlas

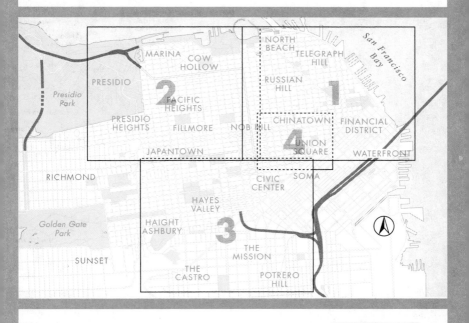

KEY

□ Hotels
▪ Restaurants
▪ Restaurant in Hotel
Embarcadero
🅱️ BART Station
Bay Area Rapid Transit

A **B** **C** **D**

1

Golden Gate
National Recreation Area

Yacht Rd.
West Harbor

Crissy
Field

Mason St.
Old Mason St.
Mason St.

Marina Blvd.

EXPLORATORIUM

Jefferson St.

**PALACE
OF FINE
ARTS**

Beach St.

MARINA

Avila St.

2

Lincoln Blvd.

Halleck St.

Gorgas Ave.

Edie Rd.

Kennedy Ave.

Palace Dr.

Lagoon

North Point St.

Capra Way

Bay St.

Francisco St.

A-16

Graham St.

Mesa St.

Funston Ave.

Letterman Dr.

Lyon St.

Baker St.

Broderick St.

Chestnut St.

Lombard St.

3

Moraga Ave.

PRESIDIO

Presidio Blvd.

Sumner Ave.

Lombard St.

**PRESIDIO OFFICERS'
CLUB & VISITOR CENTER**

MacArthur Ave.

Morton St.

Sherman Rd.

Simonds Loop

Greenwich St.

Divisadero St.

Scott St.

Filbert St.

Barnard Ave.

Presidio Blvd.

Union St.

Quarry Rd.

Portola St.

Rodriguez St.

Clark St.
Liggett St.
Sibley Rd.

Green St.

4

Julius
Kahn Playground

Vallejo St.

Broadway

Pacific Ave.

Drisco

Jackson St.

5

West Pacific Ave.

**PRESIDIO
HEIGHTS**

Washington St.

Jackson St.

Cherry St.

Maple St.

Clay St.

Spruce St.

Washington St.

Locust St.

Laurel St.

Walnut St.

Presidio Ave.

Lyon St.

Baker St.

Clay St.

Sacramento St.

Spruce

Sacramento St.

California St.

California St.

Laurel Inn

Pine St.

6

Seal Rock Inn

Jordan Ave.

Palm Ave.

Parker Ave.

Spruce St.

Heather Ave.

Iris Ave.

Manzanita Ave.

Euclid Ave.

Laurel Hill
Plgd.

Lupine Ave.

Masonic Ave.

Ella's

**SF FIRE DEPT.
MUSEUM**

Presidio Ave.

Bush St.

Sutter St.

Post St.

Pho Hoa Clement
Burma SuperStar
Ocean Restaurant
Pluto's

A **B** ▽**3** **C** **D**

Map 2

- Cow Hollow
- Fillmore
- Japantown
- Marina
- Pacific Heights
- Presidio Heights

Marina Small Craft Harbor

East Harbor

Gashouse Cove

Fort Mason

Greens

Casa Way

Rico Way

Retiro Way

Marina Blvd.

Beach St.

North Point St.

Bay St.

Russian Hill Park

Cervantes Blvd.

Alhambra St.

Mallorca Way

Toledo Way

COW HOLLOW

George R. Moscone Recreation Center

Francisco St.

Chestnut St.

Polk St.

Larkin St.

Laïola

Magnolia St.

Marina Inn

Lombard St.

Isa

Cow Hollow Motor Inn and Suites

Coventry Motor Inn

Greenwich St.

Bodega Bistro

Pagolac

Home Plate

Moulton St.

Fillmore St.

Buchanan St.

Laguna St.

Harris Pl.

Octavia St.

Del Sol

Pacific Heights Inn

Antica Trattoria

Helmand Palace

Union St.

La Folie

Terzo

Union Street Inn

Ottimista Enoteca

Green St.

Gough St.

Franklin St.

Van Ness Ave.

Betelnut

Pasta Pomodoro

Rose's Café

Pierce St.

Steiner St.

Webster St.

Broadway

Harris'

Pacific Ave.

PACIFIC HEIGHTS

Jackson St.

Bromley Pl.

Washington St.

Clay St.

Acquerello

Sacramento St.

Alta Plaza

PACIFIC MED. CTR.

Lafayette Park

Swan Oyster Depot

California St.

Cable Car

FILLMORE

Vivande Porta Via

Octavia St.

Gough St.

Franklin St.

Pine St.

Elite Café

Webster St.

Buchanan St.

Laguna St.

Bush St.

Bay Bread Boulangerie

Fern St.

Florio

Quince

Sutter St.

SPQR

Queen Anne

Majestic

Post St.

Maki

Radisson Miyako Hotel

O Izakaya

Geary St.

MT. ZION HOSP.

JAPAN CENTER, MIYAKO BUILDING

Geary St.

ST. MARY'S CATHEDRAL

Myrtle St.

Hamilton Square

St. Francis Square

Cleary Ct.

O'Farrell St.

Olive St.

JAPANTOWN

Map 3

- The Castro
- Civic Center
- Haight Ashbury
- Hayes Valley
- Mission District
- SOMA

2

Geary Blvd. ← ■ Aziza
■ Ton Kiang
■ Wooden Charcoal Barbecue House
■ Moscow and Tblisi Bakery

O'Farrell St.

Terra Vista Ave. ← ■ Cinderella Bakery and Restaurant

■ Yoshi's

Kimball Playground

St. Francis Square

Hollis

Willow St.

Ellis St.

WESTERN ADDITION

1

Fortuna Ave.
Baker St.
Joseph's Ave.
Anza Vista Ave.

Eddy St.

Turk St.

Elm St.

Pierce St.

Golden Gate Ave.

McAllister St.

← ■ Katia's

2

■ Poleng Lounge

Fulton St.

Presidio Ave.
Lyon St.
Baker St.
Broderick St.
Divisadero St.
Scott St.

Alamo Square

Steiner St.
Fillmore St.
Webster St.

Grove St.
Ivy St.
Hayes St.
Linden
Fell St.
Hickory St.
Oak St.

Grove St.

Hayes St.

■ Nopa

← ■ Park Chalet

Fell St.

Page St.

3

Panhandle

Oak St.

HAIGHT ASHBURY

Lyon St.

Page St.

Haight St.

Pierce St.

■ RNM

Rosamunde Sausage Grill ■ ■ Indian Oven
■ Thep Phanom

← ■ Cha Cha Cha

Masonic Ave.
Waller St.

Buena Vista Park

Alpine Ter.
Buena Vista Ter.

Waller St.

Lloyd St.
Carmelita St.
Potomac St.

Germania St.

Herman St.

Duboce Park

Dubuce Ave.

Belcher St.

U.S. MINT

4

Buena Vista Ave. East

Corona Heights Playground

Castro St.
Noe St.
Walter St.

14th St.

■ Home ■ ■ Chow
Market St.

Dolores St.

15th St.

Church St.
Landers St.

5

16th St.

MISSION DOLORES

■ Park Chow
■ Dragonfly
■ San Tung No. 2

← 17th St.

17th St.

Ford St.

Dorland St.

THE CASTRO

6

Market St.

18th St.

Douglass St.
Eureka St.
Diamond St.
Collingwood St.
Castro St.

18th St.

Hancock St.

19th St.

Mission Dolores Park

0 ——— 350 M
0 ——— 1,000 ft

■ Barrney's Goumet Burger

■ Incanto
■ La Ciccia ↓

A   B   C   D

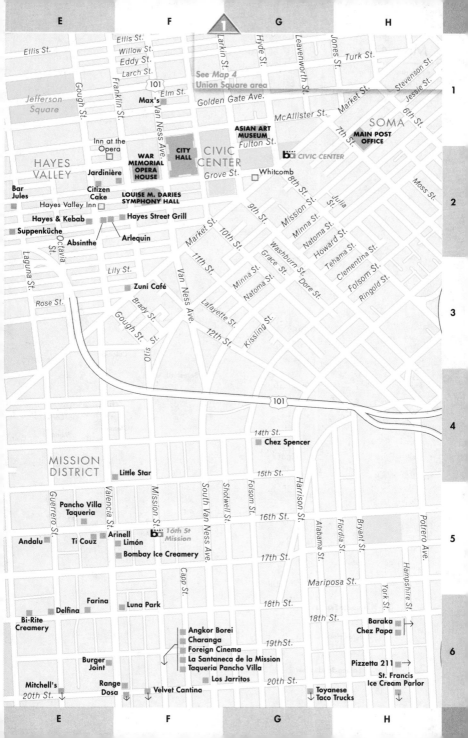

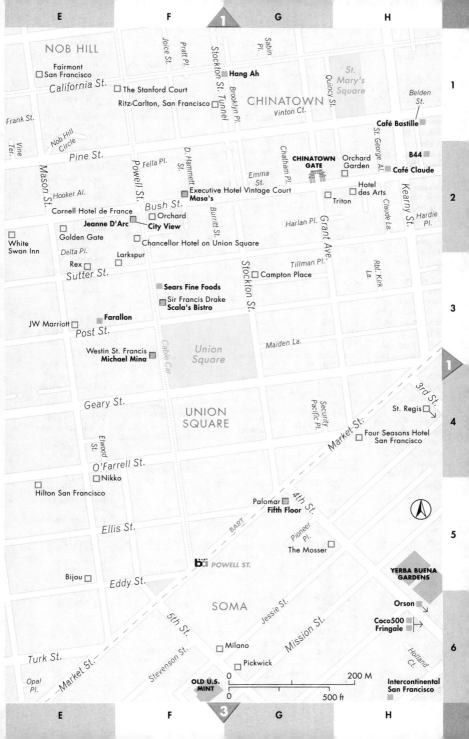

Where to Stay

Clift Hotel

WORD OF MOUTH

"San Francisco is such a beautiful city. It is really glorious. Definitely pick an area where you will be blown away by the spectacle: Nob Hill, near the Water, or the Union Square area."

—CaboVacation

Updated by
Sura Wood
Written by
Andy Moore

San Francisco is one of the country's best hotel towns, offering a rich selection of properties that satisfy most tastes and budgets. Whether you're seeking a cozy inn, a kitschy motel, a chic boutique, or a grande dame hotel, this city has got the perfect room for you.

If you're searching for a centrally located, classy hotel, check out the dramatic Clift, a property with surrealistic flavor, conjured by maverick star-designer Philippe Starck, or Hotel Monaco, a sumptuous beaux arts beauty. Both are a few blocks from Union Square, a shopper's paradise.

Now is a great time to go: upgrades and renovations are taking place at properties throughout the city, and both new and established properties are trending toward the eco-friendly, and SF hotels are "going green" in a big way. Although the Orchard Garden boasts San Francisco's first all-new green construction, many other local properties are installing ecological upgrades. Most of the city's hotels are nonsmoking—or will be soon.

Wherever you stay, be sure to ask what's included in your room rate. And when you settle into your perfect room, remember this tip: When in doubt, ask the concierge. This holds true for almost any request, whether you have special needs or burning desires (if anyone can get you tickets to a sold-out show or reservations at a fully booked restaurant, it's the concierge). You'll likely be impressed by the lengths hoteliers are willing to go to please their guests.

WHERE SHOULD I STAY?

	Neighborhood Vibe	Pros	Cons
By the airport	Construction booms near San Francisco International Airport have added several luxury hotels to this rather prosaic area.	Rates are about 20% lower than in-town hotels, and weekend prices are often slashed because clients tend to be midweek business travelers.	The drive from the airport area to downtown San Francisco takes 20 to 30 minutes, so what you gain in value you may lose in convenience.
Civic Center/ Van Ness	A wide mix of lodgings scattered throughout this area.	Asian Art Museum, opera house, symphony hall, and government offices surround this central hub. Close to busy Fillmore Street and not far from Union Square.	Away from touristy areas, public transportation can sometimes be a challenge. There's a large homeless population in the Civic Center area.
Financial District	A mini-midtown Manhattan where properties cater to business travelers.	Excellent city and bay views, which are spectacular by night. Easy access to restaurants and nightclubs.	Some streets are iffy at night. Street parking takes some work. Hotels are on the pricey side.
Fisherman's Wharf/North Beach	Mostly chain hotels by the Wharf; lodgings get funkier and smaller in North Beach.	Near attractions like Ghirardelli Square, Pier 39, and the Cannery. Cable car lines and piers for bay cruises are nearby.	City ordinances limit Wharf hotels to four stories, so good views are out. Very hilly area.
Nob Hill	Synonymous with San Francisco's high society, this area contains some of the city's best-known luxury hotels.	Many hotels boast gorgeous views and notable restaurants. Easy access to Union Square and Chinatown.	Hotels here will test your wallet, while the area's steep hills may test your endurance.
Pacific Heights, Cow Hollow, the Marina	A few tony accommodations in the quietly residential Pacific Heights. Mostly motels along Lombard Street, the major traffic corridor leading to the Golden Gate Bridge.	Away from the more tourist-oriented areas, visitors have a chance to explore where locals eat and shop. Lots of free parking.	Getting downtown can be challenging via public transportation. Some complain of the fraternity-like bar scene.
SoMa	The "new heart of the city," adjacent to the developing Mission Bay neighborhood, offers luxury high-rises, old classics, and a few bargains.	Near the cultural magnet of the San Francisco Museum of Modern Art and Yerba Buena Gardens, as well as a growing number of eateries.	Lots of construction may mean traffic snarls. As with many changing neighborhoods, street life takes many forms. Be cautious walking around at night.
Union Square/ Downtown	Union Square is Square One for visitors; you'll find a wide range of choices—and prices—for lodging.	Excellent shopping and dining. Home to the theater district, great transit access to other neighborhoods.	Often crowded and noisy. Close to Tenderloin, a still seedy part of town. Take cabs at night.

13

WHERE TO STAY PLANNER

Strategy

Where should we stay? With hundreds of San Francisco hotels, it may seem like a daunting question. But fret not—our expert writers and editors have done most of the legwork. The 90-plus selections here represent the best this city has to offer—from the best budget motels to the sleekest designer hotels. Scan "Best Bets" on the following pages for top recommendations by price and experience. Or find a review quickly in the listings. Search by neighborhood, then alphabetically. Happy hunting!

Family Travel

San Francisco has gone to great lengths to attract family vacationers, and hotels have followed the family-friendly trend. Some properties provide diversions like in-room video games; others have suites with kitchenettes and fold-out sofa beds. Most full-service San Francisco hotels provide roll-away beds, babysitting, and stroller rentals, but be sure to make arrangements when booking the room, not when you arrive. For recommendations on family-friendly hotels, see the "Room for the Kids" box in this chapter.

Reservations

Reservations are always advised, especially during the peak seasons—May through October and weekends in December. The San Francisco Convention and Visitors Bureau publishes a free lodging guide with a map and listings of San Francisco and Bay Area hotels. You can reserve a room, by phone or via the Internet, at more than 60 bureau-recommended hotels. San Francisco Reservations, in business since 1986, can arrange reservations at more than 200 Bay Area hotels, often at special discounted rates. Hotellocators.com also offers online and phone-in reservations at special rates.

Booking: Hotellocators.com (☎800/576–0003 🖷858/581–1730 ⊕www.hotellocators.com). **San Francisco Convention and Visitors Bureau** (☎415/391–2000 general information, 415/283–0177, 888/782–9673 lodging service ⊕www.sfvisitor.org). **San Francisco Reservations** (☎800/677–1500 ⊕www.hotelres.com). **Bed & Breakfast San Francisco** (☎415/899–0060 ⊕www.bbsf.com).

Parking

Several properties on Lombard Street and in the Civic Center area have free parking (but not always in a covered garage). Hotels in the Union Square and Nob Hill areas almost invariably charge $23–$50+ per day for a spot in their garages. Some hotel package deals include parking. Some B&Bs have limited free parking available, but many don't and require you to park on the street. Depending on the neighborhood and the time, this can be easy or difficult, so ask for realistic parking information when you call. Some hotels with paid parking offer a choice of valet parking with unlimited in-out privileges or self-parking (where the fee is less expensive and there's no tipping).

Facilities

In each review, we list what facilities are available, but we don't specify whether they cost extra. When pricing accommodations, always ask what's included and what entails an additional charge. All the hotels listed have private baths, central heating, and private phones unless otherwise noted. Many places don't have air-conditioning, but you probably won't need it. Even in September and October, when the city sees its warmest days, the temperature rarely climbs above 70°F.

Many hotels now have wireless Internet (Wi-Fi) available, although it's not always free. Larger hotels often have video or high-speed checkout capability, and many can arrange babysitting. Pools are a rarity, but most properties have gyms or health clubs, and sometimes full-scale spas; hotels without facilities usually have arrangements for guests at nearby gyms, sometimes for a fee.

Prices

San Francisco hotel prices, among the highest in the United States, may come as an unpleasant surprise. Weekend rates for double rooms in high season average about $132 a night citywide. Rates may vary widely according to room availability; always inquire about special rates and packages when making reservations; call the property directly, but also check its Web site and try Internet booking agencies.

The lodgings we list are the cream of the crop in each price category. Assume that prices are based on the European Plan (EP, with no meals) unless we specify that hotels operate on the Continental Plan (CP, with a Continental breakfast), Breakfast Plan (BP, with a full breakfast), Modified American Plan (MAP, with breakfast and dinner), or the Full American Plan (FAP, with all meals).

WHAT IT COSTS FOR HOTELS

¢	$	$$	$$$	$$$$
under $90	$90–$149	$150–$199	$200–$250	over $250

Prices are for two people in a standard double room in high season, excluding 14% tax.

In This Chapter:

13

BEST BETS FOR SAN FRANCISCO

Fodor's offers a selective listing of quality lodging experiences at every price range, from the city's best budget motel to its most sophisticated luxury hotel. Here, we've compiled our top recommendations by price and experience. The very best properties—in other words, those that provide a particularly remarkable experience in their price range—are designated in the listings with the Fodor's Choice logo.

Hotel Drisco, p. 256
Hotel Majestic, p. 256
Palace Hotel, p. 261
Queen Anne, p. 257

TOP B&BS

Golden Gate Hotel, p. 265
Hotel Drisco, p. 256
Washington Square Inn, p. 252

TOP SPAS

Mandarin Oriental, p. 249
St. Regis, p. 261

FODOR'S CHOICE ★

Argonaut Hotel, p. 249
Four Seasons, p. 258
Hotel Monaco, p. 267
Hotel Rex, p. 268
Mandarin Oriental, p. 249
Palace Hotel, p. 261
Ritz-Carlton, p. 253
San Remo Hotel, p. 251
Union Street Inn, p. 258

By Price

$

Cornell Hotel de France, p. 264
Cow Hollow Motor Inn, p. 254
Hotel des Arts, p. 267
Queen Anne, p. 257

$$–$$$

Beresford Arms, p. 266
Harbor Court, p. 258
Hotel Drisco, p. 256
Orchard Hotel, p. 270

$$$$

Campton Place, p. 263
Hotel Palomar, p. 259

By Experience

BUSINESS TRAVELERS

Four Seasons, p. 258
Hilton SF Financial District, p. 248
Hotel Vitale, p. 259
Le Meridien, p. 248
Hotel Nikko, p. 268

GREAT CONCIERGE

Hilton, p. 265
Hotel Triton, p. 268
JW Marriott, p. 269
Ritz-Carlton, p. 253

HISTORICAL FLAVOR

Fairmont, p. 253
Hotel Whitcomb, p. 246
Palace, p. 261

Saint Francis, p. 271
York Hotel, p. 272

JET-SETTING CLIENTELE

Clift, p. 264
Hotel Boheme, p. 250
Monaco, p. 267
Triton, p. 268
W, p. 262

MOST KID-FRIENDLY

Hilton, p. 265
Hotel del Sol, p. 254
Omni Hotel, p. 249
Seal Rock Inn, p. 247
Westin San Francisco Market Street, p. 262

MOST ROMANTIC

Fairmont Hotel, p. 253

LODGING REVIEWS (ALPHABETICAL)

BY THE AIRPORT

$$ **Embassy Suites San Francisco Airport, Burlingame.** This beige-and-orange California Mission–style hostelry is one of the most lavish hotels in the airport corridor. Set on the bay, with clear vistas of airplanes flying above San Francisco in the distance, the building's focal point is a nine-story atrium and tropical garden showcasing exotic towering palms, bamboo and banana plants, and koi-filled ponds all crowned by a waterfall. The property was renovated in 2007, and each suite has a living room with work area, flat-screen TVs, microwave, a sleeper sofa, and bedroom; kitchenettes are conveniently located between each suite's two rooms. Rates include a complimentary cooked-to-order breakfast, evening cocktails, and free access to the business center. **Pros:** Low rates, luxurious accommodations. **Cons:** No standard rooms, no concierge. ⊠*150 Anza Blvd., Burlingame,* ☎*650/342–4600* 🖷*650/343–8137* ⊕*www.sfoburlingame.embassysuites.com* ⇆*340 suites* ⌂*In-room: kitchen, refrigerator, Wi-Fi. In-hotel: restaurant, bar, pool, gym, laundry service, airport shuttle, parking (no fee), some pets allowed (fee), no-smoking rooms* ▭*AE, DC, MC, V* ⑩*BP.*

$$$–$$$$ **Sofitel–San Francisco Bay.** Set on a lagoon in a business park near several big-name corporate headquarters, this hotel is a warm, inviting oasis in an otherwise sterile area. Parisian lampposts, a "Métro" sign, and a poster-covered kiosk lend an unexpected French ambience to the public spaces, while the light, expansive, luxurious rooms have a more modern feel. Done in pale earth tones, accommodations include fine linens, French bath products, complimentary turndown service, Evian water, and fresh orchids. Many staff members speak both French and English. Bay 223 restaurant and bar completes the experience with a fine menu of artfully presented, contemporary American cuisine. **Pros:** Bilingual staff, stylish interior design, reasonable rates. **Cons:** Sterile, uninviting environs, a bit far from the city. ⊠*223 Twin Dolphin Dr., Redwood City,* ☎*650/598–9000* 🖷*650/598–0459* ⊕*www.sofitel-sanfrancisco-bay.com* ⇆*421 rooms, 42 suites* ⌂*In-room: Wi-Fi. In-hotel: restaurant, room service, bar, pool, gym, concierge, laundry service, airport shuttle, parking (no fee), some pets allowed (fee), no-smoking rooms* ▭*AE, DC, MC, V.*

CIVIC CENTER/VAN NESS

¢–$ **Hayes Valley Inn.** Offering "European charm in the heart of Hayes Valley," the modest, clean rooms of this hotel come with sinks and vanities . . . but the bathroom is down the hall. The Opera House, Davies Symphony Hall, and a chic shopping and dining district are steps away on Hayes Street. Slightly larger, corner turret rooms overlook a busy intersection. **Pros:** Inexpensive, free local calls, good location, close to shopping, restaurants, and theater. **Cons:** No in-room bathroom, some street noise. ⊠*417 Gough St., Civic Center,* ☎*415/431–9131 or 800/930–7999* 🖷*415/431–2585* ⊕*hayesvalleyinn.com* ⇆*28 rooms* ⌂*In room: no a/c, Wi-Fi. In hotel: restaurant, no elevator, laundry* *facilities, concierge, public Internet, parking (fee), some pets allowed, no-smoking rooms* ▭*AE, MC, V* ⊙*CP.*

$$$ **Hotel Kabuki.** This pagoda-style hotel is next door to Japantown and two blocks from Fillmore Street and Pacific Heights. Rooms are located in the tower and the garden wing, which has a traditional Japanese garden and waterfall. Japanese-style rooms have futon beds with tatami mats, while the Western variety have traditional beds. All rooms are decorated with gorgeous Asian furniture and original artwork, and most have their own soaking rooms, which come with a bucket, stool, and a Japanese-style tub (1 foot deeper than Western tubs). The O Izakaya Lounge serves breakfast and dinner daily, and the bar hosts karaoke on some nights. A club level offers complimentary breakfast as well as free appetizers and cocktails during happy hour. **Pros:** Japanese style, serene environment. **Cons:** Popular with the business crowd. ⊠*1625 Post St., at Laguna St., Japantown,* ☎*415/922–3200 or 800/533–4567* ⊟*415/921–0417* ⊕*www.jdvhotels.com* ⊅*204 rooms, 14 suites* △*In-room: dial-up, Wi-Fi. In-hotel: restaurant, bar, gym, laundry service, public Internet, parking (fee), no-smoking rooms* ▭*AE, D, DC, MC, V.*

$–$$ **Hotel Whitcomb.** Built in 1910, this historic hotel (formerly the Ramada Plaza) was the temporary seat of city government from 1912 to 1915 before becoming a hotel in 1916. (The mayor's office now serves as the hotel's administrative offices, and the jail cells are still intact in the hotel basement.) The expansive, well appointed lobby boasts marble balustrades and columns, carved wooden ceilings, rare Janesero paneling, Austrian crystal chandeliers, Tiffany stained glass, and a ballroom with one of the largest parquet dance floors in the city. Broad halls lead to spacious, newly refurbished rooms and baths. Northeast corner suites offer views of Market Street and the gold-encrusted dome of City Hall. Stroll out the front door to find the Civic Center MUNI and BART stations and the main public library; the Asian Art Museum, Opera House, Davies Symphony Hall and Westfield Centre are close by. **Pros:** Good location, rich architectural and historical legacy, opulent lobby, spacious rooms. **Cons:** Difficult to find street parking, area can be dodgy at night. ⊠*1231 Market St., Civic Center,* ☎*415/626–8000 or 800/227–4747* ⊟*415/861–1460* ⊕*www.hotelwhitcomb.com* ⊅*486 rooms, 12 suites* △*In room: Wi-Fi. In hotel: meeting rooms, restaurant, room service, bar, gym, laundry facilities, laundry service, concierge, public Wi-Fi, airport shuttle, parking (fee), no-smoking rooms* ▭*AE, D, DC, MC, V.*

$–$$ **Inn at the Opera.** Within walking distance of Davies Symphony Hall and the War Memorial Opera House, this homey boutique hotel caters to season-ticket holders for the opera, ballet and symphony; it has been the venue of choice for stars of the music, dance, and opera worlds, from Luciano Pavarotti to Mikhail Baryshnikov. The genteel, newly refurbished, marble-floor lobby resembles the foyer of a finely appointed mansion, and the compact standard rooms feature dark-wood furnishings, queen-size pillow-top beds with 250-thread-count sheets, and cozy terry robes. The sumptuous, romantically-lit Ovation restaurant, with its old world European charm, is an intimate gathering place for performers and audience members to congregate before and after shows. Rates include an expanded Continental breakfast buffet, and complimentary cookies and apples are available at the front desk. An Internet kiosk in the lobby ($10 per hour) is equipped with its own printer. **Pros:** Staff goes the extra mile, intimate restaurant. **Cons:** No A/C, smallish rooms and bath, sold out far in advance during opera season. ✉ *333 Fulton St., Van Ness/Civic Center,* ☎ *415/863–8400 or 800/325–2708* 📠 *415/861–0821* ⊕ *www.innattheopera.com* 🛏 *30 rooms, 18 suites* ♿ *In-room: no a/c, refrigerator, VCR (some), dial-up, Wi-Fi. In-hotel: restaurant, room service, bar, concierge, laundry service, parking (fee), no-smoking rooms* ⊟ *AE, DC, MC, V* ⍥ *CP.*

13

$$$ **Phoenix Hotel.** From the piped-in, poolside jungle beat to the trendy Bambuddha restaurant-lounge's bamboo furnishings and Southeast Asian menu, the Phoenix (a riff on a classic 1950s Miami Beach motel) evokes a kitschy dream of the tropic. It's a magnet for the hip at heart and ultra-cool—Little Richard, Elijah Wood, Sean Lennon, and members of R.E.M. and Pearl Jam have stayed here—so it's not the best choice for those seeking peace and quiet (or anyone put off by the hotel's location, on the fringes of the sketchy Tenderloin District). All suites, deluxe, and superior rooms and baths have been completely redone; the simple accommodations—decorated with bamboo furniture, batik-print bedspreads, and original pieces by local artists—face the courtyard, an azure blue-tiled pool, and a sculpture garden, where a free Continental breakfast is served. The friendly staff is as groovy and hip as you'd expect. **Pros:** Boho atmosphere, popular with musicians. **Cons:** Somewhat seedy location, no elevators. ✉ *601 Eddy St., Tenderloin,* ☎ *415/776–1380 or 800/248–9466* 📠 *415/885–3109* ⊕ *www.thephoenixhotel.com* 🛏 *41 rooms, 3 suites* ♿ *In-room: no a/c, refrigerator (some), DVD (some), dial-up, Wi-Fi. In-hotel: restaurant, bar, pool, no elevator, concierge, laundry service, public Wi-Fi, parking (no fee), no-smoking rooms* ⊟ *AE, D, DC, MC, V* ⍥ *CP.*

$–$$ **Seal Rock Inn.** About as far west as you can go in San Francisco without falling into the Pacific, this hotel within easy walking distance of the Cliff House and Ocean Beach is a welcome refuge from the hubbub of downtown. A recreation area with a small pool, Ping-Pong table, and badminton court—plus large rooms with accordion-style dividers separating a queen bed from two twins—makes it a good choice for families with kids. Recent improvements include two ADA-compliant rooms, new furniture and mattresses, renovated bathrooms and a new patio. Second-story rooms enjoy ocean views, some have kitchenettes and a little restaurant serves breakfast and lunch. **Pros:** Close to the beach, Lots of activities for kids. **Cons:** No A/C, no pets allowed. ✉ *545 Point Lobos Ave., Lincoln Park,* ☎ *415/752–8000 or 888/732–5762* 📠 *415/752–6034* ⊕ *www.sealrockinn.com* 🛏 *27 rooms* ♿ *In-room: no a/c, kitchen (some), refrigerator, ethernet. In-hotel: restaurant, pool, parking (no fee), no-smoking rooms* ⊟ *AE, DC, MC, V* ⍥ *EP.*

FINANCIAL DISTRICT

$$–$$$ **Galleria Park.** This boutique hotel, which has a dedicated clientele and is particularly packed on weekdays with corporate travelers, is close to BART, the Chinatown Gate, Union Square, and the high-end Crocker Galleria shopping complex. A recent $8 million renovation has updated and dramatically improved guest rooms, which are now decorated in chartreuse and sage, as well as modernized the meeting and fitness facilities. Complimentary morning coffee and tea and evening wine are served in the art-deco lobby in front of the pièce de résistance, a massive, hand-sculpted art-nouveau fireplace that looks like it leaped out of a fairy tale. Restored original 1911 skylights and artwork by local artists contribute to the inviting atmosphere. **Pros:** Can't beat the location, one block from BART, friendly management, quiet rooms. **Cons:** Small rooms and baths. ✉ *191 Sutter St., Financial District,* ☎ *415/781–3060 or 800/792–9639* 🖷 *415/433–4409* ⊕ *www.galleriapark.com* 📧 *169 rooms, 8 suites* ⚴ *In-room: refrigerator, ethernet, Wi-Fi. In-hotel: restaurant, room service, bar, gym, laundry service, public Internet, parking (fee), some pets allowed, no-smoking rooms* 🖃 *AE, D, DC, MC, V.*

$$$ **Hilton San Francisco Financial District.** A $45-million transformation has taken place at this stylish, luxurious hotel adjacent to Chinatown and the Financial District. The lobby's minimalist decor has a distinctly Asian flavor, and the "Seven Fifty" Mediterranean Restaurant and Lounge Room offers local sustainable regional cuisine. For personal pampering, sample the Tru day spa which provides a range of packages. Tastefully decorated, airy rooms come with blond wood Signature Serenity beds, Wi-Fi, flat-screen TVs, and large work desks with ergonomic chairs. **Pros:** Abundant parking, bay and city views. **Cons:** Congested area. ✉ *750 Kearny St., Financial District,* ☎ *415/433–6600* 🖷 *415/765–7891* ⊕ *www.sanfranciscohiltonhotel.com* 📧 *549 rooms, 7 suites* ⚴ *In room: safe, dial-up, Wi-Fi. In-hotel: room service, bar, laundry service, concierge, executive floor, parking (fee)* 🖃 *AE, D, DC, MC, V* ⦿ *BP.*

$$$–$$$$ **Le Méridien.** Across Battery Street from the Embarcadero Center complex, this hotel (formerly the Park Hyatt) is completely renovating its lounge and lobby area (as well as doing a style-makeover of its standard rooms and suites) in an effort to attract both leisure and business visitors. Australian lacewood paneling, polished granite sinks, stylish contemporary furniture, and fresh flowers outfit the spacious guest rooms. The in-room safes have interior outlets for recharging laptops and cell phones. The Park Grill serves excellent, high-end California cuisine, and the popular Bar 333 off the lobby has a Mediterranean menu and an extensive list of wines and other libations. **Pros:** Excellent service, ultraconvenient, spacious rooms, great views, top-notch concierge. **Cons:** New Age elevator soundtrack. ✉ *333 Battery St., Financial District,* ☎ *415/296–2900* 🖷 *415/296–2901* ⊕ *www.lemeridien.com/sanfrancisco* 📧 *351 rooms, 9 suites* ⚴ *In-room: safe, dial-up, Wi-Fi. In-hotel: 2 restaurants, room service, bars, gym, concierge, laundry service, public Internet, parking (fee), no-smoking rooms* 🖃 *AE, MC, V.*

$$$$ **Mandarin Oriental, San Francisco** Two towers connected by glass-enclosed
Fodor'sChoice sky bridges compose the top 11 floors of one San Francisco's tallest
★ buildings. Spectacular panoramas grace every room, and windows open
so you can hear that trademark San Francisco sound, the "ding ding"
of the cable cars some 40 floors below. The rooms, corridors, and lobby
areas are decorated in rich hues of red, gold, and chocolate brown.
The Mandarin Rooms have extra deep tubs next to picture windows
enabling guests to literally and figuratively soak up what one reader
called "unbelievable views from the Golden Gate to the Bay Bridge
and everything in between." Pamper yourself with luxurious Egyptian-
cotton sheets, two kinds of robes (terry and waffle-weave), and terry
slippers. A lovely complimentary tea and cookie tray delivered to your
room upon your arrival is one among many illustrations of the hotel's
commitment to service. The pricey mezzanine-level restaurant, Silks,
earns rave reviews for innovative American cuisine with an Asian flair.
Pros: Spectacular "bridge-to-bridge" views, attentive service. **Cons:**
Located in a business area that's quiet on weekends, restaurant is excellent but expensive (as is the hotel). ⊠*222 Sansome St., Financial District,* ☎*415/276–9600 or 800/622–0404* 🖷*415/276–9304* ⊕*www.
mandarinoriental.com/sanfrancisco* ⇗*151 rooms, 7suites* &*In-room:
safe, DVD, dial-up, Wi-Fi. In-hotel: restaurant, room service, bar, gym,
concierge, laundry service, public Internet, parking (fee), some pets
allowed (fee), no-smoking rooms* ⊟*AE, D, DC, MC, V.*

$$$–$$$$ **Omni San Francisco Hotel.** Although the lobby's glittering crystal chan-
deliers, dark mahogany paneling, and iron-and-marble staircase may
hark back to an old-fashioned gentility, this 1926 redbrick-and-stone
building is home to a modern luxury hotel. Rooms have 9-foot-high
ceilings with crown moldings and carved-mahogany furniture; sliding
doors open to reveal bathrooms with marble floors and green-and-black
granite basins. Daylight floods the corner suites, each of which has six
tall windows. More expensive Signature Rooms offer extra amenities
such as complimentary fresh seasonal fruit daily, bottled water, and
assorted business tools including color printer-copiers and personal
phone numbers. Bob's Steak and Chop House, more elegant than the
name implies, is off the lobby. **Pros:** Outstanding personalized service,
cookies and milk for the kids, immaculately clean. **Cons:** Some may
find the a/c inadequate, rooftop views are less than inspiring. ⊠*500
California St., Financial District,* ☎*415/677–9494* 🖷*415/273–3038*
⊕*www.omnisanfrancisco.com* ⇗*347 rooms, 15 suites* &*In-room:
safe, DVD (some), ethernet, Wi-Fi. In-hotel: restaurant, room service,
bar, gym, concierge, laundry service, public Internet, parking (fee),
some pets allowed (fee), no-smoking rooms* ⊟*AE, D, DC, MC, V.*

FISHERMAN'S WHARF/NORTH BEACH

$$$–$$$$ **Argonaut Hotel.** When the four-story Haslett Warehouse was a fruit-and-
Fodor'sChoice vegetable canning complex in 1907, boats docked right up against the
★ building. Today, it's a hotel with a nautical decor—anchors, ropes, com-
passes, and a row of cruise ship deck chairs in the lobby—that reflect its
unique partnership with the San Francisco Maritime National Histori-
cal Park. Spacious rooms, many with a sofa bed in the sitting area, have

13

exposed-brick walls, wood-beamed ceilings, and whitewashed wooden furniture reminiscent of a summer beach house. Windows open to the sea air and the sounds of the waterfront, and many rooms have straight ahead views of Alcatraz and the Golden Gate Bridge. Suites come with extra deep whirlpool tubs and telescopes for close-up views of passing ships. **Pros:** Bay views; bright, clean rooms; near Hyde Street cable car; sofa beds; toys for the kids. **Cons:** Nautical theme isn't for everyone, cramped public areas, service can be hit or miss, location is a bit of a hike from other parts of town. ⊠ *495 Jefferson St., at Hyde St., Fisherman's Wharf,* 🕾 *415/563–0800 or 866/415–0704* 🖷 *415/563–2800* ⊕ *www.argonauthotel.com* 🖘 *239 rooms, 13 suites* ⚑ *In-room: safe, refrigerator, VCR, ethernet. In-hotel: restaurant, room service, bar, gym, concierge, laundry service, Wi-Fi, parking (fee), some pets allowed, no-smoking rooms* ☰ *AE, D, DC, MC, V.*

$$–$$$ **Best Western Tuscan Inn.** Described by some Fodors.com users as a "hidden treasure," this hotel's redbrick facade barely hints at the Tuscan country villa that lies within. Each small, Italianate room has white-pine furniture, floral bedspreads and curtains, a completely mirrored wall, and a newly refurbished bathroom. Complimentary beverages and biscotti are laid out mornings near the fireplace in the oak-paneled lobby, where a convivial wine hour is held nightly. There's free morning limousine service to the Financial District. Café Pescatore, the Italian seafood restaurant off the lobby, provides room service for breakfast. **Pros:** Wine/beer hour, down-home feeling. **Cons:** Congested touristy area, small rooms. ⊠ *425 N. Point St., at Mason St., Fisherman's Wharf,* 🕾 *415/561–1100* 🖷 *415/561–1199* ⊕ *www.tuscaninn.com* 🖘 *209 rooms, 12 suites* ⚑ *In-room: Wi-Fi. In-hotel: restaurant, room service, bar, laundry service, public Internet, parking (fee), some pets allowed, no-smoking rooms* ☰ *AE, D, DC, MC, V.*

$$ **Hotel Bohème.** This small hotel in historic North Beach takes you back in time with cast-iron beds, large mirrored armoires, and memorabilia recalling the Beat generation—whose leading light, Allen Ginsberg, often stayed here (legend has it that in his later years he could be seen sitting in a window, typing away on his laptop computer). Screenwriters toiling nearby at Francis Ford Coppola's dream factory, American Zoetrope Studio, as well as sundry poets and artists are frequent patrons. Rooms have a bistro table, two chairs, and tropical-style mosquito netting over the bed; bathrooms have cheerful yellow tiles and tiny showers. Rooms in the rear are a refuge from the noisy crush, especially on weekends. Complimentary sherry is served in the lobby. **Pros:** North Beach location with literary pedigree. **Cons:** Street parking is scarce, lots of traffic congestion, no a/c. ⊠ *444 Columbus Ave., North Beach,* 🕾 *415/433–9111* 🖷 *415/362–6292* ⊕ *www.hotelboheme.com* 🖘 *15 rooms* ⚑ *In-room: no a/c, dial-up, Wi-Fi. In-hotel: no elevator, concierge, no-smoking rooms* ☰ *AE, D, DC, MC, V.*

$$–$$$ **Hyatt at Fisherman's Wharf.** The location is key to this hotel's popularity: it's within walking distance of tourist hot spots such as Ghirardelli Square, the Cannery, Pier 39, Aquatic Park, and Alcatraz ferries; bay cruises dock nearby; and it's across the street from a cable-car turnaround. The double-pane windows of the moderately sized, predominantly nonsmoking rooms—which have flat-screen TVs and dark-wood furniture—keep out the considerable street noise. Each floor has a laundry room. In the North Point Lounge, a domed Tiffany skylight with a seashore motif crowns a large, comfy lounge area with a fireplace and fountain. Plans to renovate the guestrooms, expand the fitness center, and redesign the lobby are in the works. **Pros:** Primo sightseeing location, close to cable car. **Cons:** Street noise, crowds. ⊠ *555 N. Point St., Fisherman's Wharf,* ☎ *415/563–1234 or 800/233–1234* 📠 *415/486–4444* ⊕ *www.fishermanswharf.hyatt.com* 🛏 *313 rooms, 8 suites* ♿ *In-room: safe, refrigerators (some), Wi-Fi. In-hotel: restaurant, bar, room service, pool, gym, concierge, laundry facilities, laundry service, public Internet, parking (fee), no-smoking rooms* ⊟ *AE, D, DC, MC, V.*

$$$ Marriott Fisherman's Wharf. Behind the hotel's sand-color facade is a lavish, low-ceiling lobby with marble floors, a double fireplace, and English club–style furniture. Rooms—which are expected be fully remodeled by mid-2009—have either a king-size bed or two double beds; all are triple-sheeted, and the abundance of extra pillows allows for lots of luxurious lounging. One hundred rooms, designed with business travelers in mind, have an extra-large desk, ergonomic chair, speakerphone, and two data ports. Restaurant Spada serves all three meals. Complimentary limo service to the Financial District is available weekday mornings. **Pros:** Near tourist hot-spots, comfortable bedding. **Cons:** Touristy area. ⊠ *1250 Columbus Ave., Fisherman's Wharf,* ☎ *415/775–7555* 📠 *415/474–2099* ⊕ *www.marriott.com* 🛏 *269 rooms, 16 suites* ♿ *In-room: safe, refrigerator, dial-up, ethernet. In-hotel: restaurant, room service, bar, gym, concierge, spa, laundry facilities, laundry service, public Internet, public Wi-Fi, parking (fee), some pets allowed (fee), no-smoking rooms* ⊟ *AE, D, MC, V.*

¢ **San Remo Hotel.** A few blocks from Fisherman's Wharf, this three-story 1906 Italianate Victorian—once home to longshoremen and Beat poets—has a narrow stairway from the street leading to the front desk and labyrinthine hallways. Rooms are small but charming, with lace curtains, forest-green-painted wood floors, brass beds, and other antique furnishings. The top floor is brighter, because it's closer to the skylights that provide sunshine to the thriving population of potted plants that line the brass-banistered hallways. About a third of the rooms have sinks, and all share spotless black-and-white-tile bathroom facilities with pull-chain toilets. A rooftop suite must be reserved three to six months in advance. Fior D'Italia, "America's Oldest Italian Restaurant," occupies the building's entire first floor. **Pros:** Inexpensive. **Cons:** Some rooms are dark, no private bath, spartan amenities.

Fodor's Choice
★

✉ *2237 Mason St., North Beach,* ☎ *415/776–8688 or 800/352–7366* 🖶 *415/776–2811* ⊕ *www.sanremohotel.com* 🛏*62 rooms with shared baths, 1 suite* ♿ *In-room: no a/c, no phone, no TV. In-hotel: no elevator, laundry facilities, public Internet, parking (fee), no-smoking rooms* ⊟ *AE, MC, V.*

$–$$ **SW Hotel.** Opened in 1913 as the Columbo Hotel, this lodging on the bustling border between Chinatown and North Beach has rooms and suites decorated in a blend of Italian and Chinese styles, with Florentine wall coverings and Ming-style furniture. Old-fashioned wooden venetian blinds cover the windows, and baths have polished granite countertops. Top-floor rooms have nice views of Coit Tower and North Beach. Be warned: The smallest rooms have teensy closets and bathrooms, so ask for the most spacious accommodations available. A multilingual staff serves morning pastries and beverages in the mezzanine area. **Pros:** Top-floor views of Coit Tower, multilingual staff, self-serve parking under building. **Cons:** Cramped closets and bathrooms. ✉ *615 Broadway, Chinatown/North Beach,* ☎ *415/362–2999 or 888/595–9188* 🖶 *415/362–1808* ⊕ *www.swhotel.com* 🛏*105 rooms, 2 suites* ♿ *In-room: no a/c (some), kitchen (some), dial-up, Wi-Fi. In-hotel: public Internet, parking (fee), no-smoking rooms* ⊟ *AE, DC, MC, V* ⍟*CP.*

$$$ **Washington Square Inn.** Overlooking the tree-lined park of its namesake and surrounded by fine shops and cafés, this gracious corner B&B sits at the foot of Telegraph Hill in the heart of North Beach. Both large and small rooms are individually decorated with Venetian and French accents; upgraded bathrooms are done in imported marble and tiles. Most rooms have gas fireplaces and beds with 400- to 600-thread-count sheets. The lobby, which has a gleaming mahogany fireplace and brass chandeliers, is the setting for free wine and antipasti in the evening. An expanded Continental breakfast is served by the front windows. **Pros:** Nice rooms, fun location. **Cons:** Some guests complain about gruff management, no a/c, street parking is difficult to come by. ✉ *1660 Stockton St., at Filbert St.,* ☎ *415/981–4220 or 800/388–0200* 🖶 *415/397–7242* ⊕ *www.wsisf.com* 🛏*15 rooms* ♿ *In-room: no a/c, dial-up, Wi-Fi. In-hotel: restaurant, no elevator, concierge, public Internet, parking (fee), no-smoking rooms* ⊟ *AE, D, DC, MC, V* ⍟*BP.*

NOB HILL

$$ **Executive Hotel Vintage Court.** This Napa Valley–inspired hotel two blocks from Union Square has inviting rooms named after California wineries. Some have sunny window seats, and all have large writing desks, dark-wood venetian blinds, and steam heat. Bathrooms are small; some have tub-showers, while others have stall showers. The Wine Country theme extends to complimentary local vintages served nightly in front of a roaring fire in the chocolate-color lobby, where long couches encourage lingering. For a superior gastronomic experience, book a table at the adjoining Masa's, one of the city's most celebrated French restaurants. **Pros:** Complimentary local wines. **Cons:** Small bathrooms, far from downtown and many tourist spots. ✉ *650 Bush St., Nob Hill,* ☎ *415/392–4666 or 800/654–1100* 🖶 *415/433–4065* ⊕ *www.vintage*

court.com ✎*106 rooms, 1 suite* ⚐*In-room: refrigerator, dial-up, Wi-Fi. In-hotel: restaurant, bar, concierge, laundry service, public Internet, parking (fee), some pets allowed (fee), no-smoking rooms* ⊟*AE, D, DC, MC, V* ⦿*CP.*

$$$$ **Fairmont San Francisco.** This hotel, which dominates the top of Nob Hill like a European palace, has a rich history that includes surviving the 1906 earthquake and hosting the signing of the United Nations Charter in 1945. Architect Julia Morgan's 1907 lobby design includes alabaster walls and gilt-embellished ceilings supported by Corinthian columns. In the main building, gracious, recently enhanced rooms done in conservative color schemes have high ceilings, fine dark-wood furniture, colorful Chinese porcelain lamps, wonderful new beds, flat-screen TVs, and marble bathrooms. Rooms in the Tower are generally larger and have better views. Amenities and special services (including free chicken soup if you're under the weather) keeps loyal guests coming back. Don't miss drinks at the recently spiffed up Tonga Room, an outsized Tiki lounge that serves blue tropical cocktails with umbrellas. **Pros:** Huge bathrooms, stunning lobby, great location. **Cons:** Some guests have complained about spotty service, hills can be challenging for those on foot. ⊠*950 Mason St., Nob Hill,* ☎*415/772–5000 or 800/257–7544* 🖷*415/772–5013* ⊕*www.fairmont.com/sanfrancisco* ✎*591 rooms, 65 suites* ⚐*In-room: safe, ethernet. In-hotel: 2 restaurants, room service, bars, gym, spa, concierge, laundry service, public Internet, parking (fee), some pets allowed (fee), no-smoking rooms* ⊟*AE, D, DC, MC, V.*

$$$$ **Ritz-Carlton, San Francisco.** A preferred destination for travel industry honchos and visitors alike, this hotel—a stunning tribute to beauty and attentive, professional service—recently completed a $12.5 million renovation of its guest rooms and meeting spaces. Ionic columns grace the neoclassic facade, crystal chandeliers illuminate Georgian antiques and museum-quality 18th- and 19th-century paintings in the lobby. All rooms have flat-screen TVs, featherbeds with 300-thread-count Egyptian cotton Frette sheets and down comforters. Club Level rooms include use of the upgraded Club Lounge, which has a dedicated concierge and several elaborate complimentary food presentations daily. The Dining Room has a seasonal menu with modern French accents. The delightful afternoon tea service in the Lobby Lounge, which overlooks the beautifully landscaped Terrace courtyard, is a San Francisco institution. **Pros:** Guests rave about the terrific service; all-day food service on club level; immaculate, beautiful surroundings. **Cons:** Expensive, hilly location. ⊠*600 Stockton St., at California St., Nob Hill,* ☎*415/296–7465* 🖷*415/291–0288* ⊕*www.ritzcarlton.com/hotels/san_francisco* ✎*276 rooms, 60 suites* ⚐*In-room: safe, refrigerator, DVD, dial-up, Wi-Fi. In-hotel: 2 restaurants, room service, bars, pool, gym, concierge, laundry service, executive floor, public Internet, parking (fee), some pets allowed, no-smoking rooms* ⊟*AE, D, DC, MC, V.*

FodorsChoice
★

$$–$$$ **The Stanford Court.** A stained-glass dome and a sweeping 360-degree mural depicting scenes of early San Francisco and the gold rush dominate the lobby of this stately-but-comfortable Marriott-operated hotel. Rooms achieve understated elegance with a mix of English-country-

manor-style furnishings accented with Asian artwork and accessories. Nice touches include 300-thread-count Frette sheets, plush robes, heated towel racks, bathroom TVs, and nightly turndown service. Fournou's Ovens—known for its Provençal decor, 54-square-foot oven, and world-class wine cellar—is usually packed for dinner. Complimentary coffee or tea is delivered to your room each morning upon request. **Pros:** Focus on comfort, classic elegance. **Cons:** Far from most popular tourist sights, some guests complain that rooms are small. ⊠*905 California St., Nob Hill,* 🕾*415/989–3500* 🖷*415/391–0513* ⊕*www. stanfordcourt.com* 🖙*393 rooms, 9 suites* ᕦ*In-room: dial-up, Wi-Fi. In-hotel: restaurant, room service, bar, gym, concierge, laundry service, public Internet, parking (fee), some pets allowed, no-smoking rooms* 🖃*AE, D, DC, MC, V.*

PACIFIC HEIGHTS, COW HOLLOW & THE MARINA

¢–$ **Coventry Motor Inn.** Among the many motels on busy Lombard Street, this is one of the cleanest, friendliest, and quietest—especially the rooms that don't face Lombard. The oak-paneled lobby is decorated with leather furniture and photographs of historic San Francisco, and the unusually spacious rooms have cheery yellow wallpaper, gold drapes, oak furniture, and well-lit dining and work areas. Many rooms have bay windows, and some on the upper floors have views of the Golden Gate Bridge. **Pros:** Clean, friendly, good value, lots of eateries nearby, free parking under building. **Cons:** Busy street, few amenities. ⊠*1901 Lombard St., Cow Hollow,* 🕾*415/567–1200* 🖷*415/921–8745* ⊕*www.coventrymotorinn.com* 🖙*69 rooms* ᕦ*In-room: dial-up, Wi-Fi. In-hotel: parking (no fee), no-smoking rooms* 🖃*AE, MC, V.*

¢–$ **Cow Hollow Motor Inn and Suites.** Rooms at this large, family-owned modern motel are more spacious than average, with sitting-dining areas, dark-wood traditional furniture, and wallpaper with muted yellow, brown, and green patterns. Resembling typical San Francisco apartments, expansive rooms feature hardwood floors, Oriental rugs, antique furnishings, marble wood-burning fireplaces, big living rooms, and fully equipped kitchens; some have views of the Golden Gate Bridge. Huge, lovely suites, overlooking the eclectic mix of shops, coffeehouses, and neighborhood businesses on Chestnut Street, have one or two bedrooms and baths. **Pros:** Rooms are the size of apartments, covered parking under building. **Cons:** Congested neighborhood has a fratty feeling. ⊠*2190 Lombard St., Marina,* 🕾*415/921–5800* 🖷*415/922–8515* ⊕*www.cowhollowmotorinn.com* 🖙*117 rooms, 12 suites* ᕦ*In-room: kitchen (some), Wi-Fi. In-hotel: restaurant, parking (no fee), no-smoking rooms* 🖃*AE, DC, MC, V.*

$$ **Hotel Del Sol.** Go tropical in the Marina district at this colorfully restored three-story 1950s motor lodge. Summer barbecues by the courtyard pool and the hotel's proximity to Funston playground make this place kid-friendly, as do free toys, games, a "pillow library," and evening cookies and milk. Since the Del Sol is only two blocks from Union Street shopping and restaurants, with easy access off Lombard Street, it will please adults, too. **Pros:** Kid friendly, plenty of nearby places to eat and shop. **Cons:** Congested area, street parking is elusive. ⊠*3100*

CLOSE UP

A Concierge's Top Tips

Concierges can be the Great Finesser of your trip: finding hard-to-get reservations or tickets, helping with business matters, and generally making your stay easier. Here's the inside scoop from a former concierge.

Be Specific. When soliciting help in choosing a restaurant, focus on what you like, not what you don't. Avoid unhelpful statements such as "Where should I eat? I don't like fish, I don't like steak, and I don't like Chinese." Instead, tell the concierge what you do like and reveal your tastes, as in, "I love candlelit French bistros, but tonight I feel like something livelier, more casual, maybe Italian." You'll always get better results.

Do your homework. Nothing drives a concierge crazier than a guest who arrives at the desk and says, "I'm in San Francisco for two weeks, and I've never been here before. What should I do?" (Fortunately you're already one step ahead by having consulted Fodor's first!)

Save big at biz hotels. If you're a weekend traveler on a mid-range budget, you can sometimes get great deals at high-end hotels that cater primarily to business travelers. The opposite is true at tourist hotels, which spike their rates on the weekends.

"Block" your room. If you want to book a particular room or room type, call the hotel on the morning of your arrival and reconfirm the arrangements with the front-office manager. Ask the manager to "block" (pre-assign) your room. This is especially important when the hotel is sold out and you're arriving late at night; otherwise you'll get the "last-sell" room—

the least popular room reserved for the last-to-arrive guest.

Call ahead for your car. When you're ready to retrieve your car from valet parking, don't expect simply to arrive in the lobby, hand over your ticket, and instantly get your vehicle. Always call at least 10 minutes beforehand, lest you be left standing in the driveway, late for dinner.

Timing is everything. If you have a complicated request, or need to have a personal conversation with the concierge, call or stop by the desk in the late morning, mid-afternoon, or evening. Concierges are busiest in the morning at check-out time, when business travelers need the most assistance, and in the late afternoon and early evening at check-in time, when guests want dinner reservations. The ideal time to chitchat is usually between noon and 4 PM, and 8 PM and 10 PM.

Tip early and often. For the best service, don't wait to tip your concierge: give half the money up front, then the other half once your request has been fulfilled. If the staff knows you're a good tipper, they'll work extra hard to ensure you get you what you want, when you want it.

Tip your concierge based on the time spent arranging your request. For simple matters that require only one phone call, such as an airport shuttle, tip $2. For restaurant recommendations and reservations that require discussion and opinion, $5 to $20, the latter for harder-to-book tables. For itinerary planning, tip $20 to $100, depending on how complicated and time-consuming the arrangements are.

–John Vlahides

13

Webster St., Marina, ☎*415/921–5520 or 877/433–5765* 📠*415/931–4137* ⊕*thehoteldelsol.com* ⇖*42 rooms, 15 suites* ♿*In room: kitchen (some), refrigerator (some), DVD, Wi-Fi. In hotel: room service, pool, children's programs (ages toddler to 10), laundry service, concierge, parking (no fee), no-smoking rooms* ▱*AE, D, DC, MC, V* ⦿*CP.*

$$–$$$ **Hotel Drisco.** Pretend you're a resident of one of the wealthiest and most beautiful residential neighborhoods in San Francisco at this understated, elegant 1903 Edwardian hotel. The quiet haven, which feels like a secluded B&B, serves as a celebrity hideaway for the likes of Ethan Hawke and Ashley Judd. Genteel furnishings and luxurious amenities like flat-screen TVs grace pale-yellow-and-white rooms, some of which have sweeping city views. Morning newspaper, plush robes, slippers, and nightly turndown service are included. A free breakfast is offered in a sunny, spacious room, and wine is set out each evening in a lovely area off the lobby. Guests have commented on the helpful and incredibly friendly staff. **Pros:** Great service, comfortable rooms, quiet residential retreat. **Cons:** Small rooms, far from Downtown. ✉*2901 Pacific Ave., Pacific Heights,* ☎*415/346–2880 or 800/634–7277* 📠*415/567–5537* ⊕*www.hoteldrisco.com* ⇖*29 rooms, 19 suites* ♿*In-room: no a/c, refrigerator, safe, DVD. In-hotel: concierge, laundry service, public Internet, no-smoking rooms* ▱*AE, D, DC, MC, V* ⦿*CP.*

$$–$$$ **Hotel Majestic.** Built in 1902 as a private residence, this five-story white Edwardian building, the city's oldest continually operating hotel, turned into a residence club two years later—movie star sisters Joan Fontaine and Olivia de Havilland, symbols of Old Hollywood royalty, once lived here. Nicolas Cage, his uncle August Coppola, and the crew of *Sweet November* are among the more contemporary moviemakers who have visited the hotel's elegant lobby, appointed with antique chandeliers, plush Victorian chairs, and hundreds of antiquarian French books. Most rooms—which have either hand-painted, four-poster or two poster twin beds—have gas fireplaces and claw-foot tubs. The hotel, which survived both of San Francisco's major 20th-century earthquakes, is legendary for its friendly ghost, the newly renovated Café Majestic, and the largest collection of exotic butterflies in northern California—on display at the café bar, where you can also order light fare. **Pros:** Quintessential SF hotel, destination café, Victorian flavor, quiet neighborhood, perfect for a romantic getaway. **Cons:** You'll need a cab to get downtown or to tourist hot spots. ✉*1500 Sutter St., Pacific Heights,* ☎*415/441–1100 or 800/869–8966* 📠*415/673–7331* ⊕*www.thehotelmajestic.com* ⇖*49 rooms, 9 suites* ♿*In-room: refrigerator (some), Wi-Fi. In-hotel: restaurant, room service, bar, concierge, laundry service, public Internet, parking (fee), no-smoking rooms* ▱*AE, D, DC, MC, V* ⦿*CP.*

$$–$$$ **Laurel Inn.** The blue-and-tan Googie-style facade of this stylish inn suggests its 1963 urban motel origins. Rooms, completely renovated in 1999 and decorated in black and taupe, are spacious and clean; all have ceiling fans, some have desks and fold-out sofas, and 18 offer convenient kitchenettes. Adjoining rooms can be connected to create a kid-friendly suite. Accommodations in the rear have cityscape views and tend to be quieter. Day passes are available to the extensive exercise

facilities at the Jewish Community Center of San Francisco, located directly across the street. The young, hip G-bar cocktail lounge boasts the best martini in town. Diverse shops and restaurants are one block away on Sacramento Street. **Pros:** Clean, spacious, kid-friendly rooms, close to Sacramento Street. **Cons:** No a/c, far from downtown. ⊠*444 Presidio Ave., Pacific Heights,* ☏*415/567–8467 or 800/552–8735* 🖶*415/928–1866* ⊕*thelaurelinn.com* 🛏*49 rooms* ⟲ *In-room: no a/c, kitchen (some), refrigerator (some), Wi-Fi. In-hotel: bar, laundry service, concierge, public Internet, parking (fee), some pets allowed, no-smoking rooms* ⊟*AE, D, DC, MC, V* ⦿*CP.*

¢–$ **Marina Inn.** Five blocks from the Marina, this four-story 1924 building feels like a B&B but is priced like a motel. English country-style rooms with vivid floral wallpaper and bedspreads are simply appointed with queen-size two-poster beds, private baths, small pinewood writing desks, and armoires. Some rooms have daybeds appropriate for a small child. The rooms facing Octavia and Lombard streets have bay windows with window seats, but they are noisier than the inside rooms. A simple Continental breakfast is served in the central sitting room. **Pros:** Cheap, daybed option for kids. **Cons:** Street-side rooms are noisy. ⊠*3110 Octavia St., at Lombard St., Marina,* ☏*415/928–1000 or 800/274–1420* 🖶*415/928–5909* ⊕*www.marinainn.com* 🛏*40 rooms* ⟲*In-room: no a/c, dial-up, Wi-Fi. In-hotel: no-smoking rooms* ⊟*AE, DC, MC, V* ⦿*CP.*

¢–$ **Pacific Heights Inn.** One of the most genteel-looking motels in town, this two-story motor court near the busy intersection of Union and Van Ness is dressed up with wrought-iron railings and benches, hanging plants, and pebbled exterior walkways facing the parking lot. Rooms, with floral bedspreads and brass beds, are on the small side; however, about half have kitchenettes, and several units are two-bedroom suites. Two rooms come with special Duxiana beds, which are especially kind to weary backs. Morning pastries and coffee are served in the lobby, along with a free newspaper. **Pros:** Kitchenettes, reasonable rates. **Cons:** Small rooms, noisy, crowded parking area. ⊠*1555 Union St., Pacific Heights,* ☏*415/776–3310 or 800/523–1801* 🖶*415/776–8176* ⊕*www.pacificheightsinn.com* 🛏*35 rooms, 5 suites* ⟲*In-room: no a/c, kitchen (some), refrigerator, Wi-Fi. In-hotel: no elevator, parking (no fee), some pets allowed (fee), no-smoking rooms* ⊟*AE, DC, MC, V* ⦿*CP.*

$–$$ **Queen Anne.** Built in the 1890s as a girls' finishing school and located in fashionable Pacific Heights, this Victorian mansion has a large comfortable parlor done up in red brocade, lace, and heirloom antiques. Original stained glass, inlaid wood floors throughout its elegant hallways, and 14 fireplaces, combine "the romantic charm of the past with present day comfort." Complimentary amenities include a Continental breakfast, daily newspaper, weekday courtesy car service downtown, and afternoon tea and sherry. The versatile parlor, salon, boardroom, library, and small covered outdoor courtyard make this a popular spot for weddings. **Pros:** Free weekday car service, character. **Cons:** Far from downtown. ⊠*1590 Sutter St., Pacific Heights,* ☏*415/441–2828 or 800/227–3970* 🖶*415/775–5212* ⊕*www.queenanne.com* 🛏*41* rooms, 7 suites ♨In-room: VCR (some), dial-up. In-hotel: laundry service, concierge, public Internet, airport shuttle, parking (fee) ▤AE, D, DC, MC, V |◎|CP.

$$$–$$$$
Fodor'sChoice
★
Union Street Inn. Precious family antiques and unique artwork helped British innkeepers Jane Bertorelli and David Coyle (former chef for the Duke and Duchess of Bedford) transform this green-and-cream 1902 Edwardian into a delightful B&B. Equipped with candles, fresh flowers, wineglasses, and fine linens, rooms are popular with honeymooners and those looking for a romantic get-away. The newly renovated Carriage House, separated from the main house by an old-fashioned English garden planted with lemon trees, is equipped with a double Jacuzzi, refinished hardwood floors, and upgraded bathrooms. An elaborate breakfast, which many guests rave about, is included, as are afternoon tea and evening hors d'oeuvres. **Pros:** Personal service, excellent full breakfast, romantic setting. **Cons:** Congested neighborhood, limited number of rooms, no a/c, no elevator. ✉2229 Union St., Cow Hollow, ☎415/346–0424 ☐415/922–8046 ⊕www.unionstreetinn.com ⬤6 rooms ♨In-room: no a/c, Wi-Fi. In-hotel: no elevator, parking (fee), no-smoking rooms ▤AE, MC, V |◎|BP.

SOMA

$$$$
Fodor'sChoice
★
Four Seasons Hotel San Francisco. Occupying floors 5 through 17 of a new skyscraper, this luxurious hotel, designated as the "heart of the city," is sandwiched between multimillion-dollar condos, elite shops, and a premier sports-and-fitness complex. Elegant rooms with contemporary artwork and fine linens have floor-to-ceiling windows overlook either Yerba Buena Gardens or the historic downtown. All have deep soaking tubs, glass-enclosed showers, and flat-screen TVs. From the contemporary street-level lobby, take the elevator to the vast Sports Club/LA, where you have free access to the junior Olympic pool, full-size indoor basketball court, and the rest of the magnificent facilities, classes, and spa services. Seasons restaurant serves high-end California cuisine, with a strong focus on seasonal and locally produced ingredients. Various packages offer focuses on art, shopping, and cooking. **Pros:** Near museums, galleries, restaurants, and clubs; terrific fitness facilities. **Cons:** Pricey. ✉757 Market St., SoMa, ☎415/633–3000 or 800/819–5053 ☐415/633–3001 ⊕www.fourseasons.com/sanfrancisco ⬤231 rooms, 46 suites ♨In-room: safe, DVD, dial-up, Wi-Fi. In-hotel: restaurant, room service, bar, pool, gym, spa, concierge, laundry service, public Internet, parking (fee), some pets allowed, no-smoking rooms ▤AE, D, DC, MC, V.

$$–$$$
Harbor Court. Exemplary service and a friendly staff earn high marks for this cozy hotel, which overlooks the Embarcadero and is within shouting distance of the Bay Bridge. Guest rooms are on the small side, but have double sets of soundproof windows and include nice touches such as wall-mounted 27-inch flat-screen TVs. Brightly colored throw pillows adorn beds with 320-thread-count sheets, and tub-showers have curved shower-curtain rods for more elbow room. Some rooms have views of the Bay Bridge and the Ferry Building. Complimentary evening wine and late-night cookies and milk are served in the lounge, where

coffee and tea are available mornings. The hotel provides free use of the adjacent YMCA and free weekday limo service within the Financial District. **Pros:** Convenient location, quiet, friendly service, cozy. **Cons:** Small rooms. ⊠*165 Steuart St., SoMa,* ☎*415/882–1300 or 866/792–6283* 📠*415/882–1313* ⊕*www.harborcourthotel.com* ⚓*130 rooms, 1 suite* ♿*In-room: dial-up. In-hotel: bar, concierge, laundry service, public Internet, public Wi-Fi, parking (fee), some pets allowed, no-smoking rooms* ▭*AE, D, DC, MC, V.*

$$ **Hotel Milano.** Adjacent to the new Westfield San Francisco Shopping Centre—whose tenants include Bloomingdale's and Nordstrom—and close to many of the museums and attractions south of Market Street, this hotel is a shopping and culture maven's delight. The eight-story hotel's stately 1913 neoclassical facade gives way to a warm, stylish lobby with a large Alexander Calder–style mobile over the lounge area. Warm earth tones complement the spacious, attractive guest rooms, which have contemporary Italian furnishings. Too much sightseeing or shopping? Ease your fatigue in the split-level fitness center on the seventh and eighth floors. **Pros:** Good value, great location close to shopping/museums, comfy beds, responsive front desk, stylish arty environs. **Cons:** Lots of hubbub and traffic, a/c is inconsistent. ⊠*55 5th St., SoMa,* ☎*415/543–8555* 📠*415/543–5885* ⊕*www.hotelmilanosf.com* ⚓*108 rooms* ♿*In-room: safe, refrigerator, dial-up, Wi-Fi. In-hotel: restaurant, room service, bar, gym, concierge, laundry service, parking (fee), no-smoking rooms* ▭*AE, D, DC, MC, V.*

$$$$ **Hotel Palomar.** The top five floors of the green-tile 1908 Pacific Place Building offer a luxurious oasis above the busiest part of town. A softly lit lounge area with plush sofas gives way to the high-end, newly renovated Fifth Floor restaurant/café, renowned for its adventurous French cuisine. Rooms have muted alligator-pattern carpeting, drapes with bold navy and cream stripes, Frette linens, flat-screen TVs, and sleek furniture echoing a 1930s sensibility. Sparkling bathrooms provide a decadent "tub menu" of L'Occitane herbal/ botanical infusions for optimal relaxation. In-room spa services such as massage, manicures, and body wraps are facilitated through Equilibrium Spa at fellow Kimpton-group property, Hotel Monaco. **Pros:** In-room spa service available, first-class restaurant, good location, refuge from downtown. **Cons:** Pricey. ⊠*12 4th St., SoMa,* ☎*415/348–1111 or 866/373–4941* 📠*415/348–0302* ⊕*www.hotelpalomar-sf.com* ⚓*185 rooms, 13 suites* ♿*In-room: safe, DVD, Wi-Fi. In-hotel: restaurant, room service, bar, gym, concierge, laundry service, public Internet, parking (fee), some pets allowed, no-smoking rooms* ▭*AE, D, DC, MC, V.*

$$$$ **Hotel Vitale.** "Luxury, naturally," the theme of this eight-story terraced bay-front hotel, is apparent in every thoughtful detail: a little vases of aromatic herbs mounted outside each room, the penthouse day spa with soaking tubs set in a rooftop bamboo forest, the aromatherapy garden off the patio of restaurant Americano, the complimentary newspaper and yoga-stretch classes available each morning. Handsome rooms have 440-thread-count sheets, twice-daily maid service, limestone-lined baths, and views of the Bay Bridge, Embarcadero, Treasure Island, or the city skyline. Wi-Fi and LCD flat-screen TVs keep businesspeople in

the loop, and spacious Family Studios have two sofa beds curtained off from the main sleeping area. **Pros:** Family friendly studios, great views, luxurious amenities throughout. **Cons:** Cramped rooms can be noisy, some guests report inconsistent service from staff. ⊠*8 Mission St., Embarcadero* ☎*415/278–3700 or 888/890–8688* 🖷*415/278–3750* ⊕*www.hotelvitale.com* ↩*190 rooms, 9 suites* &*In-room: safe, refrigerator, dial-up, Wi-Fi. In-hotel: restaurant, room service, bar, gym, spa, concierge, laundry service, public Internet, parking (fee), some pets allowed, no-smoking rooms* ☰*AE, D, DC, MC, V* ⱠⓄⱠ*EP.*

$$$–$$$$ **Intercontinental San Francisco.** The arctic-blue glass exterior and subdued, Zen-like lobby of this sparkling new hotel may be as a bland as an airport concourse, but it's merely a prelude to the spectacularly light, expansive, thoughtfully laid-out guestrooms, which have all the ultramodern conveniences. The hotel is within shouting distance of the Moscone Center, and the hotel's business is geared toward convention and corporate travelers, which, depending on occupancy, can make for lower rates on weekends. Bar 888 specializes in vintage grappas, and Luce Restaurant, trimmed in iridescent black mosaic, serves Italian/California cuisine. Be aware: the hotel, which opened February 2008, is located in a so-called "transitional" neighborhood. Stick to Fourth or Fifth Street and walk a couple of blocks to BART, shopping, or museums. **Pros:** A stone's throw from the Moscone Center, well-equipped gym, near hip clubs and edgy eateries. **Cons:** Conservative decor is a bit short on character, borders a rough neighborhood, a bit far from many major points of interest. ⊠*888 Howard St., SoMa* ☎*415/616–6500 or 888/811–4273* ⊕*www.intercontinentalsanfrancisco.com* ↩*536 rooms 14 suites* &*In-room: safe, refrigerator, Wi-Fi. In hotel: restaurant, room service, bars, gym, spa, laundry service, concierge, parking (fee), some pets allowed, no-smoking rooms* ☰*AE, D, DC, MC, V.*

$$ **The Mosser.** Originally built by patron of the arts Alice Phelan in 1913 as the Keystone, this property was purchased in 1981 by composer Charles W. Mosser and completely renovated in 2003. The result is a compatible pairing of contemporary decor and original Victorian architectural elements. Recent upgrades include the newly replaced elevator, double-pane windows and flat-screen TVs. A musical motif extends throughout: Studio Paradiso, which offers state-of-the-art recording equipment and expert technical staff, is next door, and handsomely framed lithographs of recording equipment hang on the walls of the rooms. Tastefully decorated in geometrical patterns of either olive green or dusty fuchsia, 75% of the rooms have tiled private baths with deep tubs, and 25% offer clean, convenient shared facilities on each floor. Annabelle's Bar & Bistro serves contemporary California-style cuisine for lunch and dinner. Ask for special rates at this convenient, stylish, family-owned hotel. **Pros:** Convenient location. **Cons:** About a quarter of the rooms are without private baths. ⊠*54 4th St., SoMa,* ☎*415/986–4400 or 800/227–3804* 🖷*415/495–4337* ⊕*www.the-mosser.com* ↩*166 rooms, 112 with private baths, 54 with shared bath* &*In-room: Wi-Fi. In-hotel: restaurant, bar, concierge, laundry service, parking (fee), some pets allowed (fee), no-smoking rooms* ☰*AE, D, DC, MC, V.*

$$$$ **Palace Hotel.** "Majestic" is the word that best sums up this landmark

Fodor$Choice hotel, which was the world's largest and most luxurious when it opened

★ in 1875. It was completely rebuilt after the 1906 earthquake and fire, and the carriage entrance reemerged as the grand Garden Court restaurant. Today the hotel is still graced with architectural details that recall a bygone era, like chandeliers, tall mirrored glass doors, and eight pairs of turn-of-the-century, bronze filigreed marble columns supporting a magnificent domed ceiling filtering natural light; it's a refined environment ideally suited for the high tea served on weekends and daily during holiday periods. Rooms, with twice-daily maid service and nightly turndown, have soaring 14-foot ceilings, traditional mahogany furnishings, flat-screen TVs, and marble bathrooms. The wood-paneled Pied Piper Bar is named after the delightful 1909 Maxfield Parrish mural behind the bar. **Pros:** Gracious service, close to Union Square, near BART. **Cons:** Older design, small rooms with even smaller baths, many nearby establishments closed on weekends, west-facing rooms can be warm and stuffy. ⊠ *2 New Montgomery St., SoMa,* ☎*415/512–1111 or 888/627–7196* ⊟*415/243–8062* ⊕*www.sfpalace.com* ⥺*518 rooms, 34 suites* ♿*In-room: safe, refrigerator, ethernet. In-hotel: 3 restaurants, room service, bar, pool, gym, spa, concierge, laundry service, public Wi-Fi, parking (fee), no-smoking rooms* ⊟*AE, D, DC, MC, V.*

$$$ **Pickwick.** This terra-cotta-clad neo-Gothic hotel, built in 1926, is decked out with a can't-miss-it, seven-story corner sign straight out of film noir. Next door to the Westfield San Francisco Centre, which houses Bloomingdales and Nordstrom, and convenient to Moscone Center, Yerba Buena Center, and Union Square, the hotel caters to both business and leisure travelers. Some rooms have flat screen TVs. Little Joe's offers Italian cuisine as well a traditional breakfast and lunch. Courteous multilingual staff and 24-hour concierge service offer welcome assistance. **Pros:** Multilingual staff, helpful concierge, close to Metreon and Yerba Buena District. **Cons:** Not as opulent as some other options. ⊠*85 5th St., SoMa,* ☎*415/421–7500 or 800/227–3282* ⊟*415/243–8066* ⊕*www.thepickwickhotel.com* ⥺*186 rooms, 3 suites* ♿*In-room: refrigerator (some), Wi-Fi. In-hotel: restaurant, bar, concierge, laundry service, public Wi-Fi, parking (fee), no-smoking rooms* ⊟*AE, D, DC, MC, V.*

$$$$ **St. Regis Hotel, San Francisco.** This may be the most luxurious hotel in the city. Guests often remark that it's hipper and more modern than other hotels in the St. Regis chain, though the decor is still conservative; rooms have subdued cream-color, leather-textured walls and window seats, and 85% have views of the city. The 42-inch plasma-screen TVs and cordless remotes handle everything from raising the motorized window shades to controlling the entertainment systems to providing weather and other electronic information. Rooms also have Bose sound systems, a copier/fax/printer combo, and direct phone lines. Baths, with limestone tiling and TVs, have deep soaking tubs and separate showers with shower heads that rain straight down. All suites and some rooms have 24-hour butler service. The two-level spa has nine treatment rooms, and the area around the 50-foot lap pool, filled with

13

natural light and bubbling water sounds, is a stunning essay in bright white: a Jacuzzi and sauna are in the immaculate dressing area. The showplace lobby has an elegant bar, restaurant, and a 16-foot-long, two-sided open fireplace. **Pros:** Stunning, newly furnished rooms; good location, views. **Cons:** Expensive, some guests report inconsistent service, hallway noise, long waits for room service and valet parking, some rooms and baths are on the small side. ⊠ *125 3rd St., SoMa,* ☎ *415/284–4000* 📠 *415/284–4100* ⊕ *www.stregis.com/SanFrancisco* 🛏 *214 rooms, 46 suites* ⟨⟩ *In-room: safe, refrigerator, DVD, ethernet, Wi-Fi. In-hotel: 2 restaurants, room service, bar, pool, gym, concierge, laundry service, public Internet, parking (fee), some pets allowed (fee), no-smoking rooms* ▤ *AE, D, DC, MC, V* ⊙ *EP.*

\$\$\$–\$\$\$\$ **W San Francisco.** The epitome of cool urban chic and fashion forward in design and clientele, this swanky 31-story hotel owes some of its cachet to a prime location next door to the San Francisco Museum of Modern Art. Infused with hip energy, techno-pop pulses in the lobby and café and otherworldly mobiles (which change with the seasons) hang overhead; add the mauve leather ottomans and blue velvet sofas to the mix, and you have a cross between a fashion show runway and a stage set. Compact guest rooms, some of which have upholstered window seats, come with luxurious beds, comfy pillow-top mattresses, and goose-down comforters and pillows. Sleek baths sport green glass countertops and shiny steel sinks. The glass-roof pool and hot-tub area, next to Bliss Spa, is open 24/7, as is the Whatever/Whenever concierge desk in the lobby. In the evening there's a lively bar scene, and the lobby, lit by candlelight, sets the mood for XYZ, the hotel's signature restaurant, an "in spot" which attracts celebs such as Sharon Stone and Kanye West. Upper floors boast excellent views of the Museum of Modern Art, Yerba Buena Gardens, and/or the Bay Bridge. During the week, the majority of the clientele is businesspeople, but on weekends the hotel is kid friendly, and pets are always welcome. The accommodating staff will help parents arrange for babysitting and will take your pup for a walk. Fragrances waft throughout the hotel and guest rooms, so sensitive noses should call ahead to request special preparations. **Pros:** Hip energy, cool mod sophisticated digs, in the heart of the cultural district. **Cons:** Three blocks from BART, hotel's signature scents could pose a problem for sensitive noses. ⊠ *181 3rd St., SoMa,* ☎ *415/777–5300* 📠 *415/817–7823* ⊕ *www.whotels.com* 🛏 *410 rooms, 9 suites* ⟨⟩ *In-room: safe, refrigerator, DVD, dial-up, Wi-Fi. In-hotel: restaurant, room service, bar, pool, gym, spa, concierge, laundry service, public Internet, parking (fee), some pets allowed (fee), no-smoking rooms* ▤ *AE, D, DC, MC, V.*

\$\$\$\$ **Westin San Francisco Market Street.** Rising 36 stories over the bustling downtown and SoMa areas, this hotel (formerly the Argent) revels in its views. Bright, airy rooms have floor-to-ceiling windows. Floors 16 to 34 overlook Yerba Buena Gardens, the city, bay, and the hills beyond; others peer between the tall looming edifices of the Financial District (though some of these also glimpse the Golden Gate Bridge, the bay, or Alcatraz). Back on earth, the inlaid marble lobby is home to Ducca, a new restaurant with an outdoor eating area adjacent to a landscaped piazza and the new Contemporary Jewish Museum. The hotel recently remodeled its guest rooms (adding Westin's Heavenly beds), expanded its meeting space, and added an outdoor dining and lounge space with fire pit. A room with treadmill or stationary bike is available. **Pros:** Good location, clean rooms. **Cons:** Some street noise, lots of conven-tion/corporate business. ⊠*50 3rd St., SoMa,* ☏*415/974–6400 or 877/222–6699* 🖷*415/543–8268* ⊕*www.westin.com* 🛏*641 rooms, 26 suites* ♿*In-room: safe, refrigerator (some), VCR (some), dial-up, Wi-Fi. In-hotel: restaurant, room service, bar, gym, concierge, laundry service, parking (fee), no-smoking rooms* ▤*AE, D, DC, MC, V.*

13

UNION SQUARE/DOWNTOWN

$ **Andrews Hotel.** Two blocks west of Union Square, this Queen Anne–style abode began its life in 1904 as the Sultan Turkish Baths. The lobby is dominated by a huge Elliott grandfather clock and the original cage-style elevator. Rooms and bathrooms are small, but well decorated with Victorian reproductions, old-fashioned flower curtains with lace sheers, iron bedsteads, ceiling fans, and large closets. Complimentary wine is served each evening in the lobby. Fino, the hotel restaurant, has been praised for its pizza and spaghetti carbonara. **Pros:** Intimate, decor has character, moderately priced. **Cons:** Smallish rooms and baths. ⊠*624 Post St., Union Square,* ☏*415/563–6877 or 800/926–3739* 🖷*415/928–6919* ⊕*www.andrewshotel.com* 🛏*48 rooms, 5 suites* ♿*In-room: no a/c, DVD. In-hotel: restaurant, laundry service, public Internet, parking (fee), no-smoking rooms* ▤*AE, DC, MC, V* ⦿*CP.*

$$$$ **Campton Place.** Aesthetic beauty and highly attentive service remain the hallmarks of this exquisite jewel-like, top-tier hotel. Fresh-cut orchids and Japanese floral arrangements bring natural beauty inside a hotel where you'll feel sheltered from the teeming crowds on the street. Rooms can be small but are well-laid out and elegantly decorated in a contemporary Italian style, with sandy earth tones and handsome pear-wood paneling and cabinetry. Limestone baths have deep soaking tubs; double-paned windows keep city noises at bay, a plus in this active neighborhood. The Campton Place Restaurant, whose new Indian chef serves French-infused contemporary cuisine at dinner, is famed for its lavish breakfasts. The lounge is a popular cocktail hour hangout for the downtown crowd. **Pros:** Attentive service, first-class restaurant, abundant natural light. **Cons:** Smallish rooms, pricey (but worth it). ⊠*340 Stockton St., Union Square,* ☏*415/781–5555 or 866/332–1670* 🖷*415/955–5585* ⊕*www.camptonplace.com* 🛏*101 rooms, 9 suites* ♿*In-room: safe, ethernet. In-hotel: restaurant, room service, bar, gym, concierge, laundry service, public Wi-Fi, parking (fee), some pets allowed (fee), no-smoking rooms* ▤*AE, DC, MC, V.*

$–$$ **Chancellor Hotel on Union Square.** Built to accommodate visitors to the 1915 Panama Pacific International Exposition, this busy hotel is considered by many to be one of the best buys on Union Square for comfort without extravagance. Floor-to-ceiling windows in the modest lobby overlook cable cars on Powell Street. The moderate-size Edwardian-style, rooms, some with huge walk-in closets, have high ceilings and were recently remodeled. Though a bit dated, the small clean bathrooms have deep tubs—rubber ducky included. The pleasant Restaurant Luques serves American breakfast and lunch, and complimentary coffee, tea, apples, and cookies are available round-the-clock in the lobby. **Pros:** Huge walk-in closets, great value for Union Square, clean rooms. **Cons:** Older building with dark hallways and rooms, small bathrooms, noise from cable cars. ✉*433 Powell St., Union Square,* ☎*415/362–2004 or 800/428–4748* 🖷*415/362–1403* ⊕*www.chancellorhotel.com* ➥*135 rooms, 2 suites* ♿*In-room: no a/c, safe, Wi-Fi. In-hotel: restaurant, room service, bar, concierge, laundry service, public Internet, parking (fee), no-smoking room* ▭*AE, D, DC, MC, V.*

$$$$ **Clift.** A favorite of hipsters, music industry types, and celebrities fleeing the media onslaught—security discreetly keeps photographers and other heat-seekers away—this sexy hotel, whose entrance is so nondescript you can walk right past it without a hint of what's inside, is the brainchild of Entrepreneur Ian Schrager and artist-designer Philippe Starck, known for his collection of eccentric chairs. The moody, dramatically illuminated lobby is dominated by a gigantic Napoleonic chair that could accommodate Shrek, with room to spare. This theatrical staging is enhanced by surreal seating options like a leather love seat with buffalo tusks and a miniature "drink me" chair, all surrounding a floor-to-ceiling, pitch-black fireplace. Spacious rooms—as light as the lobby is darkly intriguing—have translucent orange Plexiglas tables, high ceilings, and two huge "infinity" wall mirror. Some visitors have remarked on the thin walls and advise booking a room on an upper-level floor to avoid street noise. The art-deco Redwood Room bar, paneled with wood from a 2,000-year-old tree, is known for its "beautiful people." Asia de Cuba restaurant prepares an artful fusion of Asian and Latino cuisines. **Pros:** Good rates compared to similar top-tier hotels in SF, surreal moody interior design, ideal location for shopping and theaters, close to public transportation, discreet and helpful staff. **Cons:** Some guests note thin walls, street noise. ✉*495 Geary St., Union Square,* ☎*415/775–4700 or 800/697–1791* 🖷*415/441–4621* ⊕*www.clifthotel.com* ➥*337 rooms, 26 suites* ♿*In-room: safe, DVD, dial-up, Wi-Fi. In-hotel: restaurant, room service, bar, gym, concierge, laundry service, public Internet, parking (fee), some pets allowed (fee), no-smoking rooms* ▭*AE, D, DC, MC, V.*

$ **Cornell Hotel de France.** Discovering this French family-operated hotel is like finding a bit of Paris near Union Square. Charming hosts Claude and Micheline Lambert arrived from their native Orleans 40 years ago, and over the years have renovated and decorated each room with prints of paintings by Picasso, Chagall, and Gustave Klimt. Many savvy repeat visitors know to ask about special packages and discounted rates. Downstairs, Restaurant Jeanne d'Arc offers classic French cuisine in a medieval scene set off by stained-glass windows and artifacts depicting—who else?—Joan of Arc. **Pros:** Special packages and discounts available upon request, a little bit of France in SF. **Cons:** Several blocks from the center of things, surrounding area can be dodgy after dark. ⊠715 Bush St., Union Square, ☎415/421–3154 or 800/232–9698 ⊟415/399–1442 ⊕www.cornellhotel.com ⇩58 rooms, 5 suites ☖In-hotel: public Internet, parking (fee) ⊟AE, D, DC, MC, V ⏐◎⏐BP.

$ **Golden Gate Hotel.** Families looking for accommodations in the Union Square area will delight in this homey, family-run B&B. Built in 1913, the four-story Edwardian has front and back bay windows and an original "birdcage" elevator that transports you to hallways lined with nostalgic historical photographs. Freshly painted and carpeted guest rooms are decorated with antiques, wicker pieces, and Laura Ashley bedding and curtains. Fourteen rooms have private baths, some with claw-foot tubs. Sit in the cozy parlor by the fire and savor afternoon tea and homemade cookies. **Pros:** Friendly staff, spotless rooms, comfortable bedding, good location if you're a walker. **Cons:** Only half of the rooms have private baths. ⊠775 Bush St., Union Square, ☎415/392–3702 or 800/835–1118 ⊟415/392–6202 ⊕www.goldengatehotel.com ⇩25 rooms, 14 with bath ☖In-room: no a/c, dial-up, Wi-Fi. In-hotel: concierge, public Internet, parking (fee), some pets allowed, no-smoking rooms ⊟AE, DC, MC, V ⏐◎⏐CP.

$$$ **Hilton San Francisco.** With 1,908 renovated rooms and suites, this is the largest hotel on the West Coast. Its silvery tower rises 46 floors to a penthouse event space with awe-inspiring 360-degree panoramic views that rank among the finest in San Francisco. Handsome rooms, many with balconies and superlative views of their own, are either in the original 16-story building or in the tower, which was built in 1971. Accommodations on the 44th floor afford the most stunning views of the city and the bay. Seventy-eight ADA compliant rooms have roll-in showers. Thirty-five executive cabana-style rooms surround a sheltered courtyard by an outdoor heated swimming pool and whirlpool. "Sight and Sound" guest rooms feature plasma televisions and a custom connectivity panels for digital cameras, iPods, and video downloads. In 2008, the hotel added 13,600 square feet of event space, a Starbucks, and a new restaurant, Urban Tavern, a place to enjoy a community table, charcuterie, and a simple menu. A full-service spa, bars, and shops are also on the premises. As the hotel is located near the dicey Tenderloin area, guests are directed toward Union Square (two blocks away) when venturing out on foot after dark. **Pros:** Super views, excellent service, full-service spa. **Cons:** Area is dodgy after dark. ⊠333 O'Farrell St., Union Square, ☎415/771–1400 ⊟415/771–6807 ⊕www.sanfrancisco.hilton.com ⇩1,824 rooms, 84 suites ☖In-room: safe, refrigerator, DVD (some), ethernet. In-hotel: restaurant, room service, bars, pool, gym, spa, concierge, laundry service, executive floor, public Wi-Fi, parking (fee), no-smoking rooms ⊟AE, D, DC, MC, V.

$$$$ Hotel Adagio. The gracious, Spanish-colonial facade of this 16-story, theater-row hotel complements its chic, modern interior. Walnut furniture, bronze light fixtures, and brown and deep-orange hues dominate the decent sized, updated rooms, half of which have city views; two penthouse suites have terraces overlooking the neighborhood. The airy, newly redone lobby lounge gives way to the tony Cortez restaurant, where inventive Mediterranean-inspired cuisine is served beneath colorful, glowing sculptures. **Pros:** Close to theater district, on a bus route, good on-site restaurant. **Cons:** Street noise, side streets can be dodgy at night. ⊠550 Geary St., Union Square, ☎415/775–5000 or 800/228–8830 ⊟415/775–9388 ⊕www.thehoteladagio.com ⟿169 rooms, 2 suites ⌂In-room: safe, refrigerator, dial-up, Wi-Fi. In-hotel: restaurant, room service, bar, gym, laundry service, public Internet, parking (fee), no-smoking rooms ⊟AE, D, DC, MC, V.

$–$$ Hotel Beresford. At this relatively inexpensive hotel less than two blocks from Union Square, a white wooden horse marks the entrance to the White Horse Restaurant and pub, an authentic reproduction of an English establishment. Well-maintained rooms with traditional furniture have clean, bright bathrooms. The friendly staff assists with sightseeing arrangements, and the front desk has a large video library. **Pros:** Reasonably priced, close to Union Square, friendly staff. **Cons:** No a/c, no in-room Internet access. ⊠635 Sutter St., Union Square, ☎415/673–9900 or 800/533–6533 ⊟415/474–0449 ⊕www.beresford.com ⟿114 rooms ⌂In-room: no a/c, refrigerator, VCR (some). In-hotel: restaurant, bar, concierge, laundry service, public Internet, parking (fee), some pets allowed, no-smoking rooms ⊟AE, D, DC, MC, V �|○|CP.

$–$$ Hotel Beresford Arms. Surrounded by fancy molding and 10-foot-tall windows, the red-carpeted lobby of this ornate brick Victorian explains why the building is on the National Register of Historic Places. Rooms with dark-wood antique-reproduction furniture vary in size and setup: junior suites have sitting areas and either a wet bar or kitchenette; full suites have two queen beds, a Murphy bed, and a kitchen. All suites have a bidet in the bathroom. Continental breakfast, afternoon tea, and wine are served beneath a crystal chandelier in the lobby. **Pros:** Moderately priced, suites with kitchenettes and Murphy beds are a plus for families with kids. **Cons:** No A/C. ⊠701 Post St., Union Square, ☎415/673–2600 or 800/533–6533 ⊟415/929–1535 ⊕www.beresford.com ⟿83 rooms, 12 suites ⌂In-room: no a/c, kitchen (some), refrigerator, VCR, dial-up, Wi-Fi. In-hotel: concierge, laundry service, public Internet, parking (fee), some pets allowed, no-smoking rooms ⊟AE, D, DC, MC, V �|○|CP.

$–$$ Hotel Bijou. Dedicated to the city's cinematic history, this hotel's tasteful lobby is filled with black-and-white photographs of local movie houses and reproductions of Tamara De Lempicka's art-deco paintings. Each night, the red velvet curtains of the hotel's twenty-seat 1930s "movie palace," Le Petit Théâtre Bijou, open for guests-only, shows complimentary screenings of films shot on location in San Francisco; classic noirs such as *The Maltese Falcon have been on the bill.* Smallish but cheerful rooms are decorated with black-and-white movie stills. The convenience of this downtown location is offset by the proximity to the Tenderloin. **Pros:** Near downtown, free nightly movies. **Cons:** Close to the Tenderloin, small rooms. ⊠*111 Mason St., at Eddy St., Union Square,* ☎*415/771–1200* 🖷*415/346–3196* ⊕*www.hotelbijou.com* ⟐*65 rooms* ⟁*In-room: no a/c, Wi-Fi. In-hotel: concierge, laundry service, public Internet, parking (fee), no-smoking rooms* ▭*AE, D, DC, MC, V* ℺*CP.*

13

¢–$ **Hotel des Arts.** You'll need to climb a narrow, nondescript staircase to discover this hotel, which doubles as an art gallery. The hallways and rooms of this small, funky property have been transformed by international artists, who painted the walls and installed site-specific small sculptures. Check the Web site to scope out the painted rooms (about half have private baths); specific ones can be reserved by phone. The exhibited art is constantly rotating, so you can also let serendipity be your guide. If you're looking for a cool souvenir of your stay, select small paintings in the hallways are available for purchase. **Pros:** Art gallery atmosphere, good location. **Cons:** Only about half of the rooms have private baths. ⊠*447 Bush St., Union Square,* ☎*415/956–3232 or 800/956–4322* 🖷*415/956–0399* ⊕*sfhoteldesarts.com* ⟐*46 rooms* ⟁*In-room: refrigerator (some), Wi-Fi. In-hotel: parking (fee)* ▭*AE, D, DC, MC, V* ℺*CP.*

$$$–$$$$ **Hotel Diva.** Entering this hotel requires stepping over footprints, handprints, and autographs embedded into the sidewalk by visiting stars. With two major theaters, the Curran and Geary (home of the acclaimed American Conservatory Theater company), just across the street, this hotel has long been a magnet for actors, musicians, writers, and artists. It's definitely a hip place, and the updated rooms, especially the suites, feel urban and modern. A new digital movie system plays on flat screen TVs. Cobalt-blue carpets and brushed-steel headboards echoing the shape of ocean waves lend a nautical touch to the white-walled rooms, which have silver bedspreads and sleek steel light fixtures. Bathrooms are tiny but well equipped. A Starbucks and Colibri Mexican Bistro are in the lobby. **Pros:** Clean, safe, in the heart of the theater district, accommodating service. **Cons:** No frills, tiny bathrooms. ⊠*440 Geary St., Union Square,* ☎*415/885–0200 or 800/553–1900* 🖷*415/346–6613* ⊕*www.hoteldiva.com* ⟐*115 rooms, 1 suite* ⟁*In-room: safe, refrigerator (some), DVD, Wi-Fi. In-hotel: gym, concierge, laundry service, public Internet, parking (fee), some pets allowed (fee), no-smoking rooms* ▭*AE, D, DC, MC, V* ℺*CP.*

$$$$ **Hotel Monaco.** A cheery 1910 Beaux Arts facade and snappily dressed

Fodor'sChoice doormen welcome you into a plush lobby dominated by a French ingle-

★ nook fireplace, vaulted ceilings painted with whimsical murals of hot-air balloons, and a large metal baobab tree dedicated to hotelier Bill Kimpton. Rooms are strikingly decorated with vivid stripes and colors, Chinese-inspired armoires, canopy beds, and high-back upholstered chairs. Outer rooms feature bay-window seats overlooking the bustling theater district. If you didn't bring a pet, request a "companion gold-fish." Guests have cheered the hotel's staff for its "amazing service" and "attention to detail" and praised the ornate Grand Café and Bar, which serves French/California cuisine. Take advantage of complimentary access to the recently redone Equilibrium Spa, where you can soak, steam, or bake to our heart's content from 6 AM–10 PM. **Pros:** Amazing service, stylish, full of character, near theater district, you're never alone when you have a goldfish to keep you company. **Cons:** Close to the Tenderloin, some discount-rate rooms are small. ✉ *501 Geary St., Union Square,* ☎*415/292–0100 or 866/622–5284* 🖷*415/292–0111* ⊕*www. monaco-sf.com* ⤴*181 rooms, 20 suites* ⌂*In-room: safe, DVD, Wi-Fi. In-hotel: restaurant, room service, bar, gym, spa, concierge, laundry service, public Internet, parking (fee), some pets allowed, no-smoking rooms* ▤*AE, D, DC, MC, V.*

$$$$ **Hotel Nikko.** The vast gray-flecked white marble and gurgling fountains in the neoclassical lobby of this business traveler hotel has the sterility of an airport. Crisply designed rooms in muted tones have modern bathrooms with sinks that sit on top of black vanities and "in-vogue" separate showers and tubs. The excellent, 10,000-square-foot Club Nikko fitness facility has traditional *ofuros* (Japanese soaking tubs), his-and-hers *kamaburso* (Japanese meditation rooms), and a glass-enclosed 16-meter rooftop pool and a whirlpool. San Francisco's only cabaret theater, located on the lobby level, is a venue for national talent most evenings. **Pros:** Friendly multilingual staff, some rooms have ultramodern baths, very clean. **Cons:** Rooms and antiseptic lobby lack color, some may find the atmosphere cold, expensive parking. ✉*222 Mason St., Union Square,* ☎*415/394–1111 or 800/248–3308* 🖷*415/394–1106* ⊕*www.hotelnikkosf.com* ⤴*510 rooms, 22 suites* ⌂*In-room: refrigerator, ethernet, Wi-Fi. In-hotel: restaurant, room service, bar, pool, gym, concierge, laundry service, executive floor, public Internet, public Wi-Fi, parking (fee), some pets allowed (fee), no-smoking rooms* ▤*AE, D, DC, MC, V.*

$$ **Hotel Rex.** If this stylish literary-themed hotel—named after San Francisco Renaissance poet, translator, and essayist Kenneth Rexroth and
Fodor's Choice
★ frequented by artists and writers—had a kindred spirit, it would The New Yorker magazine. Paintings and shelves of antiquarian books line the "library," a homey lobby lounge where book readings and roundtable discussions take place. Although the small, somewhat dark, cramped rooms with restored period furnishings and striped carpeting evoke the spirit of salon society—excerpts from historic San Francisco social registers paper the elevator—they also have modern touches like a study decorated with a collection of vintage typewriters (and two high-tech workstations). California seasonal cuisine is served in the hotel's petite bistro, Andrée. **Pros:** Convenient location, literary pedigree. **Cons:** Cramped airless rooms, tiny baths and closets, musty hallways. ✉*562 Sutter St., Union Square,* ☎*415/433–4434 or 800/433–4434* 🖷*415/433–3695* ⊕*www.thehotelrex.com* ⤴*92 rooms, 2 suites* ⌂*In-room: refrigerator, Wi-Fi. In-hotel: restaurant, room service, bar, concierge, laundry service, public Internet, parking (fee), no-smoking rooms* ▤*AE, D, DC, MC, V.*

$$–$$$ **Hotel Triton.** The spirit of fun has taken up full-time residence in this Kimpton property, which has a youngish, super-friendly staff; pink and blue neon elevators; and a colorful psychedelic lobby mural depicting the San Francisco art and music scene—think flower power mixed with Andy Warhol. Playful furniture includes a green/gold metallic couch and striped carpeting, a whimsical and far-out setting for free morning coffee and tea, fresh afternoon cookies, evening wine events, and the on-call tarot reader. Smallish rooms are painted silver gray and tomato-soup red and come with ergonomic desk chairs, flat-screen TVs, and oddball light

13

fixtures; sinks are positioned outside the bathrooms, European style. Twenty-four "environmentally sensitive" rooms have water- and air-filtration systems and biodegradable soap. A 24-hour yoga channel will help you find that elusive path to inner peace. **Pros:** Attentive service, refreshingly funky atmosphere, hip arty environs, good location. **Cons:** Rooms and baths are on the small side. ☒*342 Grant Ave., Union Square,* ☎*415/394–0500 or 800/433–6611* 🖷*415/394–0555* ⊕*www. hoteltriton.com* ⤵*133 rooms, 7 suites* ⟐*In-room: refrigerator, DVD (some), Wi-Fi. In-hotel: restaurant, bar, gym, laundry service, parking (fee), some pets allowed, no-smoking rooms* ▭*AE, D, DC, MC, V.*

$$$–$$$$ **JW Marriott San Francisco.** Guests here are whisked skyward in bullet elevators from the rose-and-gray-marble foyer into this John Portman–designed, former Pan Pacific hotel. A graceful Matisse-inspired bronze sculpture encircles the fountain in the dramatically reconfigured 21-story lobby atrium. Guest rooms have new gold, olive, and maroon bedding, flat-screen televisions, versatile desks for dining or working and elegant bathrooms boast new vanities and deep soaking tubs, which many guests rave about. **Pros:** Recently renovated, convenient location, large rooms, luxurious bathrooms. **Cons:** Comfortable but lacking character. ☒*500 Post St., Union Square,* ☎*415/771–8600* 🖷*415/398–0267* ⊕*www.marriott.com/sfojw* ⤵*329 rooms, 9 suites* ⟐*In-room: safe, VCR (some), ethernet. In-hotel: restaurant, room service, bar, gym, concierge, laundry service, public Wi-Fi, parking (fee), some pets allowed (fee), no-smoking rooms* ▭*AE, D, DC, MC, V.*

$–$$ **Larkspur Union Square.** This compact boutique hotel, housed in a 1913 Edwardian building near Union Square, is now managed by the Larkspur Hospitality Company. Complimentary amenities include breakfast buffet in the Garden Room, a morning paper, and a nightly wine reception in the lobby. Rooms come with Featherborne beds, Lather natural bath and body products, and flat-screen TVs. A computer and printer are available in the library. A recent remodeling project updated 10 rooms, all of the hotel's suites, and the lobby. ADA rooms will also be available. Note that as this is a historic building, so rooms and baths can feel cramped and claustrophobic—but for travelers who want to be near Union Square, it's a relatively inexpensive option. **Pros:** Good location, moderately priced. **Cons:** Dark, airless rooms and hallways; small baths. ✉*524 Sutter St., Union Square,* 🕾*415/421–2865 or 800/919–9779* 🖷*415/398–6345* ⊕*www.larkspurhotelunionsquare. com* ⇄*109 rooms, 5 suites* ᕈ*In-room: dial-up, Wi-Fi. In-hotel: laundry service, concierge, public Wi-Fi, parking (fee), some pets allowed, no-smoking rooms* ▤*AE, D, DC, MC, V* ⑩*BP.*

$$$–$$$$ **Orchard Garden Hotel.** Feel virtuous and environmentally sensitive at the first San Francisco hotel built to environmentally stringent LEED specifications, exacting standards which mandate the use of eco-friendly features such as chemical-free cleaning agents, recycling bins, and a custom guest-room key card energy control system. Local artist Archie Held's glass water sculpture in the lobby sets the stage for the hotel's high aesthetics. The owner's collection of original artwork is scattered throughout the hotel—and rooftop garden. Amenities include complimentary car service to the Financial District. Buffet breakfast as well as lunch and dinner which can be enjoyed at Roots, a restaurant, supplied by organic and local purveyors. The simply styled rooms offer low-flow toilets, washable textiles in soothing hues of green and gold, and natural woods. **Pros:** Environmentally sensitive. **Cons:** A bit of a hike from Union Square. ✉*446 Bush St., Union Square,* 🕾*415/399– 9807, 888/717–2881* 🖷*415/393–9917* ⊕*www.theorchardgarden- hotel.com* ⇄*82 rooms, 4 suites* ᕈ*In-room: safe, refrigerator, DVD, Wi-Fi. In-hotel: restaurant, concierge, parking (fee)* ▤*AE, D, DC, V, MC* ⑩*BP.*

$$$–$$$$ **Orchard Hotel.** Unlike most other boutique hotels in the area, which sometimes occupy century-old buildings, the strictly 21st-century Orchard was built in 2000. The 104-room hotel embraces state-of-the-art technology—from CD and DVD players in each room to Wi-Fi access throughout the building—mixing cutting-edge Silicon Valley chic with classic European touches. The hotel's marble lobby, where the bronze statue "Spring Awakening" greets visitors, previews the dramatic architectural embellishments, like arched openings, vaulted ceilings, and stone floors that are found throughout the hotel. With just 12 rooms per floor, the hotel feels quite intimate; some guests have compared it to a cozy (decidedly upscale) mountain inn. Rooms, sizable by boutique hotel standards, are done in a soft palette of relaxing colors, a balm for harried shoppers returning from a busy day of retail therapy in Union Square. The hotel's restaurant, Daffodil, serves seasonal California fare for breakfast and dinner. Like its "green sister," the Orchard Garden, this one is also going for its LEED certification, giving SF visitors yet another eco-friendly option. **Pros:** Cutting-edge technology. **Cons:** Can be a bit pricey. ✉*665 Bush St., Union Square,* 🕾*415/362–8878 or 888/717–2881* 🖷*415/362–8088* ⊕*www.theor- chardhotel.com* ⇄*104 rooms, 9 suites* ᕈ*In-room: safe, DVD, Wi-Fi. In-hotel: restaurant, room service, laundry service, parking (fee), some pets allowed, no-smoking rooms* ▤*AE, D, DC, MC, V.*

$$–$$$ **Prescott Hotel.** This relatively small establishment providing extremely personalized service prides itself on offering "good taste on Union Square." One guest described the hotel as making "you feel welcomed

13

at every point of your stay." Postrio, Wolfgang Puck's award-winning restaurant, one of the most breathtaking dining rooms in the city, is attached to the lobby. The casual Postrio café bar offers three-cheese pizza, delectable sandwiches, and soups. The rooms, which were renovated in 2001, are filled with cherry furniture, handsomely decorated in dark autumn colors and have bathrooms with marble-top sinks. Free coffee and evening wine are offered by a flickering fireplace in the living room. Executive Club Level rooms include a free Continental breakfast and afternoon cocktails with Puck's pizza in the private Executive Club Level lounge. **Pros:** Good location; excellent café, bar, and restaurant on premises. **Cons:** Off-site valet service can be slow, some guests complain of street noise. ✉ *545 Post St., Union Square,* ☎ *415/563–0303 or 866/271–3632* 🖷 *415/563–6831* ⊕ *www.prescotthotel.com* 🛏 *132 rooms, 32 suites* ♿ *In-room: safe, VCR (some), Wi-Fi. In-hotel: restaurant, room service, bar, gym, concierge, executive floor, public Internet, parking (fee), some pets allowed, no-smoking rooms* ▤ *AE, D, DC, MC, V.*

$$$$ Sir Francis Drake Hotel. Beefeater-costumed doormen welcome you into the regal, dimly lit, and slightly run-down lobby of this 1928 landmark property, decked out with boldly striped banners, wrought-iron balustrades, chandeliers, Italian marble, and leather and velvet furnishings that are a little on the tired side. The cumulative effect is of a Scottish castle that's seen better days. The lobby bar, guest rooms, bathrooms, public spaces, gym, and meeting rooms are somewhat shopworn or downright shabby despite an ongoing $20 million renovation. Be advised: staff is in flux and service can be unresponsive. The trade-off is a first rate location and an establishment steeped in history, including Harry Denton's Starlight Room, on the hotel's top floor. A tribute to faded 1920s glory, it's one of the city's best known skyline bars. The hotel's surprisingly affordable restaurant, Scala's Bistro, serves better than average food in its somewhat noisy bi-level dining room. **Pros:** Can't beat the location, free in-room Wi-Fi, onsite restaurant and bar are moderately priced. **Cons:** Small baths and dated rooms, lobby furniture looks a bit tired, some complaints about unresponsive service and cleanliness. ✉ *450 Powell St., Union Square,* ☎ *415/392–7755 or 800/795–7129* 🖷 *415/391–8719* ⊕ *www.sirfrancisdrake.com* 🛏 *412 rooms, 5 suites* ♿ *In-room: DVD, Wi-Fi. In-hotel: restaurant, bar, gym, concierge, room service, laundry service, public Internet, parking (fee), some pets allowed, no-smoking rooms* ▤ *AE, D, DC, MC, V.*

$$$$ Westin St. Francis. Since its 1904 opening, this historic hotel has hosted the likes of Hirohito, Queen Elizabeth II, several U.S. presidents, and a roster of international luminaries. The site of sensational, banner headline scandals, the hotel's past is shrouded in as much infamy as stardust. This is the place where Sara Jane Moore tried to assassinate Gerald Ford, where Al Jolson died playing poker; suite 1219–1221 was the scene of massive scandal, which erupted when a 30-year-old aspiring actress died after a night of heavy boozing in the close company of silent film comedian Fatty Arbuckle. (The incident destroyed his career.) The hotel is comprised of the original building (Empire-style furnishings, Victorian moldings) and a modern 32-story tower (Asian-inspired lacquered furniture, glass elevators); guests are divided when it comes to the virtues of the modern addition vs. the historic building. The imposing facade, black-marble lobby, and gold-top columns form an impressive public space. Adding to the air of upscale sophistication is the cool chic of Michael Mina restaurant and the Oak Room Restaurant and Lounge. **Pros:** Fantastic beds, prime location, spacious rooms, some with great views. **Cons:** Some guests commented on the long wait at check-in, rooms in original building can be small, glass elevators are not for the faint of heart. ⊠*335 Powell St., Union Square,* ☎*415/397–7000 or 800/917–7458* 🖷*415/774–0124* ⊕*www.westinstfrancis.com* ♐*1,155 rooms, 40 suites* ⚷*In-room: safe, refrigerator (some), dial-up, ethernet, Wi-Fi. In-hotel: 3 restaurants, room service, bars, spa, concierge, laundry service, public Internet, parking (fee), some pets allowed, no-smoking rooms* ⊟*AE, D, DC, MC, V.*

$$$ **White Swan Inn.** A cozy library with a crackling fireplace is the heart of this inviting, English-style B&B. Comfortable chairs and sofas encourage lingering in the lounge, where wine, cheese, and tea are served in the afternoon. Sizable rooms with plaid bedspreads, floral carpeting and wallpaper, and reproduction Edwardian furniture each have a gas fireplace topped by a book-lined mantel. Some guests, however, have complained of the rooms' "thin walls" where you can "hear your neighbor's hair dryer." The popular gourmet breakfast buffet and evening turndown with chocolates extend the personal touch. **Pros:** Cozy B&B antidote to sterile chain hotels, nice lounge and patio area. **Cons:** Thin walls make for noisy rooms, nearby streets can be a bit rough at night, Union Square is a bit of a hike (about three blocks). ⊠*845 Bush St., Union Square,* ☎*415/775–1755 or 800/999–9570* 🖷*415/775–5717* ⊕*www.jdvhotels.com* ♐*25 rooms, 1 suite* ⚷*In-room: no a/c, refrigerator, VCR (some), Wi-Fi. In-hotel: restaurant, gym, concierge, laundry service, parking (fee), no-smoking rooms* ⊟*AE, D, MC, V* ⦿*BP.*

¢–$$ **York Hotel.** Hitchcock's classic thriller Vertigo was set and partially shot in this ornate "personality" hotel, which was a speakeasy during Prohibition. Kim Novak, who played the elusive Judy Barton in the film, actually stayed in Room 301 (though filming took place two floors up). Undergoing a major remodel, the hotel's exterior and interior are slated for a redesign built around the film which will extend to guest rooms, meeting rooms, corridors, fitness center, lounge, and lobby. The hotel remains open during the renovations, and will remerge as Hotel Vertigo once work is complete. A new restaurant is also in the works. Although the block includes several apartment buildings, a fancy salon, and cafés, the neighborhood is a bit dicey, so exercise caution when walking here at night. **Pros:** Tons of personality. **Cons:** Borderline neighborhood. ⊠*940 Sutter St., between Leavenworth and Hyde Sts., Tenderloin,* ☎*415/885–6800 or 800/808–9675* 🖷*415/885–2115* ⊕*www.yorkhotel.com* ♐*92 rooms, 4 suites* ⚷*In-room: no a/c, safe, dial-up, Wi-Fi. In-hotel: bar, gym, concierge, laundry service, public Internet, parking (fee), no-smoking rooms* ⊟*AE, D, DC, MC, V.*

Nightlife & the Arts

Arrow Bar

WORD OF MOUTH

"When I have to take a visitor out for a really fun night eating and drinking in the city, I always start at 16th Street and Valencia in the Mission every time. This is even true for when my parents come to town."

—KeithG

Updated by
Sura Wood

This small city packs the punch of a much larger metropolis after dark. Sophisticated, trendy, relaxed, quirky, and downright outrageous could all be used to describe San Francisco's diverse and vibrant collection of bars, clubs, and performance venues. It can be overwhelming to decide where to go in your short time here, but some neighborhood generalizations can help you find the kind of entertainment you want.

Nob Hill is noted for its old-money mansions; today's plush hotel bars and panoramic skyline lounges, the most famous being Top of the Mark, fit right in. North Beach's historic bars invoke the city's beatnik past, and its sleek lounges catch diners leaving mom-and-pop Italian restaurants. Fisherman's Wharf is probably the most touristy part of the city, but many of the hotels are here; you could also find yourself here after a trip to the Exploratorium or a ferry ride back from Alcatraz, Angel Island, or Sausalito. Singles bars in tony Union Street and the nearby Marina attract well-dressed and well-to-do crowds in their 20s and 30s. (Be sure to break out your richest-looking digs for the Marina.) South of Market—or SoMa—is a nightlife hub, with a bevy of popular dance clubs, bars, and supper clubs, as well as a few excellent live-music venues. The gay and lesbian scenes center on the Castro district and along Polk Street. Twentysomethings and alternative types should check out the ever-funky Mission District and Haight Street, although even these two neighborhoods have more upscale cocktail lounges and fewer dive bars every year.

THE 4-1-1

Entertainment information is printed in the pink Sunday "Datebook" section (www.sfgate.com/datebook) and the more-calendar-based Thursday "96 Hours" section (www.sfgate.com/96hours) in the *San Francisco Chronicle*. Also consult any of the free alternative weeklies, notably the *SF Weekly* (www.sfweekly.com), which blurbs nightclubs and music, and the *San Francisco Bay Guardian* (www.sfbg.com),

SAFETY AFTER DARK

San Franciscans sometimes seem to get a perverse thrill out of the grittiness of their city. Some of the best nightlife options are in slightly sketchy locations; in the areas we've listed below, you're better off cabbing it. Bartenders can call you a ride when you're ready to leave.

■ **Civic Center:** After the symphony, ballet, or opera, don't wander north, east, or south. The one safe corridor is west to Gough, which will bring you to Hayes Valley. Especially avoid Market Street between 6th and 10th streets.

■ **SoMa:** More than five blocks or so south of Market starts to get into an industrial no-man's land.

■ **The Tenderloin:** Plenty of locals walk to bars in the Tenderloin, but if crack addicts and sketchy dudes hanging out in front of hourly-rate motels make you uncomfortable (can't imagine why they would), you should take a cab. The edges of the Tenderloin, closer to Jones (east) or Sutter (north), aren't too bad.

■ **The Outer Mission (below 24th St.):** If you're feeling out of sorts on Mission Street between 16th and 24th streets, cut over to Valencia.

It's safe to walk around the Financial District, Union Square, Haight Street and Cole Valley, Nob Hill, the Mission (above 24th Street), and SoMa north of Howard.

14

which lists neighborhood, avant-garde, and budget events. SF Station (www.sfstation.com; online only) has an up-to-date calendar of entertainment goings-on.

HOURS

Sports bars and hotel bars tend to be open Sunday, but others may be closed. A few establishments—especially wine bars and restaurant bars—also close Monday. Last call is typically 1:30 AM; Financial District bars catering to the after-work crowd, however, may stop serving as early as 9 or 10 PM and generally close by midnight at the latest. Bands and performers usually take the stage between 8 and 11 PM. A handful of after-hours clubs are open until 4 AM or all night.

TICKETS & COVERS

The cover charge at smaller, less-popular clubs ranges from $5 to $10, and credit cards are rarely accepted. Covers at larger venues may spike to $30, and tickets usually can be purchased through Tickets. com or Ticketweb.com. Bars often have covers for live music—usually $5–$15.

LATE-NIGHT TRANSPORTATION

You're better off taking public transportation or taxis on weekend nights, unless you're heading downtown (Financial District or Union Square) and are willing to park in a lot. There's only street parking in North Beach, the Mission, Castro, and the Haight, and finding a spot can be practically impossible. MUNI stops running between 1 AM and 5 AM but has its limited Owl Service on 20 lines—including the N, L, 90, 91, 14, and 22—every 30 minutes; check www.sfmuni.com for details. You can sometimes hail a taxi on the street in well-trod nightlife locations (like North Beach or the Mission), but you can also call for one (415/626–2345 Yellow Cab, 415/648–3181 Arrow). ■TIP→ **Be aware that cabs in SF are more expensive than anywhere in the U.S.; expect to pay at least $10 to get anywhere within the city.**

WHAT TO WEAR

Except at a few skyline lounges, you're not expected to dress up. Still, San Franciscans are a stylish bunch. For women, dressed-up jeans with heels and cute tops are one popular uniform; for guys it's button-up shirts or designer tees and well-tailored jeans. Of course, stylish means a black designer outfit at one place and funky thrift-store togs at another, so you have to use your judgment.

SMOKING

By law, bars and clubs are smoke-free, except for the very few that are staffed entirely by the owners. Patios and gardens can turn into smoker's havens.

BARS & LOUNGES

Balboa Cafe. You'll spy young (thirtysomething) and upwardly mobile former frat boys and sorority girls munching on tasty burgers (considered by some to be the best in town) while trying to add a few new names to their Blackberrys. Mayor Gavin Newsom—a part-owner—has been known to drop in. ⊠*3199 Fillmore St., at Greenwich St., Marina* ☎*415/921–3944* ⊕*www.plumpjack.com.*

Bix. The retro-chic martini-bar craze keeps going strong at glam, gorgeous Bix. Jazz combos provide the backbeat for the cocktail-swilling gadabouts and nattily dressed diners who pack the small bar area of this spirited yet refined supper club. Plenty of regulars stop in just to sip the well-crafted cocktails, so you won't feel out of place if you're not eating—but you will if you're not wearing something chic. ⊠*56 Gold St., off Montgomery St., North Beach* ☎*415/433–6300* ⊕*www.bixrestaurant.com.*

Bourbon & Branch. The address and phone are unlisted, the black outer door unmarked, and when you make your reservation (required), you get a password for entry. In short, Bourbon & Branch reeks of Prohibition-era speakeasy cool. It's not exclusive, though: everyone is granted a password. The place has sex appeal, with tin ceilings, bordello-red silk wallpaper, intimate booths, and low lighting; loud conversations and cell phones are not allowed. The menu of expertly mixed cocktails and quality bourbon and whiskey is substantial, but the servers aren't always authorities. **This place is small, so couples or groups of four or less are ideal.** Your reservation dictates your exit time, which is strictly enforced. ⊠*501 Jones St., Tenderloin* ☎*No phone* ⊕*www.bourbonandbranch.com.*

★ **Buena Vista Café.** Smack-dab at the end of the Hyde Street cable-car line, the Buena Vista packs 'em in for its famous Irish coffee—which, according to owners, was the first served stateside (in 1952). The place oozes nostalgia and draws devoted locals as well as out-of-towners relaxing after a day of sightseeing. It's narrow and can get crowded,

TOP 5 BARS

■ **Cliff House:** Granted, it's pricey and the interior is ho-hum, but huge picture windows with views of the rolling Pacific create an ambience that's pure Zen.

■ **El Rio:** The perfect dive, with $2.50 drink specials, a stellar patio, and an ever-changing calendar of events (free-oyster Fridays, salsa Sundays . . .).

■ **Hôtel Biron:** Everything a small wine bar should be: intimate, stylish, and slightly hard to find, with an eclectic wine list and good small plates.

■ **Martuni's:** Expertly mixed martinis, a relaxed and friendly clientele, and the off-chance that your traveling companion might belt out a Liza Minelli tune after a few drinks. What more could you ask for?

■ **Vesuvio Café:** One of those rare bars that everyone knows about. It's in one of the most touristed parts of town, but still manages to be cool.

14

but this place is a welcome respite from the overpriced, generic tourist joints nearby. ⊠*2765 Hyde St., at Beach St., Fisherman's Wharf* ☎*415/474–5044* ⊕*www.thebuenavista.com.*

Circa. This classy lounge with shimmering chandeliers is dimly lighted, but fellow patrons will still notice the logo on your purse; dress appropriately (par for the course in the Marina). At the central, square bar, attractive yuppies sip cosmos and nibble pan-seared scallops, while skilled DJs spin downtempo electronica. This place takes tongue-in-cheek chic seriously, down to the lobster-and-truffle mac-and-cheese. As expected, there's a strong list of specialty cocktails. ⊠*2001 Chestnut St., at Fillmore St., Marina* ☎*415/351–0175* ⊕*www.circasf.com.*

Edinburgh Castle. Work off your fish-and-chips and Scottish brew with a turn at the dartboard or pool table at this dark and cavernous pub. It's popular with locals and Brits who congregate at the long bar or in the scattered seating areas, downing single-malt scotch or pints of Fuller's. Live music alternates with spoken-word sessions, weekly trivia nights, and even Scottish cultural events (January's Robert Burns celebration is a favorite). Be aware that the area around the bar is gritty. ⊠*950 Geary St., between Larkin and Polk Sts., Tenderloin* ☎*415/885–4074* ⊕*www.castlenews.com.*

Gordon Biersch Brewery and Restaurant. This giant microbrewery has outlasted the boutique-beer trend and continues to draw big after-work crowds. Part of a nationwide empire that got its start in nearby Palo Alto, Gordon Biersch is known for its German-style pilsners and brews—as well as what some have called the greatest garlic fries in creation (though regulars give the burgers at this location low marks). ■TIP➔ **The outdoor seating area has killer views of the Bay Bridge, making this an ideal spot for an afternoon drink.** ⊠*2 Harrison St., at the Embarcadero, SoMa* ☎*415/243–8246* ⊕*www.gordonbiersch.com.*

Harrington's. The epicenter for downtown festivities on St. Patrick's Day, this family-owned Irish saloon (closed Sunday) is an attitude-free place for the well-tailored-suit set to have an after-work drink the rest of the year. The restaurant serves American fare, with the occasional

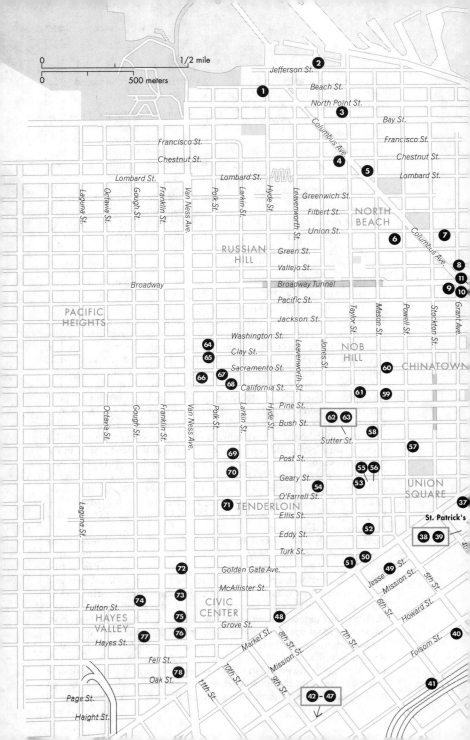

Nightlife & the Arts In & Around Downtown

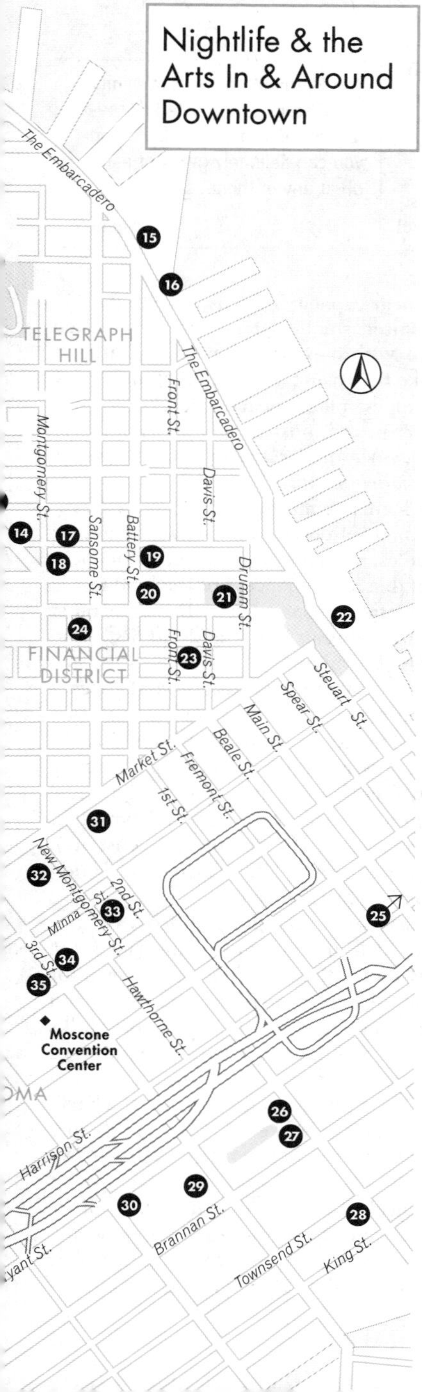

TELEGRAPH
HILL

The Embarcadero

Montgomery St.

Front St.

Davis St.

Battery St.

Sansome St.

Drumm St.

Davis St.

Front St.

FINANCIAL
DISTRICT

Steuart St.

Spear St.

Market St.

Main St.

Beale St.

Fremont St.

1st St.

New Montgomery St.

2nd St.

Minna St.

3rd St.

Hawthorne St.

♦ Moscone
Convention
Center

OMA

Harrison St.

Brannan St.

Bryant St.

Townsend St.

King St.

Irish special. It has a good selection of imported beers and a patio out back. Another local favorite, the Royal Exchange, is next door and eerily similar. ⊠ *245 Front St., near Sacramento St., Financial District* ☎ *415/392–7595.*

Jade Bar. One of the city's sexiest-looking bars, this narrow tri-level space with floor-to-ceiling windows, a 15-foot waterfall, and styl-

ish sofas and banquettes attracts near-capacity crowds, even midweek. A limited menu offers Asian-inspired small plates—such as smoked salmon served on wonton crisps with a wasabi dressing—that pair nicely with signature cocktails like the Rising Sun (a potent and fruity rum drink). This is one of the hippest places near Civic Center, so if you want to avoid the typical over-priced, post-theater spots, look no further. ⊠ *650 Gough St., between McAllister and Fulton Sts., Hayes Valley* ☎ *415/869–1900* ⊕ *www.jadebar.com.*

Laszlo. Attached to the Foreign Cinema restaurant, Laszlo is a cavernous, classy space with an open, bi-level design; movies are projected onto the walls. Dim lighting, candles, and an upscale selection of cocktails and single-malts make it suitable for romance, but the loud music and cacophonic levels of conversation keep it lively. DJs spin most nights after 9. ⊠ *2532 Mission St., between 21st and 22nd Sts., Mission* ☎ *415/401–0810* ⊕ *www.laszlobar.com*

Le Colonial. Down an easy-to-miss alley off Taylor Street is what appears to be a two-story colonial plantation house in the center of the city. Without being kitschy, the top-floor bar successfully evokes French-colonial Vietnam, thanks to creaky wooden floors, Victorian sofas, a patio with potted palms, and tasty French-Vietnamese food and tropical cocktails. When you arrive, sweep right past the café tables downstairs, past the hostess, and up the stairs to your left (dining is downstairs). The bar occasionally has live, low-key music. ⊠ *20 Cosmo Pl., Union Square* ☎ *415/931–3600* ⊕ *www.lecolonialsf.com.*

★ **MatrixFillmore.** Don a pair of Diesel jeans and a Michael Kors sweater and sip cosmos or Cabernet with the Marina's bon vivants. This is the premier spot in the "Triangle" (short for Bermuda Triangle, named for all of the singles who disappear in the bars clustered at Greenwich and Fillmore streets). Although there's a small dance floor where some folks bump and grind to high-energy DJ-spun dance tracks, the majority of the clientele usually vies for the plush seats near the central open fireplace, flirts at the bar, or huddles for romantic tête-à-têtes in the back. The singles scene can be overwhelming on weekends. ⊠ *3138 Fillmore St., between Greenwich and Filbert Sts., Marina* ☎ *415/563–4180* ⊕ *www.matrixfillmore.com.*

Nihon. Whiskey-lovers *need* to check this place out, if only to drool over the 150 or so bottles behind the bar. This place has a super-swank, youngish scene. The pricey Japanese tapas are pretty good, and whiskey pairs with sushi surprisingly well. The dramatic lighting, close quarters, and blood-red tuffets make Nihon more suitable for romance than business. ✉*1779 Folsom St., between Eire and 14th Sts. SoMa* ☎*415/552–4400* ⊕*www. nihon-sf.com.*

Perry's. It may be one of San Francisco's oldest singles bars, but Perry's still packs 'em in. You can dine on great hamburgers as well as more substantial fare while gabbing about the game with the well-

scrubbed, khaki-clad, baseball-cap-wearing crowd. ✉*1944 Union St., at Laguna St., Cow Hollow* ☎*415/922–9022* ⊕*www.perryssf.com.*

Rite Spot Cafe. A Mission tradition for more than 50 years, this classy and casual charmer is like a cabaret club in an aging mobster's garage. Quirky lounge singers and other musicians entertain most nights. A small menu of low-price sandwiches and Italian food beats your average bar fare. Rite Spot is in a mostly residential and somewhat desolate part of the Mission, so you may feel like you're entering a no-man's land. ✉*2099 Folsom St., at 17th St., Mission* ☎*415/552–6066* ⊕*www.ritespotcafe.net.*

Royal Oak. Tiffany-style lamps and cascading ferns contribute to the clubby feel of this comfortable spot, walkable to other nearby neighborhood bars. Arrive early to snag a seat on one of the antique, swoopback tufted-velvet couches. ✉*2201 Polk St., at Vallejo St., Russian Hill* ☎*415/928–2303.*

Specs Twelve Adler Museum Cafe. If you're bohemian at heart, you can groove on this hidden hangout for artists, poets, and heavy-drinking lefties. It's one of the few remaining old-fashioned watering holes in North Beach that still smacks of the Beat years and the 1960s. Though it's just off a busy street, Specs is strangely immune to the hustle and bustle outside. ✉*12 William Saroyan Pl., off Columbus Ave., between Pacific Ave. and Broadway, North Beach* ☎*415/421–4112.*

Sugar. Just trendy enough, but never pretentious, Sugar has fun cocktails (lemon drops, grape 'o' tinis), good drink specials, and a low-key vibe. DJs spin world and house music in this small, narrow neighborhood favorite. ✉*377 Hayes St., Hayes Valley* ☎*415/255–7144* ⊕*www.sugarloungesf.com.*

★ **Tosca Café.** Like Specs and Vesuvio nearby, this historic charmer holds a special place in San Francisco lore. It has an Italian flavor, with opera, big-band, and Italian standards on the jukebox, plus an antique espresso machine that's nothing less than a work of art and lived-in red leather booths. With Francis Ford Coppola's Zoetrope just across the street, celebrities and hip film industry types often stop by when they're in town; locals, like Sean Penn, have been known to shoot pool in the back room. ✉*242 Columbus Ave., near Broadway, North Beach* ☎*415/391–1244.*

21st Amendment. Possibly the best brewpub in SF, with a good range of beer types (unlike some others). The watermelon wheat gets rave reviews. The space has an upmarket warehouse feel, though exposed wooden ceiling beams, framed photos, whitewashed brick walls, and hardwood floors make it feel cozy. ✉*563 2nd St., between Federal and Brannan Sts., SoMa* ☎*415/369–0900* ⊕*www.21st-amendment.com.*

★ **Vesuvio Café.** If you're only hitting one bar in North Beach, it should be this one. The low-ceiling second floor of this raucous boho hangout, little altered since its 1960s heyday (when Jack Kerouac frequented the place), is a fine vantage point for watching the colorful Broadway-Columbus intersection. Another part of Vesuvio's appeal is its diverse, always-mixed clientele (20s to 60s), from neighborhood regulars to young couples to Bacchanalian posses of friends. ✉*255 Columbus Ave., at Broadway, North Beach* ☎*415/362–3370* ⊕*www.vesuvio.com.*

> **TAKE ME OUT AFTER THE BALLGAME**
>
> Two bars near the Giants' AT&T Park are especially popular on game day.
>
> Stylish American restaurant and trendy bar **Momo's** (✉*760 2nd St., at King St., SoMa* ☎*415/227–8660* ⊕*www.sfmomos.com*) has an outdoor patio perfect for sunny days; it's the most popular pre- and post-game bar.
>
> **Nova** (✉*555 2nd St., near Bryant St., SoMa* ☎*415/543–2282* ⊕*www.novabar.com*) fills up before and after Giants games with fans thirsty for infused-vodka drinks and other chic cocktails.

BARS WITH LIVE MUSIC

Although they're not dedicated music venues, these bars often host up-and-coming bands. Drop in, and you might discover the next Pedro the Lion or Death Cab for Cutie.

The Knockout. In a grungy but hip section of the Mission, the king of dive bars (with requisite cheap bottled beer and photo booth) is popular with the discerning hipsters who dare to venture south of César Chavez (you get the impression that they wouldn't bother hanging out in the Mission *north* of César Chavez). There's usually a cover for bands or DJs on weekends, but it's never more than $10. Gong Show Karaoke on Sunday and Bingo on Thursday keep it real. An added bonus for trekking out to the southern edge of the Mission: some of the city's best taquerías are nearby. ✉*3223 Mission St., at Valencia, Mission* ☎*415/550–6994* ⊕*www.theknockoutsf.com.*

Fodor's Choice
★ **El Rio.** A dive bar in the best sense, El Rio has a calendar chock-full of events, from free bands and films to Salsa Sunday (seasonal), that keep Mission kids coming back. Bands play several nights a week—Tuesday is generally free, Saturday brings the "big acts" ($8 cover), which are still relatively unknown local bands. No matter what day you attend, expect to find a diverse gay–straight crowd. The large patio out back is especially popular when the weather's warm. ✉*3158 Mission St., between César Chavez and Valencia Sts., Mission* ☎*415/282–3325* ⊕*www.elriosf.com.*

The Hotel Utah Saloon. This funky hipster spot offers a mix of local bands and young national touring acts performing rock, indie pop, alt-country, and everything in between. The low-ceiling performance space is small, with a few tables grouped around the stage. (Be sure to grab a Cuban sandwich from the bar before the show.) The bar area takes up about half of this joint and is just as popular as the music. Monday is open-mike night. ⊠ *500 4th St., at Bryant St., SoMa* ☎ *415/546–6300* ⊕ *www.thehotelutahsaloon.com.*

OUTDOOR BARS

You're on vacation, so there's no to reason to wait until 5 to relax with a local brew—or even indulge in Champagne and oysters. These places are perfect for having a nip while the sun's still out (some of them turn lame after dark), so get going and get your afternoon drink on!

Hog Island Oyster Bar. On a sunny day, is there anything better than sipping wine and eating oysters? Only if it's here, on a waterside patio, with the looming Bay Bridge and the Oakland and Berkeley hills as a backdrop. The oysters are from Marin County, and many of the wines are from Sonoma or Napa. ⊠ *Ferry Bldg., 1 Embarcadero Plaza, Financial District* ☎ *415/391–7117* ⊕ *www.hogislandoysters.com.*

Park Chalet. You'll feel like you're in a cabin in the woods as you relax in an Adirondack chair under a heat lamp, enclosed by the greenery of Golden Gate Park. The Park Chalet shares a building with the Beach Chalet (*below*)—but it isn't waterside, so you won't freeze if it's overcast. ⊠ *1000 Great Hwy., near Martin Luther King Jr. Dr., Golden Gate Park* ☎ *415/386–8439* ⊕ *www.beachchalet.com.*

Pier 23 Cafe. Beer arrives at your table in buckets at this waterfront bar, which has ample seating at plastic tables on a wooden deck. Although you'd expect to sit elbow-to-elbow with fishermen, you're more likely to share the space with twenty- and thirtysomethings drawn by the beer and food specials. ⊠ *Pier 23, Embarcadero* ☎ *415/362–5125* ⊕ *www. pier23cafe.com.*

Zeitgeist. It's a bit divey, a bit rock and roll, and the port-a-potties are arguably cleaner than the bathroom, but Zeitgeist is a good place to relax with a cold one or an ever-popular (and ever-strong) bloody Mary in the large beer "garden" (there's not much greenery) on a sunny day. Grill food of the burger and hot dog variety is available. If you own a trucker hat, a pair of Vans, and a Pabst Blue Ribbon T-shirt, you'll fit right in. ⊠ *199 Valencia St., at Duboce Ave. Mission* ☎ *415/255–7505.*

SKYLINE & OCEAN-VIEW BARS

San Francisco is a city of spectacular vistas. Enjoy drinks, music, and sometimes dinner with views of the city or the Pacific Ocean at any of the places below. **Don't bother going to these bars when it's foggy.**

Beach Chalet. This restaurant-microbrewery, on the second floor of a historic building filled with 1930s Works Project Administration murals,

CLOSE UP

Best Hotel Bars

Big 4 Bar. Dark-wood paneling and green leather banquettes lend a masculine feel to the bar at the Huntington Hotel, where the over-30 crowd orders scotch and Irish coffee, not mojitos and cosmopolitans. To accompany your whiskey, try the pot-pies or Irish stew. This place is a San Francisco history lesson—read up on the Big Four (four of the city's most influential pre-earthquake movers and shakers) before you go to get more out of the experience. ⊠ *The Huntington Hotel, 1075 California St., Nob Hill* ☎ *415/474–5400.*

Pied Piper Bar. Originally opened in 1875 (after being built for the then-extravagant price of $5 million), the Palace Hotel is still one of San Francisco's classiest. Suitably, this watering hole, which takes its name from the Maxfield Parrish mural *The Pied Piper of Hamelin* behind the bar, draws a very affluent and upscale clientele for its excellent two-olive martinis and other libations. ⊠ *2 New Montgomery St., at Market St., SoMa* ☎ *415/512–1111.*

Redwood Room. Opened in 1933 and updated by über-hip designer Philippe Starck in 2001, the Redwood Room at the Clift Hotel is a San Francisco icon. The entire room, floor to ceiling, is paneled with the wood from a single redwood tree, giving the place a rich, monochromatic look. The gorgeous original art-deco sconces and chandeliers still hang, but bizarre video installations on plasma screens also adorn the walls. It's packed on weekend evenings after 10 PM, when young scenesters swarm the hotel; for maximum glamour, visit on a weeknight. ⊠ *Clift Hotel, 495 Geary St., at Taylor St., Union Square* ☎ *415/929–2300 for table reservations, 415/775–4700.*

Seasons Bar. The walnut-panel walls, inlaid cherrywood floor, and elegant furnishings of the tiny lobby bar capture the aesthetic of the coolly minimalist Four Seasons. Discreet staff members in dark suits serve top-shelf (in price and quality) cocktails and salty nibbles. A piano player entertains Tuesday through Saturday evening in the lobby lounge, where you can relax on overstuffed sofas and chairs. The clientele is, as expected, generally 40-plus and business-suited. ⊠ *Four Seasons Hotel San Francisco, 757 Market St., between 3rd and 4th Sts., SoMa* ☎ *415/633–3000.*

Tonga Room. Since 1947, the Tonga Room has given San Francisco a taste of high Polynesian kitsch. Fake palm trees, grass huts, a lagoon (three-piece combos play pop standards on a floating barge), and faux monsoons—courtesy of sprinkler-system rain and simulated thunder and lightning—grow more surreal as you quaff fruity cocktails. ⊠ *Fairmont San Francisco, 950 Mason St., at California St., Nob Hill* ☎ *415/772–5278.*

W Café and XYZ Bar. Floor-to-ceiling blue velvet draperies, black-and-white terrazzo floors, and a thumpin' sound system set the aggressive see-and-be-seen tone of the lobby bar at the W Hotel, where a DJ spins hypnotic beats Wednesday through Friday evenings. Escape the ogling crowd by heading upstairs to the tucked-away XYZ Bar. ⊠ *W Hotel, 181 3rd St., at Howard St., SoMa* ☎ *415/777–5300.*

–By John A. Vlahdides and Shannon Kelly

has a stunning view of the Pacific Ocean, so you may want to time your visit to coincide with the sunset. **Get there at least 30 minutes before sunset to beat the dinner reservations.** If you come right at dinnertime or even at lunch on weekends, diners with reservations will be given first dibs on the window seats (and on tables in general). The bar is toward the back, with a so-so view of the action. The American bistro food—which, for appetizers, includes ahi tuna tartare and fried calamari—is decent, the house brews are rich and flavorful, and there's a good selection of California wines by the glass. The seasonal Oktoberfest brew is a highlight of the beer menu. The cheaper **Park Chalet** (*above*) on the ground floor has park, rather than ocean, views. ✉ *1000 Great Hwy., near Martin Luther King Jr. Dr., Golden Gate Park* ☎ *415/386–8439* ⊕ *www.beachchalet.com.*

Carnelian Room. Only the birds get a better view of the San Francisco skyline than you will from the 52nd floor of the Bank of America Building—at least when the fog's not billowing. There's no official dress code for the bar, but the adjoining restaurant, popular with jacket-and-tie-clad bankers, doesn't allow jeans. This place is sometimes closed for private events, so call ahead. ✉ *555 California St., at Kearny St., Financial District* ☎ *415/433–7500* ⊕ *www.carnelianroom.com.*

★ **Cliff House.** A bit classier than the Beach Chalet, with a more impressive, sweeping view of Ocean Beach, the Cliff House is our pick if you have to choose one oceanfront restaurant/bar. Sure, it's the site of many high-school prom dates, and you could argue that the food and drinks are overpriced, and some say the sleek facade looks like a mausoleum—but the views are terrific. The best window seats are reserved for diners, but there's a small upstairs lounge where you can watch gulls sail high above the vast blue Pacific. Come before sunset. ✉ *1090 Point Lobos, at Great Hwy., Lincoln Park* ☎ *415/386–3330* ⊕ *www.cliffhouse.com.*

★ **Harry Denton's Starlight Room.** Forget low-key drinks—the only way to experience Harry Denton's is to go for a show. Cough up the cover charge and enjoy the opulent, over-the-top decor and entertainment (some of the best cover bands in the business, usually playing Top 40 hits from the '60s, '70s, and '80s). Velvet booths and romantic lighting help re-create the 1950s high life on the 21st floor of the Sir Francis Drake Hotel, and the small dance floor is packed on Friday and Saturday nights. Jackets are preferred for men. Call ahead—it's sometimes closed for private events on weekdays. ✉ *Sir Francis Drake Hotel, 450 Powell St., between Post and Sutter Sts., Union Square* ☎ *415/395–8595* ⊕ *www.harrydenton.com.*

Top of the Mark. A famous magazine photograph immortalized this place, on the 19th floor of the Mark Hopkins InterContinental, as a hot spot for World War II servicemen on leave or about to ship out. Entertainment ranges from solo jazz piano to six-piece jazz ensembles. Cover charges and schedules vary, but tend to be around $10 beginning at 7 PM weekdays and 9 PM weekends. ✉ *Mark Hopkins InterContinental, 999 California St., at Mason St., Nob Hill* ☎ *415/616–6916* ⊕ *www.topofthemark.com.*

14

View Lounge. Art-deco-influenced floor-to-ceiling windows frame superb views on the 39th floor of the San Francisco Marriott, and a jazz trio with vocalist performs Friday and Saturday evenings. You won't feel out of place here just getting a drink or two rather than dinner. It can get quite crowded on weekends. ⊠*San Francisco Marriott, 55 4th St., between Mission and Market Sts., SoMa* ☎*415/896–1600.*

SPORTS BARS

Bus Stop. Popular with frat boys and stockbrokers alike, this Marina/ Cow Hollow favorite has 20 screens and two pool tables. If you want to meet the local diehards, this is the place. It's also one of the few spots in this neighborhood where you'll feel comfortable dressed down. Order food from neighboring restaurants; the bar provides menus. ⊠*1901 Union St., at Laguna St., Cow Hollow* ☎*415/567–6905.*

Fourth Street Bar and Deli. San Francisco may not be the best sports town in the country, but you'd never guess it by the buzzing scene at this huge, modern sports wonderland on the ground floor of the Marriott Hotel. The bar has 44 beers, 23 televisions, and all the salty, fried snacks you'll need to properly enjoy the game. ⊠*55 4th St., at Mission St., SoMa* ☎*415/442–6734.*

Greens Sports Bar. Cramped and packed to the gills with sports memorabilia, Greens is the quintessential old-school neighborhood sports bar, with 18 screens and 18 beers on tap. Seating is on stools at high bar tables, and the TVs are positioned just right for optimal viewing. Food is not served here, but the bar has delivery menus. ⊠*2239 Polk St., at Green St., Van Ness/Polk* ☎*415/775–4287.*

Knuckles Historical Sports Bar and Grill. The marble bar tops are evidence of Knuckles' historic location, in the early-20th-century Joseph Musto Marble Works building. The original exposed beams and brick remain part of the decor. Because it's in Fisherman's Wharf, this lively spot draws a healthy stream of sports-crazed tourists. The venue has 28 TVs, including a jumbo screen, and some local sports memorabilia, like a San Francisco Giants pennant from the team's Candlestick Park days. If you're hungry for more than a game, be sure to try the famous Vida Blue burger, named after the great pitcher who won three World Series championships across the bay with the Oakland Athletics in the early '70s. Knuckles also has two pool tables and a vintage shuffleboard table in the back. ⊠*555 N. Point St., Fisherman's Wharf* ☎*415/486–4346* ⊕*www.knucklessportsbar.com.*

WINE BARS

As you might expect, San Francisco has quite a few wine bars and wine connoisseurs. But the wine-bar scene is far from snobby. We've never encountered anything but helpful advice from wine-bar staff, even when making small-budget selections. Most of these spots offer tasting "flights," wines grouped together by type for contrast and comparison.

Bubble Lounge. Champagne is the specialty at this dark, upscale spot; the selection of bubbly is excellent, with more than 300 types to choose from. Upstairs, young executives nestle into wing chairs and over-stuffed couches, and downstairs there's a re-created Champagne cellar.

A full bar is available, as are sushi, caviar, desserts, and other delicate nibbles. You won't feel out of place in a suit or slinky dress and heels here. Make table reservations ($25 minimum) on weekends, or you'll be relegated to the tiny bar area. ⊠*714 Montgomery St., at Washington St., North Beach* ☎*415/434–4204* ⊕*www.bubblelounge.com.*

CAV Wine Bar & Kitchen. Pair your Napa or French wines with a salumi platter or gratinée fondue at this sleek, contemporary space. CAV has an impressive selection of wines by the glass, a better-than-average food menu, and frequent wine classes—a great way to learn the lingo before you head up to Sonoma or Napa. ⊠*1666 Market St., at Gough St., Hayes Valley* ☎*415/437–1770* ⊕*www.cavwinebar.com.*

★ **Eos Restaurant and Wine Bar.** Though it's just a few blocks away, Cole Valley is a world apart from funky, grungy Haight Street. Eos, along with the handful of restaurants and bars that line this part of Cole Street, manages to be both sophisticated and unpretentious—and truly fantastic. A narrow and romantically lighted space, with more than 400 wines by the bottle and 40-plus by the glass, offers two different wine flights—one red and one white—every month. The adjoining restaurant's excellent East-meets-West cuisine is available at the bar. ⊠*901 Cole St., at Carl St., Haight* ☎*415/566–3063* ⊕*www.eossf. com.*

The Hidden Vine. True to its name, this tiny wine bar is in a tiny alley (just north of Market Street) and down a set of stairs. The location is part of the appeal, but the wines and amuse-bouches make it truly worthwhile. A jumble of velvet chairs and love seats fills the carpeted space, and the owner, who serves most nights, acts as your sommelier. Another hidden find, Le Colonial *(above)* is just across the alley. ⊠*½ Cosmo Pl., at Taylor St., Union Square* ☎*415/673–3567* ⊕*www. thehiddenvine.com.*

★ **Hôtel Biron.** Sharing an alleylike block with the backs of Market Street restaurants, this tiny, cavelike (in a good way) find displays rotating artwork of the Mission School aesthetic on its brick walls. The clientele is well-behaved twenty- to thirtysomethings who enjoy the cramped quarters, good range of wines and prices, off-the-beaten path location, soft lighting, and hip music. If it's too crowded, CAV is just around the corner. ⊠*45 Rose St., off Market St., Hayes Valley* ☎*415/703–0403* ⊕*www.hotelbiron.com.*

London Wine Bar. America's first wine bar doesn't seem to have changed much since it opened in 1974. The place is more cozy pub than snooty wine bar, but the cellar, especially strong in selections from small California wineries, is extensive, with 30 to 40 wines available by the glass. The after-work bar is open only on weekdays, until about 9. ⊠*415 Sansome St., between Clay and Sacramento Sts., Financial District* ☎*415/788–4811.*

Nectar. Classy Nectar has reasonable tasting flights (around $20) and decent food that looks more impressive than it tastes. No complaints about the wine choices, though, which are consistently excellent. The small storefront lounge is warmly lit, with modern furnishings, including a signature beehive-shaped wine display. On weekends, the decibel

14

level rises considerably and space is at a premium. ✉ *3330 Steiner St., Marina* ☎ *415/345–1377* ⊕ *www.nectarwinelounge.com.*

CABARET

San Francisco's modest cabaret scene tends toward the outlandish—case in point, the cross-dressing, lip-synching waitresses at asiaSF. The only traditional cabaret is at the Plush Room, where old standards and new talent alike draw appreciative crowds.

asiaSF. Saucy, sexy, and fun, this is one of the hottest places in town for a drag-show virgin. (Veterans might try something more specialized, like the Stud's "Trannyshack.") The entertainment, as well as gracious food service, is provided by some of the city's most gorgeous "gender illusionists," who strut in impossibly high heels on top of the catwalk bar, vamping to tunes like "Cabaret" and "Big Spender." The creative Asian-influenced cuisine is surprisingly good. **Go on a weekday to avoid a deluge of bachelorette parties.** Make reservations, or risk being turned away. Oh, and bring a camera. ✉ *201 9th St., at Howard St., SoMa* ☎ *415/255–2742* ⊕ *www.asiasf.com.*

Fodor's Choice ★ **Club Fugazi.** Club Fugazi's claim to fame is *Beach Blanket Babylon,* a wacky musical send-up of San Francisco moods and mores that has been going strong since 1974, making it the longest-running musical revue anywhere. Although the choreography is colorful, the singers brassy, and the satirical songs witty, the real stars are the comically exotic costumes and famous ceiling-high "hats"—which are worth the price of admission alone. The revue sells out as early as a month in advance, so order tickets as far ahead as possible. Those under 21 are admitted only to the Sunday matinee. **If you don't shell out the extra $15–$20 for reserved seating, you won't have an assigned seat—so get your cannoli to go and arrive at least 30 minutes prior to showtime to get in line.** ✉ *678 Green St., at Powell St., North Beach* ☎ *415/421–4222* ⊕ *www.beachblanketbabylon.com.*

COMEDY

Despite San Francisco's diverse arts-and-entertainment landscape, its comedy scene is rather limp. Big-name acts, however, often perform at its two main comedy clubs, Cobb's and Punch Line.

Cobb's Comedy Club. Stand-up comics such as Bill Maher, Paula Poundstone, and Sarah Silverman have appeared at this club. You can also see sketch comedy and comic singer-songwriters here. Sixteen- and 17-year-olds must be accompanied by their parents; children aren't allowed. ✉ *915 Columbus Ave., at Lombard St., North Beach* ☎ *415/928–4320* ⊕ *www.cobbscomedyclub.com.*

Punch Line. A launch pad for the likes of Jay Leno and Whoopi Goldberg, this place books some of the nation's top talents. Headliners have included Dave Chappelle, Margaret Cho, and Jay Mohr. Only those 18 and over are admitted. ✉*444 Battery St., between Clay and Washington Sts., Financial District* ☎*415/397–7573* ⊕*www.punchlinecomedy club.com.*

Purple Onion. This intimate nightspot ranks right up there with Bimbo's and the Fillmore on the list of San Francisco's most famous clubs; the Onion provided an early platform for both folk-music troubadours such as the Kingston Trio and comedic acts like the Smothers Brothers. In addition to stand-up, you can catch sketch comedies, open mikes, and improv shows. ✉*140 Columbus Ave., at Broadway, North Beach* ☎*415/956–1653* ⊕*www.purpleonioncomedy.com.*

14

DANCE CLUBS

Compared to other big cities, San Francisco doesn't have many dedicated dance clubs—probably thanks in part to its 2 AM curfew. Lots of places are hit or miss—out of control one night, crickets the next. **Go on popular theme nights to avoid feeling like a private dancer.** You will rarely be denied entry based on the bouncer's whims (though we've heard of "sliding" cover scales at some clubs). Dress nicely, act nicely, and you shouldn't have any problems. Many rock, blues, and jazz clubs (*see below*) also have active dance floors; some have DJ-spun music when live acts aren't performing. For dance party news, check out the San Francisco edition of www.nitevibe.com.

Annie's Social Club. Anglophiles, unite! Once a month (usually the first Saturday), the DJs at the **Leisure** theme night crank out Brit pop. You can work on your karaoke rendition of "God Save the Queen" in the back room. Good fun! ✉*917 Folsom St., at 5th St., SoMa* ☎*415/974–1585* ⊕*www.anniessocialclub.com.*

★ **DNA Lounge.** The sounds change nightly at the venerable DNA Lounge, but this club gets a star solely for **Bootie.** Held the second Saturday of each month, this popular mashup unites hardcore and indie rockers, hip-hop devotees, and EMO fans. If a DJ mix of Gorillaz, Donna Summer, and Joy Division sounds like your bag, you're in for a treat. **Remedy,** which brings deep-house and hip-hop DJs most Friday nights, is also popular. On other nights, the place can be dead. Three bars and dance floors on two levels mean it's rarely uncomfortably crowded. ✉*375 11th St., between Harrison and Folsom Sts., SoMa* ☎*415/626–1409.*

The EndUp. Sometimes 2 AM is just too early. The EndUp is by far SF's most popular after-hours place, with possibly the best sound system in the city. **Said system is** *cranked.* **Even the cool kids wear earplugs.** It can be a bit of a meat market (which ladies can avoid on Fag Fridays), but this San Francisco insti-

SHOOK ME ALL NIGHT LONG

The EndUp is San Francisco's only serious after-hours place. It's open nonstop from 10 PM Friday until 4 AM Monday, and generally from 10 PM to 4 AM weekdays. People from all walks of life end up here.

tution doesn't adhere to any particular scene. ⊠*401 6th St., SoMa* ☎*415/646–0999* ⊕*www.theendup.com.*

Mezzanine. If you like megaclubs, then you'll dig this industrial-chic two-story club, which doubles as a gallery and performance venue. Live acts have included Mos Def, the Dandy Warhols, and Def Jux artists. The crowd is generally mixed, straight and gay. If the jam-packed dance floor (which can accommodate nearly 1,000 people) overwhelms you, head upstairs to the quietish mezzanine lounges to converse or to ogle the sexy crowd. ⊠*444 Jessie St., at 5th St., SoMa* ☎*415/625–8880* ⊕*www.mezzaninesf.com.*

★ **111 Minna Gallery.** Gallery by day, bar–dance club by night, this unpretentious warehouse space is often full of artsy young San Franciscans who prefer it to glitzier spots. The door is unmarked, and it's on a small side street just south of Mission. Dance events typically take place Wednesday through Saturday 9 PM–2 AM (though the bar opens at 5), but the dance party starts earlier on Wednesday for popular **Qoöl** (5 PM–10 PM). It's closed for private events on Monday. ⊠*111 Minna St., between 2nd and New Montgomery Sts., SoMa* ☎*415/974–1719* ⊕*www.111minnagallery.com.*

Pink. Look for a rosy lightbulb marking the entrance. Inside, the hyper-pink look might make you think of Barbie . . . or Pepto. International DJs spin regularly (mostly house music) to a crowded room. Count on a cover charge of at least $5, sometimes three times that. Doors open at 10, Tuesday through Saturday. ⊠*2925 16th St., between South Van Ness and Mission Sts., Mission* ☎*415/431–8889* ⊕*http://pinksf. com.*

Roccapulco. Salsa, salsa, salsa. With dancing and live music from big-name salsa bands on Friday and Saturday, this cavernous dance hall and restaurant knows how to pack 'em in. Pick up some moves at the Wednesday, Friday, and Saturday evening salsa lessons. The club enforces a dress code, so don't wear jeans or sneakers. This place is also a supper club serving Latin-nouveau cuisine. ⊠*3140 Mission St., between Precita and César Chavez Sts., Mission* ☎*415/648–6611* ⊕*www.roccapulco.com.*

330 Ritch Street. One of the city's best parties, the long-running **Popscene** features Brit pop, '60s soul, and New Wave every Thursday. Live acts—such as the Killers, Hot Hot Heat, and Lily Allen—are thrown into the mix. The stylish, modern space also serves pizza and has 16 beers on tap. ⊠*330 Ritch St., between 3rd and 4th Sts., SoMa* ☎*415/541–9574* ⊕*http://popscene-sf.com.*

GAY & LESBIAN NIGHTLIFE

In the days before the gay liberation movement, bars were more than mere watering holes—they also served as community centers where members of a mostly undercover minority could network and socialize. In the 1960s, the bars became hotbeds of political activity; by the 1970s other social opportunities had become available to gay men and lesbians, and the bars' importance as centers of activity decreased.

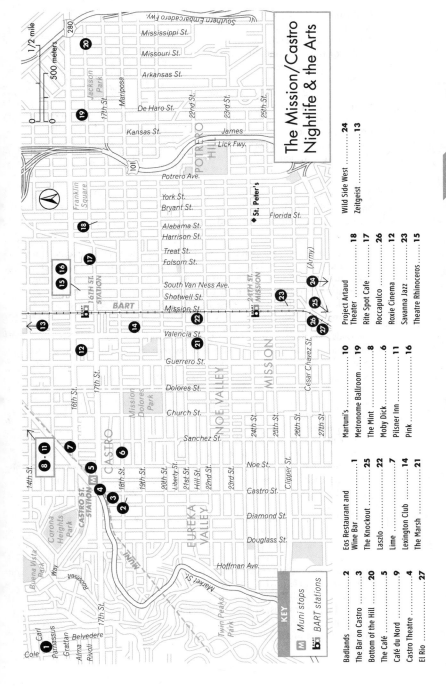

The Mission/Castro Nightlife & the Arts

KEY
Ⓜ Muni stops
🚉 BART stations

Old-timers may wax nostalgic about the vibrancy of pre-AIDS, 1970s bar life, but you can still have plenty of fun. The one difference is the one-night-a-week operation of some of the best clubs, which may cater to a different (sometimes straight) clientele on other nights. This type of club tends to come and go, so it's best to pick up one of the two main gay papers to check the latest happenings. The *Bay Area Reporter* (☎415/861–5019 ⊕*www.ebar.com*), a biweekly newspaper, lists gay and lesbian events in its calendar. The biweekly *San Francisco Bay Times* (☎415/626–0260 ⊕*www.sfbaytimes.com*) is aimed at gay and lesbian readers.

STRICTLY BALLROOM

Looking for less bump and grind? At the mellow, alcohol-free **Metronome Ballroom** (✉*1830 17th St., at De Haro St., Potrero Hill* ☎*415/252–9000*), weekend nights bring ballroom, Latin, and swing dancers for lessons, open dance, and revelry. This is also a school, so instruction in all sorts of ballroom styles is offered daily.

GAY MALE BARS

"A bar for every taste, that's the ticket" was how the curious film *Gay San Francisco* described late-1960s nightlife here. Leather bars, drag-queen hangouts, piano bars, and bohemian cafés were among the many options for gay men back then. The scene remains just as versatile today. Unless otherwise noted, there is no cover charge at the following establishments.

THE CASTRO

Badlands. Shirts off! If a sweaty muscle sandwich sounds like your idea of a good time, head to Badlands, where serious party boys come to grind to throbbing music on a packed dance floor. The lines can be ridiculous on weekends; those in the know go on Wednesday or Thursday. Tight-teed patrons range from 20s to 40s. ✉*4121 18th St., between Castro and Collingwood Sts., Castro* ☎*415/626–9320* ⊕*www.badlands-sf.com.*

The Bar on Castro. Without fail, the Bar on Castro has a healthy population of flirtatious, good-looking, twenty- and thirtysomething professionals. Not too stiff, not too wild (well, maybe a little wild)—it's sort of an everyman's—and everywoman's—gay bar. DJs spin house music, and it gets a bit dancey close to midnight; there's a smoking lounge in the back. ✉*456 Castro St., Castro* ☎*415/626–7220* ⊕*www.thebarsf. com.*

The Café. Always comfortable and often packed with a mixed gay, lesbian, and straight crowd, this is a place where you can dance to house or disco music, shoot pool, or meet guys in their 20s at the bar. The outdoor deck—a rarity—makes it a favorite destination for smokers. Weekend cover is $3; expect a line to get in. ✉*2367 Market St., at 17th St., Castro* ☎*415/861–3846* ⊕*www.cafesf.com.*

The Cinch. This Wild West–theme neighborhood bar has pinball machines, pool tables, and a smoking patio. It's not the least bit trendy, which is part of the charm for regulars. ✉*1723 Polk St., between Washington and Clay Sts., Van Ness/Polk* ☎*415/776–4162* ⊕*www. thecinch.com.*

Divas. In the rough-and-tumble Tenderloin, around the corner from the Polk Street bars, trannies (transvestites and transsexuals) and their admirers come here for the racy entertainment. (Naughty schoolgirls night is a fave.) This multilevel space has separate areas for stage performances, dancing, and quiet chats. It's not a drag bar, as there is no sense of irony or camp about the place; the girls here are charming, and the fun is in the titillation. ⌧*1081 Post St., between Larkin and Polk Sts., Tenderloin* ☎*415/474–3482* ⊕*www.divassf.com.*

★ **Eagle Tavern.** Bikers are courted with endless drink specials and, increasingly, live rock music at this humongous indoor-outdoor leather bar, one of the few SoMa bars remaining from the days before AIDS and gentrification. The Sunday-afternoon "Beer Busts" (3–6 PM) are a social high point and benefit charitable organizations. It's a surprisingly welcoming place for people from all walks of life. ⌧*398 12th St., at Harrison St., SoMa* ☎*415/626–0880* ⊕*www.sfeagle.com.*

★ **Lime.** The 1960s mod design of this chic cocktail lounge and restaurant (with rainbow-color Plexiglas at every turn) evokes L.A. more than SF, but it's the top choice for Abercrombie-wearing A-gays who swill mojitos by the bucket. There's also a diverse and delicious menu of small plates, good for sharing. ⌧*2247 Market St., between Noe and Sanchez Sts., Castro* ☎*415/621–5256.*

Lion Pub. With big comfy chairs, cascades of potted plants, and a small fireplace, this bar is so welcoming that—even though it's one of the oldest gay bars in the city—it tends to draw every sort of San Franciscan, young and old, gay and straight. Specialty drinks made with fresh-squeezed fruit juices attract cocktail connoisseurs. ⌧*2062 Divisadero St., at Sacramento St., Pacific Heights* ☎*415/567–6565.*

★ **Martuni's.** A mixed crowd enjoys cocktails in the semi-refined environment of this elegant bar at the intersection of the Castro, the Mission, and Hayes Valley; variations on the martini are a specialty. In the intimate back room, a pianist plays nightly and patrons take turns singing show tunes. It's a favorite post-theater spot—especially after the symphony or opera, which are within walking distance. ⌧*4 Valencia St., at Market St., Mission* ☎*415/241–0205.*

Moby Dick. The quintessential neighborhood watering hole, this unpretentious spot has a pool table, pinball machines, and a live "DVJ" mixing pop videos and music. A giant fish tank sits over the bar, giving shy types something to look at other than their shoes. An eclectic (in style and age) mix of casually dressed couples and guys with nothing to prove frequent this place, but there's some pick-up potential, too. ⌧*4049 18th St., at Hartford St., Castro* ☎*415/861–1199* ⊕*www.mobydicksf.com.*

N Touch. This self-proclaimed gay Asian dance club has long been popular with well-coiffed Asian–Pacific Islander men. Dancing, whether to '70s and '80s hits or contemporary house music, is accompanied by go-go dancers on Friday and Saturday nights. Monday and Tuesday are karaoke nights. ⌧*1548 Polk St., at Sacramento St., Van Ness/Polk* ☎*415/441–8413* ⊕*www.ntouchsf.com.*

Pilsner Inn. Casual and comfortable—yet still hip and cruisy—Pilsner is the type of neighborhood joint you quickly claim as your own. Kick

14

WHAT A DRAG

When it comes to men dressing as women, this city has got it down. These are the shows drag queens attend on their nights off.

Local celebrity diva Peaches Christ hosts **Midnight Mass** (⊠ *Bridge Theater, 3010 Geary Blvd., Richmond* ☎ *415/751–3213* ⊕ *www.peacheschrist.com*) on Saturday in summer and sporadically throughout the year. The "mass" includes a midnight screening of a campy cult classic (think *Showgirls* or *Mommie Dearest*), preceded by an outrageous drag show that parodies the film.

Fabulous emcee Cookie Dough presides over the Castro's **Monster Show** (⊠ *Harvey's, 500 Castro St., at 18th St., Castro* ⊕ *www.cookievision.* *com*) every Saturday at 11:30 PM. If you want to get a who's who of the SF drag scene, this is the place. The longest-running drag show in the Castro packs 'em in for events like "Old-School Divas" and "Fractured Fairy-Tales." The annual Oscar-bashing event is priceless.

You haven't lived until you've seen a transvestite called Suppositori Spelling (who looks uncannily like her namesake) crowd-surf her way to the stage, down a bottle of cough syrup, and perform a rousing—if somewhat scary—Hedwig-esque rendition of "I Will Survive." **Trannyshack** (⊠ *The Stud, 399 9th St., at Harrison St., SoMa* ☎ *415/252–7883* ⊕ *www.* *heklina.com*) is every Tuesday at midnight.

back with a pint on the fantastic year-round patio (it's covered), and enjoy eye-candy of the thirtysomething variety (ranging from conservative yuppie guys to Mission emo-boys). Pilsner Inn is technically a sports bar, which means it has a pool table and sponsors some local amateur teams. ⊠ *225 Church St at Market St., Castro* ☎ *415/621–7058* ⊕ *www.pilsnerinn.com.*

★ **The Stud.** Mingle with glam trannies, tight-teed pretty boys, ladies and their ladies, and a handful of straight onlookers who dance to the live DJ and watch world-class drag performers on the small stage. The entertainment is often campy, pee-your-pants funny, and downright talented. Each night's music is different—from funk, soul, and hip-hop to '80s tunes and disco favorites. *Trannyshack,* the city's best and longest-running drag cabaret show, starts Tuesday at midnight—it's well worth a Wednesday-morning hangover. The club is closed on Monday. ⊠ *399* SOMA *9th St., at Harrison St., SoMa* ☎ *415/863–6623* ⊕ *www.studsf.com.*

Trax. "Laid back" would be an understatement. Once inside, you won't feel like you're in a gay bar—or in San Francisco. And that's the way the regulars like it. Cheap beer specials draw people from every ilk. And though you don't have to don your cruisewear for this place, it's still social. ⊠ *1437 Haight St., Haight* ☎ *415/864–4213.*

KARAOKE BARS

★ **The Mint.** A mixed gay-straight crowd that's drop-dead serious about its karaoke (to the point where you'd think an *American Idol* casting agent was in the crowd) comes here seven nights a week. Regulars sing everything from Simon and Garfunkel songs to disco classics in front of an attentive audience. Do *not* go here unprepared! Check out the songbook online to perfect your debut before you attempt to take the mike. ✉*1942 Market St., between Duboce and Laguna Sts., Hayes Valley* ☎*415/626–4726* ⊕*www.themint.net.*

Bow Bow Cocktail Lounge. Not ready for the Mint? Stick with the rest of us at this quirky, divey karaoke bar. You can still get your kicks performing in front of a sometimes rowdy—but almost always supportive—audience of young drunks and older Asian men. Plus, where else can you get boiled eggs and hot sauce after midnight (or at all)? ✉*1155 Grant Ave. near Broadway, Chinatown* ☎*415/421–6730.*

BEYOND THE BARS

Of course, there's more to gay nightlife than the bars. Most nights **Theatre Rhinoceros** (✉*2940 16th St., Mission* ☎*415/861–5079* ⊕*www. therhino.org*) has plays and solo shows on two stages. The **San Francisco Lesbian, Gay, Bisexual and Transgender Community Center** (✉*1800 Market St., Hayes Valley* ☎*415/865–5555* ⊕*www.sfcenter.org*) is home to many social activities, from writers' groups to yoga.

14

LESBIAN BARS

For a place known as a gay mecca, San Francisco has always suffered from a surprising drought of women's bars. The Lexington Club, in the nightlife-filled Mission District, is the best-known bar. The Café *(above) is* probably the most lesbian-friendly Castro bar, though you'll find queer gals (and many more queer guys) at the Mint and the Stud, too.

The calendar at www.hillgirlz.com, one of the best places for detailed information about the city's lesbian scene, covers everything from dance events to social and political gatherings.

★ **Lexington Club.** According to its slogan, "every night is ladies' night" at this all-girl club geared to urban alterna-dykes in their 20s and 30s (think piercings and tattoos, not lipstick). Catfights are not uncommon. **The women's room has awesome graffiti.** ✉*3464 19th St., at Lexington St., Mission* ☎*415/863–2052* ⊕*www.lexingtonclub.com.*

Wild Side West. A friendly pool game is always going on at this mellow, slightly out-of-the-way neighborhood hangout, where all are welcome. Outside is a large deck and one of San Francisco's best bar gardens, where acoustic-guitar sing-alongs are not uncommon. ✉*424 Cortland Ave., Bernal Heights* ☎*415/647–3099.*

JAZZ CLUBS

Traditionally, San Francisco hasn't had world-renowned jazz clubs like, say, New York and Paris—but that began to change with the arrival of Yoshi's. The fabled Oakland-based jazz club opened a hot new outpost in San Francisco's Fillmore District at the end of 2007. Jazz fans can also get their kicks at venues ranging from mellow restaurant cocktail lounges to hip Mission District venues. Be sure to check rock, pop, folk, and blues venues for special jazz events. Most clubs charge a cover that varies with the act; call for specific details.

★ **Jazz at Pearl's.** Run by the supremely talented vocalist Kim Nalley, who headlines two or three times a week, Pearl's is San Francisco's premier jazz club. Dim lighting, plush 1930s supper-club style, and great straight-ahead jazz make it ideal for a romantic evening. A full menu is available until late. Cover is $10–$20 for the two shows each evening; the first is at 8 PM, the second around 11 PM. There is no age requirement, but there is a dress code, so don't wear jeans. ✉256 Columbus Ave., at Broadway, North Beach ☎415/291–8255 ⊕http://jazzatpearls.com.

TOP LIVE SHOWS
■ Boom Boom Room
■ City Arts & Lectures
■ Club Fugazi
■ Great American Music Hall
■ Stern Grove Festival
■ Teatro ZinZanni

Moose's. This popular North Beach restaurant has great music and a small but stylish bar area. Combos play classic jazz nightly from 7:30 to 10 PM and during Sunday brunch, starting at noon. There's no cover. ✉1652 Stockton St., near Union St., North Beach ☎415/989–7800 ⊕www.mooses.com.

Savanna Jazz. Deep in the Outer Mission, this is one of the best jazz joints in SF, an unexpected find in a neighborhood filled with hipster bars. Loungey booths and low lighting set the scene for consistently good old-school Latin and Brazilian jazz acts. Cover is generally $5–$8. ✉2937 Mission St., between 25th and 26th Sts., Mission ☎415/285–3369 ⊕www.savannajazz.com.

★ **Yoshi's.** The legendary Oakland club that has pulled in some of the world's best jazz musicians—Pat Martino, Branford Marsalis, Betty Carter, and Dizzy Gillespie, to name just a few—opened a San Francisco location in late 2007. The new club has terrific acoustics, a 9-foot Steinway grand piano (broken in by Chick Corea), and seating for 411; it's been hailed as "simply the best jazz club in the city." Yoshi's also serves Japanese food in an adjoining restaurant set in a soaring two-story space, decorated with blond wood and hanging paper lanterns (you can also order food at café tables in the club). And yes, the coupling of sushi and jazz *is* as elegant as it sounds. Sightlines are good from just about any vantage point, including the back balcony. Yoshi's is located in the Fillmore District, which was known as the "Harlem of the West" in its heyday during the 1940s and '50s. Be advised, the strip where the club is located is part of a new city redevelopment project—it's on a tough block in an even tougher neighborhood; so, take advantage of the valet parking. ✉1330 Fillmore St., at Eddy St., Japantown ☎415/655–5600 ⊕www.yoshis.com.

ROCK, POP, HIP-HOP, FOLK & BLUES CLUBS

★ **Bimbo's 365 Club.** The plush main room and adjacent lounge of this club, here since 1951, retain a retro vibe perfect for the "Cocktail Nation" programming that keeps the crowds entertained. For a taste of the old-school San Francisco nightclub scene, you can't beat this place. Indie low-fi and pop bands like Stephen Malkmus and the Jicks and Camera Obscura fill the bill. ✉*1025 Columbus Ave., at Chestnut St., North Beach* ☎*415/474-0365* ⊕*www.bimbos365club.com.*

Fodor'sChoice ★ **Boom Boom Room.** John Lee Hooker's old haunt has been an old-school blues haven for years, attracting top-notch acts from all around the country. Luck out with legendary masters like James "Super Chikan" Johnson, or discover new blues and funk artists. ✉*1601 Fillmore St., at Geary Blvd., Japantown* ☎*415/673-8000* ⊕*www.boomboom blues.com.*

★ **Bottom of the Hill.** This is a great live-music dive—in the best sense of the word—and truly the epicenter for independent rock in the Bay Area. The club has hosted some great acts over the years, including the Strokes and the Throwing Muses. Rap and hip-hop acts occasionally make it to the stage. ✉*1233 17th St., at Texas St., Potrero Hill* ☎*415/621-4455* ⊕*www.bottomofthehill.com.*

Café du Nord. You can hear some of the coolest jazz, blues, rock, and alternative sounds at this basement bar. Built in 1907, it has retained some of its original Victorian features, which contribute to the hip, vaguely illicit feel—reminiscent of its days as a speakeasy. The music, a mix of local talent and indie headliners like Kristin Hersh and Bettie Serveert, is strictly top-notch. DJ events take place a few nights a week. ✉*2170 Market St., between Church and Sanchez Sts., Castro* ☎*415/861-5016* ⊕*www.cafedunord.com.*

The Fillmore. This is *the* club that all the big names, from Coldplay to Clapton, want to play. San Francisco's most famous rock-music hall serves up a varied menu of national and local acts: rock, reggae, grunge, jazz, folk, acid house, and more. Most tickets cost $20–$30, and some shows are open to all ages. **Avoid steep service charges by buying tickets at the Fillmore box office on Sunday (10–4).** ✉*1805 Geary Blvd., at Fillmore St., Western Addition* ☎*415/346-6000* ⊕*www.the fillmore.com.*

Fodor'sChoice ★ **Great American Music Hall.** You can find top-drawer entertainment at this great, eclectic nightclub. Acts range from the best in blues, folk, and jazz to up-and-coming college-radio and American-roots artists to of-the-moment indie rock stars (OK Go, Mates of State) and the establishment (Cowboy Junkies). The colorful marble-pillared emporium (built in 1907 as a bordello) also accommodates dancing at some shows. Pub grub is available most nights. ✉*859 O'Farrell St., between Polk and Larkin Sts., Tenderloin* ☎*415/885-0750* ⊕ *http://musichallsf.com.*

The Independent. Originally called the Box for its giant cube-shaped interior, this off-the-beaten-path music venue showcases an eclectic mix of rock, heavy metal, folk, soul, reggae, hip-hop, and DJ acts. There's a big dance floor. Recent shows include Lyrics Born, Testament, and the Dears. ✉*628 Divisadero St., at Hayes St., Western Addition* ☎*415/771-1421* ⊕*www.theindependentsf.com.*

Lou's Pier 47. Nightly blues accompany the hot Cajun seafood at this waterfront spot. Bands typically start playing in the late afternoon and continue until midnight. If you're staying near the Wharf, this is your best bet for live music without having to take a taxi. ✉*300 Jefferson*

St., at Jones St., Fisherman's Wharf ☎*415/771–5687* ⊕*www.lous pier47.com.*

The Plough and Stars. This decidedly unglamorous pub, where crusty old-timers swap stories over pints of Guinness, is the city's best bet for traditional Irish music. Bay Area musicians (and, once in a while, big-name bands) perform Thursday through Saturday. Talented locals gather to play on Tuesday and Sunday *seisiúns,* informal "sessions" where musicians sit around a table and drink and eat while chiming in; anyone skilled at Irish traditional music can join in. ✉*116 Clement St., at 2nd Ave., Richmond* ☎*415/751–1122* ⊕*www.theploughand stars.com.*

Red Devil Lounge. Local and up-and-coming hip-hop, rap, funk, indie rock, and jazz acts perform at this plush, dimly lighted lounge, which also offers DJ dancing and the occasional spoken-word night. Intimate (read: tightly spaced) tables line the narrow balcony overlooking the dance floor. Call ahead for schedules. ✉*1695 Polk St., at Clay St., Van Ness/Polk* ☎*415/921–1695* ⊕*www.reddevillounge.com.*

The Saloon. Hard-drinkin' in-the-know North Beach locals favor this raucous spot, known for great blues. Get the schedule at www.sfblues. net/Saloon.html. Built in the 1860s, the one-time bordello is purported to be the oldest bar in the city. This is not the place to order a mixed drink. You've been warned. ✉*1232 Grant Ave., near Columbus Ave., North Beach* ☎*415/989–7666.*

Slim's. National touring acts—mostly along the pop-punk and hard- and alt-rock lines—are the main event at this venue, one of SoMa's most popular nightclubs. Co-owner Boz Scaggs helps bring in the crowds and famous headliners like Dressy Bessy and Dead Meadow. ✉*333 11th St., between Harrison and Folsom Sts., SoMa* ☎*415/522–0333* ⊕*www.slims-sf.com.*

Warfield. This former movie palace—a "palace" in every sense of the word—is now one of the city's largest rock-and-roll venues, with tables and chairs downstairs and theater seating upstairs. The historic venue has booked everyone from Phish and the Grateful Dead to the Pretenders and Green Day. Check schedules and buy tickets at Ticketmaster. com. ✉*982 Market St., at 6th St., Civic Center* ☎*415/775–7722.*

THE ARTS

San Francisco's symphony, opera, and ballet all perform in the Civic Center area, also home to the 928-seat Herbst Theatre, which hosts many fine soloists and ensembles. **San Francisco Performances** (✉*500 Sutter St., Suite 710,* ☎*415/398–6449* ⊕*www.performances.org*) brings an eclectic array of topflight global music and dance talents to various venues—mostly the Yerba Buena Center for the Arts, Davies Symphony Hall, and Herbst Theatre. Artists have included the Los Angeles Guitar Quartet, the Paul Taylor Dance Company, and Midori.

Nightlife: Japantown, Pacific Heights, and the Marina

14

TICKETS

The opera, symphony, the San Francisco Ballet's *Nutcracker,* and touring hit musicals are often sold out in advance. Tickets are usually available for other shows within a day of the performance.

City Box Office (✉ *180 Redwood St., Suite 100, off Van Ness Ave. between Golden Gate Ave. and McAllister St., Civic Center* ☎ *415/392–4400* ⊕ *www. cityboxoffice.com*), a charge-by-phone service, offers tickets for many performances and lectures. You can buy tickets in person at its downtown location weekdays 9:30–5:30. You can charge tickets for everything from jazz concerts to Giants games by phone or online through **Tickets.com** (☎ *800/955– 5566* ⊕ *www.tickets.com*). Half-price, same-day tickets for many local and touring stage shows go on sale (cash only) at 11 AM Tuesday through Saturday at the **TIX Bay Area** (✉ *Powell St. between Geary and Post Sts., Union Square* ☎ *415/433– 7827* ⊕ *www.theatrebayarea.org*) booth on Union Square. TIX is also a full-service ticket agency for theater and music events around the Bay Area, open 11–6 Tuesday through Thursday, Friday 11–7, Saturday 10–7, and Sunday 10–3.

LATE-NIGHT TRANSPORTATION

For information on getting around after dark, *see* Late-Night Transportation *in* Nightlife, *above.*

THE 4-1-1

The best guide to the arts is the Sunday "Datebook" section (www. sfgate.com/datebook), printed on pink paper, in the *San Francisco Chronicle.* The four-day entertainment supplement "96 Hours" (www. sfgate.com/96hours) is in the Thursday *Chronicle.* Also be sure to check out the city's free alternative weeklies, including *SF Weekly* (www. sfweekly.com) and the more avant-garde *San Francisco Bay Guardian* (www.sfbg.com).

Online, SF Station (www.sfstation.com) has a frequently updated arts and nightlife calendar. San Francisco Arts Monthly (www.sfarts.org), which is published at the end of the month, has arts features and events, plus a helpful "Visiting San Francisco?" section. For offbeat, emerging artist performances, consult CounterPULSE (www.counterpulse.org).

TOP ARTS PICKS

Berkeley Repertory Theatre. The Bay Area's most satisfying theatrical performances are just a quick BART trip away.

Castro Theatre. This dramatic art-deco palace is the perfect spot for munching buttery popcorn and watching a Judy Garland or Jimmy Stewart flick.

Yoshi's. Amazing jazz and great Japanese food in a stylish theater.

Stern Grove Festival. While away a Sunday afternoon listening to opera, jazz, rock, and other musical genres in a gorgeous eucalyptus-enclosed amphitheater.

DANCE

San Francisco has long been a hub for dancers. Isadora Duncan danced in the courtyard of the Palace of the Legion of Honor, and the San Francisco Ballet presented the American debut of the *Nutcracker* in 1944. The dot-com real estate boom displaced many troupes and forced them to disband, but dance is still a major part of the city's cultural life. Today, San Francisco is gaining recognition for its exciting modern and experimental dance companies. Local groups such as Alonzo King's Lines Ballet and ODC/San Francisco tour extensively and are well regarded by national dance critics. The San Francisco Ballet excels at both traditional and contemporary repertoires.

Dancers' Group (http://dancersgroup.org) is a Web site for dancers and dance aficionados with events and resource listings. **Voice of Dance** (http://voiceofdance.com) is a national publication with local calendars. Web-only **DanceView Times** (www.danceviewtimes.com) reviews productions and events.

14

★ **Alonzo King's Lines Ballet.** Since 1982 this company has been staging the fluid and gorgeous ballets of choreographer and founder Alonzo King, sometimes in collaboration with top-notch world musicians such as Zakir Hussain and Hamza El Din. Ballets incorporate both classical and modern techniques, with experimental set design, costumes, and music. The San Francisco season is in the spring. ☎*415/863–3040* ⊕*www.linesballet.org.*

Margaret Jenkins Dance Company. This nationally acclaimed modern troupe, founded in 1973, sometimes performs with popular local musicians such as the Kronos Quartet and the Paul Dresher Ensemble. Jenkins's highly gestural style sometimes suggests the influence of Merce Cunningham, one of her teachers in the 1960s. ☎*415/861–3940, 415/392–4400 for tickets* ⊕*www.mjdc.org.*

☾ **ODC/San Francisco.** Popular with kids, this 10-member group's annual
★ Yuletide version of *The Velveteen Rabbit* (mid-November–mid-December), at the Yerba Buena Center for the Arts, ranks among the city's best holiday-season performances. The group's main repertory season generally runs intermittently between January and June. ☎*415/863–6606* ⊕*www.odcdance.org.*

★ **San Francisco Ballet.** Under artistic director Helgi Tomasson, the San Francisco Ballet's works—both classical and contemporary—have won admiring reviews. The primary season runs from February through May. Its repertoire includes full-length ballets such as *Don Quixote* and *Sleeping Beauty*; the December presentation of the *Nutcracker* is one of the most spectacular in the nation. The company also performs bold new dances from star choreographers such as William Forsythe and Mark Morris, alongside modern classics by George Balanchine and Jerome Robbins. Tickets and information are available at the **War Memorial Opera House.** ✉ *War Memorial Opera House, 301 Van Ness Ave., Civic Center* ☎*415/865–2000* ⊕*www.sfballet.org* ☾ *Weekdays 10–4.*

Smuin Ballet/SF. Former San Francisco Ballet director Michael Smuin founded this company, which is renowned for its fluidity. It regularly integrates popular music—everything from Gershwin to the Beatles and Elton John—into its performances. ☎*415/495–2234* ⊕*www. smuinballet.org.*

FILM

The San Francisco Bay Area, including Berkeley and Marin County, is considered one of the nation's most savvy movie markets. Films of all sorts find an audience here. The area is also a filmmaking center, where documentaries and experimental works are produced on modest budgets and feature films and television programs are shot on location. In San Francisco, about a third of the theaters regularly show foreign and independent films.

San Francisco Cinematheque (☎*415/552–1990* ⊕*www.sfcinematheque. org*) showcases experimental film and digital media, with most screenings at the Yerba Buena Center for the Arts or Artists' Television Access.

MOVIE THEATERS

Many of these theaters screen high-quality independent and foreign-language films (Friday and Saturday evening shows often sell out, so consider buying tickets in advance via ⊕*www.moviefone.com* or ☎*777*–FILM[preceded by the local area code]).

The Bridge. This theater, built in 1939, has been showing films on its single screen since the 1950s. ✉*3010 Geary Blvd., at Blake St., Western Addition* ☎*415/267–4893.*

Fodor'sChoice **Castro Theatre.** Designed by art-deco master Timothy Pfleuger and
★ opened in 1922, the most dramatic movie theater in the city hosts revivals as well as foreign and independent engagements and the occasional sing-along movie musical. Parking is limited in the Castro district, so taking public transportation is advised. ✉*429 Castro St., near Market St., Castro* ☎*415/621–6120* ⊕*www.castrotheatre.com.*

The Clay. This small but comfortable and well-kept single-screen theater dates to 1910 and has first-run art-house films. ✉*2261 Fillmore St., at Clay St., Pacific Heights* ☎*415/267–4893.*

Embarcadero Center Cinemas. Shows often sell out at this modern, extremely popular five-screen theater, which has the best in first-run independent and foreign films. ✉*1 Embarcadero Center, Promenade level, Embarcadero* ☎*415/267–4893.*

Lumière. This three-screen theater tends toward experimental and foreign films, as well as documentaries. ✉*1572 California St., between Polk and Larkin Sts., Van Ness/Polk* ☎*415/267–4893.*

Opera Plaza Cinemas. The four theaters and their screens are small, but this is often the last place you can see an independent or foreign film before it ends its run in the city. It's great for indie-film-loving procrastinators, but if you arrive late for the show, you may have to sit in the front row of the tiny screening room. ✉*601 Van Ness Ave., between Turk St. and Golden Gate Ave., Civic Center* ☎*415/267–4893.*

Red Vic Movie House. An adventurous lineup of hard-to-find contemporary and classic American and foreign indies and documentaries is screened in a funky setting, which is California's only worker-owned and -operated movie house. ✉*1727 Haight St., between Cole and Shrader Sts., Haight* ☎*415/668–3994* ⊕*www.redvicmoviehouse. com.*

Roxie Cinema. Film noir and indie features and documentaries, as well as first-run movies and classic foreign cinema, are the specialties here. ✉*3117 16th St., between Valencia and Guerrero Sts., Mission* ☎*415/863–1087* ⊕*www.roxie.com.*

MUSIC

San Francisco's symphony and opera perform in the Civic Center area, but musical ensembles can be found all over the city: in churches, museums, restaurants, and parks—not to mention in Berkeley and on the Peninsula.

★ **Chanticleer.** A Bay Area treasure, this all-male a cappella ensemble stages lively and technically flawless performances that show off a repertoire ranging from sacred medieval music to show tunes to contemporary avant-garde works. ☎*415/252–8589* ⊕*www.chanticleer.org.*

42nd Street Moon. This group produces delightful "semistaged" concert performances of rare chestnuts from Broadway's golden age of musical theater, such as *L'il Abner* and *The Boys From Syracuse.* The **Eureka Theatre** (✉*215 Jackson St., between Front and Battery Sts., Financial District*) hosts most 42nd Street Moon shows. ☎*415/255–8207* ⊕*www.42ndstmoon.com.*

★ **Kronos Quartet.** Twentieth-century works and a number of premieres make up the programs for this always entertaining, Grammy Award–winning string ensemble, which spends much of the year traveling throughout the United States and abroad. ⊕*www.kronosquartet.org.*

Noontime Concerts at St. Patrick's Catholic Church. This Gothic revival church, completed in 1872 and rebuilt after the 1906 earthquake, hosts a notable chamber-music series on Wednesday at 12:30; suggested donation is $5. ✉*756 Mission St., between 3rd and 4th Sts., SoMa* ☎*415/777–3211* ⊕*www.noontimeconcerts.org.*

Old First Concerts. The well-respected Friday-evening and Sunday-afternoon series includes chamber music, choral works, vocal soloists, new music, and jazz. Tickets are $15. ✉*Old First Presbyterian Church, 1751 Sacramento St., at Van Ness Ave., Van Ness/Polk* ☎*415/474–1608* ⊕*www.oldfirstconcerts.org.*

Philharmonia Baroque Orchestra. This ensemble has been called a local baroque orchestra with a national reputation and the nation's preeminent group for performances of early music. Its season of concerts, fall through spring, celebrates composers of the 17th and 18th centuries, including Handel, Vivaldi, and Bach. ☎*415/252–1288* ⊕*www.philharmonia.org.*

★ **San Francisco Symphony.** One of America's top orchestras, the San Francisco Symphony performs from September through May, with additional summer performances of light classical music and show tunes; visiting artists perform here the rest of the year. Michael Tilson Thomas, who is known for his innovative programming of 20th-century Ameri-

CLOSE UP

Arts & Culture Beyond the City

Although most folks from outlying areas drive *into* San Francisco to enjoy the nightlife, there are plenty of reasons to head *out* of the city.

FILM

The **Pacific Film Archive** (✉ *2575 Bancroft Way, near Bowditch St., Berkeley* ☎ *510/642–0808* ⊕ *www. bampfa.berkeley.edu*), affiliated with the University of California, screens a comprehensive mix of old and first-run American and foreign films. The spectacular art-deco **Paramount Theatre** (✉ *2025 Broadway, near 19th St. BART station, Oakland* ☎ *510/465–6400* ⊕ *www.paramounttheatre.com*) screens a few vintage flicks (*The Sting, Casablanca*) every month.

PERFORMING ARTS & MUSIC

Some of the most talented practitioners of folk, blues, Cajun, and bluegrass perform at the alcohol-free **Freight & Salvage Coffee House** (✉ *1111 Addison St., Berkeley* ☎ *510/548–1761* ⊕ *www.freightandsalvage.org*). Oakland is home to **Yoshi's** (✉ *510 Embarcadero St., between Washington and Clay Sts., Oakland* ☎ *510/238–9200* ⊕ *www. yoshis.com*), one of the nation's best jazz venues.

The East Bay's **Berkeley Symphony Orchestra** (☎ *510/841–2800* ⊕ *www.berkeleysymphony.org*) has risen to considerable prominence under artistic director Kent Nagano's baton. The emphasis is on 20th-century composers. The orchestra plays a handful of concerts each year, in the University of California-Berkeley's Zellerbach Hall and in other locations around Berkeley. **The acoustics in Zellerbach Hall are notoriously dead; sit in the front or middle orchestra for the best sound.** The **Cal Performances** (☎ *510/642–9988* ⊕ *www.calperformances.org*) series, held at various venues on the University of California–Berkeley campus from September through May, offers the Bay Area's most varied bill of internationally acclaimed artists in all disciplines. The Tony Award–winning **Berkeley Repertory Theatre** (✉ *2025 Addison St., Berkeley* ☎ *510/845–4700* ⊕ *www. berkeleyrep.org*) is the American Conservatory Theatre's major rival for leadership among the region's resident professional companies. It performs an adventurous mix of classics and new plays from fall to spring in its theater complex, near BART's Downtown Berkeley station. Parking is at a premium, so plan to arrive early if you're coming by car.

can works (most notably his Grammy Award–winning Mahler cycle), is the music director, and he and his orchestra often perform with soloists of the caliber of Andre Watts, Gil Shaham, and Renée Fleming. Just to illustrate the more adventuresome side of the organization, this symphony once collaborated with the heavy-metal group Metallica. Tickets run about $15–$100.

Many members of the San Francisco Symphony perform in the **Summer in the City** (☎ *415/864–6000* ⊕ *www.sfsymphony.org*) concert series, held in the 2,400-seat Davies Symphony Hall. The schedule includes light classics and Broadway, country, and movie music. ✉ *Davies Sym-*

phony Hall, 201 Van Ness Ave., at Grove St., Civic Center ☎*415/864– 6000* ⊕*www.sfsymphony.org.*

MUSIC FESTIVALS

Hardly Strictly Bluegrass Festival. The city's top free music event, as well as one of the greatest gatherings for bluegrass, country, and roots music fans in the country, takes place from late September to early October. Roughly 50,000 folks turn out to see the likes of Willie Nelson, Emmylou Harris, Jimmie Dale Gilmore, and Del McCoury at Speedway Meadows in Golden Gate Park. ☎*No phone* ⊕*www.strictlyblue grass.com.*

Noise Pop Festival. Widely considered to be one of the country's top showcases for what's new in indie-pop and alt-rock, Noise Pop is a weeklong festival in February or March held at Slim's, the Great American Music Hall, and other cool clubs. Founded in 1993, the low-key festival has helped local fans discover such talented acts as Modest Mouse, Kristin Hersh, and Bettie Serveert. (Phone info on the event is best obtained by calling the individual venues.) ☎*415/375–3370* ⊕*www.noisepop.com.*

San Francisco Bluegrass Festival. While the Hardly Strictly Bluegrass Festival attracts both die-hard fans and casual listeners, this event targets those who can name all the players in Ralph Stanley's band. The festival takes place each February at various small venues both in and around San Francisco. Past participants have included Kenny Hall, Laurie Lewis, Jackstraw, and, yes, Ralph Stanley. ☎*No phone* ⊕*www. sfbluegrass.org.*

San Francisco Blues Festival. Billed as the country's oldest ongoing blues festival, SFBF has hosted a hall of fame's worth of blues legends over the years, including John Lee Hooker, B. B. King, Buddy Guy, and James Cotton. It's also a great place to catch rising Bay Area blues stars like J. C. Smith and Tommy Castro. The festival, which was founded by local blues historian Tom Mazzolini in 1973, is held each September at Fort Mason's Great Meadow, which has stunning views of the Golden Gate Bridge and the bay. ☎*415/979–5588* ⊕*www.sfblues.com.*

San Francisco Jazz Festival. Every year starting in October, concert halls, clubs, and churches throughout the city host this acclaimed two-week festival. The popular event, which got its start in 1983, has featured such big-name acts as Ornette Coleman, Sonny Rollins, and McCoy Tyner, as well as talked-about up-and-comers like Brad Mehldau and Chris Botti. ☎*415/398–5655* ⊕*www.sfjazz.org.*

San Francisco World Music Festival. Founded in 2000, this acclaimed festival draws musicians from around the world to various venues in the city. Unlike some so-called world music festivals, this event truly *is* a global affair, offering more than just the standard assortment of Celtic acts and Latin jazz players. The event takes place each fall, usually starting in September. ☎*415/561–6571* ⊕*www.sfworldmusicfestival. org.*

SFJAZZ Spring Season. The increasingly popular counterpart to the fall festival, the Spring Season is programmed by artistic director Joshua Redman, a saxophone colossus who grew up across the Bay in Berkeley.

Founded in 2000, the lengthy festival runs roughly from mid-March to early June and features an array of top-notch headliners. ☎*415/398–5655* ⊕*www.sfjazz.org.*

☾ **Stern Grove Festival.** The nation's oldest continual free summer music festival hosts Sunday-afternoon performances of symphony, opera, jazz, pop music, and dance. The amphitheater is in a beautiful eucalyptus grove below street level, perfect for picnicking before the show. (Dress for cool weather.) ✉*Sloat Blvd. at 19th Ave., Sunset* ☎*415/252–6252* ⊕*www.sterngrove.org.*

FodorsChoice
★

OPERA

★ **San Francisco Opera.** Founded in 1923, this world-renowned company has resided in the Civic Center's War Memorial Opera House since the building's completion in 1932. Over its split season—September through January and June through July—the opera presents about 70 performances of 10 to 12 operas. Translations are projected above the stage during almost all non-English operas. Long considered a major international company and the most important operatic organization in the United States outside New York, the opera frequently embarks on productions with European opera companies. Ticket prices are about $25–$195. The full-time box office (Monday 10–5, Tuesday–Friday 10–6) is at 199 Grove Street, at Van Ness Avenue. ✉*War Memorial Opera House, 301 Van Ness Ave., at Grove St., Civic Center* ☎*415/864–3330 tickets* ⊕*www.sfopera.com.*

SPOKEN WORD

Nearly every night of the week, aspiring and established writers, poets, and performers step up to the mike and put their words and egos on the line. Check the listings section of the free alternative weekly papers and the *San Francisco Sunday Chronicle* "Book Review" section for other options.

Cafe International. An open-mike session follows one or more featured readers here every Friday night at 8. Spoken-word performances are interspersed with acoustic musical acts. ✉*508 Haight St., at Fillmore St., Lower Haight* ☎*415/552–7390.*

FodorsChoice
★

City Arts & Lectures. Each year this program includes more than 20 fascinating conversations with writers, composers, actors, politicians, scientists, and others. The Herbst Theatre, in the Civic Center area, is usually the venue. Past speakers include Nora Ephron, Salman Rushdie, Ken Burns, and Linda Ronstadt. ☎*415/392–4400* ⊕*www.cityarts.net.*

★ **Commonwealth Club of California.** The nation's oldest public-affairs forum hosts speakers as diverse as Erin Brockovich and Bill Gates; every president since Teddy Roosevelt has addressed the club. Topics range from culture and politics to economics and foreign policy. Events are open to nonmembers; contact the club for the current schedule of events. Venues vary by speaker. Lectures are broadcast on NPR. ✉*595 Mar-*

ket St., at 2nd St., Financial District ☎415/597–6700 ⊕www.com monwealthclub.org.

★ **West Coast Live.** Billed as "San Francisco's Live Radio Show to the World," the program invites an audience to its weekly broadcasts, many at Fort Mason's Magic Theater, the Empire Plush Room, and the Freight & Salvage Coffee House in Berkeley. The ever-changing guest list includes authors, musicians, comedians, and pundits. Recent guests include Dave Barry, Charlie Owen, and Jamaica Kincaid. ☎415/664–9500 ⊕www.wcl.org.

THEATER

14

San Francisco's theaters are concentrated on Geary Street west of Union Square, but a number of additional commercial theaters, as well as resident companies that enrich the city's theatrical scene, are within walking distance of this theater row. The three major commercial theaters—Curran, Golden Gate, and Orpheum—are operated by the Shorenstein-Nederlander organization, which books touring plays and musicals, some before they open on Broadway. Theatre Bay Area (www.theatrebayarea.org) lists most Bay Area performances online.

★ **American Conservatory Theater.** Not long after its founding in the mid-1960s, the city's major nonprofit theater company became one of the nation's leading regional theaters. During its season, which runs from early fall to late spring, ACT presents approximately eight plays, from classics to contemporary works, often in rotating repertory. In December ACT stages a much-loved version of Charles Dickens's *A Christmas Carol*. The **ACT ticket office** (✉405 Geary St., Union Square ☎415/749–2228) is next door to Geary Theater, the company's home. ✉Geary Theater, 425 Geary St., Union Square ⊕www.act-sf.org.

Curran Theater. Some of the biggest touring shows mount productions at this theater, which has hosted classical music, dance, and stage performances since its 1925 opening. Shows are of the long-running Broadway musical variety, such as *Stomp* and *Jersey Boys*, and the seasonal *A Christmas Carol*. ✉445 Geary St., at Mason St., Union Square ☎415/551–2000 ⊕www.shnsf.com.

Exit Theatre. *The* place for absurdist and experimental theater, this three-stage venue also presents the annual **Fringe Festival** in September. ✉156 Eddy St., between Mason and Taylor Sts., Union Square ☎415/931–1094 ⊕www.sffringe.org.

Golden Gate Theater. This stylishly refurbished movie theater is now primarily a musical house. Touring productions of popular Broadway shows and revivals are its mainstay. ✉Golden Gate Ave. at Taylor St., Tenderloin ☎415/551–2000 ⊕www.shnsf.com.

Lorraine Hansberry Theatre. The performance of plays by black writers such as August Wilson and Langston Hughes is the raison d'être of this company. The 300-seat space is intimate. ✉620 Sutter St., at Mason St., Union Square ☎415/474–8800 ⊕www.lorrainehansberry theatre.com.

Magic Theatre. Once Sam Shepard's favorite showcase, the pint-size Magic presents works by rising American playwrights, such as Matthew Wells, Karen Hartman, and Claire Chafee. ⊠*Fort Mason, Bldg. D, Laguna St. at Marina Blvd., Marina* ☎*415/441–8822* ⊕*www.magictheatre.org.*

The Marsh. Experimental works, including one-man and one-woman shows, works in progress, and new vaudeville shows, can be seen here. ⊠*1062 Valencia St., at 22nd St., Mission* ☎*800/838–3006 tickets, 415/826–5750 information* ⊕*www.themarsh.org.*

New Conservatory Theatre Center. This three-stage complex hosts the annual **Pride Season,** focusing on contemporary gay- and lesbian-themed works, as well as other events, including educational plays for young people. ⊠*25 Van Ness Ave., between Fell and Oak Sts., Hayes Valley* ☎*415/861–8972* ⊕*www.nctcsf.org.*

Orpheum Theater. The biggest touring shows, such as *Hairspray* and *The Lion King,* are performed at this gorgeously restored 2,500-seat venue. The theater, opened in 1926 as a vaudeville stage, is as much an attraction as the shows. It was modeled after the Spanish baroque palaces and is considered one of the most beautiful theaters in the world; the interior walls have ornate cathedral-like stonework, and the gilded plaster ceiling is perforated with tiny lights. ⊠*1192 Market St., at Hyde St., Tenderloin* ☎*415/551–2000* ⊕*www.shnsf.com.*

☺ ★ **San Francisco Mime Troupe.** The politically leftist, barbed satires of this Tony Award–winning troupe are hardly mime in the Marcel Marceau sense. The group performs afternoon musicals at area parks from the July 4 weekend through September, and taking one in is a perfect way to spend a sunny summer day. ☎*415/285–1717* ⊕*www.sfmt.org.*

Fodor'sChoice ★ **Teatro ZinZanni.** Contortionists, chanteuses, jugglers, illusionists, and circus performers ply the audience as you're served a surprisingly good five-course dinner in a fabulous antique Belgian traveling-dance-hall tent. Be ready to laugh, and arrive early for a front-and-center table. Reservations are essential; tickets are \$125–\$150. Dress fancy. ⊠*Pier 29, Embarcadero at Battery St., Embarcadero* ☎*415/438–2668* ⊕*www.zinzanni.org.*

Theatre Rhinoceros. Gay and lesbian performers and playwrights are showcased in this small Mission theater. ⊠*2926 16th St., between Mission St. and South Van Ness Ave., Mission* ☎*415/861–5079* ⊕*www.therhino.org.*

★ **Yerba Buena Center for the Arts.** Across the street from the Museum of Modern Art and abutting a lovely urban garden, this performing arts complex schedules interdisciplinary art exhibitions, dance, music, film programs, and contemporary theater events. You can depend on the quality of the productions at Yerba Buena. ⊠*3rd and Howard Sts., SoMa* ☎*415/978–2787* ⊕*www.ybca.org.*

Sports & the Outdoors

Golden Gate Bridge

WORD OF MOUTH

"Saw a thread about biking over the [Golden Gate] Bridge into Sausalito and taking a ferry back. Anyone out there done this?"

—schmidtrossi

"Yes! Did it, loved it, and would do it again. I rented from Blazing Saddles, Pier 39. They were very helpful in mapping out the trail for me. I went past Sausalito and on to Tiburon, then took the ferry to Angel Island . . . then took another ferry back to SF."

—suzanne

Updated by
Fiona G.
Parrott

San Francisco's surroundings—bay, ocean, mountains, and forests—make getting outdoors outside the city a no-brainer. Muir Woods, Point Reyes, and Stinson Beach in Marin County (*see* Chapter 17) offer dozens of opportunities for exploring the natural beauty of the Bay Area. But the peninsular city—with its many green spaces, steep inclines, and catch-your-breath views—has plenty to offer itself.

Bikers and hikers traverse the majestic Golden Gate Bridge, bound for the Marin Headlands or the winding trails of the Presidio. Runners, strollers, in-line skaters, and cyclists head for Golden Gate Park's wooded paths, and water lovers satisfy their addictions by kayaking, sailing, or kite-surfing in the Bay and along the rugged Pacific coast. The monthly *Competitor Nor Cal Magazine* (⊕*www.competitornorcal. com*), available free at sporting-goods stores, tennis centers, and other recreational sites, lists running and bicycle races, and other participant sports events in northern California.

Prefer to watch from the sidelines? The Giants (baseball) and the '49ers (football) are San Francisco's professional sports teams; the Athletics (baseball) and Golden State Warriors (basketball) play in Oakland. But the city has plenty of other periodic sporting events you can watch (including the roving costume-party that is the Bay to Breakers race). For events listings and local perspectives on Bay Area sports, pick up a copy of the *San Francisco Chronicle* (⊕*www.sfgate.com*) or the *Examiner* (⊕*www.examiner.com*), both of which list schedules and scores.

BASEBALL

☾ The National League's New York Giants became the **San Francisco Giants**
Fodor'sChoice (⊠*AT&T Park, 24 Willie Mays Plaza, between 2nd and 3rd Sts., China*
★ *Basin* ☎*415/972–2000 or 800/734–4268* ⊕*http://sanfrancisco.giants. mlb.com*) when they moved to California in 1958, the same year that the Brooklyn Dodgers moved to Los Angeles. Today, the beautiful yet

classic design of the Giants' AT&T Park has created a new legion of fans—some more interested in the baseball experience than the Giants, per se. Still, buy your tickets in advance—nearly every game sells out.

GETTING TICKETS

The park is small and there are 30,000 season ticket holders (for 43,000 seats), so Giants tickets for popular games routinely sell out

the day they go on sale, and other games sell out quickly. If tickets aren't available at Tickets.com, try the Double Play Ticket Window, or even showing up on game day—there are usually plenty of scalpers, some selling at reasonable prices.

Tickets.com (☎877/473–4849 ⊕*www.tickets.com*) sells game tickets over the phone and charges a per-ticket fee of $2–$10, plus a per-call processing fee of up to $5. The **Giants Dugout** (✉*AT&T Park, 24 Willie Mays Plaza, SoMa* ☎*415/972–2000* ✉*4 Embarcadero Center, Embarcadero* ☎*415/951–8888*) sells tickets in any of its stores (check the Web site, http://sanfrancisco.giants.mlb.com/sf/ballpark/dugout_stores.jsp, for all locations); a surcharge is added at all but the ballpark store.

The Giants' Web-only **Double Play Ticket Window** (⊕*http://sanfrancisco.giants.mlb.com*) allows season ticket holders to resell their unused tickets. You won't always find a deal, but you might get a seat at an otherwise sold-out game. Click the "Tickets" menu on the home page.

BICYCLING

San Francisco is known for its treacherously steep hills, so it may be surprising to see so many cyclists. This is actually a great city for biking—there are ample bike lanes, it's not hard to find level ground with great scenery (along the water), and if you're willing to tackle a challenging uphill climb, you're often rewarded with a fabulous view—and a quick trip back down.

The **San Francisco Bicycle Coalition** (☎*415/431–2453* ⊕*www.sfbike.org*) has extensive information about the policies and politics of riding a bicycle in the city and lists local events for cyclists on its Web site. You can also download (but not print) a PDF version of the *San Francisco Bike Map and Walking Guide*.

WHERE TO RENT

Bike and Roll. You can rent bikes here for $7 per hour or $27 per day; discounted weekly rates are available. They also have complimentary maps.   ✉*734 Lombard St., North Beach* ☎*888/544–2453 or 415/771–8735* ⊕*www.bicyclerental.com*.

CLOSE UP

Where Giants Tread

The size of AT&T Park hits you immediately—the field, McCovey Cove, and the Lefty O'Doul drawbridge all look like miniature models. At only 13 acres, the San Francisco Giants' ballpark is one of the country's smallest. After Boston's Fenway, AT&T Park has the shortest distance to the wall; from home plate, it's just 309 feet to right. But there's something endearing about its petite stature—not to mention its location, with yacht masts poking up over the outfield and the blue bay sparkling beyond.

From 1960 to 2000, the Giants played at Candlestick Park (now Monster Park, the home of the NFL's '49ers). The huge, modern stadium has nice views, but it's also in one of the coldest, windiest parts of the city. (Giants' pitcher Stu Miller was famously "blown off the mound" here in 1961.)

In 2000, the Giants played their first game at AT&T Park (then Pacific Bell Park, later SBC Park—in fact, some locals jokingly call it the Phone Company Park). All told, $357 million was spent on the privately funded park, and it shows in the retro redbrick exterior, the quaint clock tower, handsome bronze statues and murals, above-average food (pad Thai, anyone?), and tiny details like baseball-style lettering on "no-smoking" signs. There isn't a bad seat in the house, and the park has an unusual level of intimacy and access. Concourses circle the field on two levels—on field level, you can stand inches from players as they exit the locker rooms. On street level, non-ticket-holders can get up close, too, outside a gate behind the visiting team's dugout.

Diehards may miss the grittiness of Candlestick, but it's hard not to love this park. It's a new stadium with an old-time aura, already a San Francisco institution.

THE FAMOUS "SPLASH HIT"
Locals show up in motorboats and inflatable rafts, with fishing nets ready to scoop up home run balls that clear the right field wall and land in McCovey Cove. Hitting one into the water isn't easy: the ball has to clear a 26-foot wall, the elevated walkway, and the promenade outside. Barry Bonds had the first splash hit on May 1, 2000.

GETTING THERE
Parking is pricey ($25 and up), and 5,000 spaces for 43,000 seats doesn't add up. Take public transportation. MUNI line N (to CalTrain/Mission Bay) stops right in front of the park, and MUNI bus lines 10, 15, 30, 42, 45, and 47 stop a block away. Or you can arrive in style—take the ferry from Jack London Square in Oakland (www.eastbayferry.com).

AT&T Park (⊠ *24 Willie Mays Plaza, SoMa* ☎ *415/972–1800* ⊕ *www.attpark. com*).

Park Tours (🎟 *$10* ⊗ *Daily at 10:30 and 12:30*).

🅒 The giant Coca-Cola bottle and mitt you see beyond the outfield are part of a **playground.** The bottle is a slide and the mitt actually has decent views of the field. It also has a mini-version of the park.

—Shannon Kelly

Bike Hut. Known for its mom-and-pop–style service, the Hut is a small rental-, repair-, and used-bike shop. Hourly rentals go for $5, daily rentals for $20. ✉ *Pier 40, SoMa* ☎ *415/543–4335* ⊕ *www.thebikehut.com.*

Blazing Saddles. This outfitter rents bikes for $7 an hour or $28 a day, and shares tips on sights to see along the paths. ✉ *2715 Hyde St., Fisherman's Wharf* ✉ *465 Jefferson St., at Hyde St., Fisherman's Wharf* ✉ *Pier 43½, near Taylor St., Fisherman's Wharf* ✉ *Pier 41, at Powell St., Fisherman's Wharf* ☎ *415/202–8888* ⊕ *www.blazingsaddles.com.*

WORD OF MOUTH

"Pacific Heights, Nob Hill, and Russian Hill can be monster climbs [so] study the terrain before you head out. Several years ago I watched the Tour de San Francisco and Lance Armstrong complained about the Fillmore Street climb—he said he might not return unless they did something about it."

–StuDudley

San Francisco Cyclery. Rent a bike for $15 for one to two hours, $20 for two to four hours, or $30 for eight hours. ✉ *672 Stanyan St., between Page and Haight Sts., Haight* ☎ *415/379–3870* ⊕ *www.sanfranciscocyclery.com* ☉ *Wed.–Mon. 10–6.*

From April through October, you can rent mountain bikes on **Angel Island** (☎ *415/435–1915* ⊕ *www.angelisland.org*) for $10 an hour or $30 a day.

THE EMBARCADERO

A completely flat, sea-level route, the Embarcadero hugs the eastern and northern bay and gives you a clear view of open waters, the Bay Bridge, and sleek high-rises. The route from Pier 40 to Aquatic Park takes about 30 minutes, and there are designated bike lanes the entire way. Along the way you can see—from east to west—the Ferry Building, the Bay Bridge, a view of Coit Tower near Pier 19 (look inland), and various ferries and historic ships. At Aquatic Park, there's a nice view of Golden Gate Bridge. If you're not tired yet, continue along the Marina and through the Presidio's Crissy Field. You may want to time your ride so you end up at the Ferry Building, where you can refuel with a sandwich, a gelato, or—why not?—fresh oysters.

Be sure to keep your eyes open along this route—cars move quickly here, and streetcars and tourist traffic can cause congestion. Near Fisherman's Wharf you can bike on the promenade, but take it slow—we've seen more than one near miss between bicyclist and pedestrian.

CAUTION Streetcar tracks can wreak havoc on skinny bike tires—and the bicyclist perched above them. Watch the ground and cross the tracks perpendicularly.

15

GOLDEN GATE PARK

A beautiful maze of roads and hidden bike paths crisscrosses San Francisco's most famous park, winding past rose gardens, lakes, waterfalls, museums, horse stables, bison, and, at the park's western edge, spectacular views of the Pacific Ocean. John F. Kennedy Drive is closed to motor vehicles on Sunday (and sometimes Saturday), when it's crowded with people-powered wheels. **Get a map of the park before you go—it's huge.**

NO UPHILL BATTLE
Don't want to get stuck slogging up 30-degree inclines? Then be sure to pick up a copy of the foldout *San Francisco Bike Map and Walking Guide* ($3), which indicates street grades by color and delineates bike routes that avoid major hills and heavy traffic. You can pick up a copy in bicycle shops, select bookstores, or at the San Francisco Bicycle Coalition's Web site (*see above*).

From the eastern entrance of the park between Oak and Fell streets, veer right to begin a 30- to 45-minute, 3-mi ride down John F. Kennedy Drive through the park to the Great Highway, where land meets ocean. Take a break and watch the waves roll in at Ocean Beach, or cross the street for a drink or a bite to eat at the casual, tree-shrouded Park Chalet (behind the Beach Chalet). Extend your ride a few more miles by turning left, riding a few blocks, and connecting with a raised bike path that runs parallel to the Pacific, winds through fields of emerald-green ice plant, and, after 2 mi, leads to Sloat Boulevard and the San Francisco Zoo. **On exceptionally windy days, expect to encounter blowing sand along this route.**

THE MARINA GREEN & GOLDEN GATE BRIDGE

★ The Marina Green, a vast lawn at the edge of the northern bayfront, stretches along Marina Boulevard, adjacent to Fort Mason. It's the starting point of a well-trod, paved bike path that runs through the Presidio along Crissy Field's waterfront wetlands, then heads for the Golden Gate Bridge and beyond. To do this ride, first take the path from Aquatic Park through Fort Mason to the Marina Green. Continue into the Presidio, and you'll eventually reach the base of the bridge, a 60-minute ride round-trip. To view the bridge from underneath, stay at water level and ride to Fort Point (where Kim Novak leaped into the drink in the film *Vertigo*).

If you want to cross the bridge, take Lincoln Boulevard to reach the road-level viewing area and continue across the bridge (signs indicate which side you must use). Once you're across, turn right on the first road leading northeast, Alexander Avenue. After a 10-minute all-downhill ride, you'll arrive on Bridgeway in downtown Sausalito, where you can rest in a café. After a little shopping, board the Blue & Gold Fleet's ferry (the ferry terminal is at the end of Bridgeway) with your bike for the half-hour ride back to Fisherman's Wharf. **If it's overcast, foggy, or windy, don't bother doing the Golden Gate Bridge bike ride—the wind can feel downright dangerous on the bridge, and the trip is only awe-inspiring when you can take in the view.**

ANGEL ISLAND STATE PARK

★ A former military garrison and a beautiful wildlife preserve, Angel Island has some steep roads and great views of the city and the bay. Bicycles must stay on roadways; there are no single-track trails on the island. A ferry operated by **Blue & Gold Fleet** (☎ *415/705–8200* ⊕ *www.blueandgoldfleet.com*) runs to the island from Pier 41 at Fisherman's Wharf and takes about 20 minutes one way; the fare is $14.50 round-trip, which includes park admission. Ferries leave once a day at 10 AM weekdays and 10:30 AM weekends, returning at around 3:30 PM; schedules change, so call for up-to-date info. Twenty-five bicycles are permitted on-board on a first-come, first-served basis. The café is closed mid-November through February, so bring your own grub. ☎ *415/435–1915* ⊕ *www.angelisland.org*.

LEGS OF STEEL

After crossing the Golden Gate, the super-fit can ride alongside triatheletes and hardcore cyclists in the Marin Headlands. Take the Alexander Avenue exit off the bridge as if you were going to Sausalito, but turn left instead and double back under the freeway. Just before the road merges with San Francisco–bound traffic, bear right and ascend the steep, rolling hills of the Marin Headlands. Follow the road to the top, where it becomes one-way and drops toward the ocean. Loop around the backside of the hills and through the tunnel, back to the bridge. On a clear day, the views along this route are stunning.

15

BOATING & SAILING

San Francisco Bay has year-round sailing, but tricky currents and strong winds make the bay hazardous for inexperienced navigators. Boat rentals and charters are available throughout the Bay Area and are listed under "Boat Renting" in the Yellow Pages.

☾ Near Fisherman's Wharf, from spring through fall, **Adventure Cat Sailing** (⊠ *Pier 39, Fisherman's Wharf* ☎ *415/777–1630 or 800/498–4228* ⊕ *www.adventurecat.com*) takes passengers aboard a 55-foot-long catamaran. The kids can play on the trampoline-like net between the two hulls while you sip drinks on the wind-protected sundeck. A 90-minute bay cruise costs $30; sunset sails with drinks and hors d'oeuvres are $45. **Rendezvous Charters** (⊠ *Pier 40, South Beach Harbor* ☎ *415/543–7333* ⊕ *www.rendezvouscharters.com*) offers individually ticketed trips on large sailing yachts, including sunset sails ($25) and Sunday brunch cruises on a schooner ($40). **Spinnaker Sailing** (⊠ *Pier 40, South Beach Harbor* ☎ *415/543–7333* ⊕ *www.spinnaker-sailing.com*) offers sailing instruction and charters private sailboats with or without a skipper (bring your logbook if you want to captain a boat yourself). Both Rendezvous and Spinnaker are south of the Ferry Building on the eastern waterfront, right next to AT&T Park, *not* next to Pier 39.

☾ If you prefer calm freshwater, you can rent rowboats ($14 per hour), pedal boats ($19 per hour), and electric motorboats ($29 per hour) at **Stow Lake** (⊠ *Off John F. Kennedy Dr., ½ mi west of 10th Ave., Golden*

Gate Park ☎415/752–0347), in Golden Gate Park. Remember to bring cash (they don't accept anything else) and bread crumbs for the ducks. The lake is open daily for boating, weather permitting, but call for seasonal hours.

> **DID YOU KNOW?**
>
> The Beatles played their last concert together at Candlestick Park on August 29, 1966.

FISHING

Fishing boats angle for salmon and halibut outside the bay or striped bass and giant sturgeon within. On land, you can cast your line at the Municipal Pier, Fisherman's Wharf, Baker Beach, or Aquatic Park. Fishing licenses are not necessary when casting from public piers. (The exception is sturgeon fishing, for which you need a Sturgeon Fishing Report Card.) Licenses are required for all other types of fishing, and can be purchased from the **California Department of Fish and Game** (⊕www.dfg.ca.gov). Non-California residents can purchase one-, two-, or 10-day licenses for $13, $19, and $39, respectively. Sportfishing charters depart daily from Fisherman's Wharf during the salmon-fishing season (March or April through October), and cost about $60 to $70.

Lovely Martha's Sportfishing (⊠Fisherman's Wharf, Berth 3 ☎650/871–1691 ⊕www.lovelymartha.com) has salmon-fishing excursions and bay cruises. **Wacky Jacky** (⊠Foot of Jones St. at Jefferson St., Fisherman's Wharf ☎415/586–9800), skippered by a straight-shootin' woman named Jacky, takes you salmon fishing in a sleek, fast, and comfortable 50-foot boat.

FOOTBALL

The **San Francisco '49ers** (⊠Monster Park, 490 Jamestown Ave., Bayview Heights ☎415/656–4900 ⊕www.sf49ers.com) play at **Monster Park** near the San Mateo County border, just north of the airport. Single-game tickets, available via **Ticketmaster** (☎415/421–8497 ⊕www.ticketmaster.com), almost always sell out far in advance. **Locals stubbornly refer to the park by its original name, Candlestick Park. In fact, if you ask people on the street how to get to Monster, many won't know (or will pretend not to know) what you're talking about. Ask how to get to Candlestick, however, and you'll be directed without prejudice.**

GOLF

You can get detailed directions to the city's public golf courses or reserve a tee time ($1 reservation fee per player) up to six days in advance through San Francisco's automated **municipal tee times reservation line** (☎415/750–4653 ⊕www.parks.sfgov.org) and online site (click on the link for "Golf Course Info").

Expect to use every club in your bag to tackle the fast, sloping greens and unpredictable winds at the challenging **Gleneagles International Golf Course** (✉*McLaren Park, 2100 Sunnydale Ave., Excelsior/Visitacion Valley* ☎*415/587–2425* ⊕*www.gleneaglesgolfsf.com*). The 9-hole, par-36 course is a little worse for wear.

Golden Gate Park Golf Course (✉*Near 47th Ave. and Fulton St., Golden Gate Park* ☎*415/751–8987*) is a 9-hole, par-27 course in lovely Golden Gate Park, just above Ocean Beach. It's a beginner's paradise, but more seasoned players might be put off by the lax play and wayward balls. There's first-come, first-served play only (no reservations).

★ **Harding Park Golf Course** (✉*99 Harding Rd., at Skyline Blvd., Lake Merced* ☎*415/664–4690* ⊕*www.harding-park.com*) has an 18-hole, par-72 course and a 9-hole, par-32 Jack Fleming–designed course. The 9-hole course has all the characteristics of a championship course, but is less difficult. Both have fantastic views. About $15 million has been invested into the place over the past few years, and it shows. Book tee times as far in advance as possible. The 18-hole, par-68 **Lincoln Park Golf Course** (✉*300 34th Ave., at Clement St., Richmond* ☎*415/221–9911* ⊕*www.lincolnparkgc.com*) offers magnificent views of the Golden Gate Bridge, but the somewhat scraggly greens don't hold up well in damp weather. Arnold Palmer Golf Management runs the challenging and well-maintained 18-hole, par-72 **Presidio Golf Course** (✉*300 Finley Rd., at Arguello Blvd., Presidio* ☎*415/561–4661* ⊕*www.presidiogolf. com*). You can book tee times online for an additional $8–$12 fee.

15

HIKING

Hills and mountains—including Mt. Tamalpais in Marin County and Mt. Diablo in the East Bay, which has the second-longest sight lines anywhere in the world after Mt. Kilimanjaro—form a ring around the Bay Area. The **Bay Area Ridge Trail** (⊕*http://ridgetrail.org*) is an ongoing project to connect all of the region's ridgelines. The trail is currently 300-mi long, but when finished it will extend 500 mi, stretching from San Jose to Napa and encompassing all nine Bay Area counties.

One of the most impressive ridgelines of the Bay Area Ridge Trail can be found on Mt. Tamalpais, in Marin County. The **Rock Spring Trail** starts at the Mountain Theater and gently climbs about 1¾ mi to the **West Point Inn**, once a stop on the Mt. Tam railroad route. Relax at a picnic table and stock up on water before forging ahead, via Old Railroad Grade Fire Road and the Miller Trail, to Mt. Tam's Middle Peak, about 2 mi uphill.

Starting from the Pan Toll Ranger Station, the precipitous **Steep Ravine Trail** brings you past stands of coastal redwoods and, in the springtime, numerous small waterfalls. Take the connecting **Dipsea Trail** to reach the town of Stinson Beach and its swath of golden sand. If you're too weary to make the 3½-mi trek back up, Golden Gate Transit Bus 63 (Saturday, Sunday, and holidays from mid-March through early December) takes you from Stinson Beach back to the ranger station.

CLOSE UP

Spa Day

Traditional sit-down Japanese showers and communal bathing are two out-of-the-ordinary features of **Kabuki Springs & Spa** (✉ *1750 Geary Blvd., Japantown* ☎ *415/922-6000* ⊕ *www.kabukisprings.com*). The renowned $130 Javanese Lulur Treatment includes a combination massage with jasmine oil, exfoliation with turmeric and ground rice, yogurt application, and a candlelight soak with rose petals. Men and women are welcome every day for private treatments, but call ahead regarding communal bathing schedules; the baths are coed only on Tuesday. Note that clothing is optional, except on coed days.

Southeast-Asian-inspired **Kamalaspa** (✉ *240 Stockton St., Union Square* ☎ *415/217-7700* ⊕ *www.kamalaspa.com*) has a full range of ayurvedic (using herbs and aromatic oils) massage and body treatments in addition to the traditional facials, pedicures, and massages. The overall experience is luxurious, expensive, and worth it.

Osento (✉ *955 Valencia St., Mission* ☎ *415/282-6333* ⊕ *www.osento.com*) is a women-only establishment. Like Kabuki, it's a Japanese-style spa with massage and day-use facilities like saunas, a communal hot tub, and an outdoor shower and sundeck. Unlike Kabuki, clothing is not allowed in certain areas, and *everyone* goes nude. It's a bit bare bones, but at

$12–$20 (sliding scale) for a day pass, it might be the best deal in town.

One downside: after experiencing the serene and luxurious **Nob Hill Spa** (✉ *1075 California St., Nob Hill* ☎ *415/345-2888* ⊕ *www.huntingtonhotel.com*) at the Huntington Hotel, you'll start to *expect* Champagne with your massage. Unique features include the eucalyptus steam bath and a gorgeous infinity pool that overlooks the city through a glass wall. After your treatments, you can hang here all day: take a yoga or Pilates class, get a green-tea body scrub, or just read on the sundeck.

All treatments at the St. Regis Hotel's très chic **Remède Spa** (✉ *125 3rd St., at Mission St., SoMa* ☎ *415/284-4060* ⊕ *www.remede.com*) incorporate a line of high-end French skin-care products. Treatments include custom skin therapy, massage, body scrubs, seaweed wraps, and a variety of mani–pedi, facial, and waxing options. Prices range from $40 for a manicure to $240 for a Shiatsu, Swedish, deep-tissue, or reflexology massage.

Elegant but casual **Spa Radiance** (✉ *3011 Fillmore St., between Union and Filbert Sts., Cow Hollow* ☎ *415/346-6281* ⊕ *www.sparadiance.com*) specializes in facials and draws the occasional celebrity. Try a vitamin-and-oxygen treatment, or the "super-duper" series—a deep-pore cleaning followed by dermabrasion.

But you don't have to leave the city for a nice hike. In the middle of San Francisco, you can climb to the top of Mt. Davidson, Bernal Heights, Corona Heights, or Buena Vista Park. Little more than undeveloped hilltops, they offer spectacular views of the city and beautiful shows of wildflowers in spring.

In the Presidio, hiking and biking trails wind through nearly 1,500 acres of woods and hills, past old redbrick military buildings and jaw-dropping scenic overlooks with bay and ocean views. Rangers and docents lead guided hikes and nature walks throughout the year. For a current schedule, pick up a copy of the quarterly *Park News* at the **Presidio Visitor Center** (⊠*Presidio Officers' Club, Bldg. 50, Moraga Ave., in Main Post area* ☎*415/561–4323* ⊕*www.nps. gov/prsf*) or go online. Stop by the **Warming Hut** (⊠*Bldg. 983, off Old Mason Rd., facing water just east of Fort Point* ☎*415/561–3040*) to refuel on snacks and to browse through the extensive selection of books (including good ones for kids) and the many ingenious gifts made from recycled materials.

> **TAKE IT TO THE BRIDGE**
>
> We prefer biking across the bridge rather than walking, but you can get the same spectacular views either way. Be sure to wear a jacket, and save this for fair-weather days. Set aside four hours if you plan to walk all the way across and back.

Fodor's Choice ★ The Presidio is part of **Golden Gate National Recreation Area (GGNRA)** (☎*415/561–4700* ⊕*www.nps.gov/goga*), which also encompasses the San Francisco coastline, the Marin Headlands, and Point Reyes National Seashore. It's veined with hiking trails, and guided walks are available. Current schedules are available at GGNRA visitor centers in the Presidio and Marin Headlands; you can also find them online at www.nps.gov/goga/parknews. For descriptions of each location within the recreation area—along with rich color photographs, hiking information, and maps—pick up a copy of *Guide to the Parks,* available in local bookstores or online from the **Golden Gate National Parks Conservancy** (☎*415/561–3000* ⊕*www.parksconservancy.org*).

The **Golden Gate Promenade** is another great walk; it passes through Crissy Field, taking in marshlands, kite-flyers, beachfront, and windsurfers, with the Golden Gate Bridge as a backdrop. The 3.3-mi walk is flat and easy—it should take about two hours round-trip. If you begin at Aquatic Park, you'll end up practically underneath the bridge at Fort Point Pier. **If you're driving, park at Fort Point and do the walk from west to east.** It can get blustery, even when it's sunny, so be sure to layer.

KAYAKING

Surrounded by water on three sides, San Francisco has plenty of opportunities for kayaking enthusiasts of all levels. **City Kayak** (⊠*Pier 39, Embarcadero at Stockton St., Fisherman's Wharf* ⊠*Pier 38, Embarcadero at Townsend St., SoMa* ☎*415/357–1010 or 650/704–8585* ⊕*www.citykayak.com*), the only kayak-rental outfit in the city, operates bay tours along the waterfront and beneath the Bay Bridge starting from $50; they also run full-moon night paddles and trips to Alcatraz. Rentals are $15 per hour for a single; $25 for a double; and $50 for a four-person kayak. Half-day trips depart at 10 AM daily. No prior experience is necessary, but you must watch an instructional video. **The Pier 39 location is for tours only, not rentals.** Trips run by **Outdoor Programs** (⊠*500 Parnassus Ave., at 3rd Ave., Inner Sunset* ☎*415/476–*

2078 ⊕*www.outdoors.ucsf.edu*) originate in either Sausalito or Mission Bay in San Francisco and range from moonlight paddles from Sausalito (with views of the San Francisco skyline) to daytime sea-kayaking classes for all levels.

Sea Trek Kayaking (☎*415/488–1000* ⊕*www.seatrekkayak.com*) has trips around Angel Island and the Golden Gate Bridge, moonlight paddles, and many trips in Marin County. Three-hour trips are $65–$75 and full-day trips are $85–$95. Most excursions leave from Sausalito (*see Chapter 17*), but Angel Island tours leave from the island.

WORD OF MOUTH

"Crissy Field . . . a perfect combination of natural beauty (the bay, the Marin headlands) and man-made beauty (the bridges, the city skyline). Where people of all kinds are out enjoying it. Add the fact that you can get a fantastic cup of coffee at the Warming Hut and I am in heaven."

–Sfmaster

RUNNING

PLACES TO RUN

The *San Francisco Bike Map and Walking Guide (see Bicycling, above)*, which indicates hill grades on city streets by color, is a great resource. Online, check the **San Francisco Road Runners Club** site (⊕*www.sfrrc.org*) for some recommended routes and links to several local running clubs.

★ The city is spectacular for running—*Runner's World* magazine named San Francisco number one in its list of the top 25 running cities in 2005. There are more than 7 mi of paved trails in and around **Golden Gate Park**; circling **Stow Lake** and then crossing the bridge and running up the path to the top of Strawberry Hill is a total of 2½ mi. An enormously popular route is the 2-mi raised bike path that runs from Lincoln Way along the ocean, at the southern border of Golden Gate Park, to Sloat Boulevard, which is the northern border of the San Francisco Zoo. (Stick to the park's interior when it's windy, as ocean gusts can kick up sand.) From Sloat Boulevard, you can pick up the **Lake Merced** bike path, which loops around the lake and the golf course, to extend your run another 5 mi. The paved path along the **Marina** runs 1½ mi (round-trip) along a flat, well-paved surface and has great bay views. You can extend your run by jogging the paths through the restored wetlands of Crissy Field (just past the yacht harbor), then up the hill to the Golden Gate Bridge: its walkway is 1.7-mi long.

EVENTS

First run in 1912, the 12K **Bay to Breakers race** (☎*415/359–2800* ⊕*www.baytobreakers.com*), held the third Sunday in May, is one of the world's oldest footraces—but in true San Francisco fashion, there's nothing typical about it. About a third of the 50,000 to 100,000 runners are serious athletes; the rest are "fun runners" who wear famously wacky costumes—or no costumes at all (there's a faithful nude contin-

A Shore Thing

Taking in a beachside sunset is the perfect way to end a busy day in the city (assuming the fog hasn't blown in for the afternoon). Always bring a sweater—even the sunniest of days can become cold and foggy without warning. Icy temperatures and treacherous currents make most waters too dangerous for swimming without a wet suit, but with a Frisbee, picnic, or some good walking shoes, you can have a fantastic day at the beach without leaving the city.

An urban beach, surrounded by Fort Mason, Ghirardelli Square, and Fisherman's Wharf, **Aquatic Park Beach** (⊕ *www.nps.gov/safr*) is a tiny, ¼-mi-long strip of sand with gentle water, bordered by docks and piers. The waters near shore are shallow, safe for kids to swim or wade, and fairly clean (admirably so, for a city). Locals—including the seemingly ubiquitous older-man-in-Speedo—come out for quick dips in the frigid water. The Golden Gate Promenade, with dog-walkers, inline-skaters, and cyclists, passes just behind the beach, so this isn't a secluded spot. Facilities include restrooms and showers.

Members of the **Dolphin Club** come every morning for a dip in the ice-cold waters of Aquatic Park; an especially large and raucous crowd braves the cold on New Year's Day.

Baker Beach (⊠ *Gibson Rd., off Bowley St., southwest corner of Presidio*), with gorgeous views of the Golden Gate Bridge and the Marin Headlands, is a local favorite and an established nudist spot. (Never seen nude Frisbee? This is the place.) The pounding surf and strong currents make swimming a dangerous prospect, but the mile-long shoreline is ideal for fishing,

building sand castles, or watching sea lions at play. On warm days, the entire beach is packed with bodies—including those nudists, who hang out at the north end. Picnic tables, grills, restrooms, and drinking water are available. Rangers give tours of the 95,000-pound cannon at Battery Chamberlin, overlooking the beach, the first weekend of every month.

Sheltered **China Beach,** one of the city's safest swimming beaches, was named for the poor Chinese fishermen who once camped here. (Some maps label it James D. Phelan Beach.) This 600-foot strip of sand, south of the Presidio and Baker Beach, has gentle waters as well as changing rooms, bathrooms, showers, grills, drinking water, and picnic tables. Despite its humble beginnings, China Beach today is bordered by the multimillion-dollar homes of the Seacliff neighborhood. The hike down to the beach is steep.

The largest—and probably best—of San Francisco's city beaches, **Ocean Beach** stretches for more than 3 mi along the Great Highway south of the Cliff House, making it ideal for long walks and runs. It isn't the cleanest shore, but it's an easy-to-reach place to chill; spot sea lions sunning themselves atop Seal Rock, at the north end of the beach; or watch daredevil surfers riding the roiling waves. Because of extremely dangerous currents, swimming isn't recommended. After the sun sets, bonfires form a string of lights along the beach in summer. (Fires are prohibited north of Fulton Street or south of Lincoln Way, the northern and southern edges of Golden Gate Park.) Restrooms are at the north end.

15

gency). The race makes its way from the Embarcadero at the bay to the Pacific Ocean, passing through Golden Gate Park.

The **San Francisco Marathon** (☎ *415/284–9653* ⊕ *www.runsfm.com*), held annually on a Sunday in late July or early August, starts and finishes at the Embarcadero. Up to 7,000 runners pass through downtown, the Marina, the Presidio, and Golden Gate Park, and cross the Golden Gate Bridge, tackling some of the city's milder hills along the way.

TENNIS

The **San Francisco Recreation and Park Department** (☎ *415/831–2700* ⊕ *www.parks.sfgov.org*) maintains 132 public tennis courts throughout the city. All courts listed here are free except for those in Golden Gate Park. **Golden Gate Park** (⊠ *John F. Kennedy Dr., near 3rd Ave.* ☎ *415/753–7131 reservations, 415/753–7001 information*) has 21 tennis courts. Court fees are $5 to $10. Call for weekend reservations. Weekdays are first-served, first-served; avoid times after 4 PM on weekdays, when school teams show up for practice. In the southeast corner of the beautiful Presidio, **Julius Kahn Park** (⊠ *W. Pacific Ave. between Spruce and Locust Sts., Presidio*) has four courts; the park and fantastic playground are great distractions for kids if the courts are full when you arrive. **Mission Dolores Park** (⊠ *18th and Dolores Sts., Castro*) has six lighted courts, available on a first-come, first-served basis. **Mountain Lake Park** (⊠ *Lake St. and 8th Ave., Richmond*), on the southern edge of the Presidio, has nice courts; it's an in-the-know tennis spot.

WHALE-WATCHING

Between January and April, hundreds of gray whales migrate along the coast; the rest of the year humpback and blue whales feed offshore at the Farallon Islands. The best place to watch them from shore is Point Reyes, in Marin County (*see* Chapter 17).

California Whale Adventures (☎ *415/760–8613*) has year-round whale-watching trips ($95) Friday through Sunday. In October, you can take a great white shark tour, and seabird tours run July through October; these tours cost $150 per person and are operated on weekends only. All trips leave from Fisherman's Wharf.

★ **The Oceanic Society** (☎ *415/474–3385* ⊕ *www.oceanicsociety.org*) operates year-round whale-watching excursions ($85 Friday, $90 weekends) with top-notch interpretation; in winter they also run half-day trips ($45 Friday, $50 weekends) from Bodega Bay and Half Moon Bay. The society also has a whale-watching hotline (☎ *415/474–0488*) and publishes the excellent *Oceanic Society Field Guide to the Gray Whale*. Most trips leave from the San Francisco Yacht Harbor, outside the harbormaster's office in the Marina district.

Shopping

City Lights Bookstore at the corner of Jack Kerouac Street and Columbus Avenue

WORD OF MOUTH

"Shop 'Til We Drop was the order of my daughter's day. We checked out shopping downtown at Union Square, Hayes Valley (boutique big bucks), Castro (mostly male boutiques and great food shops), Haight-Ashbury (of course my old hippie soul loved this very reasonable shopping mecca), Chinatown (absolutely great souvenirs)."

—joan

Updated
by Natasha
Sarkisian
By Sharron
Wood

From its swank boutiques to its funky thrift stores, San Francisco is simply one of the best shopping destinations in the United States. Deep-pocketed browsers as well as window shoppers mob the dozens of pricey shops packed into a few blocks around Union Square, while bargain hunters dig through used-record and thrift shops in the Mission District and the Haight. From the anarchist bookstore to the mouthwatering specialty food purveyors at the gleaming Ferry Building, the local shopping opportunities strikingly reflect the city's character.

Visitors with limited time often focus their energies on the high-density Union Square area, where several major department stores tower over exclusive boutiques. But if you're keen to find unique local shops, you should definitely move beyond Union Square. Each neighborhood has distinctive, gotta-have-it places.

If shopping in San Francisco has a downside, it's that real bargains can be few and far between. Sure, neighborhoods such as the Lower Haight and the Mission have thrift shops and other inexpensive stores, but you won't find many discount outlets in the city, where rents are sky-high and space is at a premium. And the 8.5% sales tax adds up for serious shoppers, though tax is waived if you arrange to have your purchases shipped to an out-of-state address.

Seasonal sales, usually in late January and late July or August, are good opportunities for finding deep discounts on fashionable clothing. The *San Francisco Chronicle* and *San Francisco Examiner* advertise sales. For smaller shops check the two free weeklies, the *San Francisco Bay Guardian* and *SF Weekly*, which can be found on street corners every Wednesday. Sample sales are usually held by individual manufacturers, so check your favorite company's site before visiting. Splendora

(⊕*www.splendora.com/cityguide/san_francisco*) is a good site to check for upcoming sales and promotions around the city.

MAJOR SHOPPING DISTRICTS

Many San Francisco neighborhoods keep their own hours, and the shops in those neighborhoods follow suit. In the Castro, for example, which is filled with restaurants and nightspots, many of the shops are open until 8 PM or later, to take advantage of the evening foot traffic. The same is generally true of the nightlife mecca of the Mission. More sedate residential neighborhoods like Noe Valley, Pacific Heights, and Union Street

tend to close up shop earlier, though, often by 6 PM and rarely past 7. (In these quieter neighborhoods, stores also tend to be closed Sunday, Monday, and sometimes even Tuesday.) Many Chinatown shops keep long hours, opening by 8 or 9 AM and staying open into the evening. Little boutiques in fashionable Hayes Valley and Jackson Square, on the other hand, usually keep shorter hours, often 10 or 11 AM to around 6 PM. And though the Union Square area attracts serious shoppers, you won't find anything to buy until around 10 AM, when most of the stores open. The neighborhoods below are profiled in alphabetical order.

THE CASTRO & NOE VALLEY

The Castro, often called the gay capital of the world, is also a major shopping destination for nongay travelers. It's filled with men's clothing boutiques and home-accessories stores geared to the neighborhood's fairly wealthy demographic. Of course, there are plenty of places hawking kitsch, too, and if you're looking for something to shock your Aunt Martha back home, you've come to the right place. Just south of the Castro on 24th Street, largely residential Noe Valley is an enclave of fancy-food stores, bookshops, women's clothing boutiques, and specialty gift stores.

CHINATOWN

The intersection of Grant Avenue and Bush Street marks the gateway to Chinatown. The area's 24 blocks of shops, restaurants, and markets are a nonstop tide of activity. Dominating the exotic cityscape are the sights and smells of food: crates of bok choy, tanks of live crabs, cages of live partridges, and hanging whole chickens. Racks of Chinese silks, colorful pottery, baskets, and carved figurines are displayed chockablock on the sidewalks, alongside fragrant herb shops where your bill might be tallied on an abacus. And if you need to knock off souvenir shopping for the kids and office-mates in your life, the dense and multiple selections of toys, T-shirts, mugs, magnets, decorative boxes, and countless other trinkets make it a quick, easy, and inexpensive proposition.

16

Shopping In & Around Downtown

Marina Blvd.

The Embarcadero

Jefferson St.
Beach St.
North Point St.
Bay St.

1
2
3
4

Francisco St.
Chestnut St.
Francisco St.
Chestnut St.
Lombard St.
Lombard St.
Lombard St.

Columbus Ave.

Greenwich St.
Filbert St.
Union St.

63
62
61

NORTH BEACH

60 **59**
58 **57**
56
54 **55**

Steiner St.
Fillmore St.
Webster St.
Laguna St.
Octavia St.
Gough St.
Franklin St.
Van Ness Ave.
Polk St.
Larkin St.
Hyde St.
Leavenworth St.

PACIFIC HEIGHTS

Broadway

RUSSIAN HILL

Green St.
Vallejo St.
Broadway Tunnel
Pacific St.
Jackson St.

5
6
7 **8** **9**
10
11

Jackson St.
Washington St.
Clay St.
Sacramento St.
California St.

See Pacific Heights Shopping detail map

Taylor St.
Mason St.
Powell St.
Stockton St.
Grant Ave.

53
37
38 **39**

NOB HILL

CHINATOWN

Van Ness Ave.
Octavia St.
Gough St.
Franklin St.

12

California St.

Pine St.
Bush St.
Sutter St.
Post St.
Geary St.
O'Farrell St.
Ellis St.
Eddy St.
Turk St.
Golden Gate Ave.
McAllister St.

13

15
14

UNION SQUARE

See Union Square Shopping detail map

Grove St.
Ivy St.

16
17
18 **19**
20 **22**
21
23
24
26 **27**
28 **29**

Hayes St.
Linden St.
Fell St.
Hickory St.

25

Laguna St.
Octavia St.
Gough St.
Franklin St.

CIVIC CENTER

Fulton St.

HAYES VALLEY

See Inset

Grove St.
Hayes St.

◆ **United Nations Plaza; Heart of the City Farmers' Market**

Mission St.
7th St.
8th St.
Howard St.
Folsom St.
Harrison St.
4th St.
5th St.
6th St.

34

33

9th St.
10th St.
11th St.
12th St.

Oak St.
Page St.
Haight St.

Buchanan St.

Market St.

30

31

32

35

16

EMBARCADERO CENTER

Four sprawling buildings of shops, restaurants, offices, and a popular independent movie theater—plus the Hyatt Regency hotel—make up the Embarcadero Center, downtown at the end of Market Street. Most of the stores are branches of upscale national chains, such as Ann Taylor, Banana Republic, and Crane & Co. It's one of the few major shopping centers with an underground parking garage and is a popular spot for Financial District workers running errands on their lunch breaks.

FISHERMAN'S WHARF

A constant throng of sightseers crowds Fisherman's Wharf, and with good reason: Pier 39, the Anchorage, Ghirardelli Square, and the Cannery are all here, each with shops and restaurants, as well as outdoor entertainment—musicians, mimes, and magicians. Best of all are the Wharf's view of the bay and its proximity to cable-car lines, which can shuttle shoppers directly to Union Square. Many of the tourist-oriented shops border on tacky, slinging the requisite Golden Gate tees, taffy, and baskets of shells, but tucked into the mix are a few fine galleries, clothing shops, and groceries that even locals will deign to visit.

> **TOP 5 LOCAL SHOPS**
>
> ■ **Cookin': Recycled Gourmet Appurtenances.** Terrific browsing through all sorts of vintage cookware.
>
> ■ **Great China Herb Co.** Like an insta-trip across the Pacific; hundreds of herbs and surprises like dried sea horses.
>
> ■ **Lululemon.** Comfy, cool loungewear, especially the perfect-fit pants.
>
> ■ **Margaret O'Leary.** Knitwear like no other; it'll last for decades.
>
> ■ **Metier.** Outstanding selection for women; a one-stop for shoes, dresses, jewelry.

THE HAIGHT

Haight Street is a perennial attraction for visitors, if only to see the sign at Haight and Ashbury streets—the geographic center of the Flower Power movement during the 1960s. Puncturing the thrill of seeing this famous intersection is the presence of the Gap and a Ben & Jerry's, but from a shopper's perspective, it's still possible to find high-quality vintage clothing, funky shoes, folk art from around the world, and used records and CDs galore in this always-busy neighborhood.

HAYES VALLEY

A community park called Hayes Green breaks up a crowd of cool shops just west of the Civic Center. Here you can find everything from hip housewares to art galleries to handcrafted jewelry. The density of unique stores—as well as the lack of chains anywhere in sight—makes it a favorite destination for many San Francisco shoppers.

JACKSON SQUARE

Clustered in the shadow of the Transamerica building, the city's finest retail antiques dealers, along with law firms and cafés, occupy three-story brick buildings, some of which date back to the city's gold rush days. A few boutiques and modern design houses have joined the mix of intimate showrooms targeting serious collectors of tribal rugs, botanical prints, and antique silver.

JAPANTOWN

Unlike the ethnic enclaves of Chinatown, North Beach, and the Mission, the 5-acre **Japan Center** (✉ *Bordered by Laguna, Fillmore, and Post Sts. and Geary Blvd.* ☎*No phone*) is under one roof. The three-block complex includes a reasonably priced public garage and three shop-filled buildings. Especially worthwhile are the Kintetsu and Kinokuniya buildings, where shops sell things like bonsai trees, tapes and records, jewelry, antique kimonos, *tansu* (Japanese chests), electronics, and colorful glazed dinnerware and teapots.

THE MARINA DISTRICT

With the city's highest density of (mostly) nonchain stores, the Marina is an outstanding shopping nexus. But it's nobody's secret—those with plenty of cash and style to burn flood the boutiques to snap up luxe accessories and housewares. Union Street and Chestnut Street in particular cater to the shopping whims of the grown-up sorority sisters and frat boys who live in the surrounding pastel Victorians.

THE MISSION

The aesthetic of the resident Pabst Blue Ribbon–downing hipsters and starving-artist types contributes to the affordability and individuality of shopping here. These night owls keep the city's best thrift stores, vintage-furniture shops, alternative bookstores, and, increasingly, small clothing boutiques afloat. As the Mission gentrifies, though, bargain hunters find themselves trekking the long blocks in search of truly local flavor. Thankfully, many of the city's best bakeries and cafés are sprinkled throughout the area.

NORTH BEACH

Although it's sometimes compared to New York City's Greenwich Village, North Beach is only a fraction of the size, clustered tightly around Washington Square and Columbus Avenue. Most of its businesses are small eateries, cafés, and shops selling clothing, antiques, and vintage wares. Once the center of the Beat movement, North Beach still has a bohemian spirit that's especially apparent at the rambling City Lights Bookstore, where Beat poetry lives on.

PACIFIC HEIGHTS

The rest of the city likes to deprecate its wealthiest neighborhood, but no one has any qualms about weaving through the mansions to come to Fillmore and Sacramento streets to shop. With grocery and hardware stores sitting alongside local clothing ateliers and international designer outposts, these streets manage to mix small-town America with big-city glitz. After you've splurged on a cashmere sweater or a handblown glass vase, an outdoor seat at Peet's or Coffee Bean is the perfect way to pass an afternoon watching the parade of Old Money, dogs, and strollers.

16

High San Francisco rents mean there aren't many discount outlets in the city, but a few do exist in the renovated warehouses south of Market Street, called SoMa. Most outlets are along the streets and alleyways bordered by 2nd, Townsend, Howard, and 10th streets. At the other end of the spectrum is the gift shop of the San Francisco Museum of Modern Art, which sells handmade jewelry, upscale and offbeat housewares, and other great gift items.

Serious shoppers head straight to Union Square, San Francisco's main shopping area and the site of most of its department stores, including Macy's, Neiman Marcus, Barney's, and Saks Fifth Avenue. Also here are the Virgin Megastore, the Disney Store, and Borders Books, Music & Cafe. Nearby are such platinum-card international boutiques as Yves Saint Laurent, Cartier, Emporio Armani, Gucci, Hermès of Paris, Louis Vuitton, and Gianni Versace.

The latest major arrival is the **Westfield San Francisco Shopping Centre** (⊠ *865 Market St., between 4th and 5th Sts., Union Square* ☎ *415/495–5656*), anchored by Bloomingdale's and Nordstrom. Besides the sheer scale of this mammoth mall, it's notable for its gorgeous atriums and its top-notch dining options (no typical food courts here—instead you'll find branches of a few top local restaurants.) The area is also home to the new Barneys CO-OP; the New York institution's SF outpost has high, urban fashion on seven exquisitely appointed floors.

Although the department stores and some boutiques may remain open until 9 PM and beyond, most retailers in the square don't open until 10 AM or later, so there isn't much advantage to docking in the neighborhood before then unless you're grabbing an early breakfast nearby.

ANTIQUES

The most obvious place to look for antiques is Jackson Square. Another option is the San Francisco Design Center, where three buildings and more than 100 showrooms display furnishings and other home design items. Although the showrooms are open to the public, many sell only to design professionals.

Antonio's Antiques. The two busily packed stories of furniture and objets d'art might include an 18th-century French harp or delicate tortoise-shell miniatures. If you like the shop's pieces, which lean toward items from the 17th and 18th centuries, you may also want to visit its larger store in SoMa, a maze of museum-quality English and French antiques. Italian pieces are housed across the street. ⊠ *701 Sansome St., at Jackson St., Financial District* ☎ *415/781–1737* ◪ *Warehouse, 701 Bryant St., at 5th St., SoMa* ☎ *415/781–1737.*

Evelyn's Antique Chinese Furniture. The precious pieces of Han dynasty pottery and 19th-century bamboo bookcases artfully arranged in the front room are only a small portion of the restored and unrestored pieces sold at this store, which they claim has the largest selection of antique Chinese furniture in the United States. In the spacious back room items both large (cabinets) and small (steel tea stoves) are stacked high. ⊠*381 Hayes St., between Franklin and Gough Sts., Hayes Valley* ☎*415/255–1815.*

★ **Forgotten Shanghai.** The Asian antiques for sale here are both beautiful and practical, with camphor-wood trunks and beautifully aged leather boxes among the treasures. ⊠*245 Kansas St., near 16th St., Potrero Hill* ☎*415/701–7707.*

Grand Central Station Antiques. This large, three-story space stocks mostly 19th- and early-20th-century European and American storage pieces—armoires, highboys, buffets, and the occasional barrister bookcase—with an emphasis on the small and practical. Service is affable. ⊠*333 9th St., between Folsom and Ringold Sts., SoMa* ☎*415/252–8155.*

Hunt Antiques. Full of fine 17th- to 19th-century period English furniture, porcelains, Staffordshire pottery, paintings, and grandfather clocks, this Jackson Square shop feels like an English town house. ⊠*478 Jackson St., between Montgomery and Sansome Sts., Financial District* ☎*415/989–9531.*

Interior Visions. The welcoming proprietor is happy to tell you about her collection of mostly 19th- and early-20th-century pieces. Among the treasures might be a French gold-velvet chaise longue from the 1930s or a turn-of-the-20th-century Belgian oak highboy. ⊠*2206 Polk St., between Vallejo and Green Sts., Russian Hill* ☎*415/771–0656.*

16

Lotus Collection. The handmade pillows, tapestries depicting iconic events in Europe, and Japanese brocades make this one of the finest collections of decorative antique textiles in the States. It's also a secret source for the city's interior designers outfitting Pac Heights mansions. ⊠*445 Jackson St., between Montgomery and Sansome Sts., Financial District* ☎*415/398–8115.*

ART GALLERIES

Art galleries are ubiquitous in San Francisco. Although most surround Union Square, Hayes Valley, near the Civic Center, has become another gallery enclave, and the Mission District and SoMa are the spots for less-expensive works by local emerging artists. The free *San Francisco Bay Area Gallery Guide,* available at most galleries, includes a handy map and addresses of galleries all over the city. For a quick overview, stop by 49 Geary Street by Union Square, which houses several of the city's best galleries. Most galleries are closed on Sunday and Monday.

Catharine Clark Gallery. Although nationally known artists display their sculpture, paintings, photographs, and installation artwork here, emerging artists with a Bay Area connection get the spotlight. ⊠*150 Minna St., between 3rd St. and New Montgomery St., SoMa* ☎*415/399–1439.*

★ **Fraenkel Gallery.** One of the world's preeminent photography galleries, Fraenkel has represented museum-caliber photographers like Richard Avedon, Garry Winogrand, and Idris Khan since 1979. They usually exhibit one or two of their artists at a time, but each July at their annual

Union Square Shopping

UNION SQUARE

exhibit entitled "Several Exceptionally Good Recently Acquired Pictures" you can see a full range of their work. ✉*49 Geary St., between Kearny St. and Grant Ave., Union Square* ☎*415/981–2661.*

Hackett-Freedman Gallery. The gallery prides itself on its friendly staff, who will educate you about the art or leave you alone—whichever you prefer. Contemporary realist works, including still lifes, landscapes, and figurative paintings, compose the core of its collection. ✉*250 Sutter St., Suite 400, between Grant Ave. and Kearny St., Union Square* ☎*415/362–7152.*

Fodor's Choice
★

Hang Art. A spirit of fun imbues this industrial-chic space, where emerging artists display their works. Prices range from a few hundred dollars to several thousand, making it an ideal place for novice art collectors to get their feet wet. A rental program lets you take a piece home before buying it. Solo exhibitions hang in the main gallery, while the annex across the street displays group shows. ✉*556 and 567 Sutter St., between Mason and Powell Sts., Union Square* ☎*415/434–4264.*

Hespe Gallery. Priced between three and 50 grand, the paintings and sculptures here by mid-career artists, especially those from California, are primarily done in an abstract style. Owner Charles Hespe is an instantly likable art enthusiast who equally delights buyers and browsers. ✉*251 Post St., Suite 420, between Stockton and Grant Sts., Union Square* ☎*415/776–5918.*

16

John Berggruen Gallery. Twentieth-century American and European paintings are displayed throughout three airy floors here. Works by Bay Area figurative artists such as Richard Diebenkorn are a specialty. ✉*228 Grant Ave., at Post St., Union Square* ☎*415/781–4629.*

John Pence Gallery. The 8,000-square-foot facility, San Francisco's largest gallery, can display more than 100 works. Drawings, paintings, and sculpture are all represented, with many of the works by important contemporary academic realists. ✉*750 Post St., between Leavenworth and Jones Sts., Tenderloin* ☎*415/441–1138.*

Meyerovich Gallery. Sculpture and works on paper by masters such as Pablo Picasso, Marc Chagall, Robert Motherwell, and Henry Moore are the attraction. Colorful, whimsical sculptures by contemporary artist Ron Tatro draw the eye from across the room. ✉*251 Post St., 4th fl., between Stockton St. and Grant Ave., Union Square* ☎*415/421–7171.*

San Francisco Camerawork. This nonprofit artists' organization holds frequently changing thematic exhibits. It's also an excellent photography resource center with a well-stocked bookstore and a reference library. The lecture program includes noted photographers and critics. ✉*657 Mission St., 2nd fl., between 2nd and New Montgomery Sts., SoMa* ☎*415/512–2020.*

Southern Exposure. One of the city's most established venues for cutting-edge art is this artist-run, nonprofit gallery in a former cannery. Juried shows and accompanying lectures and films change frequently in the spacious, high-ceiling galleries. ✉*417 14th St., at Valencia St., Mission* ☎*415/863–2141.*

Varnish Fine Art. The cast metal sculptures that are a specialty here look right at home in the artsy-industrial gallery with high corrugated metal ceilings. A wine bar on the ground floor encourages visitors to linger and look at the artwork, and if you settle into one of the couches upstairs to peruse their small library of art books you could end up pleasantly whiling away the afternoon. ⊠*77 Natoma St., between 1st and 2nd Sts., SoMa* ☎*415/222–6131.*

BEAUTY

★ **BeneFit.** You can find the locally based BeneFit line of cosmetics and skin-care products at Macy's and Sephora, but it's much more fun to come to one of the eponymous boutiques. No-pressure salespeople dab you with whimsical products such as Ooh La Lift concealer and Tinted Love, a stain for lips and cheeks. ⊠*2117 Fillmore St., between California and Sacramento Sts., Pacific Heights* ☎*415/567–0242* ⊠*2219 Chestnut St., between Scott and Pierce Sts., Marina* ☎*415/567–1173.*

Body Time. The local minichain, founded in Berkeley in 1970, emphasizes the premium-quality ingredients it uses in its natural perfumes and skin-care and aromatherapy products. The specialty: sustainably harvested essential oils that you can combine and dilute to create your own fragrances. Customers who bring back their empty bottles for refills get a discount. ⊠*1465 Haight St., at Ashbury St., Haight* ☎*415/551–1070.*

Kiehl's. Perhaps because it started out in 1851, Kiehl's possesses a nononsense appeal. Its fans swear by its high-quality, simply packaged skin- and hair-care products. This spacious store stocks a wide variety of its lotions, potions, and soaps. Not sure whether the Formula 133 Hair Conditioner and Grooming Aid is right for you? Ask for a sample. ⊠*2360 Fillmore St., between Washington and Clay Sts., Pacific Heights* ☎*415/359–9260.*

★ **Lush.** Towers of bulk soap, which can be cut to order, and mountains of baseball-size fizzing "bath bombs" are some of the first items you'll see in this tightly packed and extremely fragrant little shop. They pride themselves on using the highest-quality ingredients, and some items are so fresh (and perishable) they're stored in a refrigerator and come with an expiration date. ⊠*240 Powell St., between O'Farrell and Geary Sts., Union Square* ☎*415/693–9633* ⊠*2116 Union St., at Webster St., Cow Hollow* ☎*415/921–5874.*

Nancy Boy. The spare, white-on-white store, locally owned, sells indulgent skin- and hair-care products for men, as well as a small selection of aromatherapy items, such as soy travel candles scented with essential oils. ⊠*347 Hayes St., between Franklin and Gough Sts., Hayes Valley* ☎*415/552–3802.*

BOOKS

Alexander Book Co. The three floors of titles here are stocked with literature, poetry, and children's books, with a focus on hard-to-find works by men and women of color. ⊠*50 2nd St., between Market and Mission Sts., SoMa* ☎*415/495–2992.*

Book Passage. Windows at this modest-size bookstore frame close-up views of the Ferry Building docks and San Francisco Bay. Commuters

The Mission/
Noe Valley Shopping

POTRERO HILL

Jackson Park

Franklin Square

Mission Dolores Park

MISSION

NOE VALLEY

EUREKA VALLEY

CASTRO

St. Peter's ◆

0   1/2 mile

0   1/2 kilometer

Cool Local Souvenirs

■ Something from McEvoy Ranch's body-care line, like their olive mud soap or their gardener's hand salve, all made with locally produced, organic olive oil.

■ A book published by City Lights, like one of their new political dynamos or something old-school like Allen Ginsberg's evergreen *Howl.*

■ A candy-color, eco-chic bamboo fruit bowl by Ekobo, available at Spring.

■ A cashmere weekender cardigan from Margaret O'Leary—something to live in every Saturday.

■ A collectible bottle of California wine from K&L Wine Merchants or a rare Armagnac from D&M Wines and Liquors.

■ A vintage 1960s sundress from American Rag for something retro but not too costumey.

■ A striking porcelain tea and coffee service designed by the renowned chef Thomas Keller, found at Gump's.

–Natasha Sarkisian

snatch up magazines by the front door as they speed off to catch their ferries, while leisurely shoppers thumb through the thorough selection of cooking and travel titles. Author events typically take place several times a month. ⊠*1 Ferry Bldg., #42, Embarcadero at foot of Market St., Embarcadero* ☎*415/835–1020.*

Booksmith. Founded in 1976, this fine bookshop sells current releases, children's titles, and offbeat periodicals. Authors passing through town often make a stop at this neighborhood institution. ⊠*1644 Haight St., between Cole and Clayton Sts., Haight* ☎*415/863–8688.*

Bound Together Anarchist Book Collective. This old-school collective, in operation since 1976, stocks books on anarchist theory and practice, as well as an array of books on other forms of radicalism, gender issues, and other left-leaning topics. A portion of the revenue goes to the support of anarchist projects and the Prisoners' Literature Project. ⊠*1369 Haight St., at Masonic Ave., Haight* ☎*415/431–8355.*

Fodor'sChoice **City Lights Bookstore.** The city's most famous bookstore is where the Beat ★ movement of the 1950s was born. Neal Cassady and Jack Kerouac hung out in the basement and now regulars and tourists while hours away in this well-worn space. The upstairs room highlights impressive poetry and Beat literature collections. Poet Lawrence Ferlinghetti, the owner, remains active in the workings of this three-story place. Since publishing Allen Ginsberg's *Howl* in 1956, City Lights' press continues to publish a dozen new titles each year. ⊠*261 Columbus Ave., at Broadway, North Beach* ☎*415/362–8193.*

★ **A Different Light.** San Francisco's most extensive gay and lesbian bookstore has books by, for, and about lesbians, gay men, bisexuals, and the transgendered. Subjects run the gamut from sci-fi and fantasy to religion and film criticism. The magazine section is large. A rack in front is chock-full of flyers for local events. ⊠*489 Castro St., between Market and 18th Sts., Castro* ☎*415/431–0891.*

Dog Eared Books. An eclectic group of shoppers—gay and straight, fashionable and not—wanders the aisles of this pleasantly ramshackle bookstore. The diverse selection of publications, about 85% of them used, includes quirky selections like vintage children's books, remaindered art books, and local 'zines. A bin of free books just outside the front door is fun to browse, if only to see the odd assortment of out-of-date titles. ✉ *900 Valencia St., at 20th St., Mission* ☎*415/282–1901.*

Get Lost Travel Books, Maps & Gear. Here, travel literature is mixed in for inspiration amid the guidebooks—totaling more than 9,000 titles. The store also carries language-instruction materials, luggage, and other travel accessories. ✉ *1825 Market St., at Guerrero St., Mission* ☎*415/437–0529.*

Kinokuniya Bookstore. The selection of English-language books about Japanese culture—everything from medieval history to origami instructions—is one of the finest in the country. Kinokuniya is the city's biggest seller of Japanese-language books. Dozens of glossy Asian fashion magazines attract the young and trendy, and books and DVDs related to the Japanese anime director Hayao Miyazaki are the latest trend. ✉ *Kinokuniya Bldg., 1581 Webster St., 2nd fl., Japantown* ☎*415/567–7625.*

Modern Times Bookstore. Named after Charlie Chaplin's politically subversive film, the store stocks high-quality literary fiction and nonfiction, much of it with a political bent. There are also sections for children's books, Spanish-language titles, and magazines and local subversive 'zines. Author readings and public forums are held regularly. **If you're looking to kill a little time in the Mission before hooking up with dinner companions, this is a low-key and inviting place to hide out in the stacks.** ✉ *888 Valencia St., between 19th and 20th Sts., Mission* ☎*415/282–9246.*

★ **William Stout Architectural Books.** Architect William Stout began selling books out of his apartment 25 years ago. Today the store sources libraries from around the world and Bay Area professionals with serious minded tomes on architecture and design. Head down into the crumbling whitewashed basement for beautifully illustrated coffee-table books. Stout is also the sole distributor of the über-popular IDEO method cards, which offer and inspire design solutions. ✉ *804 Montgomery St., at Jackson St., Financial District* ☎*415/391–6757.*

CHILDREN'S CLOTHING

Dottie Doolittle. Pacific Heights mothers shop here for charming silk dresses and other special-occasion outfits for their little ones. Less pricey togs for infants, boys to size 12, and girls to size 16 are also on hand. ✉ *3680 Sacramento St., at Spruce St., Pacific Heights* ☎*415/563–3244.*

Murik. Those with fashion-forward five-year-olds will be grateful to discover this tiny shop. From Petit Bateau jumpers for infants to linen pants and ruffled shirts for your gradeschooler, the pricey garments are so adorable you might wish you could wear them yourself.

✉ *73 Geary St., between Grant Ave. and Kearny St., Union Square* ☎ *415/395–9200.*

Small Frys. The colorful cottons carried here are mainly for infants, with some articles for older children. The mix includes OshKosh and many Californian and French labels. A few shelves of toys and whimsical finger puppets round out the collection. ✉ *4066 24th St., between Castro and Noe Sts., Noe Valley* ☎ *415/648–3954.*

Yountville. Tiny silk sweaters and flouncy pink swimsuits are among the Californian and European designs at this store for infants to eight-year-olds. ✉ *2416 Fillmore St., between Jackson and Washington Sts., Pacific Heights* ☎ *415/922–5050.*

CLOTHING: MEN & WOMEN

COOL & CASUAL

AB fits. The friendly staff can help guys and gals sort through the jeans selection, one of the hippest in the city—they carry Del Forte organic denim. Indeed, the salespeople are known for being able to match the pants to the person. Though many of the same designers are stocked at both locations, the Union Square branch tends toward slightly dressier fashions. ✉ *1519 Grant Ave., between Filbert and Union Sts., North Beach* ☎ *415/982–5726* ✉ *40 Grant Ave., between O'Farrell and Geary Sts., Union Square* ☎ *415/982–5726.*

Behind the Post Office. There's no "return to sender" here, as covetable women's clothes fill this little shop. In spite of its tiny size it attracts a devoted clientele for its casual clothing, including slinky knits by Ella Moss and jeans by Citizens of Humanity. ✉ *1510 Haight St., at Ashbury St., Haight* ☎ *415/861–2507.*

★ **Blues Jean Bar.** With more than a dozen different brands of jeans on tap, this Western-theme shop takes the pain out of finding the perfect pair of denims. Simply tell the bartender the size and style you're looking for and he or she will load you up with several trendy pairs by designers such as Carpe Denim and True Religion to try on in either the "Him," "Her," or "Them" dressing rooms. ✉ *1827 Union St., between Octavia and Laguna Sts., Cow Hollow* ☎ *415/346–4280.*

Eco Citizen. The men's and women's clothes here are not just green, they're also fair-trade, organic, sustainable, and trendy—yet still basic enough to wear for more than one season (so you won't have to throw them out after two months, which makes them truly green). ✉ *1488 Vallejo St., between Polk and Larkin Sts., Russian Hill* ☎ *415/614–0100.*

RAG. To really get your pulse on the local fashion scene, seek out the Residents Apparel Gallery. Bay Area designers rent racks to showcase their deconstructed tees and socially responsible designs. Above each rack hangs a photo and a bio of the aspiring designer. ✉ *541 Octavia St., between Hayes and Grove Sts., Hayes Valley* ☎ *415/621–7718.*

Self Edge. Hanging from metal rods on perfectly separated wooden hangers are dozens of pairs of Japanese selvage denim. The industrial weight fabric that makes up these jeans will run you between $160 and $450, but they'll hem them for free with their vintage chain-stitching machine. ✉ *714 Valencia St., at 18th St. Mission* ☎ *415/558–0658.*

Three Bags Full. Everything here is hand-knit—whether it be a feather-weight cashmere shrug or a chunky wool cable sweater. Local business-women replace their stuffy suit jackets with a cozy but sleek wool or cotton blazer. ✉*2181 Union St., at Fillmore St., Cow Hollow* ☎*415/567–5753* ✉*500 Sutter St., at Powell St., Union Square* ☎*415/398–7987* ✉*3314 Sacramento St., near Fillmore St., Pacific Heights* ☎*415/923–1454.*

FLIRTY

Dema. Dema Grim's classically cut clothes in ethnic and vintage fabrics that really pop truly capture the spirit of the Mission. ✉*1038 Valencia St., between 21st and 22nd Sts., Mission* ☎*415/206–0500.*

Dish. Many of the women's clothes displayed within this spare, concrete-floor space are romantic, minus the frills. Look for the flowing dresses of local designer Erica Tanov, as well as clothes and accessories by more widely known designers like BCBG and Theory. ✉*541 Hayes St., between Laguna and Octavia Sts., Hayes Valley* ☎*415/252–5997.*

Elizabeth Charles. Parlaying the city's current obsession with the land down under, this intimate boutique stocks only Australian and New Zealand designers, with an emphasis on flowing frocks in the very finest fabrics. *2056 Fillmore St., between California and Pine Sts. Pacific Heights* ☎*415/440–2100.*

HeidiSays. Fanciful windows brimming with bright and festive prints draw passersby into this well-stocked store. Perky salespeople help you choose between Catherine Malandrino, Trina Turk, and Rebecca Taylor frocks. To complete your emblematic San Franc chic outfit, head down the street, where the Heidi empire continues with HeidiSays Casual and HeidiSays Shoes, where you can pick up lingerie, loungewear, bags, and pumps. ✉*2426, 2416, and 2105 Fillmore St., Pacific Heights* ☎*415/749–0655.*

Lemon Twist. Dannette Scheib is known for her inspired details, such as her signature tulle petticoats that go underneath her A-line skirts. Her husband Eric's T-shirts capture an urban essence in a simply stenciled telephone pole design. Their Lemon Drop baby line is both sweet and tart. **If you see a print you like on the workshop table in back, she's happy to make you a custom piece at no additional charge and ship it to you back home.** ✉*537 Octavia Blvd., between Hayes and Grove Sts., Hayes Valley* ☎*415/558–9699.*

Ooma. The delicious fashions, many made by local designers, tend toward the feminine and flirty (no men's stuff here). A wide range of jewelry and accessories complements the colorful clothes. ✉*1422 Grant Ave., between Green and Union Sts., North Beach* ☎*415/627–6963.*

Sarah Shaw. Specializing in cocktail and party dresses, this boutique racks up American designers like Wendy Hil, Trina Turk, and Robert Rodriguez. Businesswomen looking to give their corporate suits a

16

feminine spin take their cues from her inspired combinations. ✉*3095 Sacramento St., at Baker St., Presidio Heights* ☎*415/929–2990.*

HIGH DESIGN

Anica. This avant-garde women's clothing boutique—whose name means charismatic in Hindi—specializes in low-maintenance high-fashion. The designs here, from serious up-and-coming designers, actually look good off the hanger. ✉*2418 Polk St., between Filbert and Union Sts., Russian Hill* ☎*415/447–2878.*

Carrots. The former location of Ernie's (the historic restaurant made famous in Hitchcock's Vertigo) was transformed by Melissa Grimm and her sister Catie (of the Grimm family of Grimmway Farms fame—they're the world's largest grower of carrots) into a spacious emporium showcasing Bay Area superstar designers Alexander Wang and Peter Som alongside Narciso Roqriguez and Stella McCartney. The icing on the cake is a bar that serves mini carrot cupcakes. ✉*843 Montgomery St., between Gold and Jackson Sts., Jackson Square* ☎*415/834–9040*

Erica Tanov. The designer's background in lingerie and bedding guides the delicate fabrics here: wispy cashmere, silk organza and charmeuse, and linen. Sweaters tend to drape and wrap; skirts and pajama-wide pants are often brightened with florals or stripes. ✉*2408 Fillmore St., between Jackson and Washington Sts., Pacific Heights* ☎*415/674–1228.*

Harputs and Harputs Market. After selling Adidas shoes since 1968 out of its brick-and-mortar digs, Harputs recently opened the Market next store. The boutique carries the largest selection of Y-3 (a joint venture between Adidas and avant-garde designer Yohji Yamamoto) on the West Coast. In between vintage Vespas and sewing machines, you can find vintage Christian Dior shades, suits, and accessories by Comme des Garçons, and an impressive collection of vintage Ellesse fluorescent jumpsuits. Still, Harputs stays true to its roots: sneaker fanatics swoon over the display cases of rare Adidas shoes. ✉*1525–1527 Fillmore St., between Geary Blvd. and O'Farrell St., Pacific Heights* ☎*415/923–9300 or 415/922–9964.*

The Archive. The closest thing you'll get to Savile Row in San Francisco, this small and narrow cutting-edge men-only fashion boutique has everything from handmade suits to handmade large silver belt buckles from top-shelf Japanese and Italian designers. ✉*317 Sutter St., between Grant Ave. and Stockton St., Union Square* ☎*415/391–5550.*

Fodor'sChoice
★ **Margaret O'Leary.** If you can only buy one piece of clothing in San Francisco, make it a hand-loomed, locally made cashmere sweater by this Irish-born local legend. The perfect antidote to the city's wind and fog, the sweaters are so beloved by San Franciscans that some people literally never wear anything else. The Fillmore location, the larger of the two, is rounded out with a nice selection of Margaret's other favorite designers like jeans by AG Denim. Pick up an airplane wrap for your trip home and a media cozy to keep your iPod toasty, too. ✉*1 Claude La., at Sutter St., Union Square* ☎*415/391–1010* ✉*2400 Fillmore St., at Washington St., Pacific Heights* ☎*415/771–9982.*

Metier. For boutique shopping that's anything but hit or miss, browse through this unusual selection of clothes by brands like Blumarine and See by Chloe. An even more impressive selection of jewelry by artists like Cathy Waterman and Philip Crangi has won this boutique an especially loyal following. ✉*355 Sutter St., between Stockton and Grant Sts., Union Square* ☎*415/989–5395.*

Rolo. The store sells hard-to-find men's and women's denim, sportswear, shoes, and accessories with a distinct European influence, including clothes designed by Comme des Garçons, Corpus Denim, and Fred Perry. The Market Street location carries menswear only. **The branch at 1301 Howard sells past-season items at a discount of up to 50%.** ✉*2351 Market St., at Castro St., Castro* ☎*415/431–4545* ✉*1301 Howard St., at 9th St., SoMa* ☎*415/861–2097* ✉*1235 Howard St., between 8th and 9th Sts., SoMa* ☎*415/355–1122.*

TAILORED

★ **Cable Car Clothiers.** This classic British menswear store, open since 1939, is so chock-full of inventory that a whole room is dedicated to hats, pants are cataloged like papers in file cabinets, and entire displays showcase badger-bristle shaving brushes. **Their cable-car logo gear, from silk ties to pewter banks make for dashing souvenirs.** ✉*200 Bush St., at Sansome St., Union Square* ☎*415/397–4740.*

Mrs. Dewson's Hats. Although this shop was the famous purveyor of hats to nattily dressed former San Francisco mayor Willie Brown, Ruth Garland Dewson has been selling chapeaux—some of her own design—since 1978. The popular "Willie Brim" is a fur felt fedora; the brim comes in three sizes. ✉*2050 Fillmore St., at California St., Pacific Heights* ☎*415/346–1600.*

Red Lantern. Chinese fashions of centuries past get a modern updating at this pretty little boutique where luxe fabrics—silk, brocade, and faux fur—give each item a sumptuous feel. If none of the mandarin-style jackets or *cheongsams* (traditional formfitting Chinese dresses) suits you, owner Fong Chong can make clothing to order. ✉*2030-A Union St., between Webster and Buchanan Sts., Cow Hollow* ☎*415/776–8876.*

DISCOUNT CLOTHING

Christine Foley. Discounts of up to 50% apply to the hand-loomed cotton sweaters with fanciful, intricate designs. There's a particularly large selection of colorful sweaters for children. Pillows, stuffed animals, and assorted knickknacks sell at retail prices in the small storefront showroom. ✉*668 Post St., between Taylor and Jones Sts., Union Square* ☎*415/621–8126.*

★ **Jeremy's.** A discount store for people who usually wouldn't be caught dead discount shopping, this store offers steep discounts (generally 20% to 50%, with occasional clearance items even more deeply discounted) on top-notch men's and women's apparel by designers such as

16

Prada and Jil Sander. The space is cleanly organized, so you won't need to rack-rake. ✉2 S. Park Rd., at 2nd St., SoMa ☎415/882–4929.

Fodor'sChoice
★ **Loehmann's.** Renovations have tamed the chaos that used to reign among these drastically reduced designer labels, resulting in more orderly racks and more spacious changing rooms. Credit is due to their massive inventory, from gym clothes to businesswear. The racks for in-season overruns are tidier; the sections of past seasons' clothes are messier but have even deeper discounts. The shoe department is across the street from the main store. ✉222 Sutter St., at Kearny St., Union Square ☎415/982–3215.

My Roommate's Closet. Fed by more than 25 boutiques in San Francisco, New York, and Los Angeles, the Closet carries clothing and accessories by designers like Vera Wang, Chaiken, and Theory, all at less than 50% of their retail price. ✉3044 Fillmore St., at Union St., Marina ☎415/447–7703.

VINTAGE & RESALE CLOTHING

American Rag. This might be the only place in the city where a $500 Marc Jacobs frock is sold alongside a $15 vintage dress, but it certainly mirrors San Francisco's style. The large vintage section in back carriers an impressive selection of furs, sailor outfits, and Army jumpsuits. You can also rummage through shoes, sunglasses, and other accessories. ✉1305 Van Ness Ave., between Sutter and Bush Sts., Western Addition ☎415/474–5214.

Buffalo Exchange. Both men and women can find fashionable, high-quality used clothing at this national chain. Among the items: a wide selection of Levi's, leather jackets, sunglasses, and vintage lunch boxes. Some new clothes are available, too. ✉1555 Haight St., between Clayton and Ashbury Sts., Haight ☎415/431–7733 ✉1210 Valencia St., at 23rd St., Mission ☎415/647–8332.

Held Over. The extensive collection of clothing from the 1920s through 1980s is organized by decade, saving those looking for flapper dresses from having to wade through lime-green polyester sundresses of the '70s. Shoes, hats, handbags, and jewelry complete the different looks. ✉1543 Haight St., between Ashbury and Clayton Sts., Haight ☎415/864–0818.

Helpers' Bazaar. Arguably the city's best-dressed philanthropist, Joy Bianchi, along with other volunteers, runs this store to benefit the mentally disabled. A red Bill Blass cocktail dress, a Chanel suit, or a Schiaparelli hat are among the vintage masterpieces you might expect to find here—to see the good stuff, all you have to do is ask nicely. Don't miss a look at Bianchi's "mouse couture," a clever fund-raiser display in which designers like Armani and Carolina Herrera dress up 4-inch stuffed mice. ✉900 N. Point St., Ghirardelli Square, Fisherman's Wharf ☎415/441–0779.

Schauplatz. Vintage clothing from the 1920s to the 1980s can be unearthed on the racks of this narrow little store on a hip block in the Mission. Some of the dramatic women's wear—go-go boots, pillbox hats, faux Chanel suits—is suitable for streetwear or dress-up, depending on your style, while the menswear tends more toward fashionably retro jackets and button-up shirts from the classic to the gaudy. ✉*791 Valencia St., between 18th and 19th Sts., Mission* ☎*415/864–5665.*

Still Life. Boho and green are alive in well in this city—and this frame-worthy studio-sized shop captures both phenomenons with its half-vintage, half-new-hipster selections. Women's sundresses, men's tees, and baby boots sit amid the reappropriated décor, where, for example, a taxidermied elk head and laboratory supplies become display pieces. ✉*835 Divisadero St., between McAllister and Fulton Sts., Lower Haight* ☎*415/440–2499.*

★ **Shige Nishiguchi Kimonos.** Though cotton *yukatas* (casual, lightweight kimonos) are the biggest sellers, vintage silk kimonos—some of them hand-painted—and vintage *obis* (kimono sashes) are the reason this tiny shop in the Japan Center is a destination for aficionados of Japanese dress. ✉*1730 Geary Blvd., Suite 203, Japantown* ☎*415/346–5567.*

Ver Unica. Though you can find a few items from the psychedelic '60s, beautifully preserved fashions from the '40s and '50s are the best reason for visiting. You can even find purses and several pairs of hard-to-find vintage shoes to go along with that tailored jacket with the faux fur collar. ✉*437B Hayes St., between Gough and Octavia Sts., Hayes Valley* ☎*415/431–0688.*

16

DEPARTMENT STORES

Barneys New York. Barneys sets itself apart by identifying up-and-coming designers first. Fashion is taken seriously here—a pair of distressed shoes that look like they've been run over by a truck can cost you over a grand—but, it's always done with a wink and a smile, from their infamous store windows to the details of design (on the third floor copper pennies create a rack for designer ready-to-wear). As you enter Barney's six-story corner locale, a flight of stairs extends to the mezzanine where 20,000 shoes make up their infamous shoe salon. Below street level, cosmetics and fragrances reign: there are even state-of-the-art cylindrical sniffing chambers where you can sample new scents. ✉*77 O'Farrell St., at Stockton St. Union Square* ☎*415/268–3500.*

Bloomingdales. The shiny newness (the store opened in late 2006), the black-and-white checkerboard theme, the abundance of glass, and the sheer size might remind you of Vegas. The store emphasizes American designers like Diane von Furstenberg and Jack Spade. Its well-planned layout defines individual departments without losing the grand and open feel. ✉*845 Market St., between Grant Ave. and Kearny St., Union Square* ☎*415/856–5300.*

★ **Gump's.** It's a San Francisco institution, dating back to the 19th century, and it's a strikingly luxurious one. The airy store exudes a museum-like air, with its large decorative vases, sumptuous housewares, and a gobsmacking Tahitian pearl display. Locals line up to register for weddings. But it's also a great place to pick up gifts, such as their Golden Gate Bridge notecards or their silver-plated butter spreaders in a signature Gump's box. ✉*135 Post St., between Grant Ave. and Kearny St., Union Square* ☎*415/982–1616.*

Macy's. Downtown has two behemoth branches of this retailer, where you can find almost anything you could want, if only you have the patience to find it. One—with entrances on Geary, Stockton, and O'Farrell streets—houses the women's, children's, furniture, and housewares departments. With its large selection and its emphasis on American designers, like DKNY and Marc Jacobs, the department for young women stands out. The men's department occupies its own building, across Stockton Street. During the holidays, pups up for adoption bark in the ground-level windows. ⊠ *170 O'Farrell St., at Stockton St., Union Square* ☎ *415/397–3333 Men's branch:* ⊠ *50 O'Farrell St., entrance on Stockton St., Union Square* ☎ *415/397–3333.*

Neiman Marcus. The surroundings, which include a Philip Johnson–designed checkerboard facade, gilded atrium, and stained-glass skylight, are as ritzy as the goods showcased in them. The mix includes designer men's and women's clothing and accessories as well as posh household wares. **Although the prices may raise an eyebrow or two, Neiman's biannual Last Call sales—in January and July—draw a crowd.** After hitting the vast handbag salon, ladies who lunch daintily order consommé and bread laden with strawberry butter in the Rotunda Restaurant. ⊠ *150 Stockton St., at Geary Blvd., Union Square* ☎ *415/362–3900.*

★ **Nordstrom.** Somehow Nordstrom manages to be all things to all people, and this location, with spiral escalators circling a four-story atrium, is no exception. Whether you're an elegant lady of a certain age shopping for a new mink coat or a teen on the hunt for a Roxy hoodie, the salespeople are known for being happy to help. While still carrying the best selections in town of new designers like Tory Burch, their own Nordstrom brands have loyal followings. The latest addition is a Nordstrom Spa. ⊠ *San Francisco Shopping Centre, 865 Market St., between 4th and 5th Sts., Union Square* ☎ *415/243–8500.*

Saks Fifth Avenue. As the West Coast counterpart to the New York flagship, this branch claims a prime bit of Union Square territory and is filled with women carrying the latest handbags. Where the store really outshines the competition is in the incredibly well-stocked Men's Store. The impeccable service will get any casual guy into a suit and tie—and the staff can convince almost anyone to actually like dressing up. ⊠ *384 Post St., at Powell St., Union Square* ☎ *415/986–4300* ⊠ *Men's Store, 220 Post St., at Grant St., Union Square* ☎ *415/986–4300.*

FARMERS' MARKETS

Fodor's Choice
★ **Ferry Plaza Farmers' Market.** The most upscale and expensive of the city's farmers' markets, in front of the restored Ferry Building, places baked goods and fancy pots of jam alongside organic basil and heirloom tomatoes. The Saturday market is the grandest, with about 100 vendors packed both in front of and behind the building. The Tuesday and Thursday markets are smaller. At the Sunday garden market, vegetable and ornamental plants crop up next to a small selection of food items. (The Thursday and Sunday markets don't operate in winter, generally December or January through March.) **On Saturday, don't miss the coffee at Blue Bottle—and yes, the line is worth it.** ⊠ *Ferry Plaza, Embarcadero*

at north end of Market St., Financial District ☎415/291–3276 ⊕www.ferryplazafarmersmarket.com ☉ Tues. and Sun. 10–2, Thurs. 4–8, Sat. 8–2.

Heart of the City Farmers' Market. Held every Sunday and Wednesday near the Civic Center, this market sells heaps of cheap produce, along with occasional baked goods, potted herbs, and even live chickens. *United Nations Plaza, between 7th and 8th Sts., Civic Center* ☎415/558–9455 ☉ Wed. 7–5:30, Sun. 7–5.

FOOD & DRINK

16

Cowgirl Creamery Artisan Cheese. Fantastic organic-milk cheeses—such as the mellow, triple-cream Mt. Tam and *bocconcini* (small balls of fresh mozzarella)—are produced at a creamery an hour north of the city. These and other carefully chosen artisanal cheeses and dairy products, including a luscious, freshly made crème fraîche, round out the selection at the in-town store. ✉1 Ferry Bldg., #17, Embarcadero at foot of Market St., Embarcadero ☎415/362–9354.

Graffeo Coffee Roasting Company. Forget those fancy flavored coffees if you're ordering from this North Beach emporium, open since 1935. This shop, one of the best-loved coffee stores in a city that's truly devoted to its java, sells dark roast, light roast, and dark roast decaf beans only. ✉735 Columbus Ave., at Filbert St., North Beach ☎415/986–2420.

Great China Herb Co. Since 1922, this aromatic shop has been treating the city with its wide selection of ginseng, tea, and other herbs. You might even hear the click of an abacus as a purchase is tallied up. A Chinese (but English-speaking) doctor is always on hand to recommend the perfect remedy. ✉857 Washington St., between Grant Ave. and Stockton St., Chinatown ☎415/982–2195.

Harvest Market. Pasta salads, bean soups, California rolls, and other prepared foods make perfect, ready-to-eat picnic fixings. There's also a superb collection of crusty breads, cheeses, fruits, and vegetables. ✉2285 Market St., between Sanchez and Noe Sts., Castro ☎415/626–0805 ✉191 8th St., at Howard St., SoMa ☎415/621–1000.

Lucca Delicatessen. At this bit of old Italy in the upscale Marina District, take a number and wait your turn to choose from a wide selection of homemade pastas, Italian sausages, prepared salads, and imported cheeses and olive oils. ✉2120 Chestnut St., at Steiner St., Marina ☎415/921–7873.

McEvoy Ranch. The only retail outpost of this Petaluma ranch, a producer of outstanding organic, extra-virgin olive oil. Depending on seasonal availability, the store also gets olive trees, plants, and flowers in from the ranch. **If you stop by in fall or winter, don't miss the Olio Nuovo, the**

days-old green oil produced during the harvest. ⊠ *1 Ferry Bldg., #30, Embarcadero at foot of Market St., Embarcadero* ☎ *415/291-7224.*

Fodor's Choice ★

Molinari Delicatessen. Billing itself as the oldest delicatessen west of the Rockies, the store has been making its own salami, sausages, and cold cuts since 1896. Other homemade specialties include meat and cheese ravioli, tomato sauces, and fresh pastas. In-the-know locals grab a made-to-order sandwich for lunch and eat it at one of the sidewalk tables. ⊠ *373 Columbus Ave., at Vallejo St., North Beach* ☎ *415/421-2337.*

Oakville Grocery. Locals brave the tourists and make a trip down to Fisherman's Wharf just to shop here. In addition to prepared food from their wood fireplace or coffee bar, you can snap up some of their specialty foods—one of more than two dozen mustards, for example. You can't go wrong with anything in their house line of coffee, teas, oils, jams, honeys, and pasta sauces. And if you couldn't make it to Wine Country, they also carry a good selection of hard-to-find wine from small, regional wineries. ⊠ *2801 Leavenworth, at Jefferson St., Fisherman's Wharf* ☎ *415/614-1600.*

Victoria Pastry Co. In business since the early 1900s, and a throwback to the North Beach of old, this bakery has display cases full of Italian pastries, cookies, and St. Honoré cakes. ⊠ *1362 Stockton St., at Vallejo St., North Beach* ☎ *415/781-2015.*

WINES & SPIRITS

Arlequin Wine Merchant. If you like the wine list at Absinthe Brasserie, you can walk next door and pick up a few bottles from its highly regarded sister establishment. This small, nonintimidating shop carries hard-to-find wines from small producers. Why wait to taste? Crack a bottle in the patio out back. ⊠ *384 Hayes St., at Gough St., Hayes Valley* ☎ *415/863-1104.*

Cellar 360. If you can't make it to Napa, come here to browse through 6,000 square feet of wine retail space in the historic Woolen Mill building. During happy hour, tourists and locals alike pack the longest bar in the city to taste the 250 wines available. After a few glasses, you might be sold on a case . . . and if you're not: a Copia education class in their fully-equipped classroom will probably do the trick. ⊠ *900 Northpoint St., Suite F301 at Ghiradelli Square, Fisherman's Wharf* ☎ *415/440-0772.*

City Beer. Think beer isn't as sophisticated as wine? Think again. At City Beer, more than 300 beers are for sale (many refrigerated)—and with six on tap, you can imbibe while you shop. You'll get 10% off when you mix and match your six-pack with everything from Allagash Curieux, a dark beer aged in Jim Beam barrels, to Zatec, an authentic Czech beer. ⊠ *1168 Folsom St., Suite 100 between 7th and 8th Sts., SoMa* ☎ *415/503-1033.*

D&M Wines and Liquors. This family-owned liquor store appears to be like any neighborhood liquor store at first glance, but it's actually a rare and wonderful specialist. In a city obsessed with wine, these spirit devotees distinguished themselves by focusing on rare, small production Armagnac, Calvados, and Champagne. ✉*2200 Fillmore St., at Sacramento St., Pacific Heights* ☏*415/346–1325.*

★ **K&L Wine Merchants.** More than any other wine store, the Merchants has an ardent cult following around town. The friendly staffers promise not to sell what they don't taste themselves and weekly events open the tastings to customers. Their best-seller list for varietals and regions for both the under- and over-$30 categories appeal to the wine dork in everyone. ✉*638 4th St., between Brannan and Townsend Sts., SoMa* ☏*415/896–1734.*

PlumpJack Wines. A small selection of imported wines complements the well-priced, well-stocked collection of hard-to-find California wines here. Gift baskets—such as the Italian market basket, containing wine, Italian foods, and a cookbook—are popular hostess gifts. ✉*3201 Fillmore St., at Greenwich St., Cow Hollow* ☏*415/346–9870* ✉*4011 24th St., between Castro and Noe Sts., Noe Valley* ☏*415/282–3841.*

San Francisco Wine Trading Company. Owner and noted wine expert Gary Marcaletti provides the only place in the city with well-known Bay Area importer Kermit Lynch's line of wines. It also has Saturday-afternoon tastings. ✉*250 Taraval St., between Funston and 12th Aves., Ingleside* ☏*415/731–6222.*

True Sake. Though it would be reasonable to expect a Japanese aesthetic at the U.S.'s first store dedicated entirely to sake, you might instead hear dance music thumping quietly in the background while you browse. Each of the many sakes is displayed with a label describing the drink's qualities and food pairing suggestions. Should these prove insufficient, simply pick up a copy of *The Sake Handbook* or another of the sake-related publications. ✉*560 Hayes St., between Laguna and Octavia Sts., Hayes Valley* ☏*415/355–9555.*

William Glen. The more than 400 whiskies arranged along the back wall—mostly single-malt scotches—are organized by their region of origin, so you can easily distinguish those made in Islay from those from Speyside or Lowland. The charming Scottish proprietor can tell you about his favorites, help you with the selection of tartan scarves or cashmere sweaters, or even equip you with a kilt. ✉*360 Sutter St., Union Square* ☏*415/989–1030.*

Wine Club. The large selection of wines at some of the best prices in the city makes up for the bare-bones feel of this place. A self-serve wine bar tucked in the back allows you to taste a wide variety of wines for a modest fee, a great boon to those who'd like to try before they buy. A small collection of caviar and wine paraphernalia, including Riedel wineglasses, books, openers, and decanters, is also available. ✉*953 Harrison St., between 5th and 6th Sts., SoMa* ☏*415/512–9086.*

FURNITURE & HOUSEWARES

Aldea. A visit to this shop is like being in someone's home and being able to buy everything you see from the sheets, to the chairs, to the shampoo in the shower. It's the perfect place to find a hostess gift or for that corner missing something special. The aesthetic is modern, with bright references to Mexico, India, Turkey, and Japan. ✉ *3338 17th St., Suite 100B, between Valencia and Mission Sts., Mission* ☎ *415/865–9807.*

Biordi Art Imports. Hand-painted Italian pottery, mainly imported from Tuscany and Umbria, has been shipped worldwide by this family-run business since 1946. Dishware sets can be ordered in any combination. ✉ *412 Columbus Ave., at Vallejo St., North Beach* ☎ *415/392–8096.*

Candelier. This fragrant little shop on tony Maiden Lane sells every sort of candle you can imagine. Tapers, votives, and pillars are popular purchases, as are the luxury bath products and small decorative items. ✉ *33 Maiden La., between Grant Ave. and Kearny St., Union Square* ☎ *415/989–8600.*

Dandelion. The variety of housewares, bath items, books, and tchotchkes includes something for everyone on your gift list. Cocktail paraphernalia, golf-related books, luxury bath products, and indulgent food items such as Fauchon-brand black-fig preserves are only a sample of what's here. ✉ *55 Potrero Ave., at Alameda St., Potrero Hill* ☎ *415/436–9500.*

Diptyque. The original Diptyque boutique in Paris has long attracted a following of celebrities. You can find the full line of scented candles and fragrances in this chic shop that would be at home on the boulevard St-Germain. Trademark black-and-white labels adorn the popular L'eau toilet water, scented with geranium and sandalwood. Candles come in both traditional and esoteric scents, including lavender, basil, leather, and fig tree. Also available is a collection of French Mariage Frères teas. ✉ *171 Maiden La., between Grant and Stockton Sts., Union Square* ☎ *415/402–0600.*

★ **Flight 001.** Über-stylish travel accessories—retro-looking flight bags, supersoft leather passport wallets, and tiny Swiss travel alarm clocks—line the shelves of this brightly lighted shop, which vaguely resembles an airplane interior. High-tech travel gear and a small collection of guidebooks speed you on your way. ✉ *525 Hayes St., between Laguna and Octavia Sts., Hayes Valley* ☎ *415/487–1001.*

The Gardener. Artful, functional home and garden accessories are the lure here, from woven baskets and teak salad bowls to beautifully illustrated books. Although there's only a small selection of actual gardening items, such as seeds, bulbs, and tools, there are plenty of bath and body items with which to pamper yourself after a day in the yard. ✉ *1 Ferry Bldg., Embarcadero at foot of Market St., Embarcadero* ☎ *415/981–8181.*

Modern Artifacts. From Eames chairs and a Hans Wegner sofa covered in nubby fabric to a sensuous lamp designed by Italian architect Gae Aulenti, this store has all the accoutrements for a stylish modernist apartment. ✉ *1639 Market St., between Franklin and Gough Sts., Hayes Valley* ☎ *415/255–9000.*

Nest. A mix between a Parisian antiques show and a Jamaican flea market, this cozy store could get even the most monochrome New Yorker excited about color. You can turn up vibrant handmade quilts, Chan Luu jewelry, Les Indiennes hand-blocked cotton fabrics, and M. Sasek's cheerfully illustrated book, *This Is San Francisco.* ✉ *2300 Fillmore*

St., at Clay St., Pacific Heights ☎415/292–6199.

★ **Paxton Gate.** Elevating gardening to an art, this serene shop offers beautiful earthenware pots, amaryllis and narcissus bulbs, decorative garden items, and coffee-table books such as *An Inordinate Fondness for Beetles.* The collection of taxidermy and preserved bugs presents more unusual gift ideas. ✉824 Valencia St., between 19th and 20th Sts., Mission ☎415/824–1872.

La Place du Soleil. Run by a charming couple who once lived in London, this shop purveys china cups and other teatime pieces alongside the duo's favorite international candies, bath products, and decorative items. Also sharing the space are a few unique pieces of furniture, such as a 19th-century stained-pine English bookcase. ✉2356 Polk St., between Green and Union Sts., Russian Hill ☎415/771–4252.

★ **Scheuer Linens.** Designers and other fans make their way to this store, a Union Square fixture since 1953, for luxurious bed and bath items and linens. The pretty tablecloths, runners, and napkins, fragrant candles, and luxurious bath accessories are popular gifts. ✉340 Sutter St., at Stockton St., Union Square ☎415/392–2813.

16

★ **Spring.** Under the exposed beams of this loftlike space and fittingly surrounded by plants are hundreds of products for an environmentally friendly home. In true SF style, residents with sustainability concerns buy up everything from hemp dishcloths to nontoxic home-care products to organic bedding. A visit is an education on what it really means to be green. ✉2162 Polk St., at Vallejo St., Russian Hill ☎415/673–2065.

Sue Fisher King Company. When Martha Stewart or the buyers at Williams-Sonoma need some inspiration they come to see how Sue has set her sprawling table or dressed her stately bed. (Her specialty is opulent linens for every room.) When Pacific Heights residents are looking for an impeccable hostess or bridal gift, they come by for a hand-embroidered velvet pillow or a piece of Astier de Villatte white pottery. Out back is a tiny, charming garden area overflowing with plants. ✉3067 Sacramento St., between Baker and Broderick Sts., Pacific Heights ☎415/922–7276.

Therapy. Housewares range from ever-practical refrigerator magnets to downright silly items such as a soap-on-a-rope tribute to the cartoon character Strawberry Shortcake. A retro theme runs to stationery and other reasonably priced items, and the adjacent annex sells retro-style furniture. ✉545 Valencia St., between 16th and 17th Sts., Mission ☎415/865-0981.

Under One Roof. Profits from its home and garden items, gourmet foods, bath products, books, frames, cards, and silly gift items go to Northern California AIDS organizations, which makes it easy to justify buying an

Oscar Wilde action figure or a bath mat shaped like a T-bone steak. ✉ *549 Castro St., between 18th and 19th Sts., Castro* ☎ *415/503–2300.*

Worldware. Sumptuously dressed beds, overstuffed mohair sofas, and richly colored rugs from around the world are just a few of the eclectic items displayed by owner and interior designer Greg Henson in his spacious store. Luxurious bath products and small decorative items make more portable purchases. ✉ *301 Fell St., at Gough St., Hayes Valley* ☎ *415/487–9030.*

COOKWARE

City Discounts. This small restaurant-supply store sells commercial-grade pans, knives, and microplanes at a fraction of the price of what you'd pay at a national kitchenware chain store. There's a nice selection of imported Italian food and the Italian proprietess is a great help in making selections. ✉ *1542 Polk St., between Sacramento and California Sts., Russian Hill* ☎ *415/771–4649.*

Fodor'sChoice ★ **Cookin': Recycled Gourmet Appurtenances.** People trek here from all over the world for the impressive collection of indestructible vintage Le Creuset in discontinued colors. If you can't make sense of this store's jumble of used cookware—stacked ceiling high in some places—ask the helpful owner, who will likely interrogate you about what you're preparing to cook before leading you to the right section, whether that be the corner with hundreds of ramekins or the bewildering selection of garlic presses. ✉ *339 Divisadero St., between Oak and Page Sts., Western Addition* ☎ *415/861–1854.*

Sur la Table. Everything the home chef could need is here, along with some things many cooks have never heard of—such as round aspic cutters and larding needles. Cooking classes and demonstrations are often held downstairs at the Maiden Lane location. ✉ *77 Maiden La., between Grant Ave. and Kearny St., Union Square* ☎ *415/732–7900* ✉ *1 Ferry Bldg., Embarcadero at foot of Market St., Financial District* ☎ *415/262–9970.*

Williams-Sonoma. Behind the striped awnings and historic facade is the massive mothership of the Sonoma-founded kitchen store empire. La Cornue custom stoves beckon you inward and two grand staircases beckon you upward to the world of dinnerware, linens, and chefs' tools. Antique tart tins, eggbeaters, and pastry cutters from the personal collection of founder Chuck Williams line the walls. ✉ *340 Post St., in between Powell and Stockton Sts., Union Square* ☎ *415/362–9450.*

The Wok Shop. The store carries woks, of course, but also anything else you could need for Chinese cooking—bamboo steamers, ginger graters, wicked-looking cleavers—as well as accessories for Japanese cooking, including sushi paraphernalia and tempura racks. ✉ *718 Grant Ave., at Sacramento St., Chinatown* ☎ *415/989–3797.*

VINTAGE HOUSEWARES

Swallowtail. Under wall-to-wall skylights sit stuffed rams, vintage crystal goblets, Lucite chandeliers, and antique chairs reupholstered with fresh prints. Groupings of skulls and Victorian dentistry tools could inspire you to make odd collections part of your decor. ✉ *2217 Polk St., at Vallejo St., Russian Hill* ☎ *415/567–1555.*

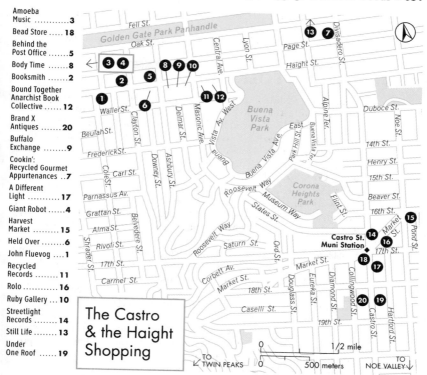

The Castro & the Haight Shopping

X-21 Modern. Furniture and decorative items of the mid-20th century fill this place. Stainless-steel desks and bookshelves are popular; the more eclectic items might include a molded-plastic chair shaped like a hand. ⊠ *890 Valencia St., at 20th St., Mission* ☎ *415/647–4211.*

Zonal. Most of the refurbished vintage steel filing cabinets, dining-room tables, desks, and even barrister bookcases were built in the 1930s and '40s. Upholstered pieces, such as a generously-sized slipper chair, are contemporary but have a sleek retro look. ⊠ *568 Hayes St., at Laguna St., Hayes Valley* ☎ *415/255–9307.*

HANDBAGS, LUGGAGE & LEATHER GOODS

Goyard. After more than a century of selling trunks, handbags, and pet leashes on the Rue St-Honoré in Paris, Goyard opened their second store here to offer San Franciscans a relatively discreet alternative to Louis Vuitton. Rather than splashing their name everywhere, they signal luxury with a signature chevron pattern. Even if you walk away empty-handed, you'll be reminded of what travel used to mean. ⊠ *345 Powell St., between Post and Geary Sts., Union Square* ☎ *415/398–1110.*

Kate Spade. Slightly retro, a bit tongue in cheek, and well-made—the formula has made these purses wildly popular among ladies of all ages. (The "baby bags" seem far too lovely for stashing diapers.) The shop also stocks a few shoes as well as cosmetics cases, date books, and note cards. ✉ *227 Grant Ave., between Post and Sutter Sts., Union Square* ☎415/216–0880.

HANDICRAFTS & FOLK ART

F. Dorian. In addition to cards, jewelry, and other crafts from Central and South America, Africa, Asia, and the Middle East—a carved wooden candleholder from the Ivory Coast is one example—this store carries brightly colored glass and ceramic works by local artisans and whimsical mobiles. ✉ *370 Hayes St., between Franklin and Gough Sts., Hayes Valley* ☎415/861–3191.

Global Exchange. A branch of the well-known nonprofit organization, the store carries handcrafted items from more than 40 countries. The staff works directly with village cooperatives and workshops. Whether you buy a Nepalese sweater, a South African wood carving, or Balinese textiles, employees explain the origin of your purchase. ✉ *4018 24th St., between Noe and Castro Sts., Noe Valley* ☎415/648–8068.

Ma-Shi'-Ko Folk Craft. Beautiful Mashiko pottery, rustic pieces fired in a wood kiln and coated with a natural glaze, are the specialty here. The wealth of unique pottery and antiques, including many ceramic vases and wooden chests, makes a visit here worth the somewhat chilly reception from the proprietor. ✉ *Kinokuniya Bldg., 1581 Webster St., 2nd fl., Japantown* ☎415/346–0748.

Polanco. Devoted to showcasing the arts of Mexico, this gallery sells everything from antiques and traditional folk crafts to fine contemporary paintings. Brightly painted animal figures and a virtual village of Day of the Dead figures share space with religious statues and modern linocuts and paintings. ✉ *393 Hayes St., between Franklin and Gough Sts., Hayes Valley* ☎415/252–5753.

Ruby Gallery. A pooch named Ruby presides over this small artists' cooperative where the jewelry, clothing, handbags, candleholders, intricately crafted cards, and other gift items are made by local artists. Hair accessories—from elegant clips studded with vintage Czech glass to barrettes fashioned out of buttons—are especially charming. ✉ *3602 20th St., at Valencia St., Mission* ☎415/550–8052 ✉ *1431 Haight St., between Masonic Ave. and Ashbury St., Haight* ☎415/554–0555.

Soko Hardware. Run in Japantown by the Ashizawa family since 1925, this shop specializes in beautifully crafted Japanese tools for gardening and woodworking. In addition to the usual hardware-store items, you can find seeds for Japanese plants and books about topics such as making shoji screens. ✉ *1698 Post St., at Buchanan St., Japantown* ☎415/931–5510.

Studio 24. The gift shop of the acclaimed Galería de la Raza sells crafts from Mexico and Central and South America. Prints and calendars by Latino artists, Day of the Dead folk art, and masks and wood carvings from Latin America are a few of the items for sale. ✉ *2857 24th St., at Bryant St., Mission* ☎415/826–8009.

Fodor's Choice ★ **Xanadu Gallery San Francisco.** The spectacular collection of international art and antiquities here includes items such as Latin American folk art and masks, sculptures, woven baskets, tapestries, and textiles from

Africa, Oceania, and Indonesia. Museum-quality pieces such as a gilt bronze figure of a lama (Tibetan Buddhist holy man) can go for nearly $100,000, but beautiful books on subjects such as Tibetan art make more affordable souvenirs. **If nothing else, the shop is worth a visit to see its Frank Lloyd Wright–designed home, where a spiral ramp recalls New York City's Guggenheim Museum.** ✉ *140 Maiden La., between Stockton St. and Grant Ave., Union Square* ☎ *415/392–9999.*

Xela Imports. Africa, Southeast Asia, and Central America are the sources for the merchandise, which includes jewelry, religious masks, fertility statuary, and decorative wall hangings. The name of the store is pronounced *shay*-la. ✉ *3925 24th St., between Sanchez and Noe Sts., Noe Valley* ☎ *415/695–1323.*

JEWELRY & COLLECTIBLES

De Vera. Nature inspires these beautiful, curious objets d'art and jewelry, such as an oversize gold rose thorn, life-size handblown glass ants, and branching coral jewelry. Some, like the cameos, are antiques to boot. ✉ *29 Maiden La., at Kearney St., Union Square* ☎ *415/788–0828.*

★ **San Francisco Museum of Modern Art Museum Store.** The shop is known for its exclusive line of watches and jewelry, as well as artists' monographs and artful housewares. Posters, calendars, children's art sets and books, and art books for adults round out the merchandise. Larger items include sleek, modernist furniture. ✉ *151 3rd St., between Mission and Howard Sts., SoMa* ☎ *415/357–4035.*

Shreve & Co. Along with gems in dazzling settings, San Francisco's oldest retail store—it's been at this location since 1852—carries lovely watches by Jaeger-LeCoultre and others. On weekends well-heeled couples crowd around the glass cases pointing at hefty diamond engagement rings. ✉ *200 Post St., at Grant Ave., Union Square* ☎ *415/421–2600.*

Tiffany & Co. This gray marble beauty towers over Union Square with almost as much leverage as its signature blue box. The company that all but invented the modern engagement ring makes more than just brides swoon with Elsa Peretti's sinuous silver and architect Frank Gehry's collection using materials like Pernambuco wood and black gold. ✉ *350 Post St., between Powell and Stockton Sts., Union Square* ☎ *415/781–7000.*

Union Street Goldsmith. Open since 1976, this local favorite prides itself on its wide selection of rare gemstones, such as golden sapphires and violet tanzanite. Custom work is a specialty, and a number of no-pressure design consultants are happy to talk with you about how to make the jewelry you're dreaming of a reality. ✉ *1909 Union St., at Laguna St., Cow Hollow* ☎ *415/776–8048.*

Velvet da Vinci. Each contemporary art piece here is one-of-a-kind or limited edition. The beautiful, unusual items might be sculpted out of resin, hammered from copper, or woven with silver wires. ✉ *2015 Polk St., between Broadway and Pacific Ave., Russian Hill* ☎ *415/441–0109.*

16

ANTIQUE JEWELRY

Brand X Antiques. The vintage jewelry, mostly from the early part of the 20th century, includes a wide selection of estate pieces and objets d'art. With rings that range from $5 to $50,000, there's something for everyone. ✉570 Castro St., at 18th St., Castro ☎415/626–8908.

Fodor'sChoice **Lang Antiques and Estate Jewelry.** Dozens of diamond bracelets in the
★ window attract shoppers to one of the city's best vintage jewelry shops, where rings, brooches, and other glittering items represent a wide spread of eras, from Victorian and Edwardian to art nouveau and Arts and Crafts. The shop has been selling fine jewelry, including engagement rings and a small number of vintage watches, since 1969. ✉323 Sutter St., at Grant Ave., Union Square ☎415/982–2213.

BEADS

Bead Store. More than a thousand kinds of strung and unstrung pieces include such stones as lapis and carnelian, Czech and Venetian glass, African trade beads, Buddhist and Muslim prayer beads, and Catholic rosaries. Silver jewelry is another specialty. ✉417 Castro St., at Market St., Castro ☎415/861–7332.

Yone. In business since 1965, the store carries so many types of beads that the owner has lost track (though it's probably somewhere between 5,000 and 10,000). Individual beads, made of glass, wood, plastic, bone, sterling silver, and countless other materials, can cost up to $100. ✉478 Union St., at Grant Ave., North Beach ☎415/986–1424.

MUSIC

Fodor'sChoice **Amoeba Music.** With more than 2.5 million new and used CDs, DVDs,
★ and records, this warehouselike store (and the original Berkeley location) carries titles you can't find on Amazon at bargain prices. No niche is ignored—from electronica and hip-hop to jazz and classical—and the stock changes daily. Weekly in-store performances attract large crowds. ✉1855 Haight St., between Stanyan and Shrader Sts., Haight ☎415/831–1200.

Aquarius Records. Owner Windy Chien carries on the tradition in this space, which was *the* punk-rock store in the 1970s. These days it carries a variety of music, including a large selection of experimental electronica, all of it hand-picked by staffers, so you can be sure you're getting the latest and hippest. ✉1055 Valencia St., between 21st and 22nd Sts., Mission ☎415/647–2272.

Recycled Records. A Haight Street landmark, the store buys, sells, and trades a vast selection of used records, including hard-to-find imports and those of obscure alternative bands. The CD collection is large, but the vinyl is the real draw. ✉1377 Haight St., between Masonic and Central Aves., Haight ☎415/626–4075.

Ritmo Latino. This is your best bet for Latin music in San Francisco, including salsa, *ranchero,* Latin jazz, *conjunto,* mariachi, and more. ✉2401 Mission St., at 20th St., Mission ☎415/824–8556.

Streetlight Records. Thousands of used CDs, with an emphasis on rock, jazz, soul, and R&B, are bought and sold here. But there's plenty of vinyl for purists. The Noe Valley branch has been a neighborhood

Japantown, Pacific Heights & Cow Hollow Shopping

staple since 1973. ⊠*3979 24th St., between Noe and Sanchez Sts., Noe Valley* ☎*415/282-3550* ⊠*2350 Market St., at Castro St., Castro* ☎*415/282-8000.*

Virgin Megastore. The huge, glitzy music store near Union Square has dozens of listening stations, extensive DVD and video game collections, and many music and pop-culture-related books. The third-floor Citizen Cupcake serves panini, sweet treats, and even sake cocktails. ⊠*2 Stockton St., at Market St., Union Square* ☎*415/397-4525.*

MEMORABILIA

San Francisco Rock Posters and Collectibles. The huge selection of rock-and-roll memorabilia, including posters, handbills, and original art, takes you back to the 1960s. Also available are posters from more-recent shows—many at the legendary Fillmore Auditorium—with such musicians as George Clinton, Porno for Pyros, and the late Johnny Cash. ⊠*1851 Powell St., between Filbert and Greenwich Sts., North Beach* ☎*415/956-6749.*

PAPER & STATIONERY

★ **Flax.** In addition to paints, brushes, and various art supplies, this sprawling creator's playground sells beautifully made photo albums and journals, fine pens and pencils, crafts kits, scads of stationery, and inspiring doodads for kids. ⊠*1699 Market St., near Valencia St., Mission* ☎*415/552-2355.*

Kozo Arts. The art of papermaking rises to new levels here. The store's specialty is silk-screened Chiyogami papers from Japan. The papers are also made into hand-bound photo albums, cards, and journals. ⊠*1969-A Union St., between Buchanan and Laguna Sts., Cow Hollow* ☎*415/351-2114.*

Lola of North Beach. For a card that is anything but Hallmark, snap up something from local letterpresses; many have San Francisco themes. A section of the intimate North Beach store is devoted to the stages of a relationship: friendship, I like you, I love you, I miss you, I'm sorry, and I'm here for you. It also carries an impressive collection of baby clothes, including some adorable tees. **The Ghirardelli Square branch flutters with more tourist-geared, SF-centric cards.** ⊠*1415 Grant Ave., at Green St., North Beach* ☎*415/781-1817* ⊠*900 N. Point St., in Ghirardelli Square, Fisherman's Wharf* ☎*415/567-7760.*

Paper Source. Beautiful handmade papers, cards, envelopes, ribbons, and bookbinding materials line the walls of this shop, which embodies the Bay Area's do-it-yourself spirit. Assembly is required here and that's the fun of it. ⊠*1925 Fillmore St., at Pine St., Pacific Heights* ☎*415/409-7710*

✉2061 *Chestnut St., between Fillmore and Steiner Sts., Marina* ☎415/614–1585.

SHOES

Twenty Two Shoes. These crumpled and distressed leather shoes—made in Italy, but designed in Oakland—have hit the feet of the Hollywood set; the line of bags is a recent addition. ✉*2277 Union St., at Steiner St., Cow Hollow* ☎415/409–2277.

Gimme Shoes. From the chunky to the sleek, the shoes carried here—including those by Robert Clergerie, Helmut Lang, Prada, and John Varvatos—are top-notch. And if $600 seems steep for pale green pumps, perhaps you haven't seen the perfect pair by Dries Van Noten. ✉*416 Hayes St., at Gough St., Hayes Valley* ☎415/864–0691 ✉*2358 Fillmore St., at Washington St., Pacific Heights* ☎415/441–3040.

★ **John Fluevog.** The selection of trendy but sturdily made footwear for men and women is one of the best in the city. Club kids go for the Canadian brand's shoes and especially their boots, handing over a pretty penny for dramatic styles such as the popular 5-inch-heel knee-high boots made out of red pony fur. ✉*1697 Haight St., at Cole St., Haight* ☎415/436–9784.

16

SPORTING GOODS

★ **Lululemon Athletica.** This yoga-inspired company makes all kinds of athletic gear with their Luon fabric—it's nonchafing, moisture wicking, preshrunk, and best of all it can be washed and dried in warm water. Their pants are known for being the best thing in town for your derriere. ✉*1981 Union St., between Laguna and Buchanan Sts., Marina* ☎415/776–5858 ✉*327 Grant Ave., between Bush and Sutter Sts., Union Square* ☎415/402–0914.

Niketown. More glitzy multimedia extravaganza than sporting-goods store, this emporium is nevertheless the best place in town to find anything and everything with the famous swoosh. ✉*278 Post St., at Stockton St., Union Square* ☎415/392–6453.

The North Face. The Bay Area–based national retailer is famous for its top-of-the-line tents, sleeping bags, backpacks, and outdoor apparel, including rugged Gore-Tex jackets and pants. ✉*180 Post St., between Kearny St. and Grant Ave., Union Square* ☎415/433–3223.

Patagonia. Technical wear for serious outdoors enthusiasts is the specialty. Along with sportswear and casual clothing, it carries activewear for backpacking, fly-fishing, kayaking, and the like. ✉*770 N. Point St., at Hyde St., Fisherman's Wharf* ☎415/771–2050.

★ **REI.** The beloved Seattle-based co-op was founded by a group of mountain climbers in 1938. In addition to carrying a vast selection of clothing and outdoor gear, the store rents camping equipment and repairs snowboards and bikes. ✉*840 Brannan St., between 7th and 8th Sts., SoMa* ☎415/934–1938.

Sports Basement. These sprawling places reward intrepid shoppers with significant discounts on name-brand sportswear, accessories, and camping and outdoor gear. Helpful salespeople, more knowledgeable than you would expect at a discount warehouse, will help you find just the right running shoes, biking shorts, or yoga tights. ⊠ *1590 Bryant St., between 15th and 16th Sts., Potrero Hill* ☎ 415/437–0100 ⊠ *610 Mason St., across from Crissy Field, Marina* ☎ 415/437–0100.

TOYS & GADGETS

★ **Apple Store San Francisco.** A shiny, stainless-steel box is the setting for San Francisco's flagship Apple store, a high-tech temple to Macs and the people who use them. Play around with iPods, laptops, and hundreds of geeky accessories; then watch a theater presentation or attend an educational workshop. ⊠ *1 Stockton St., at Market St., Union Square* ☎ 415/392–0202.

Ark Toys, Books & Crafts. The store emphasizes high-quality toys, many of which have an educational bent (books, science kits) or encourage imaginative play (dress-up costumes, paper dolls). The stock includes numerous toys manufactured in Europe. Most of the items are for toddlers through 12-year-olds. ⊠ *3845 24th St., between Church and Sanchez Sts., Noe Valley* ☎ 415/821–1257.

ATYS. Gadgets for the home and office with a sleek modern design are imported from Scandinavia, Italy, Germany, and Japan. Among the eye-catching items are a digital watch designed by Philippe Starck and Japanese knives that could be displayed as sculptures. ⊠ *2149-B Union St., between Fillmore and Webster Sts., Cow Hollow* ☎ 415/441–9220.

Chinatown Kite Shop. Kites at this family-owned business (operating since 1969) range from basic diamond shapes to box- and animal-shape configurations. Colorful dragon kites make great Chinatown souvenirs. ⊠ *717 Grant Ave., between Clay and Sacramento Sts., Chinatown* ☎ 415/989–5182.

★ **826 Valencia.** The brainchild of author Dave Eggers is primarily a center established to help kids with their writing skills via tutoring and storytelling events. But the storefront is also "San Francisco's only independent pirate supply store," a quirky space filled with eye patches, spyglasses, and other pirate-theme paraphernalia. Eggers's quarterly journal, *McSweeney's,* and other publications are available here. Proceeds benefit the writing center. ⊠ *826 Valencia St., between 18th and 19th Sts., Mission* ☎ 415/642–5905.

Exploratorium. The educational gadgets and gizmos sold here are so much fun that your kids—whether they're in grade school or junior high—might not realize they're learning while they're playing with them. ⊠ *3601 Lyon St., at Marina Blvd., Marina* ☎ 415/561–0360.

Giant Robot. This superhip spot feeds San Franciscans' passion for Asian pop cultural fluff, from Gama-Go Ninja Kitty bike messenger bags and Uglydoll keychains and figurines to Astro Boy stationery sets. Of course, the store also carries *Giant Robot* magazine, as well as a large selection of T-shirts. ⊠ *618 Shrader St., at Haight St., Haight* ☎ 415/876–4773.

Marin County, Berkeley & Oakland

Rowing, Marin County

WORD OF MOUTH

"Once you've done the city, and if you have a car, visit the Muir Woods. This is one of the greatest surprises I've had in the Bay Area! It's amazing that 30 minutes outside of the city there is a stand of giant redwoods that are more awesome than any man-made skyscraper. . . ."

—krissy66

GETTING ORIENTED

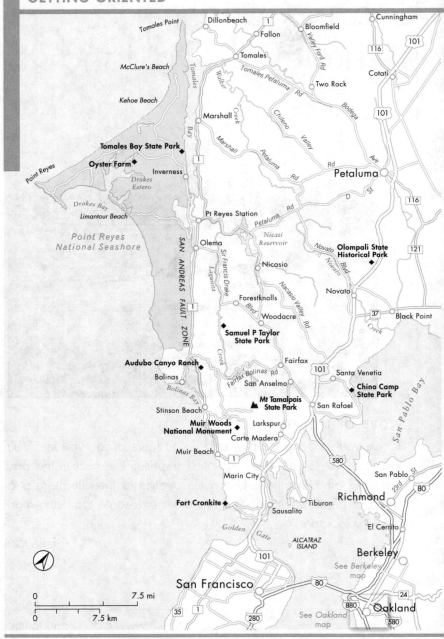

Tomales Point
Dillonbeach
Fallon
Bloomfield
Cunningham
1
116
101
McClure's Beach
Tomales
Two Rock
Tomales Petaluma Rd
Cotati
Kehoe Beach
Walker
Creek
Valley Ford Rd
Chileno
Valley
101
Marshall
Bodega
Ave
Tomales
Bay
Tomales Bay State Park
Marshall
Oyster Farm
1
Petaluma
Rd
Petaluma
Point Reyes
Inverness
Drakes
Estero
D
St.
Drakes Bay
Limantour Beach
Pt Reyes Station
Petaluma
Rd
116
*Point Reyes
National Seashore*
Olema
Nicasi
Reservoir
Novato
Olompali State
Historical Park
121
SAN
ANDREAS
Nicasio
Laguntia
Sir Francis Drake
1
Forestknolls
Nacasio Valley Rd
Novato
Blvd
Novato
37
Black Point
FAULT
Woodacre
Creek
Samuel P Taylor
State Park
ZONE
Fairfax
Santa Venetia
San Pablo Bay
Audubo Canyo Ranch
Fairfax Bolinas Rd
101
China Camp
State Park
Bolinas
San Anselmo
Creek
Bolinas Bay
Mt Tamalpais
State Park
San Rafael
Stinson Beach
Muir Woods
National Monument
Larkspur
Corte Madera
580
San Pablo St.
Muir Beach
1
Marin City
San Pablo St.
Richmond
29rd
80
Fort Cronkite
Tiburon
Sausalito
El Cerrito
Golden
Gate
ALCATRAZ
ISLAND
Berkeley
See Berkeley
map
101
280
San Francisco
80
24
880
Oakland
35
1
See Oakland
map
580

0   7.5 mi

0   7.5 km

INDEPENDENCE

GETTING ORIENTED

Cross the Golden Gate Bridge and head north to reach Marin County's rolling hills and green expanses, where residents enjoy a haute-suburban lifestyle. Farther afield, the wild landscapes of the Marin Headlands, Muir Woods, Mt. Tamalpais, Stinson Beach, and Point Reyes National Seashore await.

East of the city, across the San Francisco Bay, are Berkeley and Oakland, which most Bay Area residents refer to as the East Bay. These two towns have distinct personalities, but life here feels more relaxed than in the city—though every bit as vibrant.

Marin County. Marin is considered the prettiest of the Bay Area counties, primarily because of its wealth of open space. Anchored by water on three sides, the county is mostly parkland, including long stretches of unmolested coastline. The picturesque small towns here—Sausalito, Tiburon, Mill Valley, and Bolinas among them—may sometimes look rustic, but they're mostly in a dizzyingly high tax bracket. There's a reason people call BMWs "basic Marin wheels."

Oakland. Life in this tight-knit, harborfront city is strongly defined by a turbulent history. But the up-and-coming downtown scene and rejuvenated waterfront are signals of good things ahead.

Berkeley. This college town has long been known for its liberal ethos, stimulating university community (and perhaps even more stimulating coffee shops), and activist streak. But these days, the booming restaurant and arts scenes are luring even those who wouldn't be caught dead in Birkenstocks.

TOP 5 REASONS TO GO

Walk among giants: Walking into Muir Woods, a mere 12 mi north of the Golden Gate Bridge, is like entering a cathedral built by God.

Attend a reading: Chances are, an author you admire will be reading somewhere in the Bay Area during your trip. Berkeley draws an especially erudite crowd; Q&A sessions can feel like a grad-school discussion.

Bite into the "Gourmet Ghetto": Eat your way through this area of Berkeley, starting with a slice of pizza from the Cheeseboard.

Browse through Rockridge: Hit College Avenue, the main drag of Oakland's Rockridge neighborhood, to browse bookstores, people-watch, and get a treat at Bittersweet, the chocolate café.

Find solitude at Point Reyes National Seashore: Head here to hike beautifully rugged—and deserted—beaches.

17

BRIDGELOCK

Most San Franciscans consider the whole of the Bay Area their home and won't hesitate to drive (or bike) across the Golden Gate or Bay bridge to get in an afternoon's hike or to visit a special bistro with a mountain view. Beware traffic patterns: venturing outside the city's limits during rush hour can mean slow going. If you find your blood pressure soaring, try to focus on the spectacular views.

MARIN COUNTY, BERKELEY & OAKLAND PLANNER

Making the Most of Your Time

Berkeley is a university town, and the rhythm of the school year might affect your visit. It's easier to navigate the streets and find parking near the university between semesters, but there's also less buzz around town. Surprisingly, summer is chock-full of students attending the many summer sessions on campus. Moving-in weeks before the fall semester bring a massive influx of students *and* parents and other family members—definitely not the best time to take a campus tour.

BART trains can be packed during traditional morning and evening rush hours, but things are much less congested at other times. BART can get you from downtown San Francisco to a coffee shop in Rockridge in about 25 minutes. (It's closer to 30 minutes for farther points in Berkeley.)

It'll take about the same amount of time to reach Tiburon if traffic is clear on the Golden Gate Bridge (also depending, of course, on what part of the city you're departing from).

About the Restaurants & Hotels

The Bay Area is home to some of the most popular and innovative restaurants in the country, including Chez Panisse Café & Restaurant, in Berkeley, and Lark Creek Inn, in Larkspur—for which reservations must be made well in advance. Expect an emphasis on using locally grown produce, hormone-free meats, and California wine. The coast provides a spectacular waterfront setting for dining as well as lodging; in many instances, the views are the most important part of the experience. Keep in mind that many Marin cafés don't serve dinner, and that dinner service ends on the early side. (No 10 PM reservations in this neck of the woods.)

There aren't many hotels in Berkeley or Oakland, but Marin is a destination where hotels package themselves as cozy retreats. Summer is often booked well in advance, despite weather that is often mercurial and sometimes downright chilly. Check for special packages during this season.

Getting Around

If you don't want to worry about finding a parking space, using public transportation to reach Berkeley or Oakland is ideal; BART has several central stops in both towns. For sheer romance, nothing beats the ferry; there's service from San Francisco to Sausalito and Tiburon in Marin County, and to Alameda and Oakland in the East Bay. To visit the outer reaches of Marin, a car is essential (unless you want to spend all day on the bus).

⇨ Please see the Marin County Essentials and East Bay Essentials sections for more details.

WHAT IT COSTS				
$$$$	$$$	$$	$	¢
RESTAURANTS				
over $30	$23–$30	$15–$22	$10–$14	under $10
HOTELS				
over $250	$200–$250	$150–$199	$90–$149	under $90

Restaurant prices are per person for a main course at dinner, or the equivalent. Hotel prices are for two people in a standard double room in high season.

Updated by
Fiona G.
Parrott

It's rare for a metropolis to compete with its suburbs for visitors, but the view from any of San Francisco's hilltops shows that the Bay Area's temptations extend far beyond the city limits. To the north is Marin County, the beauty queen: small but chic villages like Tiburon and Mill Valley, plus dramatic coastal scenery. East of town are two energetic urban centers, Berkeley and Oakland. Formerly radical Berkeley is getting more glam, while Oakland is slowly shaking off its image as San Francisco's ugly stepsister.

17

Up in Marin, the birthplace of mountain biking, trail-veined Mt. Tamalpais and the woods below draw hikers and cyclists. Beaches lure families and thrill seekers, while little towns offer urbanites respite from busy city streets. In the mid-1960s and '70s, alternative-lifestyle seekers established Marin's reputation as ground zero for gurus, granola, and redwood hot tubs. Despite the influx of stock-market millionaires and chic boutiques, the counterculture identity still sticks. Immediately after crossing the Golden Gate Bridge on Highway 101 northbound, you'll pass through a tunnel whose archway is painted with a rainbow that welcomes you to magical Marin, "Land of Oz."

Meanwhile, the town often referred to as the People's Republic of Berkeley retains its liberal image, though it's drastically tamer than it was in the late 1960s. It's now as famous for chef and food activist Alice Waters (and her pricey restaurant Chez Panisse) as it is for its role as the birthplace of the Free Speech movement. Oakland is polishing some of its rough edges, too, with a successful port and a revitalized downtown, alternative arts scene, and hipster cafés and boutiques.

MARIN COUNTY

WORD OF MOUTH

"Be sure to get out onto the water. A ferry ride to Sausalito, Tiburon, or Larkspur will reward you with wonderful views and there are things to be seen at in each of those places."

–Grasshopper

Marin is quite simply a knockout—some go so far as to call it spectacular and wild. This isn't an extravagant claim since more than 40% of the county (180,000 acres), including the majority of the coastline, is parkland. The territory ranges from chaparral, grassland, and coastal scrub to broadleaf and evergreen forest, redwood, salt marsh, and rocky shoreline.

Regardless of its natural beauty, what gave the county its reputation was Cyra McFadden's 1977 book, *The Serial,* a literary soap opera that depicted the county as a bastion of hot-tubbing and "open" marriages. Indeed old-time bohemian, but also increasingly jet-set, Marinites still spend a lot of time outdoors, and surfing, cycling, and hiking are common after-work and weekend activities. Adrenaline junkies mountain bike down Mt. Tamalpais, and those who want solitude take a walk on one of Point Reyes's many empty beaches. The hot tub remains a popular destination after hours, but things have changed since the boho days. Artists and musicians who arrived in the 1960s have set the tone for mellow country towns, but Marin is now undeniably chic, with BMWs supplanting VW buses as the car of choice.

Most cosmopolitan is Sausalito, the town just over the Golden Gate Bridge from San Francisco. Across the inlet from Sausalito, Tiburon and Belvedere are lined with grand homes that regularly appear on fund-raising circuits, and to the north, landlocked Mill Valley is a hub of wining and dining and tony boutiques.

In general, the farther you get from the Golden Gate Bridge, the more country things become, and West Marin is about as far as you can get from the big city, both physically and ideologically. Separated from the inland county by the slopes and ridges of giant Mt. Tamalpais, this territory beckons to mavericks, artists, ocean lovers, and other free spirits. Stinson Beach has tempered its isolationist attitude to accommodate out-of-towners, as have Inverness and Point Reyes Station. Bolinas, on the other hand, would prefer you not know its location.

SAUSALITO

2 mi north of Golden Gate Bridge.

Bougainvillea-covered hillsides and an expansive yacht harbor give Sausalito the feel of an Adriatic resort. The town sits on the northwestern edge of San Francisco Bay, where it's sheltered from the ocean by the Marin Headlands; the mostly mild weather here is perfect for strolling and outdoor dining. Nevertheless, morning fog and afternoon winds can roll over the hills without warning, funneling through the central part of Sausalito once known as Hurricane Gulch.

South on **Bridgeway** (toward San Francisco), which snakes between the bay and the hills, a waterside esplanade is lined with restaurants on piers that lure diners with good seafood and even better views. Stairs along the west side of Bridgeway climb the hill to wooded neighborhoods filled with both rustic and opulent homes. As you amble along Bridgeway past boutiques, gift shops, and galleries, you'll notice the absence of basic services. If you need an aspirin or some groceries (or if you want to see the locals), you'll have to head to Caledonia Street, which runs parallel to Bridgeway, north of the ferry terminus and inland a couple of blocks. The streets closest to the ferry landing flaunt their fair share of shops selling T-shirts and kitschy souvenirs. Venture into some of the side streets or narrow alleyways to catch a bit more of the town's taste for eccentric jewelry and handmade crafts.

■TIP→ **The ferry is the best way to get to Sausalito from San Francisco; you get more romance (and less traffic) and disembark in the heart of downtown.**

Like much of San Francisco, Sausalito had a raffish reputation before it went upscale. Discovered in 1775 by Spanish explorers and named Sausalito (Little Willow) for the trees growing around its springs, the town served as a port for whaling ships during the 19th century. By the mid-1800s wealthy San Franciscans were making Sausalito their getaway across the bay. They built lavish Victorian summer homes in the hills, many of which still stand. In 1875 the railroad from the north connected with ferryboats to San Francisco, bringing the merchant and working classes with it. This influx of hardworking, fun-loving folk polarized the town into "wharf rats" and "hill snobs," and the waterfront area grew thick with saloons, gambling dens, and bordellos. Bootleggers flourished during Prohibition, and shipyard workers swelled the town's population in the 1940s.

Sausalito developed its bohemian flair in the 1950s and '60s, when a group of artists, led by a charismatic Greek portraitist named Varda, established an artists' colony and a houseboat community here. Today more than 450 houseboats are docked in Sausalito, which has since also become a major yachting center. Some of the houseboats are ragged, others deluxe, but all are quirky (one, a miniature replica of a Persian castle, even has an elevator inside). For a close-up view of the community, head north on Bridgeway—Sausalito's main thoroughfare—from downtown, turn right on Gate Six Road, and park where it dead-ends at the public shore. Keep a respectful distance; these are homes, after all, and the residents become a bit prickly from too much ogling.

Get your bearings and find out what's happening in town at the **Sausalito Visitors Center & Historical Exhibit** (✉*780 Bridgeway* ☎*415/332–0505*), operated by the town's historical society. It's closed Monday.

The landmark **Plaza Viña del Mar** (✉*Bridgeway and Park St.*), named for Sausalito's sister city in Chile, marks the center of town. Flanked by two 14-foot-tall elephant statues (created in 1915 for the Panama-Pacific International Exposition), the fountain is a great setting for snapshots and people-watching.

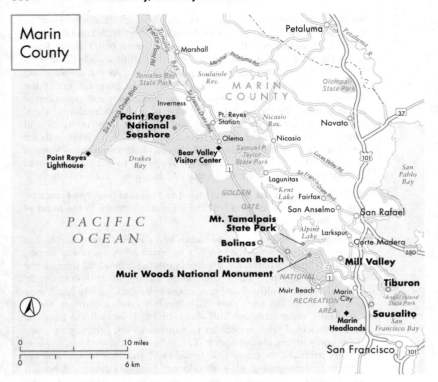

Marin County

On the waterfront between the Hotel Sausalito and the Sausalito Yacht Club is an unusual historic landmark—a **drinking fountain**. It's inscribed with HAVE A DRINK ON SALLY in remembrance of Sally Stanford, the former San Francisco madam who later became the town's mayor in the 1970s. Sassy Sally, as they called her, would have appreciated the fountain's eccentric custom attachment: a knee-level basin that reads HAVE A DRINK ON LELAND, in memory of her beloved dog.

NEED A BREAK?

Judging by the crowds gathered outside Hamburgers (⊠ *737 Bridgeway* ☎ *415/332–9471*), you'd think someone was juggling flaming torches out front. They're really gaping at the juicy hand-formed beef patties sizzling on a rotating grill. Brave the line (it moves fast), get your food to go, and head for the esplanade to enjoy the sweeping views. Hours are 11 AM to 5 PM.

An anonymous-looking World War II shipyard building holds one of Sausalito's great treasures: the sprawling (more than 1½ acres) **Bay Model** of the entire San Francisco Bay and the San Joaquin–Sacramento River delta, complete with flowing water. The U.S. Army Corps of Engineers uses the model to reproduce the rise and fall of tides, the flow of currents, and the other physical forces at work on the bay. ⊠ *2100 Bridgeway, at Marinship Way* ☎ *415/332–3870 recorded information, 415/332–3871 operator assistance* ⊕ *www.spn.usace.army.mil/bmvc*

⊠Free ⊗Memorial Day–Labor Day, Tues.–Fri. 9–4, weekends 10–5; Labor Day–Memorial Day, Tues.–Sat. 9–4.

♨ The **Bay Area Discovery Museum** fills five former military buildings with entertaining and enlightening hands-on exhibits related to science and the arts. Kids and their families can fish from a boat at the indoor wharf, imagine themselves as marine biologists in the Wave Workshop, and play outdoors at Lookout Cove, a 2½-acre bay-in-miniature made up of scaled-down sea caves, tidal pools, and even a re-created shipwreck. At Tot Zone, toddlers and preschoolers can play in an indoor-outdoor interactive area. From San Francisco, take the Alexander Avenue exit from U.S. 101 and follow signs to East Fort Baker. ⊠557 McReynolds Rd., at East Fort Baker ☎415/339–3900 ⊕www.baykidsmuseum.org ⊠$10, free 2nd Sat. each month after 1 ⊗Tues.–Fri. 9–4, weekends 10–5.

WHERE TO STAY & EAT

¢ ✕**Bridgeway Cafe.** For a straight-shooting American menu, head to this little diner-café, right on the main drag across the road from the bay. People line up on weekends for great breakfasts of pancakes and eggs and lunches of hot and cold sandwiches. Take in a view of the water or strollers while enjoying a morning croissant, well-crafted BLT, or their excellent fries. The Mediterranean dishes are also a hit—try the mixed appetizer platter or a hearty Greek salad. The café serves continuously until 5 PM. ⊠633 Bridgeway ☎415/332–3426 ⊟AE, D, MC, V ⊗No dinner.

$–$$ ✕**Fish.** If you're wondering where the locals go, this is the place. For fresh seafood, you can't beat this gleaming dockside fish house a mile north of downtown. Order at the counter, and then grab a seat by the floor-to-ceiling windows or at a picnic table on the pier, overlooking the yachts and fishing boats. Most of the sustainably caught fish is hauled in from the owner's boats, right at the dock outside. Try the ceviche, crab Louis, cioppino, barbecue oysters, or anything fresh that day that's being grilled over the oak-wood fire. Outside, kids can doodle with sidewalk chalk on the pier. ⊠350 Harbor Dr. ☎415/331–3474 ⌂Reservations not accepted ⊟No credit cards.

Fodor'sChoice

★

$$–$$$ ✕**Paradise Bay.** The views from this gem of a restaurant—which is a five-minute walk north of the tourist hub—will make you feel like you're in a secluded paradise; boats, sea kayaks, and the beautiful bay stretch before you. Outdoor seating in the Bay Area doesn't get much better than this, and the inventive, well balanced, local and organic based menu won't disappoint either. Try the Paradise Bay cioppino in a rich tomato fennel broth or the grilled organic lamb sirloin with goat cheese and garlic flan. The trio crème brûlée—espresso, mango, and coconut—is divine, as is the extensive cocktail list. This is also the perfect place for weekend brunch—the buttermilk ginger pancakes topped with banana and mango are out of this world. ⊠1200 Bridgeway, ☎415/331–3226 ⊟AE, D, MC, V

$$–$$$ ✕**Poggio.** One of the few restaurants in Sausalito to attract both food-savvy locals and tourists, Poggio serves modern Tuscan cuisine in a handsome, open-walled space that spills onto the street. Expect dishes

17

such as grilled lamb chops with roasted eggplant, braised artichokes with polenta, feather-light gnocchi, and pizzas from the open kitchen's wood-fired oven. ⊠ *777 Bridgeway* ☏ *415/332–7771* ⚓ *Reservations essential* ⊟ *AE, D, MC, V.*

$–$$$ ✕**Spinnaker.** Okay, let's not mince words: you go to Spinnaker for the view, not the food. Sure, the plain-Jane menu of seafood, steaks, and pastas is solid, but it can't compare to the spectacular waterfront setting of its contemporary glass-walled building, on a point beyond the harbor near the yacht club. If you're lucky, you can spot pelicans diving and harbor seals frolicking just outside the windows. Just don't expect to see any locals. ⊠ *100 Spinnaker Dr.* ☏ *415/332–1500* ⊟ *AE, D, DC, MC, V.*

$$–$$$ ✕**Sushi Ran.** Sushi aficionados swear this is the Bay Area's best for
★ raw fish, but don't overlook the excellent Pacific Rim fusions, a result of Japanese ingredients and French cooking techniques, served up in unusual presentations. Because Sushi Ran is so highly ranked among area foodies, book two to seven days in advance for dinner. Otherwise, expect a long wait, which you can soften by sipping one of the 45 by-the-glass sakes from the outstanding wine-and-sake bar. **If you wander in after a day of sightseeing and can't get a table, you can sup in the noisy bar.** ⊠ *107 Caledonia St.* ☏ *415/332–3620* ⊟ *AE, D, MC, V* ☻ *No lunch weekends.*

$$$$ ▦**Casa Madrona.** What began as a small inn in a 19th-century landmark house has expanded over the decades to incorporate a variety of lodgings and a full-service spa, all tiered down the hill in the center of town. The design in the original rooms and suites ranges from the cutesiness of what's called the Artist's Loft to elegant Mediterranean motifs. An adjacent three-story building contains newer rooms that are uniformly contemporary, with wet bars, sunken tubs, and bay windows; some have balconies overlooking Richardson Bay. Bay-view rooms are pricey, but the vistas are spectacular. ⊠ *801 Bridgeway,* ☏ *415/332–0502 or 800/567–9524* 🖶 *415/332–2537* ⊕ *www.casamadrona.com* ⇢ *56 rooms, 7 suites* ⚘ *In-room: no a/c, DVD (some), dial-up, Wi-Fi. In-hotel: restaurant, spa, concierge, laundry service, no-smoking rooms* ⊟ *AE, D, DC, MC, V.*

$$$$ ▦**The Inn Above Tide.** The only hotel in the Bay Area with balconies literally hanging over the water, each of its rooms has a perfect-10 view that takes in wild Angel Island as well as the city lights across the bay. In the corner Vista Suite (the most expensive room here, at nearly triple the standard-room rate), you can even watch San Francisco twinkle from the king bed. Nice touches—gardenias by the sink, large tubs, binoculars in every room, complimentary California wine and imported cheese—abound, and most rooms have wood-burning or gas fireplaces. Although it's set in the middle of town, this place is tranquil. ⊠ *30 El*

Portal, ☎*415/332–9535 or 800/893–8433* 🖷*415/332–6714* ⊕*www. innabovetide.com* ⇆*29 rooms, 2 suites* ♿*In-room: DVD, dial-up, Wi-Fi. In-hotel: concierge, laundry service, no-smoking rooms* ▤*AE, DC, MC, V* ⦿❘*CP.*

$$ **Hotel Sausalito.** Handmade furniture and tasteful original art and reproductions give this well-run inn the feel of a small European hotel. The Mediterranean-like glow comes from the soft yellow, green, and orange tones bathing the rooms, some of which have harbor or park views. Space ranges from small quarters for budget-minded travelers (a rarity in pricey Marin) to commodious suites. Best of all, it's smack-dab downtown, right next to the ferry landing and above a row of shops. ⊠*16 El Portal,* ☎*415/332–0700 or 888/442–0700* 🖷*415/332–8788* ⊕*www.hotelsausalito.com* ⇆*14 rooms, 2 suites* ♿*In-room: no a/c, VCR, dial-up, Wi-Fi. In-hotel: concierge, no-smoking rooms* ▤*AE, DC, MC, V* ⦿❘*CP.*

THE ARTS

The annual **Sausalito Art Festival** (☎*415/332–3555 or 415/331–3757* ⊕*www.sausalitoartfestival.org*), held over Labor Day weekend, attracts more than 50,000 people to the northern waterfront area; Blue & Gold Fleet ferries from San Francisco dock at the pier adjacent to the fair.

SHOPPING

Edith Caldwell Gallery. Elegant, spare, and inviting, this gallery draws passersby with its intriguing shows. You'll find a mix of figurative and still life paintings, unique objets d'art, and stunning tapestries. ⊠*819 Broadway, Sausalito* ☎*415/331–5003.*

Something/Anything Gallery. Tucked away where Broadway ends and curves toward the dock, this gallery has a huge array of jewelry and gifts, from unique watches to humorous pendants. With friendly service and carefully crafted mementos of Sausalito, it's easy to find an inexpensive souvenir. ⊠*20 Princess St., Sausalito* ☎*415/339–8831.*

TIBURON

2 mi north of Sausalito, 7 mi north of Golden Gate Bridge.

On a peninsula that was called Punta de Tiburon (Shark Point) by the Spanish explorers, this beautiful Marin County community retains the feel of a village, despite the encroachment of commercial establishments from the downtown area. The harbor faces Angel Island across Raccoon Strait, and San Francisco is directly south across the bay—which makes the views from the decks of harbor restaurants a major attraction. Tiburon is slightly more low-key than Sausalito, and the community favors Sunday brunch and cocktail hour. Since its incarnation, in 1884, when ferries from San Francisco connected the point with a railroad to San Rafael, the town has centered on the waterfront. **The ferry is the most relaxing (and fastest) way to get here whenever the weather is pleasant, particularly in summer, allowing you to avoid traffic and parking problems. Think about avoiding a midweek visit to Tiburon.**

Although there will be fewer strollers on the street, most shops close either Tuesday or Wednesday, or both.

Tiburon's narrow **Main Street** is on the bay side; you can browse the shops and galleries or relax on a restaurant's deck jutting out over the harbor.

Past the pink-brick bank building, Main Street is known as **Ark Row** (⊕*www.landmarks-society.org*) and has a tree-shaded walk lined with antiques and specialty stores.

Look closely and you can see that some of the buildings are actually old houseboats. They floated in Belvedere Cove before being beached and transformed into stores. If you're curious about architectural history, the Tiburon Heritage & Arts Commission prints a self-guided walking-tour map, which you can pick up at local businesses.

The stark-white **Old St. Hilary's Landmark and Wildflower Preserve,** an 1886 Carpenter Gothic church barged over from Strawberry Point in 1957, overlooks the town and the bay from its hillside perch. **The church is surrounded by a wildflower preserve that is spectacular in May and June, when the rare black jewel flower blooms.** Expect a steep walk uphill to reach the preserve. ⊠*201 Esperanza St., off Mar West St.* ☎*415/435–1853* ⊕*www.landmarks-society.org* ⏎*$2 suggested donation* ☉*Apr.–Oct., Wed. and Sun. 1–4 and by appointment.*

WHERE TO STAY & EAT

$–$$$ ✕ **Guaymas.** The festive Mexican restaurant at the ferry terminal claims a knockout view of the bay, handsome whitewashed adobe walls, tile floors, and a heated terrace bar—and it serves a top-notch margarita. The large open kitchen churns out a long list of fairly authentic Mexican dishes such as ceviche, *carnitas uruapan* (slow-roasted pork with salsa and black beans), mesquite-grilled fish, and tamales. **Sunday brunch is popular, so make a reservation.** ⊠*5 Main St.* ☎*415/435–6300* ⏦*Reservations essential* ▤*AE, D, DC, MC, V.*

¢–$$$ ✕ **Rooney's.** Beloved by locals, this is a Tiburon favorite. A friendly greeting will make you feel as if you're at home, as will the lanterns and polished wood floors (head inside over dining dockside). Comfort food anchors the lunch menu with choices like "New York–style" sandwiches, salads, and a few surprises such as African chicken. For dinner, choose from fresh Dungeness crab, rib-eye steak, or seasonal specials. Last orders are taken at 9 PM except on Friday and Saturday, when you have an extra half hour. ⊠*38 Main St.* ☎*415/435–1911* ▤*MC, V* ☉*No dinner Mon. and Tues.*

$$–$$$ ✕ **Sam's Anchor Cafe.** Open since 1921, this casual dockside restaurant with mahogany wainscoting is the town's most famous eatery. Today, most people flock here for the deck, where out-of-towners and old salts sit shoulder to shoulder for bay views, beer, seafood, and Ramos fizzes. The lunch menu is nothing special—burgers, sandwiches, salads, fried

fish with tartar sauce—and you'll sit on plastic chairs at tables covered with blue-and-white-checked oil cloths. At night you can find standard seafood dishes with vegetarian and meat-lovers options. Expect a wait for outside tables on weekends (there are no reservations for deck seating or weekend lunch). Mind the seagulls; they know no restraint. ⊠27 *Main St.* ☎415/435–4527 ⊟*AE, D, DC, MC, V.*

¢–$ ✕**Sweden House Bakery & Café.** A dollhouse-like, painted-wood café, this is a cozy place for pastries and coffee, a breakfast of delicious Swedish pancakes with lingonberries, or lunch (chicken salad with walnuts and Swedish meat loaf are good choices). The secluded bay-view deck is a favorite spot on sunny days. Sweden House is open until 5 weekdays, 6 on weekends, and 7 between Memorial Day and Labor Day. ⊠35 *Main St.* ☎415/435–9767 ⌑*Reservations not accepted* ⊟*MC, V* ⊗*No dinner.*

$$–$$$$ ⊡**Waters Edge Hotel.** Checking into this spacious and elegant hotel feels
★ like tucking away into a cozy retreat by the water. The views are stunning, the lighting perfect. Most rooms have a wood-burning fireplace, and many have balconies with bay views at this stylish small hotel in downtown Tiburon. Furnishings are chic and modern in cocoa and cream colors; down comforters and high-thread-count linens make the beds deliciously comfortable. High-vaulted ceilings show off the carefully placed, Asian-influenced objects, which line the hallways and front living room area. **In the morning, breakfast is delivered to your door, but take your coffee outside to the giant communal sundeck over the water; the south-facing views of San Francisco Bay are incredible.** ⊠25 *Main St.,* ☎415/789–5999 *or* 877/789–5999 🖷415/789–5888 ⊕*www.marin hotels.com* ⇌23 *rooms* ⌂*In-room: VCR, dial-up, Wi-Fi. In-hotel: concierge, laundry service, no-smoking rooms* ⊟*AE, D, DC, MC, V* ☝*CP.*

SHOPPING

The Candy Store on Main Street. If you long for sheets of candy dots or to bite the tops off wax bottles, come here to score the retro candy of your childhood. There's also ice cream, freshly made fudge, and a space-age-looking dispenser for pucker powder. ⊠7 *Main St., Tiburon* ☎415/435–0434.

Gallery 108. The window display beckons with paintings and furniture from northern China; inside, silky calligraphy brushes beg to be touched, as do the striking jewelry and imported pearls. ⊠82 *Main St., Ark Row, Tiburon* ☎415/435–2511.

MILL VALLEY

2 mi north of Sausalito, 4 mi north of Golden Gate Bridge.

One of just a few towns that are simultaneously woodsy and chic, Mill Valley has a dual personality. Here, as elsewhere in the county, the foundation is a superb natural setting. Virtually surrounded by parkland, the town lies at the base of Mt. Tamalpais, the Bay Area's tallest mountain, and includes dense redwood groves traversed by countless creeks. But this is no lumber camp. Smart restaurants and chichi bou-

17

tiques line the streets, and more rock stars than one might suspect make their homes here.

The small downtown area, no more than five blocks square, has the constant bustle of a leisure community; even at noon on a Tuesday, people are out shopping for fancy cookware and lacy pajamas.

In the center of it all is **Lytton Square,** at the corner of Miller and Throckmorton avenues, where locals and visitors congregate on weekends to socialize in the many coffeehouses.

To see one of the numerous outdoor oases that make Mill Valley so appealing, follow Throckmorton Avenue ¼ mi south from Lytton Square to **Old Mill Park,** a shady patch of redwoods that shelters a playground, a reconstructed sawmill, and a reproduction passenger car from the Mt. Tam railway. From the park, Cascade Drive winds its way past creek-side homes to the trailheads of several forest paths.

WHERE TO STAY & EAT

¢–$ ✕ **Emporio Rulli.** Take the 10-minute drive from Mill Valley to this Ital-
Fodor'sChoice ian pastry shop and café in Larkspur, and you'll swear you've passed
★ through a portal to Italy. Everything here is made from scratch, from the house-roasted coffee and fresh-baked panettone to the delicious gelato. At lunch, a small menu of daily specials rounds out the Italian sandwiches, which you can enjoy at sidewalk tables or within the gorgeous shop that spills from one elegant room to the next, decorated with dark wood, swag curtains, finial finishes, and even a Venetian mural. ⊠464 *Magnolia Ave., Larkspur* ☎415/924–7478 ⚑*Reservations not accepted* ▤*AE, MC, V* ☉*No dinner.*

$$–$$$ ✕ **Frantoio.** If you love olive oil, you'll go nuts for this cavernous trattoria, where, during olive-harvesting season (late fall into early winter), you can watch an authentic stone olive mill churn out deliciously fruity oil that fills the little bottles on every table. On the menu, look for roasted meats, fresh fish, and pizzas from the oak-wood-fired brick oven, as well as terrific house-made pastas. The place is most fun in olive season, but the food is good year-round. **Be forewarned: the giant space gets crashingly loud when full.** ⊠152 *Shoreline Hwy.* ☎415/289–5777 ▤*AE, D, DC, MC, V* ☉*No lunch.*

$$$–$$$$ ✕ **Lark Creek Inn.** Occupying a refurbished 100-year-old house sur-
★ rounded by lush, mature gardens and towering redwoods, this is one of Marin's prettiest—and best—restaurants, especially for Sunday brunch. The menu, which changes daily, is new American and highlights topnotch meats and organic produce from local farmers. The Caesar salad boasts a secret ingredient and is succulently presented with whole leaf spears. The signature dessert, butterscotch pudding, sounds humble but has a sumptuous flavor. Sit outside on the patio or inside the country-elegant dining room beneath a dramatic greenhouse ceiling. Be mindful that all this beauty of place and plate comes at a price. ⊠234 *Magnolia Ave., Larkspur* ☎415/924–7766 ⚑*Reservations essential* ▤*AE, MC, V* ☉*No lunch Mon.–Sat.*

$$–$$$ ✕ **Left Bank.** Provincial France meets Northern California at this convivial, bustling brasserie with a gigantic stone hearth and whimsical

French posters. The menu packs in hearty dishes such as bouillabaisse, braised oxtail with homemade noodles, steak and french fries, and a succulent fondue of local goat, Brie, and blue cheeses. For dessert, you'll have to go to Lyon to find better profiteroles. The service can be erratic, and the plank floors and high ceilings can make things noisy, but this place is fun. **For quieter conversation and maximum romance, sit outside on the wraparound veranda.** Check the Web site for special event dinners, such as tie-ins to celebrations of cookbooks by local writers or evenings that include live music. ⊠*507 Magnolia Ave., Larkspur* ☎*415/927–3331* ⊟*AE, MC, V.*

$$-$$$ ✕**Picco.** If you're in the mood for fantastically original food and feeling slyly glamorous, head to Picco, which prides itself on its "exotic organic flavors" and "dangerous cocktails." Dramatic lighting and modernist decor set the stage. The food shines, from a plate of miniburgers with sautéed onions and Point Reyes blue cheese to artfully presented roasted vegetables. **If there's a long wait, start with small dishes at the bar or try the Picco Pizzeria and Wineshop next door.** ⊠*320 Magnolia Ave.* ☎*415/924–0300* ⊟*AE, MC, V.*

$$-$$$$ ✕🗖**Mountain Home Inn.** Abutting 40,000 acres of state and national
★ parks, the inn sits on the skirt of Mt. Tamalpais, where you can follow hiking trails all the way to Stinson Beach. The inn's multilevel, airy wooden building nests high up in the trees, with pristine wilderness on one side and an unparalleled view of the bay on the other. Rooms are built for romance, each mixing huge views with some combination of balcony, fireplace, and whirlpool tub. **For full-moon nights book far in advance.** The on-site wine bar and dining room (closed Monday and Tuesday) serves lunch on the deck (May to October) and a terrific $38 prix-fixe dinner of American regional cuisine inside by the fire. The restaurant (reservations recommended) serves sumptuous meals with spectacular views. Top your Niman Ranch beef burger with caramelized onions, roasted red peppers, local blue cheese, and a range of other options. There's a late-afternoon American cheese tasting course, as well as an après-trek menu of small plates for hungry hikers. Dinner features modern riffs on classic American fare. ⊠*810 Panoramic Hwy.,* ☎*415/381–9000* 🖷*415/381–3615* ⊕*www.mtnhomeinn.com* ➳*10 rooms* ⚥*In-room: no a/c, no TV, Wi-Fi (some). In-hotel: restaurant, bar, no-smoking rooms* ⊟*AE, MC, V* ❑*BP.*

$$-$$$$ 🗖**Mill Valley Inn.** The only hotel in downtown Mill Valley has smart-looking rooms done up in Tuscan colors of ocher and olive, with hand-crafted beds, armoires, and lamps by local artisans. Beds are made with crisp white linens, starkly contrasting the deep browns and greens of the towering redwoods just outside the windows. There's also a small spa next door. Some rooms are not accessible via elevator. ⊠*165 Throckmorton Ave.,* ☎*415/389–6608 or 800/595–2100* 🖷*415/389–5051* ⊕*www.marinhotels.com* ➳*25 rooms, 1 suite, 2 cottages* ⚥*In-room: Wi-Fi. In-hotel: no elevator (some), laundry service, no-smoking rooms* ⊟*AE, D, DC, MC, V* ❑*CP.*

17

NIGHTLIFE & THE ARTS

The **Mill Valley Fall Arts Festival** (☎415/383–5256 ⊕ *www.mvfaf. org*) takes place in mid-September in Old Mill Park, with live music, a kids' stage, and artisans selling crafts, jewelry, and art.

SHOPPING

The area around Throckmorton Avenue in downtown Mill Valley brims with stylish and quirky stores—indies as well as chains. One of the chains, Banana Republic, actually began life here as a small safari-focused retailer.

WORD OF MOUTH

"Mountain Home Inn is perfect [since] it is just above Muir Woods, in fact there is a trail down to Muir Woods just across the street from Mountain Home. It's 1,000 feet down, over a mile, steep but the trail is good, with wooden steps . . .."

–sequoia370

Book Passage. This sprawling independent bookstore, in nearby Corte Madera, is a magnet for book lovers. The calendar of author events is packed with readings by such big names as Alice Walker, Calvin Trillin, Michael Connelly, and Peter Mayle. Pick-me-up snacks are available at the in-store café. ⊠ *The Marketplace, 51 Tamal Vista Blvd., Corte Madera* ☎415/927–0960 or 800/999–7909.

Maison Reve. French farmhouse meets contemporary style here. Clusters of interesting objects, such as vintage glass bottles, gather gracefully in vignettes. The price range is admirable, with unique finds possible at a reasonable cost. Head downstairs for charming children's gifts. ⊠ *11 Throckmorton Ave., Mill Valley* ☎415/383–9700.

THE MARIN HEADLANDS

★ The term "Golden Gate" may now be synonymous with the world-famous bridge, but it originally referred to the grassy, poppy-strewn hills flanking the passageway into San Francisco Bay. To the north of the gate lie the **Marin Headlands,** part of the Golden Gate National Recreation Area (GGNRA) and the most dramatic scenery in these parts. The raw beauty of the headlands, which consist of several small but steep bluffs, is particularly striking if you've just come from the enclosed silence of the nearby redwood groves. Windswept hills plunge down to the ocean, and creek-fed thickets shelter swaying wildflowers.

The headlands stretch from the Golden Gate Bridge to Muir Beach. Photographers flock to the southern headlands for shots of the city, with the Golden Gate Bridge in the foreground and the skyline on the horizon. Equally remarkable are the views north along the coast and out to sea, where the Farallon Islands are visible on clear days. **Almost any of the roads, all very windy, offer great coast views, especially as you drive at higher elevations. You'll see copious markers for scenic spots.**

The headlands' strategic position at the mouth of San Francisco Bay made them a logical site for World War II military installations. Today you can explore the crumbling concrete batteries where naval guns protected the approaches from the sea; kids especially love climbing on these structures. The headlands' main attractions are centered on Forts Barry and Cronkhite, which lie just across Rodeo Lagoon from each other. Fronting the lagoon is Rodeo Beach, a dark stretch of sand that attracts sand-castle builders and dog owners.

⚠ Note: the beaches at the Marin Headlands aren't safe for swimming. The giant cliffs are steep and unstable, so hiking down them can be dangerous. Stay on trails. Head farther north, to Muir Beach and beyond, for better ocean access.

The **Marin Headlands Visitor Center** (⊠ *Fort Barry, Field and Bunker Rds., Bldg. 948* ☎*415/331–1540* ⊕*www.nps.gov/goga/marin-headlands. htm*), open daily 9:30–4:30, sells a useful guide to historic sites and wildlife and has exhibits on the area's history and ecology. Pick up the park newspaper, which lists a calendar of events, including a schedule of guided walks. Kids will enjoy the "please touch" educational sites and small play area inside.

☼ At the end of Conzelman Road, in the southern headlands, is the **Point ★ Bonita Lighthouse,** a restored beauty that still guides ships to safety with its original 1855 refractory lens. Half the fun of a visit is the steep ½-mi walk from the parking area down to the lighthouse, which takes you through a rock tunnel and across a suspension bridge. Signposts along the way detail the bravado of surfmen, as the early lifeguards were called, and the tenacity of the "wickies," the first keepers of the light. ⊠*End of Conzelman Rd.* ☎*Free* ☉*Sat.–Mon. 12:30–3:30.*

If you're an art lover, stop by the **Headlands Center for the Arts** (⊠*944 Fort Barry* ☎*415/331–2787* ⊕*www.headlands.org* ☉ *Weekdays 10– 5, Sun. noon–5*), where you can see contemporary art in a rustic natural setting. All but one of the center's nine converted military buildings are usually closed to the public, but you can visit the main building (the former barracks) to see several changing installations. The downstairs "archive room" features an odd assortment of objects found and created by residents, such as natural rocks, interesting glass bottles filled with collected items, and unusual masks. Stop by the industrial gallery space, two flights up, to see what the resident visual artists are up to—most of the work is quite contemporary. The center also hosts biweekly public programs, from artist talks to open studios. Call for current schedules.

Small but scenic, **Muir Beach,** a rocky patch of shoreline off Route 1 in the northern headlands, is a good place to stretch your legs and gaze out at the Pacific. Locals often walk their dogs here, and anglers and boogie boarders share the gentle surf. Families and cuddling couples come for picnicking and sunbathing. At one end of the sand is a cluster of waterfront homes, and at the other are the bluffs of Golden Gate National Recreation Area.

WHERE TO STAY & EAT

$$–$$$$ ✕▥ **Pelican Inn.** From its slate roof to its whitewashed plaster walls, this ★ inn looks so Tudor that it's hard to believe it was built in the 1970s. The Pelican is English to the core, with its smallish guest rooms upstairs

(no elevator), high half-tester beds draped in heavy fabrics, and bangers and grilled tomatoes for breakfast. Downstairs, the little pub pours ales and ports, and "the snug" is a private fireplace lounge for overnight guests. At dinner in the tavernlike or solarium dining rooms ($$–$$$), keep it simple with fish-and-chips, roasted hen, or prime rib and focus on the well-crafted wine list. Lunch is served, too...a good thing, since your nearest alternatives are miles away via slow, winding roads. ⊠*10 Pacific Way, off Rte. 1, Muir Beach* ☎*415/383–6000* 🖷*415/383–3424* ⊕*www.pelicaninn.com* ⏃*7 rooms* ⏃*In-room: no a/c, no phone, no TV. In-hotel: restaurant, bar, no elevator* 🖃*MC, V* ⦿*BP.*

¢ ▦**Marin Headlands Hostel.** As hostels go, it's hard to beat this beautifully located, well-maintained property in a valley on the north side of the headlands. This is also the only lodging in the GGNRA that isn't a campsite. Accommodations, inside the old military infirmary, consist of private rooms with space for up to five, or shared dorm-style rooms that sleep six to 22 people in bunk beds. Cook your own food in the communal kitchen and eat at a table in the giant common area near the woodstove; big windows look out onto stands of pine and eucalyptus. Couples can share rooms in a separate two-story house made cozy with couches in some rooms, comfortable wooden tables, and forest views. Don't miss the map of the world, which reaches over a corner and across two walls in the main house. ⊠*941 Fort Barry,* ☎*415/331–2777* ⊕*www.norcalhostels.org/marin* ⏃*7 private rooms, 8 dormitory rooms, all with shared bath* ⏃*In-room: no a/c, no phone, no TV. In-hotel: no elevator, laundry facilities, no-smoking rooms* 🖃*D, MC, V.*

MUIR WOODS NATIONAL MONUMENT

Fodor'sChoice
★ *12 mi northwest of the Golden Gate Bridge.*

One hundred fifty million years ago ancestors of redwood and sequoia trees grew throughout the United States. Today the *Sequoia sempervirens* can be found only in a narrow, cool coastal belt from Monterey to Oregon. The 550 acres of Muir Woods National Monument contain some of the most majestic redwoods in the world—some nearly 250 feet tall and 1,000 years old. The stand was saved from destruction in 1905, when it was purchased by a couple who donated it to the federal government. Three years later it was named after naturalist John Muir, whose environmental campaigns helped to establish the national park system. His response: "This is the best tree lover's monument that could be found in all of the forests of the world. Saving these woods from the ax and saw is in many ways the most notable service to God and man I have heard of since my forest wandering began."

Muir Woods, part of the Golden Gate National Recreation Area, is a pedestrian's park. The trails vary in difficulty and distance. Beginning from the park headquarters, a 2-mi, wheelchair-accessible **loop trail** crosses streams and passes ferns and azaleas, as well as magnificent redwood groves. Among the most famous are **Bohemian Grove** and the circular formation called **Cathedral Grove**. On summer weekends visitors oohing and aahing in a dozen languages line the trail. If you prefer a little more serenity, consider the challenging **Dipsea Trail,** which climbs west from the forest floor to soothing views of the ocean and the Golden Gate Bridge. For a complete list of trails, check with rangers, who can also help you pick the best one for your ability level.

■TIP➜ **The weather in Muir Woods is usually cool and often wet, so wear warm clothes and shoes appropriate for damp trails.** Picnicking and camping aren't allowed, and pets aren't permitted. Parking can be difficult here—the lots are small and the crowds are large—so try to come early in the morning or late in the afternoon. The **Muir Woods Visitor Center** has a wide selection of books and exhibits on redwood trees and the history of Muir Woods.

To get here from San Francisco, take U.S. 101 north across the Golden Gate Bridge to the Mill Valley/Stinson Beach exit and then follow signs to Highway 1 north. On weekends, Memorial Day through Labor Day, Golden Gate Transit operates a free shuttle from Mill Valley every half hour. Park in Marin City at the Gateway Shopping Center (look for lighted signs directing you from U.S. 101) or at the Manzanita Park-and-Ride, at the Highway 1 exit off U.S. 101 (look for the lot under the elevated freeway), or take connecting bus service from San Francisco with Golden Gate Transit. At this writing, there were plans to expand the service to year-round operation; call ahead. ⊠*Panoramic Hwy. off Hwy. 1, approximately 12 mi north of Golden Gate Bridge* ☎*415/388–2595 park information, 415/921–5858 shuttle information* ⊕*www.nps.gov/muwo* 🎟️*$5* ☉*Daily 8* AM–*sunset.*

17

MT. TAMALPAIS STATE PARK

16 mi northwest of Golden Gate Bridge.

Although the summit of Mt. Tamalpais is only 2,571 feet high, the mountain rises practically from sea level, dominating the topography of Marin County. Adjacent to Muir Woods National Monument, Mt. Tamalpais State Park affords views of the entire Bay Area and the Pacific Ocean to the west. The mountain was sacred to Native Americans, who saw in its profile—as you can see today—the silhouette of a sleeping Indian maiden. Locals fondly refer to it as the "Sleeping Lady." For years the 6,300-acre park has been a favorite destination for hikers. There are more than 200 mi of trails, some rugged but many developed for easy walking through meadows, grasslands, and forests and along creeks. Mt. Tam, as it's called by locals, is also the birthplace (in the 1970s) of mountain biking, and today many spandex-clad bikers whiz down the park's winding roads.

The park's major thoroughfare, the Panoramic Highway, snakes its way up from U.S. 101 to the **Pantoll Ranger Station** (✉ *3801 Panoramic Hwy., at Pantoll Rd.* ☎ *415/388–2070* ⊕ *www.parks.ca.gov*). The office is staffed sporadically, depending on funding, but if you leave a phone message, a ranger will call you back (within several days) during business hours. From the ranger station, the Panoramic Highway drops down to the town of Stinson Beach. Pan Toll Road branches off the highway at the station, connecting up with Ridgecrest Boulevard. Along these roads are numerous parking areas, picnic spots, scenic overlooks, and trailheads. Parking is free along the roadside, but there's a fee at the ranger station and at some of the other parking lots.

> WORD OF MOUTH

"If it's a nice day, the road to Muir Woods and Stinson Beach will be very crowded. I would simply spend the day on Point Reyes and count on spending a long time on the highway for the return to SF."

—mkessler

STINSON BEACH

20 mi northwest of Golden Gate Bridge.

Stinson Beach is the most expansive stretch of sand in Marin County. It's as close (when the fog hasn't rolled in) as you can get to the stereotypical feel of a Southern California beach. ⚠ Swimming here is recommended only from early May through September, when lifeguards are on duty, because the undertow can be strong and shark sightings, although infrequent, aren't unusual. There are several clothing-optional areas (such as Red Rock Beach). On any hot summer weekend every road to Stinson Beach is jam-packed, so factor this into your plans. The town itself is very down to earth—like tonier Mill Valley, but more relaxed.

WHERE TO STAY & EAT

$–$$$ ✕ **Parkside Cafe.** Most people know the Parkside for its beachfront snack bar (cash only), but inside is the best restaurant in Stinson Beach. The food is classic Cal cuisine, with appetizers such as day-boat scallops ceviche and mains such as lamb with goat-cheese-stuffed red peppers. Breakfast, a favorite among locals, is served until 2 PM. Eat on the sunny patio, which is sheltered from the wind by creeping vines, or by the fire in the contemporary dining room. ✉ *43 Arenal Ave.* ☎ *415/868–1272* ▭ *MC, V.*

$–$$ ✕ **Sand Dollar.** The town's oldest restaurant still attracts all the old salts from Muir Beach to Bolinas, but these days they sip whiskey over an up-to-date bar or beneath market umbrellas on the spiffy deck. The food is good—panfried sand dabs (small flatfish) and pear salad with blue cheese—but the big draw is the lively atmosphere. Musicians play weekends in summer, and on sunny afternoons, the deck gets so packed that people sit on the fence rails, sipping beer. ✉ *3458 Rte. 1* ☎ *415/868–0434* ▭ *AE, MC, V* ☺ *No lunch Tues. Nov.–Mar.*

¢–$$$ ⚏**Stinson Beach Motel.** Built in the 1930s, this motel surrounds three courtyards that burst with flowering greenery. Rooms are immaculate, simple, and summery, with freshly painted walls, good mattresses, and some kitchenettes. The motel is on the main drag, so it's convenient to everything in town, but it can get loud on busy summer weekend days. **Room 3 has the most privacy, though all rooms face a central courtyard, not the street.** Weekday room rates ($85–$125) are a bargain for the north coast. ⊠*3416 Hwy. 1,* ☎*415/868–1712* 🖷*415/868–1790* ⊕*www. stinsonbeachmotel.com* ⇦*7 rooms* ⌂*In-room: no a/c, no phone, kitchen (some). In-hotel: no elevator* ⊟*D, MC, V.*

BOLINAS

7 mi north of Stinson Beach.

The tiny town of Bolinas wears its 1960s idealism on its sleeve, attracting potters, poets, and peace lovers to its quiet streets. With a funky gallery, a general store selling organic produce, a café, and an offbeat saloon, the main thoroughfare, Wharf Road, looks like a hippie-fied version of Main Street USA. Although privacy-seeking locals openly dislike tourism and have torn down signs to the town, Bolinas isn't difficult to find: heading north from Stinson Beach on Route 1, make a left at the first road just past the Bolinas Lagoon (Bolinas-Olema Road), and then turn left at the stop sign. **The road dead-ends smack-dab in the middle of the tiny town, so drive slowly lest you find yourself in a confrontation with an angry local.**

WHERE TO EAT

$–$$ ✕**Coast Cafe.** Decked out in a nautical theme with surfboards and buoys, the dining room at the casual Coast serves dependably good American fare, including specials such as shepherd's pie, pot roast, local fresh fish, grass-fed steaks, and gorgeous salads. It's also open for breakfast on weekends. ⊠*46 Wharf Rd.* ☎*415/868–2298* ⊟*AE, D, DC, MC, V.*

POINT REYES NATIONAL SEASHORE

Fodor'sChoice   *Bear Valley Visitor Center is 12 mi north of Bolinas.*

★

One of the Bay Area's most spectacular treasures and the only national seashore on the West Coast, the 66,500-acre **Point Reyes National Seashore** (⊕*www.nps.gov/pore*) encompasses hiking trails, secluded beaches, and rugged grasslands as well as **Point Reyes,** a triangular peninsula that juts into the Pacific. The town itself is a quaint, one-main-drag affair, with a charming bakery, some good gift shops with imported goods, and a few places to eat. It's nothing fancy, but that's part of its relaxed charm.

In the southernmost part of Point Reyes National Seashore, accessed through Bolinas, is the free **Point Reyes Bird Observatory** (*[PRBO]* ⊠*Mesa Rd.* ☎*415/868–0655* ⊕*www.prbo.org*). Those not interested in birds might find it ho-hum, but birders adore it. The compact visitor center, open daily 9–5, is small yet has excellent interpretive exhibits,

17

including a comparative display of real birds' talons. What really warrants a visit, though, are the surrounding woods, which harbor nearly 225 bird species. As you hike the quiet trails through forest and along ocean cliffs, you're likely to see biologists banding birds to aid in the study of their life cycles.

Mile-long **Duxbury Reef** is the largest shale intertidal reef in North America. Look for starfish, barnacles, sea anemones, purple urchins, limpets, sea mussels, and the occasional abalone. But check a tide table (www.wrh.noaa.gov/mtr/marine.php) or the local papers if you plan to explore the reef—it's accessible only at low tide. To get here, take Mesa Road and turn left onto Overlook Drive and then right on Elm Avenue.

The **Bear Valley Visitor Center** (⊠ *Bear Valley Rd. west of Rte. 1* ☎*415/464–5100*), open weekdays 9–5 and weekends 8–5, has informative exhibits about the park wildlife. Rangers here dispense information about beaches, whale-watching, hiking trails, and camping. The infamous San Andreas Fault runs along the eastern edge of the park and up the center of Tomales Bay; take the short **Earthquake Trail** from the visitor center to see the impact near the epicenter of the 1906 earthquake that devastated San Francisco. A ½-mi path from the visitor center leads to **Kule Loklo,** a brilliantly reconstructed Miwok village that sheds light on the daily lives of the region's first inhabitants. From here, trails also lead to the park's free campgrounds (camping permits are required).

⟳ The **Point Reyes Lighthouse** (⊠ *Western end of Sir Francis Drake Blvd.*
★   ☎*415/669–1534* ⊘*Thurs.–Mon. 10–4:30; weather lens room 2:30–4, except during very windy weather*), in operation since December 1, 1870, is one of the premier attractions of the Point Reyes National Seashore. It occupies the tip of Point Reyes, 22 mi from the Bear Valley Visitor Center, a scenic 45-minute drive over hills scattered with old cattle ranches. The lighthouse originally cast a rotating beam lighted by four wicks that burned lard oil. Keeping the wicks lighted and the lens soot-free in Point Reyes's perpetually foggy climate was a constant struggle that reputedly drove the early attendants to alcoholism and insanity. On busy whale-watching weekends (late December through mid-April), parking at the forged-iron-plate lighthouse may be restricted by park staff; on these days buses shuttle visitors from the Drakes Beach lot to the top of the stairs leading down to the lighthouse (bus $5, admission free). Once there, consider whether you have it in you to walk down—and up—the 308 steps to the lighthouse. The view from the bottom is worth the effort, but the whales are visible from the cliffs above the lighthouse. ▪TIP➜ **In late winter and spring, wildlife enthusiasts should make a stop at Chimney Rock, just before the lighthouse, and take the short walk to the Elephant Seal Overlook.** Even from up on the cliff, the males look enormous as they spar for the resident females.

WHERE TO STAY & EAT

¢–$ ✕**Pine Cone Diner.** For California country-kitchen cooking, you can't beat the Pine Cone. A block off the main drag, this oh-so-cute diner serves great traditional breakfasts as well as Mexican specialties such as huevos rancheros. At lunch expect hearty homemade soups, crunchy salads, and thick sandwiches, all made with local, organic ingredients. The dinner menu has a good selection of comfort food. **Kids love the outdoor picnic tables.** ⊠60 4th St., Point Reyes Station ☎415/663–1536 ⊟No credit cards ⊗No dinner.

$–$$$ ✕**Station House Cafe.** In good weather hikers fresh from the park fill the garden to enjoy alfresco dining, and on weekends there's not a spare seat on the banquettes in the wide-open dining room. The focus is on traditional American food—fresh popovers hit the table as soon as you arrive—and there's a little of everything on the menu. Grilled salmon, barbecued oysters, and burgers are all predictable hits. The place is also open for breakfast, and there's a full bar, too. ⊠11180 Rte. 1, Point Reyes Station ☎415/663–1515 ⊟AE, D, MC, V ⊗Closed Wed.

¢–$ ✕**Tomales Bay Foods and Indian Peach Food.** A renovated hay barn off
★ the main drag houses this collection of food shops, a favorite stopover among Bay Area foodies. Watch workers making Cowgirl Creamery cheese; then buy some at a counter that sells exquisite artisanal cheeses from around the world. Tomales Bay Foods showcases local organic fruits and vegetables and premium packaged foods, and the kitchen at Indian Peach Food turns the best ingredients into creative sandwiches, salads, and soups. You can eat at a small café table or on the lawn, or take it away for a picnic. The shops are open until 6 PM. ⊠80 4th St., Point Reyes Station ☎415/663–9335 cheese shop, 415/663–8478 deli ⊟MC, V ⊗Closed Mon. and Tues.

$$ ✕🏠**Olema Inn & Restaurant.** Built in 1876, the inn retains all of its 19th-century architectural charm but has been decorated in a sophisticated, uncluttered style. The spartan, understated rooms have antique armoires and sumptuous beds with crisp linens; the white-tile baths have gleaming fixtures. But the main attraction is the top-notch Northern California cooking served in the restaurant ($$$, reservations essential). The preparations of organic, local, and free-range ingredients include fresh oysters, pork chops with apple-cider glaze, and house-made ricotta gnocchi. ■TIP➔**Come on Monday, locals' night, when the place hops with live music and you can browse through a delectable small-plates menu.** ⊠10000 Sir Francis Drake Blvd., Olema ☎415/663–9559 ⊟415/663–8783 ⊕www.theolemainn.com ⏴6 rooms ⟀In-room: no a/c, no phone. In-hotel: no elevator, some pets allowed, no-smoking rooms ⊟AE, MC, V ⊗No lunch weekdays. Closed Tues.

$$$–$$$$ 🏠**Blackthorne Inn.** There's no other inn quite like the Blackthorne, a combination of whimsy and sophistication tucked on a hill in the woods. The giant tree-house-like structure has spiral staircases, a 3,500-square-foot deck, and a fireman's pole. The solarium was made with timbers from San Francisco wharves, and the outer walls are salvaged doors from a railway station. The best room is aptly named the Eagle's Nest, perched as it is in the glass-sheathed octagonal tower that crowns the inn. ⊠266 Vallejo Ave., Inverness Park ☎415/663–8621

⊕*www.blackthorneinn.com* ⤴*3 rooms, 1 suite* ⚬*In-room: no a/c, no phone, no TV. In-hotel: restaurant, no elevator, no kids under 14, no-smoking rooms* ▤*MC, V* ⟰*BP.*

$$ **Inverness Valley Inn.** Nestled within a 15-acre valley on the north end of town, this secluded getaway offers private cabins with plenty of room and peace and quiet. All of the cabins have their own entrances with patios that are perfect for sunset barbeques and leisurely breakfasts. The cabins are modern and well-lit, with large windows and impressive skylights. They're ideal for families who want extra space and a kitchen (or kitchenette) for cooking. In the back of the property there are chickens, sheep, and goats for those in need of a taste of farm life. ⊠*13275 Sir Francis Drake Blvd., Inverness* ☎*415/669–7250* ⊕*www.invernessvalleyinn.com* ⤴*20 cabins* ⚬*In-room: kitchen, Wi-Fi. In-hotel: tennis courts, pool, spa, no elevator, some pets allowed, no-smoking rooms* ▤*AE, MC, V*

$–$$ **Motel Inverness.** This roadside row of rooms has everything a small-town motel should offer: friendly management; spotless, thoughtfully maintained accommodations (some quite small); and extras that add real value. Some rooms have a small kitchen with cooking utensils. The lodge, a window-lined common room with skylighted cathedral ceiling, has a fireplace, big-screen TV, billiards table, kitchenette, and well-maintained fish tank. Sliding glass doors open to a deck overlooking Tomales Bay. For $400, you can have the two-story suite (sleeps four) and its two decks, full kitchen, fireplace, and jetted tub; $500 rents you the ornate Dacha, a three-bedroom Russian-style house on stilts over the bay. ⊠*12718 Sir Francis Drake Blvd., Inverness* ☎*415/669–1081 or 888/669–6909* ⎙*415/669–1906* ⊕*www.motelinverness.com* ⤴*7 rooms, 2 suites, 1 house* ⚬*In-room: no a/c, no phone, kitchen (some). In-hotel: no elevator, no-smoking rooms* ▤*MC, V.*

$$ **Ten Inverness Way.** This is the kind of down-to-earth place where you sit around after breakfast and share tips for hiking Point Reyes. The living room of this low-key inn has a stone fireplace and library. Some rooms have dormer ceilings with skylights; patchwork quilts, folksy murals, and well-worn antiques are among the homespun touches. Wine and cheese and fresh-baked cookies are nice extras. **The innkeepers also lead guided hikes of the park.** No children under 12, except in the suite. ⊠*10 Inverness Way, Inverness* ☎*415/669–1648* ⎙*415/669–7403* ⊕*www.teninvernessway.com* ⤴*4 rooms, 1 suite* ⚬*In-room: no a/c, no phone, no TV. In-hotel: restaurant, no elevator, no kids under 12, no-smoking rooms* ▤*D, MC, V* ⟰*BP.*

SPORTS & THE OUTDOORS

Blue Waters Kayaking (⊠*12938 Sir Francis Drake Blvd., Inverness* ☎*415/669–2600* ⊕*www.bwkayak.com*) rents kayaks and offers tours and lessons. **Five Brooks Stable** (⊠*8001 Hwy. 1, Olema* ☎*415/663–1570* ⊕*www.fivebrooks.com*) rents horses and equipment. Trails from the stables wind through Point Reyes National Seashore and along the beaches. Rides run from one to six hours and cost $50–$240.

MARIN COUNTY ESSENTIALS

To research prices, get advice from other travelers, and book travel arrangements, visit www.fodors.com.

BOAT & FERRY TRAVEL

The Golden Gate Ferry crosses the bay to Sausalito from the south wing of San Francisco's Ferry Building (at Market Street and the Embarcadero). Blue & Gold Fleet ferries depart daily for Sausalito and Tiburon from Pier 41 at Fisherman's Wharf; weekday commuter ferries leave from the Ferry Building for Tiburon. The trip to Sausalito takes 30 minutes; to Tiburon takes 20 minutes. Seas can be choppy, but the ride is not long, and you can expect more crowds on weekends and during peak commute times.

The Angel Island–Tiburon Ferry sails across the strait to the island daily April through September and weekends the rest of the year.

Boat & Ferry Lines **Angel Island–Tiburon Ferry** (☎ 415/435–2131 ⊕ www.angel islandferry.com). **Blue & Gold Fleet** (☎ 415/705–5555 ⊕ www.blueandgoldfleet. com). **Golden Gate Ferry** (☎ 415/923–2000 ⊕ www.goldengateferry.org).

BUS TRAVEL

Golden Gate Transit buses travel to Sausalito, Tiburon, and Mill Valley from 1st and Mission streets as well as from other points in San Francisco. For Mt. Tamalpais State Park, take Bus 10, 70, or 80 to Marin City; in Marin City transfer to Golden Gate Transit Bus 63 (weekends and holidays, mid-March through early December only). To reach points in West Marin (i.e., Bolinas, Point Reyes Station, and the edge of Mt. Tamalpais State Park) on weekdays only, take West Marin Stagecoach vans from Marin City; call for routes and schedules. San Francisco Muni Bus 76 runs hourly from 4th and Townsend streets to the Marin Headlands Visitor Center on Sunday and major holidays only. The trip takes roughly 45 minutes.

Bus Lines **Golden Gate Transit** (☎ 415/923–2000 ⊕ www.goldengate.org). **San Francisco Muni** (☎ 415/673–6864 ⊕ www.sfmuni.com). **West Marin Stagecoach** (☎ 415/526–3239 ⊕ www.marin-stagecoach.org).

SIGHTSEEING GUIDES

Blue & Gold Fleet has a one-hour narrated tour of the San Francisco Bay, for $22, with frequent daily departures from Pier 39 in San Francisco. Super Sightseeing offers a four-hour bus tour of Muir Woods. The tour, which stops in Sausalito en route, leaves at 9 AM and 2 PM daily from North Point and Taylor Street at Fisherman's Wharf and costs $46 ($45 senior citizens, $24 ages 5–11); 24-hour advance reservations are recommended. Great Pacific Tour Co. runs four-hour morning and afternoon tours of Muir Woods and Sausalito for $49 ($47 senior citizens, $39 ages 5–11), with hotel pickup in 14-passenger vans with excellent interpretation.

By Bus & Van **Blue & Gold Fleet** (☎ 415/705–5555 ⊕ www.blueandgoldfleet.com). **Great Pacific Tour Co.** (☎ 415/626–4499 ⊕ www.greatpacifictour.com). **Super Sightseeing** (☎ 415/777–2288 or 888/868–7788 ⊕ www.supersightseeing.com).

VISITOR INFORMATION
Information **Marin County Visitors Bureau** (✉ *1013 Larkspur Landing Circle, Larkspur* ☎ *866/925-2060* ⊕ *www.visitmarin.org*). **Mill Valley Chamber of Commerce** (✉ *85 Throckmorton Ave.* ☎ *415/388-9700* ⊕ *www.millvalley.org*). **Sausalito Chamber of Commerce** (✉ *780 Bridgeway* ☎ *415/332-0505 or 415/331-7262* ⊕ *www.sausalito.org*). **Tiburon Peninsula Chamber of Commerce** (✉ *96-B Main St.* ☎ *415/435-5633* ⊕ *www.tiburonchamber.org*).

THE EAST BAY

OAKLAND

Directly east of Bay Bridge.

Often overshadowed by San Francisco's beauty and Berkeley's offbeat antics, Oakland's allure lies in its amazing diversity. Here you can find a Nigerian clothing store, a beautifully renovated Victorian home, a Buddhist meditation center, and a lively salsa club, all within the same block. Oakland's multifaceted nature reflects its colorful and often tumultuous history. Once a cluster of Mediterranean-style homes and gardens that served as a bedroom community for San Francisco, the city became a hub of shipbuilding and industry almost overnight when the United States entered World War II. New jobs in the city's shipyards and factories attracted thousands of workers, including some of the first female welders, and the city's neighborhoods were imbued with a proud but gritty spirit. In the 1960s and '70s this intense community pride gave rise to such militant groups as the Black Panther Party and the Symbionese Liberation Army, but they were little match for the economic hardships and racial tensions that plagued Oakland. In many neighborhoods the reality was widespread poverty and gang violence—subjects that dominated the songs of such Oakland-bred rappers as the late Tupac Shakur.

Today Oakland is a mosaic of its past. The affluent have once again flocked to the city's hillside homes as a warmer, more spacious, and more affordable alternative to San Francisco, and a constant flow of newcomers—many from Central America and Asia—ensures continued diversity, vitality, and growing pains. Many neighborhoods to the west and south of downtown remain run-down and unsafe, but a renovated downtown area—including one of the most vibrant arts scenes in the Bay Area—and the thriving though sterile Jack London Square have injected new life into the city. The national visibility from the 1998 election of former California governor Jerry Brown as Oakland mayor (his term ended in early 2007) further invigorated the city's rising spirits.

Everyday life here revolves around the neighborhood, with a main business strip attracting both shoppers and strollers. In some areas, such as high-end Piedmont and Rockridge, you'd swear you were in Berkeley or San Francisco's Noe Valley or Cow Hollow. These are perfect places for browsing, eating, or just relaxing between sightseeing trips to Oakland's architectural gems, rejuvenated waterfront, and numerous green spaces. Between Rockridge and Piedmont and to the west, you can find the Temescal district, along Telegraph Avenue just south of 51st Street, which is starting to attract a small collection of eateries and shops.

❹ One of Oakland's top attractions,
☺ the **Oakland Museum of California**
★ is an excellent introduction to a tour of California, and its detailed exhibits on the state's art, history, and natural wonders can help fill the gaps on a brief visit. You can travel through the state's myriad

WORD OF MOUTH

"I believe the downtown/historic area of Oakland is undergoing/ has undergone a bit of a renaissance—galleries, restaurants, etc. . . . I'm not referring to Jack London Square, which does have the dubious honor of being home to the oldest bar in California. Anyone know if that's true? That tiny old place that slants?"

–Leely

ecosystems in the Natural Sciences Gallery, from the sand dunes of the Pacific to the coyotes and brush of the Nevada border. Kids love the lifelike wild-animal exhibits, especially the snarling wolverine, big-eyed harbor seal, and trove of hidden creatures. The rambling Cowell Hall of California History includes everything from Spanish-era armor to a small but impressive collection of vintage vehicles, including a gorgeous, candy-apple-red "Mystery" car from the 1960s and a gleaming red, gold, and silver fire engine that battled the flames in San Francisco in 1906. The Gallery of California Art holds an eclectic collection of modern works and early landscapes. Of particular interest are paintings by Richard Diebenkorn, Joan Brown, Elmer Bischoff, and David Park, all members of the Bay Area Figurative School, which flourished here after World War II. Fans of Dorothea Lange won't want to miss the gallery's comprehensive collection of her work. The museum also has a sculpture garden with a view of the Oakland and Berkeley hills in the distance. ✉*1000 Oak St., at 10th St.* ☎*510/238–2200* ⊕*www. museumca.org* ✉*$8, free 2nd Sun. of month* ☉ *Wed.–Sat. 10–5, until 9 1st Fri. of month, Sun. noon–5.*

❸ The 155-acre **Lake Merritt** (✉*Bordered by Lakeshore Ave. on south, Lakeside Dr. on west, Harrison St. on north, and Bellevue Ave. on east*), a natural saltwater lake, sits in the middle of downtown Oakland. Joggers and power-walkers charge along the 3-mi path that encircles the lake, crew teams often glide across the water, and boatmen guide snuggling couples in authentic Venetian gondolas. **California gondoliers** (✉*568 Bellevue Ave., Lake Merritt* ☎*866/737–8494* ⊕*www. gondolaservizio.com*) is by the sign that says "Sailboat House, Gondola Servizio." Fares start at $45 per couple for 30 minutes.

Lakeside Park, which surrounds the north side of Lake Merritt, has several outdoor attractions, including a children's park. The **Rotary**
❷ Nature Center and Waterfowl Refuge is the nesting site of herons, egrets, geese, and ducks in spring and summer. Migrating birds pass through from September through February, and you can watch the birds being fed daily at 3:30 (year-round). ✉*600 Bellevue Ave.* ☎*510/238–3739*

17

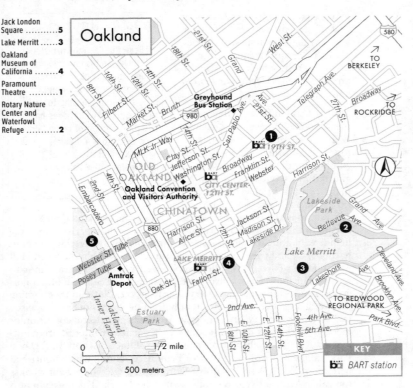

⊕ *www.oaklandnet.com/parks/Facilities/points_lakeside_park.asp*
🎫 *Free* ⊙ *Daily 10–5.*

★ Given Oakland's reputation for Victorian and Craftsman homes, newcomers are generally surprised by the profusion of art-deco architecture in the downtown neighborhood around the 19th Street BART station.

❶ Some of these buildings have fallen into disrepair, but the **Paramount Theatre,** perhaps the most glorious example of art-deco architecture in the city, if not the entire Bay Area, still operates as a venue for concerts and performances of all kinds, from the Oakland Ballet to Tom Waits and Elvis Costello. You can take a two-hour tour of the building, which starts near the box office on 21st Street at 10 AM on the first and third Saturday of each month. Just behind the Paramount on Telegraph Avenue, the Fox Theater, another art-deco landmark, was saved from the wrecking ball and is being lovingly restored. ✉*2025 Broadway* ☎*510/465–6400* ⊕*www.paramounttheatre.com* 🎫*Tour $5.*

❺ Shops, restaurants, small museums, and historic sites line **Jack London Square,** which is named after one of California's best-known authors; London wrote *The Call of the Wild, The Sea Wolf,* and many other books. When he lived in Oakland, he spent many a day boozing and brawling in the waterfront area. The tiny, wonderful **Heinold's First and**

Last Chance Saloon (⊠*48 Webster St.* ☎*510/839–6761*) was one of London's old haunts. It has been serving since 1883, although it's a little worse for the wear since the 1906 earthquake. The Klondike cabin in which London spent a summer in the late 1890s was moved from Alaska and reassembled here, next door to Heinold's saloon, in 1970. The square also contains a bronze bust of London. ■TIP➔ **Since it's on the waterfront, the square is an obvious spot for tourists to visit and is worth a peek if you take a ferry that docks here; to really get a feel for Oakland, though, you're better off browsing downtown, or at least in Rockridge.** ⊠*Embarcadero at Broadway* ☎*866/295–9853* ⊕*www.jacklondonsquare.com.*

Bordered by 7th, 10th, Clay, and Washington streets in the shadow of the convention center and towering downtown hotels, **Old Oakland** was once a booming business district. Today the restored Victorian storefronts lining these four blocks house restaurants, cafés, shops, and galleries, and a lively three-block farmers' market takes place Friday morning. Architectural consistency distinguishes the area from surrounding streets and lends it a distinct neighborhood feel. **Ratto's International Market** (⊠*827 Washington St.* ☎*510/832–6503*), the Italian grocer that's been dishing up meat, cheese, imported sweets, and liquor to the neighborhood since 1897, has fresh deli sandwiches. **Pacific Coast Brewing Company** (⊠*906 Washington St.* ☎*510/836–2739*) is a homey place for some pub grub and a microbrew. The block-long Swan's Marketplace houses shops and the **Housewives Market** (⊠*907 Washington St.*), an old-fashioned market with stalls for meat, seafood, and even a sausage maker.

Across Broadway from Old Oakland but worlds apart, **Chinatown** is a densely packed, bustling neighborhood. Unlike its San Francisco counterpart, Oakland's Chinatown makes no concessions to tourists; you won't find baskets of trinkets lining the sidewalk and souvenir displays in the shop windows. Supermarkets such as **Yuen Hop Noodle Company and Asian Food Products** (824 Webster St.), open since 1931, overflow with goodies. The line for sweets, breads, and towering cakes snakes out the door of **Napoleon Super Bakery** (810 Franklin St.). The sprawling and always lively **Jade Villa** (800 Broadway; *see* Where to Stay & Eat, *below*) is a favorite spot for dim sum.

The upscale neighborhood of **Rockridge** is one of Oakland's most desirable places to live. Explore the tree-lined streets that radiate out from College Avenue just north and south of the Rockridge BART station for a look at California bungalow architecture at its finest.

College Avenue is the main shopping drag in Rockridge. By day it's crowded with shoppers buying fresh flowers, used books, and clothing; by night the same folks are back for dinner and locally brewed ales in the numerous restaurants and pubs. The hub of College Avenue life in Rockridge is **Market Hall** (⊠*5655 College Ave.* ☎*510/652–4680* ⊕*www.rockridgemarkethall.com*), an airy European-style marketplace with pricey specialty-food shops. The avenue ends at the California College of the Arts campus.

17

WHERE TO STAY & EAT

$$ ╳**Doña Tomás.** A neighborhood favorite, this spot in Oakland's up-and-coming Temescal district serves seasonal Mexican fare to a hip but low-key crowd. Mexican textiles and art adorn walls in two long rooms; there's also a vine-covered patio. Banish all images of taquería grub and tuck into starters such as quesadillas filled with butternut squash and goat cheese and entrées such as *albondigas en sopa de zanahoria* (pork-and-beef meatballs in puree-of-carrot soup). A fine selection of tequilas rounds out the offerings. ⊠*5004 Telegraph Ave.* ☎*510/450–0522* ☐*AE, MC, V* ⊘*Closed Sun. and Mon. No lunch.*

¢–$ ╳**Jade Villa.** Live-lobster tanks and a red-velvet wall hung with gold Chinese characters serve as the only decor in this sprawling dining room, which is packed to capacity on weekends. Locals revere the dim sum offerings, especially the shrimp-stuffed mushrooms and barbecue pork buns, delivered continually on carts by sometimes brusque, sometimes smiling waitresses. If you don't speak Chinese, it helps to have the Chinese–English dim sum menu handy for pointing. The dim sum is also available to go from the counter off the patio. A full menu is available as well. ⊠*800 Broadway* ☎*510/839–1688* ☐*AE, D, MC, V.*

$$–$$$ ╳**Jojo.** A staid, mostly 40s-plus crowd gathers in the warm glow of soft lighting and butter-yellow walls to feast on a short list of French favorites at this petite eatery. The menu varies by the season; starters might include a tart filled with crab and goat cheese or mussels steamed with rosé and shallots. Entrées are generous and include a surprisingly light wild-mushroom savory bread pudding and a flatiron steak with anchovy-mustard butter. ⊠*3859 Piedmont Ave.* ☎*510/985–3003* ☐*AE, DC, MC, V* ⊘*Closed Sun. and Mon.*

¢–$ ╳**L'Amyx Tea Bar.** Light through the large windows bathes the blond wood tables, comfy chairs, and long bar, all filled with absorbed students, chatting friends, and tired shoppers in need of a boost. A small area in the back sells first-rate tea accoutrements, but sink into a couch or private nook to bask in much more than the usual cuppa. Try a tea smoothie or a herbal remedy such as Tealaxation. ⊠*4179 Piedmont Ave.* ☎*510/594–8322* ☐*MC, V.*

$–$$$ ╳**Luka's Taproom & Lounge.** Luka's is a real taste of downtown Oakland: hip and urban, with an unpretentious vibe. Diners nibble on *frites* any Belgian would be proud of and entrées like *choucroute garni*, sauerkraut with duck confit, ham hock, and pork shoulder. The brews draw 'em in, too—you'd be hard pressed to find a larger selection of Belgian beer this side of the pond—and the DJs in the adjacent lounge keep the scene going late. ⊠*2221 Broadway, at West Grand Ave.* ☎*510/451–4677* ☐*AE, MC, V* ⊘*No lunch Sat.*

$$–$$$ ✕**Oliveto Cafe & Restaurant.** Respected chef Paul Bertolli is at the helm of this locally renowned eatery that anchors Market Hall in the Rockridge neighborhood. The first-class dining room ($–$$$) upstairs serves straightforward Italian cuisine; the menu changes daily but might include house-made duck prosciutto, pan-seared swordfish, or spit-roasted leg of lamb. Downstairs, in the terra-cotta-walled café ($–$$), everything from a morning espresso to pizza to a full-blown Italian meal (at half the upstairs price) can be enjoyed at one of the small tables or at the bar. ⊠*5655 College Ave.* ☎*510/547–5356 or 510/547–4382* ☐*AE, MC, V* ⊗*No lunch weekends in restaurant.*

$ ⊡**Executive Inn & Suites.** This two-building hotel is convenient to both the Oakland airport and downtown Oakland. To make up for its removed location, the property offers free shuttle service to the Oakland airport, BART stations, and Jack London Square. Rooms in the older building are renovated but those in the newer one are generous in size and have extra-large desks, kitchen areas, and large whirlpool tubs. Each room has either a patio or a balcony, and an in-room ethernet connection (there's also Wi-Fi in the lobby). South-facing rooms overlook the peaceful waters of the Oakland Estuary; north-facing rooms have a freeway view and can be noisy. ⊠*1755 Embarcadero, off I–880 at 16th St. exit,* ☎*510/536–6633 or 800/346–6331* ☐*510/536–6006* ⊕*www.executiveinnoakland.com* ⊅*147 rooms, 81 suites* ⅏*In-room: safe (some), refrigerator, ethernet. In-hotel: restaurant, bar, pool, gym, concierge, laundry facilities, laundry service, public Wi-Fi, airport shuttle, parking (no fee), no-smoking rooms* ☐*AE, D, DC, MC, V* ❚⊙❚*CP.*

$$ ⊡**Washington Inn Hotel.** This stylish four-story brick hotel sits across the street from the convention center, in the heart of Old Oakland. In operation since 1905, the hotel has up-to-the-minute decor; red couches brighten the spacious lobby, which has Wi-Fi access. Elegant touches include intricately molded ceiling tiles and a wrought-iron elevator, a relic of the building's early days. Guest rooms are chic but on the small side. Rooms overlooking the atrium lobby are the quietest (and smallest); corner rooms get the most sunlight. ⊠*495 10th St., at Washington St.,* ☎*510/452–1776* ☐*510/452–4436* ⊕*www.thewashingtoninn. com* ⊅*41 rooms, 6 suites* ⅏*In-room: safe, VCR. In-hotel: restaurant, bar, gym, laundry service, public Internet, parking (fee), no-smoking rooms* ☐*AE, D, DC, MC, V* ❚⊙❚*CP weekends, BP weekdays.*

$$–$$$ ⊡**Waterfront Plaza Hotel.** One of Oakland's more appealing neighborhoods is home to this thoroughly modern waterfront hotel. Rooms in the hotel's five-story section overlook Jack London Square and have shared balconies; those in the three-story building each have a private balcony facing the water. Throughout the hotel, some rooms have fireplaces. Location is the reason to choose this hotel and the only thing that justifies its prices; service can be occasionally impatient. ⊠*10 Washington St., Jack London Sq.,* ☎*510/836–3800 or 800/729–3638* ☐*510/832–5695* ⊕*www.waterfrontplaza.com* ⊅*143 rooms* ⅏*In-room: safe, VCR (some), Wi-Fi. In-hotel: restaurant, room service, bar, pool, gym, concierge, laundry service, public Wi-Fi, parking (fee), no-smoking rooms* ☐*AE, D, DC, MC, V.*

17

NIGHTLIFE & THE ARTS

Oakland is where practicing artists have turned to for cheaper rent and loft spaces. Oakland's underground arts scene—visual arts, indie music, spoken word, film—is definitely buzzing.

Fodor'sChoice ★ **Café van Kleef.** When Dutch artist Peter van Kleef first opened his gallery in this downtown space, the booze flowed freely—and free, for lack of a liquor license. That gallery has morphed into this candle-lighted, funky café-bar that crackles with creative energy. Van Kleef has a lot to do with the convivial atmosphere; the garrulous owner loves sharing tales about his quirky, floor-to-ceiling collection of mementos, including what he claims are Cassius Clay's boxing gloves and Dorothy's ruby slippers. The café also has a consistently solid calendar of live music, heavy on the jazz side. And the drinks may not be free anymore, but they're quite possibly the stiffest in town. ⊠*1621 Telegraph Ave., between 16th and 17th Sts.* ☎*510/763–7711* ⊕*www.cafevankleef.com.*

Mama Buzz Café. At this well-worn café-gallery, a kind of living room for the indie arts crowd, you can get the lowdown on one of the most diverse arts communities around. In addition to coffee and light fare, the calendar includes poetry readings, live-music events, art exhibits, and hard-to-categorize events such as Punk Rock Haircut Night (get a new do, cheap), the Knitty Gritty knitting circle, and the Left-Wing Letter Bee. The owners publish the 'zine *Kitchen Sink.* ⊠*2318 Telegraph Ave.* ☎*510/465–4073* ⊕*www.mamabuzzcafe.com.*

The Parkway Speakeasy Theater. Billing itself as the "anti-multiplex," this movie theater feels like a college experience, when everyone crowded into a dorm lounge for communal watching. Pick up a beer or glass of wine, served alongside pizza and snacks, and then sprawl on a love seat or cozy recliner as you settle in for a first-run or indie film or any of the eclectic series that the Parkway dreams up. ⊠*1834 Park Blvd.* ☎*510/848–1994* ⊕*www.picturepubpizza.com.*

Fodor'sChoice ★ **Yoshi's.** Oma Sosa and Charlie Hunter are among the musicians who play at Yoshi's, one of the area's best jazz venues. Monday through Saturday, shows start at 8 PM and 10 PM; Sunday shows usually start at 2 PM and 8 PM. The cover runs from $10 to $30. ⊠*510 Embarcadero St., between Washington and Clay Sts.* ☎*510/238–9200* ⊕*www.yoshis.com.*

SPORTS & THE OUTDOORS

BASEBALL The American League's **Oakland A's** (⊠*McAfee Coliseum, 7000 Coliseum Way, off I–880, north of Hegenberger Rd.* ☎*510/638–4627* ⊕*oakland.athletics.mlb.com*), formally the Oakland Athletics, play at the **McAfee Coliseum.** Same-day tickets usually can be purchased at the stadium box office (Gate D), but advance purchase is recommended. On Wednesday, entry is a bargain at $2 and you can buy a hot dog for a dollar. To get to the game, take a BART train to the Coliseum/Oakland Airport Station.

BASKETBALL The National Basketball Association's **Golden State Warriors** (⊠ *Oakland Arena, 7000 Coliseum Way, off I–880, north of Hegenberger Rd.* ☎*510/986–2200 or 888/479–4667* ⊕*www.nba.com/warriors*) play at the **Oakland Arena** from November through April. Basketball tickets are available through **Ticketmaster** (☎*415/421–8497* ⊕*www.ticketmaster.com*). You can take a BART train to the game. Get off at the Coliseum/Oakland Airport Station.

FOOTBALL The National Football League's **Oakland Raiders** (⊠ *McAfee Coliseum, 7000 Coliseum Way, off I–880, north of Hegenberger Rd., Oakland* ☎*510/864–5000* ⊕*www.raiders.com*) play at **McAfee Coliseum.** Tickets, sold through **Tickets.com** (☎*510/762–2277* ⊕*www.tickets.com*), are usually available, except for high-profile games.

SHOPPING

College Avenue is great for upscale strolling, shopping, and people-watching. The streets around Lake Merritt and the Grand Lake have more casual fare and smaller boutiques.

Diesel. Wandering bibliophiles collect armfuls of the latest fiction and nonfiction here. The loftlike space, with its high ceilings and spare design, encourages airy contemplation, and on chilly days (a rarity) there's a fire going in the hearth. Keep an eye out for their excellent reading series. ⊠*5433 College Ave., Oakland* ☎*510/653–9965.*

Maison d'Etre. Close to the Rockridge BART station, this store crystallizes the funky-chic shopping scene of Rockridge. Look for impulse buys like whimsical watches, imported fruit tea blends, and a basket of funky slippers near the back. ⊠*5640 College Ave., Oakland* ☎*510/658–2801.*

17

BERKELEY

2 mi northeast of Bay Bridge.

The birthplace of the Free Speech Movement, the radical hub of the 1960s, the home of arguably the nation's top public university, and the city whose government condemned the bombing of Afghanistan—Berkeley is all of those things. The city of 100,000 facing San Francisco across the bay is also culturally diverse, a breeding ground for social trends, a bastion of the counterculture, and an important center for Bay Area writers, artists, and musicians. Berkeley residents, students, and faculty spend hours nursing various coffee concoctions while they read, discuss, and debate at any of the dozens of cafés that surround the campus. Oakland may have Berkeley beat when it comes to cutting-edge arts, and the city may have forfeited some of its renegade 1960s spirit, as some residents say, but unless a guy in a hot-pink satin body suit, skull cap, and cape rides a unicycle around *your* town, you'll likely find that Berkeley remains plenty offbeat.

It's the quintessential university town, and many who graduated years ago still bask in daily intellectual conversation, great weather, and good food. Residents will walk out of their way to go to the perfect bread shop or consult with their favorite wine merchant. And every September, residents gently lampoon themselves during the annual "How Berkeley Can You Be?" parade and festival where they celebrate their tie-dyed past and consider its new incarnations.

The state legislature chartered the **University of California** (⊕ *www.berkeley. edu*) in 1868 as the founding campus of the state university system and established it five years later on a rising plain of oak trees split by Strawberry Creek. Frederick Law Olmsted, who designed New York City's Central Park, proposed the first campus plan. University architects over the years have included Bernard Maybeck as well as Julia Morgan, who designed Hearst Castle at San Simeon. The central campus occupies 178 acres, bound by Bancroft Way to the south, Hearst Avenue to the north, Oxford Street to the west, and Gayley Road to the east. With more than 30,000 students and a full-time faculty of 1,400, the university, known simply as "Cal," is one of the leading intellectual centers in the United States and a major site for scientific research.

❶ The **Berkeley Visitor Information Center** (⊠ *University Hall, Room 101, 2200 University Ave., at Oxford St.* ☎ *510/642–5215* ⊗ *Weekdays 8:30–4:30*) is the starting point for the free, student-guided tours of the campus, which last 1½ hours and start at 10 on weekdays. (Weekend tours depart from Sather Tower, *below.*)

❷ Student-guided campus tours leave from **Sather Tower,** the campus landmark popularly known as the Campanile, at 10 on Saturday and 1 on Sunday. The 307-foot structure, modeled on St. Mark's Tower in Venice and completed in 1914, can be seen for miles. The carillon is played daily at 7:50 AM, noon, and 6 PM and for an extended 45-minute concert Sunday at 2. Take the elevator up 175 feet; then walk another 38 steps to the observation deck for a view of the campus and a close-up look at the iron bells, each of which weighs up to 10,500 pounds. ⊠ *South of University Dr.* ☜ *$2* ⊗ *Weekdays 10–4, Sat. 10–5, Sun. 10–1:30 and 3–5.*

❸ **Sproul Plaza** (⊠ *Telegraph Ave. and Bancroft Way*), just inside the U.C. Berkeley campus border on Bancroft Way, was the site of several free-speech and civil-rights protests in the 1960s. Today a lively panorama of political and social activists, musicians, and students show off Berkeley's flair for the bizarre. Preachers orate atop milk crates, amateur entertainers bang on makeshift drum sets, and protesters distribute leaflets about everything from marijuana to the Middle East. No matter what the combination, on weekdays when school is in swing, it always feels like a carnival. ■ TIP➔ **Walk through at noon for the liveliest show of student spirit.**

❹ The collection of the **Phoebe A. Hearst Museum of Anthropology** counts almost 4 million artifacts, of which fewer than 1% are on display at any time. The Native Californian Cultures gallery showcases items related to the native peoples of California. Changing exhibits may cover the archaeology of ancient America or spotlight the museum's especially strong ancient Egyptian holdings. Mood music enhances the experience. ⊠ *Kroeber Hall, Bancroft Way, at end of College Ave.*

☎ *510/642–3682* ⊕ *hearstmuseum.berkeley.edu* ✉ *Free; guided tour $5* ⊙ *Wed.–Sat. 10–4:30, Sun. noon–4.*

❺ The **University of California, Berkeley Art Museum & Pacific Film Archive** has an interesting collection of works that spans five centuries, with an emphasis on contemporary art. Changing exhibits line the spiral ramps and balcony galleries. Look for the museum's enormous orange-red statue of a man hammering, which can be seen from the outside when strolling by its floor-to-ceiling windows. Don't miss the museum's series of vibrant paintings by abstract expressionist Hans Hofmann in the main gallery. On the ground floor, the Pacific Film Archive has a library and hosts discussions and programs about historic and contemporary films, but the exhibition theater is across the street at 2575 Bancroft Way, near Bowditch Street. The downstairs galleries, which house rotating exhibits, are always free. The museum's raw foods café is famous, and you can also find some cooked options, too. ✉ *2626 Bancroft Way, entrance to theater at 2575 Bancroft Way between College and Telegraph* ☎ *510/642–0808, 510/642–1124 film-program information* ⊕ *www.bampfa.berkeley.edu* ✉ *$8* ⊙ *Wed. and Fri.–Sun. 11–5, Thurs. 11–7.*

❻ At the fortresslike **Lawrence Hall of Science**, a dazzling hands-on science center, kids can look at insects under microscopes, solve crimes using chemical forensics, and explore the physics of baseball. On weekends there are special lectures, demonstrations, and planetarium shows. The museum runs a popular (and free) stargazing program, which is held on the first and third Saturday of each month, weather permitting. (Call for times.) ✉ *Centennial Dr. near Grizzly Peak Blvd.* ☎ *510/642–5132* ⊕ *www.lawrencehallofscience.org* ✉ *$11* ⊙ *Daily 10–5.*

South of campus, along College Avenue between Ashby Avenue and Claremont, shops and cafés pack the area known as **Elmwood,** a local favorite for browsing. Generations of Berkeleyites have enjoyed BLTs and sundaes at the counter of **Ozzie's Soda Fountain** (✉ *2900 College Ave.* ☎ *510/841–0989),* the last pharmacy soda fountain in the Bay area, open since 1921 inside the Elmwood Pharmacy. The menu tops out at $5. **Nabolom Bakery** (✉ *2708 Russell St.* ☎ *510/845–2253),* which has been around since 1976, is a workers' collective where politics and delicious pastries collide. Shingled houses line tree-shaded streets nearby.

Telegraph Avenue is Berkeley's student-oriented thoroughfare and the best place to get a dose of the city's famed counterculture. On any given day you might encounter a troop of chanting Hare Krishnas or a drumming band of Rastafarians. First and foremost, however, Telegraph is a place for socializing and shopping, the only uniquely Berkeley shopping experience in town and a definite don't-miss. **Take care when wandering the street at night, things can feel a bit edgy. Nearby People's Park, mostly harmless by day, is best avoided at night.** Cafés, bookstores, poster shops, and street vendors line the avenue. T-shirt vendors and tarot-card readers come and go on a whim, but a few establishments— **Rasputin Music** (No. 2401), **Amoeba Music** (No. 2455), and **Moe's**

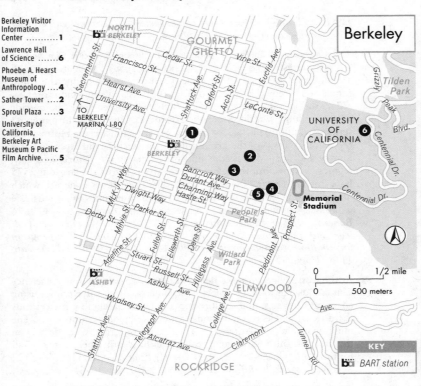

Books (No. 2476)—are neighborhood landmarks. Allen Ginsberg wrote his acclaimed poem "Howl" at **Caffe Mediterraneum** (No. 2475), a relic of 1960s-era café culture.

An industrial area on **4th Street** north of University Avenue has been converted into a pleasant shopping stretch with popular eateries and shops selling handcrafted and eco-conscious goods. About six blocks long, this compact area is busiest on bright weekend afternoons. Popular destinations are Cody's bookstore and the Crate and Barrel Outlet along with a mini-slew of upscale boutiques and wonderful paper stores.

Northwest of the U.C. Berkeley campus, **Walnut Square,** at Walnut and Vine streets, has coffee shops and an eclectic assortment of boutiques proffering such goodies as holistic products for your pet, African masks, and French children's clothing. Around the corner on Shattuck Avenue is Chez Panisse Café & Restaurant, at the heart of what is locally known as the **Gourmet Ghetto,** a three-block stretch of specialty shops and eateries. Your senses will immediately perk up as you enter the upscale market **Epicurious Garden** (⊠1509–1513 Shattuck Ave.), which has everything from impeccable sushi to gelato. Outside, you can find a terraced garden—the only place to sit—that winds up four levels and ends at the Imperial Tea Court. The restaurant Taste anchors this zone; it offers a rechargeable wine-tasting card that guests use to help themselves to one-ounce automated pours from new wine selections.

NEED A BREAK?

With a jazz combo playing in the storefront and a long line snaking down the block, Cheeseboard Pizza (⊠ *151 Shattuck Ave.* 🕾 *510/549–3055* 🕙 *Tues.–Fri. 11:30–2, until 3 on Sat., also 4:30–7*) counts out the pulse of the Gourmet Ghetto. This cooperatively owned, take-out spot (if you're lucky, you can grab one of the few inside tables) is an institution, drawing devoted customers with the smell of just-baked garlic, fresh vegetables, and perfect sauces. The jovial worker-owners serve up just one freshly baked pizza daily—always vegetarian—and you can find surprises such as fresh corn, zucchini, or a small lime wedge to squeeze over your slice. Next door at the bakery–cheese shop, customers take a playing card instead of a number and are served in suites. It can get crowded, and jokers are wild.

Vine Street is another culinary destination. In a historic building **Vintage Berkeley** (⊠ *2113 Vine St.* 🕾 *510/665–8600*) gathers locals in its large front garden for nightly wine-tastings of California wines from smaller vineyards. Take the stairs up to the top floor of Walnut Square to find **Love at First Bite** (⊠ *1510 Walnut St., Suite G* 🕾 *510/848–5727*) a cupcakery showcasing scrumptious confections. **Twig & Fig** (⊠ *210 Vine St., Suite B* 🕾 *510/848–5599*) invites you in for a peek at its three rhythmically clacking letterpresses. Stop in for one-of-a-kind papery gifts and publications such as *Inside the Brambles,* a local's guide to Tilden Park. Of all the coffeehouses in caffeine-crazed Berkeley, the one that deserves a pilgrimage is **Peet's** (⊠ *2124 Vine St.* 🕾 *510/841–0564*). When this, the original, opened at Vine and Walnut streets in 1966, the unparalleled coffee was roasted in the store and brewed by the cup. Named after the Dutch last name of the founder, Peet's has since expanded, but this isn't a café where you can sit on sofas or order quiche. It's strictly coffee, tea, and sweets to go.

17

OFF THE BEATEN PATH

Scharffen Berger Factory. A cloud of chocolate-scented vapor welcomes you to the factory tour. You can get a history lesson on cocoa and the company's relatively recent debut and success. Suit up with ear protection and a hairnet, then file in to see where the magic happens. Happily, you can get generous tastings throughout the talk. Tour reservations are required, so call in advance and arrive 10 minutes before start time. At the shop you can snap up special annual chocolate bars. ⊠ *914 Heinz Ave.* 🕾 *510/981–4066* ⊕ *www.scharffenberger.com* 🕙 *Mon.– Sat. 10–6, Sun. 10–5. Tours daily 10:30–3:30 on half-hr* 🎫 *Free.*

WHERE TO STAY & EAT

Dining in Berkeley is a low-key affair; even in the finest restaurants—and some are quite fine—most folks dress casually. Late diners be forewarned: Berkeley is an "early to bed" kind of town. For inexpensive lodging, investigate University Avenue, west of campus. The area is noisy, congested, and somewhat dilapidated but does include a few decent motels and chain properties. All Berkeley lodgings, except for the swanky Claremont, are strictly mid-range.

¢–$ ✕**Bette's Oceanview Diner.** Buttermilk pancakes are just one of the specialties at this 1930s-inspired diner, complete with checkered floors and burgundy booths. Huevos rancheros and lox and eggs are other breakfast options; kosher franks, generous slices of pizza, and a slew of sandwiches are available for lunch. The wait for a seat can be quite long; thankfully, 4th Street was made for strolling. **If you're starving, head to Bette's to Go, next door, for takeout.** ✉*1807 4th St.* ☎*510/644–3230* ⌃*Reservations not accepted* ▤*MC, V* ◷*No dinner.*

$$–$$$$ ✕**Café Rouge.** You can recover from 4th Street shopping in this spacious two-story bistro, complete with zinc bar, skylights, and festive lanterns. The short, seasonal menu ranges from the sophisticated, such as rack of lamb and juniper-berry-cured pork chops, to the homey, such as spit-roasted chicken or pork loin, or cheddar-topped burgers. If you visit by day, be certain to peek at their own meat market in the back. ✉*1782 4th St.* ☎*510/525–1440* ▤*MC, V* ◷*No dinner Mon.*

$–$$$ ✕**César.** Suitably keeping near-Spanish hours for the Spanish cuisine here, dinners are served late at César, whose kitchen closes at 11:30 PM on Friday and Saturday and at 11 PM the rest of the week. Couples spill out from its street-level windows on warm nights, or rub shoulders at the polished bar or center communal table. Founded by a trio of former Chez Panisse chefs, César is like a first cousin to Chez Panisse, each restaurant recommending the other if there's a long wait ahead. For tapas and perfectly grilled bocadillos (small sandwiches), there's no better choice. The bar also makes a mean martini and has an impressive wine list. **Come early to get seated quickly and also to hear your tablemates; the room gets loud when the bar is in full swing.** ✉*1515 Shattuck Ave.* ☎*510/883–0322* ⌃*Reservations not accepted* ▤*MC, V.*

$$$–$$$$ ✕**Chez Panisse Café & Restaurant.** At Chez Panisse, even humble pizza
FodorsChoice is reincarnated in new ways, with innovative toppings of the fresh-
★ est local ingredients. The downstairs portion of Alice Waters's legendary eatery is noted for its formality and personal service. Here, the daily-changing multicourse dinners are prix-fixe ($$$$), with the cost slightly lower on weekdays. Upstairs, in the informal café, the crowd is livelier, the prices are lower ($$), and the ever-changing menu is à la carte. The food is simpler, too: penne with new potatoes, arugula, and sheep's-milk cheese; fresh figs with Parmigiano-Reggiano cheese and arugula; and grilled tuna with savoy cabbage, for example. Legions of loyal fans insist Chez Panisse lives up to its reputation and delivers a dining experience well worth the price. Visiting foodies won't want to miss a meal here, upstairs or down; be sure to make reservations a few weeks ahead of time to avoid disappointment. And, yes, it's that good. ✉*1517 Shattuck Ave., north of University Ave.* ☎*510/548–5525 restaurant, 510/548–5049 café* ⌃*Reservations essential* ▤*AE, D, DC, MC, V* ◷*Closed Sun. No lunch in restaurant.*

$$–$$$ ✕**Lalime's.** The food served in this charming, flower-covered house
★ reflects the entire Mediterranean region. The menu, in constant flux and unfailingly great, depends on the availability of fresh seasonal ingredients. Choices might include grilled ahi tuna or creamy Italian risotto.

The light colors of the dining room, which has two levels, help to create a cheerful mood. A star in its own right, Lalime's is a good second choice if Chez Panisse is booked. *1329 Gilman St.* ☎*510/527–9838* ✍*Reservations essential* ⊟*AE, DC, MC, V* ⊘*No lunch.*

¢–$ ✗**Picante Cocina Mexicana.** A barn-like space full of cheerful Mexican tiles and folk art masks, Picante is a find for anyone seeking good Mexican food for a song. The *masa* (flour) is freshly ground for the tortillas and tamales, the salsas are complex, and the combinations are inventive. Try tamales filled with butternut squash and chilies or a simple taco of roasted poblanos and sautéed onions; we challenge you to finish a plate of super nachos. Order at the counter and grab a table inside or on the back patio. ⊠*1328 6th St.* ☎*510/525–3121* ✍*Reservations not accepted* ⊟*MC, V.*

¢–$$ ✗**Rick & Ann's.** Haute comfort food is the signature here. Their brunches are legendary for quality and value, and customers line up outside the door before the restaurant opens on the weekend. If you come during prime brunch time, expect a long wait, but their soft-style eggs are worth it. Pancakes, waffles, and French toast are more flavorful than usual with variations such as potato-cheese and orange-rice pancakes. Lunch and dinner offer burgers, favorites such as Mom's macaroni and cheese, and chicken potpie, but always with a festive twist. Reservations are accepted 48 hours in advance for dinner and for lunch parties of six or more, but you can't book a table for brunch. ⊠*2922 Domingo Ave.* ☎*510/649–8568* ⊟*MC, V* ⊘*No dinner Mon. and Tues.*

$$$$ ⬚**Claremont Resort and Spa.** Straddling the Oakland–Berkeley border,
Fodor'sChoice the hotel beckons like a gleaming white castle in the hills. Traveling
★ executives come for the business amenities, including T-1 Internet connections, guest e-mail addresses, and oversize desks. The Claremont also draws honeymooners and leisure travelers with its luxurious suites, therapeutic massages, and personalized yoga workouts at the on-site spa. The rooms on the spa-side of the hotel glow with new fixtures and furniture. Some offer spa tubs and, if you're high enough up, spectacular Bay views. **Another advantage: the scents wafting upwards from the spa treatment rooms.** ⊠*41 Tunnel Rd., at Ashby and Domingo Aves.,* ☎*510/843–3000 or 800/551–7266* ☐*510/843–6629* ⊕*www.claremontresort.com* ⇨*249 rooms, 30 suites* ⚘*In-room: safe, refrigerator (some), VCR, ethernet. In-hotel: 2 restaurants, bars, tennis courts, pools, gym, spa, concierge, children's programs (ages 6 wks–10 yrs), laundry service, public Internet, parking (fee), no-smoking rooms* ⊟*AE, D, DC, MC, V.*

$ ⬚**French Hotel.** The only hotel in north Berkeley, one of the best walking neighborhoods in town, this three-level brick structure has a cer-

17

tain *pensione* feel—guests check in at a counter at the back of the café, and the only public space in the hotel is the hallway to the elevator. Rooms have pastel or brick walls and cherrywood armoires and writing tables. Balconies make the rooms seem larger than their modest dimensions. The bedspreads and decor are '70s-chic, but you couldn't ask for a more central location. A ground-floor café, serving arguably the best latte in town, buzzes day and night with overflow from the Gourmet Ghetto (Chez Panisse is across the street). ⊠ *1538 Shattuck Ave.,* ☎ *510/548–9930* 🖷 *510/548–9930* 🛏 *18 rooms* ⅋ *In-room: no a/c. In-hotel: restaurant, concierge, parking (no fee), Wi-Fi, no-smoking rooms* 🖃 *AE, D, MC, V.*

$ 🖵 **Holiday Inn Express.** Convenient to the freeway and 4th Street shopping, this inviting, peach-and-beige-hue hotel offers lots of bang for the buck. The two-story property is surprisingly elegant; high ceilings lend the lobby and rooms an airy quality. Each room has a small kitchen area with a refrigerator, microwave, sink, and cabinets. The hotel also offers a free breakfast bar, a small but well-equipped gym, and free access to a business center. ⊠ *1175 University Ave.,* ☎ *510/548–1700 or 866/548–1700* 🖷 *510/548–1705* ⊕ *www.hiexberkeley.com* 🛏 *31 rooms, 19 suites* ⅋ *In-room: refrigerator, VCR, ethernet. In-hotel: gym, laundry facilities, laundry service, parking (no fee), no-smoking rooms* 🖃 *AE, D, DC, MC, V* ⅋①CP.

$$ 🖵 **Hotel Durant.** Long the mainstay of parents visiting their children at U.C. Berkeley, this hotel is a good option for those who want to be a short walk from campus and the restaurants and shops of Telegraph Avenue. The rooms, updated in 2006 with new bathrooms and dark wood set against deep jewel tones, are small without feeling cramped. The historic photos of Berkeley highlight the hotel's storied past, and the central location is perfect for the car-less. The hotel bar, Henry's, is where U.C. Berkeley sports fans congregate to watch football games. **Guests receive free passes to the extensive Cal Recreational Sports Facility, known as RSF.** ⊠ *2600 Durant Ave.,* ☎ *510/845–8981* 🖷 *510/486–8336* ⊕ *www.hoteldurant.com* 🛏 *139 rooms, 5 suites* ⅋ *In-room: no a/c, refrigerator (some), ethernet. In-hotel: restaurant, room service, bar, concierge, laundry service, public Internet, parking (fee), no-smoking rooms* 🖃 *AE, D, DC, MC, V.*

NIGHTLIFE & THE ARTS

Berkeley Repertory Theatre. One of the region's highly respected resident professional companies and a Tony Award winner for Outstanding Regional Theatre (in 1997), the theater performs classic and contemporary plays from autumn to spring. Well-known pieces such as *Mother Courage* and *Oliver Twist* mix with edgier fare. The theater's complex is near BART's downtown Berkeley station. ⊠ *2025 Addison St.* ☎ *510/845–4700* ⊕ *www.berkeleyrep.org.*

Berkeley Symphony Orchestra. The ensemble has risen to considerable prominence under artistic director Kent Nagano. The works of 20th-century composers, from Messiaen to Zappa, are a focus, but more traditional pieces are also performed. The orchestra plays a handful of concerts each year, in Zellerbach Hall and other locations around Berkeley. ⊠ *University of California, Zellerbach Hall, Telegraph Ave.*

and Bancroft Way ☎*510/841–2800* ⊕*www.berkeleysymphony.org.*

★ **Cal Performances.** The series, running from September through May at various U.C. Berkeley venues, offers the Bay Area's most varied bill of internationally acclaimed artists in all disciplines, from classical soloists to the latest jazz, world-music, theater, and dance ensembles. Look for frequent campus colloquia or preshow talks featuring Berkeley's professors. ⊠*University of California, Zellerbach Hall, Telegraph Ave. and Bancroft Way* ☎*510/642–9988* ⊕*www.calperfs.berkeley.edu.*

WORD OF MOUTH

"There are great art movie houses in Berkeley. There is also very good theatre. You might check out either Berkeley Rep Theatre or Aurora Theatre to see what they are playing."

–PamSF

Fodor's Choice
★ **Freight & Salvage Coffee House.** Some of the most talented practitioners of folk, blues, Cajun, and bluegrass perform in this alcohol-free space, one of the finest folk houses in the country. Most tickets are less than $20. ⊠*1111 Addison St.* ☎*510/548–1761* ⊕*www.thefreight.org.*

SHOPPING

Fodor's Choice
★ **Amoeba Music.** Heaven for audiophiles, this legendary Berkeley favorite is *the* place to go for new and used CDs, records, cassettes, and DVDs. The dazzling stock includes thousands of titles for all music tastes—no matter what you're looking for, you can probably find it here. The store even has it's own record label. There are now branches in San Francisco and Hollywood, but this is the original. ⊠*2455 Telegraph Ave., at Haste St.* ☎*510/549–1125.*

Body Time. The local chain, founded in Berkeley in 1970, emphasizes the premium-quality ingredients it uses in its natural perfumes and skin-care and aromatherapy products. Sustainably harvested essential oils that you can combine and dilute to create your own personal fragrances are the specialty. Its distinct Citrus, Lavender-Mint, and China Rain scents are all popular Berkeley favorites. ⊠*2509 Telegraph Ave., at Dwight Way* ☎*510/548–3686.*

Fodor's Choice
★ **Cody's Books.** Known for its frequent readings by internationally renowned authors, Cody's closed its famous Telegraph branch. The 4th Street location carries on its spirit in an airy, loftlike space where you can find everything from inventive wrapping paper and stationery to the latest literary rage and gorgeous art books. ⊠*1730 4th St.* ☎*510/559–9500.*

Kermit Lynch Wine Merchant. A Berkeley institution, Kermit Lynch's friendly salespeople can direct you to the latest bargains from France. Lynch's newsletters describing his finds are legendary, as is his friendship with Alice Waters of Chez Panisse. Responsible for taking American appreciation of French wine to another level, the shop is a great place to peruse as you educate your palate. ⊠*1605 San Pablo Ave., at Dwight Way* ☎*510/524–1524.*

Moe's Books. The spirit of Moe—the cantankerous, cigar-smoking proprietor—lives on in this four-story house of books. Students and professors come here for used books, including large sections of literary

17

and cultural criticism, art books, and literature in foreign languages. ■TIP→ **Wear good shoes and eat lunch first; you won't want to come out for hours.** ✉ *2476 Telegraph Ave., near Haste St.* ☎ *510/849–2087.*

Rasputin Music. A huge selection of new music for every taste draws crowds to this megastore. In any other town (without an Amoeba Music store), its stock of used CDs and vinyl would certainly be unsurpassed. ✉ *2401 Telegraph Ave., at Channing Way* ☎ *800/350–8700 or 510/848–9004.*

EAST BAY ESSENTIALS

BOAT & FERRY TRAVEL

The Alameda/Oakland Ferry runs several times daily between San Francisco's Ferry Building or Pier 39, Alameda, and the Clay Street dock near Oakland's Jack London Square; one-way tickets are $5.50. The trip lasts 30 to 45 minutes, depending on your departure point, and leads to the heart of Oakland's gentrified shopping and restaurant district. Arriving in Oakland by boat conveys a historic sense of the city's heyday as a World War II–era shipbuilding center. Purchase tickets on board.

Contacts Alameda/Oakland Ferry (☎ *510/522–3300* ⊕ *www.eastbayferry. com*).

BUS TRAVEL

Although Bay Area Rapid Transit (BART) travel is often cheaper and more convenient, buses run frequently between San Francisco's Trans-Bay Terminal (at 1st and Mission streets) and the East Bay. AC Transit's F and FS lines stop near the university and 4th Street shopping in Berkeley. Lines C and P travel to Piedmont in Oakland. The O bus stops at the edge of Chinatown near downtown Oakland.

Contacts AC Transit (☎ *817–1717 after any Bay Area area code* ⊕ *www. actransit.org*).

TRAIN TRAVEL

BART (Bay Area Rapid Transit, formally) trains make stops in downtown Berkeley and in several parts of Oakland, including Rockridge. Use the Lake Merritt station for the Oakland Museum and southern Lake Merritt; the Oakland City Center–12th Street station for downtown, Chinatown, and Old Oakland; and the 19th Street station for the Paramount Theatre and the north side of Lake Merritt. From the Berkeley (not North Berkeley) station, walk a block up Center Street to get to the western edge of campus. Both trips take 30 to 45 minutes one way from the center of San Francisco.

Contacts BART (☎ *510/465–2278* ⊕ *www.bart.gov*).

VISITOR INFORMATION

Information Berkeley Convention and Visitors Bureau (✉ *2015 Center St. 94704* ☎ *510/549–7040* ⊕ *www.visitberkeley.com*). **Oakland Convention and Visitors Bureau** (✉ *463 11th St. 94607* ☎ *510/839–9000* ⊕ *www.oaklandcvb.com*).

The Wine Country

Keyes Vineyard, Howell Mountain, Napa Valley

WORD OF MOUTH

"I don't necessarily agree with the notion that larger wineries should be skipped. For a well-rounded Wine Country experience, you want a good mixture of different kinds of wineries, both large and small."

—TravelDiva

GETTING ORIENTED

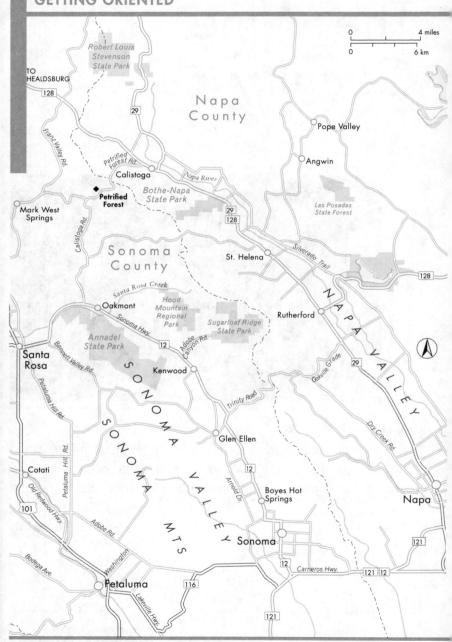

Napa County

Sonoma County

Robert Louis Stevenson State Park

TO HEALDSBURG
128

Pope Valley

Angwin

Franz Valley Rd.

Petrified Forest Rd.
Calistoga
29

Napa River

Petrified Forest

Bothe-Napa State Park

Las Posadas State Forest

Mark West Springs

Calistoga Rd.

29
128

St. Helena

Silverado Trail

128

Santa Rosa Creek

Oakmont

Sonoma Hwy.

Hood Mountain Regional Park

Sugarloaf Ridge State Park

Rutherford

NAPA VALLEY

Annadel State Park

Bennett Valley Rd.

Santa Rosa

Petaluma Hill Rd.

12

Adobe Canyon Rd.

Kenwood

Trinity Road

Oakville Grade

29

Dry Creek Rd.

S O N O M A

S O N O M A   V A L L E Y

Cotati

Petaluma Hill Rd.

Old Redwood Hwy.
101

Glen Ellen
12

Arnold Dr.

Boyes Hot Springs

Napa

121

Adobe Rd.

M T S

Sonoma

12

Bodega Ave.

Washington

Petaluma
116

Lakeville Hwy.

Carneros Hwy.
121 12

121

0 ___ 4 miles
0 ___ 6 km

GETTING ORIENTED

The Napa and Sonoma valleys run roughly parallel, north-west to southeast, and are separated by the Mayacamas Mountains. Northwest of the Sonoma Valley are several more important viticultural areas in Sonoma County, including Dry Creek, Alexander Valley, and the Russian River Valley. The Carneros region, which spans southern Sonoma and Napa counties, is just north of San Pablo Bay, and the closest of all these wine regions to San Francisco. For details on getting to Napa and Sonoma from San Francisco and the East Bay, *see By Car in the Wine Country Essentials.*

Napa Valley. Big names all around, from high-profile winer-ies to world-renowned chefs. Napa, the valley's oldest town, sweet-life St. Helena, and down-to-earth Calistoga all make good home bases here. (Calistoga has the extra draw of local thermal springs.) Yountville has become a culinary boom-town, while the tiny communities of Oakville and Rutherford are surrounded by major vintners like Robert Mondavi and Francis Ford Coppola. Rutherford in particular is the source for outstanding cabernet sauvignon.

Sonoma Valley. Historic attractions and an unpretentious attitude. The town of Sonoma, with its atmospheric central plaza, is rich with 19th-century buildings. Glen Ellen, mean-while, has a special connection with author Jack London.

Elsewhere in Sonoma. The winding, rural roads here feel a world away from Napa's main drag. The lovely Russian River, Dry Creek, and Alexander valleys are all excellent places to seek out pinot noir, zinfandel, and chardonnay. (The wind-ing, rural roads here feel a world away from the main drag through Napa.) The small town of Healdsburg is getting lots of attention lately, thanks to its terrific restaurants, B&Bs, and chic boutiques.

5 HIDDEN PLEASURES OF THE WINE COUNTRY

Biking. Cycling is one of the best ways to see the Wine Country—the Russian River and Dry Creek valleys are particularly beautiful. Just remember that drinking and riding are a dangerous mix!

Browsing the farmers' mar-kets. Almost every town in Napa and Sonoma has a seasonal farm-ers' market, each rounding up an amazing variety of local produce. Most markets run from spring through early fall, usually on Sat-urday mornings and sometimes on Tuesday evenings, too.

Touring the di Rosa Preserve. Though this art and nature pre-serve is just off the busy Carneros Highway, it's a relatively unknown treasure. The galleries and gar-dens are filled with hundreds of artworks. Book a two-hour tour to get the insider's look.

Canoeing on the Russian River. Trade in your car keys for a paddle and glide down the Russian River. May through October is the best time to be on the water.

Cocktails at Cyrus. Think it's vir-tually sacrilege to drink anything other than wine in this neck of the woods? Bartender Scott Beattie will change your mind. At the bar of Healdsburg's hottest restaurant, he mixes superb, inventive drinks with house-made infused syrups and seasonal ingredients like local Meyer lemons.

18

WINE COUNTRY PLANNER

Getting Around	Timing
Driving your own car is by far the best way to explore the Wine Country. Well-maintained roads zip through the centers of the Napa and Sonoma valleys, while scenic routes thread through the backcountry. Distances between towns are fairly short and you can sometimes drive from one end of the Napa or Sonoma Valley to the other in less than an hour—if there's no significant traffic. (However, it's not quite as easy as you might think to get between the two valleys, since they're divided by the Mayacamas Mountains.) This may be a relatively rural area, but the usual rush hours still apply, and high-season weekend traffic can be excruciatingly slow, especially on Route 29. ■TIP→ **If you're wine-tasting, either select a designated driver or be very careful of your wine intake. Those sips add up.** Local cops are quick with DUIs. For more details, *see the Wine Country Essentials* at the end of this chapter.	"Crush," the term used to indicate the season when grapes are picked and crushed, usually takes place in September or October, depending on the weather. From September until November the entire Wine Country celebrates its bounty with street fairs and festivals. The Sonoma County Harvest Fair, with its famous grape stomp, is held the first weekend in October. Golf tournaments, wine auctions, and art and food fairs occur throughout the fall.
	In season (April through October), Napa Valley draws crowds of tourists, and traffic along Route 29 from St. Helena to Calistoga is often backed up on weekends. The Sonoma Valley, Santa Rosa, and Healdsburg are less crowded. In season and over holiday weekends it's best to book lodging, restaurant, and winery reservations at least a month in advance. Many wineries give tours at specified times and require appointments.
	To avoid crowds, visit the Wine Country during the week and get an early start (most wineries open around 9 or 10). Because many wineries close as early as 4 or 4:30—and almost none are open past 5—you'll need to get a reasonably early start if you want to fit in more than one or two, especially if you're going to enjoy the leisurely lunch customary in the Wine Country. Summer is usually hot and dry, and autumn can be even hotter, so pack a sun hat if you go during these times.

About the Hotels

Napa and Sonoma know the tourism ropes well; their inns and hotels range from low-key to utterly luxurious and generally maintain high standards. Most of the bed-and-breakfasts are in historic Victorian and Spanish buildings and the breakfast part of the equation often involves fresh local produce. The newer hotels tend to have a more modern, streamlined aesthetic, and many have state-of-the-art spas with massage treatments or spring-water pools. Many hotels and B&Bs have excellent restaurants on their grounds, and all that don't are still just a short car ride away from gastronomic bliss.

However, all of this comes with a hefty price tag. As the cost of vineyards and grapes has risen, so have lodging rates. Santa Rosa, the largest population center in the area, has the widest selection of moderately priced rooms. Try there if you've failed to reserve in advance or have a limited budget. In general, all accommodations in the area often have lower rates on weeknights, and prices are about 20% lower in winter.

On weekends, two- or even three-night minimum stays are commonly required, especially at smaller inns and B&Bs. If you'd prefer to stay a single night, though, innkeepers are usually more flexible in winter. Many B&Bs book up long in advance of the summer and fall seasons, and they're often not suitable for children.

WINE COUNTRY COSTS

	$$$$	$$$	$$	$	¢
Restaurants					
	over $30	$23–$30	$15–$22	$10–$14	under $10
Hotels					
	over $400	$300–$400	$250–$299	$200–$249	under $200

Restaurant prices are per person for a main course at dinner, or for a prix-fix if a set menu is the only option. Hotel prices are for two people in a standard double room in high season.

About the Restaurants

Star chefs from around the world have come into the Wine Country's orbit, drawn by the area's phenomenal produce, artisanal foods, and wines. These days, some visitors come to Napa and Sonoma as much for the restaurants' tasting menus as for the wineries' tasting rooms.

Although excellent meals can be found virtually everywhere in the region, the small town of Yountville has become a culinary crossroads under the influence of chef Thomas Keller. If a table at Keller's famed French Laundry is out of reach, keep in mind that he's also behind a number of more modest restaurants in town. And the buzzed-about restaurants in Sonoma County, including Cyrus and Farmhouse Inn, offer plenty of mouthwatering options.

Such high quality often means high prices, but you can also find appealing, inexpensive eateries. High-end delis serve superb picnic fare, and brunch is a cost-effective strategy at pricey restaurants.

With few exceptions (which are noted in individual restaurant listings), dress is informal. Where reservations are indicated as essential, you may need to make them a week or more ahead. In summer and early fall you may need to book several weeks ahead.

18

Updated by
Sharron Wood

Life is good in California Wine Country. Eating and, above all, drinking are cultivated as high arts. Have you been day-dreaming about driving through vineyards, stopping here and there for a wine tasting or a picnic? Well, that fantasy is a common reality here.

It's little wonder that so many visitors to San Francisco take a day or two—or five or six—to unwind in the Napa and Sonoma valleys. They join the locals in the tasting rooms, from serious wine collectors making their annual pilgrimages to wine newbies who don't know the difference between a merlot and mourvèdre but are eager to learn.

The state's wine industry is booming, and the Napa and Sonoma valleys have long led the field. For instance, in 1975 Napa Valley had no more than 20 wineries; today there are more than 250. A recent up-and-comer is the Carneros region, which overlaps Napa and Sonoma counties at the head of the San Francisco Bay. (As it turns out, chardonnay and pinot noir grapes thrive on its cool, windy hillsides.)

In the past decade, many individual grape growers have started producing their own wines instead of selling their crops to larger wineries. These small "boutique" wineries are turning out excellent, reasonably priced wines that have caught the attention of connoisseurs and critics. Meanwhile, the larger wineries continue to consolidate land and expand their grape varietals.

Great dining and wine go hand in hand, and the local viticulture has naturally encouraged a robust passion for food. Several outstanding chefs have taken root here, sealing the area's reputation as one of the best restaurant destinations in the country. The lust for fine food doesn't stop at the doors of the bistros, either. Whether you visit an artisanal olive oil producer, nibble locally made cheese, or browse the fresh vegetables in the farmers' markets, you'll soon see why Napa and Sonoma are considered a foodie paradise.

Napa and Sonoma counties are also rich in history. In the town of Sonoma, for example, you can explore buildings from California's Spanish and Mexican past. Some wineries, such as Napa Valley's Beringer, have cellars or tasting rooms dating back to the late 1800s. The town of Calistoga is a flurry of Steamboat Gothic architecture, gussied up with the fretwork favored by late-19th-century spa goers. Modern architecture is the exception rather than the rule, but one standout example is the postmodern extravaganza of Clos Pegase winery in Calistoga.

Binding all these temptations together is the sheer scenic beauty of the place. Much of Napa Valley's landscape unspools in orderly, densely planted rows of vines. Sonoma's vistas are broken by rolling hills or stands of ancient oak and madrone trees. Even the climate cooperates, as the warm summer days and refreshingly cool evenings that make the area one of the world's best grape-growing regions make perfect weather for traveling, too. If you're inspired to dig further into the Wine Country, get ahold of the in-depth *Compass American Guide: California Wine Country*, fifth edition.

THE NAPA VALLEY

Napa Valley rules the roost of American wine production. With more than 250 wineries and many of the biggest brands in the business, there are more high-profile places here than anywhere else in the state. Vastly diverse soils and microclimates give Napa vintners the chance to make a tremendous variety of wines. But what's the area like beyond the glossy advertising and well-known names?

Most communities here are small, quirky towns with restored, gingerbread-frilled Victorian buildings. Napa itself, at the bottom of the valley, has been sprucing up its historic downtown. Compact Yountville, in the lower Napa Valley, is a culinary boomtown, while St. Helena, in the middle of the valley, attracts big spenders with elegant shops and restaurants. Calistoga, near the north border of Napa County, feels a bit like an Old West frontier town, with wooden-plank storefronts and a more casual feel than many other Wine Country towns.

18

NAPA

46 mi from San Francisco via I–80 east and north, Rte. 37 west, and Rte. 29 north.

The town of Napa is the valley's largest, and many visitors who get a glimpse of the strip malls and big-box stores from Highway 29 speed right past on the way to the smaller and more seductive Yountville or Calistoga. But if you take the time to explore, you can discover that Napa no longer entirely merits its dowdy reputation. Though the tourists have yet to arrive in droves, Napa's top-notch restaurants attract food-savvy valley residents, and the shops in the pedestrian-friendly downtown area are more down-to-earth than the pricey boutiques of, say, St. Helena. And although there are still some empty storefronts, Napa definitely has the air of a work in progress. The continual reno-

Continued on page 416

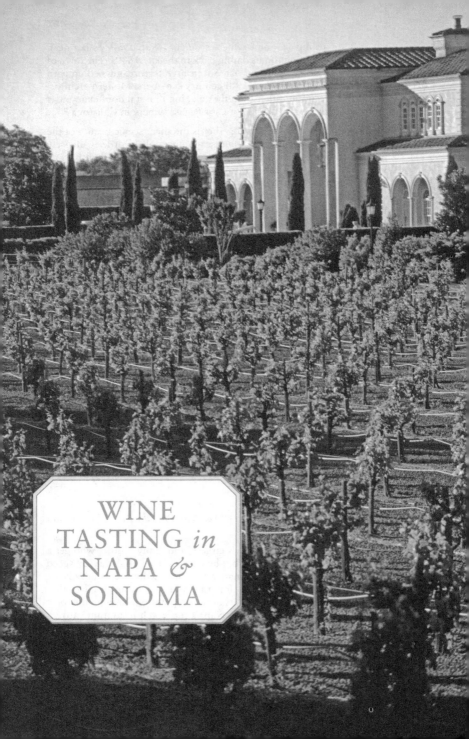

WINE
TASTING *in*
NAPA *&*
SONOMA

The tantalizing pop of a cork. Roads unspooling through hypnotically even rows of vines. Sun glinting through a glass of sparkling wine or garnet-colored cabernet. If these are the stuff of your daydreams, you won't be disappointed when you get to Napa and Sonoma. Their vineyard-blanketed hills, shady town squares, and ivy-draped wineries—not to mention the luxurious restaurants, hotels, and spas—really *are* that captivating.

(opposite page) Rows of vines in front of the opulent Ferrari-Carano Winery (top) Chardonnay grapes from Yountville (bottom) Bottles from Beringer Vineyards in St. Helena

VISITING WINERIES

Napa and Sonoma are outstanding destinations for both wine newcomers and serious wine buffs. Tasting rooms range from modest to swanky, offering everything from a casual conversation over a few sips of wine to in-depth tours of winemaking facilities and vineyards. And there's a tremendous variety of wines to taste. The one constant is a deep, shared pleasure in the experience of wine tasting. Are you ready to indulge?

Wineries in Napa and Sonoma range from faux châteaux with vast gift shops to rustic converted barns where you might have to step over the vintner's dog in the doorway. Many are regularly open to the public, usually daily from around 10 AM to 5 PM. Others require advance reservations to visit, and still others are closed to the public entirely. When in doubt, call ahead.

There are many, many more wineries in Napa and Sonoma than we could possibly include here. Free maps pinpointing most of them are widely available, though; ask the staff at the tasting rooms you visit or look for the ubiquitous free tourist magazines.

Pick a designated driver before setting out for the day. Although wineries rarely advertise it, many will provide a free non-alcoholic drink for the designated driver; it never hurts to ask.

Fees. In the past few years, tasting fees have skyrocketed. Most Napa wineries charge $10 to $20 to taste four or so wines, though $30 or even $40 fees aren't unheard of. Sonoma wineries are often a bit cheaper, in the $5 to $15 range, and you'll still find the occasional freebie.

Some winery tours are free, in which case you're usually required to pay a separate fee if you want to taste the wine. If you've paid a fee for the tour—often $10 to $20—your wine tasting is usually included in that price.

MAKING THE MOST OF YOUR TIME

■ **Call ahead.** Some wineries require reservations to visit or tour. If you have
your heart set on visiting a specific
place, double-check their availability.

■ **Come on weekdays**, especially if you're
visiting during high season (May to
November), to avoid traffic-clogged
roads and crowded tasting rooms. For
more info on the best times of year to
visit, see this chapter's Planner.

■ **Get an early start.** Tasting rooms are
often deserted before 11 AM or so, when
most visitors are still lingering over a
second cup of coffee. If you come early,
you'll have the staff's undivided attention. And don't feel self-conscious about
tippling before noon! Here, no one will
raise an eyebrow.

■ **Consider skipping Napa.** If you've got
less than two days to spend in the Wine
Country, dip into the Carneros area or
the Sonoma Valley rather than Napa
Valley or northern Sonoma County.
Though the scenery might be less dra-

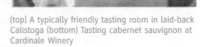

(top) A typically friendly tasting room in laid-back
Calistoga (bottom) Tasting cabernet sauvignon at
Cardinale Winery

matic, these regions are only about an
hour and half away from the city...if
you don't hit traffic.

■ **Divide your attention.** If you're lucky
enough to have three nights or more
here, split your overnights between
Napa and Sonoma to easily see the best
that both counties have to offer.

Pouring a glass of cabernet sauvignon at the Robert Mondavi Winery tasting room

AT THE BAR

In most tasting rooms, you'll be handed a list of the wines available that day. The wines will be listed in a suggested tasting order, starting with the lightest-bodied whites and progressing to the most intense reds. If you can't decide which wines to choose, tell the server what types of wines you usually like and ask for a recommendation.

The server will pour you an ounce or so of each wine you select. As you taste it, feel free to take notes or ask questions. Don't be shy—the staff are there to educate you about their wine. If you don't like a wine, or you've simply tasted enough, feel free to pour the rest into one of the dump buckets on the bar.

TOURS

Tours tend to be the most exciting (and the most crowded) in September and October, when the harvest and crushing are underway. Tours typically last from 30 minutes to an hour and give you a brief overview of the winemaking process. At some of the older wineries, the tour guide might focus on the history of the property.

■ TIP→ If you plan to take any tours, wear comfortable shoes, since you might be walking on wet floors or stepping over hoses or other equipment.

MONEY-SAVING TIPS

■ Many hotels distribute coupons for free or discounted tastings to their guests—don't forget to ask.

■ If you and your travel partner don't mind sharing a glass, servers are happy to let you split a tasting.

■ Some wineries will refund all or part of the tasting fee if you buy a bottle, making it so much easier to rationalize buying that $80 bottle of cabernet.

■ Almost all wineries will also waive the fee if you join their wine club program. However, this typically commits you to buying a certain number of bottles of their wine for a period of time, so be sure you really like their wines before signing up.

TOP 2-DAY ITINERARIES

First-Timer's Napa Tour

Start: Downtown Napa at Copia: The American Center for Wine, Food, and the Arts.

Get underway with a half-hour Winetasting 101 class. The $15 fee is offset by the passport you'll get that grants discounts at participating local wineries. Have lunch in the Copia café.

Rubicon Estate, Rutherford.

The tour here is a particularly fun way to learn about the history of Napa wine-making—and you can see the old, atmospheric, ivy-covered château.

Frog's Leap, Rutherford.
Friendly, unpretentious, and knowledgeable staff makes this place great for wine newbies. (Make sure you get that advance reservation lined up.)

Dinner & Overnight: St. Helena. Spluge at Meadowood Resort with dinner at Terra. Save at El Bonita

Domaine Carneros

di Rosa Preserve

Old Sonoma Rd.

121
12

NAPA

29

NAPA COUNTY

Robert Mondavi

Far Niente

Yountville

Oakville

KEY
— First-Timer's Napa Tour
— Wine Buff's Tour

Silverado Trail

Stag's Leap Wine Cellars

Wine Buff's Tour

Start: Stag's Leap Wine Cellars, Yountville.
Famed for its cabernet sauvignon and Bordeaux blends.

Beaulieu Vineyard, Rutherford.
Pony up the extra fee to visit the reserve tasting room to try their flagship cabernet sauvignon.

Caymus Vineyards, Rutherford.
The low-key tasting room is a great place to learn more about Rutherford and Napa cabernet artistry. Reserve in advance.

Dinner & Overnight: Yountville. Have dinner at one of the Thomas Keller restaurants. Splurge at the Villagio Inn & Spa; save at Maison Fleurie.

Next Day: Robert Mondavi, Oakville.

Spring for the reserve room tasting so you can sip the top-of-the-line wines, especially

Motel with dinner at Taylor's.

Next Day: Poke around St. Helena's shops, then drive to Yountville for lunch.

di Rosa Preserve, Napa.
Call ahead to book a one- or two-hour tour of the acres of gardens and galleries, which are chock-full of thousands of works of art.

Domaine Carneros, Napa.
Toast your trip with a glass of outstanding bubbly.

Sonoma Backroads

Start: Iron Horse Vineyards, Russian River Valley.
Soak up a view of vine-covered hills and Mount St. Helena while sipping a sparkling wine or pinot noir at this beautifully rustic spot.

Hartford Family Winery, Russian River Valley.
A terrific source for pinot noir and chardonnay, the stars of this valley.

Dinner & Overnight: Forestville. Splurge at either the Farmhouse or Applewood Inn, each of which has a top-notch restaurant. Save at the Sebastopol Inn.

Next Day: Westside Road, Russian River Valley.

This scenic route, which follows the river, is crowded with worthwhile wineries like Gary Farrell and Rochioli—but it's not crowded with visitors. Pinot fans will find a lot to love. Picnic at Rochioli, which has the best views.

Matanzas Creek Winery, near Santa Rosa.
End on an especially relaxed note with a walk through their lavender fields (best in June).

the stellar cabernet. Head across Highway 29 to the Oakville Grocery to pick up a picnic lunch.

Far Niente, Oakville.
You have to reserve in advance and the fee for the tasting and tour is steep, but the payoff is an especially intimate winery experience. You'll taste

excellent cabernet and chardonnay, then end your trip on a sweet note with a dessert wine.

WINE TASTING 101

TAKE A GOOD LOOK.

Hold your glass by the stem, raise it to the light, and take a close look at the wine. Check for clarity and color. (This is easiest to do if you can hold the glass in front of a white background.) Any tinge of brown usually means that the wine is over the hill or has gone bad.

BREATHE DEEP.

1. Sniff the wine once or twice to see if you can identify any smells.

2. Swirl the wine gently in the glass. Aerating the wine this way releases more of its aromas. (It's called "volatilizing the esters," if you're trying to impress someone.)

3. Take another long sniff. You might notice that experienced wine tasters spend more time sniffing the wine than drinking it. This is because this step is where the magic happens. The number of scents you might detect is almost endless, from berries, apricots, honey, and wildflowers to leather, cedar, or even tar. Does the wine smell good to you? Do you detect any "off" flavors, like wet dog or sulfur?

AT LAST! TAKE A SIP.

1. Swirl the wine around your mouth so that it makes contact with all your taste buds and releases more of its aromas. Think about the way the wine feels in your mouth. Is it watery or rich? Is it crisp or silky? Does it have a bold flavor, or is it subtle? The weight and intensity of a wine are called its body.

2. Hold the wine in your mouth for a few seconds and see if you can identify any developing flavors. More complex wines will reveal many different flavors as you drink them.

SPIT OR SWALLOW.

The pros typically spit, since they want to preserve their palate (and sobriety!) for the wines to come, but you'll find that swallowers far outnumber the spitters in the winery tasting rooms. Whether you spit or swallow, notice the flavor that remains after the wine is gone (the finish).

Swirl

Sniff

Sip

DODGE THE CROWDS

To avoid bumping elbows in the tasting rooms, look for wineries off the main drags of Highway 29 in Napa and Highway 12 in Sonoma. The back roads of the Russian River, Dry Creek, and Alexander valleys, all in Sonoma, are excellent places to explore. In Napa, try the northern end. Also look for wineries that are open by appointment only; they tend to schedule visitors carefully to avoid a big crush at any one time.

HOW WINE IS MADE

CRUSHING
Harvested grapes go into a stemmer-crusher, which separates stems from fruit and crushes the grapes to release "free-run" juice.

PRESSING
Remaining juice gently extracted from grapes. Usually done by pressing grapes against the walls of a tank with an inflatable bladder.

FERMENTING
Extracted juice (and also grape skins and pulp, when making red wine) goes into stainless-steel tanks or oak barrels to ferment. During fermentation, sugars convert to alcohol.

AGING
Wine stored in stainless-steel or oak casks or barrels to develop flavors.

RACKING
Wine transferred to clean barrels; sediment removed. Wine may be filtered and fined (clarified) to improve its clarity, color, and sometimes flavor.

BOTTLING
Wine bottled either at the winery or at a special facility, then stored again for bottle-aging.

WHAT'S AN APPELLATION?

A specific region with a particular set of grape-growing conditions, such as soil type, climate, and elevation, is called an appellation. What makes things a little confusing is that appellations, which are defined by the Alcohol and Tobacco Tax and Trade Bureau, often overlap. California is an appellation, for example, but so is the Napa Valley. Napa and Sonoma counties are each county appellations, but they, too, are divided into even smaller regions, usually called subappellations or AVAs (American Viticultural Areas). You'll hear a lot about these AVAs from the staff in the tasting rooms; they might explain, for example, why the Russian River Valley AVA is such an excellent place to grow pinot noir grapes. By law, if the label on a bottle of wine lists the name of an appellation, then at least 85% of the grapes in that wine must come from that appellation.

vations of historic buildings such as the glamorous 1880 Napa Valley Opera House mean that Napa is a town to watch.

Many visitors choose to stay in Napa after experiencing hotel sticker shock; prices in Napa are marginally more reasonable than elsewhere. If you set up your home base here, you'll undoubtedly want to spend some time getting out into the beautiful countryside, but don't neglect attractions in town as well. You could easily spend a full day checking out the various programs at Copia: The American Center for Wine, Food, and the Arts, or whiling away the afternoon in the shops, cafés, or wine bars.

★ The majestic château of **Domaine Carneros** looks for all the world like it belongs in France, and in fact it does: it's modeled after Champagne Taittinger's Château de la Marquetterie, an 18th-century castle near Epernay, France. Carved into the hillside beneath the winery, Domaine Carneros's cellars produce dry, delicate sparkling wines reminiscent of those made by Taittinger and use only grapes grown locally in the Carneros wine district. On weekends you can sample a variety of wines standing at the tasting bar ($11); every day of the week, however, the winery sells full glasses, flights, and bottles of their wines and serves them with hors d'oeuvres to those seated in the Louis XV–inspired salon or on the terrace overlooking the vineyards. Though this makes a visit here a tad more expensive than most stops on a winery tour, it's also one of the most opulent ways to enjoy the Carneros district. ✉ *1240 Duhig Rd.* ☎ *707/257–0101* ⊕ *www. domainecarneros.com* 🍷 *Tasting $6.25–$15, tour $25* ☉ *Daily 10–6; tour daily at 11, 1, and 3.*

Fodor'sChoice
★ When you're driving along the Carneros Highway on your way to Napa from San Francisco, it would be easy to zip by one of the region's best-kept secrets: the **di Rosa Preserve**. Metal sculptures of sheep grazing in the grass mark the entrance to this sprawling, art-stuffed property. Thousands of 20th-century artworks by hundreds of Northern California artists crop up everywhere—in galleries, in the former di Rosa residence, on every lawn, in every courtyard, and even on the lake. If you stop by without a reservation, you can only gain access to the Gatehouse Gallery, where there's a small collection of riotously colorful figurative and abstract sculpture and painting. ■TIP→**For the full effect, reserve ahead for a one-hour tour of the grounds, or opt for the two-hour tour, which allows more time to browse the main gallery.** ✉ *5200 Carneros Hwy.* ☎ *707/226–5991* ⊕ *www.dirosapreserve.org* 🍷 *$3, tours $10–$15* ☉ *Tues.–Fri. 9:30–3, Sat. by reservation; call for tour times.*

With its modern, minimalist look in the tasting room, which is dug into a Carneros hilltop, and contemporary sculptures and fountains on the property, **Artesa Vineyards & Winery** is a far cry from the many faux French châteaus and rustic Italian-style villas in the region. Although the Spanish owners once made sparkling wines, now they produce primarily still wines, including some well-regarded cabernet sauvignons, chardonnays, and pinot noirs. Two rooms off the tasting room display exhibits on the Carneros region's history and geography, as well as antique wine-making tools. ☒*1345 Henry Rd., north of Old Sonoma Rd. and Dealy La.* ☎*707/224–1668* ⊕*www.artesawinery.com* ☒*Tasting $10–$15, tour free* ⊙*Daily 10–5; tour daily at 11 and 2.*

★ **Copia: The American Center for Wine, Food & the Arts,** named after the goddess of abundance, is a shrine to American food and wine. A permanent exhibit called "Forks in the Road" explores the American relationship to food and wine in past decades, from TV dinners to haute cuisine. All sorts of garden tours, video screenings, food- and wine tastings, and tours are scheduled daily (pick up a list from the information desk). Purchase a card at the front desk in order to taste wines at ten different "Wine Stations"; here you can taste the favorite wines of Copia staffers, compare the same varietal grown in different parts of the world, or even find out what a "corked" wine—one that has been contaminated by mold in its cork—smells like. ■TIP➔**Call in advance or check their Web site for information on wine-maker dinners and luncheon seminars.** For an extra fee, you can get a fantastic opportunity to learn about the culinary arts from some of the area's best chefs and vintners. The Oxbow Public Market—a collection of artisanal food merchants, casual restaurants, and stands selling local produce—is next door. ☒*500 1st St.* ☎*707/259–1600* ⊕*www.copia.org* ☒*Free* ⊙*Wed.–Mon. 10–5.*

Luna Vineyards was established in 1995 by veterans of the Napa wine industry intent on making less-conventional wines, particularly Italian varieties. (Their whites are styled after those from Friuli, the reds after those from Tuscany.) A spacious tasting room with high ceilings, warmed by an enormous fireplace in cool weather, is a lovely spot for tasting their pinot grigio, merlot, sangiovese, cabernet, pinot noir, and a late-harvest dessert wine of sémillon and sauvignon blanc called Mille Baci ("a thousand kisses" in Italian). ☒*2921 Silverado Trail* ☎*707/255–2474* ⊕*www.lunavineyards.com* ☒*Tasting $12–$30, tour $5* ⊙*Daily 10–5; tour by appointment.*

Austere **Clos du Val** doesn't seduce you with dramatic architecture or lush grounds, but it doesn't have to: the wines, crafted by winemaker John Clews, have a wide following, especially among those who are patient enough to cellar the wines for a number of years. Though Clews's team makes great zinfandel, pinot noir, and chardonnay, the real claim to fame is the reserve cabernet. If you don't mind spending a bit more, try to visit on a weekend, when they pour reserve and library wines. Anyone is welcome to try a hand at the boccie-style game of pétanque. ☒*5330 Silverado Trail* ☎*707/259–2200* ⊕*www.closduval. com* ☒*Tasting $10–$20* ⊙*Daily 10–5; tour by appointment.*

FodorśChoice ★ The **Hess Collection Winery and Vineyards** is a delightful discovery on Mt. Veeder 9 mi northwest of the city of Napa. (Don't give up; the road leading to the winery is long and winding.) The simple, rustic limestone structure, circa 1903, contains Swiss owner Donald Hess's personal art collection, including mostly large-scale works by such contemporary European and American artists as Robert Motherwell, Francis Bacon, and Frank Stella. Cabernet sauvignon is the real strength here, though

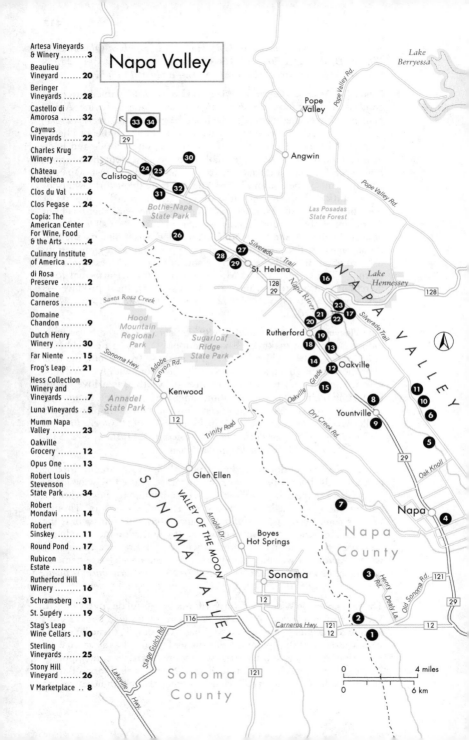

Napa Valley

Hess also produces some fine chardonnays. Self-guided tours of the art collection and guided tours of the winery's production facilities are both free. ⊠*4411 Redwood Rd., west of Rte. 29* ☎*707/255–1144* ⊕*www.hesscollection.com* ⊡*Tasting $10–$25* ⊙*Daily 10–5, tasting until 4; guided tours daily, hourly 10:30–3:30.*

WHERE TO STAY & EAT

$$$ ✕**Angèle.** An 1890s boathouse with a vaulted wood-beam ceiling sets the scene for romance at this cozy French bistro. Though the style is casual—tables are fairly close together and the warm, crusty bread is plunked right down on the paper-topped tables—the food is always well executed. Look for classic French dishes like beef bourguignonne, a rib-eye steak with red wine sauce and french fries, or a starter of ris de veau (veal sweetbreads). In fair weather, the outdoor tables are as charming as those inside. ⊠*540 Main St.* ☎*707/252–8115* ▤*AE, D, DC, MC, V.*

$$ ✕**Bistro Don Giovanni.** Dramatic flower arrangements and a roaring fire ★ in cool weather brighten this lively bistro. The Cal-Italian food is simultaneously inventive and comforting: risotto with chanterelles, artichokes, and pancetta; pizza with caramelized onions and Gongonzola; and rabbit braised in cabernet. Dishes roasted in the wood-burning oven are a specialty. Fodors.com Travel Talk Forum users suggest snagging a table on the covered patio near the fireplace for a "more intimate and quiet" experience. ⊠*4110 Howard La./Rte. 29* ☎*707/224–3300* ▤*AE, D, DC, MC, V.*

$$ ✕**Boon Fly Cafe.** Part of the Carneros Inn complex, west of downtown Napa, this small spot has a rural charm–meets–industrial chic theme. Outside, rocking chairs and swings occupy the porch of a modern red barn; inside, things get sleek with high ceilings and galvanized steel tabletops. The small menu of modernized American classics includes dishes such as braised short ribs with mashed potatoes and roasted cipollini onions and flatbread topped with bacon, Point Reyes blue cheese, and sautéed mushrooms. If there's a wait for a table, never fear: belly up to the wine bar, where you can find a good selection of reasonably priced glasses. ⊠*4048 Sonoma Hwy.* ☎*707/299–4872* ⚭*Reservations not accepted* ▤*AE, D, MC, V.*

$ ✕**Bounty Hunter.** A triple threat: Bounty Hunter is a wine store, wine ★ bar, and restaurant. You can stop by for just a glass of wine from their impressive list—a frequently changing list of 40 available by the glass in both 2- and 5-ounce pours, 400 by the bottle—but it's best to come with an appetite. There's a small selection of delicious salads and sandwiches, while meltingly tender barbecue comes from the smoker and grill just outside the back door. For something lighter, try the artichoke dip or a charcuterie plate. The space is casually chic, with pressed-tin ceilings and marble-topped café tables. **It's open until midnight on Friday and Saturday, making it a popular spot among locals for a late-night bite.** ⊠*975 1st St.* ☎*707/226–3976* ⚭*Reservations not accepted* ▤*AE, MC, V.*

$$$ ✕**Ubuntu.** Wine Country foodies are abuzz over this Napa newcomer, Fodors Choice a "vegetable restaurant" that draws heavily on local farms and its own ★ biodynamic gardens. Though vegetarian restaurants can sometimes seem ascetic—this one is even attached to a yoga studio, whose students

18

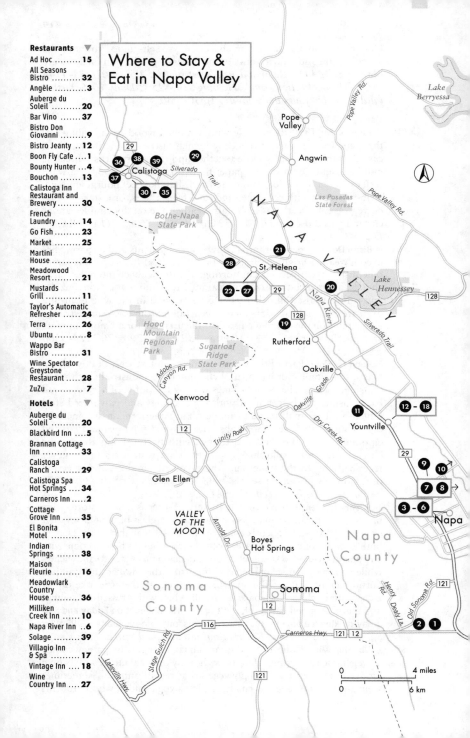

Where to Stay & Eat in Napa Valley

can be faintly seen through translucent windows—this one is anything but. Each of chef Jeremy Fox's gorgeously composed plates reveals a unique combination of flavors, from the marcona almonds generously dusted with lavender sugar and sea salt, to the grits served with barbecued Brussels sprouts and a celery root salad. Innovative desserts, like the "Bowl of Frosted Feuilletine," which mimics a tiny bowl of cereal topped with caramelized bananas and warm malted milk, prove that the restaurant doesn't take itself too seriously. The dining room strikes a New-Age-chic-meets-Wine-Country-rustic pose, with extremely high ceilings, parchment-colored lamps, fieldstone walls, and a long communal table. ⊠*1140 Main St.* ☎*707/251–5656* ▤*AE, D, MC, V.*

$$ ✕**ZuZu.** Ocher-color walls, a weathered wood bar, a faded tile floor, and hammered-tin ceiling panels set the scene for a menu composed almost entirely of tapas. These little dishes, so perfect for sharing, and Latin jazz on the stereo help make this place a popular spot for festive get-togethers. Diners down *cava* (Spanish sparkling wine) or sangria with dishes such as white anchovies with endive, ratatouille, and salt cod with garlic croutons. Reservations aren't accepted, so expect a wait on weekends, when local twentysomethings flood the zone. ⊠*829 Main St.* ☎*707/224–8555* ⌦*Reservations not accepted* ▤*AE, MC, V* ☾*No lunch weekends.*

¢–$$$ 🛏*Blackbird Inn.* Arts and Crafts style infuses this 1905 building, from the lobby's enormous fieldstone fireplace to the lamps that cast a warm glow over the impressive wooden staircase. The style is continued in the attractive guest rooms, with sturdy turn-of-the-20th-century oak beds and matching night tables, which nonetheless are updated with spacious, modern bathrooms, most with spa bathtubs. The inn is within walking distance of Napa's historic, restaurant-rich downtown area. It tends to book up quickly, so reserve well in advance. Pros: Gorgeous architecture and period furnishings, convenient to downtown Napa, free DVD library. Cons: Must be booked well in advance, some rooms are on the small side. ⊠*1755 1st St.* ☎*707/226–2450 or 888/567–9811* ⊕*www.blackbirdinnnapa.com* ⇖*8 rooms* ♿*In-room: DVD, Wi-Fi. In-hotel: no elevator, no-smoking rooms* ▤*AE, D, DC, MC, V* ⍾*CP.*

$$$$ 🛏*Carneros Inn.* Freestanding board-and-batten cottages with rocking chairs on each porch are simultaneously rustic and chic at this luxurious property. Inside, each cottage is flooded with natural light but still manages to maintain privacy worthy of a paparazzi-ducking celebrity, with windows and French doors leading to a private garden. Flat-panel TVs, ethereal beds topped with Frette linens and pristine white down comforters, and spacious bathrooms with heated slate floors and large indoor-outdoor showers may make it difficult to summon the will to leave the cottage and enjoy the hilltop infinity swimming pool and hot tub. In addition to two restaurants open the public, the Hilltop Dining Room, with views of the neighboring vineyards, is open to guests only. Pros: Cottages afford lots of privacy, huge bathrooms, hip, young feel. Cons: A long drive from destinations up-valley, limited storage space. ⊠*4048 Sonoma Hwy.* ☎*707/299–4900* ⊕*www.thecarnerosinn.com* ⇖*76 rooms, 10 suites* ♿*In-room: safe, refrigerator, DVD, Wi-Fi. In-*

FodorsChoice
★

18

hotel: 3 restaurants, room service, bar, pool, gym, spa, bicycles, no elevator, laundry service, concierge, public Wi-Fi, some pets allowed (fee), no-smoking rooms ☰AE, D, DC, MC, V.

$$$$ 🏠**Milliken Creek Inn.** Soft jazz and sunset wine and cheese set a romantic mood in the intimate lobby, with its terrace overlooking the Napa River and a lush lawn. The chic rooms take a page from the style book of British-colonial Asia, with a khaki-and-cream color scheme, rattan furniture, hydrotherapy spa tubs, and some of the fluffiest beds in the Wine Country. A tiny deck overlooking the river is the spot for massages and private yoga classes. All of the treatment rooms at the serene spa, including one used for popu-

lar couple's treatments, have river views. Pros: Cloudlike beds, serene hotel-guests-only spa, breakfast delivered to your room (or wherever you'd like to eat on the grounds). Cons: Expensive, high-tech spa tubs can be confusing, some rooms have small bathrooms. ✉*1815 Silverado Trail* ☎*707/255–1197 or 800/835–6112* ⊕*www.millikencreekinn.com* ⛵*12 rooms* ⚷*In-room: refrigerator, DVD, Wi-Fi. In-hotel: room service, spa, no elevator, concierge, no kids under 16, no-smoking rooms* ☰*AE, D, DC, MC, V* ⋈*CP.*

$–$$$ 🏠**Napa River Inn.** Almost everything's close at hand here: this waterfront inn is part of a complex of restaurants, shops, a gallery, and a spa, all within easy walking distance of downtown Napa. Guest rooms spread through three neighboring buildings. Those in the 1884 Hatt Building, in Victorian style, are arguably the most romantic, with deep red walls, original architectural details such as maple hardwood floors, and old-fashioned slipper tubs. Brighter colors dominate in the rooms of the Plaza and Embarcadero buildings, many of which have river views. Baked goods from the neighboring bakery are delivered to your door for breakfast. Pros: New pedestrian walkway connects the hotel to downtown Napa, unusual pet-friendly policy, wide range of room sizes and prices. Cons: River views could be more scenic (there's a major road across the river), construction project nearby. ✉*500 Main St.* ☎*707/251–8500 or 877/251–8500* ⊕*www.napariverinn.com* ⛵*65 rooms, 1 suite* ⚷*In-room: safe, refrigerator, DVD (some), Wi-Fi. In-hotel: 4 restaurants, room service, bar, gym, spa, bicycles, laundry service, concierge, public Internet, airport shuttle, some pets allowed (fee), no-smoking rooms* ☰*AE, D, DC, MC, V* ⋈*CP.*

NIGHTLIFE & THE ARTS

The interior of the 1879 Italianate Victorian **Napa Valley Opera House,** which had its grand reopening in 2003, isn't quite as majestic as the facade, but the intimate 500-seat venue is still an excellent place to see all sorts of performances, from Pat Metheny and Mandy Patinkin to various dance companies and even the occasional actual opera. ⊠*1030 Main St.* ☎*707/226–7372* ⊕*www.napavalleyoperahouse.org.*

BICYCLING ## SPORTS & THE OUTDOORS

Thanks to the long country roads that wind through the region, bicycling is a popular pastime. The Silverado Trail, with its gently rolling hills, is more scenic than Route 29, which nevertheless tempts some bikers with its pancake-flat aspect.■**TIP**➡**There are almost no designated bike lanes in Wine Country, though, so when cycling on the shoulders of the roads be sure to pay attention to traffic.**

Napa Valley Bike Tours (⊠*6488 Washington St., Yountville* ☎*707/944–2953 or 800/707–2453*) rents bikes (with helmets), including tandem bikes, for $30–$65 per day and will deliver bikes to many hotels in the Napa Valley if you're renting at least two bikes for a full day. One-day winery tours are $139, including lunch and van support.

YOUNTVILLE

13 mi north of the town of Napa on Rte. 29.

These days Yountville is something like Disneyland for the foodie set. It all started with Thomas Keller's French Laundry, long regarded as one of the best restaurants in the United States, and the only spot in all of Northern California to wrest a coveted three-star ranking from Michelin when they published their first guide to the San Francisco Bay Area in 2006. Now Keller is also behind two more casual restaurants just a few blocks away from his mothership, and a third on the drawing board—and that's only the beginning. You could stay here for a week and not exhaust all the options in this tiny town with a big culinary reputation.

Yountville is full of small inns and fancy hotels that cater to those who prefer not to have to drive after an extravagant meal. It's also well located for excursions to many big-name Napa wineries, especially those in the Stags Leap District, where big, bold cabernet sauvignons helped put the Napa Valley on the wine-making map.

In between bouts of eating and drinking, you might stop by **V Marketplace** (⊠*6525 Washington St.* ☎*707/944–2451*). The vine-covered brick complex, which once housed a winery, livery stable, and distillery, currently contains a smattering of clothing boutiques, art galleries, and jewelry stores, but as of this writing a large new retail space selling wines, house-made cured meats, and housewares was in the works. Across Highway 29 from downtown Yountville, in the Veterans Home, is the nifty **Napa Valley Museum** (⊠*55 Presidents Circle* ☎*707/944–0500* ⊕*www.napavalleymuseum.org* ⊠*$4.50* ⊙ *Wed.–Mon. 10–5*). The interactive displays on wines and wine making are particularly

CLOSE UP

Winespeak

You might hear wine connoisseurs tossing around terms like "Brett effect" and "*botrytis*," but don't let that turn you off. Like any activity, wine making and wine tasting have specialized vocabularies, and most of the terms are actually quite helpful, once you have them down. Here's a handful of core terms to know:

Aroma and bouquet. Aroma is the fruit-derived scent of young wine. It diminishes with fermentation and becomes a more complex **bouquet** as the wine ages.

Body. The wine's density as experienced by the palate. (A full-bodied wine makes the mouth literally feel full.) You'll also hear the word **mouthfeel** when tasters size up the texture of wine in their mouths.

Bordeaux blend. A red wine blended from varietals native to France's Bordeaux region—cabernet sauvignon, cabernet franc, malbec, merlot, and petit verdot.

Corked. When a bottle's cork spoils and the wine inside takes on a musty flavor, the wine is corked.

Estate bottled. A wine entirely made by one winery at a single facility. The grapes must come from the winery's own vineyards within the same appellation (and this must be printed on the label).

Finish. The flavors that remain in the mouth after swallowing wine. A long finish is a good thing.

Flight. A few wines specially selected for tasting together.

Horizontal tasting. A tasting of several different wines of the same vintage.

Library wine. An older vintage that the winery has put aside to sell at a later date.

Oaky. A vanilla–woody flavor that develops when wine is aged in oak barrels. Leave a wine too long in a new oak barrel and that oaky taste overpowers the other flavors.

Reserve wine. Fuzzy term used by vintners to indicate a wine is better in some way (through aging, source of the grapes, etc.) than others from their winery.

Rhône blend. A wine made from grapes hailing from France's Rhône Valley, such as marsanne, roussanne, syrah, cinsault, mourvèdre, or viognier.

Tannins. You can tell when they're there, but their origins are still a mystery. These natural grape compounds produce a sensation of drying or astringency in the mouth. Tannins settle out as wine ages; they're a big player in many red wines.

Terroir. French word that translates as "soil." Typically used to describe the unique environment (climate, soil, etc.) that influence the grapes and thus the wine.

Vertical tasting. A tasting of several wines of different vintages, generally starting with the youngest and proceeding to the oldest.

Vintage. The grape harvest of a given year, and the year in which the grapes are harvested. (A vintage date on a bottle indicates the year in which the grapes were harvested, not the year in which the wine was bottled.)

Oh, and that Brett effect? That's the funky flavor a certain yeast strain can cause in wine. Some like a mild Brett effect, but it's usually considered a fault in the wine.

engaging; for instance, you can test your knowledge of wine terms and food-and-wine pairings. The rotating shows upstairs, focusing on fine art and local history, are also worth a look.

French-owned **Domaine Chandon** claims one of Yountville's prime pieces of real estate, on a knoll west of downtown where whimsical sculptures sprout out of the lawn and ancient oaks shade the winery. Tours of the sleek, modern facilities are available for $7, but the highlight is a tasting. The top-quality sparklers are made using the laborious *méthode champenoise* (which means, among other things, that the bubbly undergoes a second fermentation in the bottle before the bottles are "riddled," or turned every few days over a period of weeks, to nudge the sediment into the neck of the bottle). To complete the decadent experience, you can order hors d'oeuvres to accompany the wines in the tasting room. ⊠ *1 California Dr., west of Rte. 29* ☎ *707/944–2280* ⊕ *www.chandon.com* 🍷 *Tasting $7–$30* ⊙ *Daily 10–6; tours May–Dec., Mon.–Thurs. 11, 1, 3, and 5, Fri.–Sun., 11, noon, 1, 2, 3, 4, and 5; Jan.–Apr., weekdays 11, 1, and 3, weekends 11, 1, 3, and 5.*

It was the 1973 cabernet sauvignon produced by **Stag's Leap Wine Cellars** that put the winery—and the California wine industry—on the map by placing first in the famous Paris tasting of 1976. A visit to the winery is a no-frills affair; visitors in the small, spare tasting room are clearly serious about tasting wine and aren't interested in distractions like a gift shop. It costs a hefty $40 to taste the top-of-the-line wines, including their limited-production estate-grown cabernets, some of which sell for well over $100. If you're interested in more modestly priced wines, try the $15 tasting, which usually includes a sauvignon blanc, chardonnay, merlot, and a cabernet. ⊠ *5766 Silverado Trail* ☎ *707/265–2441* ⊕ *www.cask23.com* 🍷 *Tasting $15–$40, tour $40* ⊙ *Daily 10–4:30; tour by appointment.*

Robert Sinskey Vineyards makes well-regarded chardonnay, cabernet, and merlot, but is best known for its intense, brambly pinot noir. The influence of Robert's wife, Maria Helm Sinskey—a chef and cookbook author—is evident at the back of the dramatic, high-ceiling tasting room, where there's an open kitchen. Tours of the cave and cellar wind up with a flight of wines, but for the best sense of how Sinskey wines pair with food, reserve a spot on the culinary tour, which includes cheese and charcuterie served with the wines. ⊠ *6320 Silverado Trail* ☎ *707/944–9090* ⊕ *www.robertsinskey.com* 🍷 *Tasting $20, tours $30–$50* ⊙ *Daily 10–4:30; 1-hr tours by appointment.*

WHERE TO STAY & EAT

$$$$

Fodor's Choice

★

✕ **Ad Hoc.** When superstar chef Thomas Keller opened this relatively casual spot in 2006, he meant to run it for only six months until he opened a burger joint in the same space—but locals were so charmed by the homey food that they clamored for the stopgap to stay. Now a single, seasonal fixed-price menu ($48) is served nightly. The selection might include a juicy pork loin and buttery polenta, served family style, or a delicate panna cotta with a citrus glaze. The dining room is warmly low-key, with zinc-topped tables, wine served in tumblers, and rock and jazz on the stereo. If you just can't wait to know what's going be served before you visit, you can call a day in advance for the menu. ✉6476 *Washington St.* ☎*707/944–2487* ▤*AE, MC, V* ◷*No lunch.*

$$ ✕**Bistro Jeanty.** Philippe Jeanty's menu draws its inspiration from the cooking of his French childhood. His traditional cassoulet will warm those nostalgic for France, and the bistro classic *steak frites* might be served with a decadent béarnaise sauce. The scene here is Gallic through and through, with a small bar and a handful of tables in two crowded rooms. ▪TIP➔**The best seats are in the back room, near the fireplace.** ✉*6510 Washington St.* ☎*707/944–0103* ▤*AE, MC, V.*

$$$ ✕**Bouchon.** The team that brought French Laundry to its current pinnacle is behind this place, where everything from the snazzy zinc bar to the elbow-to-elbow seating to the traditional French onion soup could have come straight from a Parisian bistro. *Boudin noir* (blood sausage) with potato puree and leg of lamb with white beans and piquillo peppers are among the hearty dishes served in the high-ceiling room. The noise level booms during peak hours, so ask for one of the (very few) outside tables if you prefer a bit more peace and quiet. ▪TIP➔**Late-night meals from a limited menu are served until 12:30 AM—a rarity in the Wine Country, where it's often difficult to find a place to eat after 10 PM.** ✉*6534 Washington St.* ☎*707/944–8037* ▤*AE, MC, V.*

$$$$ ✕**French Laundry.** An old stone building houses the most acclaimed restaurant in Napa Valley—and, indeed, one of the most highly regarded in the country. The restaurant's two prix-fixe menus ($240), one of which is vegetarian, vary but the "oysters and pearls," a silky sabayon of pearl tapioca with oysters and sevruga caviar, is a signature starter. Some courses rely on luxe ingredients like foie gras, while others take humble foods like fava beans and elevate them to art. Reservations at French Laundry are hard won and not accepted more than two months in advance. **Call two months ahead to the day at 10 AM on the dot. Didn't get a reservation? Call on the day you'd like to dine here to be considered if there's a cancellation.** Gentlemen, a jacket is required. ✉*6640 Washington St.* ☎*707/944–2380* ⊕*Reservations essential* ▤*AE, MC, V* ◷*Closed 1st 2 wks in Jan. No lunch Mon.–Thurs.*

Fodor's Choice ★

$$–$$$ ✕**Mustards Grill.** There's not an ounce of pretension at Cindy Pawlcyn's longtime Napa favorite, despite the fact that it's booked solid every day and night with fans of her hearty cuisine. The menu mixes updated renditions of traditional American dishes such as baby back pork ribs and lemon meringue pie with innovative choices such as sweet corn tamales with tomatillo-avocado salsa and pumpkin seeds. A black-and-white marble tile floor and upbeat artwork set a scene that one Fodors.com reader describes as "pure fun, if not fancy." ✉*7399 St. Helena Hwy./Rte. 29, 1 mi north of town* ☎*707/944–2424* ⊕*Reservations essential* ▤*AE, D, DC, MC, V.*

¢–$$ ▦**Maison Fleurie.** If you'd like to be within easy walking distance of most of Yountville's best restaurants, and possibly score a great bargain, look into this casual, comfortable inn. Rooms share a French country style (think floral bedspreads and blooming trompe l'oeil paintings) but vary dramatically in size and amenities. The largest have a private entrance, deck, fireplace, and spa bathtub. **For a much lower rate you can**
★

get a tiny but well-kept room—and save for a French Laundry meal instead. Pros: Smallest rooms are some of the most affordable in town, free bike rental, refrigerator stocked with free soda. Cons: Breakfast room can be crowded at peak times, bedding could be nicer. ✉ *6529 Yount St.* ☎ *800/788–0369* ⊕ *www.maisonfleurienapa.com* ➥ *13 rooms* ♿ *In-room: refrigerator (some), DVD (some), no TV (some), Wi-Fi. In-hotel: pool, bicycles, no elevator, no-smoking rooms* ▤ *AE, D, DC, MC, V* ¶⊙¶ *CP.*

$$$–$$$$
★

☆ **Villagio Inn & Spa.** Luxury here is about calm, not bling. Stroll past the fountains and clusters of low buildings to reach the pool, where automated misters cool the sunbathers. Streamlined furnishings, subdued color schemes, and high ceilings enhance a sense of spaciousness in the guest rooms. Each room also has a fireplace and, beyond louvered doors, a balcony or patio. A brand-new spa, completed in 2008, has huge "spa suites" big enough for small groups, as well as individual treatment rooms, spread out over 13,000 square feet. Rates include afternoon tea, a bottle of wine, and a generous buffet breakfast—and as the hotel's near the town center, you'll be right near all those outstanding restaurants. Pros: Decadent buffet breakfast, brand-new spa, steps away from Yountville's best restaurants. Cons: Can be bustling with large groups, some exterior rooms get highway noise. ✉ *6481 Washington St.* ☎ *707/944–8877 or 800/351–1133* ⊕ *www.villagio.com* ➥ *86 rooms, 26 suites* ♿ *In-room: refrigerator, DVD, Wi-Fi. In-hotel: room service, tennis courts, pool, spa, bicycles, no elevator, concierge, laundry service, no-smoking rooms* ▤ *AE, D, DC, MC, V* ¶⊙¶ *CP.*

$$$–$$$$

☆ **Vintage Inn.** Rooms in this luxurious inn are housed in two-story villas scattered around a lush, landscaped 3½-acre property. French fabrics and plump upholstered chairs outfit spacious, airy guest rooms with vaulted beamed ceilings, all of which have a private patio or balcony, a fireplace, and a whirlpool tub in the bathroom. Some private patios have vineyard views. You're treated to a bottle of wine, a buffet breakfast, and afternoon tea and scones. Pros: Spacious bathrooms, lavish breakfast buffet, luscious bedding. Cons: Some exterior rooms get highway noise, pool area is smaller than the one at its sister property, the Villagio Inn & Spa. ✉ *6541 Washington St.* ☎ *707/944–1112 or 800/351–1133* ☎ *707/944–1617* ⊕ *www.vintageinn.com* ➥ *68 rooms, 12 suites* ♿ *In-room: refrigerator, DVD, Wi-Fi. In-hotel: room service, bar, tennis courts, pool, bicycles, no elevator, concierge, laundry service, some pets allowed (fee), no-smoking rooms* ▤ *AE, D, DC, MC, V* ¶⊙¶ *CP.*

18

OAKVILLE

2 mi west of Yountville on Rte. 29.

There are three reasons to visit the town of Oakville: its grocery store, its scenic mountain road, and its magnificent, highly exclusive wineries.

The **Oakville Grocery** (✉ *7856 St. Helena Hwy./Rte. 29* ☎ *707/944–8802*), built in 1881 as a general store, carries a surprisingly wide range of unusual and chichi groceries and prepared foods despite its tiny size. Despite the maddening crowds that pack the narrow aisles on weekends, it's still a fine place to sit on a bench out front and sip an espresso between winery visits.

Along the mountain range that divides Napa and Sonoma, the **Oakville Grade** (✉ *West of Rte. 29*) is a twisting half-hour route with breathtaking views of both valleys. Although the surface of the road is good, it can be difficult to negotiate at night, and the continual curves mean that it's not ideal for those who suffer from motion sickness.

The combined venture of the late California winemaker Robert Mondavi and the late French baron Philippe de Rothschild, **Opus One** produces only one wine: a big, inky Bordeaux blend that was the first of Napa's ultra-premium wines, fetching unheard-of prices before it was overtaken by cult wines like Screaming Eagle. The winery's futuristic limestone-clad structure, built into the hillside, seems to be pushing itself out of the earth. Although the tour, which focuses on why it costs so much to produce this exceptional wine, comes off as a bit snooty—one Fodors.com reader calls it "stuffy"—the facilities are undoubtedly impressive, with gilded mirrors, exotic orchids, and a large semicircular cellar modeled on the Château Mouton Rothschild winery in France. You can also taste without the tour ($30), as long as you've called ahead for a reservation. ✉ *7900 St. Helena Hwy./Rte. 29* ☎ *707/944–9442* ⊕ *www.opusonewinery.com* ✉ *Tour $35* ⊙ *Daily 10–4; tasting and tour by appointment.*

The arch at the center of the sprawling Mission-style building at **Robert Mondavi** perfectly frames the lawn and the vineyard behind, inviting a stroll under the lovely arcades. If you've never been on a winery tour before, the comprehensive 70- to 90-minute tour, followed by a seated tasting, is a good way to learn about oenology, as well as the late Robert Mondavi's role in California wine making. You can also head straight for one of the two tasting rooms. Serious wine lovers should definitely consider springing for the $30 reserve room tasting, where you can enjoy four generous tastes of Mondavi's top-of-the-line wines, including the reserve cabernet that cemented the winery's reputation. Concerts, mostly jazz and R&B, take place in summer on the lawn; call ahead for tickets. ✉ *7801 St. Helena Hwy./Rte. 29* ☎ *888/766–6328* ⊕ *www.robertmondaviwinery.com* ✉ *Tasting $5–$30, tour $25* ⊙ *Daily 10–5; tours daily on the hr 10–4.*

FodorsChoice ★ Though the fee for the combined tour and tasting is one of the highest in the valley, **Far Niente** is especially worth visiting if you're tired of elbowing your way through crowded tasting rooms and are looking for a more personal experience. Here you're welcomed by name and treated to a glimpse of one of the most beautiful Napa

---

ATTENTION CAR BUFFS!

On Far Niente's winery tour you can salivate over the founder's classic race car collection, which includes a 1961 Corvette roadster, a stately, swoopy 1954 Jaguar, and a rare, bright yellow 1951 Ferrari 340 America. Even if you don't visit them at their home base, you might get lucky and spot one on the road—some of the cars from the collection are driven in the area.

properties. Small groups are shepherded through the historic 1885 stone winery for a session on the labor-intensive method for making Far Niente's well-regarded cabernets and chardonnays. The next stop is the Carriage House, where you can see the founder's gleaming collection of classic race cars. The tour ends with a seated tasting of wines and cheeses, capped by a sip

of the spectacular Dolce, a late-harvest dessert wine made by Far Niente's sister winery. ⊠*1 Acacia Dr.* ☎*707/944–2861* ⊕*www.farniente. com* ⊠*$50* ⊙*Tasting and tour by appointment.*

RUTHERFORD

1 mi northwest of Oakville on Rte. 29.

From a fast-moving car, Rutherford is a quick blur of vineyards and a rustic barn or two, but don't speed by this tiny hamlet. With its singular microclimate and soil, this is an important viticultural center, with more big-name wineries than you can shake a corkscrew at. Cabernet sauvignon is king here. The well-drained, loamy soil is ideal for those vines, and since this part of the valley gets plenty of sun, the grapes develop exceptionally intense flavors. The late, great winemaker André Tchelistcheff's claimed that "it takes Rutherford dust to grow great cabernet."

★ But it's not all grapevines here—you can switch your fruit focus to olives at **Round Pond.** This small farm grows five varieties of Italian olives and three types of Spanish olives. Within an hour of being handpicked (sometime between October and February), the olives are crushed in the mill on the property to produce pungent, peppery oils that are later blended and sold. Call a few days in advance to arrange a tour of the mill followed by an informative tasting, during which you can sample several types of oil, both alone and with Round Pond's own red wine vinegars and other tasty foods. ⊠*877 Rutherford Rd.* ☎*877/963–9364* ⊕*www.roundpond.com* ⊠*Tour $20* ⊙*Tour by appointment.*

It's the house *The Godfather* built. Filmmaker Francis Ford Coppola began his wine-making career in 1975, when he bought part of the historic, renowned Inglenook estate. He eventually reunited the original Inglenook land and snagged the ivy-covered 19th-century château to boot. In 2006 he renamed the property **Rubicon Estate,** intending to focus on his premium wines, including the namesake cabernet sauvignon–based blend. (The less-expensive wines, along with movie memorabilia, are showcased at Coppola's second winery in Sonoma County's Geyserville.) A visit here starts at a cool $25, but this price tag is tied to smooth orchestration. The fee covers valet parking, a tour of the château and discussion of the estate's history, and a tasting in the opulent, high-ceiling tasting room. Greeters explain the other offerings with

18

additional fees, such as food-and-wine pairings and more in-depth tours. ⊠*1991 St. Helena Hwy./Rte. 29* ☎*707/963–9099* ⊕*www.rubiconestate.com* ☜*$25* ⊙*Daily 10–5; tour daily at 10:30, 11:30, 12:30, 1:30, and 2:30.*

Though you might be tempted to enter the beautifully restored 1882 Queen Anne Victorian at **St. Supéry** to look for the tasting room, in fact the wines are being poured in the building behind it, a bland, unappealing, officelike structure. You'll likely forgive the atmospheric lapse once you taste their fine sauvignon blancs, merlots, chardonnays, and cabernet sauvignons. An excellent, free self-guided tour also allows you a peek at the barrel and fermentation rooms, as well as a gallery of rotating art exhibits. At the "Smell-a-Vision" station you can test your ability to identify different smells that might be present in wine. ⊠*8440 St. Helena Hwy. S/Rte. 29* ☎*707/963–4507* ⊕*www.stsupery.com* ☜*Tasting $15–$20, tour $20* ⊙*Daily 10–5; tour at 1 and 3.*

The cabernet sauvignon produced at ivy-covered **Beaulieu Vineyard** is a benchmark of the Napa Valley. The legendary André Tchelistcheff, who helped define the California style of wine making, worked his magic here from 1938 until his death in 1973. This helps explain why Beaulieu's flagship Georges de Latour Private Reserve Cabernet Sauvignon still garners high marks from major wine publications. The zinfandels, merlots, and chardonnays being poured in the main tasting room are notably good. Still, it's worth paying the few extra dollars to taste that special cabernet in the more luxe, less crowded reserve tasting room. ⊠*1960 St. Helena Hwy./Rte. 29* ☎*707/967–5200* ⊕*www.bvwines.com* ☜*Tasting $10–$30* ⊙*Daily 10–5.*

Fodor'sChoice ★ **Frog's Leap** is the perfect place for wine novices to begin their education. The owners, the Williams family, maintain a goofy sense of humor about wine that translates into an entertaining yet informative experience. They also happen to produce some very fine zinfandel, cabernet sauvignon, merlot, chardonnay, sauvignon blanc, and a rosé called, simply enough, "Pink." They pride themselves on the sustainability of their operation, and the tour guides can tell you about their organic farming and solar power techniques. The winery includes a red barn built in 1884, an ecofriendly visitor center, and, naturally, a frog pond topped with lily pads. ⊠*8815 Conn Creek Rd.* ☎*707/963–4704* ⊕*www.frogsleap.com* ☜*Tasting and tour free* ⊙*Mon.–Sat. 10–4; tastings and tour by appointment.*

Caymus Vineyards is run by wine master Chuck Wagner, who started making wine on the property in 1972. His family, however, had been farming in the valley since 1906. Today their cabernet is the winery's claim to fame, a ripe, fairly high alcohol wine that's known for its consistently high quality. ■ TIP→ **Though there's no tour and you have to reserve to taste, it's worth planning ahead to visit because the small, low-key seated tasting is a great opportunity to learn about the valley's cabernet artistry.** ⊠*8700 Conn Creek Rd.* ☎*707/967–3010* ⊕*www.caymus.com* ☜*Tasting $25* ⊙*Sales daily 10–4; tastings by appointment.*

Mumm Napa Valley is one of California's best-known sparkling-wine producers. But enjoying the bubbly from the glass-walled tasting room or on the terrace overlooking a vineyard isn't the only reason to visit. There's also an excellent photography gallery with 27 Ansel Adams prints and rotating exhibits. You can even take that glass of wonderfully crisp Brut Prestige with you as wander. ⊠*8445 Silverado Trail* ☎*707/967–7700* ⊕*www.mummnapavalley.com* ⊠*Tasting $6–$25, tour free* ⊙*Daily 10–5; tour daily on the hr 10–3.*

Perched on a hill overlooking the valley, **Rutherford Hill Winery** is a merlot lover's paradise in a cabernet sauvignon sea. When the winery's founders were deciding what grapes to plant, they discovered that the climate and soil conditions of their vineyards resembled those of Pomerol, a region of Bordeaux where merlot is king. The wine caves here are some of the most extensive of any California winery—nearly a mile of tunnels and passageways. You can get a glimpse of the tunnels and the 8,000 barrels inside on the tours, then cap your visit with a picnic in their oak, olive, or madrone orchards. ⊠*200 Rutherford Hill Rd., east of Silverado Trail* ☎*707/963–1871* ⊕*www.rutherford hill.com* ⊠*Tasting $15, tour $20* ⊙*Daily 10–5; tour daily at 11:30, 1:30, and 3:30.*

WHERE TO STAY & EAT

$$$$
★ ✕🏠**Auberge du Soleil.** Taking a cue from the olive-tree-studded landscape, this renowned hotel cultivates a Mediterranean look. It's luxury as simplicity: earth-tone tile floors, heavy wood furniture, and terracotta colors. The spare style is backed with lavish amenities, though, such as plasma TVs, private terraces, and truly grand bathrooms, many with whirlpool tubs and extra-large showers with multiple shower heads. However, some fodors.com users suggest that at these prices—some of the highest in all the Wine Country—service could be better. The Auberge du Soleil restaurant has an impressive wine list and serves a Mediterranean-inflected menu that relies largely on local produce. Be sure to ask for a table on the terrace in fair weather. The bar serves less expensive fare until 11 PM nightly. Pros: Stunning views over the valley, spectacular pool and spa areas, the most expensive suites are fit for a superstar. Cons: Prices are stratospheric, rooms in the main house get some noise from the bar and restaurant. ⊠*180 Rutherford Hill Rd., off Silverado Trail north of Rte. 128* ☎*707/963–1211 or 800/348–5406* ⊕*www.aubergedusoleil.com* ⇤*34 rooms, 18 suites* ⚁*In-room: safe, refrigerator, DVD, Wi-Fi. In-hotel: 2 restaurants, room service, bar, tennis court, pool, gym, spa, concierge, no-smoking rooms* ▤*AE, D, DC, MC, V.*

18

ST. HELENA

2 mi northwest of Oakville on Rte. 29.

Downtown St. Helena is a microcosm of the good life. Sycamore trees arch over Main Street (Route 29), a funnel of outstanding restaurants and tempting boutiques. At the north end of town looms the hulking stone building of the Culinary Institute of America. Weathered stone and brick buildings from the late 1800s give off that gratifying whiff of history.

By the time pioneer winemaker Charles Krug planted grapes in St. Helena around 1860, quite a few vineyards already existed in the area. Today the town is hemmed in by wineries, and you could easily spend days visiting vintners within a few miles. If you're looking for a break from sipping, drive 3 mi north of town, off Highway 29, to visit the **Bale Grist Mill State Historic Park,** where the 19th-century mill buildings are open daily and the water mill is in operation on weekends. Hiking trails lead from the mill through parkland.

Fodor'sChoice   When visiting **Stony Hill Vineyard,** it's easy to imagine that this is what
★   the Napa Valley was like 20 years ago, before many of the wineries started building glitzy visitor centers and charging tasting fees. When you call to make a reservation for a tour and tasting, you'll get directions for following the unmarked road that winds up the hill north of St. Helena to their secluded property. From this perch, you can have beautiful views of the valley floor in between stands of old oak and cypress trees. The tour is casual and conversational—the guide relies on questions from visitors instead of reciting a canned spiel. The visit ends with a tasting of their excellent unoaked chardonnay. If you're lucky, you might get a nip of their dry gewürztraminer or riesling, though they're often sold out. ⊠*3331 St. Helena Hwy. N/Rte. 29* ☎*707/963–2636* ⊕*www.stonyhillvineyard.com* 🖼*Tasting and tour free* ☉*Tasting and tour by appointment only.*

The first winery founded in the Napa Valley, **Charles Krug Winery,** opened in 1861 when Count Haraszthy lent Krug a small cider press. Today the Peter Mondavi family runs it. At this writing, tours have been suspended indefinitely because a major earthquake retrofit project is in the works, but you can still come for tastings. Though they are best known for their lush red Bordeaux blends, their zinfandel is also good—or go for something unusual with their New Zealand–style sauvignon blanc. Its zingy flavor of citrus and tropical fruit is rare in wines from this area. ⊠*2800 N. Main St.* ☎*707/963–5057* ⊕*www. charleskrug.com* 🖼*Tasting $10–$20* ☉*Daily 10:30–5.*

Arguably the most beautiful winery in Napa Valley, the 1876 **Beringer Vineyards** is also the oldest continuously operating property. In 1884 Frederick and Jacob Beringer built the Rhine House Mansion to serve as Frederick's family home. Though it was closed for renovations at this writing, it is expected to reopen in late 2008 for reserve tastings amid the Belgian art-nouveau hand-carved oak and walnut furniture and stained-glass windows (other tastings will probably continue in the original stone winery—please call the winery for an update before you visit). Because of its big reputation and lovely grounds the winery gets crowded in high season. ■TIP→**If you're looking for an undiscovered gem, pass this one by, but first-time visitors to the valley will learn a lot about the history of wine making in the region on the introductory tour.** Longer tours, which might pass through a demonstration vineyard or end with a seated tasting in the wine-aging tunnels, are also offered a few times a day. ⊠*2000 Main St./ Rte. 29* ☎*707/963–4812* ⊕*www. beringer.com* ☒*Tasting $10–$25, tours $15–$35* ⊙*May 30–Oct. 23, daily 10–6; Oct. 24–May 29, daily 10–5; tour daily 10:45, 1:30, and 2.*

The West Coast headquarters of the **Culinary Institute of America,** the country's leading school for chefs, are in the **Greystone Winery,** a national historic landmark and an imposingly large stone building.

The campus consists of 30 acres of herb and vegetable gardens and a Mediterranean-inspired restaurant, which is open to the public. Also on the property are a well-stocked culinary store that tempts aspiring chefs with gleaming gadgets and a quirky corkscrew display. One-hour cooking demonstrations take place one to three times a day Friday through Monday; call for times and to reserve a spot. ⊠*2555 Main St.* ☎*707/967–1100* ⊕*www.ciachef.edu* ☒*Free, demonstrations $15* ⊙*Restaurant Sun.–Thurs. 11:30–9, Fri. and Sat. 11:30–10; store and museum daily 10–6.*

WHERE TO STAY & EAT

$$ ✕ **Go Fish.** Prolific restaurateur Cindy Pawlcyn and superstar chef Vic-
★ tor Scargle are the big names behind one of the few restaurants in the Wine Country to specialize in seafood. You can either sit at the long marble bar and watch the chefs whip up inventive sushi rolls and raw bar bites, or head into the dining room to study the mouthwatering menu. The large, lively space works an modern-chic look, with stainless-steel lamps and comfortable banquettes. You might try olive oil-poached haddock, clam chowder, or a rich crab-cake sandwich served on a brioche bun. ⊠*641 Main St.* ☎*707/963–0700* ⊟*AE, D, DC, MC, V.*

$$ ✕ **Market.** The fieldstone walls and friendly service would set a homey mood here even if the menu didn't present comfort food's greatest hits, from fried chicken with mashed potatoes to the signature macaroni and cheese. A top-notch team, with experience working at some of San Francisco's finest restaurants, has made this an exceedingly popular spot. ⊠*1347 Main St.* ☎*707/963–3799* ⊟*AE, MC, V.*

$$$$ ✕ **Martini House.** Beautiful and boisterous, St. Helena's most stylish restaurant fills a converted 1923 Craftsman-style home, where earthy colors are made even warmer by the glow of three fireplaces. Woodsy ingredients such as chanterelles or juniper berries might accompany sweetbreads or a hearty grilled loin of venison. Inventive salads and delicate desserts such as the blood orange sorbet demonstrate chef-owner Todd Humphries' range. In warm weather, angle for a table on the patio, where lights sparkle in the trees. If you don't have a reservation, ask for a seat at the bar downstairs, where you can order from

18

either the bar menu or the full menu. ✉*1245 Spring St.* ☎*707/963–2233* 💳*AE, D, DC, MC, V* 🕓*No lunch Mon.–Thurs.*

¢ ✕**Taylor's Automatic Refresher.** A slick 1950s-style outdoor hamburger
★ stand goes upscale at this hugely popular spot, where locals are willing to brave long lines to order juicy burgers, root beer floats, and garlic fries. There are also plenty of choices you wouldn't have found 50 years ago, such as the ahi tuna burger and chicken club with pesto mayo. Arrive early or late for lunch, or all the shaded picnic tables on the lawn might be filled with happy throngs. Another branch of Taylor's opened in downtown Napa's Oxbow Public Market in 2008. ✉*933 Main St.* ☎*707/963–3486* 💳*AE, MC, V.*

$$$ ✕**Terra.** The look may be old-school romance, with candlelit tables
Fodor$Choice in an 1884 fieldstone building, but the cooking is deliciously of the
★ moment. Chef Hiro Sone juices up Italian and southern-French cuisine with unexpected twists, in dishes such as sweetbreads with braised endive, burdock, and black truffle sauce. A few, like the sake-marinated black cod in a shiso broth, draw on Sone's Japanese background. Inventive desserts, courtesy of Sone's wife, Lissa Doumani, might include a maple sugar crème brûlée served in a baked apple. Servers gracefully and unobtrusively attend to every dropped fork or half-full water glass; they're head and shoulders above the enthusiastic but inexpert staff you can find at many other local restaurants. ✉*1345 Railroad Ave.* ☎*707/963–8931* 🍴*Reservations essential* 💳 *AE, DC, MC, V* 🕓*Closed Tues. and 1st 2 wks in Jan. No lunch.*

$$$ ✕**Wine Spectator Greystone Restaurant.** The Culinary Institute of America runs this place in the handsome old Christian Brothers Winery. Century-old stone walls house a cavernous and bustling restaurant, with several cooking stations in full view; on busy nights you might find the hard-at-work chefs more entertaining than your dinner partner. The menu has a Mediterranean spirit and emphasizes locally grown produce. Typical main courses include pan-seared scallops with a white bean puree and winter-vegetable potpie. ✉*2555 Main St.* ☎*707/967–1010* 💳*AE, D, DC, MC, V.*

$$$$ ✕🏨**Meadowood Resort.** Everything at Meadowood seems to run seam-
Fodor$Choice lessly, starting with the gatehouse staff who alert the front desk to arriv-
★ als, so that a receptionist is ready for each guest. A rambling lodge and several bungalows are scattered across the sprawling property. Guest rooms have views over these wooded grounds from expansive windows. The supremely comfortable beds defy you to get up and pursue the golf, tennis, hiking, or other activities on offer. The elegant but unstuffy dining room, overhauled in 2006, is becoming a destination restaurant for its splurge dishes (think lobster and squab salad with zinfandel-onion marmalade) and expert service. Pros: Sites of one of Napa's best restaurants, lovely hiking trail on the property, serene atmosphere. Cons: Very expensive, Wi-Fi can be dodgy in spots. ✉*900 Meadowood La.* ☎*707/963–3646 or 800/458–8080* 📠*707/963–5863* 🌐*www.meadowood.com* 🛏*40 rooms, 45 suites* 🍴*In-room: refrigerator, DVD, Wi-Fi. In-hotel: 2 restaurants, room service, bar, golf course, tennis courts, pools, gym, no elevator, children's programs (ages 6–12), concierge, no-smoking rooms* 💳*AE, D, DC, MC, V.*

¢–$$ El Bonita Motel. Only in St. Helena would a basic room in a roadside motel cost around $200 a night in high season. Still, for budget-minded travelers the tidy rooms here are pleasant enough, and the landscaped grounds and picnic tables elevate the property over similar places. There's even a small sauna next to the hot tub and swimming pool, which is heated year-round. ■TIP→**Family-friendly pluses include roll-away beds and cribs for a modest extra charge. Its location right on Route 29 makes it convenient, but light sleepers should ask for rooms farthest from the road.** Pros: Cheerful rooms, hot tub, microwaves and mini-refrigerators. Cons: Road noise is a problem in some rooms. ⊠*195 Main St./Rte. 29* ☎*707/963–3216 or 800/541–3284* 🖷*707/963–8838* ⊕*www.elbonita.com* ⇔*38 rooms, 4 suites* ⊲*In-room: kitchen, refrigerator, Wi-Fi. In-hotel: pool, no elevator, public Internet, some pets allowed (fee), no-smoking rooms* ▤*AE, D, DC, MC, V* ⏏*CP.*

$$$–$$$$ Wine Country Inn. A pastoral landscape of hills surrounds this peaceful New England–style retreat. Rooms are comfortably done with homey furniture like four-poster beds topped with quilts, and many have a wood-burning or gas fireplace, a large jetted tub, or a patio or balcony overlooking the vineyards. A hearty breakfast is served buffet-style in the sun-splashed common room, and wine and appetizers are available in the afternoon next to the wood-burning cast-iron stove. Though it's not the most stylish lodging in the area, the thoughtful staff and the vineyard views from many rooms encourage many people to return year after year. Pros: Free shuttle to selected restaurants (reserve early), lovely grounds, swimming pool is heated year-round. Cons: Some rooms let in noise from neighboring rooms, some rooms could use updating. ⊠*1152 Lodi La., east of Rte. 29* ☎*707/963–7077* 🖷*707/963–9018* ⊕*www.winecountryinn.com* ⇔*24 rooms, 5 suites* ⊲*In-room: refrigerator (some), no TV, Wi-Fi. In-hotel: pool, no elevator, concierge, no-smoking rooms* ▤*MC, V* ⏏*BP.*

SHOPPING

Dean & Deluca (⊠*607 St. Helena Hwy. S/Rte. 29* ☎*707/967–9980*), a branch of the famous Manhattan store, is crammed with everything you need in the kitchen—including terrific produce and deli items—as well as a huge wine selection. Many of the cheeses sold here are produced locally. The airy **I. Wolk Gallery** (⊠*1354 Main St.* ☎*707/963–8800*) has works by established and emerging American artists—everything from abstract and contemporary realist paintings to high-quality works on paper and sculpture. **Footcandy** (⊠*1239 Main St.* ☎*707/963–2040*) will thrill foot fetishists with its provocative displays of precarious stilettos and high-heeled boots. The **Spice Islands Marketplace** (⊠*Culinary Institute of America, 2555 Main St.* ☎*888/424–2433*) is the place to shop for all things related to preparing and cooking food, from cookbooks to copper bowls. Italian ceramics, tableware, cutlery, and other high-quality home accessories fill **Vanderbilt & Company** (⊠*1429 Main St.* ☎*707/963–1010*). Chocolates handmade on the premises are displayed like miniature works of art at **Woodhouse Chocolate** (⊠*1367 Main St.* ☎*707/963–8413*).

18

CALISTOGA

3 mi northwest of St. Helena on Rte. 29.

With false-fronted shops, 19th-century hotels, and unpretentious cafés lining Lincoln Avenue, the town's main drag, Calistoga has a slightly rough-and-tumble feel that's unique in the Napa Valley. It comes across as down-to-earth, less showy or touristy than some of the polished towns to the south. And it's easier to find a bargain here, making it a handy home base for exploring the surrounding vineyards and backroads.

Ironically, Calistoga was developed as a swell, tourist-oriented getaway. In 1859, maverick entrepeneur Sam Brannan founded the Calistoga Hot Springs Resort, intending to use the area's natural hot springs as the basis of "the Saratoga of California." (He reputedly tripped up the pronunciation of the phrase at a formal banquet—it came out "Calistoga"—and the name stuck.) Brannan's gamble didn't pay off as he'd hoped, but the hotels and bathhouses won a local following. The slightly scruffy spas on the edges of town are still going strong, as visitors dip in the mud baths or indulge in massages.

Indian Springs has welcomed clients to mud baths, mineral pools, and steam rooms, all supplied with mineral water from its three geysers, since 1871. You can choose from the various spa treatments and volcanic-ash mud baths, or soak in the toasty Olympic-size mineral-water pool. If you're planning several sessions, you might want to overnight in one of the lodge rooms or bungalows ($–$$). Reservations are recommended for spa treatments. ⊠ *1712 Lincoln Ave./Rte. 29* ☎ *707/942–4913* ⊕ *www.indianspringscalistoga.com* ⊙ *Daily 9–8.*

Fodor'sChoice
★
Schramsberg, hidden on the hillside near Route 29, is one of Napa's oldest wineries and produces a variety of bubblies made using the traditional *méthode champenoise* process. If you want to taste, you must tour first, but what a tour: in addition to seeing the winery's historic architecture, you can get to tour the cellars dug in the late 19th century by Chinese laborers, where a mind-boggling 2 million bottles are stacked in gravity-defying configurations. The tour fee includes generous pours of three very different sparkling wines, as well as one still wine. ⊠ *1400 Schramsberg Rd.* ☎ *707/942–4558* ⊕ *www. schramsberg.com* ⊠ *Tasting and tour $25* ⊙ *Tastings and tours by appointment.*

The tasting room at **Dutch Henry Winery** isn't much more than a nook in the barrel room between towering American and French oak barrels full of their excellent cabernet sauvignon, merlot, and zinfandel. The winery produces about 6,000 cases annually—sold mostly on-site and through their wine club—which explains the simple facilities, but the wines are truly top-notch. Also look for good chardonnay and merlot, and an inky syrah that's grown on the estate. ⊠ *4300 Silverado Trail* ☎ *707/942–5771* ⊕ *www.dutchhenry.com* ⊠ *Tasting $10* ⊙ *Daily 10–5; tasting by appointment.*

The approach to **Sterling Vineyards** is the most spectacular in the valley. Instead of driving up to their tasting room, you board an aerial tramway to reach the pristine, white, Mediterranean-style buildings perched on a hilltop about a mile south of Calistoga. The views from the winery are superb, although the quality of the wines doesn't necessarily match the vista. ⊠ *1111 Dunaweal La., east of Rte. 29* ☎ *707/942–3300* ⊕ *www.sterlingvineyards.com* ✉ *$20, including tramway, self-guided tour, and tasting* ⊙ *Daily 10:30–4:30.*

★ Designed by postmodern architect Michael Graves, the **Clos Pegase** winery is a one-of-a-kind "temple to wine and art" packed with unusual art objects from the collection of owner and publishing entrepreneur Jan Shrem. After tasting the wines, which include a bright sauvignon blanc and mellow pinot noir, merlot, and cabernet, be sure to check out the surrealist paintings near the main tasting room and at the curvaceous Henry Moore sculpture in the courtyard. ⊠ *1060 Dunaweal La., east of Rte. 29* ☎ *707/942–4981* ⊕ *www.clospegase.com* ✉ *Tasting $10, tour free* ⊙ *Daily 10:30–5; tour daily at 11 and 2.*

Château Montelena is an architectural mash-up. The 19th-century, vine-covered building suggests France, but the lake below it is surrounded by Chinese-inspired gardens and dotted with islands topped by Chinese pavilions. For the best view of the quirky combination, take the pathway down to the lake. From here the château, with its little turrets and ornamental crenellations, looks like it's straight out of a fairy tale. In the tasting room, make a beeline for the bright chardonnay and the estate-grown cabernet sauvignon. ⊠ *1429 Tubbs La.* ☎ *707/942–5105* ⊕ *www.montelena.com* ✉ *Tasting $15–$25* ⊙ *Daily 9:30–4.*

18

Robert Louis Stevenson State Park encompasses the summit of **Mount St. Helena.** It was here, in the summer of 1880, in an abandoned bunkhouse of the Silverado Mine, that Stevenson and his bride, Fanny Osbourne, spent their honeymoon. The stay inspired Stevenson's *The Silverado Squatters,* and Spyglass Hill in *Treasure Island* is thought to be a portrait of Mount St. Helena. The park's approximately 3,600 acres are mostly undeveloped except for a fire trail leading to the site of the bunkhouse—which is marked with a marble tablet—and to the summit beyond. ■TIP➔**If you're planning on attempting the hike to the top, bring plenty of water and dress appropriately: the trail is steep and lacks shade in spots, but the summit is often cool and breezy.** ⊠ *Rte. 29, 7 mi north of Calistoga* ☎ *707/942–4575* ⊕ *www.parks.ca.gov* ✉ *Free* ⊙ *Daily sunrise–sunset.*

★ Possibly the most astounding sight in all of Napa Valley is your first glimpse of the **Castello di Amorosa,** which looks for all the world like a medieval castle, complete with drawbridge and moat, a chapel, stables, and secret passageways. The brainchild of Daryl Sattui, who also owns several properties in Tuscany, it shows Sattui's passion for Italy and for medieval architecture down to the last obsessive detail: some of the 107 rooms contain replicas of 13th-century frescos, and the dungeon has an actual iron maiden torture device from Nuremberg, Germany. Opened in 2007 after 14 years of construction, the winery immediately started attracting large crowds lured by the astonishing architecture (you must pay for a tour to get beyond the tasting room). The Italian-style wines, however, available at the winery only, are excellent as well. ⊠*4045 North St., Helena Hwy.* ☎*707/967–6272* ⊕*www.castellodiamorosa. com* ⌯*Tasting $10–$20, tour $25–$35 weekdays, $30–$40 weekends* ⊙*Daily 9:30–6; tours by appointment.*

🖢 The **Petrified Forest** contains the remains of the volcanic eruptions of Mount St. Helena 3.4 million years ago. The force of the explosion uprooted the gigantic redwoods, covered them with volcanic ash, and infiltrated the trees with silica and minerals, causing petrifaction. The 20-minute walk around the property, following signs explaining the process of petrification, is a good way to stretch your legs after a morning in the car, though the site isn't worth a long detour. For the best experience, call ahead to reserve a spot on a meadow hike, which leads through the woodland until you have a view of Mount St. Helena. ⊠*4100 Petrified Forest Rd., 5 mi west of Calistoga* ☎*707/942–6667* ⊕*www.petrifiedforest.org* ⌯*$6* ⊙*Memorial Day–Labor Day, daily 9–7; Labor Day–Memorial Day, daily 9–5.*

WHERE TO STAY & EAT

$$$ ✕**All Seasons Bistro.** Bistro cuisine takes a California spin in this sun-filled space, where tables topped with flowers sit upon a black-and-white checkerboard floor. The seasonal menu might include organic greens or roasted monkfish with fennel and carrots. Homey desserts include crème brûlée and warm chocolate torte. You can order reasonably priced wines from their extensive list, or buy a bottle at the attached wineshop and have it poured at your table. Attentive service contributes to the welcoming atmosphere. ⊠*1400 Lincoln Ave.* ☎*707/942–9111* ▤*AE, D, MC, V* ⊙*Closed Mon.; no lunch Tues.–Thurs.*

$$ ✕**Bar Vino.** In 2006 Calistoga got a little more urbane with the addition of this Italian-inflected wine bar in the Mount View Hotel. With red-leather seats, stainless-steel light fixtures, and a marble bar indoors and café seating out, it's a stylish, modern spot for a glass of wine, with many from small producers you probably haven't heard of. Small plates that could come have straight from Tuscany—olives, mozzarella with an artichoke tapenade, risotto croquettes, a selection of salumi—are great for sharing. A handful of well-executed large plates, like the pappardelle with Italian sausage and sun-dried tomatoes and cumin-seared tuna, round out the menu. ⊠ *1457 Lincoln Ave.* ☎*707/942–9900* ▤*AE, MC, V* ⊙*No lunch.*

$$$ ✕**Calistoga Inn Restaurant and Brewery.** On pleasant days this riverside restaurant and its sprawling, tree-shaded patio comes into their own. At lunchtime, casual plates like a smoked turkey and Brie sandwich or a Chinese chicken salad are light enough to leave some energy for an afternoon of wine tasting. At night, when there's often live music played on the patio during the warm months, you'll find heartier dishes such as flatiron steak or grilled Sonoma duck breast with a mushroom marsala sauce. Service can be a bit lackadaisical, so order one of the house-made brews and enjoy the atmosphere while you're waiting. ⊠*1250 Lincoln Ave.* ☎*707/942–4101* ▤*AE, MC, V.*

$$ ✕**Wappo Bar Bistro.** Though the setting is homey, with wooden booths inside and an arbor shading the patio, the eclectic food moves beyond the familiar. The menu covers the map, with dishes ranging from *vatapa*, a Brazilian seafood stew thickened with peanuts and coconut milk, to Thai coconut curry with prawns and vegetables. A generous platter of Turkish *meze* (appetizers) makes an excellent dinner, if you're not inclined to share. At times the restaurant can seem understaffed, so be prepared for a wait—which is more enjoyable if you've snagged a table under the vine-covered patio trellis. ✉*1226 S. Washington St.* ☎*707/942–4712* ▤*AE, MC, V* ⊗*Closed Tues.*

¢ 🖼**Brannan Cottage Inn.** The pristine Victorian cottage with lacy white fretwork, large windows, and a shady porch is the only one of Sam Brannan's 1860 resort cottages still standing on its original site. Each room has individual touches such as a four-poster bed, a claw-foot tub, or a velvet settee. Pros: Innkeepers go the extra mile, most rooms have fireplaces. Cons: Owners' dog may be a problem for those with allergies, rooms look a bit worn. ✉*109 Wapoo Ave.* ☎*707/942–4200* ⊕*www.brannancottageinn.com* ⇆*6 rooms* ⌂*In-room: no phone, refrigerator, no TV (some), Wi-Fi. In-hotel: no elevator, some pets allowed (fee), no-smoking rooms* ▤*AE, MC, V* ⦿*BP.*

$$$$ 🖼**Calistoga Ranch.** A sister property of Auberge du Soleil in Rutherford, this posh resort shares a similar wide-open-spaces feel. Spacious
★ cedar-shingle bungalows throughout the wooded property have outdoor living areas, and even the restaurant, spa, and reception area have outdoor seating areas and fireplaces. Though the service is friendly and the lodges are luxurious, with sybaritic outdoor showers in every room, the overall result still has a casual ranchlike feel rather than the refined sheen of some similarly priced places. Pros: Romantic outdoor showers for two, feels like a luxurious country retreat, excellent spa. Cons: Very expensive, innovative indoor/outdoor organization works better in fair weather than in rain or cold. ✉*580 Lommel Rd.,* ☎*707/254–2800 or 800/942–4220* ⊕*www.calistogaranch.com* ⇆*46 rooms* ⌂*In-room: safe, refrigerator, DVD, ethernet, Wi-Fi. In-hotel: restaurant, room service, bar, pool, gym, spa, bicycles, no elevator, concierge, some pets allowed (fee), no-smoking rooms* ▤*AE, D, MC, V.*

¢ 🖼**Calistoga Spa Hot Springs.** Though the rooms are standard motel issue, their well-equipped kitchenettes and the property's four outdoor heated mineral pools make this a popular spot for those who want to enjoy Calistoga's famed waters on a budget. An on-site spa offers mud baths and other services at reasonable rates. The location on a quiet street one block from Calistoga's main drag is another plus. ■TIP➔**Fodors.com users suggest staking out a prime lounging spot next to the pools before the day-trippers are admitted each morning.** Pros: A rare family-friendly spot in Napa Valley, unpretentious atmosphere. Cons: Children at the mineral pools can spoil the tranquillity; kitchenettes lack a microwave; drab, dated rooms. ✉*1006 Washington St.* ☎*707/942–6269* ⊕*www.calistogaspa.com* ⇆*51 rooms, 1 suite* ⌂*In-room: kitchen. In-hotel: pools, gym, spa, no elevator, laundry facilities, no-smoking rooms* ▤*MC, V.*

18

Best Wine Country Spas

Wine Country spas have a natural edge on the treatments you can find elsewhere in the country. First, there are the natural mud baths and mineral water sources, concentrated particularly in northern Napa Valley's Calistoga. Admittedly, not everyone is enamored with dipping themselves in a thick, muddy paste. A mud bath sometimes smells sulfurous or peaty, and it takes a minute to get used to the intense heat as you submerge yourself. Once you've lounged in it for several minutes, though, you may never want to leave, especially if an attendant has cooled your forehead with an icy wash cloth. Second, there are all those grapes, which are increasingly incorporated into treatments and products like grape-seed scrubs. Below are some of the best spas of the bunch.

■ **Calistoga Spa Hot Springs.** Though its surroundings are less luxurious than some, this is the best choice if you have several hours to lounge around. If you're booking any treatment at least a day in advance, you can pay $5 and get all-day pool access as well. You can relax in four pools of varying size and temperature until you decide on a favorite. ⊠ *1006 Washington St., Calistoga* ☎ *707/942–6269* ⊕ *www.calistogaspa.com.*

■ **Dr. Wilkinson's.** The oldest spa in Calistoga. Although it's perhaps the least chic of the bunch, it's still well-loved for its reasonable prices and its friendly, unpretentious vibe. They use a mix of volcanic ash and peat moss in their mud baths. ⊠ *1507 Lincoln Ave., Calistoga* ☎ *707/942–4102* ⊕ *www.drwilkinson.com.*

■ **Fairmont Sonoma Mission Inn & Spa.** The highest sybaritic profile in the Wine Country. The vast complex covers every amenity you could want in a spa, including several pools and Jacuzzis fed by local thermal mineral springs. ⊠ *100 Boyes Blvd./Rte. 12, Boyes Hot Springs* ☎ *707/938–9000* ⊕ *www.sonomamissioninn.com.*

■ **Health Spa Napa Valley.** Focuses on health and wellness, with personal trainers and an outdoor pool in addition to the usual spa fare. The grape-seed mud wrap, during which you're slathered with mud mixed with crushed Napa Valley grape seeds, is a more decadent alternative to a mud bath. ⊠ *1030 Main St., St. Helena* ☎ *707/967–8800* ⊕ *www.napavalleyspa.com.*

■ **Kenwood Inn & Spa.** The prettiest spa setting in the Wine Country, thanks to the vineyards across the road and the Mediterranean style of the inn. It specializes in Caudalie's "vinotherapie" treatments, with massages, scrubs, and facials based on grape extracts. ⊠ *10400 Sonoma Hwy./Rte. 12, Kenwood* ☎ *707/833–1293* ⊕ *www.kenwoodinn.com.*

■ **Lavender Hill Spa.** Freestanding bathhouses with two whirlpool tubs make this a particularly good spot for couples. Its small size and lavender gardens make for a tranquil visit. ⊠ *1015 Foothill Blvd., Calistoga* ☎ *707/942–4495* ⊕ *www.lavenderhillspa.com.*

■ **Spa at Villagio.** Opened in 2008, this 13,000-square-foot spa with fieldstone walls and a Mediterranean theme has all the latest gadgets. Huge spa suites—complete with flat-panel TV screens, wet bars, and steam showers—are perfect for couples and groups. ⊠ *6481 Washington St., Yountville* ☎ *707/948–5050.*

$$$ 🏠**Cottage Grove Inn.** A long driveway lined with 16 freestanding cottages, each shaded by elm trees, looks a bit like Main Street USA, but inside the skylit buildings have all the perks you could want for a romantic weekend away. Each has overstuffed chairs in front of a wood-burning fireplace, flat-panel TVs, and an extra-deep two-person whirlpool tub. Each cottage also has its own variation on the overall comfy-rustic look, with telltale names like Fly Fishing Cottage and Provence. Spas and restaurants are within walking distance. Rates include afternoon wine and cheese. Pros: Wicker chairs on each shady porch, board games in the lobby, bathtubs so big you could swim in them. Cons: No pool, decor may be a bit frumpy for some. ✉*1711 Lincoln Ave.* ☎*707/942–8400 or 800/799–2284* ⊕*www.cottage grove.com* 🛏*16 rooms* ⚒*In-room: safe, refrigerator, DVD, ethernet, Wi-Fi. In-hotel: no elevator, public Internet, no-smoking rooms* ⊟*AE, D, DC, MC, V* ⦿*CP.*

$–$$ 🏠**Indian Springs.** This old-time spa has welcomed clients to its mud
★ baths, mineral pool, and steam room, all supplied with mineral water from its four geysers, since 1871. Rooms in the recently renovated lodge, though quite small, are beautifully done up a simple Zen style, with Asian-inspired furnishings, Frette linens on the bed, and flat-panel televisions. The cottages dotted around the property have anything from a small kitchenette to a fully equipped kitchen, encouraging longer stays (book well in advance for these). A boccie ball court, shuffleboard, and croquet lawn outside your door provide entertainment when you're not indulging in various spa treatments and volcanic-ash mud baths, or soaking in the toasty Olympic-size mineral-water pool. Pros: Lovely grounds with outdoor seating areas, stylish for the price, enormous mineral pool. Cons: Lodge rooms are small, oddly uncomfortable pillows. ✉*1712 Lincoln Ave.* ☎*707/942–4913* ⊕*www.indian springscalistoga.com* 🛏*24 rooms, 17 suites* ⚒*In room: no phone, Wi-Fi, kitchen (some), refrigerator (some). In-hotel: tennis court, pool, spa, no elevator, no-smoking rooms* ⊟*D, MC, V. 707/942–4913*

$–$$ 🏠**Meadowlark Country House.** Twenty hillside acres just north of down-
Fodor'sChoice town Calistoga surround this decidedly laid-back and sophisticated
★ inn that's particularly popular with gay and lesbian travelers but welcoming to all. Rooms in the main house and guest wing each have their own charms: one has a deep whirlpool tub looking onto a green hillside, and others have a deck with a view of the mountains. Many rooms have fireplaces, and most have whirlpool tubs large enough for two. A spacious two-story guesthouse opens directly onto the clothing-optional pool, hot tub, and sauna area (open to all guests). Fodors.com readers point out that "Kurt and Richard are delightful, helpful hosts." Pros: Sauna next to the pool and hot tub, welcoming vibe attracts diverse guests, some of the most gracious innkeepers in Napa. Cons: Clothing-option pool policy isn't for everyone. ✉*601 Petrified Forest Rd.* ☎*707/942–5651 or 800/942–5651* ⊕*www.meadowlarkinn.com* 🛏*5 rooms, 5 suites* ⚒*In-room: no phone, kitchen (some), refrigerator (some), DVD (some), VCR (some), Wi-Fi. In-hotel: pool, no elevator, some pets allowed, no-smoking rooms* ⊟*AE, MC, V* ⦿*BP.*

18

UP, UP & AWAY

Thought those vineyards were beautiful from the highway? Top that with a bird's-eye view! Several companies offer hot-air ballooning trips over Napa and Sonoma. Rides usually cost between $200 and $250, last about an hour, and include brunch or lunch after the flight. (Many companies drop their rates a bit in the off-season.) Flights take off at the crack of dawn, literally, and you can watch the huge, rainbow-colored balloons inflate as the aircraft is readied.

■ **Balloons Above the Valley**
(☎ 707/253–2222, 800/464–6824 in CA ⊕ www.balloonrides.com).

■ **Bonaventura Balloon Company**
(☎ 707/944–2822 or 800/359–6272 ⊕ www.bonaventuraballoons.com).

■ **Napa Valley Balloons**
(☎ 707/944–0228, 800/253–2224 in CA ⊕ www.napavalleyballoons.com).

$$$$ – ⬚Solage. A resort for sociable sorts who like to lounge at the bar overlooking the large pool or play a game of boccie after lunch at the indoor-outdoor restaurant, this Calistoga newcomer sprawls over 22 acres. The cottages don't look particularly luxurious from the outside, but inside they flaunt a Napa-Valley-barn-meets-San-Francisco-loft aesthetic, with high ceilings, polished concrete floors, recycled walnut furniture, and all-natural fabrics in soothing muted colors. Sports and fitness are a high priority here: in addition to a large, well-equipped spa and "mud bar" where you can indulge in decadent variation on the mud bath, there's a packed schedule of fitness activities, with everything from yoga to Pilates to biking and hiking excursions. ■ TIP→**If you want to be in the middle of the action, ask for a room facing the pool. For more seclusion, ask for one of the quieter rooms near the oak grove.** Pros: Great service, bike cruisers parked at every cottage for guests' use, separate pools for kids and adults. Cons: New landscaping looks a little bleak, some rooms don't have tubs. ⊠755 Silverado Trail ☎866/942–7442 ⊕www.solagecalistoga.com ➴89 rooms ⌂In-room: safe, refrigerator, DVD, Wi-Fi, restaurant, room service, bar, pools, gym, spa, bicycles, no elevator, laundry service, concierge, no-smoking rooms ▤AE, D, DC, MC, V.

SPORTS & THE OUTDOORS

Calistoga Bikeshop (⊠1318 Lincoln Ave. ☎866/942–2453) rents bicycles, including tandem bikes. Their Calistoga Cool Wine Tour package includes free tastings at a number of small wineries in the area. Best of all, they'll pick up any wine you purchase along the way if you've bought more than will fit in the handy bottle carrier on your bike.

SHOPPING

Enoteca Wine Shop (⊠1348B Lincoln Ave. ☎707/942–1117), on Calistoga's main drag, conveniently displays almost all of their wines with extensive tasting notes, which makes it easier to choose from among their unusually fine collection, which includes both hard-to-find bottles from Napa and Sonoma and many French wines. Locally handcrafted beeswax candles are for sale at **Hurd Beeswax Candles** (✉ *1255 Lincoln Ave.* ☎ *707/963–7211*). Unusual tapers twisted into spiral shapes are a specialty. The **Wine Garage** (✉ *1020 Hwy. 29* ☎ *707/942–5332*) is the stop for bargain hunters, since each of their bottles goes for $25 or less. It's a great way of discovering the work of smaller wineries producing undervalued wines.

THE SONOMA VALLEY

Although the Sonoma Valley may not have quite the cachet of the neighboring Napa Valley, wineries here entice with their unpretentious attitude and smaller crowds. The Napa-style glitzy tasting rooms with enormous gift shops and high tasting fees are the exception here. Sonoma's landscape seduces, too, its roads gently climbing and descending on their way to wineries hidden from the road by trees.

The scenic valley, bounded by the Mayacamas Mountains on the east and Sonoma Mountain on the west, extends north from San Pablo Bay nearly 20 mi to the eastern outskirts of Santa Rosa. The varied terrain, soils, and climate (cooler in the south because of the bay influence and hotter toward the north) allow grape growers to raise cool-weather varietals such as chardonnay and pinot noir as well as merlot, cabernet sauvignon, and other heat-seeking vines. The valley is home to dozens of wineries, many of them on or near Route 12, a California Scenic Highway that runs the length of the valley.

SONOMA

18

14 mi west of Napa on Rte. 12; 45 mi from San Francisco, north on U.S. 101, east on Rte. 37, and north on Rte. 121/12.

Founded in the early 1800s, Sonoma is the oldest town in the Wine Country, and one of the few where you can find some attractions not related to food and wine. The central **Sonoma Plaza** dates back to the mission era; surrounding it are 19th-century adobes, atmospheric hotels, and the swooping marquee of the 1930s Sebastiani Theatre. On summer days the plaza is a hive of activity, with children blowing off steam in the playground while their folks stock up on picnic supplies and browse the boutiques surrounding the square.

On your way into town from the south, you pass through the Carneros wine district, which straddles the southern sections of Sonoma and Napa counties.

A tree-lined driveway leads to **Lachryma Montis,** which General Mariano G. Vallejo, the last Mexican governor of California, built for his large family in 1852. The Victorian Gothic house, insulated with adobe, represents a blend of Mexican and American cultures. Opulent furnishings, including white-marble fireplaces and a French rosewood piano, are particularly noteworthy. Free tours are occasionally conducted by docents on the weekend. ✉ *W. Spain St., near 3rd St.* W ☎ *707/938–9559* 🖥 *$2, tour free* ☉ *Daily 10–5.*

Reminiscent of a Tuscan villa, with its ocher-color buildings surrounded by olive trees, sprawling **Viansa** focuses on Italian varietals such as sangiovese, barbera, pinot grigio, and vernaccia. Fodor's readers are generally split when summing up the charms of the winery. Some love the market on the premises that sells sandwiches and deli foods to complement the Italian-style wines, as well as a large selection of dinnerware, cookbooks, and condiments. Others find the cavernous size of the market and the crowds that tend to congregate here off-putting. Regardless, the picnic area that overlooks the wetlands below is a fine place to enjoy a glass of wine while bird-watching (only food and wines sold on the premises are permitted). ⊠ *25200 Arnold Dr.* ☎ *707/935–4700* ⊕ *www.viansa.com* 🍷 *Tasting $5–$20, tour $5 (tasting fee additional)* ☉ *Daily 10–5; tour daily at 11, 2, and 3.*

The **Robledo Family Winery,** founded by Reynaldo Robledo Sr., a former migrant worker from Michoacán, Mexico, is truly a family affair. You're likely to encounter one of the charming Robledo sons in the tasting room, where he'll proudly tell you the story of the immigrant family while pouring tastes of their sauvignon blanc, pinot noir, merlot, cabernet sauvignon, and other wines, including a chardonnay that comes from the vineyard right outside the tasting room's door. All seven Robledo sons and two Robledo daughters, as well as matriarch Maria, are involved in the winery operations. If you don't run into them on your visit to the winery, you can see their names and pictures on the bottles of wine, such as the "Dos Hermanas" late-harvest dessert wine, or the port dedicated to Maria Robledo. ⊠ *21901 Bonness Rd.* ☎ *707/939–6903* ⊕ *www.robledofamilywinery.com* 🍷 *Tasting $5–$10* ☉ *Mon.–Sat. 10–5, Sun. 11–4.*

The Spanish hacienda–style architecture recalls the native country of the Ferrer family, who make both sparkling and still wines at **Gloria Ferrer Caves and Vineyards.** The sparkling wines here, all made in the brut style, are aged in a *cava,* or cellar, where several feet of earth maintain a constant temperature. Call the day of your visit after 9:45 AM to find out when tours are being offered that day. ⊠ *23555 Carneros Hwy./Rte. 121* ☎ *707/996–7256* ⊕ *www.gloriaferrer.com* 🍷 *Tasting $2–$10, tour $10* ☉ *Daily 10–5.*

Originally planted by Franciscans of the Sonoma Mission in 1825, the **Sebastiani Vineyards** were bought by Samuele Sebastiani in 1904. Although the winery is best known for its red wines, you can also find some unusual whites here, like a white pinot noir. You might think you've entered a boutique when you've walked in the door, since the grape-theme table linens and ceramic serving platters for sale take up more room than the wine bar itself; head to the back of the room to find the pours. In addition to the regularly scheduled historical tours of the winery, a trolley tour offers an informative glimpse of the vineyards Friday and Saturday at 2. ⊠ *389 4th St. E* ☎ *707/938–5532* ⊕ *www.sebastiani.com* 🍷 *Tasting $5–$10, tour $5, $7.50 for trolley tour* ☉ *Daily 10–5; tours daily at 11, 1, and 3.*

Buena Vista Carneros Estate is the oldest continually operating winery in California. It was here, in 1857, that Count Agoston Haraszthy de Mokcsa laid the basis for modern California wine making, bucking the conventional wisdom that vines should be planted on well-watered ground by instead planting on well-drained hillsides. Chinese laborers dug tunnels 100 feet into the hillside, and the limestone they extracted was used to build the main house, which is now surrounded by redwood and eucalyptus trees and a picnic area. If you're a bit peckish, consider paying a bit more ($20) for a tasting of five wines, which are paired with cheeses or other nibbles. ⊠*18000 Old Winery Rd., off Napa Rd., follow signs from plaza* ☎*707/938–1266 or 800/678–8504* ⊕*http://buenavistacarneros.com* ⊠*Tasting $5–$10* ☉*Daily 10–5.*

Ravenswood, whose tasting room is housed in a stone building covered in climbing fig vines, has a punchy three-word mission statement: "no wimpy wines." They generally succeed, especially with their signature big, bold zinfandels, which are sometimes blended with petit syrah, carignane, or other varietals. Be sure to taste their merlot and early harvest gewürtztraminer, too. Tours include barrel tastings of wines in progress in the cellar. ⊠*18701 Gehricke Rd., off E. Spain St.* ☎*707/938–1960* ⊕*www.ravenswood-wine.com* ⊠*Tasting $10–$15, tour $15* ☉*Daily 10–5; tour at 10:30.*

Gundlach-Bundschu may look like a stern gun bunker at first glance, but it's a lot of fun to visit. They let their hair down here, with pop or rock playing on the tasting room's sound system instead of the typical soft classical music. But they're serious about wine and craft some outstanding reds, like cabernet sauvignon, tempranillo, syrah, and zinfandel, all grown in the Rhinefarm Vineyard on the estate. Climb up the hill from the tasting room and you can find a breathtaking valley view (and a perfect picnic spot). In summer, check their Web site for information about the musical and theatrical performances that take place on their outdoor stage. ⊠*2000 Denmark St.* ☎*707/938–5277* ⊕*www.gunbun.com* ⊠*Tasting $5–$10* ☉*Daily 11–4:30.*

WHERE TO STAY & EAT

$$ ✕**Cafe La Haye.** In a postage-stamp-size kitchen, skillful chefs turn out half a dozen main courses that star on a small but worthwhile seasonal menu emphasizing local ingredients. Chicken, beef, pasta, and fish get deluxe treatment without fuss or fanfare. Mussels in an aromatic garlic and fennel broth frequently crop up, for instance, and the daily risotto special is always good. The tiny dining room is hung with large, abstract paintings. ⊠*140 E. Napa St.* ☎*707/935–5994* ▭*AE, MC, V* ☉*Closed Sun. and Mon. No lunch.*

$–$$ ✕**Della Santina's.** A longtime favorite with a charming brick patio out back serves the most authentic Italian food in town. (The Della Santina family, which has been running the restaurant since 1990, hails from Lucca, Italy.) Daily fish and veal specials join classic northern Italian pastas such as linguine with pesto and lasagna Bolognese. Of special note are the roasted meat dishes and, when available, petrale sole and sand dabs. ⊠*133 E. Napa St.* ☎*707/935–0576* ▭*AE, D, MC, V.*

18

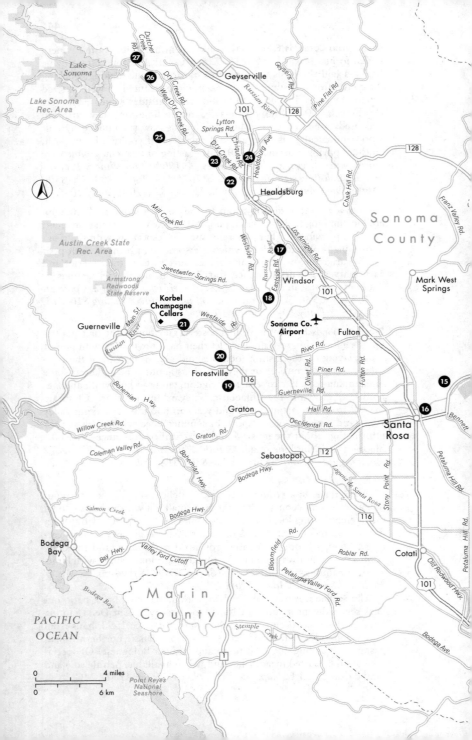

Sonoma County

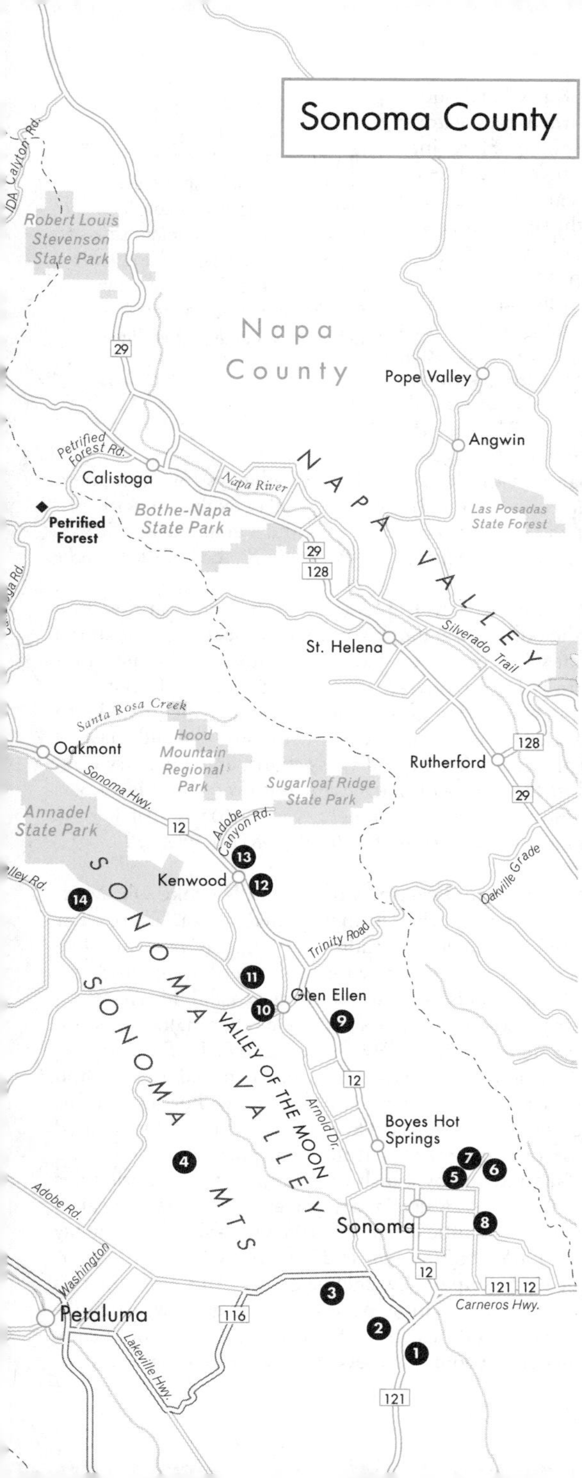

Napa County
NAPA VALLEY
Robert Louis Stevenson State Park
Calistoga
Petrified Forest
Petrified Forest Rd.
Bothe-Napa State Park
Napa River
Pope Valley
Angwin
Las Posadas State Forest
St. Helena
Silverado Trail
Rutherford
Oakville Grade
Santa Rosa Creek
Oakmont
Hood Mountain Regional Park
Sugarloaf Ridge State Park
Sonoma Hwy.
Annadel State Park
Adobe Canyon Rd.
Kenwood
Trinity Road
Glen Ellen
SONOMA VALLEY
VALLEY OF THE MOON
SONOMA MTS
Arnold Dr.
Boyes Hot Springs
Sonoma
Adobe Rd.
Washington
Petaluma
Lakeville Hwy.
Carneros Hwy.
29
128
12
116
121

Arrowood Vineyards & Winery **9**
Benziger Family Winery **10**
Buena Vista Carneros Estate **6**
De Loach Vineyards **4**
Dry Creek Vineyard **22**
Ferrari-Carano Winery **27**
Gary Farrell Winery **21**
Gloria Ferrer Caves and Vineyards **2**
Gundlach-Bundschu **8**
Hartford Family Winery **20**
Iron Horse Vineyards **19**
J Vineyards and Winery **17**
Jack London State Historic Park **11**
Kenwood Vineyards **13**
Kunde Estate Winery & Vineyards **12**
Ledson Winery & Vineyards **15**
Luther Burbank Home and Gardens **16**
Matanzas Creek Winery **14**
Michel-Schlumberger **25**
Preston Vineyards' **26**
Quivira **23**
Ravenswood **7**
Robledo Family Winery **3**
Rochioli Vineyards and Winery **18**
Sebastiani Vineyards **5**
Simi Winery **24**
Viansa **1**

$$ ╳**The Girl & the Fig.** Chef Sondra Bernstein has turned the historic barroom of the Sonoma Hotel into a hot spot for inventive French cooking. You can always find something with the signature figs in it here, whether it's a fig and arugula salad or an aperitif of sparkling wine with a fig liqueur. Also look for duck confit with French lentils, a burger with matchstick fries, or pastis-scented steamed mussels. The wine list is notable for its emphasis on Rhône varietals, and the *salon de fromage*—a counter in the bar area—sells artisanal cheese platters for eating here and cheese by the pound to go. Brunch is a Sunday exclusive, with rib-sticking dishes such as hanger steak and eggs and a goat cheese frittata. ⊠*Sonoma Hotel, Sonoma Plaza, 110 W. Spain St.* ☎707/938–3634 ⊟*AE, D, MC, V.*

> **WORD OF MOUTH**
>
> "If you are starting your trip in San Francisco, it might be useful and amusing to visit a couple of wine bars in the city before striking out for the wine country. You could identify and sample some favorite wines and earmark [the California wineries] for visiting later in your trip."
>
> –dovima

$$ ╳**Harvest Moon Cafe.** It's easy to feel like one of the family at this little
★   restaurant with the odd, zigzagging layout. Diners seated at one of the two tiny bars chat with the servers like old friends, but the husband-and-wife team in the kitchen are serious about the food. They're not exactly breaking new culinary ground here; the daily menu sticks to homey dishes like a fat grilled pork chop with cabbage and mashed potatoes, seared ahi tuna with sautéed swiss chard, and a chicory Caesar salad dusted generously with Parmesan. But everything is so perfectly executed and the vibe so genuinely warm, that a visit here is deeply satisfying. ⊠*487 W. 1st St.* ☎707/933–8160 ⊟*AE, D, MC, V* ☺ *No lunch.*

$ ╳**La Casa.** Red tile floors and ceramics on the walls evoke Old Mexico at this spot around the corner from Sonoma's plaza. There's bar seating, a patio, and large menu of traditional Mexican favorites, like enchiladas suizas (chicken enchiladas with a salsa verde), burritos, and fish tacos. Though the food is fairly standard, the casual, festive atmosphere and margaritas sold by the glass and the pitcher make it a popular stop. ⊠*121 E. Spain St.* ☎707/996–3406 ⊟*AE, D, DC, MC, V.*

$$ ╳**LaSalette.** Chef-owner Manuel Azevedo, born in the Azores and raised in Sonoma, serves dishes inspired by his native Portugal in this warmly decorated spot a few steps off Sonoma's plaza. Boldly flavored dishes such as *porco à alentejana,* a traditional pork with clams and tomatoes, might be followed by a dish of rice pudding with dried figs or a port from the varied list. **A small menu of crepes, omelets, and baked goods like decadent** *sonhos* **(little cream-filled donuts) is served on Sunday morning.** ⊠*452 E. 1st St.* ☎707/938–1927 ⊟*AE, MC, V.*

$$$$ ╳**Santé.** Under the leadership of new chef de cuisine Andrew Cain, this
★   elegant dining room in the Sonoma Mission Inn is gaining a reputation as a destination restaurant with its focus on seasonal- and locally sourced ingredients. The room is understated, with high-backed ban-

CLOSE UP

Who's Who in the Grape World

Well over 50 different varieties of grapes are grown in the California Wine Country. Although you don't need to be on a first-name basis with them all, you'll see the following dozen again and again as you visit the wineries.

WHITES

■ **Chardonnay.** Now as firmly associated with California wine making as it is with Burgundy, its home. California chardonnays spent many years chasing big, buttery flavor, but the current trend is toward more restrained wines.

■ **Gewürztraminer.** Cooler California climes such as the Russian River Valley are great for growing this German-Alsatian grape, which is turned into a boldly perfumed, fruity wine.

■ **Riesling.** Can produce wines with brisk acidity and a lush floral or fruity bouquet. In California's Anderson and Alexander valleys, late-harvest dessert wines are often made with this cool-weather grape.

■ **Sauvignon Blanc.** Hails from Bordeaux and the Loire Valley. Wines made from this grape vary widely, from herbaceous to tropical-fruity.

■ **Viognier.** Until the early 1990s this was rarely planted outside France's Rhône Valley, but today it's one of the hottest white wine varietals in California. Usually made in a dry style, the best viogniers have an intense fruity or floral bouquet.

REDS

■ **Cabernet Franc.** Though this Bordeaux grape is extremely important in California wine making, you'll rarely see it standing alone. A slightly softer, less tannic cousin of cabernet sauvignon, it's often blended with that grape to round out the rough edges.

■ **Cabernet Sauvignon.** The king of California red wine grapes; originally from Bordeaux. The best examples, like those from the Rutherford or Oakville AVAs, are big, bold, and often quite tannic, which means they usually require years in the cellar to reach their peak.

■ **Merlot.** A blue-black Bordeaux variety. In California it makes soft, fruity, full-bodied wine. Was well on its way to being the most popular red until anti-merlot jokes (popularized by the hit movie *Sideways*) damaged its rep . . . for now.

■ **Pinot Noir.** The darling of grape growers in cooler parts of Napa and Sonoma, such as the Carneros region and the Russian River Valley—but also called the "heartbreak grape" since it's hard to cultivate. At its best it has an addictively subtle earthy quality.

■ **Sangiovese.** Slow-ripening Tuscan grape that does well in warm areas. Because there are many different clones of this varietal, sangioveses can vary from simple and light to complex and earthy.

■ **Syrah.** A big red from France's Rhône Valley. With good tannins it can become a full-bodied beauty, but without them it can be flabby and forgettable. Also known as shiraz, particularly when it's grown in Australia.

■ **Zinfandel.** Often thought of as a quintessential California grape. Rich, jammy, and often spicy, zinfandel wines can be quite high in alcohol.

18

quettes and matching drapes in rich earth tones and softly lit chandeliers—but the food is anything but. Dishes like the crispy pork belly with braised collard greens, endive marmalade, and mustard sauce are complex without being fussy; a starter of macaroni and cheese with chunks of lobster and a shaving of black truffles on top is pure decadence. A decadent brunch is served on weekends. ⊠ *Fairmont Sonoma Mission Inn & Spa, 100 Boyes Blvd./Rte. 12, at Boyes Blvd., 2 mi north of Sonoma, Boyes Hot Springs* ☎707/939–2415 ☲*AE, D, DC, MC, V* ⊘*No lunch.*

$$$–$$$$ 🏨 **The Fairmont Sonoma Mission Inn & Spa.** The real draw at this Mission–style resort is the extensive, swanky spa, easily the biggest in the Wine Country. There's a vast array of massages and treatments, some using locally sourced grape and lavender products. The indoor and outdoor thermal soaking pools draw on the property's own mineral water sources. (It's a co-ed spa, and there are several treatments designed for couples.) The focus on fitness and rejuvenation extends to a 7,087-yard golf course winding through trees and vineyards, a changing schedule of fitness classes, and guided hiking and biking excursions each morning. The guest rooms aren't terribly large but are supremely comfortable; some have fireplaces and patios or balconies. The staff stays on top of every detail. Pros: Enormous spa, excellent on-site restaurant, free shuttle to downtown. Cons: Not as intimate as some similarly priced places, valet parking costs $20. ⊠*100 Boyes Blvd./Rte. 12, 2 mi north of Sonoma, Boyes Hot Springs* ☎707/938–9000 🖷707/938–4250 ⊕*www.fairmont.com/sonoma* ➹*168 rooms, 60 suites* ᗒ*In-room: safe, refrigerator, ethernet (some), Wi-Fi (some). In-hotel: 2 restaurants, room service, bars, golf course, tennis courts, pools, gym, spa, bicycles, concierge, laundry service, some pets allowed, no-smoking rooms* ☲*AE, D, DC, MC, V.*

¢–$$ 🏨 **Inn at Sonoma.** They don't skimp on the little luxuries here: wine and cheese is served every evening in the lobby and the cheerfully painted rooms are equipped with Wi-Fi and warmed by gas fireplaces. In the closets you can find fluffy terry robes, which come in handy for trips to the hot tub on the inn's upper level. A teddy bear perched on each feather comforter–topped bed holds a remote control to a small TV. Though the inn is just off heavily trafficked Broadway, good soundproofing makes it quieter than many of the hotels on Sonoma Plaza. (The town square is a five-minute walk away.) Though rooms are not particularly large, you'd be hard-pressed to find this much charm for the price elsewhere in town. Pros: Last-minute specials are a great deal, free soda in the lobby, lovely hot tub, a short walk from the plaza. Cons: Staff is friendly but seems inexperienced. ⊠*630 Broadway* ☎707/939–1340 ⊕*www.innatsonoma.com* ➹*19 rooms* ᗒ*In-room:*

DVD, Wi-Fi. In-hotel: bicycles, no-smoking rooms ▭*AE, D, DC, MC, V* ⏺*CP.*

¢ ▦**Vineyard Inn.** Built as a roadside motor court in 1941, this inn with red-tile roofs brings a touch of Southwestern style to an otherwise lackluster and somewhat noisy location at the junction of two main highways. It's across from two vineyards and is the closest lodging to Infineon Raceway, a major car and motorcycle racetrack. Though the rooms, which have queen- or king-size beds, are rather small, a good breakfast in a pleasant tiled room, a convenient location, and a modest price make it a fine home base for those who'd rather spend their money elsewhere. ■TIP➔**The inn sometimes closes for a few weeks during slow season, so check the schedule if you're booking a room in December or January.** Pros: Attractive courtyard, friendly innkeepers. Cons: Next to two busy highways, you'll need to drive everywhere. ⊠*23000 Arnold Dr., at junction of Rtes. 116 and 121* ☎*707/938–2350 or 800/359–4667* ⊕*www.sonomavineyardinn.com* ⇨*19 rooms, 2 suites* ♿*In-room: Wi-Fi. In-hotel: pool, no elevator, no-smoking rooms* ▭*AE, MC, V* ⏺*CP.*

NIGHTLIFE & THE ARTS

The **Sebastiani Theatre** (⊠*476 1st St. E* ☎*707/996–2020*), built on Sonoma's plaza in 1934 by Italian immigrant and entrepreneur Samuele Sebastiani, schedules first-run films, musical performances, and sometimes quirky theatrical performances.

Hit the **Swiss Hotel**'s bar (⊠*18 W. Spain St.* ☎*707/938–2884*) to sip a Glariffee, a cold and potent cousin to Irish coffee that's unique to this 19th-century spot.

SHOPPING

Sonoma Plaza is the town's main shopping magnet, with tempting boutiques and specialty food purveyors facing the square or just a block or two away. **Sign of the Bear** (⊠*Sonoma Plaza, 435 1st St. W* ☎*707/996–3722*) sells the latest and greatest in kitchenware and cookware, as well as a few Wine Country–theme items, like lazy Susans made from wine barrels. The **Sonoma Cheese Factory and Deli** (⊠*Sonoma Plaza, 2 Spain St.* ☎*707/996–1931*), run by the same family for four generations, makes Sonoma Jack cheese and the tangy Sonoma Teleme. It has everything you could possibly need for a picnic.

GLEN ELLEN

7 mi north of Sonoma on Rte. 12.

Craggy Glen Ellen epitomizes the difference between the Napa and Sonoma valleys. Although small Napa towns such as St. Helena get their charm from upscale boutiques and restaurants lined up along well-groomed sidewalks, in Glen Ellen the crooked streets are shaded with stands of old oak trees and occasionally bisected by the Sonoma and Calabasas creeks.

18

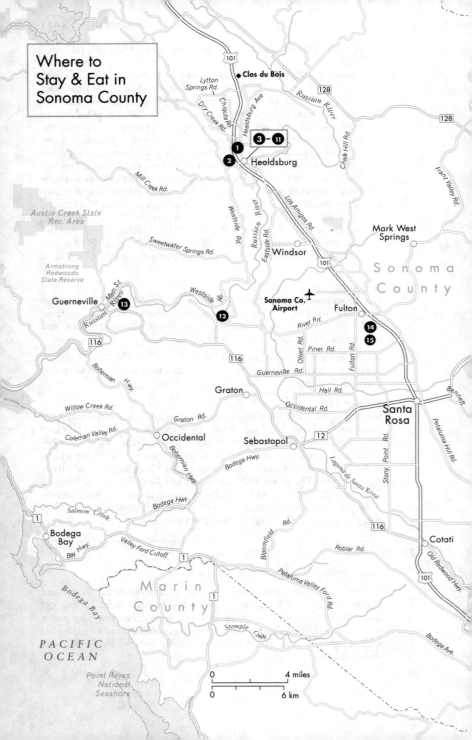

Where to Stay & Eat in Sonoma County

◆ Clos du Bois

Lytton Springs Rd.

Chiquita Rd.

Dry Creek Rd.

Healdsburg Ave.

Russian River

128

128

Franz Valley Rd.

Chalk Hill Rd.

③ — ⑪

① Healdsburg

②

Mill Creek Rd.

Westside Rd.

Russian River

Eastside Rd.

Los Amigos Rd.

Mark West Springs

Austin Creek State Rec. Area

Sweetwater Springs Rd.

Windsor

101

Sonoma County

Armstrong Redwoods State Reserve

Main St.

Westside Rd.

Sonoma Co. Airport

River Rd.

Fulton

Guerneville ⑬

Russian River

⑫

Olivet Rd.

Piner Rd.

Fulton Rd.

⑭

⑮

116

116

Guerneville Rd.

Bohemian Hwy.

Graton

Hall Rd.

Santa Rosa

Willow Creek Rd.

Graton Rd.

Occidental Rd.

Bennett

Coleman Valley Rd.

Occidental

Sebastopol

Bohemian Hwy.

12

Stony Point Rd.

Petaluma Hill Rd.

Salmon Creek

Bodega Hwy.

Bodega Bay

Bay Hwy.

Bodega Hwy.

Laguna de Santa Rosa

116

Cotati

Valley Ford Cutoff

1

Bloomfield Rd.

Roblar Rd.

Old Redwood Hwy.

101

Bodega Bay

Marin County

Petaluma Valley Ford Rd.

Bodega Ave.

PACIFIC OCEAN

1

Stemple Creek

Point Reyes National Seashore

0 ———— 4 miles

0 ———— 6 km

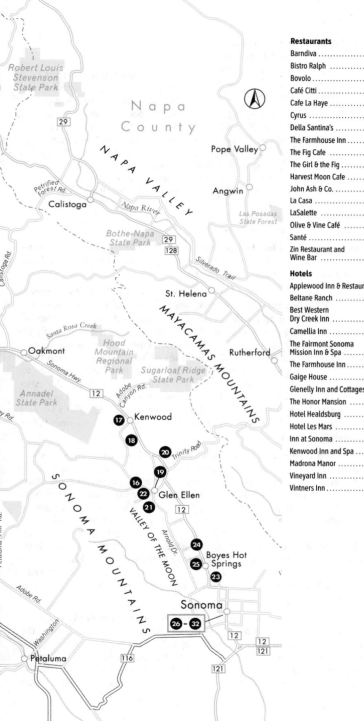

18

Jack London, who epitomizes Glen Ellen's rugged spirit, lived in the area for many years, and the town commemorates him with place-names and nostalgic establishments.

In the Jack London Village complex, **Figone's Olive Oil Co.** (✉ *14301 Arnold Dr.* ☎ *707/938–3164*) not only carries many local olive oils, serving bowls, books, and dining accessories but also presses fruit for a number of local growers, usually in the late fall. You can taste a selection of olive oils that have surprisingly different flavors.

Built in 1905, the **Jack London Saloon** (✉ *13740 Arnold Dr.* ☎ *707/996–3100* ⊕ *www.jacklondonlodge.com*) is decorated with photos of London and other London memorabilia.

In the hills above Glen Ellen—known as the Valley of the Moon—lies **Jack London State Historic Park,** where you could easily spend the afternoon hiking along the edge of vineyards and through stands of oak trees. Several of the author's manuscripts and a handful of personal effects are on view at the House of Happy Walls museum, once the home of London's widow. The ruins of Wolf House—which London designed and mysteriously burned down just before he was to move in—are a short hike away from the House of Happy Walls. Also restored and open to the public are a few farm outbuildings. London is buried on the property. ✉ *2400 London Ranch Rd.* ☎ *707/938–5216* 🚗 *Parking $6* ◷ *Park Nov.–Mar., daily 9:30–5; Apr.–Oct., daily 9:30–7. Museum daily 10–5.*

Arrowood Vineyards & Winery is neither as old nor as famous as some of its neighbors, but winemakers and critics are quite familiar with the wines produced here by Richard Arrowood, especially the chardonnays, cabernet sauvignons, and syrahs. A wraparound porch with wicker chairs invites you to linger outside the tasting room, built to resemble a New England farmhouse. A stone fireplace in the tasting room makes this an especially enticing destination in winter. ■ TIP➜ **Call at least a week or so in advance if you'd like to take a tour; they're only offered twice a day, and they tend to fill up quickly.** ✉ *14347 Sonoma Hwy./Rte. 12* ☎ *707/935–2600* ⊕ *www.arrowoodvineyards. com* 🍷 *Tasting $5–$10, tour $20–$30, includes tasting* ◷ *Daily 10–4:30; tour by appointment.*

★ One of the best-known local wineries is **Benziger Family Winery,** on a sprawling estate in a bowl with 360-degree sun exposure. Among the first wineries to identify certain vineyard blocks for particularly desirable flavors, Benziger is noted for its merlot, pinot blanc, chardonnay, and fumé blanc. The tours here are especially interesting (they're first come, first served). On a tram ride through the vineyards, guides explain the regional microclimates and geography and give you a glimpse of the extensive cave system. Tours depart several times a day, weather permitting, but are sometimes fully booked during the high season. **Arrive before lunch for the best shot at joining a tour—and bring a picnic, since the grounds here are lovely.** ⊠*1883 London Ranch Rd.* ☎*707/935–3000* ⊕*www.benziger.com* ⊟*Tasting $5–$15, tour $15* ⊘*Daily 10–5.*

WHERE TO STAY & EAT

$$ ✕**The Fig Cafe.** Celadon booths, yellow walls, and a sloping high ceil-
★ ing make this cozy, casual restaurant feel summery and airy even in the middle of winter. Artisanal cheese plates and fried calamari are popular appetizers, followed by comfort-food entrées such as braised pot roast and grilled hanger steak. Don't forget to look on the chalkboard for frequently changing desserts, such as chocolate and orange pots de crème and an apple and pear crisp. Brunch on Saturdays and Sundays features breakfast classics like French toast and eggs Florentine, in addition to some items from the regular dinner menu. ■TIP➔**The unusual no-corkage-fee policy makes it a great place to drink the wine you just discovered down the road.** ⊠*13690 Arnold Dr.* ☎*707/938–2130* ⊟*AE, D, MC, V* ⚑*Reservations not accepted* ⊘*No lunch weekdays.*

$ ✕**Olive & Vine Café.** The menu changes every day at this casual lunch-only café with wooden farmhouse tables. Take a look at the menu on the blackboard, which is likely to include panini like a barbecued pork sandwich with caramelized onions or inventive seasonal dishes like a refreshing watermelon gazpacho. But be sure to ask, too, about the items in the refrigerated case, like an updated three-bean salad or miniature pizzas with house-made tomato sauce. Though it's a good stop for picnic packers, you can eat in the dining room, a soaring barnlike space in the Jack London Village complex, or tote your dishes out to the deck, where tables overlook a creek. ⊠*14301 Arnold Dr.* ☎*707/996–9150* ⚑*Reservations not accepted* ⊟*MC, V* ⊘*No dinner.*

¢–$ ▦**Beltane Ranch.** On a slope of the Mayacamas range a few miles from
★ Glen Ellen, this 1892 ranch house stands in the shade of magnificent oak trees. The charmingly old-fashioned rooms, each individually decorated with antiques, have separate entrances, and some open onto a wraparound balcony ideal for whiling away lazy afternoons. The detached cottage, once the gardener's quarters, has a small sitting room and a fireplace. Pros: Bountiful breakfast, reasonably priced, beautiful grounds with ancient oak trees. Cons: Downstairs rooms get some noise from upstairs rooms, credit cards are not accepted. ⊠*11775 Sonoma Hwy./Rte. 12* ☎*707/996–6501* ⊕*www.beltaneranch.com* ⊅*3 rooms, 3 suites* ⚘*In-room: no a/c, no phone, no TV, Wi-Fi. In-hotel: tennis court, no elevator* ⊟*No credit cards* ❙◯❙*BP.*

$$$–$$$$ ▦**Gaige House.** Gorgeous orchids and Asian objets d'art are just a few
Fodor'sChoice of the little luxuries in this understated B&B. Rooms in the main house,
★ an 1890 Queen Anne, are mostly done in pale colors and each has its advantages. An upstairs room has wraparound windows to let in floods of light, for instance, while the lavish creekside cottages have a pronounced Japanese influence, with massive granite soaking tubs overlooking private atriums. In addition to the main pool and hot tub,

18

surrounded by magnolia trees, a second, private hot tub is available to those who sign up. Though the staffers are helpful, service never seems fussy, and there's a bottomless jar of cookies offered in the kitchen. Pros: Beautiful lounge areas, cottages are very private. Cons: Sound carries in the main house, a few rooms are on the small side. ✉ *13540 Arnold Dr.* ☎ *707/935–0237 or 800/935–0237* 🖷 *707/935–6411* ⊕ *www. gaige.com* ⟿ *12 rooms, 11 suites* ♿ *In-room: safe, refrigerator (some), DVD, Wi-Fi. In-hotel: pool, spa, no elevator, no kids under 12, no-smoking rooms* ▭ *AE, D, DC, MC, V.*

⟨ 🏨 **Glenelly Inn and Cottages.** On a quiet side street a few blocks from the town center, this sunny little establishment has a long history as a getaway. It was built as an inn in 1916, and the rooms, each individually decorated, tend toward a simple country style. Many have four-poster beds and touches such as a wood-burning stove or antique oak dresser; some have whirlpool tubs. All have puffy down comforters. Breakfast is served in front of the common room's fireplace, as are cookies or other snacks in the afternoon. ■TIP➔**Innkeeper Kristi Hallamore Jeppesen has two children of her own, so this is an unusually kid-friendly inn.** Pros: Children are welcome, quiet location, hot tub in a pretty garden. Cons: Some may not appreciate the presence of children, less expensive rooms are on the small side. ✉ *5131 Warm Springs Rd.* ☎ *707/996–6720* ⊕ *www.glenelly.com* ⟿ *8 rooms, 2 suites* ♿ *In-room: no a/c (some), no phone (some), refrigerator (some), DVD, Wi-Fi. In-hotel: no elevator, laundry facilities, some pets allowed, no-smoking rooms* ▭ *AE, D, MC, V* ⦿*BP.*

KENWOOD

3 mi north of Glen Ellen on Rte. 12.

Blink and you might miss tiny Kenwood, which consists of little more than a few restaurants and shops and a historic train depot, now used for private events. But hidden in this pretty landscape of meadows and woods at the north end of Sonoma Valley are several good wineries, most just off the Sonoma Highway.

On your way in to **Kunde Estate Winery & Vineyards,** you pass a terrace flanked with a reflecting pool and fountains, virtually coaxing you to stay for a picnic with views over the vineyard. The tour of the grounds includes its extensive caves, some of which stretch 175 feet below a syrah vineyard. Kunde is perhaps best known for its chardonnays, which range from crisp ones aged in stainless-steel tanks to toastier ones that have spent time in French oak barrels. Tastings might include sauvignon blanc, cabernet sauvignon, and zinfandel as well. If you skip the tour, take a few minutes to wander around the demonstration vineyard outside the tasting room. In the months before crush (usually in September), you can taste the different grapes on the vines and see if you can taste the similarities between the grapes and wines you just tasted. ✉ *9825 Sonoma Hwy./Rte. 12* ☎ *707/833–5501* ⊕ *www. kunde.com* ▤ *Tasting $10–$20, tour free* ⊙ *Daily 10:30–4:30, tours on the hr Fri.–Sun. 11–3.*

Kenwood Vineyards makes some good value-priced red and white wines, as well as some showier cabernet sauvignons and zinfandels, many of which are poured in the tasting room housed in one of the original barns on the property. The best of these come from Jack London's old vineyard, in the Sonoma Mountain appellation, above the fog belt of the Sonoma Valley (Kenwood has an exclusive lease). But the crisp sauvignon blanc is what keeps wine connoisseurs coming back for more. ■TIP→ **Free tastings are a boon to those discovering that all those $10 tasting fees are starting to add up.** ✉*9592 Sonoma Hwy./Rte. 12* ☎*707/833–5891* ⊕*www.kenwoodvineyards.com* ✆*Tasting free–$5* ☉*Daily 10–4:30.*

The outrageously ornate French Normandy castle visible from Route 12 might attract you even before you know that the **Ledson Winery & Vineyards** produces exceptional pinot noirs, merlots, zinfandels, and cabernet francs, as well as a wide variety of other reds and whites, all of which are available only at the winery and a small number of restaurants. The castle, intended as the Ledson family's opulent home when its construction began in 1989, is now a warren of tasting rooms, special event spaces, and a small food market for picnic supplies. ✉*7335 Sonoma Hwy./Rte. 12* ☎*707/537–3810* ⊕*www.ledson.com* ✆*Tasting $5–$15, no tour* ☉*Daily 10–5.*

WHERE TO STAY & EAT

$ ✕**Café Citti.** Opera tunes in the background and a friendly staff (as well as a roaring fire when the weather's cold) keep this no-frills roadside café from feeling too spartan. Order dishes such as roast chicken, pasta, and slabs of tiramisu from the counter and they're delivered to your table. An ample array of prepared salads and sandwiches means they do a brisk business in takeout for picnic packers. ✉*9049 Sonoma Hwy./Rte. 12* ☎*707/833–2690* ⊟*MC, V.*

$$$$ 🏨**Kenwood Inn and Spa.** Buildings resembling graceful old haciendas
★ and mature fruit trees shading the courtyards convey the sense that this inn has been here for more than a century. French doors opening onto terraces or balconies, fluffy featherbeds, and wood-burning fireplaces give the uncommonly spacious guestrooms, many with tile floors, a particularly romantic air. A swimming pool, Jacuzzis, and saunas pepper three atmospheric courtyards, and you could easily spend an afternoon padding from one to another in your robe and slippers. The intimate but well-equipped spa draws on the local preoccupation, using the Caudalie line of grape-derived products and treatments. Pros: Large rooms, lavish furnishings, very romantic. Cons: Expensive, restaurant isn't quite up to the level of the inn. ✉*10400 Sonoma Hwy.* ☎*707/833–1293* ⊕*www.kenwoodinn.com* ⇥*29 rooms* ♿*In-room: no TV, Wi-Fi. In-hotel: restaurant, bar, pool, spa, no elevator, concierge, laundry service, public Wi-Fi, no kids under 18, no-smoking rooms.*

18

ELSEWHERE IN SONOMA COUNTY

At nearly 1,598 square mi, there's much more to Sonoma County than the day-tripper favorites of Sonoma, Glen Ellen, and Kenwood. North of this trio of oenophile hotbeds is Healdsburg, a lovely small town with a rapidly rising buzz. The national media has latched onto it for its swank hotels and remarkable restaurants, and more and more Fodors. com readers recommend it as an ideal home base for wine tasting.

Within easy striking distance of Healdsburg are some of the Wine Country's most scenic vineyards, in the Alexander, Dry Creek, and Russian River valleys. And these lookers also happen to produce some of the country's best pinot noir, cabernet sauvignon, zinfandel, and sauvignon blanc. Though these regions are hardly unknown names, their quiet, narrow roads feel a world away from Highway 29 in Napa.

The western stretches of Sonoma county, which reach all the way to the Pacific Ocean, are sparsely populated in comparison to the above destinations, with only the occasional vineyard popping up in between isolated ranches. This chapter focuses on the wine-growing regions of Sonoma, but if you want to explore elsewhere in Sonoma (Bodega Bay to whale-watch, for example), contact the local visitor bureau for more information.

SANTA ROSA

8 mi northwest of Kenwood on Rte. 12.

Santa Rosa, the Wine Country's largest city, isn't likely to charm you with its office buildings, department stores, and almost perpetual snarl of traffic along U.S. 101. It is, however, home to a couple of interesting cultural offerings. Its chain motels and hotels are also handy if you're finding that everything else is booked up, especially since Santa Rosa is roughly equidistant from Sonoma, Healdsburg, and the Russian River Valley, three of the most popular wine-tasting destinations.

The **Luther Burbank Home and Gardens** commemorates the great botanist who lived and worked on these grounds and single-handedly developed the modern techniques of hybridization. The 1.6-acre garden and a greenhouse show the results of some of Burbank's experiments to develop spineless cacti, fruit trees, and flowers such as the Shasta daisy. In the music room of his house, a modified Greek Revival structure that was Burbank's home from 1884 to 1906, a dictionary lies open to a page on which the verb "burbank" is defined as "to modify and improve plant life." If you show up during the gift shop's open hours, it's worth the small fee ($5) to rent the interesting, self-guided audio tour. ⊠*Santa Rosa and Sonoma Aves.* ☎*707/524–5445* ⊕*www. lutherburbank.org* ⊠*Gardens free, guided tour of house and greenhouse $5* ☉ *Gardens daily 8–dusk; museum and gift shop Apr.–Oct., Tues.–Sun. 10–4; tour Apr.–Oct., Tues.–Sun. 10–3:30.*

Fodors Choice ★ The visitor center at beautiful **Matanzas Creek Winery** sets itself apart with an understated Japanese aesthetic, with a tranquil fountain and a koi pond. Best of all, huge windows overlook a vast field of lavender plants. ■TIP➡**The best time to visit is in June, when the lavender blooms and perfumes the air.** The winery specializes in three varietals—sauvignon blanc, merlot, and chardonnay—though in 2005 they also started producing a popular dry rosé. After you taste the wines, ask for the self-guided garden-tour book before taking a stroll. ✉*6097 Bennett Valley Rd.* ☎*707/528–6464 or 800/590–6464* ⊕*www.matanzascreek. com* 🍷*Tasting $5–$10, tour free* ⊙*Daily 10–4:30; tour weekdays at 10:30 and 2:30, Sat. at 10:30, by appointment.*

WHERE TO STAY & EAT

$$$$ ✕**John Ash & Co.** Patio seating, vaulted ceilings, and a cozy indoor fireplace make this spacious restaurant with vineyard views a good choice for romantics. The contemporary dishes draw from both Italian and French cuisine, but the ingredients are largely local (a few even come from gardens on the property). Hog Island oysters come from Tomales Bay and in season you might find local king salmon with a miso crust and shiitake mushrooms. The wine list is impressive even by Wine Country standards, and the bar opens early—at 4 PM, 3 PM Friday through Sunday—serving a smaller menu. ✉*4330 Barnes Rd., River Rd. exit west from U.S. 101* ☎*707/527–7687* ▤*AE, D, DC, MC, V* ⊙*No lunch.*

$$$ 🏨**Vintners Inn.** On a property that includes about 80 acres of vineyards—the grapes are used by the inn's owners, who also own the winery Ferrari-Carano—this French provincial-style inn is notably calm and quiet, considering how close it is to U.S. 101 and downtown Santa Rosa. The spacious guest rooms, spread among three separate two-story buildings, all have a patio or balcony; many also have woodburning fireplaces and views of the vineyards. An attractive event center designed to resemble a winery is a popular spot for weddings and meetings. Pros: Comfortable king-size beds with feather mattress toppers, spacious rooms, jogging path through the vineyards. Cons: You can hear the freeway from the hot tub, some of the furnishings a bit dated, there's a fee if you want a DVD player in most rooms. ✉*4350 Barnes Rd., River Rd. exit west from U.S. 101,* ☎*707/575–7350 or 800/421–2584* 📠*707/575–1426* ⊕*www.vintnersinn.com* 🛏*38 rooms, 6 suites* ♿*In-room: safe, refrigerator, DVD (some), Wi-Fi. In-hotel: restaurant, room service, bar, gym, no elevator, concierge, laundry service, public Wi-Fi, no-smoking rooms* ▤*AE, D, DC, MC, V* ⎯◎⎯*BP.*

NIGHTLIFE & THE ARTS

The **Wells Fargo Center for the Arts** (✉*50 Mark West Springs Rd.* ☎*707/546–3600*) presents concerts, plays, and other performances by locally and internationally known artists—everyone from Dolly Parton to the Jazz at Lincoln Center Orchestra. For symphony, ballet, and other live theater performances throughout the year, call the **Spreckels Performing Arts Center** (✉*5409 Snyder La.* ☎*707/588–3400*) in Rohnert Park, a short drive from downtown Santa Rosa.

18

RUSSIAN RIVER VALLEY

5 mi northwest of Santa Rosa.

The Russian River flows all the way from Mendocino to the Pacific Ocean, but in terms of wine making, the Russian River Valley is centered on a triangle with points at Healdsburg, Guerneville, and Sebastopol. Tall redwoods shade many of the two-lane roads that access this scenic area, where, thanks to the cooling marine influence, pinot noir and chardonnay are the king and queen of grapes.

Behind the bar in the tasting room, a dramatic steel sculpture studded with illuminated chunks of glass suggests a bottle of bubbly, cluing you in to the raison d'être of **J Vineyards and Winery** before your first sip. Their dry sparkling wines are made from pinot noir and chardonnay grapes planted in their Russian River vineyards. Still wines—made with the same varietals, as well as pinot gris and a few other grapes— are also good, if perhaps not as impressive as the sparklers, which have wonderfully complex fruit and floral aromas and good acidity. Although you can sample their wines on their own at the tasting bar, for a truly decadent experience make a reservation for the "Bubble Room Experience," where sparklers are served with treats that might include caviar. Rervations aren't necessary to taste on the terrace, open May through October, where artisanal cheeses and charcuterie plates are served. ⊠*11447 Old Redwood Hwy.* ☎*707/431–3646* ✍*Tasting $10–$55* ⊕*www.jwine.com* ☉*Daily 11–5; Bubble Room Fri.–Mon. 11–4.*

★ Down a one-lane country road from Forestville, **Iron Horse Vineyards** makes rich, creamy sparkling wines as well as estate chardonnays and pinot noirs. Three hundred acres of rolling, vine-covered hills, barnlike winery buildings, and an outdoor tasting area with a view of Mount St. Helena make for a beautifully rustic stop. Tours are available by appointment on weekdays at 10 AM. ⊠*9786 Ross Station Rd., near Sebastopol* ☎*707/887–1507* ⊕*www.ironhorsevineyards.com* ✍*Tasting $10, tour free* ☉*Daily 10–3:30; tour by appointment.*

Rochioli Vineyards and Winery claims one of the prettiest picnic sites in the area, with tables overlooking vineyards, which are also visible from the airy little tasting room hung with modern artwork. Production is small—about 14,000 cases annually—and fans on the winery's mailing list snap up most of the bottles, but the wines are still worth a stop. Because of the cool growing conditions in the Russian River Valley, the flavors of their chardonnay and sauvignon blanc are intense and complex. It's their pinot, though, that is largely responsible for the winery's stellar reputation; it helped cement the Russian River's reputation as a pinot powerhouse. ⊠*6192 Westside Rd.* ☎*707/433–2305* ✍*Tasting* *free* ⊙ *Thurs.–Mon. 11–4, Tues –Wed. by appointment; closed last two weeks of Dec. and first week of Jan.*

Fans of pinot noir will surely want to stop at **Hartford Family Winery,** a surprisingly opulent winery off a meandering country road in Forestville. Here grapes from the coolest areas of the Russian River Valley, Sonoma coast, and other regions are turned into chardonnays, old-vine zinfandels, and single-vineyard pinots, the latter with unusual aging potential. ⊠ *8075 Martinelli Rd.* ☎ *707/887–1756* ⊕ *www.hartford wines.com* 🍷 *Tasting $5–$15* ⊙ *Daily 10–4:30.*

Pass through an impressive metal gate and wind your way up a steep hill to reach **Gary Farrell Winery,** a spot with knockout views. The winery built its reputation on pinot noir, but now zinfandel is the star, especially the spicy, full-bodied zin from the Dry Creek Valley's Maple Vineyard. The winery also makes a fine cabernet sauvignon, sauvignon blanc, merlot, and chardonnay. ⊠ *10701 Westside Rd.* ☎ *707/473–2900* ⊕ *http://garyfarrellwines.com* 🍷 *Tasting $10, tour $15–$25* ⊙ *Daily 11–4; tours by appointment.*

Just far enough off the beaten track to feel like a real find, **De Loach Vineyards** produces a variety of Russian River Valley sauvignon blancs, gewürztraminers, merlots, and old-vine zinfandels but is best known for chardonnay and, especially, their pinot noir. Some of the pinot is made using open-top wood fermentation vats that are uncommon in Sonoma but have been used in France for centuries. (Some think that they intensify a wine's flavor.) Tours focus on the estate vineyards outside the tasting room door, where you can learn about the labor-intensive biodynamic and organic farming methods used here. ⊠ *1791 Olivet Rd.* ☎ *707/526–9111* ⊕ *www.deloachvineyards.com* 🍷 *Tasting $10* ⊙ *Daily 10–5; tours daily by appointment.*

OFF THE BEATEN PATH

Korbel Champagne Cellars. To be called Champagne, a wine must be made in the French region of Champagne—otherwise it's just sparkling wine. Whatever you call it, Korbel produces a tasty, reasonably priced bubbly and still wines, as well as its own brandy, which is distilled on the premises. The wine tour, one of the best in Sonoma County, clearly explains the process of making sparkling wine and takes you through the winery's ivy-covered 19th-century buildings. If you've already had the process of wine making explained to you one too many times, a tour of the rose garden, where there are more than 250 varieties of roses, may be a welcome break. Garden tours are given Tuesday through Sunday, mid-April through mid-October, at 11, 1, and 3. ⊠ *13250 River Rd., Guerneville* ☎ *707/824–7000* ⊕ *www.korbel.com* 🍷 *Tasting and tour free* ⊙ *Oct.–Apr., daily 9–4:30; May–Sept., daily 9–5; tour Oct.–Apr., daily on the hr 10–3; May–Sept., weekdays 10, 11, 12, 1, 2, 3, and 3:45, weekends at 10, 11, noon, 12:45, 1:30, 2:15, 3, and 3:45.*

18

WHERE TO STAY & EAT

$$$$
Fodor's Choice
★

✗ **The Farmhouse Inn.** From the personable sommelier who arrives at the table to help you pick wines from the excellent list (one of only about a hundred Master Sommeliers working in the United States) to the maître d' who serves local and European cheeses from the cart with a flourish, the staff match the quality of the outstanding French-inspired cuisine. The signature dish, "rabbit, rabbit, rabbit," a rich trio of confit of leg, rabbit loin wrapped in applewood-smoked bacon, and roasted rack of rabbit with a mustard cream sauce, is typical of the dishes that are simultaneously rustic and refined. A hand-painted mural surrounds the tranquil, country-style dining room.

■ **TIP** → **Dinner here has become a particularly hot item since the restaurant was awarded a Michelin star in 2007, so reserve well in advance.** ✉ *7871 River Rd., Forestville* ☎ *707/887–3300 or 800/464–6642* ◿ *Reservations essential* ⊟ *AE, D, DC, MC, V* ☉ *Closed Tues. and Wed. No lunch.*

¢–$$$ ✕▣ **Applewood Inn & Restaurant.** On a knoll in the shelter of towering

Fodor'sChoice   redwoods, this romantic inn has two distinct types of accommodations.

★   Those in the original Belden House, where cozy chairs around a river-rock fireplace encourage loitering in the lounge area, are comfortable but modest in scale. Most of the 10 rooms in the newer buildings are larger and airier, decorated in sage green and terra-cotta tones. Readers rave about the accommodating service, soothing atmosphere, and the earthy Cal-Italian cuisine served in the restaurant ($$$) built to recall a French barn. In winter, up the romance factor by asking for a table near the fireplace. Pros: Quiet, secluded location; decadent breakfast; eager-to-please staff. Cons: only basic spa treatments and facilities. ✉ *13555 Rte. 116, Guerneville* ☎ *707/869–9093 or 800/555–8509* ⊕ *www.applewoodinn.com* ⇜ *19 rooms* ⚷ *In-room: no a/c (some), Wi-Fi. In-hotel: restaurant, pool, spa, no elevator, no-smoking rooms* ⊟ *AE, MC, V* ◖⨀ *BP.*

$$–$$$$ ▣ **The Farmhouse Inn.** This pale yellow 1873 farmhouse and adjacent

★   cottages offer individually decorated rooms with comfortable touches such as down comforters, whirlpool tubs, and CD players. ■ **TIP** → **Most rooms have wood-burning fireplaces and even their own private little saunas, which makes this place especially inviting during the rainy winter months.** It's worth leaving your supremely comfortable bed for the sumptuous breakfasts here. The inn's restaurant is one of the most highly regarded in the Wine Country (*see above*). A new building, reminiscent of an old barn that was once on the property, is scheduled to open in 2009 and will almost double the number of available rooms. Pros: Saunas in many rooms, one of Sonoma's best restaurants is on site. Cons: Rooms closest to the street get a bit of road noise. ✉ *7871 River Rd., Forestville* ☎ *707/887–3300 or 800/464–6642* 🖷 *707/887–3311* ⊕ *www.farmhouseinn.com* ⇜ *8 rooms, 2 suites* ⚷ *In-room: refrigerator, DVD, Wi-Fi. In-hotel: restaurant, pool, spa, no elevator, concierge, no-smoking rooms* ⊟ *AE, D, DC, MC, V* ◖⨀ *BP.*

SPORTS & THE OUTDOORS

At **Burke's Canoe Trips** (✉ *River Rd. and Mirabel Rd., 1 mi north of Forestville* ☎ *707/887–1222*), you can rent a canoe for a leisurely paddle 10 mi downstream to Guerneville. A shuttle bus will return you to your car at the end of the day. May through October is the best time for boating.

HEALDSBURG

17 mi north of Santa Rosa on U.S. 101.

The buzz on Healdsburg is amplifying—especially among the platinum-card set who rave about relative newcomers like Cyrus and Hotel Les Mars. But you don't have to be a tycoon to stay here and enjoy the town. For every ritzy restaurant there's a great, low-key bakery or B&B. A whitewashed bandstand on the Healdsburg plaza hosts free summer concerts, where you might hear anything from bluegrass to Sousa marches. Add to that the fragrant magnolia trees shading the square and the bright flower beds, and the whole thing is as pretty as a Norman Rockwell painting.

The countryside around Healdsburg is a fantasy of pastoral bliss—beautifully overgrown and in constant repose. Alongside the relatively untrafficked roads, country stores offer just-plucked fruits and vine-ripened tomatoes. Wineries here are barely visible, tucked behind groves of eucalyptus or hidden high on fog-shrouded hills.

WHERE TO STAY & EAT

$$$ ✕**Barndiva.** This hip spot trades in the homey vibe of so many Wine Country spots for a nightclub feel. Dance music plays in the background while servers ferry inventive (if pricey) specialty cocktails. The food is as stylish as the well-dressed couples cozying up next to one another on the banquette seats. Dishes, divided on the menu into "Light," "Spicy," and "Comfort" categories, are well executed and beautifully presented. For instance, you might try "Spicy" calamari with lime aioli or short ribs with mashed potatoes from the "Comfort" column. During warmer months the beautiful patio more than doubles the number of seats. Service is friendly rather than expert. ✉*231 Center St.* ☎*707/431–0100* ⊟*AE, MC, V* ⊘*Closed Mon. and Tues. No lunch Wed.*

$$$ ✕**Bistro Ralph.** Bistro Ralph may no longer be the hottest restaurant in Healdsburg, as it was in the 1990s, but chef Ralph Tingle's homey cuisine clearly has a timeless appeal because his restaurant is still packed every night it's open. Typical dishes from the weekly changing menu include osso buco with saffron risotto and sautéed mahimahi with hedgehog mushrooms. The stark industrial space includes a gracefully curved wine rack, concrete floors, and a painted brick wall. Take a seat at the bar and chat with the locals, who love this place just as much as out-of-towners do, especially for their wicked martinis that are almost big enough to swim in. ✉*109 Plaza St., off Healdsburg Ave.* ☎*707/433–1380* ⊟*MC, V* ⊘*Closed Sun.*

$ ✕**Bovolo.** Husband and wife team John Stewart and Duskie Estes serve what they call "slow food . . . fast." Though you might pop into this casual café at the back of the Plaza Farms market for a half hour, the

18

staff will have spent hours curing the meats that star in the small menu of salads, pizzas, and sandwiches. For instance, at lunch you might order the Salumist's Salad, which mixes a variety of cured meats with greens, white beans, and a tangy vinaigrette, or a thin-crusted pizza topped with house-made Italian pork sausage and roasted peppers. At dinner, a set three-course menu ($27) is also available, which typically features a hearty main course like braised rabbit. ⊠ *106 Matheson St.* ☎ *707/431–2962* ⊴ *Reservations not accepted* ⊟ *MC, V* ☺ *June– Sept., Fri.–Tues. 9–9, Wed.–Thurs. 9–6; Oct.–May, Mon., Tues., Thurs. 9–6, Fri.–Sun. 9–9, closed Wed.*

$$$$
Fodor's Choice
★

✕ **Cyrus.** Hailed as the best thing to hit the Wine Country since French Laundry when it opened in 2005, Cyrus has earned its stripes by racking up awards and the raves of guests. From the moment a cart with Champagne and caviar is wheeled up to your table to the minute your dessert plates are whisked away, you'll be carefully tended by polished servers and an expert sommelier. The formal dining room, with its vaulted Venetian-plaster ceiling, is a suitably plush setting for chef Douglas Keane's creative, subtle cuisine. Keane has a notably free hand with decadent ingredients like truffles. Three-, four-, and five-course tasting menus can be constructed any way you like—you can even order four desserts, the waiter enthuses. Most opt to work their way through savories first, such as a terrine of foie gras with curried apple compote and duck with tamarind-glazed eggplant, before finishing up with an espresso gelato with an almond dacquoise. If you've failed to make reservations, you can order any of their dishes à la carte at the bar. ⊠ *29 North St.* ☎ *707/433–3311* ⊴ *Reservations essential* ⊟ *AE, DC, MC, V* ☺ *No lunch.*

$$

✕ **Zin Restaurant and Wine Bar.** Concrete walls and floors and large canvases on the walls give the restaurant a casual, industrial, and slightly artsy feel. The American cuisine—such as smoked pork chop with homemade applesauce or the red beans and rice with andouille sausage—is hearty and highly seasoned. Portions are large, so consider sharing if you hope to save room for one of the decadent desserts, like the bread pudding with bourbon sauce. As you might have guessed, zinfandel is the drink of choice here: roughly half of the 100 or so bottles on the wine list are zins. ⊠ *344 Center St.* ☎ *707/473–0946* ⊟ *AE, MC, V* ☺ *No lunch weekends.*

¢–$

▦ **Camellia Inn.** In another of Healdsburg's 19th-century Victorians, this colorful B&B sits on a quiet residential street just a block from the town's main square. It's been run by the same family for more than 25 years. The parlors downstairs are chockablock with ceramics and other decorative items, while rooms are individually decorated with antiques, such as an impressive mid-19th-century tiger-maple bed from Scotland. ▪ TIP→ **There's one cozy budget room with a private bath that's across the hallway.** Pros: Reasonable rates for the neighborhood, a rare family-friendly inn, within easy walking distance of dozens of restaurants. Cons: Some rooms feel a little tired, some may find the look too frilly. ⊠ *211 North St.* ☎ *707/433–8182 or 800/727–8182* 🖷 *707/433–8130* ⊕ *www.camelliainn.com* ⇥ *8 rooms, 1 suite* ♿ *In-room: no TV. In-hotel: pool, no elevator, no-smoking rooms* ⊟ *AE, D, MC, V* ⦿ *BP.*

$$$–$$$$ ✕▥ **Hotel Healdsburg.** Across the street from Healdsburg's tidy town plaza, this spare, sophisticated hotel caters to travelers with an urban sensibility. Unadorned olive green walls, dark hardwood floors, and clean-lined furniture fill the guest rooms; the beds are some of the most comfortable you can find anywhere. Spacious bathrooms continue the sleek style with monochromatic tiles and deep soaking tubs that are all right angles. The attached restaurant, Dry Creek Kitchen ($$$–$$$$), is one of the best in Healdsburg. Celebrity chef Charlie Palmer is the man behind seasonal dishes that largely rely on local ingredients, like a spice-crusted Sonoma duck breast with fava beans and fennel, plus a wine list covering the best Sonoma vintners. Pros: Some rooms overlook the town plaza, free valet parking, extremely comfortable beds. Cons: Least expensive rooms are on the small side, street noise can be a problem. ✉25 Matheson St. ☎707/431–2800 or 800/889–7188 ⊕www.hotelhealdsburg.com ⇩45 rooms, 10 suites ☖In-room: safe, refrigerator, DVD, ethernet, Wi-Fi (some). In-hotel: restaurant, room service, bar, pool, gym, spa, concierge, laundry service, some pets allowed (fee), no-smoking rooms ▭AE, MC, V ⲓⲟⲓCP.

$–$$$ ▥ **The Honor Mansion.** Each room is unique at this photogenic 1883
★ Italianate Victorian. Rooms in the main house preserve a sense of the building's heritage, while the larger suites out back are comparatively understated. Luxurious touches such as lovely antiques are found in every room, and suites have the added advantage of a deck; some even have private outdoor hot tubs. Fodors.com readers rave about the attentive staff, who "think of things you don't even know you want." Pros: Beautiful, tranquil grounds; personable innkeepers; homemade sweets available at all hours. Cons: Almost a mile from Healdsburg's plaza, on a moderately busy street. ✉14891 Grove St. ☎707/433–4277 or 800/554–4667 ⊕www.honormansion.com ⇩5 rooms, 8 suites ☖In-room: refrigerator, DVD (some), Wi-Fi. In-hotel: tennis court, pool, no elevator, no-smoking rooms ▭AE, MC, V ◷Closed 1 wk around Christmas ⲓⲟⲓBP.

$$$$ ▥ **Hotel Les Mars.** In 2005, posh Healdsburg got even more chichi with the opening of this opulent hotel. Guest rooms are spacious and elegant enough for French nobility, with 18th- and 19th-century antiques and reproductions and gas-burning fireplaces. Most of the gleaming, white marble bathrooms have spa tubs in addition to enormous showers. And when you return at night to a box of chocolate truffles and crawl into your canopy bed covered in pristine Italian linens, you might wonder when you've ever had it so good. Rooms on the third floor have soaring ceilings that make them feel particularly large, while the second-floor rooms have a slightly more understated style. Wine and cheese are served every evening in the library, sumptuously paneled with hand-carved black walnut. Pros: Large rooms, just off Healdsburg's plaza, impeccable service, Bulgari bath products. Cons: Very expensive, no parking lot. ✉27 North St. ☎707/433–4211 ⊕www.lesmarshotel.com ⇩16 rooms ☖In-room: safe, DVD, Wi-Fi. In-hotel: restaurant, bar, pool, gym, laundry service, no-smoking rooms ▭AE,DC, MC, V ⲓⲟⲓCP.

18

$$–$$$$ 🏠 **Madrona Manor.** The oldest continuously operating inn in the area, this 1881 Victorian mansion, surrounded by 8 acres of wooded and landscaped grounds, is straight out of a storybook. Rooms in the three-story mansion, the carriage house, and the two separate cottages are splendidly ornate, with mirrors in gilt frames and paintings covering every wall. Candlelight dinners are served in the formal dining rooms nightly (except Monday and Tuesday). Pros: Old-fashioned, romantic ambience; pretty veranda perfect for a cocktail. Cons: Pool heated May through October only, decor might be too fussy for some. ✉ *1001 Westside Rd., central Healdsburg exit off U.S. 101, then left on Mill St.* ☎ *707/433–4231 or 800/258–4003* 🌐 *www.madronamanor.com* ➪ *17 rooms, 5 suites* 🛏 *In-room: no TV, Wi-Fi. In-hotel: restaurant, bar, pool, no elevator, no-smoking rooms* 🚬 *AE, MC, V* ⎟O⎟*BP.*

> **FARMERS' MARKET**
>
> During two weekly **Healdsburg farmers' markets,** you can buy locally made goat's cheese, fragrant lavender, and olive oil in addition to the usual produce. On Saturday the market takes place one block west of the town plaza, at the corner of North and Vine streets, from 9 AM to noon, May through November. The Tuesday market, run from June through October, takes place on the plaza itself from 4 to 6:30 PM.

SHOPPING

Oakville Grocery (✉ *124 Matheson St.* ☎ *707/433–3200*) has a bustling Healdsburg branch filled with wine, condiments, and deli items. A terrace with ample seating makes a good place for an impromptu picnic, but you might want to lunch early or late to avoid the worst crowds. For more artisanal foods, pop into **Plaza Farms** (✉ *106 Matheson St.* ☎ *707/433–2345*), where the olive oil producer Da Vero shares a market hall with a few other shops selling locally-made or hard-to-fine imported products.

DRY CREEK & ALEXANDER VALLEYS

On the west side of U.S. 101, Dry Creek Valley remains one of the least-developed appellations in Sonoma. Zinfandel grapes flourish on the benchlands, whereas the gravelly, well-drained soil of the valley floor is better known for chardonnay and, in the north, sauvignon blanc. The wineries in this region tend to be smaller, which makes them a good bet on summer weekends, when larger spots and those along the main thoroughfares tend to be filled to the gills with tourists.

The Alexander Valley, which lies east of Healdsburg, is similarly rustic, and you can see as many folks cycling along Highway 28 here as you can behind the wheel of a car. The largely family-owned wineries often produce zinfandel and chardonnay, which grow particularly well here.

Giuseppe and Pietro Simi, two brothers from Italy, began growing grapes in Sonoma in 1876, making **Simi Winery,** in the Alexander Valley, one of the oldest in the Wine Country. Though operations are strictly

Best Wine Country Festivals

■ **Napa Valley Mustard Festival, Feb.–Mar.** When Napa is at its least crowded, and wild mustard blooms in between the vines, locals celebrate wine, food, and art with exhibitions, auctions, dinners, and cooking competitions at venues throughout the valley. *707/944–1133; http://mustard-festival.org*

■ **Russian River Wine Road Barrel Tasting Weekends, Mar.** For two weekends in March, more than 100 Russian River wineries open their cellars to visitors who want to taste the wine in the barrels, getting a preview of what's to come. *707/433–4335; www.wineroad.com*

■ **Sonoma Jazz + Festival, late May** Headlining jazz performers play in a 3,000-person tent in downtown Sonoma, while smaller music, food, and wine events take place around town. *866/468–8355; www.sonoma-jazz.org*

■ **Auction Napa Valley, early June** The world's biggest charity wine auction is one of Napa's glitziest nights. Dozens of events hosted by various wineries culminate in an opulent dinner and auction. *707/963–3388; www.napavintners.com*

■ **Sonoma County Hot Air Balloon Classic, July** Dozens of colorful hot-air balloons are sent aloft in Windsor, bright and early on two consecutive mornings in July. Spectators gather in Keiser Community Park to enjoy the show. *707/837–1884; www.schabc.org*

■ **Sonoma County Harvest Fair, early Oct.** This festival celebrates both the wine-making and agricultural sides of Sonoma County, with wine tastings, cooking demos, livestock shows, crafts, carnival rides, and local entertainers filling the Sonoma County Fairgrounds in Santa Rosa. *707/545–4203; www.harvestfair.org*

18

high-tech these days, the winery's tree-studded entrance area and stone buildings recall a more genteel era. Chardonnay is a specialty here, and the cabernet sauvignon is also very good. ⊠ *16275 Healdsburg Ave., Dry Creek Rd. exit off U.S. 101* ☎ *707/433–6981* ⊕ *www.simiwinery.com* ⊠ *Tasting $5–$14, tour $10* ⊙ *Daily 10–5; tours at 11 and 2.*

Dry Creek Vineyard, where fumé blanc is the flagship wine, also makes well-regarded zinfandels and a zesty dry chenin blanc that critics often claim is one of the best white wine values in Sonoma. After picking up a bottle you might want to picnic beneath the flowering magnolias and soaring redwoods. Conveniently, a general store and deli with plenty of picnic fixings is just steps down the road. ⊠ *3770 Lambert Bridge Rd.* ☎ *707/433–1000* ⊕ *www.drycreekvineyard.com* ⊠ *Tasting $5–$15* ⊙ *Daily 10:30–4:30.*

An unassuming winery in a wood-and-cinder-block barn, **Quivira** produces some of the most interesting wines in Dry Creek Valley. Though it's known for its dangerously drinkable and fruity Steelhead Red, a red blend made mostly of zinfandel, the intensely flavored syrahs and petite sirahs are also worth checking out. Redwood and olive trees shade the picnic area. ⊠ *4900 W. Dry Creek Rd.* ☎ *707/431–8333* ⊕ *www.quivira wine.com* ⊠ *Tasting $5* ⊙ *Daily 11–5; tours by appointment.*

Fodor'sChoice

★

Down a narrow road at the westernmost edge of the Dry Creek Valley, **Michel-Schlumberger** is one of Sonoma's finest producers of cabernet sauvignon, aptly described by the winery's tour guide as a "full, rich big mouthful of wine." The tour is unusually casual and friendly. You might wander up a gravel pathway into the edge of their lovely benchland vineyards before swinging through the barrel room in the California Mission–style building that once served as the home of the winery's founder, Jean-Jacques Michel. A tasting comes with a sampling of their coveted cabernet, plus some very fine chardonnay, syrah, and pinot noir. ⊠*4155 Wine Creek Rd.* ☎*707/433–7427 or 800/447–3060* ⊕*www.michelschlumberger.com* ⊠*Tasting $5, tour $15* ☉*Tours at 11 and 2, by appointment.*

Known for its Disney-esque Italian villa, which has as many critics as it does fervent fans for its huge size and general over-the-topness, **Ferrari-Carano Winery** produces mostly chardonnays, fumé blancs, merlot, zinfandel, and cabernet sauvignons. Though whites have traditionally been the specialty here, the reds are now garnering more attention. Tours cover not only the wine-making facilities and underground cellar but also the manicured gardens, where you can see a cork tree and learn about how cork is harvested. ⊠*8761 Dry Creek Rd., Dry Creek Valley* ☎*707/433–6700* ⊕*www.ferrari-carano.com* ⊠*Tasting $5–$15, tour free* ☉*Daily 10–5; tour Mon.–Sat. at 10, by appointment.*

Fodor'sChoice

★

Once you wind your way down **Preston Vineyards'** long driveway, flanked by vineyards and punctuated by the occasional olive tree, you'll be welcomed by the sight of a few farmhouses encircling a shady yard prowled by several friendly cats. In summer, a small selection of organic produce grown in their gardens is sold from an impromptu stand on their front porch, and house-made bread and olive oil are available year-round. Their down-home style is particularly in evidence on Sundays, the only day of the week that tasting room staffers sell a 3-liter bottle of Guadagni Red, a zinfandel, cinsault, carignane, and mourvèdre blend filled from the barrel right in front of you. Owners Lou and Susan Preston are committed to organic growing techniques and use only estate-grown grapes in their wines. ⊠*9282 West Dry Creek Rd.* ☎*707/433–3372* ⊕*www.prestonvineyards.com* ⊠*$5* ☉*Daily 11–4:30.*

WHERE TO STAY

¢–$$$ ▦ **Best Western Dry Creek Inn.** The lackluster location of this Spanish Mission–style motel near U.S. 101 nevertheless means quick access to downtown Healdsburg and other Wine Country hotspots. Deluxe rooms are slightly more spacious and muted in color than the standard rooms, but both types are kept spotless. The more expensive rooms in the Tuscan building, which opened in 2007, are considerably more upscale, with amenities like flat-panel TVs, spa tubs, and patios. A casual family restaurant is next door. Pros: Free Wi-Fi, free laundry facilities, frequent discounts available on their Web site. Cons: Thin walls, basic furnishings in standard rooms. ⊠*198 Dry Creek Rd., Healdsburg* ☎*707/433–0300 or 800/222–5784* ⊕*www.drycreekinn. com* ⊟*163 rooms* ⌂*In-room: refrigerator, DVD (some), ethernet* *(some), Wi-Fi. In-hotel: restaurant, pool, gym, laundry facilities, some pets allowed (fee), no-smoking rooms ⊟AE, D, DC, MC, V ⎮◎⎮CP.*

WINE COUNTRY ESSENTIALS

To research prices, get advice from other travelers, and book travel arrangements, visit www.fodors.com.

TRANSPORTATION

BY AIR

If you'd like to bypass San Francisco or Oakland you can fly directly to the small Charles M. Schulz Sonoma County Airport (STS) in Santa Rosa on Horizon Air, which has direct flights from Los Angeles, Portland, Las Vegas, and Seattle. Rental cars are available from Avis, Enterprise, and Hertz at the airport.

BY BUS

Bus travel is an inconvenient way to explore Wine Country. Service is infrequent and the buses can only get you to Santa Rosa or the town of Vallejo, south of Napa—neither of which is close to the vineyards. Sonoma County Transit offers daily bus service to points all over the county. VINE (Valley Intracity Neighborhood Express) provides bus service within the city of Napa and between other Napa Valley towns.

Bus Lines **Greyhound** (☎ *800/231–2222*). **Sonoma County Transit** (☎ *707/576– 7433 or 800/345–7433*). **VINE** (☎ *707/255–7631*).

18

BY CAR

Five major roads cut through the Napa and Sonoma valleys. U.S. 101 and Routes 12 and 121 travel through Sonoma County. Route 29 heads north from Napa. The 25-mi Silverado Trail, which runs parallel to Route 29 north from Napa to Calistoga, is Napa Valley's more scenic, less-crowded alternative to Route 29.

■ TIP➜ Remember, if you're wine-tasting, either select a designated driver or be very careful of your wine intake. (When you're taking just a sip or two of any given wine, it can be hard to keep track of how much you're drinking.) Also, keep in mind that you'll likely be sharing the road with cyclists; keep a close eye on the shoulder.

When calculating the time it will take you to drive between Napa and Sonoma valleys, remember that the Mayacamas Mountains are between the two. If it's not too far out of your way, you might want to travel between the two valleys along Highway 12/121 to the south, or along Highway 128 to the north, to avoid the slow, winding drive on the Oakville Grade, which connects Oakville, in Napa, and Glen Ellen, in Sonoma.

From San Francisco to Napa: Cross the Golden Gate Bridge, then go north on U.S. 101. Next go east on Route 37 toward Vallejo, then north on Route 121, also called the Carneros Highway. Turn left (north) when Route 121 runs into Route 29. This should take about 1½ hours when traffic is light.

From San Francisco to Sonoma: Cross the Golden Gate Bridge, then go north on U.S. 101, east on Route 37 toward Vallejo, and north on Route 121, aka the Carneros Highway. When you reach Route 12, take it north. If you're going to any of the Sonoma County destinations north of the valley, take the U.S. 101 all the way north through Santa Rosa to Healdsburg. This should take about an hour, not counting substantial traffic.

From Berkeley and other East Bay towns: Take Interstate 80 north to Route 37 west, then on to Route 29 north. To head up the Napa Valley, continue on Route 29; to reach Sonoma County, turn off Route 29 onto Route 121 heading north. Getting from Berkeley to Napa will take at least 45 minutes, from Berkeley to Sonoma at least an hour.

CONTACTS & RESOUCES

BED & BREAKFAST ASSOCIATIONS

Bed & Breakfast Association of Sonoma Valley (✉ *214 Napa St. E., Sonoma* 🕾 *707/938–9513 or 800/969–4667* ⊕ *www.sonomabb.com*). **The Wine Country Inns of Sonoma County** (🕾 *800/946–3268* ⊕ *www.winecountryinns.com*).

EMERGENCIES

The best-equipped emergency room and trauma center in the Wine Country is at **Santa Rosa Memorial Hospital** (✉ *1165 Montgomery Dr., Santa Rosa* 🕾 *707/546–3210*). **Walgreens** (✉ *4610 Sonoma Hwy., Santa Rosa* 🕾 *707/538–0964*) pharmacy is open 24 hours a day.

TOURS

Full-day guided tours of the Wine Country usually include lunch and cost about $60–$90 per person. Reservations are usually required.

Beau Wine Tours (✉ *21707 8th St. E, Sonoma* 🕾 *707/938–8001* ⊕ *www.beauwinetours.com*) organizes personalized tours of Napa and Sonoma in their limos, vans, and shuttle buses. **Gray Line** (✉ *Pier 43½ Embarcadero, San Francisco* 🕾 *415/434–8687 or 888/428–6937* ⊕ *www.grayline.com*) has a tour that covers both southern Napa and Sonoma valleys in a single day, with a stop for lunch in Yountville. **Great Pacific Tour Co.** (✉ *518 Octavia St., Hayes Valley, San Francisco* 🕾 *415/626–4499* ⊕ *www.greatpacifictour.com*) operates full-day tours of Napa and Sonoma, including a restaurant or picnic lunch, in passenger vans that seat 14. In addition to renting bikes by the day, **Wine Country Bikes** (✉ *61 Front St., Healdsburg* 🕾 *707/473–0610* ⊕ *www.winecountrybikes.com*) organizes both one-day and multiday trips throughout Sonoma County.

VISITOR INFORMATION

Information **Napa Valley Conference and Visitors Bureau** (✉ *1310 Napa Town Center, Napa* 🕾 *707/226–7459* ⊕ *www.napavalley.com*). **Russian River Wine Road** (✉ *Box 46, Healdsburg* 🕾 *707/433–4335 or 800/723–6336* ⊕ *www.wineroad.com*). **Sonoma County Tourism Bureau** (✉ *420 Aviation Blvd., Suite 106, Santa Rosa* 🕾 *707/539–7282 or 800/576–6662* ⊕ *www.sonomacounty.com*). **Sonoma Valley Visitors Bureau** (✉ *453 1st St. E, Sonoma* 🕾 *707/996–1090* ⊕ *www.sonomavalley.com*).

San Francisco Essentials

PLANNING TOOLS, EXPERT INSIGHT, GREAT CONTACTS

There are planners and there are those who, excuse the pun, fly by the seat of their pants. We happily place ourselves among the planners. Our writers and editors try to anticipate all the issues you may face before and during any journey, and then they do their research. This section is the product of their efforts. Use it to get excited about your trip to San Francisco, to inform your travel planning, or to guide you on the road should the seat of your pants start to feel threadbare.

GETTING STARTED

We're really proud of our Web site: Fodors.com is a great place to begin any journey. Scan Travel Wire for suggested itineraries, travel deals, restaurant and hotel openings, and other up-to-the-minute info. Check out Booking to research prices and book plane tickets, hotel rooms, rental cars, and vacation packages. Head to Talk for on-the-ground pointers from travelers who frequent our message boards.

▌ RESOURCES

ONLINE TRAVEL TOOLS

ALL ABOUT SAN FRANCISCO

Start your search for all things SF by following the links option from **www. sfcityscape.com**. This comprehensive Web site posts a link to every local publication, cultural institution, and government agency in the Bay Area.

For a snappy view of city trends, with gossip on everything from the city's best ice cream to concerts, check out **www.sfist. com**. For local politics and news, there's the online presence of the major daily newspaper, **www.sfgate.com/chronicle** as well as **www.fogcityjournal.com**. Current arts and cultural events are detailed on the extensive events calendar of **www. sfstation.com** or the *San Francisco Chronicle* newspaper's online entertainment Web site, **www.sfgate.com/eguide**.

You can browse articles from *San Francisco*, a monthly glossy, at **www.sanfran.com**. The annual summer issues on "bests" (restaurants, activities, and so on) are handy overviews. *SF Weekly*'s site, **www.sfweekly.com**, makes for good browsing.

Where's the Wi-Fi? Although San Francisco's mayor, Gavin Newsom, promised to establish free, citywide wireless Web connections, he hasn't set a deadline. Click on **www.wififreespot.com/ca.html** to see where you can log on in the Bay Area for free.

Safety   Transportation Security Administration (TSA ⊕ www.tsa.gov).

VISITOR INFORMATION

The San Francisco Convention and Visitors Bureau can mail you brochures, maps, and festivals and events listings. Once you're in town, you can stop by their info center near Union Square. Information about the Wine Country, redwood groves, and northwestern California is available at the California Welcome Center on Pier 39.

City San Francisco Convention and Visitors Bureau (✉ 201 3rd St., Suite 900, San Francisco ☎ 415/391–2000, 415/392–0328 TDD ⊕ www.onlyinsanfrancisco.com). **San Francisco Visitor Information Center** (✉ Hallidie Plaza, lower level, 900 Market St., Union Sq. ☎ 415/391–2000, 415/392–0328 TDD ⊕ www. onlyinsanfrancisco.com).

▌ THINGS TO CONSIDER

GEAR

When packing for a vacation in the Bay Area, prepare for major temperature swings. An hour's drive can take you up or down as much as 30°F in summer, and the variation from day to night in a single location is often very noticeable. Take along sweaters, jackets, and clothes for layering as your best insurance for coping with temperature differences. Include shorts or cool cottons for summer, and pack a bathing suit (many lodgings have pools and hot tubs). Bear in mind, however, that the city can be chilly any time of year but especially in summer, when the fog roils and descends and the wind kicks up in the afternoon. People aren't kidding when they talk about putting on their coats in June.

BOOKING YOUR TRIP

ONLINE

You really have to shop around. A travel wholesaler such as Hotels.com or Hotel-Club.net can be a source of good rates, as can discounters such as Hotwire or Priceline, particularly if you can bid for your hotel room or airfare. Indeed, such sites sometimes have deals that are unavailable elsewhere. They do, however, tend to work only with hotel chains (which makes them just plain useless for getting hotel reservations outside of major cities) or big airlines (so that often leaves out upstarts like jetBlue and some foreign carriers like Air India). Also, with discounters and wholesalers you must generally prepay, and everything is nonrefundable. And before you fork over the dough, be sure to check the terms and conditions, so you know what a given company will do for you if there's a problem and what you'll have to deal with on your own.

Booking engines like Expedia, Travelocity, and Orbitz are actually travel agents, albeit high-volume, online ones. And airline travel packagers like American Airlines Vacations and Virgin Vacations—well, they're travel agents, too. But they may still not work with all the world's hotels.

An aggregator site will search many sites and pull the best prices for airfares, hotels, and rental cars from them. Most aggregators compare the major travel-booking sites such as Expedia, Travelocity, and Orbitz; some also look at airline Web sites, though rarely the sites of smaller budget airlines. Some aggregators also compare other travel products, including complex packages—a good thing, as you can sometimes get the best overall deal by booking an air-and-hotel package.

Aggregators Kayak (⊕www.kayak.com) looks at cruises and vacation packages. **Mobissimo** (⊕www.mobissimo.com) examines airfare, hotels, cars, and tons of activities. **Qixo** (⊕www.qixo.com) compares cruises, vacation packages, and even travel insurance. **Sidestep** (⊕www.sidestep.com) compares vacation packages and lists travel deals and some activities. **Travelgrove** (⊕www.travelgrove.com) compares cruises and vacation packages and lets you search by themes.

Booking Engines Cheap Tickets (⊕www.cheaptickets.com) is a discounter. **Expedia** (⊕www.expedia.com) is a large online agency that charges a booking fee for airline tickets. **Hotwire** (⊕www.hotwire.com) is a discounter. **lastminute.com** (⊕www.lastminute.com) specializes in last-minute travel; the main site is for the U.K., but it has a link to a U.S. site. **Luxury Link** (⊕www.luxurylink.com) has auctions (surprisingly good deals) as well as offers on the high-end side of travel. **Onetravel.com** (⊕www.onetravel.com) is a discounter for hotels, car rentals, airfares, and packages. **Orbitz** (⊕www.orbitz.com) charges a booking fee for airline tickets, but gives a clear breakdown of fees and taxes before you book. **Priceline.com** (⊕www.priceline.com) is a discounter that also allows bidding. **Travel.com** (⊕www.travel.com) allows you to compare its rates with those of other booking engines. **Travelocity** (⊕www.travelocity.com) charges a booking fee for airline tickets, but promises good problem resolution.

Online Accommodations Hotelbook.com (⊕www.hotelbook.com) focuses on independent hotels worldwide. **Hotel Club** (⊕www.hotelclub.net) is good for major cities and some resort areas. **Hotels.com** (⊕www.hotels.com) is a big Expedia-owned wholesaler that offers rooms in hotels all over the world. **Quikbook** (⊕www.quikbook.com) offers "pay when you stay" reservations that allow you to settle your bill when you check out, not when you book; best for trips to U.S. and Canadian cities.

Other Resources Bidding For Travel (⊕www.biddingfortravel.com) is a good place to figure out what you can get and for how much before you start bidding on, say, Priceline.

WITH A TRAVEL AGENT

If you use an agent—brick-and-mortar or virtual—you'll pay a fee for the service. And know that the service you get from some online agents isn't comprehensive. For example, Expedia and Travelocity don't search for prices on budget airlines like jetBlue, Southwest, or small foreign carriers. That said, some agents (online or not) *do* have access to fares that are difficult to find otherwise, and the savings can more than make up for any surcharge.

Agent Resources **American Society of Travel Agents** (☎703/739-2782 ⊕www. travelsense.org) .

■ ACCOMMODATIONS

Be sure you understand the hotel's cancellation policy. Some places allow you to cancel without any kind of penalty—even if you prepaid to secure a discounted rate—if you cancel at least 24 hours in advance. Others require you to cancel a week in advance or penalize you the cost of one night. Small inns and B&Bs are most likely to require you to cancel far in advance. Most hotels allow children under a certain age to stay in their parents' room at no extra charge, but others charge for them as extra adults; find out the cutoff age for discounts.

■TIP➔Assume that hotels operate on the European Plan (EP, no meals) unless we specify that they use the Breakfast Plan (BP, with full breakfast), Continental Plan (CP, Continental breakfast), Full American Plan (FAP, all meals), Modified American Plan (MAP, breakfast and dinner) or are all-inclusive (AI, all meals and most activities).

BED & BREAKFASTS

Here's your chance to inhabit one of the city's lovely Victorian homes. San Francisco has plenty of bed-and-breakfasts, small inns, and romantic cottages. For a full list of options plus photographs, check Bed & Breakfast San Francisco.

The company has the most uncluttered Web site and the clearest map of San Francisco neighborhoods.

Reservation Services **Bed & Breakfast. com** (☎512/322-2710 or 800/462-2632 ⊕www.bedandbreakfast.com) also sends out an online newsletter. **Bed & Breakfast Inns Online** (☎615/868-1946 or 800/215-7365 ⊕www.bbonline.com). **Bed & Breakfast San Francisco** (☎415/899-0060 or 800/452-8249 ⊕www.bbsf.com). **BnB Finder.com** (☎212/432-7693 or 888/547-8226 ⊕www. bnbfinder.com).

■ AIRLINE TICKETS

The least expensive airfares to San Francisco are priced for round-trip travel and must usually be purchased in advance. Airlines generally allow you to change your return date for a fee; most low-fare tickets, however, are nonrefundable. (But if you cancel, you can usually apply the fare to a future trip, within one year, to any destination the airline flies.) Depending on the price difference, you might consider flying into Oakland or San Jose. Oakland's a relatively easy-to-use alternative since there's public transportation between the airport and downtown San Francisco. Getting to San Francisco from San Jose, though, can be time-consuming via public transportation, or costly unless you plan to rent a car.

■ RENTAL CARS

When you reserve a car, ask about cancellation penalties, taxes, drop-off charges (if you're planning to pick up the car in one city and leave it in another), and surcharges (for being under or over a certain age, for additional drivers, or for driving across state or country borders or beyond a specific distance from your point of rental). All these things can add substantially to your costs. Request car seats and extras such as GPS when you book.

Rates are sometimes—but not always—better if you book in advance or reserve through a rental agency's Web site. There are other reasons to book ahead, though: for popular destinations, during busy times of the year, or to ensure that you get certain types of cars (vans, SUVs, exotic sports cars).

■TIP➔**Make sure that a confirmed reservation guarantees you a car. Agencies sometimes overbook, particularly for busy weekends and holiday periods.**

Car rental costs in San Francisco vary seasonally but generally begin at $30 a day and $150 a week for an economy car with air-conditioning, automatic transmission, and unlimited mileage. This doesn't include tax on car rentals, which is 8.5%. If you dream of driving with the top down, or heading out of town to ski the Sierra, consider renting a specialty vehicle. Most major agencies have a few on hand, but the best overall service is with two locally owned agencies: Specialty Rentals and City Rent-a-Car. The former specializes in high-end vehicles and arranges for airport pickup and drop-off. City Rent-a-Car also arranges airport transfers but also delivers cars to Bay Area hotels. Both agencies also rent standard vehicles at prices competitive with those of the majors.

In San Francisco you must be at least 20 years old to rent a car, but some agencies won't rent to those under 25; check when you book.

ALTERNATIVE RENTALS

City Car Share, Flex Car, and Zip Car are membership organizations for residents who need a car only for short-term use. They're especially useful if you only want to rent a car for part of the day (say four to six hours), find yourself far from the airport, or if you're younger than most rental agencies' 25-years-or-older requirement. The membership fee often allows you to use their service in several metropolitan areas. If using such a ser-vice, you can rent a car by the hour as well as by the day.

Two companies, Electric Time Car Rentals and GoCar, rent electric vehicles at Fisherman's Wharf and Union Square. These cars can travel between 25 and 35 mph and are very handy for neighborhood-based sightseeing, but they're not allowed on the Golden Gate Bridge.

Electric Time Car Rentals has two-seat and four-seat cars with detachable roofs, locked storage boxes, and GPS audio tours of the city. They're at Anchorage Alley in Fisherman's Wharf. The GoCars are electric, two-seater, three-wheeled, open convertibles with roll bars (so drivers must wear helmets). Their vehicles also have computerized navigation and audio guides. You can pick up a GoCar at two locations: Fisherman's Wharf and Union Square.

Automobile Associations U.S.: **American Automobile Association** ([AAA] ☎415/565–2141 ⊕www.aaa.com); most contact with the organization is through state and regional members. **National Automobile Club** (☎800/622–2136 ⊕www.thenac.com); membership is open to California residents only.

Local Agencies A-One Rent-a-Car (☎415/771–3978). **City Car Share** (☎415/995–8588 or 510/352–0323 ⊕www.citycarshare.org). **City Rent-a-Car** (☎415/861–1312 or 415/359–1331). **Electric Time Car Rentals** (☎415/674–8800 ⊕www.etcars.com). **Flex Car** (☎415/282–3539 ⊕www.flexcar.com). **GoCar** (☎800/914–6227 ⊕www.gocarsf.com). **Specialty Rentals** (☎415/701–1600 or 800/400–8412 ⊕www.specialtyrentals.com). **Super Cheap Car Rental** (☎650/777–9993 ⊕www.supercheapcar.com). **Zip Car** (☎415/495–7478 ⊕www.zipcar.com).

Major Agencies Alamo (☎800/462–5266 ⊕www.alamo.com). **Avis** (☎800/331–1212 ⊕www.avis.com). **Budget** (☎800/527–0700 ⊕www.budget.com). **Hertz** (☎800/654–3131 ⊕www.hertz.com). **National Car Rental** (☎800/227–7368 ⊕www.nationalcar.com).

TRANSPORTATION

San Francisco is built on the grid system. Market Street, which runs diagonally southwest to northeast, divides several neighborhoods. If a street begins at Market, that's where the numbering of its addresses begins.

Throughout the city, as you move from one block to the next, the addresses on most streets increase by 100. To find the block number you're in, look at the top of the white street signs at intersections. You'll see a multiple of 100, with an arrow pointing to the next-highest block.

With a numbered road, you need to know whether it's called an avenue or a street. "The Avenues" begin one block west of Arguello Boulevard and run north–south through the Richmond and Sunset districts, in the western part of the city. Numbered *streets,* however, begin downtown, south of Market Street, and continue south and west through Potrero Hill, the Mission, the Castro, and Noe Valley.

▌ BY AIR

Nonstop flights from New York to San Francisco take about 5½ hours, and with the 3-hour time change, it's possible to leave JFK by 8 AM and be in San Francisco by 10:30 AM. Some flights may require a midway stop, making the total excursion between 8 and 9½ hours. Nonstop times are approximately 1½ hours from Los Angeles, 3 hours from Dallas, 4½ hours from Chicago, 4½ hours from Atlanta, 11 hours from London, 12 hours from Auckland, and 13½ hours from Sydney. Travel time from Melbourne is about 16 hours. There is no nonstop service from Melbourne to San Francisco.

Heavy fog is infamous for causing chronic delays into and out of San Francisco. If you're heading to the East or South Bay, make every effort to fly into Oakland or San Jose airport, respectively. Oakland International Airport, which is easy to navigate and accessible by public transit, is a good alternative to San Francisco International Airport.

Airline Security Issues Transportation Security Administration (⊕ www.tsa.gov) has answers for almost every question that might come up.

AIRPORTS

The major gateway to San Francisco is San Francisco International Airport (SFO), 15 mi south of the city. It's off U.S. 101 near Millbrae and San Bruno. Oakland International Airport (OAK) is across the bay, not much farther away from downtown San Francisco (via I–80 east and I–880 south), but rush-hour traffic on the Bay Bridge may lengthen travel times considerably. San Jose International Airport (SJC) is about 40 mi south of San Francisco; travel time depends largely on traffic flow, but plan an hour and a half with moderate traffic.

At all three airports security check-in can take 15–30 minutes at peak travel times.

▌TIP➔**Count yourself lucky if you have a layover at SFO's International Terminal. During its 2005 renovation, SFO brought in branches of some top local eateries. The food's far better than standard airport fare; you'll find Italian pastries from Emporio Rulli, burgers from Burger Joint or Lori's Diner, sushi from Ebisu, and much more.**

Airport Information San Francisco International Airport ([SFO] ☎650/761–0800 ⊕www.flysfo.com). **Oakland International Airport** ([OAK] ☎510/577–4000 ⊕www. flyoakland.com). **San Jose International Airport** ([SJC] ☎408/277–4759 ⊕www.sjc.org).

GROUND TRANSPORTATION

FROM SAN FRANCISCO INTERNATIONAL AIRPORT

Transportation signage at the airport is color-coded by type and is quite clear. A taxi ride to downtown costs $35–$40. Airport shuttles are inexpensive and generally efficient. Lorrie's Airport Service and SuperShuttle both stop at the lower level near baggage claim, and take you anywhere within the city limits of San Francisco. They charge $15–$17, depending on where you're going. Lorrie's also sells tickets online, at a $2 discount each way; you can print them out before leaving home. SuperShuttle offers discounts for more than one person traveling in the same party ($16 for the first passenger, $16 each additional), but only if you're traveling to a residential address.

Shuttles to the East Bay, such as BayPorter Express, also depart from the lower level; expect to pay around $35. Inquire about the number of stops a shuttle makes en route to or from the airport; some companies, such as East Bay Express, have nonstop service, but they cost a bit more. Marin Door to Door operates van service to Marin County for $25 to $35 for the first passenger, $12 each additional; you must make reservations by noon the day before travel. Marin Airporter buses cost $17–$20 and require no reservations but stop only at designated stations in Marin; buses leave every 30 minutes, on the half hour and hour, from 5 AM to midnight.

You can take BART directly to downtown San Francisco; the trip takes about 30 minutes and costs less than $5.50. (There are both manned booths and vending machines for ticket purchases.) Trains leave from the international terminal every 15 minutes on weekdays and every 20 minutes on weekends.

Another inexpensive way to get to San Francisco is via two SamTrans buses: No. 292 (55 minutes, $1.50 from SFO, $3 to SFO) and the KX (35 minutes, $4; only one small carry-on bag permitted). Board the SamTrans buses on the lower level.

To drive to downtown San Francisco from the airport, take U.S. 101 north to the Civic Center/9th Street, 7th Street, or 4th Street/Downtown exit. If you're headed to the Embarcadero or Fisherman's Wharf, take I–280 north (the exit is to the right, just north of the airport, off U.S. 101) and get off at the 4th Street/King Street exit. King Street becomes the Embarcadero a few blocks east of the exit. The Embarcadero winds around the waterfront to Fisherman's Wharf.

FROM OAKLAND INTERNATIONAL AIRPORT

A taxi to downtown San Francisco costs $35–$40. By airport regulations, you must make reservations for shuttle service. BayPorter Express and other shuttles serve major hotels and provide door-to-door service to the East Bay and San Francisco. SuperShuttle operates vans to San Francisco and Oakland. Marin Door to Door serves Marin County for a flat $45 for the first passenger, $12 each additional; make reservations by noon the day before travel.

The best way to get to San Francisco via public transit is to take the AIR BART bus ($3) to the Coliseum/Oakland International Airport BART station (BART fares vary depending on where you're going; the ride to downtown San Francisco costs $3.55).

If you're driving from Oakland International Airport, take Hegenberger Road east to I–880 north to I–80 west over the Bay Bridge. This will likely take at least an hour.

FROM SAN JOSE INTERNATIONAL AIRPORT

A taxi to downtown San Jose costs about $15; a trip to San Francisco runs about $110. South & East Bay Airport Shuttle transports you to the South Bay and East Bay; a ride to downtown San Jose costs $39 for the first passenger, $9 each additional, and a van to San Francisco costs $89 for the first passenger, $9 each additional. Reservations are required to the airport, but not from the airport; call from baggage claim before you collect your luggage. Reservations are also required for VIP Airport Shuttle, which has service to downtown San Francisco for $89 for the first three passengers, $7 each additional; to downtown San Jose costs $19.

To drive to downtown San Jose from the airport, take Airport Boulevard east to Route 87 south. To get to San Francisco from the airport, take Route 87 south to Interstate 280 north. The trip will take roughly two hours.

At $7.25 for a one-way ticket, there is no question that Caltrain provides the most affordable option for traveling between San Francisco and San Jose's airport. However, the Caltrain station in San Francisco at 4th and Townsend streets is not in a conveniently central location. It's on the eastern side of the South of Market neighborhood and not easily accessible by other public transit. You'll need to take a taxi or walk from the nearest bus line. It takes 90 minutes to reach Santa Clara station, from which a free shuttle runs every 15 minutes, whisking you to and from the San Jose International Airport in 15 minutes.

Contacts **American Airporter** (☎415/202-0733 ⊕www.americanairporter.com). **Bay-Porter Express** (☎415/467-1800 ⊕www.bayporter.com). **Caltrain** (☎800/660-4287 ⊕www.caltrain.com). **East Bay Express Airporter** (☎510/526-0304). **Lorrie's Airport Service** (☎415/334-9000 ⊕www.gosfovan.com). **Marin Airporter** (☎415/461-4222 ⊕www.marinairporter.com). **Marin Door to Door** (☎415/457-2717 ⊕www.marindoortodoor.com). **SamTrans** (☎800/660-4287 ⊕www.samtrans.com). **South & East Bay Airport Shuttle** (☎408/559-9477). **SuperShuttle** (☎800/258-3826 or 415/558-8500 ⊕www.supershuttle.com). **VIP Airport Shuttle** (☎800/235-8847, 408/885-1800, or 408/986-6000 ⊕www.yourairportride.com).

FLIGHTS

Of the major carriers, Alaska, American, Continental, Delta, Mexicana, Southwest, and United all fly into San Francisco, Oakland, and San Jose airports. Harmony Airways, jetBlue, Primaris, and US Airways service Oakland. Frontier, Hawaiian, Horizon Air, and Northwest fly into SFO and San Jose. Virgin Atlantic and the budget-conscious Midwest Express fly into SFO.

Airline Contacts **Alaska Airlines** (☎800/252-7522 or 206/433-3100 ⊕www.alaskaair.com). **American Airlines** (☎800/433-7300 ⊕www.aa.com). **ATA** (☎800/435-9282 or 317/282-8308 ⊕www.ata.com). **Continental Airlines** (☎800/523-3273 for U.S. and Mexico reservations, 800/231-0856 for international reservations ⊕www.continental.com). **Delta Airlines** (☎ 800/221-1212 for U.S. reservations, 800/241-4141 for international reservations ⊕www.delta.com). **jetBlue** (☎800/538-2583 ⊕www.jetblue.com). **Northwest Airlines** (☎800/225-2525 ⊕www.nwa.com). **Southwest Airlines** (☎ 800/435-9792 ⊕www.southwest.com). **United Airlines** (☎ 800/864-8331 for U.S. reservations, 800/538-2929 for international reservations ⊕ www.united.com). **US Airways** (☎800/428-4322 for U.S. and Canada reservations, 800/622-1015 for international reservations ⊕www.usairways.com). Smaller Airlines **Frontier Airlines** (☎800/432-1359 ⊕www.frontierairlines.com). **Midwest Airlines** (☎800/452-2022 ⊕www.midwestairlines.com).

▌BY BART

Bay Area Rapid Transit (BART) trains, which run until midnight, travel under the bay via tunnel to connect San Francisco with Oakland, Berkeley, Pittsburgh/Bay Point, Richmond, Fremont, Dublin/Pleasanton, and other small cities and towns in between. Within San Francisco, stations are limited to downtown, the Mission, and a couple of outlying neighborhoods.

Trains travel frequently from early morning until evening on weekdays—after 8 PM weekdays—and on weekends there's often a 20-minute wait between trains on the same line. Trains also travel south from San Francisco as far as Millbrae. BART trains connect downtown San Francisco to San Francisco International Airport; a ride is $5.35.

Intracity San Francisco fares are $1.50; intercity fares are $2.65–$5.60. BART bases its ticket prices on miles traveled and does not offer price breaks by zone. A monthly ticket, called a Fast Pass, is available for $48 and can be used on BART and on all Muni lines (including cable cars) within city limits. The easy-to-read maps posted in BART stations list fares based on destination, radiating out from your starting point of the current station.

During morning and evening rush hour, trains within the city are crowded—even standing room can be hard to come by. Cars at the far front and back of the train are less likely to be filled to capacity. Smoking, eating, and drinking are prohibited on trains and in stations.

Contacts Bay Area Rapid Transit ([BART] ☎415/989–2278 or 650/992–2278 ⊕www. bart.gov).

▌BY BOAT

Several ferry lines run out of San Francisco. Blue & Gold Fleet operates a number of lines, including service to Sausalito ($9 one-way) and Tiburon ($9 one-way). Tickets are sold at Pier 41 (between Fisherman's Wharf and Pier 39), where the boats depart. There are also weekday Blue & Gold commuter ferries to Tiburon ($9) and Vallejo ($12.50) from the San Francisco Ferry Building. Alcatraz Cruises, owned by Hornblower Yachts, operates the ferries to Alcatraz Island ($24.50 including audio tour and National Park Service ranger-led programs) from Pier 33, about a half-mile east of Fisherman's Wharf ($2 shuttle buses serve several area hotels and other locations). Boats leave 10 times a day (14 times a day in summer) and the journey itself is 30 minutes. Allow roughly 2½ hours for a round-trip jaunt. Golden Gate Ferry runs daily to and from Sausalito and Larkspur (each costs $7.10 one-way), leaving from Pier 1, behind the San Francisco Ferry Building. The Alameda/Oakland Ferry operates daily between Alameda's Main Street Ferry Building, Oakland's Jack London Square, and San Francisco's Pier 41 and the Ferry Building ($6 one-way); some ferries go only to Pier 41 or the Ferry Building, so ask when you board. Purchase tickets on board.

Information Alameda/Oakland Ferry (☎510/522–3300 ⊕www.eastbayferry.com). **Alcatraz Cruises** (☎415/981–7625 ⊕www. alcatrazcruises.com). **Blue & Gold Fleet** (☎415/705–5555 ⊕www.blueandgoldfleet. com). **Golden Gate Ferry** (☎415/923–2000 ⊕www.goldengateferry.org). **San Francisco Ferry Building** (✉Foot of Market Street on Embarcadero).

▌BY BUS

The San Francisco Municipal Railway, or Muni, operates light-rail vehicles, the historic F-line streetcars along Fisherman's Wharf and Market Street, trolley buses, and the world-famous cable cars. Light rail travels along Market Street to the Mission District and Noe Valley (J line), the Ingleside District (K line), and the Sunset District (L, M, and N lines); during peak hours (Mon.–Fri., 6 AM–9 AM and 3 PM–7 PM) the J line continues around the Embarcadero to the Caltrain station at 4th and King streets. The new T line light rail runs from the Castro, down Market Street, around the Embarcadero, and south past Hunters Point and Monster Park to Sunnydale Avenue and Bayshore Boulevard. Muni provides

24-hour service on select lines to all areas of the city.

On buses and streetcars, the fare is $1.50. Exact change is required, and dollar bills are accepted in the fare boxes. For all Muni vehicles other than cable cars, 90-minute transfers are issued free upon request at the time the fare is paid. Transfers are valid for two additional transfers in any direction. Cable cars cost $5 and include no transfers (*see By Cable Car, below*).

One-day ($11), three-day ($18), and seven-day ($24) Passports valid on the entire Muni system can be purchased at several outlets, including the cable-car ticket booth at Powell and Market streets and the visitor information center downstairs in Hallidie Plaza. A monthly ticket, called a Fast Pass, is available for $45 and can be used on all Muni lines (including cable cars) and on BART within city limits. The San Francisco CityPass, a discount ticket booklet to several major city attractions, also covers all Muni travel for seven consecutive days.

The San Francisco Municipal Transit and Street Map ($2.50) is a useful guide to the extensive transportation system. You can buy the map at most bookstores and at the San Francisco Visitor Information Center, on the lower level of Hallidie Plaza at Powell and Market streets.

During football season, Muni runs a special weekend shuttle to Candlestick Park for $7 round-trip.

Outside the city, AC Transit serves the East Bay, and Golden Gate Transit serves Marin and Sonoma counties.

Bus & MUNI Information **AC Transit** (☎510/839–2882 ⊕www.actransit.org). **Golden Gate Transit** (☎415/923–2000 ⊕www.goldengate.org). **San Francisco Municipal Railway System** ([Muni] ☎415/673–6864 ⊕www.sfmuni.com).

BY CABLE CAR

Don't miss the sensation of moving up and down some of San Francisco's steepest hills in a clattering cable car, the only moving thing listed on the National Register of Historic Places. As it pauses at a designated stop, jump aboard and wedge yourself into any available space. Then just hold on.

The fare (for one direction) is $5 (Muni Passport holders pay a $1 supplement). You can buy tickets on board (exact change isn't necessary) or at the kiosks at the cable-car turnarounds at Hyde and Beach streets and at Powell and Market streets.

The heavily traveled Powell–Mason and Powell–Hyde lines begin at Powell and Market streets near Union Square and terminate at Fisherman's Wharf; lines for these routes can be long, especially in summer. The California Street line runs east and west from Market and California streets to Van Ness Avenue; there is often no wait to board this route.

BY CAR

Driving in San Francisco can be a challenge because of the one-way streets, snarly traffic, and steep hills. The first two elements can be frustrating enough, but those hills are tough for unfamiliar drivers.

Be sure to leave plenty of room between your car and other vehicles when on a steep slope. This is especially important when you've braked at a stop sign on a steep incline. Whether with a stick shift or an automatic transmission, every car rolls backward for a moment once the brake is released. So don't pull too close to the car ahead of you. When it's time to pull forward, keep your foot on the brake while tapping lightly on the accelerator. Once the engine is engaged, let up on the brake and head uphill.

■ TIP→ **Remember to curb your wheels when parking on hills—turn wheels away from the curb when facing uphill, toward the curb when facing downhill. You can get a ticket if you don't do this.**

Market Street runs southwest from the Ferry Building, then becomes Portola Drive as it nears Twin Peaks (which lie beneath the giant radio-antennae structure, Sutro Tower). It can be difficult to drive across Market. The major east–west streets north of Market are Geary Boulevard (it's called Geary Street east of Van Ness Avenue), which runs to the Pacific Ocean; Fulton Street, which begins at the back of the Opera House and continues along the north side of Golden Gate Park to Ocean Beach; Oak Street, which runs east from Golden Gate Park toward downtown, then flows into northbound Franklin Street; and Fell Street, the left two lanes of which cut through Golden Gate Park and empty into Lincoln Boulevard, which continues to the ocean.

Among the major north–south streets are Divisadero, which becomes Castro Street at Duboce Avenue and continues to just past César Chavez Street; Van Ness Avenue, which becomes South Van Ness Avenue when it crosses Market Street; and Park Presidio Boulevard, which empties into 19th Avenue.

GASOLINE

Gas stations are hard to find in San Francisco; look for the national franchises on major thoroughfares such as Market Street or California Street. Once you find one, prepare for sticker shock—the fuel is notoriously expensive here.

Aside from their limited numbers and high costs, all else is standard operation at these service stations. All major stations accept credit and ATM cards; self-service pumps are the norm. Most gas stations are open seven days a week until 11 PM or midnight. Many national franchises on well-traveled streets are open 24/7. Local independent stations are likely to close on Sundays or by 9 PM.

PARKING

San Francisco is a terrible city for parking. In the Financial District and Civic Center neighborhoods, parking is forbidden on most streets between 4 PM and 6 PM. Check street signs carefully to confirm, because illegally parked cars are towed immediately. Downtown parking lots are often full, and most are expensive. The city-owned Sutter-Stockton, Ellis-O'Farrell, and 5th-and-Mission garages have the most reasonable rates in the downtown area. Large hotels often have parking available, but it doesn't come cheap; many charge in excess of $40 a day for the privilege.

Garages **Ellis-O'Farrell Garage** (⊠123 O'Farrell St., at Stockton St., Downtown ☎415/986–4800 ⊕www.eofgarage.com). **Embarcadero Center Garage** (⊠1–4 Embarcadero Center, between Battery and Drumm Sts., Financial District ☎800/733–6318 ⊕www.embarcaderocenter.com). **5th-and-Mission Garage** (⊠833 Mission St., at 5th St., SoMa ☎415/982–8522 ⊕www.fifthandmission.com). **Opera Plaza Garage** (⊠601 Van Ness Ave., at Turk St., Civic Center ☎415/771–4776). **Pier 39 Garage** (⊠Embarcadero at Beach St., Fisherman's Wharf ☎415/705–5418 ⊕www.pier39.com). **Portsmouth Square Garage** (⊠733 Kearny St., at Clay St., Chinatown ☎415/982–6353 ⊕www.portsmouthsquaregarage.com). **766 Vallejo Garage** (⊠766 Vallejo St., at Powell St., North Beach ☎415/989–4490). **Sutter-Stockton Garage** (⊠444 Stockton St., at Sutter St., Downtown ☎415/982–7275). **Wharf Garage** (⊠350 Beach St., at Taylor St., Fisherman's Wharf).

ROAD CONDITIONS

Although rush "hour" is 6–10 AM and 3–7 PM, you can hit gridlock on any day at any time, especially over the Bay Bridge and leaving and/or entering the city from the south. Sunday-afternoon traffic can be heavy as well, especially over the bridges.

The most comprehensive and immediate traffic updates are available through the city's 511 service, either online at www.511.org (where Web cams show you the traffic on your selected route) or by calling 511. On the radio, tune into an all-news radio station such as KSFO 560 AM, KCBS 740 AM, and KNBR 680/1050 AM.

Be especially watchful of nonindicated lane changes. There's a lot of construction going on in the SoMa neighborhood and the waterfront area in the southeast, but this doesn't create too many traffic problems.

San Francisco is the only major American city uncut by freeways. To get from the Bay Bridge to the Golden Gate Bridge, you'll have to take surface streets, specifically Van Ness Avenue, which doubles as U.S. Hwy 101 through the city.

ROADSIDE EMERGENCIES

Dial 911 to report accidents on the road and to reach police, the highway patrol, or the fire department.

Emergency Services **AAA** (☎415/565–2012).

RULES OF THE ROAD

To encourage carpooling during heavy traffic times, some freeways have special lanes for so-called high-occupancy vehicles (HOVs)—cars carrying more than one or two passengers. Look for the white-painted diamond in the middle of the lane. Road signs next to or above the lane indicate the hours that carpooling is in effect. If you're stopped by the police because you don't meet the criteria for travel in these lanes, expect a fine of more than $200.

In July 2008, state law banned drivers from using handheld mobile telephones while operating a vehicle (but that bad habit will surely be hard to shake). The use of seat belts in both front and back seats is required in California. The speed limit on city streets is 25 mph unless oth-

erwise posted. A right turn on a red light after stopping is legal unless posted otherwise, as is a left on red at the intersection of two one-way streets. Always strap children under 80 pounds or age eight into approved child-safety seats.

▌ BY TAXI

Taxi service is notoriously bad in San Francisco, and hailing a cab can be frustratingly difficult in some parts of the city, especially on weekends. Popular nightspots such as the Mission, SoMa, North Beach, the Haight, and the Castro have a lot of cabs but a lot of people looking for taxis, too. Midweek, and during the day, you shouldn't have much of a problem—unless it's raining. In a pinch, hotel taxi stands are an option, as is calling for a pick-up. But be forewarned: taxi companies frequently don't answer the phone in peak periods. The absolute worst time to find a taxi is Friday afternoon and evening; plan well ahead, and if you're going to the airport, make a reservation or book a shuttle instead. Most taxi companies take advance reservations for airport and out-of-town runs but not in-town transfers.

Taxis in San Francisco charge $3.10 for the first 1/5 mi (one of the highest base rates in the U.S.), 45¢ for each additional 1/5 mi, and 45¢ per minute in stalled traffic. There is no charge for additional passengers; there is no surcharge for luggage. For trips outside city limits, multiply the metered rate by 1.5.

Taxi Companies **City Wide Cab** (☎415/920–0700). **DeSoto Cab** (☎415/970–1370). **Luxor Cab** (☎415/282–4141). **Veteran's Taxicab** (☎415/648–1313). **Yellow Cab** (☎415/333–3333).

Complaints **San Francisco Police Department Taxi Detail** (☎415/553–1447).

■ BY TRAIN

Amtrak trains travel to the Bay Area from some cities in California and the United States. The *Coast Starlight* travels north from Los Angeles to Seattle, passing the Bay Area along the way, but contrary to its name, the train runs inland through the Central Valley for much of its route through Northern California; the most scenic stretch is in Southern California, between San Luis Obispo and Los Angeles. Amtrak also has several routes between San Jose, Oakland, and Sacramento. The *California Zephyr* travels from Chicago to the Bay Area and has spectacular alpine vistas as it crosses the Sierra Nevada mountains. San Francisco doesn't have an Amtrak train station but does have an Amtrak bus station, at the Ferry Building, which provides service to trains in Emeryville, just over the Bay Bridge. Shuttle buses also connect the Emeryville train station with downtown Oakland, the Caltrain station, and other points in downtown San Francisco.

Caltrain connects San Francisco to Palo Alto, San Jose, Santa Clara, and many smaller cities en route. In San Francisco, trains leave from the main depot, at 4th and Townsend streets, and a rail-side stop at 22nd and Pennsylvania streets. One-way fares are $2.25–$11, depending on the number of zones through which your travel tickets are valid for four hours after purchase time. A ticket is $5.75 from San Francisco to Palo Alto, at least $7.50 to San Jose. You can also buy a day pass ($4.50–$22) for unlimited travel in a 24-hour period. Trips last 1 to 1¾ hours; it's worth waiting for an express train. On weekdays, trains depart three or four times per hour during the morning and evening, twice per hour during daytime noncommute hours, and as little as once per hour in the evening. Weekend trains run once per hour. The system shuts down at midnight. There are no onboard ticket sales. You must buy tickets before board-ing the train or potentially pay a $250 fine for fare evasion.

INFORMATION

Amtrak (☎800/872-7245 ⊕www.amtrak. com). **Caltrain** (☎800/660-4287 ⊕www. caltrain.com). **San Francisco Caltrain Station** (✉700 4th St., at King St. ☎ 800/660-4287).

ON THE GROUND

▌ DAY TOURS & GUIDES

For walking tour recommendations, *see* the Experience San Francisco chapter.

BOAT TOURS

Blue & Gold Fleet operates a bay cruise that lasts about an hour. Tickets may be purchased at Pier 39, near Fisherman's Wharf. The tour, on a ferryboat with outside seating on the upper deck, loops around the bay, taking in the Bay Bridge, Alcatraz Island, and the Golden Gate Bridge. An audiotape tells you what you're seeing. Discounts are available for tickets purchased online.

Information **Blue & Gold Fleet** (☎415/705–5555 ⊕www.blueandgoldfleet.com).

BUS & VAN TOURS

In addition to bus and van tours of the city, most tour companies run excursions to various Bay Area and Northern California destinations, such as Marin County and the Wine Country, as well as to farther-flung areas, such as Monterey and Yosemite. City tours generally last 3½ hours and cost $40–$45. The bigger outfits operate large buses, which tend to be roomy. Service is more intimate with the smaller companies, however, because they can fit only about 10 people per vehicle; the vans can be a little tight, but with the driver–guide right in front of you, you're able to ask questions easily and won't have to worry about interrupting someone on a microphone, as is the case with the big companies.

Great Pacific Tours is the best small company and conducts city tours in passenger vans (starting at $44). Super Sightseeing is also locally owned and operates tours in 28- and 50-passenger buses. For about $15 to $20 more, both companies can supplement a city tour with a bay cruise. Super Sightseeing can also add a trip to Alcatraz for $16.

Information **Great Pacific Tours** (☎415/626–4499 ⊕www.greatpacifictour.com). **Super Sightseeing** (☎415/777–2288 or 888/868–7788 ⊕www.supersightseeing.com).

CREDIT CARDS

Throughout this guide, the following abbreviations are used: **AE**, American Express; **D**, Discover; **DC**, Diners Club; **MC**, MasterCard; and **V**, Visa.

Reporting Lost Cards **American Express** (☎800/528–4800 in U.S. ⊕www.americanexpress.com). **Diners Club** (☎800/234–6377 in U.S. ⊕www.dinersclub.com). **Discover** (☎800/347–2683 in U.S. ⊕www.discovercard.com). **MasterCard** (☎800/627–8372 in U.S. ⊕www.mastercard.com). **Visa** (☎800/847–2911 in U.S. ⊕www.visa.com).

▌ SAFETY

San Francisco is generally a safe place for travelers who observe all normal urban precautions. First, avoid looking like a tourist. Dress inconspicuously, remove badges when leaving convention areas, and know the routes to your destination before you set out. Use common sense and, unless you know exactly where you're going, steer clear of certain neighborhoods late at night: the Tenderloin, Civic Center plaza, parts of the Mission (around 14th Street, for example, or south of 24th to César Chavez Street), and the Lower Haight should be avoided, especially if you're walking alone.

Like many larger cities, San Francisco has many homeless people. Although most are no threat, some are more aggressive and can persist in their pleas for cash until it feels like harassment. If you feel uncomfortable, don't reach for your wallet.

INDEX

NOTES

ABOUT OUR WRITERS

A veteran Fodor's writer, Berkeley-based writer and editor Denise M. Leto roams the city out of sheer love for SF, exploring everything from the hidden stairways of Russian Hill to the mural-splashed alleys of the Mission. She updated all the neighborhood chapters and the Experience chapter in this edition. She also wrote our special features on cable cars, Chinatown, Golden Gate Park, and Alcatraz.

Fiona G. Parrott is a freelance writer who was born and raised in Mill Valley, California. She spent her childhood exploring the raw wilderness of Marin County and her later years exploring the culinary and musical delights of San Francisco, Berkeley, and Oakland. At present she divides her adventure time between wilderness and cityscape, researching and writing about the Bay Area's cutting edge hotspots. She's been a waitress, vet, actor, bartender, watermelon picker, latrine builder, and university lecturer, but writing for Fodor's has been one of her most exciting jobs. She updated the Sports & Outdoors and Marin, Berkeley & Oakland chapters, as well as San Francisco Essentials. In recent years Fiona also contributed to Fodor's Scotland and Fodor's Great Britain.

Shopping updater Natasha Sarkisian is acting managing editor at San Francisco magazine. She's thankful to live in a city where there's a "dangerous store" for everyone and she constantly helps friends solve their gift-giving dilemmas.

Sharon Silva, a writer and editor specializing in food books, lives in San Francisco. She is a longtime Fodor's contributor, covering the city's restaurant scene for our Where to Eat chapter.

A longtime Fodor's contributor, Sharron Wood simply adores San Francisco, from its flourishing food, wine, and cocktail culture to its perpetually perfect weather. When she's not exploring the Wine Country, she's writing about the city's nightlife, editing cookbooks, developing recipes, or plying her friends with cocktails in her Mission District apartment.

Bay Area writer Sura Wood lost her heart in San Francisco when she was eight, and she's never stopped loving the city. An arts journalist for the last fifteen years, she's written with gusto about San Francisco's food, fashion, hotels, nightlife, art, and architecture for the Fodor's website. She updated our Where to Stay and Nightlife & the Arts chapters and Eye on Architecture feature for this year's guide.